Get the eBook FREE!

(PDF, ePub, Kindle, and liveBook all included)

We believe that once you buy a book from us, you should be able to read it in any format we have available. To get electronic versions of this book at no additional cost to you, purchase and then register this book at the Manning website.

Go to https://www.manning.com/freebook and follow the instructions to complete your pBook registration.

That's it!
Thanks from Manning!

Praise for the First Edition

Elasticsearch in Action *has excellent in-depth coverage of using Elasticsearch to its full potential.*

—Paul Stadig

Elasticsearch is a complex topic, and this book is the best resource. I highly recommend it!

—Daniel Beck, juris GmbH

A great book to have when one starts working with Elasticsearch.

—Tanguy Leroux, software engineer, Elastic

The best Elasticsearch book. I do not need to search any further.

—Koray Güclü

This book will become your indispensable guide for tackling the challenges of semi-structured data.

—Artur Nowak, CTO, Evidence Prime

An accessible beginner's guide for a modern large-scale search system.

—Sen Xu, Sr. Software Engineer, Twitter

Took me from confused to confident in a week.

—Alan McCann, CTO, Givsum.com

Elasticsearch in Action
Second Edition

Elasticsearch in Action

SECOND EDITION

MADHUSUDHAN KONDA
Foreword by SHAY BANON

MANNING
SHELTER ISLAND

For online information and ordering of this and other Manning books, please visit
www.manning.com. The publisher offers discounts on this book when ordered in quantity.
For more information, please contact

> Special Sales Department
> Manning Publications Co.
> 20 Baldwin Road
> PO Box 761
> Shelter Island, NY 11964
> Email: orders@manning.com

Manning Publications Co.
20 Baldwin Road
PO Box 761
Shelter Island, NY 11964

Development editor:	Ian Hough
Technical development editor:	Al Krinker
Review editor:	Aleksandar Dragosavljević
Production editor:	Keri Hales
Copy editor:	Tiffany Taylor
Proofreader:	Jason Everett
Technical proofreader:	Simon Hewitt
Typesetter and cover designer:	Marija Tudor

ISBN 9781617299858
Printed in the United States of America

In loving memory of my Dad.

We miss you!

Love,
Kondas

brief contents

contents

foreword

I have been a big fan of Manning *In Action* books over the years, and they have been a significant part of my professional career. I love how the books focus on practical, useful, hands-on advice about the various technologies I use, both for work and in open source.

It was in that same spirit that I sat down to write Elasticsearch many years ago. I got into search while trying to build a recipe application for my wife as she was studying to be a chef. I open-sourced the code I wrote to implement it, thus taking my first step into the open source world. And a few years later, I sat down to write Elasticsearch, trying to create a useful, practical, easy-to-use search engine—search in action, if you will.

Fast-forward to 2023, and I'm delighted to see that Elasticsearch has gained traction and has its own addition to the *In Action* series, which you are now holding in your hands or looking at in digital form. I am sure you will enjoy reading the book and learning about Elasticsearch. Madhu is passionate about both search and Elasticsearch, and it comes across in the depth and breadth of this book, the enthusiastic tone, and the hands-on examples.

I hope that after learning about Elasticsearch, you will take what you have read and put it "in action." After all, search is everywhere, in everything we do, which is why I fell in love with it so many years ago.

—SHAY BANON, FOUNDER OF ELASTICSEARCH

preface

The late 1990s found me at IIT Kharagpur in India, where I was pursuing my master's degree and simultaneously immersing myself in the fascinating realm of the Java language (version 1, to be precise!). It was a solitary journey, although I enjoyed using an object-oriented language for the first time, each code compilation failure signifying a duel between my terminal and me. There were no fancy IDEs in those days; we typed in a vi editor and then compiled. (There was a rudimentary IDE called Java WorkShop from Sun Microsystems, but it was not without wrinkles and bugs.) And unlike in the present era, which is replete with resources like Google, Stack Overflow, and GitHub, there were no digital avenues to probe for solutions or discover if other programmers were encountering similar challenges. Then my best friend Amar, who was studying at IISc, Bangalore, introduced me to a new entity in the search arena: Google.

To a naïve young student, the concept of reaching out to a virtual community of coders grappling with similar issues was a novelty. So, I decided to explore this new avenue. I remember being intrigued by the simplicity of Google's design, its non-eyesore white background dotted with primary colors, as I navigated pages in search of answers. The early version of the search engine was far from the sophisticated tool we know today, but it was an encouraging beacon during those challenging times. (Anyone who has experienced Java 1.x can understand the trials involved.) That moment marked a significant turning point in my journey.

While Google's search capabilities were revolutionary for many of us, its adoption within client settings and organizations was somewhat slower. Projects I was involved in at that time had databases serving as the backbone for search applications. While functional, these setups fell considerably short of what we now recognize as the capabilities of modern search engines. The search mechanisms were clunky and unwieldy, lacked performance, and posed maintenance challenges. However, my affinity for streamlined architecture never wavered, remaining a guiding light in my quest for efficient and effective solutions.

My journey into the world of Elasticsearch began in 2015, around the same time big data became mainstream. I was working on Enterprise Java Beans (EJBs), using application server beasts like JBoss and WebLogic that favored monolith architectures, and I was instantly drawn to Elasticsearch's simplified architecture—especially its programming-language-agnostic support, out-of-the-box functionality, performance, and excellent documentation. It took me a couple of years to embrace Elasticsearch's full potential and adopt it in its entirety.

Despite Elasticsearch's simplicity and robust capabilities, I realized that the learning curve was steep, and its intricate internal mechanisms warranted guided navigation through the myriad features and inherent challenges. Understanding the countless features and labyrinth of documentation required hand-holding. This realization led me to approach Andy Waldron at Manning.

Creating a book is an endeavor that often requires late nights, sacrificed weekends, and holidays spent at the writing desk. It's a colossal task that could never see fruition without the unwavering support of family. And in this case, it was a two-year journey marked by relentless focus and determination to bring this book into your hands.

While I am typically reserved about my achievements, I can't help but acknowledge the hard work that went into this particular project. It deserves a self-issued pat on the back. Over the course of these two years, not a single day was clouded by self-doubt, and that's a feat worth celebrating.

Now, as you read *Elasticsearch in Action, Second Edition* I feel a profound sense of gratitude and delight. I appreciate your purchase and am excited for you to embark on this journey into the world of Elasticsearch.

As big data and cloud computing have grown with unprecedented momentum over the last decade, so have the depth and breadth of Elasticsearch's capabilities. Its relevance has continued to expand, reflecting the evolving demands and opportunities of these dynamic technological landscapes. Its advanced features, including multi-language analyzers, geospatial and time-series storage, anomaly detection using machine learning algorithms, graph analytics, auto-complete and fuzzy searching, root cause analysis using log stores, rich visualizations of data, complex aggregations, and many more, make Elasticsearch a must-have tool for most organizations and businesses.

I sincerely hope you enjoy reading this book as much as I've enjoyed writing it!

acknowledgments

A book is never born from thin air! It is an embodiment of dedication, the outcome of endless hours spent in meticulous planning, steadfast dedication, and tireless effort. This process has been a joint endeavor involving the unending and loving support of my family, the teamwork and expertise of the Manning staff, the encouragement of friends and colleagues, and, of course, the continued interest and support of readers like you. We all stuck together for two years, dedicated and determined, focused and fervent, with one aim: to produce *Elasticsearch in Action*. And we did it!

I must give my sincere and heartfelt thanks to my wife, Jeannette D'Souza, who has been a rock of support throughout this journey. Her endless patience, understanding, and encouragement have been an unwavering beacon during the long nights and demanding moments. She has been not just a partner but also a pillar of strength and resilience, transforming this arduous process into a journey of love and determination. For this, and for everything else that she is, I am eternally grateful.

Equally, I extend heartfelt gratitude to my son, Josh, whose love and unconditional, unquestioning support have been a wellspring of strength during these challenging times. His understanding (when I missed out on summers and holidays) and encouragement brought this book to life.

My profound gratitude to my mom, who resided with me for half a year during this process. Her caring presence manifested in loving gestures, from serving early morning coffee to preparing hearty breakfasts, mouthwatering savories, and delightful snacks. Her support has truly been a source of comfort and strength.

My heartfelt appreciation goes to my two brothers, niece, and immediate family. Their understanding and support have given me strength even when my writing obligations resulted in less frequent communication. Their consistent encouragement serves as the fuel that propels my endeavors, keeping the engine of my creativity running smoothly.

I must express my deepest gratitude to Venkat Subramaniam. His esteemed stature as an author is only outmatched by his willingness to help me and others. He lent his wisdom to my earlier chapters, providing invaluable advice that truly helped to connect with the reader. Regardless of how packed his schedule was, Venkat always found the time to assist me. His support has been instrumental, and for this, I can't thank him enough.

Without the invaluable guidance and unyielding support of Andy Waldron, my editor at Manning, this book would never have made it from concept to reality. His expertise and encouragement have been instrumental in the journey of this book toward the light of publication.

A special note of appreciation is due to Ian Hough, my developmental editor, whose patience and editorial acumen were nothing short of extraordinary. His ability to strategically oversee the planning of each chapter, ensuring that I remained on course, was instrumental in shaping this book. Even when timelines slipped, his understanding was commendable. His contributions have truly been invaluable.

My developmental copy editor, Frances Buran, worked magic in every part of the book. She relentlessly improved the writing quality, making sure my non-native language sounded good on the page.

Sincere and special thanks to copy editor Tiffany Taylor, whose linguistic expertise has been invaluable in ensuring grammatical precision and coherence throughout the book. Her meticulous efforts have significantly enhanced the clarity and readability of this work. She caught my silly and embarrassing mistakes instantly. Tiffany managed to complete the final editing efficiently and effectively.

I would like to sincerely thank Melena Selic, Marina Matesic, Rebecca Rinehart, Aria Ducic, and Susan Honeywell at Manning for making this book such a high-quality product. Without your unending help and guidance, the book would not have been possible. Huge thanks as well to the production staff at Manning for their hard work in creating this book.

My thanks to Al Krinker, my technical development editor, who reviewed each chapter with fresh eyes and a fresh perspective. Al jumped into each chapter almost the minute it reached him, so I was able to review his feedback while the chapters were fresh in my mind.

I also want to thank Simon Hewitt and Simone Cafiero for their timely technical feedback and for checking and testing the code. Their input was invaluable.

My appreciation, as well, to a few of my friends and colleagues: Herodotos Koukkides, Semi, Jason Dynes, and George Theofanous. There are a few others that I cannot name, but they have been instrumental in my journey! Thank you from the bottom of my heart!

If there's a group to whom I feel most indebted, it's undoubtedly my reviewers and readers. They played a critical role in refining the quality of this book. I extend my most sincere appreciation to the following reviewers: Adam Wan, Alan Moffet, Alessandro

Campeis, Andrei Mihai, Andres Sacco, Bruno Sonnino, Dainius Jocas, Dan Kacenjar, Edward Ribeiro, Fernando Bernardino, Frans Oilinki, George Onofrei, Giampiero Granatella, Giovanni Costagliola, Hugo Figueiredo, Jaume López, Jim Amrhein, Kent Spillner, Manuel R. Ciosici, Milorad Imbra, Dale S. Francis, Muneeb Shaikh, Paul Grebenc, Raymond Cheung, Richard Vaughan, Sai Gummaluri, Sayeef Rahim, Sergio Fernandez Gonzalez, Simone Cafiero, Simone Sguazza, Srihari Sridharan, Sumit K Singh, Vittorio Marino, and William Jamir Silva. Their invaluable feedback has greatly contributed to shaping this book into the resource it is today. Their insights and perspectives have been absolutely indispensable.

about this book

Who should read this book

This book will be an invaluable resource for anyone looking to gain an in-depth understanding of Elasticsearch and its practical applications. In particular, the following will benefit from reading *Elasticsearch in Action*:

- Developers, architects, analysts, managers, or product owners who are beginners in the realm of Elasticsearch and wish to understand its basic workings
- Data scientists who wish to implement Elasticsearch in their data pipelines for real-time analysis and processing of data
- System administrators who maintain large databases and would like to use Elasticsearch to enhance data retrieval efficiency and overall system performance
- IT consultants or technical advisors who need to understand Elasticsearch so they can recommend it in client projects and make strategic IT decisions
- Tech-savvy business owners who want to understand how Elasticsearch can enhance their operational efficiency or provide additional value to their customers
- Students and academic researchers in computer science, data science, or related fields who are studying big data technologies and are interested in learning about search technologies
- Individuals who handle large sets of data and are keen on using Elasticsearch to enhance their search capabilities, including full-text, fuzzy, term-level searches, and other complex search features
- Aspiring Elasticsearch architects, developers, or analysts aiming to design and develop microservices communicating with Elasticsearch clusters

How this book is organized: A road map

Although this book is not divided into parts, the chapters follow a clear linear progression, beginning with an introduction to Elasticsearch from a feature and architecture perspective:

- Chapter 1 embarks on a journey through the world of search, retracing the steps from rudimentary database-backed systems to the sophisticated search engines that are the norm today. We shine a spotlight on Elasticsearch, a powerful, versatile modern search engine that has redefined the capabilities of search functions, bringing to the forefront its distinct features, real-world applications, and widespread adoption.

  We also look ahead to the transformative potential of general artificial intelligence tools. We examine the exciting possibilities of technologies like ChatGPT, exploring how they could reshape the search space and redefine our interactions with information in the future.

- Chapter 2 dives headfirst into Elasticsearch, providing hands-on experience with indexing and retrieving documents using the document APIs. We also execute search queries using the search APIs. The chapter takes you through essential search criteria, from pattern matching to phrase searches, spelling corrections, range results, multi-field searches, and more. A glimpse at advanced queries further enriches the learning experience. The chapter concludes with a look at data sorting, result pagination, highlighting, and other impressive functionalities that elevate the user's search capabilities.

- Chapter 3 demystifies the architecture of Elasticsearch, guiding you through its foundational components and the intricate processes that enable searching and indexing. This exploration covers fundamental concepts that power the search engine, including the inverted index, relevancy, and text analysis. We also explore clustering and the distributed nature of the Elasticsearch server.

- Chapter 4 explores mapping schemas, data types, and mapping APIs, providing a detailed overview of data handling in Elasticsearch. The chapter looks at how mapping schemas enhance search accuracy and efficiency, thoroughly examining dynamic and explicit mapping. The exploration extends to core data types, including `text`, `keyword`, `date`, and `integer`. The chapter concludes with advanced data types such as `geo_point`, `geo_shape`, `object`, `join`, `flattened`, and more.

- Chapter 5 offers a comprehensive discussion of single- and multi-document APIs and their associated operations. This chapter provides a practical understanding of indexing, retrieving, updating, and deleting documents using these APIs. It also explores the reindexing feature.

- Chapter 6 zooms in on indexing operations using the indexing APIs. It also guides you through the foundational configurations of an index, including settings, mapping, and aliases. This exploration provides an understanding of creating customized indexes tailored for production scenarios. The chapter also looks at working with index templates, discussing the mechanics of index and composable templates. The final section investigates index lifecycle management.

- Chapter 7 immerses us in text analysis, examining how full text is tokenized and normalized using Elasticsearch's analyzer modules. We look at the mechanics of text analysis, exploring built-in analyzers like the `standard`, `simple`, `keyword`, and language analyzers. This chapter will empower you with the knowledge to create custom analyzers.

Chapters 8 through 13 are dedicated to search:

- Chapter 8 lays the groundwork for understanding the fundamentals of search, explaining the mechanics of how search requests are processed and responses generated. We introduce two primary types of search: URL request and Query DSL. We also examine cross-cutting features like highlighting, sorting, pagination, and others, providing a comprehensive introduction to Elasticsearch's search functionality.

- Chapter 9 explores the realm of term-level queries, which are specifically designed for structured data. The chapter offers a detailed examination of various types of term-level queries, including range, prefix, wildcard, and fuzzy queries.

- Chapter 10 looks at full-text queries designed specifically for searching unstructured data. The chapter examines the mechanics of using full-text search APIs, employing a variety of queries including match family queries, query strings, fuzzy queries, and simple string queries, among others.

- Chapter 11 navigates the intricate world of compound queries, highlighting the Boolean query as a versatile tool for crafting advanced search queries. We look at the use of conditional clauses like `must`, `must_not`, `should`, and `filter` to structure leaf queries into more complex, compound queries. The chapter concludes with a detailed examination of boosting and `constant_score` queries.

- Chapter 12 introduces specialized queries, including `distance_feature`, `percolator`, `more_like_this`, and `pinned`. The chapter examines the unique benefits of each type of query, such as the `distance_feature` query's ability to prioritize results closer to a given location and the `more_like_this` query's function of finding similar-looking documents. The `percolator` query, which alerts users to newly available results, is also examined in detail.

- Chapter 13 offers a detailed examination of aggregations. We explore metrics aggregations, generating statistics like sum, average, minimum, maximum, top hits, and mode. The chapter also highlights the use of bucket aggregations in collecting aggregated data into sets of buckets. We also look at pipeline aggregations, which provide advanced statistical analytics like derivatives and moving averages.

The last two chapters round out the book with a focus on administration and performance:

- Chapter 14 examines the administrative side of productionizing Elasticsearch. This includes understanding how to scale the cluster under various loads, communication between nodes, and shard sizing. The chapter also explores the crucial concept of snapshotting, providing practical examples of taking a snapshot and retrieving data from it when needed. Advanced configurations and the cluster master concept are also thoroughly examined.
- Chapter 15 dives into troubleshooting a poorly performing or issue-ridden Elasticsearch cluster. The chapter examines common causes, such as search and speed bottlenecks, unstable and unhealthy clusters, and circuit breakers, among others. This chapter will equip you with the knowledge to diagnose and address performance issues, ensuring that your Elasticsearch cluster runs smoothly and efficiently.

The book also has three appendixes:

- Appendix A is a practical guide to installing Elasticsearch and Kibana in your local environment.
- Appendix B examines ingest pipelines, a key component of data preprocessing in Elasticsearch, and how to configure and use them in various scenarios.
- Appendix C covers Elasticsearch's interoperability with various programming languages through clients such as Java, Python, JavaScript, C#, and others, offering examples and best practices.

About the code

One of the primary goals of this book is to provide a seamless hands-on experience by including easily executable code. After several iterations, a decision was made to host all the queries, written and executed on Kibana, in a text file on GitHub. These queries are captured as Query DSL-based JSON code. The aim is to provide a straightforward process where you can copy the text file from GitHub and paste it into your Kibana Dev Tools application for immediate execution.

To further aid in your learning journey, sample data files and, when necessary, mappings for these indexes are provided in a dedicated datasets folder. This approach ensures a practical, learner-friendly experience that allows you to engage directly with the material and apply your newfound knowledge.

The source code is available on GitHub (https://github.com/madhusudhan konda/elasticsearch-in-action) and the book's website (https://www.manning.com/books/elasticsearch-in-action-second-edition). The folders are as follows:

- *kibana_scripts*—Query DSL scripts for each chapter.
- *datasets*—Mappings and sample data sets required for the book chapters.
- *code*—Java and Python code.

- *docker*—Docker files to run the services on the local environment. For example, elasticsearch-docker-8-6-2.yml hosts two services: Elasticsearch and Kibana. So when you execute the `docker-compose up` command, it starts both Elasticsearch and Kibana in the Docker container.
- *appendices*—Given the pace of Elasticsearch development, this book will need to be updated. New features will be provided as appendixes to the book on GitHub. I will add and modify content as new releases surface.

Elasticsearch releases occur pretty frequently—we were on version 7.x when I started writing this book, and the version was 8.7 as the book was preparing to go to print. And I expect a few more major and minor releases from Elastic by the time you read this! It would be a huge task to update the code base whenever a new release comes out. I will try to keep the code updated, but I will also be more than happy for contributors to maintain the codebase. So, please reach out to me if you'd like to be a contributor to this project.

This book contains many examples of source code, both in numbered listings and in line with normal text. In both cases, source code is formatted in a `fixed-width font like this` to separate it from ordinary text.

In many cases, the original source code has been reformatted; we've added line breaks and reworked indentation to accommodate the available page space in the book. In rare cases, even this was not enough, and listings include line-continuation markers (➥). Additionally, comments in the source code have often been removed from the listings when the code is described in the text. Code annotations accompany many of the listings, highlighting important concepts.

liveBook discussion forum

Purchase of *Elasticsearch in Action, Second Edition* includes free access to liveBook, Manning's online reading platform. Using liveBook's exclusive discussion features, you can attach comments to the book globally or to specific sections or paragraphs. It's a snap to make notes for yourself, ask and answer technical questions, and receive help from the author and other users. To access the forum, go to https://livebook .manning.com/book/elasticsearch-in-action-second-edition. You can also learn more about Manning's forums and the rules of conduct at https://livebook.manning.com/ discussion.

Manning's commitment to our readers is to provide a venue where a meaningful dialogue between individual readers and between readers and the author can take place. It is not a commitment to any specific amount of participation on the part of the author, whose contribution to the forum remains voluntary (and unpaid). We suggest you try asking the author some challenging questions lest his interest stray! The forum and the archives of previous discussions will be accessible from the publisher's website as long as the book is in print.

about the author

MADHUSUDHAN KONDA is a seasoned technologist with an unwavering commitment to simplifying the intricate, steering the big picture, and diving into the new frontiers of programming languages and advanced frameworks. His passion for technology is not just a profession, but also a lifelong journey of exploration and learning. He thrives on the art of translating complex issues into simpler, more manageable solutions, providing a clear compass in the ever-evolving tech landscape.

Throughout his 25-year career, Madhu has donned many hats, including those of a solution architect, lead/principal engineer, and others. However, his roles have always been underscored by a fervent desire to share knowledge and nurture his colleagues in their understanding of programming languages, frameworks, and emerging technologies.

Madhu's expertise has been instrumental in architecting and delivering high-caliber solutions for a host of clients ranging from banks like Credit Suisse, UBS, Mizuho, Deutsche Bank, and Halifax to energy and aviation leaders British Petroleum and British Airways, among others.

His proficiency extends beyond leading and delivering software projects from inception to completion and architecting solutions for complex business issues. Madhu is a strategist and visionary, known for his adeptness in crafting strategic roadmaps, cost-efficient architectures, and product designs. His leadership style combines mentorship with thought leadership, always pushing boundaries and inspiring teams to reach their potential. He takes pride in teaching and training professionals ranging from beginners to seniors as well as mentoring and guiding juniors.

In addition to his impressive career, Madhu is a celebrated author. His books and video courses on Java, Spring, and the Hibernate ecosystem have been warmly received, further highlighting his commitment to fostering a culture of learning and exploration in the world of technology. He is an enthusiastic blogger, always trying to pen insightful pieces that go beyond technology, delving into the crucial realm of engineers' soft skills.

In his pursuit of clarity and conciseness, Madhu persistently strives to distill complex technological concepts into digestible content. His philosophy centers on simplifying intricate ideas to a level that even a 10-year-old could comprehend, thereby making advanced technology accessible and understandable to all.

about the cover illustration

The figure on the cover of *Elasticsearch in Action, Second Edition* is "A Man from Croatia," taken from an album of Croatian traditional costumes from the mid-nineteenth century by Nikola Arsenovic.

In those days, it was easy to identify where people lived and what their trade or station in life was just by their dress. Manning celebrates the inventiveness and initiative of the computer business with book covers based on the rich diversity of regional culture centuries ago, brought back to life by pictures from collections such as this one.

Overview *1*

This chapter covers

- Setting the scene for modern search engines
- Introducing Elasticsearch
- Understanding Elasticsearch's core areas, use cases, and prominent features
- The Elastic Stack: Beats, Logstash, Elasticsearch, and Kibana

The explosion of data in recent years has led to a new normal in terms of the standards expected of search and analytics functionality. As organizations amass data, the ability to find the "needle in the haystack" is a paramount necessity. In addition to search, being able to zoom out and aggregate data using analytical functionality has become a mandatory requirement for organizations. The last decade has seen exponential adoption of modern search and analytics engines. One such modern search engine is Elasticsearch.

Elasticsearch is a powerful and popular open source distributed search and analytics engine. It is built on top of the Apache Lucene library and can perform near-real-time search and analytics on structured and unstructured data. It is designed to handle large amounts of data efficiently.

Elasticsearch has come a long way in enabling organizations to utilize its powerful features in the search and analytics space. In addition to search and analytics use cases, it is used for application and infrastructure log analytics, enterprise security and threat detection, application performance and monitoring, distributed datastores, and more.

In this chapter, we examine the search space in general and skim over the evolution of search, from a traditional database-backed search to current modern search engines and their many convenient features. Along the way, we introduce Elasticsearch, the ultra-fast open source search engine, and examine its features, use cases, and customer adoption.

We also take a quick look at how generative artificial intelligence (AI) tools are beginning to unravel and disrupt the search space. With the advent of ChatGPT, a race to embrace AI and become the leader in the search space has begun. We dedicate a section to introducing the current players and exploring the future of AI-led search engines.

1.1   What makes a good search engine?

Let's take a moment to consider what makes a search engine "good" in terms of everyday experience. To help picture this, let's consider an experience I had with a bad search engine.

Recently my family adopted a puppy, Milly (that's her, pictured!). As we are first-time owners of a pup, we started searching online for dog food. I browsed my preferred grocer's website, but to my disappointment, the search results were not what I was looking for. The list of results included "poop bags" (the last thing you expect when searching for dog food) and other non-relevant products. The website also didn't have filters, dropdowns, or price-range selectors; it was just a plain page showing the search results, with clunky pagination enabled.

Not happy with my current grocer's search (curiosity overtook me—I was eager to find out how other search engines were implemented), I took my search to other grocers. One website presented a pet harness, while others were more hit and miss, including a search that showed me a baby's lunch box!

Not only did I get poor results from my search, but the search engines behind these supermarkets also didn't provide suggestions while I typed; nor did they correct my input when I misspelled *dog food* as *dig fod* (we are spoiled by Google when it comes to suggestions and corrections—we expect every search engine to have features similar to Google's). Most didn't bother suggesting alternatives or similar items. Some of the results weren't relevant (i.e., based on relevancy—although this can be forgiven, as not all search engines are expected to produce relevant results). One grocer returned 2,400 results for a simple search!

Not pleased with the results from the various supermarkets, I headed to Amazon, the popular online shop, where I encountered a *good* search engine. The second I started typing *dog*, a dropdown showed me suggestions (see the figure next to this paragraph). By default, an initial search on Amazon returns relevant (pretty close to what we're searching for) results. Using the Sort by Featured option, we can change the sort order (low to high prices or vice versa, etc.) if need be. Once the initial search is carried out, we can also drill down into other categories by selecting the department, average customer review, price range, and so on. I even tried a wrong spelling: *dig food*. Amazon asked me if I meant *dog food*. Clever, eh?

In the current digital world, search is in the spotlight. Organizations are adopting search without a second thought because they understand the business value a search engine offers and the varied use cases it can address. In the next section, we explore the exponential growth of search engines and how technology has enabled the creation of cutting-edge search solutions.

1.2   Search is the new normal

With the exponential growth of data (terabytes to petabytes to exabytes), the need for a tool that enables successful searches in needle-in-a-haystack situations is imperative. What was once touted as a simple search is now necessary functionality for most organizations' survival toolkits. Organizations are expected to provide a search function by default so customers can type in a search bar or navigate search drilldowns to locate what they need in a jiffy.

It is increasingly difficult to find websites and applications that don't have a humble search bar with a little magnifying glass. Providing full-fledged search is a competitive advantage.

Today, modern search engines strive for speed and relevancy as well as providing advanced functionality packaged in a rich set of business and technical features. Elasticsearch is one such modern search engine, embracing search and analytics with speed and performance at its heart. When dealing with search engines such as Elasticsearch, you'll come across data and search variants: structured and unstructured data and their respective searches. It is important to be familiar with these types of data in order to understand the search landscape. We look at them briefly in the next section.

1.2.1   Structured vs. unstructured (full-text) data

Data predominantly comes in two flavors: structured and unstructured. The fundamental differentiator between these two categories is the way the data is stored and analyzed. Structured data follows a predefined schema/model, while unstructured data is free-form, unorganized, and schema-free.

STRUCTURED DATA

Structured data is very organized, has a definite shape and format, and fits predefined data type patterns. It follows a defined schema and is easily searchable because it is well organized. The data in a database is considered structured data because before it is stored in the database, it is expected to follow a strict schema. For example, data representing dates, numbers, or Booleans must be in a specific format.

Queries against structured data return results in exact matches. That is, we are concerned with finding documents that match the search criteria—but not how well they match. Such search results are binary: we either have a result or have no result—there's no "maybe" result. For example, it doesn't make sense to expect "maybe" canceled flights when searching for "canceled flights in the last month." There may be zero or more, but the search should not return "close match to canceled flights" results.

We do not worry about *how well documents match*—just that they match at all. Hence, no relevancy score (a positive number given to each result that indicates how closely the result matches the query) is attached to the results. A traditional database search is this sort: fetch all the flights that were canceled in the last month, weekly bestseller books, the activity of a logged-in user, and so on.

> **DEFINITION** *Relevancy* refers to the degree to which a search engine's results match a user's query. It's a mechanism for indicating how closely the results match the original query. The search engine uses relevance algorithms to determine which documents are closely related to the user's query (that is, how relevant they are) and produces a positive number called a *relevancy score* for each result based on how closely the result matches the query. The next time you search on Google, look closely at the search results: the top results are very closely related to what you are looking for, and hence we can say they are *more relevant* than the bottom entries in the list of results. Google internally assigns a relevancy score to each result and most likely sorts them by this score: the higher the score, the more relevant the result, and hence the more likely it is to be at the top of the page.

UNSTRUCTURED DATA

Unstructured data, on the other hand, is unorganized and follows no schema or format. It has no predefined structure. Unstructured data is the bread and butter of most modern search engines. Examples include blog posts, research articles, emails, PDFs, audio and video files, and so on.

> **NOTE** In addition to structured and unstructured data, there's another category: semi-structured data. This data falls pretty much in between structured and unstructured data. It is nothing but unstructured data with some metadata describing it.

For unstructured data, Elasticsearch offers full-text search capabilities that allow us to search for specific terms or phrases within large amounts of unstructured text. Full-text (unstructured) queries try to find results that are relevant to the query. That is, Elasticsearch searches all the documents that are most suited for the query. For example, if a user searches for the keyword *vaccine*, the search engine not only retrieves documents related to vaccination but also throws in relevant documents about inoculations, jabs, and other vaccine-related terms.

Elasticsearch employs a similarity algorithm to generate a relevance score for full-text queries. The score is a positive floating-point number attached to the results, with the highest-scored document indicating more relevance to the query criteria.

Elasticsearch handles both structured and unstructured data efficiently. One of its key features is its ability to index and search both structured and unstructured data in the same index. This allows us to search and analyze both types of data together and gain insights that would be difficult to obtain otherwise.

1.2.2 *Search supported by a database*

Old-fashioned search was mostly based on traditional relational databases. Older search engines were based on layered architectures implemented in multi-tiered applications, as shown in figure 1.1.

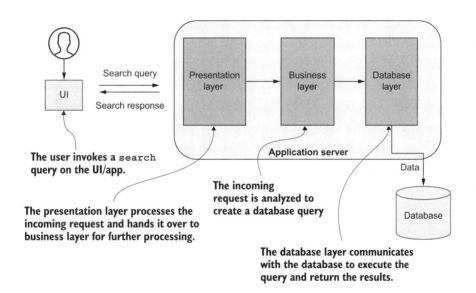

Figure 1.1 Search based on a traditional database

Queries written in SQL using clauses like *where* and *like* provided the foundation for search. These solutions are not necessarily performant and efficient for searching full-text data to provide modern search functionality.

Having said that, some modern databases (Oracle and MySQL, for example) support full-text searching (queries against free text like a blog post, movie review, research article, etc.), but they may struggle to provide efficient searches in near-real time on heavy loads. See the sidebar "Full-text searching with databases" for more details.

The distributed nature of a search engine like Elasticsearch provides instant scalability that most databases are not designed for. A search engine developed with a backing database (with no full-text search capabilities) may not be able to provide *relevant* search results for queries, let alone cope with volumetric growth and serve results in real time.

> **Full-text searching with databases**
>
> Relational databases like Oracle and MySQL support full-text search functionality, albeit with less functionality than a modern full-text search engine like Elasticsearch. They are fundamentally different when it comes to storing and retrieving data, so you must be sure to prototype your requirements before choosing one of them. Usually, if the schemas are not going to change or data loads are low, and you already have a database engine with full-text search capabilities, beginning with full-text search on a database may make sense.

1.2.3 *Databases vs. search engines*

When building a search service on a traditional database, we need to consider and understand whether our requirements can be satisfied by the database efficiently and effectively. Most databases are designed to store large amounts of data but, unfortunately, are not well-suited for use as full-text search engines, for several reasons:

- *Indexing and search performance*—Full-text search requires efficient indexing and performant search and analytical capabilities, which traditional databases are not optimized for. Databases may struggle with indexing large volumes of data and, as a result, may exhibit poor query performance. Search engines like Elasticsearch and Solr are specifically designed to handle large amounts of text data and provide search results in near-real time. Search engines can handle large-scale data, indexing it and searching it much faster than traditional databases, as they are pretty much designed from the ground up for optimized search operations. Unfortunately, relational databases lack advanced search features such as fuzzy logic, stemming, synonyms, and so on.

- *Search*—Searching with traditional databases is more or less based on the exact matching of data values. While this is suitable for non-search-related find operations on structured data, it is a definite no-no for natural language queries, which are often complex. User queries are often misspelled, misconstructed grammatically, or incomplete and may contain synonyms and other language structures that databases fail to understand

  In natural language queries, users may not use the exact terms they are searching for (spelling mistakes), and unfortunately, traditional databases are not designed to support misspelled user input. This feature is supported by the fuzzy matching search function (words that are similar but not exactly the same) in modern search engines

In traditional databases, data is often *normalized*, meaning it is spread across multiple tables and columns. This can make it difficult to search for data across multiple fields in a single query. Traditional databases are not designed to handle the types of unstructured and semi-structured data that are common in full-text search scenarios.

– *Text analysis and processing*—Search engines must often handle multiple languages and character sets, which traditional databases may not support. Search engines perform text analysis and processing to extract meaning from text, but traditional databases are not designed or optimized for this purpose.

– *Scalability and flexibility*—Full-text search engines are designed to handle large amounts of data and high query loads. Traditional databases can have scalability problems when dealing with large amounts of text data.

Search engines are designed from scratch to handle unstructured data, while databases are optimized for handling structured data. These limitations make traditional databases less suitable for use as full-text search engines; specialized search engine technologies such as Elasticsearch, Solr, Lucene, etc., are often used to provide advanced search functionality for text data.

> **NOTE** Many databases have added text search capabilities to their feature sets. However, they still may not be able to deliver performance, scalability, and functionality on par with specialized full-text search engines.

Nothing is stopping us from embracing both worlds: in some use cases, a combination of traditional databases and search engines can be employed. For example, a database can be used for transactional purposes and a search engine for search and analytics. But our focus in this book is search engines—and Elasticsearch in particular. In the next section, we review the era of modern search engines before we introduce Elasticsearch.

1.3 Modern search engines

Modern search engines are trying hard to meet ever-growing business requirements by embracing new and exciting features every day. Cheap hardware combined with the explosion of data is leading to the emergence of these modern search beasts. Let's consider present-day search engines and the features and functionality they offer. We can summarize what a good modern search engine should provide as follows:

- First-class support for full-text (unstructured) and structured data
- Type-ahead suggestions, auto-correction, and "did-you-mean" recommendations
- Forgiveness for users' spelling mistakes
- Search capabilities on geolocations
- Easy scalability, either up or down, based on fluctuating demand
- Blazing performance: speedy indexing and search capabilities
- Architecture that provides a high-availability, fault-tolerant distributed system
- Support for machine learning functionalities

In this section, we briefly discuss the high-level features of a modern search engine. Then the following section introduces a couple of search engines available in the market, including Elasticsearch.

1.3.1 *Functionality*

Modern search engines were developed to satisfy full-text search requirements while also providing other advanced functions. They are designed to provide fast and relevant search results to users by indexing and searching large volumes of text data (going forward, we will drop the word *modern* when mentioning search engines).

Search engines can quickly index large amounts of text data and make it searchable. This process typically involves breaking the text data into tokens and building an inverted index, which maps each token to the documents that contain it.

Search engines are also expected to perform advanced text analysis and processing, such as synonyms, stemming, stop words, and other natural language processing techniques, to extract meaning from text and improve search results. They can process user queries and rank search results based on various factors such as relevance and popularity. They can also handle high query loads and large amounts of data and can scale horizontally by adding more nodes to a cluster.

Finally, search engines provide advanced analytics capabilities, looking at the data to provide summaries, conclusions, and intelligence for businesses. They also support rich visualizations, near-real-time search, performance monitoring, and machine learning-based insights.

1.3.2 *Popular search engines*

While a handful of search engines are available in the market, I'll mention just three of them, all of which are built on top of Apache Lucene. The following sections look at Elasticsearch, Solr, and OpenSearch.

ELASTICSEARCH

Shay Banon, founder of Elastic, developed a search product called Compass in early 2000. It was based on an open source search engine library called Apache Lucene (https://lucene.apache.org). Lucene is Doug Cutting's full-text search library, written in Java. Because it's a library, we must import it and integrate it with an application using its APIs. Compass and other search engines use Lucene to provide a generalized search engine service so we don't have to integrate Lucene from scratch into applications. Shay eventually decided to abandon Compass and focus on Elasticsearch because it had more potential.

APACHE SOLR

Apache Solr is an open source search engine that was built on Apache Lucene in 2004. Solr is a strong competitor to Elasticsearch and has a thriving user community, and it is closer to open source than Elasticsearch (Elastic moved from Apache to Elastic License and Server Side Public License ([SSPL] in early 2021). Both Solr and Elasticsearch excel at full-text searching; however, Elasticsearch may have an edge when it comes to analytics.

While both products compete in almost all functionality, Solr is a favorite for large, static datasets working in big data ecosystems. Obviously, we have to run through prototypes and analysis to pick a product; the general trend is for projects that are integrating with a search engine for the first time to consider Elasticsearch due to its topclass documentation, community, and nearly no-hurdle startup. You must make a detailed comparison of your intended use cases for the search engine before adopting and embracing one.

AMAZON OPENSEARCH

Elastic changed its licensing policy in 2021. The licensing, which applies to Elasticsearch release versions 7.11 and above, has been moved from open source to a dual license under an Elastic License and SSPL. This license allows the community to use the product for free, as expected, but managed service providers can no longer provide the products as services. There was a spat between Elastic and Amazon Web Services (AWS) when AWS created a forked version of Elasticsearch—called Open Distro for Elasticsearch—and offered it as a managed service. This spat led to the change in the license, which eventually led to OpenSearch's birth.

As Elastic moved from the open source licensing model to the SSPL model, a new product called OpenSearch (https://opensearch.org) was developed to fill the gaping hole left by the new licensing agreement. The base code for OpenSearch was created from the open source Elasticsearch and Kibana version 7.10.2. The product's first General Availability version 1.0 was released in July 2021. Watch out for OpenSearch becoming a competitor to Elasticsearch in the search engine space.

Now that we have a fair understanding of what a modern search engine is and the shape of the search landscape, let's jump into an overview of Elasticsearch.

1.4 Elasticsearch overview

Elasticsearch is an open source search and analytics engine. Developed in Java, it is an ultra-fast, highly available search engine built on the popular full-text library Apache Lucene (https://lucene.apache.org). Elasticsearch wraps around the powerful functionality of Lucene by providing a distributed system with RESTful interfaces. Lucene is the powerhouse of Elasticsearch, and Kibana is the administrative UI to manage and work with Elasticsearch. We work with Kibana's code editor (Dev Tools) throughout this book.

Full-text searching is where Elasticsearch excels as a modern search engine. It can retrieve relevant documents in response to a user's search criteria at an awesome speed. We can search for exact terms, too, like keywords, dates, or a range of numbers or dates. Elasticsearch is packed with top-notch features such as relevancy, "did-you-mean" suggestions, auto-completion, fuzzy and geospatial searching, highlighting, and more.

In addition to being a frontrunner in providing near-real-time search capabilities, Elasticsearch stands tall in statistical aggregations on big data. Of course, we must consider the use case before embracing the product, as Elasticsearch may not be the best fit for every use case (refer to section 1.4.3 to learn about the use cases). Out of the box, Elasticsearch also boasts commendable features such as application performance monitoring, predictive analytics and outlier detection, and security threat monitoring and detection.

Elasticsearch focuses on finding a deeper meaning in the data that's been collected. It can aggregate data, perform statistical calculations, and find intelligence within the data. We can create rich visualizations and dashboards and share them with others using Kibana tooling. Elasticsearch can find averages, sums, means, and modes as well as undertaking complex analytics such as bucketing data in histograms and other analytical functions.

Furthermore, Elasticsearch runs supervised and unsupervised machine learning algorithms on our data. Models help to detect anomalies, find outliers, and forecast events. In supervised learning mode, we can provide training sets so the model learns and makes predictions.

Elasticsearch also comes with the capability to observe applications and their health by monitoring performance metrics such as the memory and CPU cycles of the web servers in a network. It lets us sift through millions of web server logs to find or debug application issues. Elasticsearch also invests time and resources in building security solutions: for example, alerting us to security threats, IP filtering, endpoint prevention, and more.

1.4.1   Core areas

Elastic, the company behind Elasticsearch, has been positioning itself predominantly in three core areas: search, observability, and security, as shown in figure 1.2. Let's look at each of these areas in turn.

Elastic Enterprise Search
Workplace, website, and app search

Elastic Observability
Unified logs, metrics, and APM data

Elastic Security
SIEM, endpoint, and threat hunting

Figure 1.2   Core application areas of Elastic, the company behind Elasticsearch

ELASTIC ENTERPRISE SEARCH

Whether letting users search across varied content providers (like Slack, Confluence, Google Drive, and others) or enabling search capabilities for our applications, apps, and websites, the Elastic Enterprise Search suite helps build models and a customized search engine.

Search can be integrated deep into a multitude of applications in various domains—business, infrastructure, applications, and so on. Users can create a web application backed by Elasticsearch, a mobile app supported by Elasticsearch, or a server-side search service with Elasticsearch as the spine for search capabilities. Later in this book, we work on examples of integrating with Elasticsearch as a search server for applications.

ELASTIC OBSERVABILITY

Applications running on infrastructure produce a lot of metrics that are usually used for application observability and monitoring. We can use Elasticsearch in the observability space: the state of applications, servers, racks, and modules can all be monitored, logged, tracked, and alerted. We can also use the Elastic tools to perform application management and monitoring on a large scale.

ELASTIC SECURITY

Elastic enters the realm of security by enabling threat detection and prevention and providing advanced features such as the capability of removing malware at the source, encryption at rest, and more. As a security information and event management (SIEM) tool, Elastic is positioning itself to protect organizations with its advanced security toolkits.

1.4.2 Elastic Stack

Elasticsearch is the core of the search engine, and a handful of Elastic products complement it. The suite of products is called the Elastic Stack and includes Kibana, Logstash, Beats, and Elasticsearch. (It was formally called ELK Stack but was renamed Elastic Stack after Beats was introduced into the product suite.)

The combination of these four products helps build an enterprise application by integrating, consuming, processing, analyzing, searching, and storing various data sets from disparate sources. As demonstrated in figure 1.3, Beats and Logstash bring the data into Elasticsearch, while Kibana is the visual UI that works on that data.

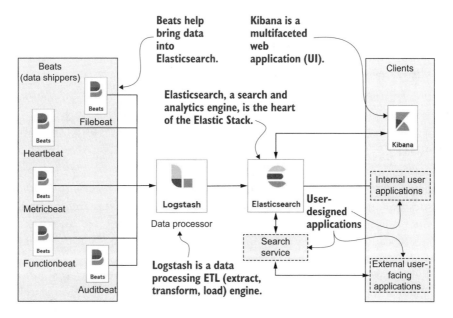

Figure 1.3 The Elastic Stack: Beats, Logstash, Elasticsearch, and Kibana

Before we move on to look at use cases for Elasticsearch, let's briefly go over these essential moving parts at a high level. Other than Elasticsearch, we do not discuss this stack of products in this book.

BEATS

Beats are single purpose data shippers; they load data from out various external systems and pump it into Elasticsearch. Various types of beats are available out of the box. These include Filebeat, Metricbeat, Heartbeat, etc., and each performs a specific data consumption task. These are single-purpose components: for example, Filebeats are designed for file-based transports and Metricbeats for vital machine and operating system memory and CPU information. The beats' agents are installed on the servers so they can consume data from their source and send it to their destination.

LOGSTASH

Logstash is an open source data-processing engine. It extracts data originating from multiple sources, processes it, and sends it to a variety of target destinations. During the processing of the data, Logstash transforms and enriches the data. It supports a myriad of sources and destinations including files, HTTP, JMS, Kafka, Amazon S3, Twitter, and dozens of others. It promotes a pipeline architecture, and every event that goes through the pipeline is parsed as per the preconfigured rules, thus creating a real-time pipeline for data ingestion.

KIBANA

Kibana is a multipurpose web console that provides a host of options such as executing queries; developing dashboards, graphs, and chart visualizations; and creating dropdowns and aggregations. However, we can use any REST client to talk to Elasticsearch to invoke the APIs, not just Kibana. For example, we can invoke APIs using cURL, Postman, or native language clients.

1.4.3   *Elasticsearch use cases*

Pinpointing Elasticsearch for a particular use case or domain is difficult. It is omnipresent in many areas from search to analytics to machine learning jobs. It is widely used across a multitude of industries, including finance, defense, transport, government, retail, cloud, entertainment, space, and more. Let's take a high-level glance at how Elasticsearch can be used in an organization.

SEARCH ENGINE

Elasticsearch has become the go-to technology for its full-text search capabilities. The product is not limited to full-text searching but can also be used for structured data and geolocation-based searches. Broadly speaking, customers use Elasticsearch in three domains: App Search, Enterprise Search, and Site Search.

In *App Search*, Elasticsearch serves as a backbone, providing search and analytical capabilities for applications. A search service backed up by Elasticsearch can be designed as a microservice that serves the application's search requirements, such as searching for customers, orders, invoices, emails, and so on.

In most organizations, data is scattered across many data stores, applications, and databases. For example, organizations are often integrated with Confluence, intranet spaces, Slack, email, databases, cloud drives (iCloud drive, Google Drive, etc.), and others. Collating and searching through vast amounts of data with integrations to varied sources is a challenge for these organizations. This is where Elasticsearch can be employed for *Enterprise Search* and data organization.

If we have an online business website amassing data, providing search is something of a bare necessity for attracting customers and keeping them happy. *Site Search* is a software-as-a-service (SaaS) offering from Elastic that, once enabled, crawls through the given site pages, fetching data and building indices backed by Elasticsearch. Once the crawling and indexing are complete, the site can be integrated easily with the search facility. The Site Search module also helps create a search bar and the code snippet related to it. The website administrator can copy the snippet of generated code onto their homepage to enable a search bar instantly, thus making the website fully functional with integrated search.

BUSINESS ANALYTICS

Organizations capture tons of data from various sources, and that data often holds the key to survival and success. Elasticsearch can help extract trends, statistics, and metrics from data, giving organizations knowledge about their operations, sales, turnover, profits, and many other features for timely management.

SECURITY ANALYTICS AND THREAT AND FRAUD DETECTION

Data security and potential breaches of it are nightmares for organizations. Elasticsearch's security analytics help organizations analyze every bit of information—be it from applications, a network, endpoints, or the cloud. This analysis can provide insights into threats and vulnerabilities and let the organization hunt for malware and ransomware, thus alleviating the risk of falling prey to hackers.

LOGGING AND APPLICATION MONITORING

Applications spit out a lot of data in the form of application logs and metrics. These logs provide insights into the health of the application. With the advent of the cloud and the microservices world, logs are scattered across services, and meaningful analysis is a cumbersome affair. Elasticsearch is our friend here. One of the popular use cases for Elasticsearch is indexing logs and analyzing them for application errors and debugging purposes.

Elasticsearch is a powerful and flexible search and analytics engine, but it's not suitable for every use case. Let's briefly go over the issues we may encounter and use cases for which Elasticsearch is the wrong choice.

1.4.4 Unsuitable Elasticsearch uses

Not every use case can be satisfied by Elasticsearch. It is a powerful and flexible search and analytics engine, but unfortunately, this tool has limitations that we must consider before choosing it for our requirements. Here are a few scenarios where Elasticsearch may be an incorrect or inefficient solution:

- *Relational data*—Elasticsearch is not the right tool to accommodate search over data that has relationships and needs to perform complex database joins. Elasticsearch is not designed to handle complex relational data structures. If your data is relationship-heavy, a relational database like MySQL or PostgreSQL may be a better fit. Most modern databases (MySQL, PostgreSQL, etc.) also offer full-text search capabilities, although the features are not as advanced as in a modern search engine like Elasticsearch.

- *Transactional data*—Elasticsearch is an "eventually consistent" search engine, which makes it unsuitable for applications that require immediate consistency, such as financial transactions. For these types of use cases, consider using a traditional relational database or a NoSQL database like MongoDB.

- *Geospatial data*—While Elasticsearch has built-in support for geospatial data, it may not be the most efficient solution for large-scale geospatial analytics. For these use cases, consider using a dedicated geospatial database like PostGIS or a geospatial analytics platform like ArcGIS.

- *High-write workloads*—Elasticsearch can handle high-read workloads, but it is not optimized for high-write workloads. If you need to index large amounts of data in real time, consider using a dedicated indexing engine like Apache Flume or Apache Kafka.

- *Online analytical processing (OLAP) data*—If you need to perform complex multi-dimensional analysis on large data sets, a traditional OLAP database like Microsoft Analysis Services or IBM Cognos may be a better fit than Elasticsearch.

- *Large binary data*—While Elasticsearch can handle large amounts of text data, it may not be the best solution for indexing and searching large binary data like videos or images. For these use cases, consider using a dedicated binary data store like Hadoop Distributed File System (HDFS), Amazon S3, or Azure Files.

- *Real-time analytics*—Elasticsearch is great for performing real-time search and analytics on large data sets, but it may not be the most efficient solution for real-time data processing and analytics. Instead, consider a specialized real-time analytics platform like Apache Spark or Apache Flink.

- *Latency-sensitive applications*—Although Elasticsearch is designed to handle high-volume search and analytical queries, it can still have latency issues when dealing with large amounts of data. For applications that require sub-millisecond response times, a specialized search engine like Apache Solr or a columnar database like Apache Cassandra may be a better fit.

- *Other types*—Elasticsearch is not a preferred solution for time-series data, graph data, in-memory data, and various other types of data. If you need to store and analyze time-series data, a specialized time-series database like InfluxDB or TimescaleDB may be a better fit. Similarly, a graph database such as Neo4j may help you tackle graph data.

It's important to evaluate your specific use case and requirements before choosing Elasticsearch as your technology and tool. In the next section, we discuss common misconceptions about Elasticsearch as a tool, a technology, and a search solution.

1.4.5 *Misconceptions*

A major misconception about Elasticsearch is mistaking it for a traditional relational database. It's also a common misunderstanding that setting up Elasticsearch is easy, while in reality, many tweaks are required to set up a decent-sized cluster. In addition, Elasticsearch is often thought of as a technology used for text search, when in fact it can be used for a wide range of search and analytics use cases. The following list summarizes some common misconceptions about Elasticsearch:

- *Elasticsearch is easy to set up and manage.* While Elasticsearch is relatively straightforward to set up and get started with, it can be challenging to manage and scale as data grows and use cases increase. Although everything works out of the box, making an engineer's life easy, taking Elasticsearch into the production environment requires effort. We may need to tweak the configuration and fine-tune the memory, manage node failures, or even scale the cluster to handle petabytes of data as our data grows.

- *Elasticsearch is a relational database.* Elasticsearch is *not* a relational database and does not support traditional relational database features like transactions, foreign keys, and complex join operations. For example, we can't enforce referential integrity or perform complex join operations in Elasticsearch. If you need these features, a proven relational database like MySQL or PostgreSQL is definitely your solution.

- *Elasticsearch can handle all types of data.* Elasticsearch is versatile and can handle a wide range of data types, but it is not designed to handle every type of data with equal ease. For example, it may not be the best solution for real-time data processing and analytics or for handling large binary data. If you need to store and process large binary data like videos or images, consider using a dedicated binary data store like HDFS or Amazon S3.

- *Elasticsearch is only for text search.* While Elasticsearch is great for text search, it can also perform complex analytics on structured and unstructured data. For example, we can use Elasticsearch to perform aggregations, analyze log data, and visualize data using Kibana.

- *Elasticsearch can replace all other technologies.* Elasticsearch is a powerful and flexible technology, but it is not a one-size-fits-all solution and or the best choice for every use case. It can never replace a traditional relational database, for example.

- *Elasticsearch is always faster than other technologies.* Elasticsearch is designed for high performance and is expected to perform well under heavy loads. However, there's only so much Elasticsearch can do, and its performance primarily depends on how well the platform engineers fine-tune it.

- *Elasticsearch deals with big data only.* Elasticsearch can handle petabytes of data in large data sets, but it is equally performant when dealing with small data sets on the order of a few gigabytes. For example, we can use Elasticsearch to search and analyze data for an organization's small email database or a startup company without much effort.

These are just a few examples of misconceptions about Elasticsearch. As mentioned earlier, you must carefully evaluate your specific requirements and use case before choosing Elasticsearch or any other technology.

1.5   *Popular adoption*

A long list of organizations use Elasticsearch for everything from searching to business analysis, log analytics, security alert monitoring, and application management, as well as using it as a document store. Let's consider some of these organizations and how they put Elasticsearch to use in their operations.

Uber powers its rider and event prediction using Elasticsearch. It does so by storing millions of events, searching through them, and analyzing the data at a near-real-time rate. Uber predicts demand based on location, time, day, and other variables, including taking past data into consideration. This helps Uber deliver rides pretty.

Netflix adopted the Elastic Stack to provide customer insights to its internal teams. It also uses Elasticsearch for log event analysis to support debugging, alerting, and managing its internal services. Email campaigns and customer operations are all backed by the Elasticsearch engine. The next time you receive an email from Netflix mentioning a newly added movie or TV series, keep in mind that the campaign analytics behind that simple email were all supported by Elasticsearch.

PayPal embraced Elasticsearch as a search engine to allow customers to store and search through their transactions. The company has implemented transaction search features along with analytics for use by merchants, end customers, and developers.

Similarly, the online e-commerce company eBay adopted Elasticsearch to support full-text searching by end users. As users, we are using Elasticsearch directly when searching through eBay's inventory. The company also uses the Elastic Stack for analytics, log monitoring, and storing transactional data in a document store.

GitHub, a popular code repository for developers, indexes its 8 million (and counting) code repositories—consisting of over 2 billion documents—with Elasticsearch to enable a powerful search experience for its users. Similarly, Stack Overflow uses Elasticsearch to provide developers with quick and relevant answers, and Medium (a popular blog platform) uses the Elastic Stack to serve reader queries in a near-real-time mode.

Before we wind up this chapter, it's only fair to touch on a recent trending topic: generative artificial intelligence (AI) tools such as OpenAI's ChatGPT and Google's Bard. The introduction of these tools will change the search space dramatically, in my opinion. Let's discuss their effects on modern search, including search engines like Elasticsearch.

1.6   *Generative AI and modern search*

Unless you are living in a cave, you have undoubtedly heard about a recent internet revolution: ChatGPT. ChatGPT is a generative AI tool that was developed and released by the OpenAI team in November 2022. In my 25 years of IT experience, I've never seen a tech tool light up the internet like ChatGPT. Is isn't often that a technically superior tool lands in the hands of the general public that can help them in unimaginable ways, such as creating a travel itinerary for a summer trip to Athens, summarizing a legal document in layman's terms, developing a self-help plan for losing weight, analyzing code for security and performance bugs, designing an application's data models, comparing and contrasting technologies for a specific use case, writing complaint letters to the Twitter CEO and much more.

ChatGPT (https://chat.openai.com) is a conversational agent (chatbot) built on a GPT (generative pretrained transformer) architecture, and it is capable of generating human-like text based on user prompts. It is an instance of a large language model (LLM) designed for conversation with a specific goal of generating safe, relevant content while engaging in a meaningful dialogue. The model is fed vast amounts of text data and learns to predict the next word in a sentence. It is trained using a diverse range of internet text, but it can also be fine-tuned with specific datasets for various tasks. Through this process, the model learns parts and parcels of human language text: grammar, punctuation, syntax, facts about the world, and some degree of reasoning ability.

> **NOTE** *LLM* is a broad term that refers to any large-scale model trained to understand or generate human-like text. These models are characterized by their vast number of parameters and their ability to handle a wide range of natural language processing tasks. LLMs can be based on various architectures and training methods.

With the release of ChatGPT to the public, a sudden race in the space of search using AI emerged overnight. ChatGPT has become a disruptor to many industries and is no less a threat to Google search. AI-backed tools similar to ChatGPT will disrupt many industries in the coming years. Under tremendous pressure—and possibly to save its search leader status—Google decided to unleash its version of conversational generative AI: its agent called Bard (https://bard.google.com) was made publicly available in May 2023.

In the meantime, Microsoft committed to investing $10 billion in ChatGPT, over and above its initial investment of $3 billion since 2019. Microsoft's Edge browser is integrated with ChatGPT via the Bing search engine, which also was made publicly available in May 2023. In addition, Microsoft rolled out AI-powered Microsoft 365 apps, so the AI agent is available in Microsoft Word, Excel, email, and other tools. Meta's LLaMA is another tool that has begun competing in the generative AI race.

The GPT-3 and -4 models were trained on billions of digital copies of books, articles, papers, blogs, and so on. The GPT-4 model was fed with data until September 2021 (it can't retrieve data after that date). Although there is no internet access for GPT-4 to fetch real-time information, as I write this, OpenAI just released a beta version of a web browser version for its Plus subscribers. So, I expect an internet-enabled generative AI assistant from OpenAI to be available to the general public soon.

Search engineers are being asked fundamental questions, including how generative AI agents will change the course of search. Let's answer this question by asking

ChatGPT how AI agents can complement or help modern search or change its direction. These are the areas where tools like generative AI will reshape the search space:

- *Intuitive Search*—Search queries will become more conversational and intuitive. Generative AI models like GPT-4 have an advanced understanding of natural language, enabling them to interpret complex queries more effectively. Users will no longer need to rely on specific keywords or phrases; they can simply ask questions as they would in a conversation with another person. This will allow for more accurate and relevant search results, as AI can better comprehend the context and intent of the query. With the introduction and release of highly capable generative AI agents and models, there is a greater scope to significantly reshape full-text search capabilities provided by modern search engines like Elasticsearch. We can expect to see several key changes that will redefine the search experience for both users and developers as this technology is increasingly integrated into search platforms.

- *Personalized search*—With the incorporation of generative AI, search results can become more personalized and adaptive. Search engines will be able to learn many valuable data points from users' preferences, behavior, and search history, which in turn will help engines tailor results to meet individual users' needs. As the AI gathers more data, it will continually refine its understanding of what users are looking for, leading to an increasingly customized search experience.

- *Predictive search*—Generative AI has the potential to make search engines more proactive in anticipating user needs. Instead of merely responding to queries, AI-driven search engines may be able to predict what information users are interested in, based on their previous interactions or current context. This will allow search platforms to proactively offer relevant suggestions, increasing the value of the search experience and reducing the need for users to perform additional queries.

- *Advanced search*—Generative AI will enable search engines to provide more diverse and rich search results. By understanding the context and semantics of a query, AI-driven search engines can generate content summaries and relevant visualizations and even synthesize new information to help answer a user's question. This will lead to a more comprehensive and informative search experience that goes beyond merely linking to existing content.

In my mind, the introduction of generative AI will revolutionize full-text search capabilities, making search engines more conversational, personalized, adaptive, and proactive. This will not only enhance the user experience but also offer new opportunities for businesses and developers to create innovative search applications and services. Teams are working hard to adopt the upcoming changes in the search space with the advent of AI. So, expect a search space revolution!

This chapter laid the groundwork for using Elasticsearch by introducing its search capabilities and looking at how searching has become an integral part of numerous applications. In the next chapter, we install, configure, and run Elasticsearch and

Kibana, and we play with Elasticsearch by indexing a few documents and running search queries and analytics. Stay tuned!

Summary

- Search is the new normal and the most sought-after functionality for organizations, enabling competitive advantage.
- Search engines built using relational databases as the backend used to serve our search purposes but can't fulfill the full-fledged search functionality found in modern search engines.
- Modern search engines provide multifaceted, full-text search capabilities and multifold benefits from basic search to advanced search and analytical functions, all with split-second performance. They are also expected to handle terabytes to petabytes of data and scale if needed.
- Elasticsearch is an open source search and analytics engine built over Apache Lucene. It is a highly available server-side application developed in Java.
- Because Elasticsearch was designed as a programming-language-agnostic product, communication with the server takes place over HTTP using rich RESTful APIs. These APIs receive and send data in JSON format.
- The Elastic Stack is a suite of products composed of Beats, Logstash, Elasticsearch, and Kibana. Beats are single-purpose data shippers, Logstash is a data-processing ETL (extract, transform, load) engine, Kibana is the administrative UI tool, and Elasticsearch is the heart and soul of the stack.
- The Elastic Stack enables an organization to position itself in three core areas: search, observability, and security.
- Elasticsearch has become popular over the last few years due to its structured/unstructured search and analytics capabilities; rich set of RESTful APIs; its schema-free nature; and performance, high-availability, and scalability characteristics.
- AI-powered search is here. With the advent of generative AI and ChatGPT, the search space will be explored further, and search will become more intuitive and predictive.

Getting started

This chapter covers

- Indexing sample documents with Elasticsearch
- Retrieving, deleting, and updating documents
- Searching with basic to advanced queries
- Running aggregations on data

This chapter is all about experiencing a taste of Elasticsearch. Elasticsearch is a Java binary that is available to download from the Elastic company's website. Once the server is installed and up and running, we can load in our business data, which is analyzed and persisted by Elasticsearch. After priming Elasticsearch with the data, we can execute search queries as well as aggregations on that data.

Although any client capable of invoking REST calls (cURL, Postman, programming SDKs, etc.) can talk to Elasticsearch, we use Kibana as our preferred client throughout this book. Kibana is a rich UI web application from Elastic. It is a visual editor that comes with all the bells and whistles to help discover, analyze, manage, and maintain our cluster and data. With Kibana, we get abundant capabilities such as advanced analytical and statistical functions, rich visualizations and dashboards, machine learning models, and more. As Elasticsearch exposes all its functionality via RESTful APIs, we can construct queries using these APIs in the Kibana editor and communicate with the server over HTTP.

To execute the samples in this chapter, you need a running environment with Elasticsearch and Kibana. If you haven't set up that environment yet, follow the instructions in Appendix A to download and install your software and bring up the Elasticsearch server and Kibana UI.

> **NOTE** Installing Elasticsearch and Kibana can come in multiple flavors, from downloading the binaries and uncompressing and installing them onto your local machine in a traditional way to using a package manager, Docker, or even the cloud. Choose the appropriate flavor of installation for development to get started.

Copy the full code to your Kibana editor

To make the coding exercises easy, I've created a ch02_getting_started.txt file under the kibana_scripts folder at the root of the repository. Copy the contents of this file as is to your installation of Kibana. You can work through the examples by executing the individual code snippets while alongside following along with the chapter's contents.

Finally, we zoom out and analyze the data by executing two types of aggregations: metric and bucket. With these aggregation types, we use queries to fetch metrics such as average, sum, minimum and maximum values, and so on. Once you have the applications running, let's get started with Elasticsearch.

2.1 *Priming Elasticsearch with data*

A search engine can't work on thin air! It needs data as its input so it can produce results as output when queried. We need to dump our data into Elasticsearch, which is the first step in priming the engine. But before we start storing data in Elasticsearch, let's get to know the sample application we work with in this chapter.

For our examples, we need a basic understanding of the problem domain and the data model. Let's assume we are building an online bookstore; obviously, we are not architecting the whole application—we are only interested in the data model part for our discussion. We go over the details of this fictitious bookstore in the next section as a prerequisite for our objective of working with Elasticsearch.

2.1.1 *An online bookstore*

To demonstrate Elasticsearch's features, let's use a fictional bookstore that sells technical books online. All we want to do is to create an inventory of books and write some queries to search through them.

NOTE The code presented in this chapter is available in the book's GitHub repository (http://mng.bz/2Dyw) and on the book's website (www.manning .com/books/elasticsearch-in-action-second-edition). Follow the instructions listed in the repository to index the data.

The data model for our bookstore application is simple. We have a book as our entity, with a few properties such as title, author, and so on as described in table 2.1. We do not need to complicate things by creating elaborate entities; instead, we'll focus on the goal of getting hands-on experience with Elasticsearch.

Table 2.1 Data model for a book entity

Field	Explanation	Example
title	Title of a book	"Effective Java"
author	Author of the book	"Joshua Bloch"
release_date	Data of release	01-06-2001
amazon_rating	Average rating on Amazon	4.7
best_seller	Flag that qualifies the book as a best seller	true

prices	Inner object with individual prices in three currencies	"prices":{
		    "usd":9.95,
		    "gbp":7.95,
		    "eur":8.95
		}

Elasticsearch is a document data store, and it expects documents to be presented in JSON format. Because we need to store our books in Elasticsearch, we must model our entities as JSON-based documents. We can represent a book in a JSON document as shown in figure 2.1.

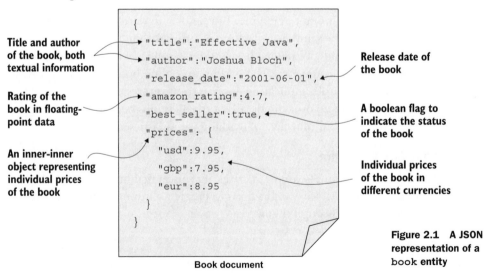

Book document

Figure 2.1 A JSON representation of a book entity

The JSON format represents data in simple name-value pairs. For our example, the book's title (name) is *Effective Java,* and its author (as a value) is Joshua Bloch. We can add additional fields (including nested objects) to the document: for example, we've added `prices` as a nested object.

Now that we have an idea of our bookstore and its data model, it is time to start populating Elasticsearch with a set of books to create an inventory. We do this in the next section.

2.1.2 Indexing documents

To work with the server, we need to get the client's data indexed into Elasticsearch. There are a few ways we can bring the data into Elasticsearch in the real world: creating an adapter to pipe the data from a relational database, extracting the data from a file system, streaming events from a real-time source, and so on. Whichever choice we make for our data source, we invoke Elasticsearch's RESTful APIs from the client application to load the data into Elasticsearch.

Any REST-based client (cURL, Postman, advanced REST client, HTTP module for JavaScript/NodeJS, programming language SDKs, etc.) can help us talk to Elasticsearch via the API. Fortunately, Elastic has a product that does exactly this (and more): Kibana. Kibana is a web application with a rich user interface, allowing users to index, query, visualize, and work with data. *This is our preferred option, and we use Kibana extensively in this book.*

> **RESTful access**
>
> Communication with Elasticsearch takes place via JSON-based RESTful APIs. In the current digital world, you are highly unlikely to find a programming language that doesn't support accessing RESTful services. In fact, designing Elasticsearch with APIs exposed as JSON-based RESTful endpoints was a smart choice, because it enables programming-language-agnostic adoption.

DOCUMENT APIs

Elasticsearch's document APIs help with creating, deleting, updating, and retrieving documents. The APIs are accessible via HTTP transport using RESTful actions. That is, to index a document, we need to use an HTTP PUT or POST (more on POST later) on an endpoint. Figure 2.2 shows the syntax of the full URL format for an HTTP PUT method.

As you can see, the URL is composed of several elements:

- An HTTP action such as PUT, GET, or POST
- Server's hostname and port
- Index name
- Document API's endpoint (_doc)
- Document ID
- Request body

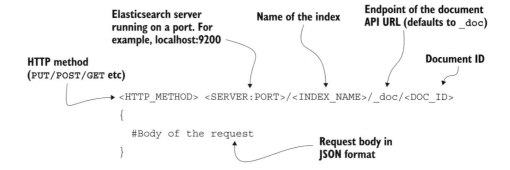

Figure 2.2   Elasticsearch URL invocation endpoint using an HTTP method

The Elasticsearch API accepts a JSON document as the request body, so the book we want to index should accompany this request. For example, the following code block indexes a book document with ID 1 to a books index.

Listing 2.1   Indexing a book document into the books index

```
PUT books/_doc/1                        ◁———————————  The index is books, and
{                                                     the document ID is 1.
  "title":"Effective Java",
  "author":"Joshua Bloch",
  "release_date":"2001-06-01",
  "amazon_rating":4.7,
  "best_seller":true,                   The body of the request
  "prices": {                           consists of JSON data.
    "usd":9.95,
    "gbp":7.95,
    "eur":8.95
  }
}
```

It can be a bit overwhelming if you are seeing a request like this for the first time, but trust me—it is not that difficult once you dissect it. The first line is the command that tells Elasticsearch what to do with the request. We say to put the book document (which is attached as a body to the request) into an index (imagine an index as a table in a database; it's a collection to hold all book documents) called books. Finally, the primary key of the book is represented by the ID 1.

We can also use cURL (if you are not aware of cURL, it's a command-line data transfer tool, usually used to talk to various services exposed on the internet) for the same request to persist the book document into Elasticsearch. This is discussed next.

USING CURL

We can also use cURL to work with Elasticsearch and index our book document into our books index. Note that we prefer Kibana over cURL in this book, so all the code is presented in scripts executable with the Kibana code editor. The full cURL command is shown in figure 2.3 (Kibana hides the full URL).

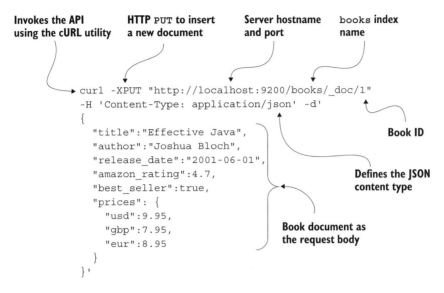

Figure 2.3 Elasticsearch URL invocation endpoint using cURL

As you can see, cURL expects us to provide request parameters such as the content type, document, and so on. Because the cURL commands are terminal commands (command-line invocation), preparing the request is cumbersome and, at times, error-prone.

Fortunately, Kibana lets us drop the server details, content types, and other parameters, so the invocation looks something like that shown in figure 2.4. As I mentioned, in this book we stick with Kibana to interact with Elasticsearch.

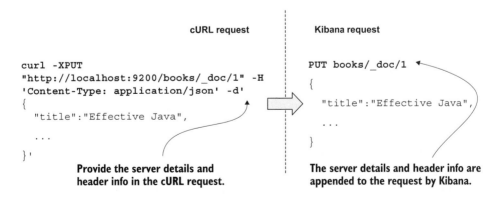

Figure 2.4 Transitioning from a cURL command to Kibana's request command

It's time to index our first document. Let's jump to the next section for the action.

2.1.3   *Indexing our first document*

To use Kibana to index documents, we'll go to Kibana's Dev Tools application for executing queries. We spend a lot of time on the Dev Tools page, so by the end of this book, you'll be quite familiar with it!

Assuming Elasticsearch and Kibana are running on your local machine, go to the Kibana dashboard at http://localhost:5601. In the top-left corner is a main menu with links and sublinks. For our purposes, navigate to Management > Dev Tools, as shown in figure 2.5.

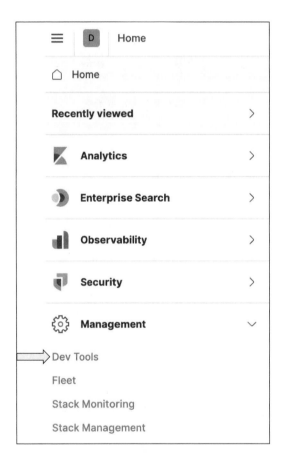

Figure 2.5   Accessing the Kibana Dev Tools navigation page

As this may be your first time accessing this page, let me explain the components. When we navigate to this page (see figure 2.6), the code editor opens, showing two panes. On the left pane, we write code with special syntax provided by Elasticsearch. Once we write a code snippet, we can invoke the URL in the snippet by clicking the Play button in the middle of the page (a right-pointing triangle).

Execute the query by clicking the Play button.

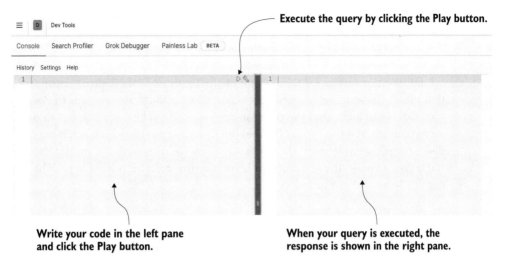

Write your code in the left pane and click the Play button.

When your query is executed, the response is shown in the right pane.

Figure 2.6   Kibana's Dev Tools code editor

Kibana must be connected to an Elasticsearch instance (the instance details are defined in the Kibana configuration file) before it's ready for action. Kibana uses the server's details to wrap the code snippet with the appropriate Elasticsearch URLs and send it to the server for execution.

To index our document for Elasticsearch, let's create a code snippet (the code was given in listing 2.1). Figure 2.7 shows the indexing request and a response.

Request

```
PUT books/_doc/1
{
  "title":"Effective Java",
  "author":"Joshua Bloch",
  "release_date":"2001-06-01",
  "amazon_rating":4.7,
  "best_seller":true,
  "prices": {
    "usd":9.95,
    "gbp":7.95,
    "eur":8.95
  }
}
```

Response

```
{
  "_index" : "books",
  "_type" : "_doc",
  "_id" : "1",
  "_version" : 1,
  "result" : "created",
  "_shards" : {
    "total" : 2,
    "successful" : 1,
    "failed" : 0
  },
  "_seq_no" : 0,
  "_primary_term" : 1
}
```

The indexing request with our book document sent to Elasticsearch

Response confirming the creation of our document in the books index with an ID of 1

Figure 2.7   Indexing a document in Kibana (left), and the response from Elasticsearch (right)

When the code is ready, click the Play button (figure 2.6). Kibana sends this request to the Elasticsearch server. After receiving the request, Elasticsearch processes it (figure 2.7), stores the message, and sends the response back to the client (Kibana). You can view the response on the right-hand panel in the editor.

The response is a JSON document. In figure 2.7, the `result` property indicates that the document was created successfully. You should also see a HTTP status code of "200 OK" indicating that the request was successful. The response has some additional metadata (such as the index, ID, and document version), which is self-explanatory. We discuss the constituents of the requests and responses in detail in upcoming chapters, but let me explain the request and response flow on a high level here. The overall process is illustrated in figure 2.8.

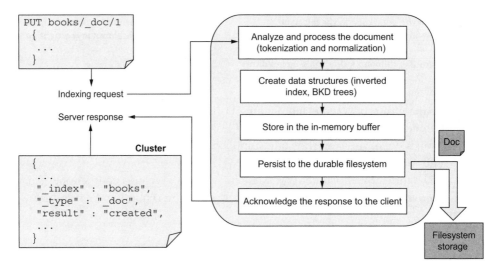

Figure 2.8   Elasticsearch's request and response flow at a high level

The flow steps are as follows:

1   Kibana posts the request to the Elasticsearch server with the required input parameters.
2   On receiving the request, the server
    –   Analyzes the document data and, for speedier access, stores it in an inverted index (a high-performing data structure that is the heart and soul of the search engine)
    –   Creates a new index (note that we did not create the index up front) and stores the document
    –   Creates the required mappings and data schemas
    –   Sends a response back to the client
3   Kibana receives the response and displays it in the right panel (figure 2.6) for our consumption.

We've indexed our first document for Elasticsearch! Indexing a document is similar to inserting a record in a relational database.

CONSTITUENTS OF THE REQUEST

The request we sent (PUT books/_doc/1) needs a bit of distilling. There are five parts to this request, and we quickly go over them here (if you wish, you can skip this section for now and come back to it once you've read the rest of the chapter):

- PUT *method*—PUT is an HTTP verb (also known as a *method*) that indicates we are sending a request to the server to create a resource (a book document, in this case). Elasticsearch uses the HTTP protocol for its RESTful API invocations, so we expect PUT, POST, GET, DELETE, and other standard HTTP methods in the request URL syntax.
- books *index*—The books part of our URL is called an *index:* a bucket for collecting all book documents. It is similar to a table in a relational database. Only book documents are stored in this books index (although books index is expected to hold only book documents, in theory, there's nothing stopping us indexing other types, too—it is our responsibility to not mix up types).
- _doc *endpoint*—The endpoint is a constant part of the path that's associated with the operation being performed. In earlier versions of Elasticsearch (version < 7.0), _doc's place used to be filled by a document's mapping type. The mapping types were deprecated, and _doc replaced them as a generic constant endpoint path in the URL (see the sidebar "Document types and the _doc endpoint" for more).
- *Document ID*—The number 1 in our URL represents the document's ID. It is like a primary key for a record in a database. We use this identifier to retrieve the document.
- *Request body*—The body of the request is the JSON representation of the book data. Elasticsearch expects all data to be sent as JSON-formatted documents. It also supports nested objects sent in JSON's nested objects format.

> **Document types and the _doc endpoint**
>
> Prior to the 7.x version of Elasticsearch, an index could hold multiple types of entities (for example, a books index could hold not just books but also book reviews, book sales, bookshops, and so on). Having all types of documents in a single index led to complications. Field mappings were shared across multiple types, leading to errors as well as data sparsity. To avoid problems with types and their management, Elastic decided to remove the types.
>
> In earlier versions, the invocation URL with a type looked like this: *<index_name>*/ *<type>*/*<id>* (for example, books/book/1). The types were deprecated in version 7.x. Now an index is expected to be dedicated to one and only one type: _doc is an endpoint etched into the URL. We learn about the removal of types in chapter 5.

The gist is that we used an HTTP PUT method to index a document with an ID of 1 into the books index for Elasticsearch. When indexing our first document, did you notice that we didn't create a schema? We indexed the document by invoking the API, but Elasticsearch never asked us to define a data schema before indexing the data.

Unlike a relational database, Elasticsearch doesn't ask us to create the schema beforehand (this is called being *schema-less*) and is happy to derive the schema from the first document it indexes. It also creates the index (the books index, to be precise).

The bottom line is that Elasticsearch doesn't like to get in our way during development. That said, we must follow the best practice of creating our own schemas beforehand in production environments; more on this as we progress through the book.

In this section, we successfully indexed a document. Let's follow the same process and index a couple more documents.

2.1.4 Indexing more documents

For the upcoming examples to work, we need a few more documents to index. Head over to Kibana's code editor, and write the following code for two more documents.

Listing 2.2 Two more book documents to index

```
PUT books/_doc/2                    ◁──────────────────────   Second book
{                                                             document
  "title":"Core Java Volume I - Fundamentals",
  "author":"Cay S. Horstmann",
  "release_date":"2018-08-27",
  "amazon_rating":4.8,
  "best_seller":true,
  "prices": {
    "usd":19.95,
    "gbp":17.95,
    "eur":18.95
  }
}                              │ Third book
PUT books/_doc/3    ◁──────┘   document
{
  "title":"Java: A Beginner's Guide",
  "author":"Herbert Schildt",
  "release_date":"2018-11-20",
  "amazon_rating":4.2,
  "best_seller":true,
  "prices": {
    "usd":19.99,
    "gbp":19.99,
    "eur":19.99
  }
}
```

Execute the queries in this listing to index them into the books index. Now that we have few documents indexed, let's find out how we can retrieve or search them.

2.2 Retrieving data

We primed our server, albeit with a very limited set of documents. It is time to spring into action to check how we can retrieve, search, and aggregate these documents. From the next section onward, we get hands-on by executing queries and retrieving data.

Let's start with a basic requirement of finding out the total number of books we have in stock (in the books index, in this case). Elasticsearch exposes a _count API to satisfy this requirement. It is pretty straightforward, as we see in the next section.

2.2.1   *Counting documents*

Knowing the total number of documents in an index is a requirement fulfilled by the _count API. Invoking the _count endpoint on the books index results in the number of documents persisted in that index.

Listing 2.3   Counting documents using the `_count` API

```
GET books/_count        ◁──┐   Counting the
                            │   number of books
```

This should return the response shown the in figure 2.9.

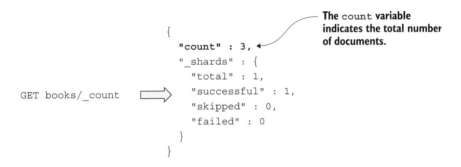

Figure 2.9   The JSON response for a _count API invocation

The highlighted count variable indicates the total number of documents in the books index. We can also use the same API to fetch from multiple indices at once, by adding comma-separated indices such as GET books1,books2/_count. (Note that if you execute this query right now, the system will throw an index_not_found_exception indicating that the books2 index doesn't exist.)

We can fetch the number of documents in *all* indices, too, by issuing a GET _count call. This returns all the documents available, including system and hidden indices. In the next section, we use APIs to retrieve documents.

2.2.2   *Retrieving documents*

Just as we deposit money in our bank account, we indexed documents into Elasticsearch earlier. We now need to access these documents (just like we withdraw money from our bank account).

Every document that is indexed has a unique identifier; some identifiers are provided by us, and others are generated by Elasticsearch. Operations to retrieve documents depend on access to the document IDs. These are the operations we cover in this section:

- Getting a single document, given an ID
- Getting multiple documents, given a set of IDs
- Getting all the documents at once (no IDs, no search criteria)

We can fetch a single document from Elasticsearch by invoking a document API call given an ID, and we can use another API query (`ids`) to fetch multiple documents. We also go over using the `_search` API to retrieve all the documents at once.

RETRIEVING A SINGLE DOCUMENT

Similar to fetching a record from a database using a primary key, retrieving the document from Elasticsearch is straightforward, as long as we have the document's ID. To do that, we issue a GET command in the Kibana console with the API URL and document ID. The generic format for retrieving the documents with an identifier is GET `<index>/`
`_doc/<id>`. To retrieve a single document, issue a GET command, providing the ID 1.

Listing 2.4   Retrieving an individual document by its ID

```
GET books/_doc/1
```

If this command is executed successfully, you will see a response on the right-hand side of the code editor, as shown in figure 2.10.

The response contains two pieces of information: the original document, under the `_source` tag, and the metadata of this document (such as index, id, found,

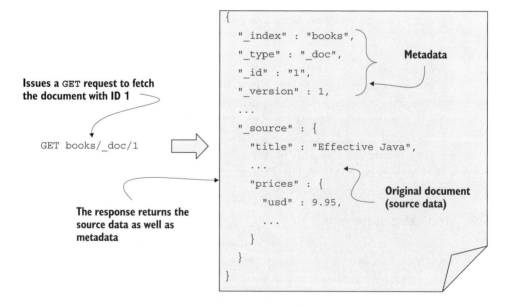

Figure 2.10   Fetching a book document by ID

version, etc.). If we don't want all the metadata but just the original source, re-run the query by changing the _doc endpoint with _source: GET books/_source/1.

RETRIEVING MULTIPLE DOCUMENTS BY ID

When we need to retrieve a set of documents given a set of identifiers, we can use an ids query. The query fetches the documents given a set of document IDs. It's a much simpler way to fetch them all at once, given a list of document IDs.

One thing to note, though, is that unlike other queries that use document APIs to fetch documents, the ids query uses a search API—specifically, a _search endpoint. Let's see that in action.

> **NOTE**   Elasticsearch provides a domain specific language (DSL) for writing queries, commonly called Query DSL. It is a simple JSON-based query writing language, extensively used to write queries in Kibana. Most queries in this chapter (and the rest of the book) are based on Query DSL.

Listing 2.5   Fetching multiple documents using an ids query

```
GET books/_search
{
  "query": {
    "ids": {
      "values": [1,2,3]
    }
  }
}
```

The request body in the query is constructed using a query object, which has an inner object named ids. The document IDs are the values provided in the query as an array. The response indicates the successful hits (results), as shown in figure 2.11, returning the three documents with those IDs.

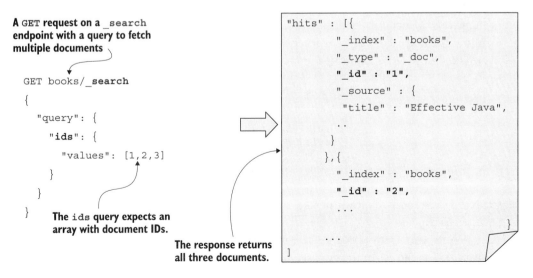

Figure 2.11   Retrieving documents with a set of IDs using an ids query, which invokes a _search endpoint

Suppressing the original source data in the response

Sometimes we can avoid clogging the network and wasting bandwidth by not retrieving source data that is not required. For example, imagine if our source document has 500 fields but not all of them are relevant to retrieve. We can control what fields are sent to the client and which are not by tweaking the fields in a response.

We can also set the flag `"_source": false` on the request to completely suppress sending the source data in the response. The flag is set at the root level (the same as at the query level):

```
GET books/_search
{
  "_source": false,          ◁─┐  Suppressing
  "query": {                   │  the source
    "ids": {
      "values": [1,2,3]
    }
  }
}
```

Of course, this way of retrieving the documents is cumbersome. Imagine if we wanted to retrieve 1,000 documents with 1,000 IDs! Well, fortunately, we don't need to use an `ids` query. Instead, we can utilize other search features that we go over later in the book.

So far, we've looked at a document API that fetches documents using IDs. This is not exactly a search feature but rather data retrieval. Elasticsearch provides a myriad of search features to fetch results based on various conditions and criteria. We have dedicated several chapters to search, from basic to advanced, later in the book. But as curious developers, we want to see high-level search queries in action, don't we? Let's discuss the set of queries based on search functions.

RETRIEVING ALL DOCUMENTS

In the previous section, we worked with the basic _search endpoint. Using the same syntax, we can write a query to fetch *all* the books from our index.

> **Listing 2.6 Retrieving all documents from the `books` index**

```
GET books/_search     ◁─┐  The URL doesn't
                        │  need a body.
```

As you can see, when you search for all records, you don't need to attach the body to the query (see the sidebar on the `match_all` query, which explains this query's syntax). The response, shown in figure 2.12, returns the three documents in our `books` index as expected.

Don't worry if you are baffled with the query syntax or the response fields. We cover the semantics in the coming chapters.

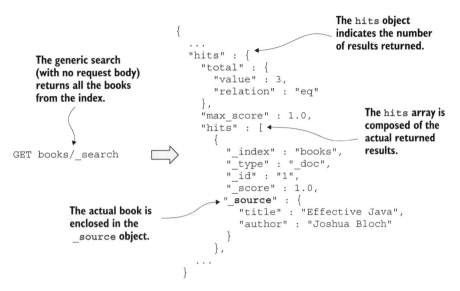

Figure 2.12 Retrieving all documents using the search API

Generic search is a short form of the match_all query

The query GET books/_search that you saw previously is a short form of a special query named match_all. Usually, a request body is added to the URL with a query clause, such as the one in listing 2.5. When we omit the query body while invoking the _search endpoint, it is an instruction to Elasticsearch that the query is a match_all query—which means *match everything*. The full query is shown here, but we rarely need to write the body if we are planning to fetch all records without any query clauses:

```
GET books/_search
{
  "query": {
    "match_all": { }
  }
}
```

However, if we need to boost the scores of all the results for whatever reason, we can create the match_all query and declare an additional Boost parameter:

```
GET books/_search
{
  "query": {
    "match_all": {
        "Boost":2                    All results will
    }                                have a score of 2
  }
}
```

The takeaway point is that whenever we invoke a _search endpoint without a body, it's a match_all query.

So far, we've seen queries that don't really exhibit the full power of Elasticsearch; they just fetch data without much intelligence. Occasionally, we may want to issue a query with criteria: for example, searching for first edition books by a particular author with an overall rating higher than four stars. The real power of Elasticsearch is hidden in the flexibility and depth of its search functionality. The next few sections look at this at a high level.

2.3 Full-text search

Once you've indexed a number of documents, it's important to be able to find those that meet specific criteria. Elasticsearch provides search functionality to search unstructured text in the name of full-text queries.

> **NOTE** Unstructured text (also called full text), just like natural language, doesn't adhere to a particular schema or model like structured text. Modern search engines work hard on full text to draw relevant results. Elasticsearch provides a rich set of matches and other queries to work with full-text data.

2.3.1 Match query: Books by an author

Say, for example, that a reader visiting our bookstore wants to find all titles authored by Joshua Bloch. We can construct the query using the _search API with a match query: a _match query helps search for words across unstructured or full text. The following query searches for books authored by "Joshua."

Listing 2.7   Querying for books authored by a specific author

```
GET books/_search
{
  "query": {
    "match": {
      "author": "Joshua"
    }
  }
}
```

In the request body, we create a query object defining a match query. In this query clause, we ask Elasticsearch to *match all documents authored by Joshua across all books in our index*. Read the query as if you are reading prose in plain English, and try to digest the essence of it.

Once the query is sent, the server analyzes the query, matches the query with its internal data structures (inverted indexes), fetches the document(s) from the file store, and returns them to the client. In this example, the server finds the single book authored by Joshua Bloch and returns it, as shown in figure 2.13.

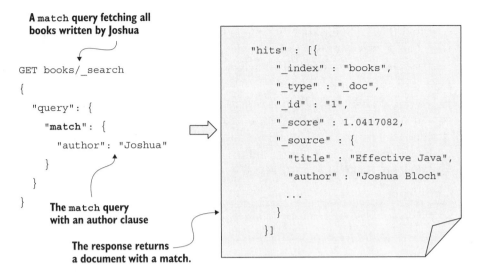

A `match` query fetching all
books written by Joshua

```
GET books/_search
{
  "query": {
    "match": {
      "author": "Joshua"
    }
  }
}
```

The `match` query
with an author clause

The response returns
a document with a match.

```
"hits" : [{
    "_index" : "books",
    "_type" : "_doc",
    "_id" : "1",
    "_score" : 1.0417082,
    "_source" : {
        "title" : "Effective Java",
        "author" : "Joshua Bloch"
        ...
    }
}]
```

Figure 2.13 Fetching books authored by Joshua

Prefix queries

You can rewrite the query from listing 2.7 with varied combination searches, such as lowercase name, mixed-case name, and so on:

```
"author":"JoShUa"
"author":"joshua" (or "JOSHUA")
"author":"Bloch"
```

All these queries will succeed, but searching for a shortened name will fail:

```
"author":"josh"
```

To return such regex-type queries, we use a `prefix` query. We can change a `match` query to a `prefix` query as follows to fetch a shortened name:

```
GET books/_search
{
  "query": {
    "prefix": {
      "author": "josh"
    }
  }
}
```

The query value must be lowercase because a `prefix` query is a term-level query.

2.3.2 *Match query with the AND operator*

If we tweak the query by changing the name to "Joshua Doe," what result do you expect? We don't have any books written by Joshua Doe, so the query shouldn't return any results, right? That's not the case: the book written by Joshua Bloch will still be returned. The reason is that the engine is searching for all books written by Joshua *or* Doe. The OR operator is used implicitly in this case.

Let's see how we search for books with an *exact* full name by using an operator. Let's take an example of a query that searches for author Joshua Schildt (mixing up Joshua's first name and Herbert's last name). Obviously, we know our index doesn't contain a book written by that fictitious author. If you run the query in listing 2.7 with "Joshua Schildt," you should get two books as a result (because Elasticsearch searches for books written by Joshua OR Schildt): one by Joshua Bloch and another by Herbert Schildt. This modified query is shown next.

Listing 2.8   Searching for books written by a fictitious author

```
GET books/_search
{
  "query": {
  "match": {
    "author": "Joshua Schildt"          ◁──┐  Searching for a fictitious
  }                                          │  author will yield two books.
  }
}
```

We can tweak this query to define a parameter called operator and explicitly set it to AND, as the following listing shows. There's a slight change to the query in that we need to add an object consisting of query and operator to the author object (unlike in listing 2.7, where we simply provided the query value to the field).

Listing 2.9   Query with an AND operator to fetch exact matches

```
GET books/_search
{
  "query": {
    "match": {                    The author field now has
      "author": {     ◁──┘        inner properties defined.
        "query": "Joshua Schildt",        ◁──┤ Our query
        "operator": "AND"     ◁──┐  The AND operator
      }                          │  (default is OR)
    }
  }
}
```

Executing the query yields no results (no books written by Joshua Schildt).

By the same logic, if we wish to fetch a book with an exact title, say *Effective Java*, figure 2.14 shows the code. We would get a list of all the books that have either of the words Effective OR Java in the title field if we did not change the operator. By providing an AND operator to join both words, the query finds books with both search words in the title field.

```
                              GET books/_search
                              {
                                "query": {
                                  "match": {
A match query fetching a specific        "title": {
title. The and operator searches
for a title with both words in the          "query": "Effective Java",
title ("Effective and Java").              "operator": "and"
                                  }
                                }
                              }
                            }
```

Figure 2.14 Fetching an exact match for a title using the and operator

Before we execute search queries that are a bit more involved, we need to do one little thing: index more documents. We only have three documents so far, and it would be helpful to have more for any meaningful queries. Elasticsearch provides a convenient bulk API (_bulk) to index documents in bulk. Let's take a short detour to index a few more documents, this time using the _bulk API.

2.3.3 Indexing documents using the _bulk API

We need to add more documents to our store as we start warming up to a variety of search queries. We can follow the same process of using document APIs as we did in section 2.1.2. However, as you can imagine, loading a lot of documents individually is a cumbersome process.

Fortunately, there's a handy _bulk API that lets us index documents simultaneously. We can use either Kibana or cURL to execute the _bulk API when indexing multiple documents, but the methods have differences in their data formats. We discuss the _bulk API at length in chapter 5; here, we briefly go over some highlights.

> **Bulk operation overrides existing data**
>
> If you perform the _bulk operation on books, it indexes them into the existing index (books) created at the beginning of the chapter. The new book documents have fields such as price, rating, and others; the object structure is enriched by these additional properties and differs from the earlier one.
>
> If you don't want the existing books index to be touched, you can create a new index (books_new, perhaps) to avoid overriding the existing index. To do this, modify the index name in the bulk data file with the following line:
>
> {"index":{"_index":"books_new","_id":"1"}}

(continued)

Make sure all the index lines are updated, not just the top one. Alternatively, you can remove the `_index` field completely and add `"index"` to the URL:

```
POST books_new/_bulk
{"index":{"_id":"1"}}
..
```

The example in the text updates the existing `books` index rather than creating a new one, so all the queries in this chapter are performed on the updated `books` index.

The example uses the data sets provided with this book, which are available at GitHub (https://github.com/madhusudhankonda/elasticsearch-in-action) and the book's website (https://www.manning.com/books/elasticsearch-in-action-second-edition). Copy the contents of the books-kibana-dataset.txt file, and paste it into Kibana's Dev Tools. Figure 2.15 shows part of the file's contents.

```
1  POST _bulk
2  {"index":{"_index":"books","_id":"1"}}
3  {"title": "Core Java Volume I - Fundamentals","author": "Cay S. Horstmann","edition": 11, "synopsis": "Java
     reference book that offers a detailed explanation of various features of Core Java, including exception
     handling, interfaces, and lambda expressions. Significant highlights of the book include simple language,
     conciseness, and detailed examples.","amazon_rating": 4.6,"release_date": "2018-08-27","tags": ["Programming
     Languages, Java Programming"]}
4  {"index":{"_index":"books","_id":"2"}}
5  {"title": "Effective Java","author": "Joshua Bloch", "edition": 3,"synopsis": "A must-have book for every Java
     programmer and Java aspirant, Effective Java makes up for an excellent complementary read with other Java books
     or learning material. The book offers 78 best practices to follow for making the code better.", "amazon_rating"
     : 4.7, "release_date": "2017-12-27", "tags": ["Object Oriented Software Design"]}
```

Figure 2.15 Bulk indexing documents using the `_bulk` endpoint

Execute the query, and you should receive an acknowledgment indicating that all the documents were successfully indexed.

Weird-looking bulk indexing document formats

If you look closely at the documents that are loaded using `_bulk`, you will notice some weird syntax. Every two lines correspond to one document, like this:

```
{"index":{"_id":"1"}}
{"brand": "Samsung","name":"UHD","size_inches":65,"price":1400}
```

The first line is metadata about the record, including the operation (`index`, `delete`, `update`) we are about to execute (`index`, in this case), the document ID, and the index where the record is going. The second line is the actual document. We revisit this format in chapter 5 when we discuss document operations.

Now that we have indexed a few more documents, we can get back on track and experiment with some other search features. Let's begin by searching for a word across multiple fields.

2.3.4 *Searching across multiple fields*

When a customer searches for something in a search bar, the search isn't necessarily restricted to just one field. For example, suppose we want to search for all documents where the word *Java* appears: not just in the title field, but also in other fields like synopsis, tags, and so on. To do this, we can enable a *multi-field* search.

Let's see an example of a query to search for *Java* in two fields: title and synopsis. Similar to the match query we saw earlier, Elasticsearch provides the multi_match query that will serve our purpose. We need to provide the search words in the inner query object, along with the fields we are interested in.

> **Listing 2.10 Searching across multiple fields**

```
GET books/_search
{
  "query": {
    "multi_match": {          ◁──┘ Multi_match query that searches
                                   across multiple fields
      "query": "Java",        ◁──┤ Search words
      "fields": ["title","synopsis"]  ◁──┐ Searches across
    }                                      two fields
  }
}
```

When we execute this multi-field query, our results with the *Java* search word appear in both the title and synopsis fields. But say we want to bump up the priority of a result based on a particular field. For example, if *Java* is found in the title field, we want to boost that search result so it is three times as important and relevant while keeping the other documents at a normal priority. To do so, we can use the (naturally) boosting feature (users may be happy to see documents at the top of the list that have the search word in the title).

> **Relevancy scores**
>
> Full-text query results have numerical scoring values for documents, expressed as a _score attribute attached to the individual results. The _score is a positive floating-point number indicating how relevant the resultant document is to the query. The first document returned will have the highest score, and the last document will have the lowest. This is the *relevancy score*, and it indicates how well the documents matched the query. The higher the score, the greater the match.
>
> Elasticsearch has an algorithm called Okapi Best Match 25 (BM25), which is an enhanced term frequency/inverse document frequency (TF/IDF) similarity algorithm that calculates the relevancy scores for the results and sorts them in that order when presenting them to the client.

In the next section, we see how we can boost results in action.

2.3.5   *Boosting results*

We want to give a higher priority (relevance) to certain fields when issuing a query against multiple fields. This way, even if the user doesn't explicitly specify what fields should be boosted, we can provide the best results. Elasticsearch lets us boost the priority of fields in our queries by providing a boost factor next to the fields. For example, to increase the `title` field by a factor of three, we set the boost on the field to `title^3` (the field name followed by caret symbol and a boost factor).

> **Listing 2.11   A `multi_match` query that boosts a field's importance**

```
GET books/_search
{
  "query": {
    "multi_match": {          ⟵  Searches through
      "query": "Java",             multiple fields
      "fields": ["title^3","synopsis"]    ⟵  A caret followed by the boost number
    }                                         indicates the field being boosted.
  }
}
```

The results will show that the weight of the `title` field's score has increased. This means we bumped the document to a higher position by boosting its score.

We may wish to search for a phrase: for example, "how is the weather in London this morning" or "recipe for potato mash." To do so, we use another type of query called `match_phrase`—coming up next.

2.3.6   *Search phrases*

At times we wish to search for a sequence of words exactly in a given order, like finding all books that have the phrase "must-have book for every Java programmer" in the `synopsis` field. We can write a `match_phrase` query for this purpose.

> **Listing 2.12   Searching for books with an exact phrase**

```
GET books/_search
{
  "query": {
    "match_phrase": {          ⟵  match_phrase query that fetches an exact
      "synopsis": "must-have book for every Java programmer"    ⟵  match of a phrase (sequence of words)
    }                                                               Phrase to search
  }                                                                 for in each book's
}                                                                   synopsis field
```

This query searches for that sequence of words in the `synopsis` field across all our books and returns the book *Effective Java*:

```
"hits" : [{
  "_score" : 7.300332,
```

```
 "_source" : {
 "title" : "Effective Java",
 "synopsis" : "A must-have book for every Java programmer and Java ...",
}]}
```

The highlighted portion proves that the query successfully grabbed the book we are looking for.

Highlighting the results

Let's see how to highlight a portion of text in the returned document that matches our original query. For example, when we search for a word or a phrase on a blog site, the site usually shows the matching text with some sort of highlighting using colors or shading. The figure shows highlighting in action: we are searching for "match phrase" in Elasticsearch's documentation site.

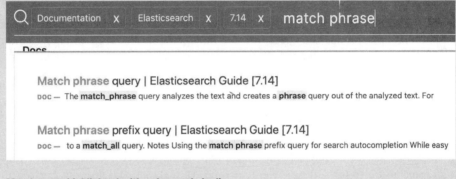

Matches are highlighted with colors and shading.

We can achieve the same effect for our results using a convenient feature called *highlighting*. To do this, we modify our search query by providing a `highlight` object in the request body at the same level as the `query` object:

```
GET books/_search
{
  "query": {
    "match_phrase": {
      "synopsis": "must-have book for every Java programmer"
    }
  },
  "highlight": {            The highlight object at the
    "fields": {            same level as the query object
      "synopsis": {}            Field(s) we wish
    }                           to highlight
  }
}
```

In the `highlight` object, we can set the fields to which we want to apply a highlight. For example, here we tell the engine to set the highlights on the `synopsis` object.

(continued)

The final outcome is something like this, where matches highlighted with an HTML markup tag (em) indicate words that are emphasized:

```
"hits" : [
  "_source" : {
    ...
    "title" : "Effective Java",
    "synopsis" : "A must-have book for every Java programmer
  },
  "highlight" : {
    "synopsis" : [
    "A <em>must</em>-<em>have</em> <em>book</em> <em>for</em>
<em>every</em> <em>Java</em> <em>programmer</em> and Java aspirant.."]}}
]
```

We can rely on match_phrase for exact phrase searches. But what happens if we leave out one or two words of the phrase? For example, does the query work if we ask it to search for "must-have book Java programmer" (dropping the words for and every)? The query won't yield results if you re-run it after removing those two words. Fortunately, we can ask Elasticsearch politely by setting a slop parameter on the match_phrase query. This is discussed in the next section.

2.3.7 *Phrases with missing words*

The match_phrase query expects a full phrase: a phrase that isn't missing any words. However, users may not always input exact phrases. To handle this, Elasticsearch's solution is to set a slop parameter on the match_phrase query: a positive integer indicating how many words the phrase is missing when searching. The following query has a slop of 2, indicating that the search query can expect up to two words to be either missing or not in order when the query is executed.

> **Listing 2.13   Matching a phrase with missing words (using slop)**

```
GET bsExecuting this query will return our book, as expected. You can
    experiment with other values of slop with the books dataset in the
    repository.
```

2.3.8 *Handling spelling mistakes*

Sometimes users enter incorrect spellings in their search criteria. Search engines are forgiving; they return results in spite of spelling errors. Modern search engines embrace spelling issues and provide the functionality to support them graciously. Elasticsearch works pretty hard to find similarity between the words using the *Levenshtein edit distance algorithm.*

Elasticsearch handles spelling mistakes by using a match query with a fuzziness setting. If fuzziness is set to 1, one spelling mistake (one letter misplaced, omitted, or added) can be forgiven. For example, if a user searches for "Komputer", by default the query shouldn't return any results, as "Komputer" is misspelled. This can be rectified by writing the following `match` query.

Listing 2.14   **Matching a phrase with a misspelling (using fuzziness)**

```
GET books/_search
{
  "query": {
    "match": {
      "tags": {
        "query": "Komputer",         ⟵┐ Incorrectly
        "fuzziness": 1        ⟵      │ spelled query
      }                              Handling one spelling mistake
    }                               by setting fuzziness to 1
  }
}
```

> **Fuzziness and Levenshtein's edit distance**
>
> Fuzzy queries search for terms that are similar to the query by employing something called *Levenshtein's edit distance*. In the previous example, we need to replace the single letter *K* with *C* to find documents that match the query. The edit distance is a mechanism to change one word into another by making single-character changes. The fuzziness function doesn't just change a word; it inserts and deletes characters to match the words. For example, "Komputer" can be changed to "Computer" by replacing a single letter. Check out this paper on Code Project to learn more about Levenshtein's edit distance: http://mng.bz/pPo2.

So far, we've been looking at searching unstructured (full-text) data by employing full-text queries. In addition to full-text queries, Elasticsearch supports queries for searching structured data: *term-level queries*. Term-level queries help us search for structured data like numericals, dates, IP addresses, and so on. We look at these queries in the next few sections.

2.4   *Term-level queries*

Elasticsearch has a separate type of query, the term-level query, to support querying structured data. Numbers, dates, ranges, IP addresses, and so on belong to the structured text category. Elasticsearch treats structured and unstructured data differently: unstructured (full-text) data is analyzed, while structured fields are stored as is.

Let's revisit our `book` document and cast an eye on the `edition`, `amazon_rating`, and `release_date` fields (highlighted in bold).

Listing 2.15   **A sample `book` document**

```
{
  "title" : "Effective Java",
  "author" : "Joshua Bloch",
```

```
"synopsis" : "A must-have book for every Java programmer and Java, ...",
"edition" : 3,
"amazon_rating" : 4.7,
"release_date" : "2017-12-27",
...
}
```

When we index the document for the first time, because we do not create an index up front, Elasticsearch deduces the schema by analyzing the values of the fields. The `edition` field, for example, is represented as a numeric (non-text) field and hence is derived as a `long` data type by the engine.

Using similar logic, the `amazon_rating` field is determined to be a `float` data type because the field includes decimal values. Finally, the `release_date` is determined to be a `date` data type because the value is represented in ISO8601 date format (`yyyy-MM-dd`). All three fields are categorized as *non-text* fields, meaning the values are not tokenized (not split into tokens) and not normalized (no synonyms or no root words) but are stored as they are.

Term-level queries produce binary output: results are fetched if the query matches the criteria; otherwise, no results are sent. These queries do not consider *how well the documents match (relevancy)*; instead, they concentrate on whether the query has a match. As relevancy is not considered, term-level queries do not produce a relevancy score. Let's look at a few term-level queries in the next two sections.

2.4.1   *The term query*

A `term` query is used to fetch exact matches for a value provided in the search criteria. For example, to fetch all third edition books, we can write a `term` query as the next listing shows.

Listing 2.16   Fetching third edition books

```
GET books/_search
{
  "_source": ["title","edition"],          ◁──┐ We return just two fields in
  "query": {                                    the response document.
    "term": {                               ◁──── Declares the query
      "edition": {                                as a term-level query
        "value": 3        ◁──┐ Provides the field and
      }                       value as search criteria
    }
  }
}
```

This query returns all third edition books (our index includes only one: *Effective Java*), as shown here:

```
"hits" : [{
  ...
  "_score" : 1.0,
  "_source" : {
```

```
        "title" : "Effective Java",
        "edition" : 3,
        ...
    }
}]
```

If you look carefully at the result, the score is 1.0 by default because term-level queries are not concerned with relevancy, as I mentioned earlier.

2.4.2 *The range query*

A `range` query fetches results that match a range: for example, fetching flights between 1:00 a.m. and 1:00 p.m. or finding a list of teenagers between ages 14 and 19. The `range` query can be applied to dates, numerals, and other attributes, making it a powerful companion when searching for range data.

Continuing our book example, we can use a `range` query to fetch all books with an `amazon_rating` greater than or equal to 4.5 stars and less than or equal to 5 stars.

> **Listing 2.17 A `range` query to fetch books rating 4.5 to 5 stars**

```
GET books/_search
{
  "query": {                    Range query
    "range": {         <──────  declaration      Range to
      "amazon_rating": {              <────────  match
        "gte": 4.5,                        <───  gte: greater than
        "lte": 5          <──────                or equal to
      }                    lte: less than
    }                      or equal to
  }
}
```

This `range` query will fetch three books, because we have three books whose ratings are greater than or equal to 4.5 (I've omitted the output for brevity).

There are a handful of term-level queries, including `terms`, `IDs`, `exists`, `prefix`, and others. We go over them in more detail in chapters 8–10.

So far, we've gone through queries that may be helpful when fetching results based on basic criteria: match on a title, search for a word in multiple fields, find the top-rated sellers, and so on. But in reality, queries can be as complex as you can imagine: for example, fetching first edition books authored by Joshua with a rating greater than 4.5 and published after 2015. Fortunately, Elasticsearch has advanced query types that we can use for complex criteria searches in the form of *compound queries*. Let's look at an example of a compound query in the next section.

2.5 *Compound queries*

Compound queries in Elasticsearch provide a mechanism to create sophisticated search queries. They combine individual queries, called *leaf queries* (like the ones we've seen so far), to build powerful, robust queries that cater to complex scenarios.

(We discuss compound queries at a high level here, but we discuss them in detail in chapter 11.)

The compound queries are as follows:

- Boolean (`bool`)
- Constant score (`constant_score`)
- Function score (`function_score`)
- Boosting (`boosting`)
- Disjunction max (`dis_max`)

Of these, the `bool` query is the most commonly used, so we look at the `bool` query in action here.

2.5.1   Boolean (bool) query

A Boolean (`bool`) query is used to create sophisticated query logic by combining other queries based on Boolean conditions. A `bool` query expects the search to be built using a set of four clauses: `must`, `must_not`, `should`, and `filter`. The following listing shows the format of a `bool` query.

Listing 2.18   Format of a `bool` query with the expected clauses

```
GET books/_search
{
  "query": {
    "bool": {              ◁──┐ A bool query is a combination
      "must": [{ }],              of conditional boolean clauses.
      "must_not": [{ }],   ◁──────────────  The criteria must
      "should": [{ }],     ◁────────        match the documents.
      "filter": [{ }]      ◁──┐             The criteria must not match
    }                         │             (no score contribution).
  }                    The query
}                      should match.
         The query must match
         (no score contribution).
```

As you can see, the `bool` query expects one or more of the clauses `must`, `must_not`, `should`, and `filter` to define the criteria (see table 2.2). More than one criterion can be expressed with a combination of these clauses.

Table 2.2   Boolean (`bool`) query clauses

Clause	Explanation
`must`	The `must` clause means the search criteria in a query *must* match the documents. A positive match bumps up the relevancy score. We build a `must` clause with as many leaf queries as possible.
`must_not`	In a `must_not` clause, the criteria *must not* match the documents. This clause does not contribute to the score (it is run in a filter execution context; more on contexts in chapter 11).

Table 2.2   Boolean (`bool`) query clauses (continued)

Clause	Explanation
should	It is not mandatory for a criterion defined in the `should` clause to match. However, if it matches, the relevancy score is bumped up.
filter	In the `filter` clause, the criteria must match the documents, similar to the `must` clause. The only difference is that the score is irrelevant in the `filter` clause (it is run in a filter execution context).

Let's say our requirement is to search for books that meet these criteria:

- Authored by Joshua
- Rating greater than 4.7
- Published after 2015

We need to employ a `bool` query to combine these criteria into a query with the help of some of the clauses from table 2.2. In the following sections, we construct the compound `bool` query for our search criteria. Rather than introducing you to the full query in one go (which might be overwhelming), we break it into the individual search criteria before putting it all together. To begin, the next section introduces the `must` clause to fetch the authors.

2.5.2   *The must clause*

We want to find all books authored by Joshua, so we can create a `bool` query with a `must` clause. Inside the `must` clause, we write a `match` query that searches for books written by Joshua (we looked at `match` queries in section 2.2.3). Here's the code.

Listing 2.19   A `bool` query with a `must` clause for matching

```
GET books/_search
{
  "query": {
    "bool": {            ◁─┐ A bool
      "must": [{           query    must clause: the documents
        "match": {               ◁── must match the criteria.
          "author": "Joshua Bloch"   ◁─┐ One of the queries (a match query)
        }                              matching books written by Joshua
      }]
    }
  }
}
```

Notice that the `bool` query is enclosed in the `query` object. It has a `must` clause that, in turn, takes multiple queries as an array: here, matching all books written by Joshua Bloch. The query should return two books (*Effective Java* and *Java Concurrency in Practice*), indicating that these are the only two books by Joshua Bloch in our store of documents.

What does it mean when we say that the must clause accepts a set of multiple queries as an array? It means we can add queries to the must clause to make it much more sophisticated. As an example, the following code includes a must clause with two leaf queries: a match query searching for the author and a match_phrase query searching for a phrase.

> **Listing 2.20 A must clause with multiple leaf queries**

```
GET books/_search
{
  "query": {
    "bool": {
      "must": [{                          ◁─┐ must query with
        "match": {                             two leaf queries
          "author": "Joshua Bloch"    ◁─┐ match query finding books
        }                                  authored by Joshua
      },
      {
        "match_phrase": {     ◁─┐ A second query searching
          "synopsis": "best Java programming books"    for a phrase in a field
        }
      }]
    }
  }
}
```

Let's move on and add a must_not clause, which creates a negation criteria.

2.5.3 *The must_not clause*

Let's improve our criteria. We shouldn't fetch Joshua's books if the ratings are below 4.7. To satisfy this condition, we use a must_not clause with a range query that sets the rating to less than (lt) 4.7. The following listing demonstrates the must_not clause, along with the must clause from the original query.

> **Listing 2.21 A bool query with must and must_not clauses**

```
GET books/_search
{
  "query": {                                       must clause that
    "bool": {                                       searches for
      "must": [{ "match": { "author": "Joshua" } }],  ◁─┘ Joshua's books
      "must_not": [{ "range": { "amazon_rating": { "lt": 4.7}}}]   ◁─
    }
  }
}
                                    must_not clause with a range query
                                    that excludes books with lower ratings
```

This query results in only one book, *Effective Java*. Joshua Bloch's other book (*Java Concurrency in Practice*) is dropped from the list because it does not fit the must_not criterion (its rating is 4.3, which is less than the prerequisite of 4.7).

In addition to searching for books written by Joshua with a rating no less than 4.7, we can add another condition to check whether the books match a tag (say, `tag = "Software"`). If it's a match, we expect the score to increase; otherwise, it has no effect on the result. For this, we use the `should` clause, discussed in the next section.

2.5.4 The should clause

The `should` clause behaves like an `OR` operator. That is, if the search words are matched against the `should` query, the relevancy score is bumped up. If the words do not match, the query does not fail; the clause is ignored. The `should` clause is more about increasing the relevancy score than affecting the results.

The next listing adds the `should` clause to the `bool` query. It tries to match the search text if documents have a `Software` tag.

Listing 2.22 Using a `should` query to increase relevancy

```
GET books/_search
{
  "query": {
    "bool": {
      "must": [{"match": {"author": "Joshua"}}],
      "must_not":[{"range":{"amazon_rating":{"lt":4.7}}}],
      "should": [{"match": {"tags": "Software"}}]      should clause with
    }                                                  a match query
  }
}
```

This query returns the result (omitted here) with an increased score: 2.267993, compared to an earlier score of 1.9459882 (you can run the queries to observe the scores).

If you are curious, change the query to include a non-matching word (`tags` equals `"Recipes"`, for example) and retry the query. The query will not fail, but the score will be the same, which proves that the `should` query affects only the scores.

Continuing with the flow, the final clause is `filter`, which works exactly like the `must` clause but doesn't affect the score. Let's see it in action in the next section.

2.5.5 The filter clause

Let's improve our query a bit more, this time by filtering out books published before 2015 (that is, we don't want any books to appear in our resultset that were published before 2015). We use a `filter` clause for this purpose, and any results that don't match the filter criteria are dropped. The following query adds the `filter` clause with a `release_date` clause.

Listing 2.23 A `filter` clause, which doesn't affect relevancy

```
GET books/_search
{
  "query": {
```

```
"bool": {
  "must": [{"match": {"author": "Joshua"}}],
  "must_not":[{"range":{"amazon_rating":{"lt":4.7}}}],
  "should": [{"match": {"tags": "Software"}}],
  "filter":[{"range":{"release_date":{"gte": "2015-01-01"}}}] }
}
}
```

◁──────┐
**filter clause with
a range query**

This query returns only one book, *Effective Java*, as this is the only book in our index that matches all three clauses in the `bool` query. If you run this query in Kibana, notice the unchanged score in the output. The `filter` clause does not affect the score: it runs in a *filter* context, meaning the scores are not altered (more on contexts in chapter 8).

Finally, we also want to find Joshua's third edition books. To do this, we update our `filter` clause to have a `term` query.

Listing 2.24   The `bool` query with the additional `filter` clause

```
GET books/_search
{
  "query": {
    "bool": {
      "must": [{"match": {"author": "Joshua"}}],
      "must_not":[{"range":{"amazon_rating":{"lt":4.7}}}],
      "should": [{"match": {"tags": "Software"}}],
      "filter":[
        {"range":{"release_date":{"gte": "2015-01-01"}}},
        {"term": {"edition": 3}}        ◁──┐  term query in
      ]}                                   │  the filter clause
    }
  }
}
```

This query is a combination of full-text and term-level queries, all working in unison to satisfy our complex requirements. The `bool` query is a Swiss Army knife search tool. We dedicate a lot of time to discussing various compound queries, options, and tips in chapter 11, to enhance our knowledge of this toolkit.

So far, we have scratched the surface by implementing a few searches. The other aspect of search is analytics. Elasticsearch helps derive statistics and aggregations including visual representations of data using bar charts, heat maps, maps, tag clouds, and many more.

While searching helps us find a needle in a haystack, aggregations zoom out to establish a summary of our data, like the total number of server errors in the last hour, average book sales in the third quarter, movies classified by their gross earnings, and so on. We look at aggregations and other functions in chapter 13, but here we check out some high-level examples.

2.6   Aggregations

Up to this point, we've searched for documents from a given corpus of documents. The other side of the coin is analytics. Analytics enables organizations to find insights into the data by looking at the big picture and analyzing the data from a very high level to draw conclusions about it. We use aggregation APIs to provide analytics in Elasticsearch.

Aggregations fall into three categories:

- *Metric aggregations*—Simple aggregations like `sum`, `min`, `max`, and `avg`. They provide an aggregate value across a set of document data.
- *Bucket aggregations*—Aggregations that collect data into "buckets," segregated by intervals such as days, age groups, and so on. These help us build histograms, pie charts, and other visualizations.
- *Pipeline aggregations*—Aggregations that work on the output from other aggregations.

We go over a few examples of metric and bucket aggregations in the coming pages, but we save the in-depth coverage (including working with pipeline aggregations) until chapter 13.

Similar to searching, we use the `_search` endpoint for aggregations. However, we use a new object called `aggs` (short for `aggregations`) in the request in place of the `query` object we've used so far. To reveal the true power of Elasticsearch, we can combine both search and aggregations in a single query.

To demonstrate aggregations effectively, we need to switch gears and index a new set of data: COVID-related data for 10 countries. The covid-26march2021.txt file to index the data using the _bulk API is available with the book's files; here's a snippet of it.

Listing 2.25   Bulk indexing COVID-related data

```
POST covid/_bulk
{"index":{}}
{"country":"USA","date":"2021-03-26","deaths":561142,"recovered":23275268}
{"index":{}}
{"country":"Brazil","date":"2021-03-26","deaths":307326,"recovered":10824095}
...
```

The `_bulk` API indexes our 10 documents into a newly created `covid` index. As we aren't concerned with the document IDs, we let the system generate a random ID for each of them—hence the empty index name and ID in the `index` action of the API: (`{"index":{}}`). Now that we have a set of documents in our covid index, let's carry out some basic aggregation tasks, starting with metric aggregations.

2.6.1   *Metrics*

Metric aggregations are simple aggregations that we use often in our daily lives: for example, what is the average height of the students in a class? What's the minimum hedge trade? What are the gross earnings of a movie? Elasticsearch provides quite a few such metrics, most of which are self-explanatory.

Before we look at the metrics in action, let's quickly go over the syntax for aggregations. Aggregation queries are written using the same Query DSL syntax as search queries; figure 2.16 shows an example. The notable point is that `aggs` is the root-level object, with an `avg` (average) metric defined on an `amazon_rating` field. Once this query is executed, it returns the aggregated results to the user. Let's jump right into executing some metric aggregations.

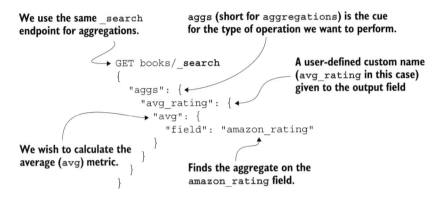

Figure 2.16   Query DSL syntax for finding an average rating aggregation

FINDING THE TOTAL NUMBER OF CRITICAL PATIENTS (SUM METRIC)

Going back to our COVID data, suppose we want to find the total number of critical patients across all 10 countries. For that, we use the following `sum` metric.

Listing 2.26   Fetching the total number of critical patients

```
GET covid/_search
{
  "aggs": {                    Aggregation query
    "critical_patients": {     using the aggs object    User-defined name of the
      "sum": {                                           aggregation request
        "field": "critical"                  The sum metric adds up the
      }                                       number of critical patients.
    }
  }              Field on which the
}                aggregation is applied
```

With this snippet, we create an aggregation-type query; aggs is the cue for Elasticsearch that this is an aggregation task. The sum metric is the type of aggregation we intend to carry out. Here we are asking the engine to find the total number of critical patients by adding the number for each of the countries. The response is something like this:

```
"aggregations" : {
  "critical_patients" : {
    "value" : 44045.0
  }
}
```

The total number of critical patients is returned under our report's name (`critical_patients`) in the response. Note that the response consists of all the documents returned, if we do not ask explicitly to suppress them. We can set `size=0` at the root level to stop the response from containing the original source documents:

```
GET covid/_search
{
  "size": 0,
  "aggs": {
    ...
  }
}
```

Now that we know how aggregations work for a `sum` metric, let's go over a couple of the others.

USING OTHER METRICS

In a similar vein, if we want to find the highest number of deaths across all countries in our COVID data, we can use a `max` aggregation.

Listing 2.27   Using the `max` metric

```
GET covid/_search
{
  "size": 0,
  "aggs": {
    "max_deaths": {
      "max": {
        "field": "deaths"
      }
    }
  }
}
```

This query returns the highest number of deaths among the 10 countries in our data set:

```
"aggregations" : {
  "max_deaths" : {
    "value" : 561142.0
  }
}
```

Similarly, we can find the minimum (`min`), average (`avg`), and other metrics. But there's a statistical function that returns all of these basic metrics together: the `stats` metric.

Listing 2.28   Returning all statistics with the `stats` metric

```
GET covid/_search
{
  "size": 0,
  "aggs": {
    "all_stats": {
```

```
      "stats": {
        "field": "deaths"
      }
    }
  }
}
```

The stats query returns all
five core metrics at once.

This `stats` query returns `count`, `avg`, `max`, `min`, and `sum`, all in one shot. Here's the response from our initial `stats` query:

```
"aggregations" : {
  "all_stats" : {
    "count" : 10,
    "min" : 30772.0,
    "max" : 561142.0,
    "avg" : 163689.1,
    "sum" : 1636891.0
  }
}
```

> **NOTE** If you are curious, swap the `stats` query with an `extended_stats` query and check the result. You'll see a lot more stats, including variance, standard deviation, and others. I'll leave it to you to experiment (the code is available with the book's files).

Now that we know what metric aggregations are all about, let's briefly look at another type of aggregations: bucket aggregations.

2.6.2   *Bucket aggregations*

A bucket aggregation (or simply *bucketing*) segregates data into various groups or *buckets*. For example, we can add groups like these to our buckets: a survey of adult groups by age bracket (20–30, 31–40, 41–50), movies by review ratings, or number of new houses constructed per month.

Elasticsearch provides at least two dozen aggregations out of the box, each having its own bucketing strategy. What's more, we can nest aggregations under the main buckets. Let's look at a couple of bucketing aggregations in action.

HISTOGRAM BUCKETS

The `histogram` bucketing aggregation creates a list of buckets representing a numerical value by going over all the documents. For example, if we want to categorize countries by the number of critical patients in buckets of 2,500, we can write the following query.

Listing 2.29   Countries by critical patients in buckets of 2,500

```
GET covid/_search
{
  "size": 0,
  "aggs": {
    "critical_patients_as_histogram": {
```

User-defined name
of the report

```
        "histogram": {
            "field": "critical",
            "interval": 2500
        }
      }
    }
  }
```

Type of bucketing aggregation:
histogram chart, in this case

Bucket interval

Field on which the
aggregation is applied

The response is something like the following, where each bucket has a key and a value:

```
"aggregations" : {
  "critical_patients_as_histogram" : {
    "buckets" : [{
      "key" : 0.0,
      "doc_count" : 4
    },
    {
      "key" : 2500.0,
      "doc_count" : 3
    },
    {
      "key" : 5000.0,
      "doc_count" : 0
    },
    {
      "key" : 7500.0,
      "doc_count" : 3
    }]
  }
}
```

The first bucket has four documents (countries) with a number of critical patients up to 2,500. The second bucket has three countries with a number of critical patients between 2,500 and 5,000, and so on.

RANGE BUCKETS

The `range` bucketing aggregation defines a set of buckets based on predefined ranges. For example, say we want to segregate the number of COVID casualties by country (casualties up to 60,000, 60,000–70,000, 70,000–80,000, and 80,000–120,000). We can define those ranges as shown here.

Listing 2.30   Casualties in custom ranges using `range` bucketing

```
GET covid/_search
{
  "size": 0,
  "aggs": {
    "range_countries": {
      "range": {
        "field": "deaths",
        "ranges": [
          {"to": 60000},
          {"from": 60000,"to": 70000},
```

range bucketing
aggregation

Field on which to
apply the aggregation

Defines the custom
ranges as an array

```
          {"from": 70000,"to": 80000},
          {"from": 80000,"to": 120000}
        ]
      }
    }
  }
}
```

We define a `range` aggregation bucket type with a set of custom ranges. Once the query is executed, the resulting buckets show the keys with the custom bucket ranges and the number of documents for each range:

```
"aggregations" : {
  "range_countries" : {
    "buckets" : [{
      "key" : "*-60000.0",
      "to" : 60000.0,
      "doc_count" : 1
    },{
      "key" : "60000.0-70000.0",
      "from" : 60000.0,
      "to" : 70000.0,
      "doc_count" : 0
    },{
      "key" : "70000.0-80000.0",
      "from" : 70000.0,
      "to" : 80000.0,
      "doc_count" : 2
    },{
      "key" : "80000.0-120000.0",
      "from" : 80000.0,
      "to" : 120000.0,
      "doc_count" : 3
    }]
  }
}
```

The results indicate that one country has up to 60,000 casualties, three countries a number of casualties between 80,000 and 12,0000, and so on.

We can perform a rich set of aggregations on our data using out-of-the-box statistical functions. We run through these in chapter 13; until then, hold tight.

We've barely scratched the surface of what Elasticsearch offers; we explore much more functionality in the coming chapters. For now, it's time to call it a wrap. In the next chapter, we examine the architecture of Elasticsearch, the mechanics of search, its moving parts, and much more.

Summary

- Elasticsearch provides a set of document APIs for indexing data, and Kibana's Dev Tools console helps with writing indexing queries for persistence.
- To retrieve a document using a single document API, we issue a GET command on the index with an ID (GET <index_name>/_doc/<ID>).

- To retrieve multiple documents, if the document identifiers are available, we can use an `ids` query.
- Elasticsearch exposes a wide set of search APIs, including basic and advanced queries.
- Full-text queries search through unstructured data to find relevant documents.
- Term queries search through structured data like numbers and dates to find documents that match.
- Compound queries allow us to compile leaf queries and create a more advanced set of queries. The `bool` query, one of the compound queries, provides a mechanism to create an advanced query with multiple clauses (for example, `must`, `must_not`, `should`, and `filter`). These clauses help us create sophisticated queries.
- Whereas a search looks for matching documents based on given criteria, analytics lets us aggregate data by providing statistical functions.
- Metric aggregations fetch common aggregations like `max`, `min`, `sum`, and `avg`.
- Bucketing aggregations segregate documents into various groups (buckets) based on certain criteria.

Architecture 3

This chapter covers

- High-level architecture and Elasticsearch's building blocks
- Search and indexing mechanics
- Understanding how an inverted index works
- Relevancy and similarity algorithms
- Routing algorithms

In chapter 2, we played with fundamental Elasticsearch features: we indexed documents, executed search queries, walked through analytical functions, and more. We briefly played with the server, without knowing much about its internals. The good news is that we don't need to break a sweat to get started with Elasticsearch. It is easy to use at a simple level but takes time to master.

Of course, Elasticsearch, like any other search engine, requires deep dives to become a master of the technology. That said, the product is designed to work out of the box with intuitive APIs and tools, and we can use the software without much prerequisite knowledge. Before we get carried away with the easy-to-use, hands-on aspects of Elasticsearch, it will benefit us in the long run to understand the high-level architecture, the inner workings of the server, and the dichotomy of its moving parts.

Getting a grip on the server is highly recommended for engineers wishing to use Elasticsearch effectively and efficiently. We may need to debug why query results are not what we expect. We may be tasked with finding the reasons for performance degradation arising from the exponential growth of indexed data. The cluster may become unstable due to memory problems, leading to a 2:00 a.m. production call. Or the business requirements may call for a custom language analyzer to integrate the application with another country's language.

As engineers, we are expected to be able to fine-tune queries or tweak administrative features or spin up an Elasticsearch multicluster farm for a business need. And to gain such knowledge, we must master the technology by understanding its internal workings—its bolts and bearings—which is what this chapter is all about.

In this chapter, we talk through the building blocks of Elasticsearch and gain a better understanding of how the searching and indexing process works behind the scenes. We learn about fundamentals that underlie the search engine, such as inverted indexes, relevancy, and text analysis. Finally, we explore the clustering and distributed nature of the Elasticsearch server. First, let's look at how the Elasticsearch engine works from a high level.

3.1   *A high-level overview*

Elasticsearch is a server-side application capable of running on anything from personal PCs to a farm of computers serving gigabytes, terabytes, or petabytes of data. It was developed using the Java programming language with Apache Lucene under the hood.

Apache Lucene, a high-performance, full-text searching library developed in Java, is well-known for its powerful searching and indexing features. However, Lucene is not a complete application that we can simply download, install, and work with. As it is a library, we are expected to integrate applications with it via programming interfaces. Elasticsearch does exactly that: it wraps Lucene as its core full-text search library, building a distributed and scalable server-side application. Elasticsearch built a programming language-agnostic application with Lucene as the centerpiece for serving full-text searches.

Elasticsearch is more than just a full-text search engine, however. It has grown into a popular search engine with aggregations and analytics that serve various use cases (application monitoring, log data analytics, web app search functions, security event capturing, machine learning, and more). It is a performant, scalable, modern search engine with high availability, fault tolerance, and speed as its primary goals.

Just as a bank account is useless without money in it, Elasticsearch is nothing without data: the data that goes into Elasticsearch and the data that comes out. Let's spend some time looking at how Elasticsearch treats this data.

3.1.1   *Data in*

Elasticsearch needs data before it can provide answers to queries. Data can be indexed into Elasticsearch from multiple sources and in various ways: extracted from a database, copied from file systems, loaded from other systems (including real-time streaming systems), and so on.

Figure 3.1 shows data being ingested into Elasticsearch via three data sources:

- *Database*—Applications usually store data in a database as an authoritative system of record. We can prime Elasticsearch with data fetched from a database on a batch or near-real-time basis. As the data shape in a database may not be exactly what Elasticsearch expects, we can use an extract, transform, load (ETL) tool (such as Logstash—a data processing tool from the Elastic suite) to transform and enrich the data before it is indexed into Elasticsearch.

- *File store*—Applications, virtual machines (VMs), databases, and other systems spit out tons of logs and metrics data. This data is important for analyzing errors, debugging applications, tracing user requests, and auditing. It can be held in physical hardware storage or cloud locations like AWS S3 or Azure files/blobs. This data must be brought into Elasticsearch for search, analytics, and storage. We can use tools such as Filebeat (a data shipper with the sole aim of getting data from files into destinations like Elasticsearch) or Logstash to dump data into Elasticsearch for search, debug, and analysis purposes.

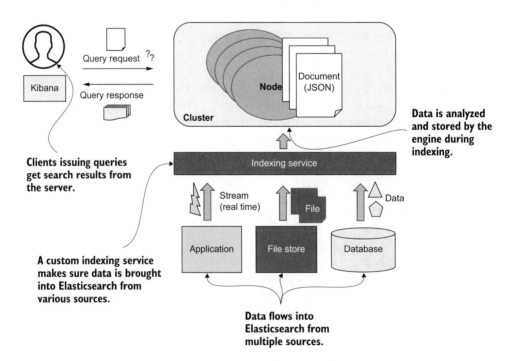

Figure 3.1   Priming Elasticsearch with data

- *Applications*—Some applications like eBay, Twitter, transport sites (trains and planes), and pricing/quotes engines emit events as streams of data, usually in real time. We can use Elastic Stack components like Logstash or build in-house, real-time streaming libraries that publish data to Elasticsearch; this data is then used for search functionality.

Elasticsearch expects data to come from persistent storage or in real time to be analyzed and processed internally. The analysis process in the form of search and analytics helps retrieve data efficiently. In a typical setup, organizations use ETL tools to transport data into Elasticsearch. The ingested data is searchable once it makes it through the Elasticsearch store.

3.1.2   Processing data

The basic unit of information in Elasticsearch is represented by a JSON document. For example, we can create a news article as a JSON document for a magazine, as the following listing shows.

Listing 3.1   Typical news article represented as a JSON document

```
{
  "title":"Is Remote Working the New Norm?",
  "author":"John Doe",
  "synopsis":"Covid changed lives. It changed the way we work..",
  "publish_date":"2021-01-01",
  "number_of_words":3500
}
```

COLLECTING DATA

Just as we store data in a relational database, we need to persist (store) data in Elasticsearch. Elasticsearch stores all its data on disk using optimized and compressed techniques. In addition to our business data, Elasticsearch has its own data related to cluster state, transnational information, and so on that needs storage.

If you installed Elasticsearch using a binary (zipped version), it has a folder called data under the installation folder. Data folders can be mounted as network file systems, defined as mount paths, or declared by the `path.data` variable. Regardless of the installation mechanism, Elasticsearch stores data on the optimized file system.

Going a bit further into data folders, Elasticsearch categorizes data per node and per data type. Each node has a dedicated folder with a set of buckets containing related data. Elasticsearch creates a set of buckets (called *indexes* in Elasticsearch lingo) based on each type of data. Simply put, an index is a logical collection of documents. It's a bucket to hold our business data.

For example, news articles may be housed in a bucket called `news` and trades in an index called `trades`, and movies may be split across genre-based indexes such as `classic_movies`, `comedy_movies`, `horror_movies`, and so on. All documents of a particular type (say, cars, trades, or students) end up in their own index. We can create as many indexes as we wish, based on our requirements (keeping in mind memory/size limitations).

> **An index in Elasticsearch is like a table in a database**
>
> In a relational database, we define a table to hold our records. Extending this concept, an index in Elasticsearch is equivalent to a table in a database; Elasticsearch allows us to create a schema-free index (meaning we don't need to create a schema based on our data model beforehand, unlike in a database, where a table cannot exists without a schema), which helps with indexing free-form text.
>
> An *index* is a logical collection holding documents in shards. *Shards* are running instances of Apache Lucene. (Understanding the mechanics is a rabbit hole and may seem overwhelming—hang on tight, because we cover shards and other moving parts shortly.)

TYPES OF DATA

Data comes in various types: dates, numbers, strings, Booleans, IP addresses, locations, and so on. Elasticsearch lets us index documents by supporting rich data types. A process called *mapping* converts JSON data types into appropriate Elasticsearch data types. Mapping uses a schema definition to let Elasticsearch know how to handle our data fields. For example, the `title` and `synopsis` fields in the news article document in listing 3.1 are text fields, while `published_date` is a date field and `number_of_words` is a numeric field.

While indexing data, Elasticsearch analyzes incoming data field by field. It analyzes each field using advanced algorithms based on mapping definitions. It then stores these fields in efficient data structures such that the data is in a form to be searched and analyzed for our purposes. Full-text fields undergo an additional process called *text analysis*, which is the heart and soul of a modern search engine like Elasticsearch. Text analysis (discussed in the next section) is a crucial step in getting our raw data into a form that enables Elasticsearch to retrieve data efficiently while supporting a myriad of queries.

ANALYZING DATA

Data represented as text is analyzed during the text analysis phase. The text is broken down into words (called *tokens*) using a set of rules. Fundamentally, two processes happen during the analysis process: tokenization and normalization.

Tokenization is the process of breaking text into tokens based on a set of rules. As shown in table 3.1, text in the `synopsis` field is broken down into individual words (tokens) separated by a whitespace delimiter (this is done by a `standard` tokenizer—a built-in software component that breaks text into tokens based on predefined rules).

Table 3.1 Untokenized vs. tokenized `synopsis` field

Untokenized `String` (before tokenization)	`Peter Piper picked a peck of Pickled-peppers!`
Tokenized `String` (after tokenization)	`[peter,piper,picked,a,peck,of,pickled,peppers]` Notes: the tokens were lowercased, and the hyphen and exclamation point were removed.

If we search for *Peter* and *Peppers*, for example, we expect the document to match our search criteria. It would be difficult to match search criteria if text was dumped in as is without being converted to tokens.

While we've separated the words based on whitespace in the example in table 3.1, a few tokenizer variants available in Elasticsearch can help us extract tokens based on digits, nonletters, stop words, and so on; we are not limited to whitespace. For example, suppose we want to search our data in other ways. Continuing the same example, users could use any of the following search text:

- "Who is Peter Piper?"
- "What did Peter pick?"
- "Has Peter picked pickled peppers?"
- "Peter Pickle Peppers"
- "Chili pickles" (our search will return this document on this query)

During tokenization, Elasticsearch persists the tokens (individual words) but doesn't enhance, enrich, or transform them. That is, the tokens are persisted as is. If we search for "pickled peppers", we'll probably get this Peter Piper document, although the relevance score (which tells us how closely the result of a search matches the query criteria) may be a bit low. However, searching for "chili capsicum" may yield no results (the other name for a pepper is capsicum). Unless we have enriched tokens, there's no easy way to answer the search for such text—and that's why we have another process called normalization that works on these tokens.

Normalization helps build a rich user experience by creating additional data around tokens. It is a process of reducing (stemming) tokens to root words or creating synonyms for them. For example:

- The `peppers` token can be stemmed to create alternate words like *capsicum*.
- The `Piper` token can be stemmed to produce *Bagpiper*.

Normalization can also help build a list of synonyms for tokens, again enriching the user's search experience. For instance, a list of synonyms for *work* may include *working, office work, employment*, or *job*; and *authoring, authored*, and *authored by* all relate to *author*.

Along with the tokens, root words, synonyms, and so on are stored in an advanced data structure called an *inverted index*. Let's take an example of a single word, *vaccine*. It can be analyzed and stored in the inverted index against several root words or synonyms like *vaccination, vaccinated, immunization, immune, inoculation, booster jab*, and so forth.

When a user searches for *immunization*, for example, documents with *vaccine* or related words may pop up, as these words are related to each other. If you search for "where can I get immunization for covid" on Google, there is a high likelihood that your results will be *vaccine* related. When I tried this search, Google returned the expected results (see figure 3.2).

Figure 3.2   Search results (as expected) from Google

We learn about this analysis phase in chapter 7. Once data has been analyzed, it is sent to a particular data node for persistence. Usually, text analysis, persistence activities, data replication, and so on are carried out in a fraction of a second, so the data is ready for consumption in less than a second after it is indexed (a service level agreement [SLA] that Elasticsearch vouches for). The next step after data processing in Elasticsearch is data retrieval in the form of search and analytics, which we discuss in the next section.

3.1.3   *Data out*

After data is collected, analyzed, and stored in Elasticsearch, it is retrieved via search and analytical queries. Search fetches matching data for a specified query, while analytics gathers data to form summarized statistics. Search looks not just for exact word-to-word matches but also for root words, synonyms, spelling mistakes, and more. The advanced features of full-text queries are what make modern search engines like Elasticsearch as preferred choices for search.

When a search query is issued, if the field is a full-text field, it undergoes an analysis phase similar to that performed when the field was indexed. That is, the query is tokenized and normalized using the same analyzers associated with that field. The respective tokens are searched and matched in the inverted index, and results based on the matches are relayed back to the client. For example, if a field is set with a French analyzer, the same analyzer is used during the search phase. This guarantees that words indexed and inserted into inverted indexes are also matched while searching.

As in any application, a bunch of building blocks make up the Elasticsearch server. We discuss those in the next section, and we work extensively with them throughout this book.

3.2 The building blocks

In the last chapter, we indexed sample documents and carried out searches on them. However, we pushed the discussion of components like indexes, documents, shards, and replicas to a later time—and that time is here. These components make up Elasticsearch and are the building blocks of the search engine. Let's examine them in detail and learn their significance.

3.2.1 Documents

A *document* is the basic unit of information indexed by Elasticsearch for storage. Each document's individual fields are analyzed for faster searches and analytics. Elasticsearch expects documents in JSON format. JSON is a simple human-readable data format that has gained popularity in recent years. It represents data as key-value pairs: for example {"name":"John Doe"}. When we communicate with Elasticsearch over RESTful APIs, we send queries to Elasticsearch as JSON objects. Elasticsearch, in turn, serializes these JSON documents and stores them in its distributed document store once they are analyzed.

PARSING DOCUMENT DATA

Our data, represented as JSON documents, is parsed by Elasticsearch during the indexing process. For example, figure 3.3 represents a JSON document for a student object.

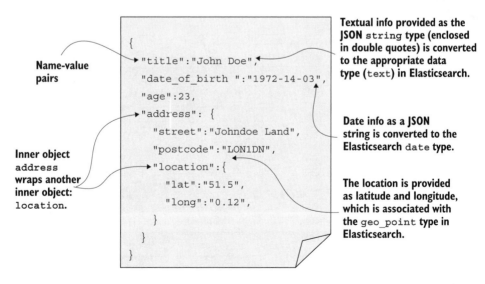

Figure 3.3 A student document represented in JSON format

We describe the attributes of the student using name-value pairs. Name fields are always strings in quotes, and values conform to JSON's data types (`int`, `string`, `boolean`, and so on). The inner objects can be represented as nested objects, which JSON supports, such as the `address` field for the `student` document. Note that JSON doesn't have a date type defined, but industry practice is to provide the date and time data as a string (preferably in ISO 8601 format: `yyyy-MM-dd`, or with a time component, `yyyy-MM-ddThh:mm:ss`). Elasticsearch parses stringified date information to extract data based on the schema definition.

Elasticsearch uses the JSON parser to unmarshal data into appropriate types based on mapping rules available on the index. Each index has a set of mapping rules that Elasticsearch applies when a document is being indexed or a search query is executed. We learn more about mapping in chapter 4.

Elasticsearch reads values from the JSON document and converts them into specific data types for analysis and storing. Just as JSON supports data nesting (a top-level object consisting of a next-level object wrapped up again with another object underneath), Elasticsearch also supports nested data structures.

RELATIONAL DATABASE ANALOGY

If you have some understanding of relational databases, the analogy shown in figure 3.4 may help. Remember, Elasticsearch can be used as a storage server (although I wouldn't suggest using a primary storage service—we discuss the reasons later) just like any database. Comparing and contrasting Elasticsearch against a database is fair. The JSON document from figure 3.3 is equivalent to a record in the table of a relational database (figure 3.4).

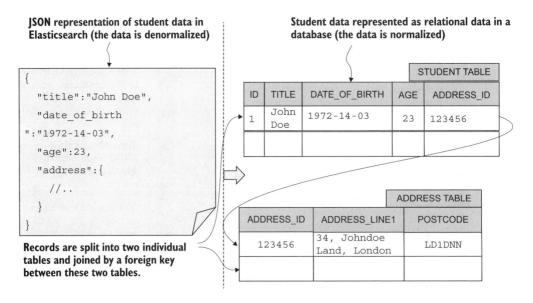

Figure 3.4 A JSON document vs. a relational database table structure

The data is pretty much the same except for how it is formed, formatted, and stored in these structures: database structures are relational, while those in Elasticsearch are denormalized and nonrelational. A document in Elasticsearch consists of self-contained information with no relations.

As you can see on the right side in figure 3.4, the STUDENT and ADDRESS tables are related by the foreign key ADDRESS_ID, which appears in both tables. Elasticsearch doesn't have the concept of relationships (or, shall we say, a limited scope of relationships is supported), so the entire student document is stored in a single index. The inner objects (address field in figure 3.4) are in the same index as the main fields.

> **NOTE** Data in Elasticsearch is denormalized to assist with speedy search and retrieval, unlike in a relational database, where data is normalized in various forms. While you can create parent-child relationships to some extent in Elasticsearch, doing so can lead to bottlenecks and performance degradation. If your data is expected to be relational, Elasticsearch may not be the right solution.

Just as we can insert multiple records in a table, we can index several JSON documents into Elasticsearch. However, unlike in a relational database, where we must create the table schema up front, Elasticsearch (like other NoSQL databases) lets you insert documents without a predefined schema. This *schema-less* feature comes in handy during testing and development but can also be a problem in production environments.

DOCUMENT OPERATION APIS

As a standard across Elasticsearch, indexing documents is expected to use clearly defined document APIs. There are two types of document APIs: those that work on a single document and those that work on multiple documents at once (batches). We can index or retrieve documents one by one using single-document APIs or batch them up using multidocument APIs (exposed as RESTful APIs over HTTP). These are briefly described here:

- *Single-document APIs*—Perform actions on individual documents, one by one. More like CRUD-related operations (create, read, update, and delete), these APIs let us get, index, delete, and update documents.
- *Multiple-document APIs*—Work with multiple documents at once. They allow us to delete and update multiple documents with a single query, index in bulk, and reindex data from source index to target index.

Each API has a specific usage, as we discuss in detail in chapter 5.

While we are on the subject of documents, one thing often comes up: document types. Although document types are deprecated and removed from version 8.x, they may appear on your radar when working with Elasticsearch and confuse you, especially with older (version 5.x or less) versions of Elasticsearch. So, let's take a moment to understand what they are and their current state before learning about indexes.

Removal of types

The data we persist has a specific shape: a movie document has properties related to a movie, data for a car has properties related to cars, and an employee document has data relevant to the context of employment and business. We index these JSON documents into respective buckets or collections: movie documents consisting of movie data need to be held in an index named `movies`, for example. Thus we index a document of type `Movie` into a `movies` index, `Car` into a `cars` index, and so on. That is, a movie document that we index into Elasticsearch has a type called `Movie`. Likewise, all car documents fall under the `Car` type, employee documents under the `Employee` type, and so on.

Prior to version 5.x, Elasticsearch allowed users to index multiple types of documents in a single index. That is, a `car` index could include types like `Cars`, `Peformance-Cars`, `CarItems`, `CarSales`, `DealerShowRooms`, `UsedCars`, or even `Customers`, `Orders`, and so on. While this sounds like a good plan to hold all car-related models in one place, there is a limitation.

In a database, the columns in a table are independent of each other. Unfortunately, that's not the case for Elasticsearch. Document fields may be various types, but they exist in the same index. That means a field in one type having a `text` data type cannot have a different type, such as `date`, in another index. This is because of the way Lucene maintains field types in an index. Because Lucene manages fields on an index level, there is no flexibility to declare two fields of different data types in the same index.

A single type per index was introduced beginning with version 6.0, so, for example, the `cars` index is expected to hold just `car` documents. When indexing a `car` document, the index name should be followed by the type: for example, `PUT cars/car/1` indexes a car document with ID `1` and puts it into a `cars` index.

However, the APIs were upgraded beginning with version 7.0.0: the document type is replaced by the default document type `_doc`, which is now a permanent fixture in the URL as an endpoint. Hence, the URL is `PUT cars/_doc/1`. As the figure shows, Elasticsearch allows us to use the types, but it throws a warning (as shown on the right in the figure) if our version is pre-8.x, advising us to use typeless endpoints.

The URL includes the type (`car`) of the document (which is deprecated and removed in version 8.0).

```
PUT cars/car/1
{
  "make":"Toyota",
  "model":"Avensis"
}
```

> **V7.0: The explicit type is replaced with an endpoint named** `_doc` **(not the document type).**

```
PUT cars/_doc/1
{
  ...
}
```

```
#! [types removal] Specifying types in document
index requests is deprecated, use the typeless
endpoints instead (/{index}/_doc/{id},
/{index}/_doc, or /{index}/_create/{id}).

  {
    "_index" : "cars",
    "_type" : "car",
    "_id" : "1",
    "_version" : 1,
    "result" : "created",
    "_shards" : {
      "total" : 2,
      "successful" : 1,
      "failed" : 0
    },
    "_seq_no" : 0,
    "_primary_term" : 1
  }
```

While using the type is allowed up to version 7.x (you will receive a warning as shown here), it is advisable to drop the type completely.

Warning using pre-version-8 typed document indexing

Always model your data so that each index has one particular data shape. When we index a document, we create a one-to-one mapping between the document and the index. That is, one index can only have one document type. We follow this principle throughout the book.

Now that we know our data is presented as JSON documents to be stored in Elasticsearch, the next logical step is to find out where these documents are stored. Just like a table in a database that hosts records, a special bucket (collection) called an *index* holds all documents of a particular shape in Elasticsearch. Details are in the next section.

3.2.2 Indexes

We need a container to host our documents in the store. For this, Elasticsearch creates an index as a logical collection of documents. Just as we keep paper documents in a filing cabinet, Elasticsearch keeps data documents in an index, except the index is not a physical storage place; it is a logical grouping. It is composed of (or backed up by) *shards.* Figure 3.5 shows a `cars` index composed of three shards on three nodes (a *node* is an instance of Elasticsearch), one shard per node.

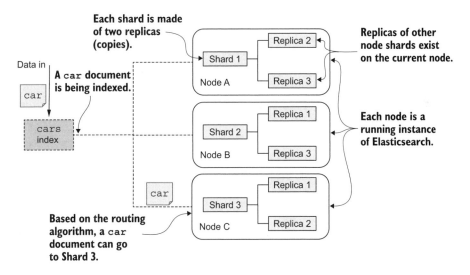

Figure 3.5 An index designed with three shards and two replicas per shard

In addition to having three shards, the index is declared to have *two replicas per shard,* both hosted on other nodes. That leads to a question: what is a shard?

Shards are the physical instances of Apache Lucene, the workhorses behind the scenes in getting our data in and out of storage. In other words, shards take care of the physical storage and retrieval of our data.

NOTE Starting with version 7.x, any index created is set to be backed up by a single shard and a replica by default. The index's shards and replicas can be configured and customized based on data size needs. While replicas can be resized, the number of shards cannot be modified on a live index.

Shards can be categorized as primary and replicas. *Primary* shards hold documents, whereas *replica* shards (or simply *replicas*), as the name suggests, are copies of primary shards. We can have one or more replicas for each shard. We can also have no replicas, but such a design is not advisable for production environments—in real-world production environments, we create multiple replicas for each shard. Replicas hold data copies, increasing the system's redundancy and thus helping speed up search queries. We learn more about shards and replicas in the next section.

An index can hold any number of documents (but as we discussed earlier, only one document type), so it is advisable to find an optimum size for your needs (we discuss shard sizing in chapter 14). Each index can either exist on a single node or be distributed across multiple nodes in the cluster. Using the design in figure 3.6 (one index with one shard and two replicas), every document we index will be stored as three copies: one in a shard and two copies on the replicas.

NOTE Optimal index sizing must be carried out before setting up the index. The size depends on the data we may have to serve today as well as the estimated size for the future. Replicas create additional copies of data, so be sure you create capacity considering this. We look at index sizing in chapter 14.

Every index has properties like mappings, settings, and aliases. Mapping is a process of defining schema definitions, while settings let us configure the shards and replicas. Aliases are alternate names given to a single index or a set of indexes. A few settings, such as the number of replicas, can be set dynamically; but other properties, like the number of shards, cannot be changed when the index is in operation. We should ideally create templates for the configuration of any new indexes.

We use RESTful APIs to work on indexes: creating and deleting indexes, changing their settings, closing and opening them, reindexing data, and other operations. We work through these APIs extensively in chapter 6.

3.2.3   *Data streams*

Indexes (such as `movies`, `movie_reviews`, etc.) hold and collect data. Over time, they can become huge as more data is accumulated and stored. Adding nodes can alleviate this problem by distributing shards across more nodes. The expectation is that such data doesn't need to be rolled over into newer indexes periodically (hourly, daily, or monthly). Keeping this in mind, let's look at a different type of data: time-series data.

As the name indicates, time-series data is time-sensitive and time-dependent. Take the example of logs generated by an Apache web server, shown in figure 3.6.

```
83.149.9.216 - - [17/May/2015:10:05:03 +0000] "GET /presentations/logstash-monitorama-2013/images/kibana-search.png HTTP/1.1" 200 203023
"http://semicomplete.com/presentations/logstash-monitorama-2013/" "Mozilla/5.0 (Macintosh; Intel Mac OS X 10_9_1) AppleWebKit/537.36 (KHTML, like Gecko)
Chrome/32.0.1700.77 Safari/537.36"
83.149.9.216 - - [17/May/2015:10:05:43 +0000] "GET /presentations/logstash-monitorama-2013/images/kibana-dashboard3.png HTTP/1.1" 200 171717
"http://semicomplete.com/presentations/logstash-monitorama-2013/" "Mozilla/5.0 (Macintosh; Intel Mac OS X 10_9_1) AppleWebKit/537.36 (KHTML, like Gecko)
Chrome/32.0.1700.77 Safari/537.36"
83.149.9.216 - - [17/May/2015:10:05:47 +0000] "GET /presentations/logstash-monitorama-2013/plugin/highlight/highlight.js HTTP/1.1" 200 26185
"http://semicomplete.com/presentations/logstash-monitorama-2013/" "Mozilla/5.0 (Macintosh; Intel Mac OS X 10_9_1) AppleWebKit/537.36 (KHTML, like Gecko)
Chrome/32.0.1700.77 Safari/537.36"
83.149.9.216 - - [17/May/2015:10:05:12 +0000] "GET /presentations/logstash-monitorama-2013/plugin/zoom-js/zoom.js HTTP/1.1" 200 7697
"http://semicomplete.com/presentations/logstash-monitorama-2013/" "Mozilla/5.0 (Macintosh; Intel Mac OS X 10_9_1) AppleWebKit/537.36 (KHTML, like Gecko)
Chrome/32.0.1700.77 Safari/537.36"
83.149.9.216 - - [17/May/2015:10:05:07 +0000] "GET /presentations/logstash-monitorama-2013/plugin/notes/notes.js HTTP/1.1" 200 2892
"http://semicomplete.com/presentations/logstash-monitorama-2013/" "Mozilla/5.0 (Macintosh; Intel Mac OS X 10_9_1) AppleWebKit/537.36 (KHTML, like Gecko)
Chrome/32.0.1700.77 Safari/537.36"
83.149.9.216 - - [17/May/2015:10:05:34 +0000] "GET /presentations/logstash-monitorama-2013/images/sad-medic.png HTTP/1.1" 200 430406
"http://semicomplete.com/presentations/logstash-monitorama-2013/" "Mozilla/5.0 (Macintosh; Intel Mac OS X 10_9_1) AppleWebKit/537.36 (KHTML, like Gecko)
Chrome/32.0.1700.77 Safari/537.36"
83.149.9.216 - - [17/May/2015:10:05:57 +0000] "GET /presentations/logstash-monitorama-2013/css/fonts/Roboto-Bold.ttf HTTP/1.1" 200 38720
"http://semicomplete.com/presentations/logstash-monitorama-2013/" "Mozilla/5.0 (Macintosh; Intel Mac OS X 10_9_1) AppleWebKit/537.36 (KHTML, like Gecko)
Chrome/32.0.1700.77 Safari/537.36"
```

Figure 3.6   Sample Apache web server log file

Logs are continuously written to the current day's log file. Each log statement has an associated timestamp. At midnight, the file is backed up with a date stamp, and a new file is created for the new day. The log framework initiates the rollover automatically during the day cutover.

If we wish to hold log data in Elasticsearch, we need to rethink the strategy for indexing data that changes/rolls over periodically. We can write an index-rollover script that rolls over the indexes every day at midnight—but there's more to this than just rolling over data. For example, we also need to direct search requests against a single *mother* index rather than multiple rolling indexes. That is, we don't want to issue queries like `GET index1,index2,index3/_search`, specifying individual indexes; instead, we want to invoke `GET myalias/search`, returning data from all underlying indexes. We create an alias for this purpose in chapter 6.

> **DEFINITION**   An *alias* is an alternate name for a single index or a set of multiple indexes. The ideal way to search against multiple indexes is to create an alias pointing to them. When we search against an alias, we are essentially searching against all the indexes managed by this alias.

This leads us to an important concept called a *data stream*: an index mechanism to hold time-series data. This is discussed in the next section.

TIME-SERIES DATA

Data streams accommodate time-series data in Elasticsearch—they let us hold data in multiple indexes but allow access as a single resource for search and analytical related queries. As discussed earlier, data tagged to a date or time axis, such as logs, automated car events, daily weather forecasts, pollution levels in a city, Black Friday sales by hour, and so on, is expected to be hosted in timed indexes. On a high level, these indexes are called *data streams*. Behind the scenes, each data stream has a set of indexes for each time point. These indexes are auto-generated by Elasticsearch and are hidden.

Figure 3.7 shows an example data stream for ecommerce order logs generated and captured daily. It also shows that the order data stream consists of auto-generated hidden indexes by day. The data stream itself is nothing more than an alias for the time-series (rolling) hidden indexes behind the scenes. While search/read requests span all of the data stream's backing hidden indexes, indexing requests are only directed to the new (current) index.

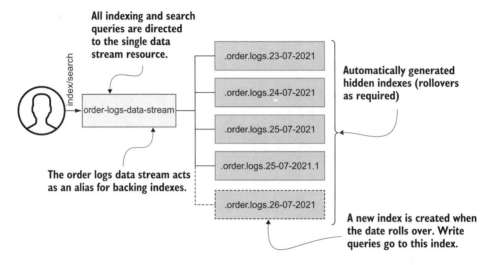

Figure 3.7   A data stream consists of automatically generated hidden indexes.

Data streams are created using a matching indexing template. *Templates* are blueprints consisting of settings and configuration values used for creating resources like indexes. Indexes created from a template inherit the settings defined in the template. We look at developing data streams with indexing templates in chapter 6.

In the last couple of sections, we briefly explained that indexes and data streams are distributed across shards and replicas. Let's dig deeper into these components.

3.2.4   *Shards and replicas*

Shards are software components that hold data, create support data structures (like inverted indexes), manage queries, and analyze data in Elasticsearch. They are instances of Apache Lucene allocated to an index during index creation. During the process of indexing, a document travels through to the shard. Shards create immutable file segments to hold the document in a durable file system.

Lucene is a high-performance engine for indexing documents efficiently. A lot goes on behind the scenes when indexing a document, and Lucene does this very efficiently. For example, documents are initially copied into an in-memory buffer on the shard and then written to writable segments before being merged and finalized to the underlying file system store. Figure 3.8 shows the inner workings of a Lucene engine during indexing.

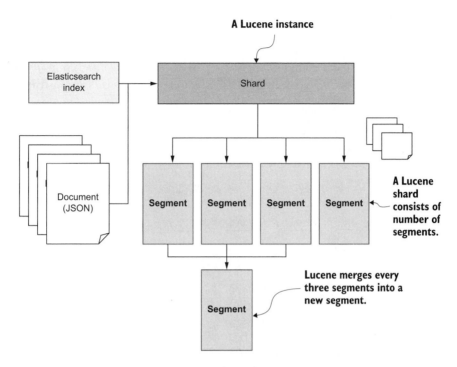

Figure 3.8 Lucene's mechanism for indexing documents

Shards are distributed across the cluster for availability and failover. On the other hand, replicas allow redundancy in the system. Once an index is in operation, shards cannot be relocated, as doing so would invalidate the existing data in an index.

As duplicate copies of shards, replica shards provide redundancy and high availability in an application. By serving read requests, replicas enable distributing the read load during peak times. A replica is not co-located on the same node as the respective shard, as that would defeat the purpose of redundancy. For example, if the node crashed, you would lose all the data from the shard and its replica if they were co-located. Hence shards and their respective replicas are distributed across different nodes in the cluster.

DEFINITIONS A *cluster* is a collection of nodes. A *node* is an instance of an Elasticsearch server. For example, when we start an Elasticsearch server on our machine, we are essentially creating a node. This node joins a cluster by default. Because the cluster has only this node, it is called a *single-node cluster*. If we start more instances of the server, they will join this cluster, provided the settings are correct.

DISTRIBUTION OF SHARDS AND REPLICAS

Each shard is expected to hold a certain amount of data. As we know, data is spread across multiple shards on multiple nodes. Let's see how shards are distributed when we start new nodes or diminish when we lose nodes.

Suppose we have created an `virus_mutations` index to hold COVID virus mutation data. According to our strategy, this index will be provided with three shards. (Chapter 6 covers the mechanics of creating an index with a certain number of shards and replicas; for now, let's continue the discussion of how shards are distributed.)

Health status of a cluster

Elasticsearch uses a simple traffic light system based on indicators to let us know a cluster's health at any given time. A cluster has the following three possible states:

- *RED*—The shards have not yet been assigned, so not all data is available for querying. This usually happens when the cluster is starting up, during which time the shards are in a transient state.
- *YELLOW*—Replicas are not yet assigned, but all the shards have been assigned and are in action. This is likely to occur when the nodes hosting the replicas have crashed or are just coming up.
- *GREEN*—This is the happy state when all shards and replicas are assigned and serving as expected.

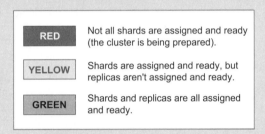

RED	Not all shards are assigned and ready (the cluster is being prepared).
YELLOW	Shards are assigned and ready, but replicas aren't assigned and ready.
GREEN	Shards and replicas are all assigned and ready.

Indicating the health of shards with a traffic light signal board

Elasticsearch exposes cluster APIs to fetch cluster-related information, including cluster health. We can use a `GET _cluster/health` endpoint to fetch the health indicator; the next figure shows the result of such a call.

`GET _cluster/health`

```
{
    "cluster_name" : "elasticsearch",
    "status" : "red",
    "timed_out" : false,
    "number_of_nodes" : 1,
    "number_of_data_nodes" : 1,
    "active_primary_shards" : 25,
    "active_shards" : 25,
    "unassigned_shards" : 24
    ...
}
```

Fetching the status of a cluster by invoking the cluster's health endpoint

We can also use a _cat (compact and aligned text API) API call to fetch the cluster's health. We can invoke this API directly in a browser rather than in Kibana, if needed. For example, invoking GET localhost:9200/_cat/health fetches the cluster's health by invoking the call on the server (localhost is where the Elasticsearch URL is running on the 9200 port).

When we start our first node (Node A), not all of the shards have been created for the index. This usually happens when the server is just starting up. Elasticsearch highlights this state of cluster as RED, indicating that the system is unhealthy (see figure 3.9).

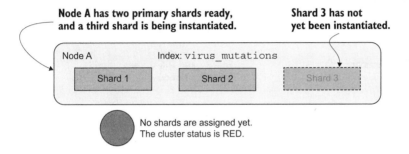

Figure 3.9   The engine is not ready and has a RED status because the shards are not yet fully instantiated.

Once Node A comes up, based on the settings, three shards are created on this node for the virus_mutations index (see figure 3.10). Node A joins a newly created single-node cluster by default. Indexing and searching operations can begin immediately, as all three shards are created successfully. No replicas have been created yet, however. Replicas, as you know, are data copies and used for backup. Creating them on the same node wouldn't be the right thing to do (if this node crashed, the replica would also be lost).

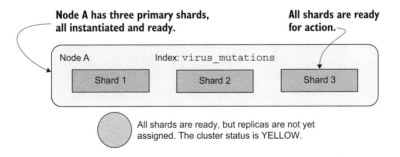

Figure 3.10   A single node with three shards joining a single-node cluster

Because the replicas aren't yet instantiated, there is a high chance that we will lose data if anything happens to Node A. Due to this risk, the cluster's health status is set to YELLOW.

We know that all the shards are on a single node, and if this node crashes for any reason, we will lose everything. To avoid data loss, we decide to start a second node to join the existing cluster. Once the new node (Node B) is created and added to the cluster, Elasticsearch distributes the original three shards as follows:

1 Shard 2 and Shard 3 are removed from Node A.

2 Shard 2 and Shard 3 are added to Node B.

This move distributes our data across the cluster by adjusting the shards, as figure 3.11 shows.

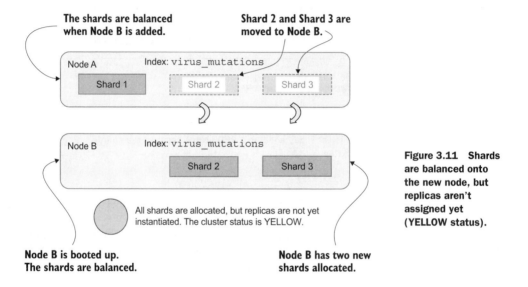

Figure 3.11   Shards are balanced onto the new node, but replicas aren't assigned yet (YELLOW status).

As soon as the shards are distributed after we add Node B, the cluster status turns YELLOW.

> **NOTE** Elasticsearch exposes the cluster's health via an endpoint: `GET _cluster/health`. This endpoint fetches the cluster's details, including the cluster name, status of the cluster, number of shards and replicas, and so on.

When the new node springs into life, in addition to distributing shards, replicas are instantiated. A clone of each shard is created, and data is copied to these clones from the respective shards. As mentioned earlier, the replicas do not sit on the same node as the primary shard. Replica 1 is a copy of Shard 1, but it is created and available on Node B. Similarly, Replica 2 and Replica 3 are copies of Shard 2 and Shard 3, respectively, which are on Node B, but the replicas are available on Node A (figure 3.12).

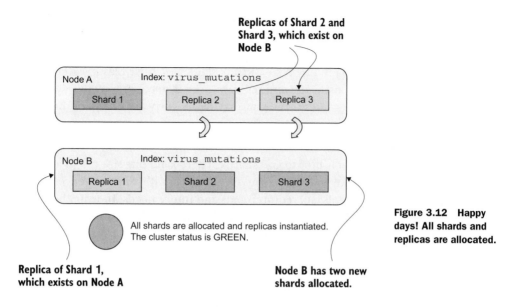

Figure 3.12   Happy days! All shards and replicas are allocated.

The primary and replica shards are all assigned and ready. The cluster status is now GREEN.

REBALANCING SHARDS

There's always a risk of hardware failures. In our example, what happens if Node A crashes? If Node A disappears, Elasticsearch readjusts the shards by promoting Replica 1 to Shard 1, because Replica 1 is a copy of Shard 1 (see Figure 3.13).

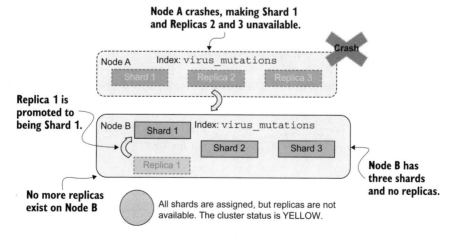

Figure 3.13   Replicas are lost (or promoted to shards) when a node crashes.

Now Node B is the only node in the cluster, and it has three shards. As the replicas no longer exist, the cluster's status is set to YELLOW. Once DevOps brings up Node A, the shards will be rebalanced and reassigned, and replicas will be instantiated, so the system will try to attain a healthy GREEN state. Note that Elasticsearch manages such disasters and can exist with minimal resources if needed, to avoid downtime, and it does so behind the scenes without us having to worry about any of those operational headaches.

SHARD SIZING

A common question is how to size shards. There is no one-size-fits-all answer. To get a conclusive result, we must perform sizing trials (with due diligence) based on the organization's current data requirements and future needs. Industry best practice is to size an individual shard as no more than 50 GB, but I have seen shards up to 400 GB in size. GitHub's indexes are spread across 128 shards, each 120 GB. I advise making shards between 25 GB and 40 GB, keeping the node's heap memory in mind. If we know that a `movies` index may hold up to 500 GB of data, it is best to distribute this data among 10 to 20 shards distributed across multiple nodes.

There is one more parameter to consider when sizing shards: heap memory. As we know, nodes have limited computing resources, such as memory and disk space. Each Elasticsearch instance can be tweaked to use heap memory based on available memory. I advise hosting up to 20 shards per gigabyte of heap memory. By default, Elasticsearch is instantiated with 1 GB memory, but the setting can be changed by editing the jvm.options file in the config directory of the installation. Tweak the `Xms` and `Xmx` properties of the JVM to set the heap memory based on your availability and needs.

The takeaway is that shards hold our data, so we must do the initial legwork to get the sizing right. Sizing depends on how much data the index holds (including future requirements) and how much heap memory we can allocate to a node. Every organization must have a strategy for shards before onboarding data. It is imperative to balance data requirements and the optimal number of shards.

Shards cannot be modified on a live index

The number of shards cannot be changed once the index is created and is in operation. When we create an index, Elasticsearch associates a single shard with a single replica by default (before version 7, the default was five shards and one replica). While the number of shards is written in stone, the number of replicas can be changed using the index settings API during the course of the index's life. Documents are housed in a particular shard according to the routing algorithm:

```
shard_number = hash(document_id) % number_of_primary_shards
```

The algorithm depends directly on the number of shards, so changing that number during a live run will modify the current document's location and corrupt it. This in turn will compromise the inverted index and retrieval process. There's a way out, though: reindexing. By reindexing, we can change the shard settings if necessary. We learn about the reindexing mechanism in detail in chapter 5.

We learn about shard sizing in chapter 14. Shards and replicas make nodes, and nodes form clusters. Let's learn about these in the next section.

3.2.5   *Nodes and clusters*

When you launch Elasticsearch, it boots up a single instance called a *node*. Each node hosts a set of shards and replicas (the instances of Apache Lucene). The index, a logical collection to hold our data, is created across these shards and replicas. Figure 3.14 shows a single node forming a cluster.

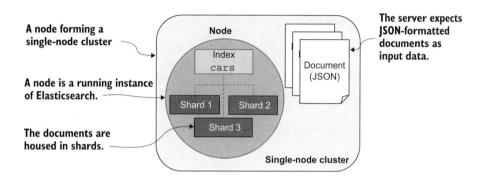

Figure 3.14   A single-node Elasticsearch cluster

While you can start multiple nodes on the same machine—thus creating a multi-node cluster—doing so is not advisable. Replicas will never be created on the same machine where their respective shards exist, leading to a situation with no backup of our data. This leaves the cluster in an unhealthy YELLOW state. To start another node on the same machine, all we need to do is make sure the data and log paths are different (check out the sidebar "Additional node on a personal machine" for details).

SINGLE-NODE CLUSTERS

When you boot up a node for the first time, Elasticsearch forms a new cluster, commonly called a *single-node cluster*. While we can use a single-node cluster for development purposes, it is far from a production-grade setup. A typical production environment has a farm of data nodes forming clusters (single or multiple) based on the data and application search requirements. If we start another node in the same network, the newly instantiated node joins the existing cluster, provided the `cluster` `.name` property points to the single-node cluster. We discuss production-grade setup in chapter 14.

> **NOTE**   A property file named elasticsearch.yml (in the *<INSTALL_DIR>*/config directory) mentions a property called `cluster.name`, which dictates the name of our cluster. This is an important property as all nodes with the same name join together and form a cluster. For instance, if we expect a 100-node

cluster, all 100 nodes should have the same `cluster.name` property. The default cluster name for an out-of-the-box server is `elasticsearch`, but it is a best practice to configure a unique name for the cluster.

The cluster can be ramped up by scaling up (vertical scaling) or scaling out (horizontal scaling). When additional nodes are booted up, they can join the same cluster as existing nodes as long as the `cluster.name` property is the same. Thus, a group of nodes can form a multi-node cluster, as shown in figure 3.15.

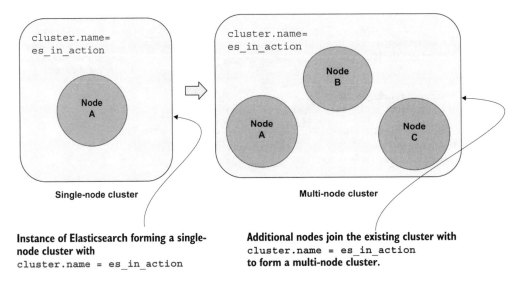

Single-node cluster   **Multi-node cluster**

Instance of Elasticsearch forming a single-node cluster with
`cluster.name = es_in_action`

Additional nodes join the existing cluster with
`cluster.name = es_in_action`
to form a multi-node cluster.

Figure 3.15 Cluster formation from a single node to a multiple-node cluster

Adding more nodes to the cluster not only creates redundancy and makes the system fault tolerant but also brings huge performance benefits. When we add more nodes, we create more room for replicas. Remember that the number of shards cannot be changed when the index is in operation. So, what's the benefit of shards adding nodes? Usually, data is reindexed from an existing index into a new index. This new index is configured with a new number of shards, taking the additional new nodes into consideration.

Manage node disk space judiciously

To improve read performance, we can add replicas, but with them come greater memory and disk space requirements. While it is not unusual to create clusters containing terabytes or even petabytes when working with Elasticsearch, we must consider our data sizing requirements.

For example, if we have a *three-shards-and-15-replicas-per-shard* strategy, with each shard sized at 50 GB, we must ensure that all 15 replicas have enough capacity not only to store documents on disk but also for heap memory:

- Shard memory: 3 × 50 GB/shard = 150 GB
- Replica memory per shard: 15 × 50 GB/replica = 750 GB/per shard
- (Replica memory for 3 shards = 3 × 750 GB = 2250 GB)
- Total memory for both shards and replicas on a given node = 150 GB + 750 GB = 900 GB
- (Grand total for 20 nodes = 18 TB)

A whopping 18 TB is required for one index with a *three-shards-and-15-replicas-per-shard* strategy. In addition to this initial disk space, we need further disk space to run the server smoothly. So, we must work through the capacity requirements judiciously. We discuss how to set up clusters with memory and disk space in chapters 14 and 15.

MULTI-NODE MULTICLUSTERS

We briefly looked at a node as an instance of an Elasticsearch server. As stated earlier, when we start the Elasticsearch application, we are essentially initializing a node. By default, this node joins a one-node cluster. We can create a cluster of any number of nodes based on our data requirements. We can also create multiclusters, as shown in figure 3.16, but doing so depends on an organization's use cases.

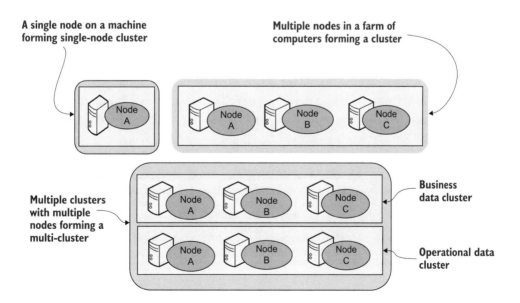

Figure 3.16 Varied cluster configurations

An organization may have different types of data, such as business-related data (invoices, orders, customer information, etc.) and operational information (web server and database server logs, application logs, application metrics, etc.). Bundling all sorts of data into a single cluster is not unusual, but it may not be a best practice. It may be a better strategy to create multiple clusters for varied data shapes, with customized configurations for each cluster. For example, a business-critical data cluster may be running on an on-premises cluster with greater memory and disk space options configured, while an application-monitoring data cluster has a slightly different setup.

Additional node on a personal machine

If you are running a node on your personal laptop or PC, you can instantiate an additional node from the same installation folder. Rerun the shell script by passing two additional parameters: the `path.data` and `path.logs` options, pointing to the respective directories, as shown here:

```
$>cd <INSTALL_DIR>/bin
$>./elasticsearch -Epath.data=../data2 -Epath.logs=../log2
```

This command spins up an additional node with the given data and log folders. If you now issue the `GET _cat/nodes` command, a second node should appear in the list.

Each node needs to work with specific responsibilities at times. Some may need to worry about data-related activities such as indexing and caching, while others may be required to coordinate a client's requests and responses. Some tasks may also include node-to-node communications and cluster-level management. To enable such responsibilities, Elasticsearch has a set of roles for nodes to undertake a specific set of responsibilities when assigned to that role. We discuss node roles in the next section.

NODE ROLES

Every node plays multiple roles, from being a coordinator to managing data to becoming a master. The developers of Elasticsearch keep fiddling with nodes, so you may see new roles appear now and then. Table 3.2 lists the node roles that we can categorize.

Table 3.2   Node roles and responsibilities

Role	Description
Master node	Its primary responsibility is cluster management.
Data node	Responsible for document persistence and retrieval.
Ingest node	Responsible for the transformation of data via pipeline ingestion before indexing.
Machine learning node	Handles machine learning jobs and requests.
Transform node	Handles transformation requests.
Coordination node	This is the default role. It takes care of incoming client requests.

The node roles are as follows:

- *Master node*—Involved in high-level operations such as creating and deleting indexes, node operations, and other admin-related jobs for cluster management. These admin operations are lightweight processes; hence, one master is enough for an entire cluster. If this master node crashes, the cluster elects one of the other nodes as the master, so the baton passes. Master nodes don't participate in document CRUD operations, but the master node knows the location of the documents.
- *Data node*—Where indexing, searching, deleting, and other document-related operations happen. These nodes host indexed documents. Once an index request is received, the data nodes jump into action to save the document to its index by calling a writer on the Lucene segment. As you can imagine, they talk to the disk frequently during CRUD operations; hence, they are disk I/O- and memory-intensive operations.

NOTE Specific variants of the data node role are used when we deploy multi-tiered deployments: the `data_hot`, `data_cold`, `data_warm`, and `data_frozen` roles. We go over them in chapter 14.

- *Ingest node*—Handles ingest operations such as transformations and enrichment before indexing kicks in. Documents ingested via a pipeline operation (for example, processing Word or PDF documents) can be put through additional processing before being indexed.
- *Machine learning node*—As the name indicates, executes machine learning algorithms and detects anomalies. It is part of a commercial license, so you must purchase an X-Pack license to enable machine learning capabilities.
- *Transform node*—The latest addition to the list. A transform node is used for aggregated summaries of data. It is required for carrying out transform API invocations to create (transform) new indexes that are pivoted based on existing indexes.
- *Coordinating node*—While roles are assigned to a node by the user on purpose (or by default), there's one special role that all nodes take on, regardless of user intervention: coordinating node (or coordinator). As the name suggests, the coordinator looks after client requests end to end. When a request is made of Elasticsearch, one of these nodes picks up the request and dons the coordinator's hat. After accepting the requests, the coordinator asks the other nodes in the cluster to process the request. It awaits the response before collecting and collating the results and sending them back to the client. It essentially acts as a work manager, distributing incoming requests to appropriate nodes and responding to the client.

CONFIGURING ROLES

When we start up Elasticsearch in development mode, the node is by default set with `master`, `data`, and `ingest` roles (and each node is by default a coordinator—there is no special flag to enable or disable a coordinating node). We can configure these roles based on our needs: for example, in a cluster of 20 nodes, we can enable 3 nodes as master nodes, 15 as data nodes, and 2 as ingest nodes.

To configure a role on a node, all we need to do is tweak the `node.roles` setting in the elasticsearch.yml configuration file. The setting takes in a list of roles: for example, setting `node.roles: [master]` enables the node as a master node. Multiple node roles can be set, as shown in the following example:

```
node.roles: [master, data, ingest, ml]    ⬅── This node has four roles: master,
                                               data, ingest, and machine learning.
```

Remember, we mentioned that the coordinator role is the default role provided to all nodes. Although we set up four roles in the example (`master`, `data`, `ingest`, and `ml`), this node still inherits a `coordinator` role.

We can specifically assign just a `coordinator` role to a node by simply omitting any `node.roles` values. In the following snippet, we assign the node nothing but the `coordinator` role, meaning this node doesn't participate in any activities other than coordinating requests:

```
nodes.roles : [ ]    ⬅── Leaving the roles array empty
                         sets the node as a coordinator.
```

There is a benefit to enabling nodes as dedicated coordinators: they perform as load balancers, working through requests and collating the result sets. However, the risk outweighs the benefits if we enable many nodes as just coordinators.

In our earlier discussions, I mentioned that Elasticsearch stores analyzed full-text fields in an advanced data structure called an inverted index. If there's one data structure that any search engine (not just Elasticsearch) depends on heavily, that's the inverted index. It is time to examine the internal workings of an inverted index, to solidify our understanding of the text analysis process, storage, and retrieval.

3.3   *Inverted indexes*

If you look at the back of any book, usually you'll find an index that maps keywords to the pages where they are found. This is nothing but a physical representation of an inverted index.

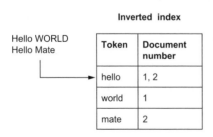

Similar to navigating to pages based on the page numbers associated with the keyword you are searching for in a book, Elasticsearch consults the inverted index for search words and document associations. When the engine finds document identifiers for these search words, it returns the full document(s) by querying the server to return them to the client. Elasticsearch uses a data structure called an *inverted index* for each full-text field during the indexing phase, as figure 3.17 illustrates.

Figure 3.17   An inverted index data structure

At a high level, an inverted index is a data structure much like a dictionary, but with both the words and lists of documents the words are present in. This inverted index is the key to faster retrieval of documents during the full-text search phase. For each document that consists of full-text fields, the server creates a respective inverted index.

> **NOTE** Block k-dimensional (BKD) trees are special data structures used to hold non-text fields like numeric and geoshapes.

We've learned a bit of theory about inverted indexes, but now let's look at a simple example of how they work. Say we have two documents with one text field, `greeting`:

```
//Document 1
{
  "greeting":"Hello, WORLD"
}
//Document 2
{
  "greeting":"Hello, Mate"
}
```

In Elasticsearch, the analysis process is a complex function carried out by an analyzer module. The analyzer module is further composed of character filters, a tokenizer, and token filters. When the first document is indexed, as in the `greeting` field (a text field), an inverted index is created. Every full-text field is backed up by an inverted index. The value of the greeting "Hello, World" is analyzed, tokenized, and normalized into two words—*hello* and *world*—by the end of the process. But there are a few steps in between.

Let's look at the overall process (figure 3.18). The input line `<h2>Hello WORLD</h2>` is stripped of unwanted characters such as HTML markup. The cleaned-up data is split into tokens (most likely individual words) based on whitespace, thus forming

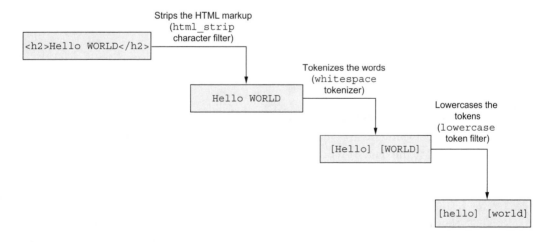

Figure 3.18   Text analysis procedure where Elasticsearch processes text

Hello WORLD. Finally, token filters are applied so that the sentence can be transformed into tokens: [hello] [world]. By default, Elasticsearch uses a standard analyzer to lowercase the tokens, as is the case here. Note that the punctuation (comma) was also removed during this process.

After these steps, an inverted index is created for this field. It is predominantly used in full-text search functionalities. In essence, it is a hash map with words as keys pointing to documents where these words are present. It consists of a set of unique words and the frequency with which those words occur across all documents in the index.

Let's revisit our example. Because document 1 ("Hello WORLD") was indexed and analyzed, an inverted index was created with the tokens (individual words) and the documents they occur in; see table 3.3.

Table 3.3   Tokenized words for the "Hello, World" document

Word	Frequency	Document ID
hello	1	1
world	1	1

The words *hello* and *world* are added to the inverted index along with the document IDs where these words are found (of course, document ID 1). We also note the frequency of the words across all documents in this inverted index.

When the second document ("Hello, Mate") is indexed, the data structure is updated (table 3.4).

Table 3.4   Tokenized words for the "Hello, Mate" document

Word	Frequency	Document ID
hello	2	1,2
world	1	1
mate	1	2

When updating the inverted index for the word *hello*, the document ID of the second document is appended, and the frequency of the word increases. All tokens from the incoming document are matched with keys in the inverted index before being appended to the data structure (like *mate* in this example) as a new record if the token is seen for the first time.

Now that the inverted index has been created from these documents, when a search for *hello* comes along, Elasticsearch will consult this inverted index first. The inverted index points out that the word *hello* is present in document IDs 1 and 2, so the relevant documents will be fetched and returned to the client.

We have oversimplified the inverted index here, but that's all right, as our aim is to gain a basic understanding of the data structure. If we now search for *hello mate*, for example, both documents 1 and 2 are returned, but document 2 probably has a higher relevancy score than document 1 because the contents of document 2 match the query.

While an inverted index is optimized for faster information retrieval, it adds complexity to analysis and requires more space. The inverted index grows as indexing activity increases, thus consuming computing resources and heap space. We will not work directly with the data structure, but understanding the basics helps.

The inverted index also helps deduce relevancy scores; it provides the frequency of terms, which is one of the ingredients in calculating the relevancy score. We've used the term *relevancy* for a while, and it is time to understand what it is and what algorithms a search engine like Elasticsearch uses to fetch relevant results for the user. We discuss concepts related to relevancy in the next section.

3.4 Relevancy

Modern search engines not only return results based on query criteria but also analyze and return the most *relevant* results. If you are a developer or DevOps engineer, you have most likely used Stack Overflow to search for answers to technical problems. Searching on Stack Overflow never disappoints me (at least, in most cases). The results I get for a query are close to what I'm looking for. The results are sorted in a decent order, from highly relevant results at the top to the least relevant ones at the bottom. It would be highly unlikely for the results of a query not to satisfy your requirements—but you might not return to Stack Overflow if the results were all over the place.

3.4.1 Relevancy scores

Stack Overflow applies a set of relevancy algorithms to search and sort the results it returns to the user. Similarly, Elasticsearch returns results for full-text queries sorted, by a *relevancy score*.

Relevancy is a positive floating-point number that determines the ranking of search results. Elasticsearch uses the Best Match 25 (BM25) relevancy algorithm by default to score return results so the client can expect relevant results. It's an advanced version of the previously used term-frequency/inverse document frequency (TF/IDF) similarity algorithm (see the next section for more about relevancy algorithms).

If we are searching for, say, *Java* in the title of a book, a document containing more than one occurrence of the word *Java* in the title is more relevant than documents where the title has one or no occurrence. Look at the example results in figure 3.19, retrieved by Elasticsearch for a query searching for the keyword *Java* in a title (the full example is provided in the book's repository).

```
GET books/_search
{
  "_source": "title",
  "query": {
    "match": {
      "title": "Java"
    }
  }
}
```

```
"hits" : {
    ...
    "max_score" : 0.33537668,

    "hits" : [{
        "_score" : 0.33537668,
        "_source" : { "title" : "Effective
Java" }
        },
        {
        "_score" : 0.30060259,
        "_source" : { "title" : "Head First
Java" }
        },
        {
        "_score" : 0.18531466,
        "_source" : { "title" : "Test-Driven:
TDD and Acceptance TDD for Java Developers"}
        }...]
    }
```

Figure 3.19   Relevant results for *Java* in a title search

The first result shows a higher relevancy score (0.33537668) than the second and third results. All the titles include the word *Java*, so to calculate the relevancy score, Elasticsearch uses the field-length norm algorithm: the search word in the first title (*Effective Java*, containing two words) is more relevant than the search word in the second title (*Head First Java*, consisting of three words). The max_score is the highest of all the available scores, usually the score of the first document.

Relevancy scores are generated based on the similarity algorithms employed. In this example, Elasticsearch by default applied the BM25 algorithm to determine the scores. This algorithm depends on term frequency, inverse document frequency, and field length, but Elasticsearch allows much more flexibility: it provides a handful of algorithms in addition to BM25. These algorithms are packaged in a module called similarity, which ranks matching documents. Let's look at some of these similarity algorithms.

3.4.2   *Relevancy (similarity) algorithms*

Elasticsearch employs several relevance algorithms, the default being BM25. BM25 and TF-IDF are both relevance algorithms used in Elasticsearch for scoring and ranking documents. They differ in how they calculate term weights and document scores.

- *TF-IDF (Term Frequency-Inverse Document Frequency)*. The TF-IDF algorithm is a traditional weighting scheme that assigns a weight to a term in a document based on its term frequency (TF) and inverse document frequency (IDF). TF is the number of times a term appears in a document, while IDF is a measure of how common or rare a term is across the entire set of documents. The terms that occur more frequently in a specific document and less frequently in the entire collection should be considered more relevant as per TF-IDF algorithm.

- *BM25 (Best Matching 25) algorithm.* The BM25 relevancy algorithm is an improvement over the TF-IDF algorithm. It introduces two important modifications to the base algorithm in that it uses a nonlinear function for term frequency to prevent highly repetitive terms from receiving excessively high scores. It also employs a document length normalization factor to counter the bias towards longer documents. In the TF-IDF algorithm, longer documents are more likely to have higher term frequencies, which means they may receive unduly credit with higher scores. BM25's job is to avoid such bias.

So, both BM25 and TF-IDF are relevancy algorithms used in Elasticsearch. BM25 is considered an improvement over TF-IDF due to its term frequency saturation and document length normalization features. As a result, the BM25 is expected to be more accurate and return relevant search results.

Elasticsearch provides a module called `similarity` that lets us apply the most appropriate algorithm if the default isn't suited to our requirements.

Similarity algorithms are applied per field by using mapping APIs. Because Elasticsearch is flexible, it also allows customized algorithms based on our requirements. (This is an advanced feature, so unfortunately we do not discuss it much in this book.) Table 3.5 lists the algorithms available out of the box.

Table 3.5 Elasticsearch's similarity algorithms

Similarity algorithm	Type	Description
Okapi BM25 (default)	`BM25`	An enhanced TF/IDF algorithm that considers field length in addition to term and document frequencies
Divergence from Randomness (DFR)	`DFR`	Uses the DFR framework developed by its authors, Amati and Rijsbergen, which aims to improve search relevance by measuring the divergence between the actual term and an expected random distribution. Terms that occur more often in relevant documents than in a random distribution are assigned higher weights when ranking search results.
Divergence from Independence (DFI)	`DFI`	A specific model of the DFR family that measures the divergence of the actual term frequency distribution from an independent distribution. DFI aims to assign higher scores to documents by comparing the observed term frequencies with those expected in a random, uncorrelated term frequency.
LM Dirichlet	`LMDirichlet`	Calculates the relevance of documents based on the probability of generating the query terms from the document's language model
LM Jelinek-Mercer	`LMJelinek-Mercer`	Provides improved search result relevance compared to models that do not account for data sparsity
Manua		Creates a manual script
Boolean similarity	`boolean`	Does not consider ranking factors unless the query criteria are satisfied

In the next section, we briefly review the BM25 algorithm, which is a next-generation enhanced TF/IDF algorithm.

THE OKAPI BM25 ALGORITHM

Three main factors are involved in associating a relevancy score with the results: term frequency (TF), inverse document frequency (IDF), and field-length norm. Let's look at these factors briefly and learn how they affect relevancy.

Term frequency represents the number of times the search word appears in the current document's field. If we search for a word in a title field, the number of times the word appears is denoted by the term frequency variable. The higher the frequency, the higher the score.

Say, for example, that we are searching for the word *Java* in a title field across three documents. When indexing, we created the inverted index with similar information: the word, the number of times that word appears in that field (in a document), and the document IDs. We can create a table with this data, as table 3.6 shows.

Table 3.6   **Term frequency for a search keyword**

Title	Frequency	Doc ID
Mastering Java: *Learning Core Java and Enterprise Java With Examples*	3	25
Effective Java	1	13
Head First Java	1	39

Java appears three times in the document with ID 25 and one time in the other two documents. Because the search word appears more often in the first document (ID 25), it is logical to consider that document our favorite. Remember, the higher the frequency, the greater the relevance.

While this number seems to be a pretty good indication of the most relevant document in our search result, it is often not enough. Another factor, *inverse document frequency*, when combined with TF, produces improved scores.

The number of times the search word appears across the whole set of documents (i.e., across the whole index) is the *document frequency*. If the document frequency of a word is high, we can deduce that the search word is common across the index. If the word appears multiple times across all the documents in an index, it is a common term and, accordingly, not that relevant.

Words that appear often are not significant: words like *a, an, the, it,* and so forth are common in natural language and hence can be ignored. The inverse of the document frequency (*inverse document frequency*) provides a higher significance for uncommon words across the whole index. Hence, *the higher the document frequency, the lower the relevancy, and vice versa.* Table 3.7 shows the relationship between word frequency and relevance.

Table 3.7 Relationship between word frequency and relevance

Word frequency	Relevancy
Higher term frequency	Higher relevancy
Higher document frequency	Lower relevancy

Stop words

Words such as *the, a, it, an, but, if, for*, and *and*, are called *stop words* and can be removed by using a stop filter plugin. The default `standard` analyzer doesn't have the `stopwords` parameter enabled (the `stopwords` filter is set to `_none_` by default), so these words are analyzed. However, if our requirement is to ignore these words, we can enable the stop words filter by adding the parameter `stopwords` set to `_english_`, as shown here:

```
PUT index_with_stopwords
{
  "settings": {
    "analysis": {
      "analyzer": {
        "standard_with_stopwords_enabled": {
          "type": "standard",
          "stopwords": "_english_"
        }
      }
    }
  }
}
```

We learn about customizing analyzers in chapter 7.

Until version 5.0, Elasticsearch used the TF-IDF similarity function to calculate scores and rank results. The TF-IDF function was deprecated in favor of the BM25 function. The TF-IDF algorithm didn't consider the field's length, which skewed the relevancy scores. For example, which of these documents do you think is more relevant to the search criteria?

- A field with 100 words, including 5 occurrences of a search word
- A field with 10 words, including 3 occurrences of the search word

Logically, it may be obvious that the second document is the most relevant as it has more search words in a shorter length. Elasticsearch improved its similarity algorithms by enhancing TF-IDF with an additional parameter: field length.

The *field-length norm* provides a score based on the length of the field: the search word occurring multiple times in a short field is more relevant. For example, the word *Java* appearing once over a long synopsis may not indicate a useful result. On the other hand, as shown in table 3.8, the same word appearing twice or more in the title field (with fewer words) says that the book is about the Java programming language.

Table 3.8 Comparing different fields to gather similarity

Word	Field length	Frequency	Relevant?
Java	Synopsis field with a length of 100 words	1	No
Java	Title field with a length of 5 words	2	Yes

In most cases, the BM25 algorithm is adequate. However, if we need to swap BM25 with another algorithm, we can do so by configuring it using the indexing APIs. Let's go over the mechanics of configuring the algorithm as needed.

CONFIGURING SIMILARITY ALGORITHMS

Elasticsearch allows us to plug in other similarity algorithms if the default BM25 doesn't suit our requirements. Two similarity algorithms are provided out of the box without further customization: BM25 and boolean. We can set the similarity algorithm for individual fields when we create the schema definitions using index settings APIs, as shown in figure 3.20.

> **NOTE** Working with similarity algorithms is an advanced topic. While I advise you to read this section, you can skip it and revisit it when you wish to know more.

```
PUT index_with_different_similarities
{
  "mappings": {                          ─── Creates an index with two
    "properties": {                          fields
      "title":{
        "type": "text",
        "similarity": "BM25"  ◄──────── The title field is defined with a
      },                                 BM25 (default) similarity explicitly.
      "author":{
        "type": "text",                  The author field is defined
        "similarity": "boolean"   ─── with a boolean similarity
      }                                  function.
    }
  }
}
```

Figure 3.20 Setting fields with different similarity functions

In the figure, an index index_with_different_similarities is being developed with a schema that has two fields: title and author. The important point is the specification of two different algorithms attached to these two fields independently: `title` is associated with the BM25 algorithm, while `text` is set with `boolean`.

Each similarity function has additional parameters, and we can alter them to reflect precise search results. For example, although the BM25 function is set by default with the optimal parameters, we can easily modify the function using the index settings API. We can change two parameters in BM25 if we need to: `k1` and `b`, described in table 3.9.

Table 3.9 Available BM25 similarity function parameters

Property	Default value	Description
k1	1.2	Nonlinear term frequency saturation variable
b	0.75	TF normalization factor based on the document's length

Let's look at an example. Figure 3.21 shows an index with a custom similarity function, where the core BM25 function is amended with our own settings for `k1` and `b`.

```
PUT my_bm25_index         Configures an index with specific
{                         BM25 parameters
  "settings": {
    "index":{
      "similarity":{
        "custom_BM25":{        Creates a custom
          "type":"BM25",       similarity function with a
          "k1":"1.1",          modified BM25 algorithm
          "b":"0.85"
        }
      }                        Sets the k1 and b values
    }                          based on our requirements
  }
}
```

Figure 3.21 Setting custom parameters on the BM25 similarity function

Here, we are creating a custom similarity type—a tweaked version of BM25, which can be reused elsewhere. (It's more like a data type function, predefined and ready to be attached to attributes.) Once this similarity function is created, we can use it when setting up a field, as shown in figure 3.22.

```
PUT books/_mapping
{
  "properties":{
    "synopsis":{
      "type":"text",
      "similarity":"custom_BM25"
    }
  }
}
```

Creates an index with fields and their types

The synopsis field is now created with a modified BM25 similarity algorithm.

Figure 3.22   Creating a field in an index with a custom BM25 similarity function

We create a mapping definition, assigning our custom similarity function (custom_BM25) to a synopsis field. When ranking results based on this field, Elasticsearch considers the provided custom similarity function to apply the scores.

> ### Similarity algorithms are beasts
>
> Information retrieval is a vast and complex subject. The algorithms involved in scoring and ranking results are advanced and complicated. While Elasticsearch provides a few similarity algorithms as plug-and-play, you may need a deeper understanding when working with them. Once you have tweaked the configurational parameters of these scoring functions, be sure you have tested and tried every possible combination.

You may wonder how Elasticsearch can retrieve documents in a fraction of a second. How does it know where in these multiple shards the document exists? The key is the routing algorithm, discussed next.

3.5   *Routing algorithm*

Every document has a permanent home: that is, it must belong to a particular primary shard. Elasticsearch uses a *routing algorithm* to distribute the document to the underlying shard when indexing.

Routing is a process of allocating a home for a document to a certain shard, with each document stored in one and only one primary shard. Retrieving the same document is easy, because the same routing function is used to find the shard to which that document belongs.

The routing algorithm is a simple formula that Elasticsearch uses to deduce the shard for a document during indexing or searching:

```
shard_number = hash(id) % number_of_shards
```

The output of the routing function is a shard number. It is calculated by hashing the document's ID and finding the remainder of the hash when divided (using the modulo operator) by the number of shards. The hash function expects a unique ID, generally a document ID or a custom ID provided by the user. Documents are evenly distributed, so there is no chance of one of the shards being overloaded.

Notice that the formula depends directly on the `number_of_shards` variable. That means we cannot change the number of shards once an index is created. If we could change the settings (say, changing the number of shards from two to four), the routing function would break for the existing records, and data wouldn't be found. This is why Elasticsearch doesn't let us change the shards once an index is set up.

What if we have not anticipated data growth, and the shards are exhausted by a spike in data? All is not lost. There's a way out: *reindexing* our data. Reindexing effectively creates a new index with appropriate settings and copies the data from the old index to the new index.

> ## Replicas can be altered on an operational index
>
> While the number of shards cannot be changed when the index is in operation, we can alter the number of replicas if needed. Remember, the routing function is a function of the number of primary shards, not replicas. If we need to change the shard number, we must close the indexes (closed indexes block all read and write operations), change the shard number, and reopen the indexes. Alternatively, we can create a new index with a new set of shards and reindex the data from the old index to the new index.

One of the major goals of Elasticsearch is scalability of the engine. In the next section, we look at Elasticsearch's scalability at a high level: how to scale, how vertical and horizontal scaling work, and the reindexing process. We do not dive into the nitty gritty of scaling solutions here because we come back to this discussion in chapter 14.

3.6 Scaling

When Shay Banon and his team rewrote Elasticsearch from the ground up, one of their goals was ensuring that the server scales effortlessly. That is, if the data increases or the query load escalates, adding additional nodes should solve the problem. Of course, there are other solutions, such as vertical scaling, performance tuning, and more. There are two primary schools of scaling, based on need: scaling horizontally and scaling vertically. Elasticsearch supports both of them.

3.6.1 Scaling up (vertical scaling)

In a vertical scaling scenario, we do not buy additional VMs from our cloud provider but instead add computing resources, such as extra memory, CPU, and I/O, to the existing machines. For example, we may increase the CPU cores, double memory, and so on.

There is also another way to enhance the power of the cluster. Because we now have room, we can install additional nodes on the machine, thus creating multiple nodes in the single (fat) machine.

Remember that scaling up requires the cluster to be shut down, so our application may experience downtime unless we lean on a traditional disaster recovery (DR) model. This brings up our secondary or backup system, which services clients while the primary system is undergoing maintenance.

However, this sort of scaling has a potential risk. If the whole machine crashes in an emergency or due to a hardware failure, data may be lost, because all the nodes hosting the data exist on the same machine. Of course, we have backups, so restoration is possible, but it's painful. Our replicas are hosted on the same machine, albeit different nodes, which is asking for trouble.

3.6.2 Scaling out (horizontal scaling)

Alternatively, we can scale our environment out (horizontally). Instead of attaching additional RAM and memory to the existing machines, we can throw in a number of new machines (probably VMs with less resource power than the fat machines used for vertical scaling) to form a horizontally scaled farm.

These new VMs are booted up as new nodes, thus joining the existing Elasticsearch cluster. As soon as the new nodes join the cluster, Elasticsearch, being a distributed architected engine, instantly distributes data to them. Creating VMs is easy, especially using modern infrastructure as code (IaC) tools like Terraform, Ansible, Chef, and so on, so this approach tends to be favored by many DevOps engineering teams.

Let's wrap up this chapter here. It is your guide to understanding the fundamentals of Elasticsearch: its moving parts, low-level blocks, and search concepts. We talk more about the concepts and fundamentals, along with examples, in the next two chapters, so stay tuned.

Summary

- Elasticsearch expects data to be brought in to be indexed. Data sources can include simple files, databases, live streams, Twitter, and so on.
- In the indexing process, data undergoes a rigorous analysis phase, during which advanced data structures like inverted indexes are created.
- Data is retrieved or searched via the search APIs (along with the document APIs for single document retrieval).
- Incoming data must be wrapped up in a JSON document. Because the JSON document is the fundamental data-holding entity, it is persisted to shards and replicas.
- Shards and replicas are Apache Lucene instances whose responsibility is to persist, retrieve, and distribute documents.
- When we start up the Elasticsearch application, it boots up as a one-node, single-cluster application. Adding nodes expands the cluster, making it a multi-node cluster.
- For faster information retrieval and data persistence, Elasticsearch provides advanced data structures like inverted indexes for structural data (such as textual information) and BKD trees for nonstructural data (such as dates and numbers).
- Relevancy is a positive floating-point score attached to retrieved document results. It defines how well the document matches the search criteria.

- Elasticsearch uses the Okapi Best Match (BM) 25 relevancy or similarity algorithm, an enhanced version of the term frequency/inverse document frequency similarity algorithm.
- You can scale Elasticsearch up or out, based on your requirements and available resources. Scaling up beefs up existing machines (adding additional memory, CPU, RAM, etc.), while scaling out spins up more virtual machines (VMs), allowing them to join the cluster and share the load.

Mapping 4

Data is like a rainbow—it comes in all sorts of "colors." Business data has various shapes and forms represented as textual information, dates, numbers, inner objects, Booleans, geolocations, IP addresses, and so on. In Elasticsearch, we model and index data as JSON documents, with each document consisting of a number of fields and every field containing a certain type of data. For example, a movie document may consist of a title and synopsis represented as textual data, a release date as a date, and gross earnings as floating-point data.

In earlier chapters, when we indexed sample documents, we did not bother about the data types of the fields. Elasticsearch derived these types implicitly by looking at each field and the type of information in it. Elasticsearch created a schema without us having to do any up-front work, unlike in a relational database.

It is mandatory to have the table schema defined and developed in a database before retrieving or persisting data. But we can prime Elasticsearch with documents without defining a schema for our data model. This schema-free feature helps developers get up and running with the system from day one. However, best practice is to develop a schema up front rather than letting Elasticsearch define it for us, unless our requirements do not need one.

Elasticsearch expects us to provide clues about how it should treat a field when indexing data. These clues are either provided by us in the form of a schema definition while creating the index or implicitly derived by the engine if we allow it to do so. This process of creating the schema definition is called *mapping*.

Mapping allows Elasticsearch to understand the shape of the data so it can apply a set of predefined rules on fields before indexing them. Elasticsearch also consults the manual of mapping rules to apply full-text rules on text fields. Structured fields (exact values, like numbers or dates) have a separate set of instructions enabling them to be part of aggregations and sorting and filtering functions, in addition to being available for general searches.

In this chapter, we set the context for using mapping schemas, explore the mapping process, and work with data types, looking at how to define them using the mapping APIs. Data that is indexed for Elasticsearch has a definite shape and form. Meticulous shaping of data lets Elasticsearch do a faultless analysis, providing the end user with precise results. This chapter discusses the treatment of data in Elasticsearch and how mapping schemas help us avoid hindrances and obtain accurate searches.

> ### 100 m run or 400 m hurdles?
>
> This chapter deals with dozens of hands-on examples around both core and advanced data types. While I advise you to read about them in the given order, if you are just starting with Elasticsearch and wish to focus on the beginner elements, you can skip section 4.6 and revisit it when you are more confident and want to learn more.
>
> If all you want is a 100 m run rather than 400 m hurdles, read the chapter up to the core data types (section 4.4) and then feel free to jump to the next chapter.

4.1 Overview of mapping

Mapping is a process of defining and developing a schema definition representing a document's data fields and their associated data types. Mapping tells the engine the shape and form of the data that's being indexed. Because Elasticsearch is a document-oriented database, it expects a single mapping definition per index. Every field is treated according to the mapping rule. For example, a string field is treated as a text field, a number field is stored as an integer, a date field is indexed as a date to allow for date-related operations, and so on. Accurate and error-free mapping allows Elasticsearch to analyze data faultlessly, aiding search-related functionalities, sorting, filtering, and aggregation.

NOTE To simplify the coding exercises, I've created a ch04_mapping.txt file under the kibana_scripts folder at the root of the book's repository (http://mng.bz/OxXo). Copy the contents of this file to Kibana as is. You can work through the examples by executing the individual code snippets while following the chapter's content.

4.1.1   *Mapping definition*

Every document consists of a set of fields representing business data, and every field has one or more specific data types associated with it. The *mapping definition* is the schema of the fields and their data types in a document. Each field is stored and indexed in a specific way based on data type. This helps Elasticsearch support many search queries such as full-text, fuzzy, term, and geo.

In programming languages, we represent data with specific data types (strings, dates, numbers, objects, etc.). It is a common practice to let the system know the types of variables during compilation. In a relational database, we define a table schema with appropriate field definitions to persist the records, and it is mandatory for the schema to exist before we start our persistence in the database.

Elasticsearch understands the data types of the fields while indexing documents and stores the fields into appropriate data structures (for example, an inverted index for text fields and block k-dimensional (BKD) trees for numerical fields) for data retrieval. Indexed data with precisely formed data types leads to accurate search results and helps sort and aggregate the data.

Figure 4.1 shows the anatomy of the mapping schema for an index. As you can see, the index consists of a mapping object made up of individual fields and their types enclosed in a properties object.

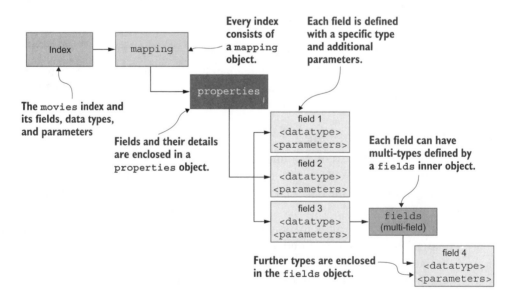

Figure 4.1   Anatomy of a mapping schema

4.1.2 Indexing a document for the first time

Let's find out what happens if we index a document without creating the schema up front. Suppose we want to index a `movie` document, as shown in the following listing.

Listing 4.1 Indexing a document with ID 1 into a `movies` index

```
PUT movies/_doc/1
{
  "title":"Godfather",          ⟵  Title of
  "rating":4.9,                     the movie    Rating given
                                ⟵                to the movie
  "release_year":"1972/08/01"   ⟵
}                                                Movie's release year
                                                 (note the date format)
```

This is the first document sent to Elasticsearch to be indexed. Remember, we didn't create an index (`movies`) or schema for this document data before document ingestion. Here's what happens when this document hits the engine:

1 A new index (`movies`) is created automatically with default settings.
2 A new schema is created for the `movies` index using data types (discussed shortly) deduced from this document's fields. For example, `title` is set to the `text` and `keyword` types, `rating` to `float`, and `release_year` to a `date` type.
3 The document is indexed and stored in the Elasticsearch data store.
4 Subsequent documents are indexed without undergoing the previous steps because Elasticsearch consults the newly created schema for further indexing.

Elasticsearch does some groundwork behind the scenes when performing these steps to create a schema definition with field names and additional information. We can use the mapping API to dynamically fetch the schema definition that Elasticsearch created. The response to a GET command is shown in figure 4.2.

```
GET movies/_mapping

...
    "properties" : {
      "rating" : {"type" : "float"},        Due to the rating value of 4.9, a
                                             floating-point number, the type is
      "release_year" : {                     determined to be float.
        "type" : "date",
        "format" : "yyyy/MM/dd HH:mm:ss||yyyy/MM/dd||epoch_millis"
      },
                                             As the release_year value is
      "title" : {                            in year format (ISO format), the
        "type" : "text",                     type is determined to be date.
        "fields" : {             The title is textual
          "keyword" : {          information, so a text
            "type" : "keyword",  data type is assigned.
            "ignore_above" : 256
          }
        }
      }                          The fields object indicates the
    }                            second data type defined for the
  }                              same title field (multiple data       Figure 4.2 Movie index
}                                types).                               mapping derived from
                                                                       document values
```

Elasticsearch uses *dynamic mapping* to deduce the data types of fields when a document is indexed for the first time by looking at the field values and deriving these types. Each field has a specific data type defined: the `rating` field is declared to be a `float`, `release_year` a `date` type, and so on. Elasticsearch dynamically determined that the type of the `title` field is `text` based on its string value (`"Godfather"`). Because the field is stamped as a `text` type, all full-text-related queries can be performed on this field.

An individual field can also be composed of other fields, representing multiple data types. In addition to creating the `title` field as a `text` type, Elasticsearch did something extra: using the `fields` object, it created an additional `keyword` type for the `title` field, thus making `title` a *multi-typed* field. However, it must be accessed using `title.keyword`.

Multi-typed fields can be associated with multiple data types. In our example, by default, the `title` field is mapped to `text` as well as the `keyword` type. `keyword` fields are used for exact value searches. Fields with this data type are left untouched and don't go through an analysis phase: they are not tokenized, synonymized, or stemmed. See section 4.7 for more about multi-typed fields.

> ### Analysis of keyword fields
>
> Fields declared as the `keyword` data type use a special analyzer called `noop` (the no-operation analyzer), and `keyword` data is not touched during the indexing process. This keyword analyzer spits out the entire field as one big token.
>
> By default, `keyword` fields are not normalized, as the `normalizer` property on the `keyword` type is set to `null`. But we can customize and enable `normalizer` on the `keyword` data type by setting filters such as `german_normalizer`, `uppercase`, and so on. Doing so indicates that we want the `keyword` field to undergo normalization before indexing.

The process by which Elasticsearch deduces a mapping from field values is called *dynamic mapping* (more in the next section). While dynamic mapping is intelligent and convenient, be aware that it can also get schema definitions wrong. Elasticsearch can only go so far when deriving a schema based on our document's field values. It may make incorrect assumptions, leading to erroneous index schemas that can produce incorrect search results.

We have learned that Elasticsearch derives and determines the data types of fields and creates a schema for us dynamically if the schema doesn't exist when the first document comes through for indexing. In the next section, we discuss how Elasticsearch determines types and the downsides of dynamic mapping.

4.2 *Dynamic mapping*

When we index a document for the first time, both the mapping and the index are created automatically. The engine doesn't complain if we don't provide the schema up front—Elasticsearch is forgiving on that count. We can index a document without letting the engine know anything about the fields' data types. Consider a movie document consisting of a few fields, shown in figure 4.3.

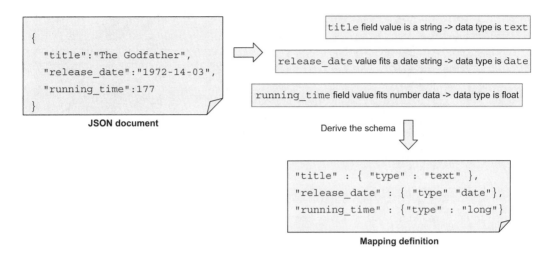

Figure 4.3 **Dynamically deriving the indexing schema**

Reading the fields and values in this document, Elasticsearch infers the data types automatically:

- The `title` field value is a string, so Elasticsearch maps the field to a `text` data type.
- The `release_date` field value is a string, but the value matches an ISO 8601 date format, so it is mapped to a `date` type.
- The `rating` field is a number, so Elasticsearch maps it to a `float` data type.

Because we do not explicitly create the mapping but instead let Elasticsearch derive the schema on the fly, this type of mapping is called *dynamic mapping*. This feature is handy during application development or in testing environments.

How does Elasticsearch know the data type of the `rating` field is a `float` type? For that matter, how does Elasticsearch deduce any of the types? Let's look next at the mechanism and rules of how types are derived by Elasticsearch.

4.2.1 *The mechanism for deducing types*

Elasticsearch analyzes field values and guesses the equivalent data type based on those values. When the incoming JSON object is parsed, the `rating` value of 4.9, for example, resembles a floating-point integer in programming language lingo. This "guess-work" is pretty straightforward; hence, Elasticsearch stamps the `rating` field as a `float` field.

While deducing a number type may be easy, how about the type of the `release_year` field? This field value is compared and matched to one of the two default date formats: `yyyy/MM/dd` or `yyyy-MM-dd`. If it matches, it is assigned a `date` data type.

> ### Date format during dynamic mapping
>
> Elasticsearch can deduce that a field is a `date` type if the values in the JSON document are provided in the format `yyyy-MM-dd` or `yyyy/MM/dd`, although the latter isn't an ISO date format. However, this flexibility is available only for dynamic mapping cases.
>
> If we declare a field as a `date` type explicitly (using explicit mapping—more on this later), then unless we provide a custom format, the field adheres by default to the `strict_date_optional_time` format. This format conforms to an ISO date format: `yyyy-MM-dd` or `yyyy-MM-ddTHH:mm:ss`.

This guesswork is adequate for most cases but falls short if the data is slightly off the default track. Consider the `release_year` field in our movie document. If our document has a value for `release_year` in a different format (say, `ddMMyyyy` or `dd/MM/yyyy`), the dynamic mapping rule breaks down. Elasticsearch considers that value a `text` field rather than a `date` field.

Similarly, let's try indexing another document with the `rating` field set to 4 (we intend to provide ratings as decimal numbers). Elasticsearch determines that this field is a `long` data type as the value fits its "long" data type rule. Although we want the `rating` field to host floating-point data, Elasticsearch fell short in determining the appropriate type. Looking at the value (4), it assumed that the field's data type is `long`.

In both cases, we have a schema with incorrect data types. Having incorrect types can cause problems in an application, making fields ineligible for sorting, filtering, and aggregating data. But this is the best that Elasticsearch can do when we use its dynamic mapping feature.

> ### Bring your data—make your schema
>
> While Elasticsearch is clever enough to derive mapping information based on our documents, so we don't have to worry about schemas, there is a chance that things will go badly and we will end up with an incorrect schema definition. Having a bad schema is asking for trouble.
>
> Because we generally understand our domains well and know our data models inside and out, my advice is not to let Elasticsearch create schemas, especially in production environments. Instead, it's best to create our schemas up front, usually by creating a mapping strategy across the organization using mapping templates (we work through some mapping templates in chapter 6). Of course, if your use case includes data without a standard format, dynamic mapping can be a big help.

So far, we've looked at dynamic mapping and seen that although this feature is attractive, it does have limitations, as discussed in the next section.

4.2.2 Limitations of dynamic mapping

There are some limitations to letting Elasticsearch derive the document schema. Elasticsearch can misinterpret document field values and derive an incorrect mapping that voids the field's eligibility for appropriate search, sort, and aggregation capabilities. Let's find out how Elasticsearch determines data types incorrectly and thus aids in formulating inaccurate and erroneous mapping rules.

DERIVING AN INCORRECT MAPPING

Suppose we intend to provide a field with numeric data but that the data will be wrapped as a string (for example, `"3.14"`—note the quotes). Unfortunately, Elasticsearch treats such data incorrectly: in this example, it expects the data type to be `text`, not `float` or `double`.

Let's modify the `student` document we looked at in chapter 3 and add a field: the student's age. It sounds like a number, but we're indexing it as a `text` field by wrapping the value in quotes.

Listing 4.2   **Adding an age field with text values to the `student` document**

```
PUT students_temp/_doc/1                    ◁───┐
{                                                │
  "name":"John",                                 │
  "age":"12"   ◁───┐  The age variable's value is │
}                  │  set as a string (in quotes). │   First document
                                                 │
PUT students_temp/_doc/2  ◁───┐  Second          │
{                             │  document         │
  "name":"William",                              │
  "age":"14"                                  ◁──┘
}
```

Notice that the `age` field's value is enclosed in quotes, so Elasticsearch treats it as a text field (although it includes numbers). After these two documents are indexed, we can write a search query to sort students by ascending or descending age (see figure 4.4). The response indicates that the operation is not allowed; let's see why.

Because the `age` field of a `student` document is indexed as a `text` field (by default, any string field is mapped to a `text` field during the dynamic mapping process), Elasticsearch cannot use that field in sorting operations. Sorting functionality is not available on `text` fields by default.

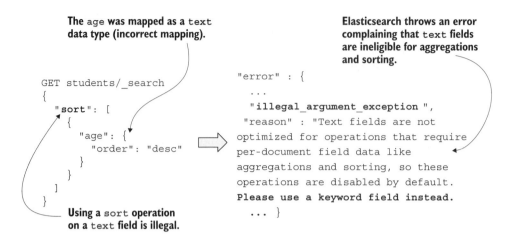

Figure 4.4   A sort operation on a text field results in an error.

If we try to sort on a `text` field, Elasticsearch throws an error message saying that the field isn't optimized for sorting. If we want to override this behavior and sort `text` fields, we can do so by setting `fielddata` to `true` when defining the schema:

```
PUT students_with_fielddata_setting
{
  "mappings": {
    "properties": {
      "age": {
        "type": "text",
        "fielddata": true
      }
    }
  }
}
```

A word of advice: field data is stored on the cluster's heap memory in a *field data cache*. Enabling `fielddata` leads to expensive computations, which may in turn lead to performance issues on the cluster. I suggest using `keyword` fields rather than enabling `fielddata` (see the next section).

FIXING SORTING USING KEYWORD TYPES

Fortunately, Elasticsearch can create any field as a multi-field with `keyword` as the second type by default. Going with this default feature, the `age` field is tagged as a multi-field, thus creating `age.keyword` with `keyword` as the data type. To sort students, all we need to do is change the field name from `age` to `age.keyword`.

Listing 4.3   Modified `sort` query sorting on the `age.keyword` field

```
GET students_temp/_search          Uses the _search API
{                                   to fetch all documents
```

```
"sort": [
   {
      "age.keyword": {
         "order": "asc"
      }
   }
]
}
```

Sorting function

age.keyword is the name of the field.

Sorts the data in ascending order

This query sorts all students in ascending order by age. The query runs successfully because age.keyword is a keyword type field on which we can apply a sorting function. By default, we sort on the second data type (age.keyword) created by Elasticsearch.

> **NOTE** In the example, age.keyword is the default name provided by Elasticsearch during dynamic mapping which is derived implicitly. Whereas, we have full control over creating fields, their names, and their types when defining mapping schemas explicitly.

Treating a field as a text type instead of a keyword unnecessarily affects the engine as data is analyzed and broken down into tokens.

DERIVING INCORRECT DATE FORMATS

Another potential problem with dynamic mapping is that date formats may be determined incorrectly if not provided in Elasticsearch's default date format (yyyy-MM-dd or yyyy/MM/dd). A date is considered a text type if we post it in the United Kingdom's dd-MM-yyyy format or the United States' MM-dd-yyyy format. We cannot perform date math on fields associated with non-date data types. Such fields are also ineligible for sorting, filtering, and aggregations.

> **NOTE** There is no date type in JSON, so it's up to consuming applications to decode the value and determine whether it is a date. When working with Elasticsearch, we provide data in a string format for these fields: for example, "release_date" : "2021-07-28".

The takeaway when working with dynamic mapping features is that there is a scope for erroneous mapping by Elasticsearch. Preparing our schema based on field values may not always fit the bill. So, the general advice is to develop the schema based on our data model requirements rather than relying on the mercy of the engine.

To overcome those limitations, we can choose an alternative: *explicit mapping*, where we define our schema and create it before the indexing process kicks in. We discuss explicit mapping in the next section.

4.3   *Explicit mapping*

In the previous section, we discussed Elasticsearch's schema-less dynamic mapping. Elasticsearch is intelligent enough to derive mapping information based on our documents, but we can end up with an incorrect schema definition. Fortunately, Elasticsearch provides ways for us to dictate the mapping definitions.

The following are two approaches to explicitly create (or update) a schema. Figure 4.5 demonstrates using both APIs to create a `movies` index:

- *Indexing APIs*—We can create a schema definition at the time of index creation using the `create index` API (not the `mapping` API) for this purpose. The `create index` API expects a request consisting of the required schema definition as a JSON document. The new index and its mapping definitions are created simultaneously.
- *Mapping APIs*—As our data model matures, we will sometimes need to update the schema definition with new attributes. Elasticsearch provides a `_mapping` endpoint to carry out this action, allowing us to add fields and their data types.

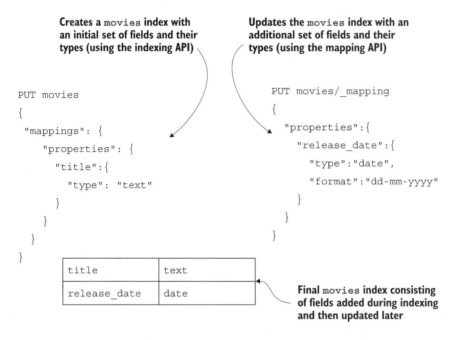

Figure 4.5   Creating and updating a schema using the indexing and mapping APIs

The next section looks at these two methods. We'll follow an example in which we are working with employee data.

4.3.1   *Mapping using the indexing API*

Creating a mapping definition at the time of index creation is relatively straightforward. We simply issue a PUT command followed by the index name and pass the `map-pings` object with all the required fields and their details as the body of the request (see figure 4.6).

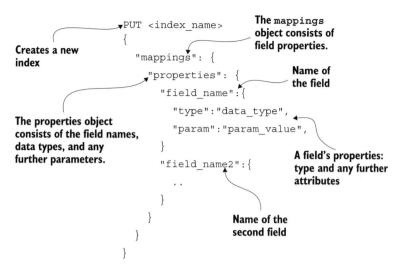

Figure 4.6 Creating a mapping definition during index creation

Now that we know the theory behind using the mapping API for creating a schema, let's put it to work by developing a mapping schema for an `employee` model, as in the following listing. Employee information is modeled with fields such as `name`, `age`, `email`, and `address`.

We index the document containing these fields into an `employees` index by invoking the mapping API over an HTTP PUT action. The request body is encapsulated with properties for our fields.

Listing 4.4 Creating the schema up front

```
PUT employees
{
  "mappings": {
    "properties": {
      "name":{ "type": "text"},          The name field is
      "age": {"type": "integer"},        a text data type.
      "email": {"type": "keyword"},      The age field is
      "address":{                        a number type.
        "properties": {                  Address object in an inner
          "street":{ "type":"text" },    object with further fields
          "country":{ "type":"text" }
        }
      }
    }
  }
}
```

The email field is a keyword type.

Inner object properties

Once the script is ready, execute this command in Kibana's Dev Tools. You should receive a successful response in the right pane, indicating that the index was created.

We now have an `employees` index with the expected schema mapping. In this example, we dictated the types to Elasticsearch; now we are in control of the schema.

Did you notice the `address` field in listing 4.4? It is an `object` type consisting of additional fields: `street` and `country`. However, the `address` field type has not been mentioned as `object`, although we said it was an `object` that encapsulates other data fields. This is because the `object` data type is deduced by Elasticsearch for any inner objects by default—hence we didn't mention it explicitly. Also, the subfield `properties` object wrapped in the `address` helps define further attributes of the inner object.

Now that our `employees` index is in production, suppose we are given a new requirement: management wants us to extend the model to include a few more attributes such as department, phone number, and others. To fulfill this requirement, we must add these fields using the mapping API on a live index. We go over this topic briefly in the next section.

4.3.2   *Updating schema using the mapping API*

As our project matures, the data model will undoubtedly change, too. Continuing with our employee document, let's add `joining_date` and `phone_number` attributes:

```
{
  "name":"John Smith",
  "joining_date":"01-05-2021",
  "phone_number":"01234567899"
  ...
}
```

The joining date is a `date` type as we want to do date-related operations, such as sorting employees by this date. The phone number is expected to be stored as is (we don't want the data to be tokenized—more on this in the coming sections), so it fits the `keyword` data type. To amend the existing `employees` schema definition with these additional fields, we invoke a `_mapping` endpoint on the existing index, declaring the new fields in the request object.

Listing 4.5   Updating the existing index with additional fields

```
PUT employees/_mapping          ◁──┐ _mapping endpoint to
{                                   │ update the existing index
  "properties":{
    "joining_date":{            ◁──┐ The joining date field
      "type":"date",               │ is a date type.
      "format":"dd-MM-yyyy"
    },
    "phone_number":{
      "type":"keyword"          ◁──┐ Phone numbers
    }                              │ are stored as is.
  }
}
```

Expected date format ┌──▷ (points to `"format":"dd-MM-yyyy"`)

If you look at the request body closely, the `properties` object is defined at the root level. This is unlike the earlier method of creating a schema using the indexing API, where the `properties` object was wrapped in the root-level `mappings` object.

UPDATING AN EMPTY INDEX

We can also use the same principle of updating the schema on an empty index. An *empty index* is created without schema mapping (for example, executing the `PUT books` command creates an empty `books` index).

Similar to how we updated the index in listing 4.5 by calling the `_mapping` endpoint with the required schema definition, we can use the same approach for the empty index. The following snippet updates the schema on the `departments` index with an additional field.

Listing 4.6 Updating the mapping schema of an empty index

```
PUT departments                         Creates an empty
                                        index first
PUT departments/_mapping                   Uses the mapping API to
{                                          update an empty index
  "properties":{
    "name":{
      "type":"text"                      The name field is
    }                                    declared as a text type.
  }
}
```

So far, we've seen the additive case of updating the schema with additional fields. But what if we want to change the data types of the existing fields? Suppose we want to change a field's type from `text` to `keyword`. Can we update the mapping just as easily as we added fields? The short answer is no. Elasticsearch doesn't allow us to change or modify the data types of existing fields. Instead we have to do a bit more work, as discussed in the next section.

4.3.3 Modifying existing fields is not allowed

Once an index is live (created with data fields and operational), any modifications of existing fields on the live index are prohibited. For example, if a field was defined as a `keyword` data type and indexed, it cannot be changed to a different data type (say, from `keyword` to `text`). There is a good reason for this. Data is indexed using existing schema definitions and, hence, stored in the index. Searching on that field data fails if the data type has been modified, which leads to an erroneous search experience. To avoid search failures, Elasticsearch does not allow us to modify existing fields.

Well, you may ask, what is the alternative? Business requirements change, as do technical requirements. How can we fix data types (which may have been created incorrectly) on a live index?

We can use *reindexing*. Reindexing operations source data from the original index to a new index (which can have updated schema definitions). The idea is as follows:

1 Create a new index with the updated schema definitions.

2 Copy the data from the old index into the new index using the reindexing APIs. The new index with new schema is ready to use once reindexing is complete. The index is open for both read and write operations.

3 When the new index is ready, our application switches over to it.

4 We remove the old index once we confirm that the new index works as expected.

Reindexing is a powerful operation and is discussed in detail in chapter 5, but let's take a quick look at how the API works. Suppose we wish to migrate data from an existing (`source`) index to a target (`dest`) index. We issue a reindexing call, as shown in listing 4.7.

NOTE These indices do not exist yet. This listing is only FYI.

Listing 4.7 Migrating data between indexes using reindexing API

```
POST _reindex
{
  "source": {"index": "orders"},
  "dest": {"index": "orders_new"}
}
```

The new `orders_new` index is created with the changes to the schema, and then the data from the old index (`orders`) is migrated to this newly created index with updated declarations.

NOTE If your application is rigidly coupled with an existing index, moving to the new index may require a code or configuration change. The ideal way to avoid such situations is to use aliases. *Aliases* are alternate names given to indexes. Aliasing helps us switch between indexes seamlessly with zero downtime. We look at aliases in chapter 6.

Sometimes data have incorrect types when documents are indexed. For example, a `rating` field of type `float` may receive a value enclosed as a string: `"rating": "4.9"` instead of `"rating":4.9`. Fortunately, Elasticsearch is forgiving when it encounters mismatched values for data types. It proceeds with indexing the document by extracting the value and storing it in the original data type. We discuss this mechanism in the next section.

4.3.4 *Type coercion*

Sometimes JSON documents contain incorrect values that differ from those in the schema definition. For example, an integer-defined field may be indexed with a string value. Elasticsearch tries to convert such inconsistent types, thus avoiding indexing problems. This process is known as *type coercion*. For example, say we've defined the `age` field of a car to be an integer type:

```
"age":{"type":"short"}
```

Ideally, we index our documents with of `age` as an integer value. However, a user may accidentally set the value of `age` as a string type (`"2"`) and invoke the call.

> **Listing 4.8 Setting a string value for a numeric field**

```
PUT cars/_doc/1
{
  "make":"BMW",
  "model":"X3",            An integer input
  "age":"2"          ◁──┘ as a string
}
```

Elasticsearch indexes this document without any errors. Although the `age` field is expected to contain an integer, Elasticsearch *coerces* the type for us to avoid errors. The coercion only works if the parsed value of the field matches the expected data type. In this case, parsing `"2"` results in 2, which is a number.

So far, we've talked a lot about mapping and data types without putting much emphasis on data types. Designing your schema with appropriate data types is crucial in optimizing the search experience. We need to understand data types, their characteristics, and when to use them. Unlike a database or programming language, Elasticsearch comes with a long list of data types, catering to almost every data shape and form. The next section looks at data types in detail.

4.4 Data types

Similar to a variable's data type in a programming language, fields in a document have a specific data type associated with them. Elasticsearch provides a rich list of data types, from simple to complex to specialized. The list of these types keeps growing, so watch for more.

Elasticsearch provides over two dozen different data types, so we have a good selection of appropriate data types based on our specific needs. Data types can be broadly classified in the following categories:

- *Simple types*—Common data types representing strings (textual information), dates, numbers, and other basic data variants. Examples are `text`, `boolean`, `long`, `date`, `double`, and `binary`.
- *Complex types*—Created by composing additional types, similar to an object construction in a programming language where objects can hold inner objects. Complex types can be flattened or nested to create even more complex data structures based on the requirements. Examples are `object`, `nested`, `flattened`, and `join`.
- *Specialized types*—Used predominantly for specialized cases such as geolocation and IP addresses. Examples are `geo_shape`, `geo_point`, and `ip`, and range types such as `date_range` and `ip_range`.

NOTE The full range of types is available from the official documentation: http://mng.bz/yQpe.

Every field in a document can have one or more associated types based on the business and data requirements. Table 4.1 provides a list of common data types with some examples.

Table 4.1 Common data types with examples

Type	Description	Examples
text	Represents textual information (such as string values); unstructured text	Movie title, blog post, book review, log message
integer, long, short, byte	Represents a number	Number of infectious cases, flights canceled, products sold, book's rank
float, double	Represents a floating-point number	Student's grade point average, moving average of sales, reviewer average ratings, temperature
boolean	Represents a binary choice: true or false	Is the movie a blockbuster? Are COVID cases on the rise? Has the student passed the exam?
keyword	Represents structured text: text that must not be broken down or analyzed	Error codes, email addresses, phone numbers, Social Security numbers
object	Represents a JSON object	(In JSON format) employee details, tweets, movie objects
nested	Represents an array of objects	Employee address, email routing data, a movie's technical crew

As you can imagine, this is not a comprehensive list of data types. This book is written for version 8.6, and nearly 40 data types are defined by Elasticsearch. Elasticsearch defines types microscopically in some cases to optimize search queries. For example, text types are further classified into more specific types such as search_as_you_type, match_only_text, completion, token_count, and others.

Elasticsearch also tries to group data types in families to optimize space and performance. For example, the keyword family has keyword, wildcard, and constant_keyword data types. Currently this is the only family group; we can expect more in the near future.

> **Single field with multiple data types**
>
> In programming languages like Java and C#, we can't define a variable with two different types. However, there is no such restriction in Elasticsearch. Elasticsearch is pretty cool when it comes to representing a field with multiple data types, allowing us to develop the schema the way we want to.
>
> For example, we may want the author of a book to be both a text type and a keyword type. Each field has a specific characteristic, and keywords will not be analyzed, meaning the field is stored as is. We can also have more types—for example, the author field can be declared as a completion type in addition to the other two types.

In the next few sections, we review these data types, their characteristics, and their usage. But before we work with data types in detail, we need to understand how to create mapping definitions. Section 4.3 digs deeper into working with mapping features, but for now we briefly look at a mechanism to create a mapping definition as it is a prerequisite for the next sections.

Developing mapping schemas

When we indexed a movie document (listing 4.1), Elasticsearch created a schema dynamically (figure 4.2), deriving types by analyzing field values. We are now at a point where we would like to create our schema definitions. Elasticsearch uses an indexing API to create these definitions, so let's check it out with an example.

Suppose we wish to create a student with `name` and `age` fields that have the data type `text` and `byte`, respectively (the next section introduces these data types). We can create the `students` index with these mapping definitions up front, thus taking control of creating the schema. The figure demonstrates this succinctly, with the mapping definition execution on the left-hand side and fetching the definition on the right-hand side.

```
PUT students
{
    "mappings": {
        "properties": {
            "name":{
                "type": "text"
            },
            "age":{
                "type": "byte"
            }
        }
    }
}
```

The `students` index is defined with a schema consisting of `name` (`text`) and `age` (`byte`).

```
GET students/_mapping
```

Fetches the mappings for the students index

```
{
    "students" : {
        "mappings" : {
            "properties" : {
                "age" : {
                    "type" : "byte"
                },
                "name" : {
                    "type" : "text"
                }
            }
        }
    }
}
```

The `students` mapping definition

Mapping definition (left) and retrieving the schema (right)

We create the index with a request containing a set of field properties wrapped in a `mappings` object. We invoke the `_mapping` endpoint on the index to check the definition of the schema (shown on the right-hand side).

Now that we know how to create schemas at a high level, we are ready to examine the core data types.

4.5   Core data types

Elasticsearch provides a set of core data types to represent data, including `text`, `keyword`, `date`, `long`, and `boolean`. We need a basic understanding of core data types before we can understand the advanced types and dynamic and explicit mapping. In the next few sections, we look at the core basic data types with examples.

> **NOTE** To avoid bloating the chapter, the code for some of the examples can be found on GitHub (http://mng.bz/GyBR) and the book's website (https://www.manning.com/books/elasticsearch-in-action-second-edition).

4.5.1   The text data type

If there's one type of data that search engines must do well, it is the *full-text* data type. Human-readable text, also called *full text* or *unstructured text* in search engine lingo, is the bread and butter of a modern search engine. We consume a lot of textual information in the current digital world: news items, tweets, blog posts, research articles, and much more. Elasticsearch defines a dedicated data type to handle full-text data: the `text` data type.

Any field stamped with the `text` data type is analyzed before it is persisted. During the analysis process, analyzers massage (enrich, enhance, and transform) textual data into various forms and store them in internal data structures for easy access.

As we saw in our earlier examples, setting the type is straightforward. Use this syntax in your mapping definition: `"field name":{ "type": "text" }`. We worked through an example in section 4.2.2, so we won't repeat that exercise. Instead, let's look at how Elasticsearch treats `text` fields during indexing.

ANALYZING TEXT FIELDS

Elasticsearch supports both types of text data—structured and unstructured. Unstructured text is full-text data, usually written in a human-readable language (English, Chinese, Portuguese, etc.). Efficient and effective search on unstructured text makes a search engine stand out.

Unstructured text undergoes an analysis process whereby data is split into tokens, characters are filtered out, words are reduced to their root word (stemmed), synonyms are added, and other natural language processing rules are applied. We dedicate chapter 7 to text analysis, but let's quickly see an example of how Elasticsearch handles full text. The following text is a user's review of a movie:

```
"The movie was sick!!! Hilarious :) :) and WITTY ;) a KiLLer 👍"
```

When this document is indexed, it undergoes an analysis based on the analyzer. Analyzers are text-analysis modules that analyze incoming text to tokenize and normalize it. By default, Elasticsearch uses a *standard analyzer,* and analyzing the review comment involves the following steps (figure 4.7):

1 Tags, punctuation, and special characters are stripped away using character filters. This is how the review looks after this step:

```
The movie was sick Hilarious and WITTY a KiLLer 👍
```

2 The sentence is broken down into tokens using a tokenizer:

```
[the, movie, was, sick, Hilarious, and, WITTY, a, KiLLer, 👍]
```

3 The tokens are changed to lowercase using token filters:

```
[the, movie, was, sick, hilarious, and, witty, a, killer, 👍]
```

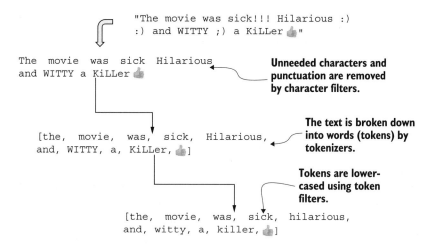

```
"The movie was sick!!! Hilarious :)
 :) and WITTY ;) a KiLLer 👍"
```

The movie was sick Hilarious
and WITTY a KiLLer 👍

Unneeded characters and punctuation are removed by character filters.

```
[the, movie, was, sick, Hilarious,
and, WITTY, a, KiLLer, 👍]
```

The text is broken down into words (tokens) by tokenizers.

```
[the, movie, was, sick, hilarious,
and, witty, a, killer, 👍]
```

Tokens are lower-cased using token filters.

Figure 4.7 Processing a full-text field during indexing with the standard analyzer module

These steps may vary, depending on your analyzer. For example, if you choose an English analyzer, tokens are reduced to root words (stemmed):

```
[movi,sick,hilari, witti, killer, 👍]
```

Did you notice the stemmed words `movi`, `hilari`, and `witti`? They are not real words per se, but incorrect spellings don't matter as long as all derived forms can match the stemmed words.

> **NOTE** We can use the `_analyze` API exposed by Elasticsearch to test how text is analyzed. This API helps us understand the inner workings of the analyzers and supports building complex and custom analyzer modules for various language requirements.

The code is available on the GitHub repository. Feel free to experiment with running analyzers on text data.

Stemming

Stemming is a process of reducing words to their root words. For example, *fighter*, *fight*, and *fought* can all be reduced to one word: *fight*. Similarly, *movies* can be reduced to *movi* and *hilarious* to *hilari*, as in the previous examples.

> **(continued)**
>
> Stemmers are language dependent. For example, we can employ a French stemmer if the chosen language of the documents is French. Stemmers are declared via token filters when composing the analyzer module during the text analysis phase in Elasticsearch.

The same process is retriggered during execution of search queries on the same field. Chapter 7 is dedicated to the analysis of full text and discusses the intricacies of analyzers and how Elasticsearch manages full-text data.

We mentioned earlier that Elasticsearch defines types microscopically: for example, further classifying `text` fields into more specific types such as `search_as_you_type`, `match_only_text`, `completion`, `token_count`, and others. Let's examine these specialized text types briefly in the next few sections to see how Elasticsearch puts extra emphasis and effort into full text.

THE TOKEN_COUNT DATA TYPE

A specialized form of the `text` data type, `token_count`, defines a field that captures the number of tokens in that field. For example, if we have defined a book's `title` as a `token_count`, we can retrieve all books based on the number of tokens a book has. Let's create a mapping for this by creating an index with a `title` field.

> **Listing 4.9 Index with a `token_count` data type for the `title` field**

```
PUT tech_books
{
  "mappings": {
    "properties": {          The field's
      "title": {             name
        "type": "token_count",        The title's data type
        "analyzer": "standard"        is token_count.
      }                      The analyzer is expected
    }                        to be provided.
  }
}
```

As you can see, `title` is defined as a `token_count` type. The analyzer is expected to be provided, so we set the standard analyzer on the `title` field. Now, let's index three technical books—this one and my future (hopefully) books—before searching for them based on the title's token count feature.

> **Listing 4.10 Indexing three new documents into the `tech_books` index**

```
PUT tech_books/_doc/1
{
  "title":"Elasticsearch in Action"
}
```

```
PUT tech_books/_doc/2
{
  "title":"Elasticsearch for Java Developers"
}

PUT tech_books/_doc/3
{
  "title":"Elastic Stack in Action"
}
```

Now that the `tech_books` index contains a few books, let's put the `token_count` type to use. The following `range` query fetches books with titles composed of more than three words (`gt` is short for greater than) but fewer than or equal to five words (`lte` is short for less than or equal to).

Listing 4.11 `range` query fetching books with a certain number of words

```
GET tech_books/_search
{
  "query": {
   "range": {
     "title": {
       "gt": 3,
       "lte": 5
      }
     }
    }
}
```

The `range` query fetches books based on the number of words in the title. It retrieves *Elasticsearch for Java Developers* (four tokens) and *Elastic Stack in Action* (four tokens) but omits *Elasticsearch in Action* (three tokens).

We can also combine the `title` field as a `text` type and a `token_type`, as Elasticsearch allows a single field to be declared with multiple data types (multi-fields—discussed in detail in section 4.7). The following listing creates a new index (`tech_books2`) using this technique.

Listing 4.12 Adding `token_count` as an additional data type to a `text` field

```
PUT tech_books2
{
  "mappings": {
    "properties": {
      "title": {              The title field is defined
        "type": "text",       as text data type.
        "fields": {                    The title field is declared to
          "word_count": {              have multiple data types.
            "type": "token_count",     word_count is the
            "analyzer": "standard"     additional field.
          }                                It is mandatory to
        }                                  provide the analyzer.
      }
```

The type of
word_count

```
          }
        }
      }
    }
}
```

Because the `word_count` field is an inner attribute of the `title` field, we can use a `term` query (a type of query run on structured data such as numbers, dates, Booleans, etc.).

```
GET tech_books/_search
{
  "query": {                    We are using
    "term": {            ←───   a term query.
      "title.word_count": {   ←──┐  The name
        "value": 4              │  of the field
      }
    }
  }
}
```

We use `<outer_field>.<inner_field>` as the `word_count` field's name, so `title.word_count` is the accessor of the field.

In addition to `token_count`, the `text` type has other descendants, such as `search_as_you_type` and `completion`. For space reasons, we won't discuss them in this book. Let's continue learning about common data types, with `keyword` being next in line.

4.5.2   *The keyword data types*

The `keyword` family of data types comprises `keyword`, `constant_keyword`, and `wildcard`. Let's look at these types.

THE KEYWORD TYPE

Structured data, such as PIN codes, bank accounts, and phone numbers, doesn't need to be searched as partial matches or produce relevant results. The results tend to provide binary output: a result is returned if there is a match, or no result is returned. This type of query doesn't care how well the document is matched, so we don't expect relevance scores associated with the results. Such structured data is represented as a `keyword` data type in Elasticsearch.

The `keyword` data type leaves fields untouched. The field is untokenized and not analyzed. The advantage of `keyword` fields is that they can be used in data aggregations, range queries, and filtering and sorting operations on data. To set a `keyword` type, use this format:

```
"field_name":{ "type": "keyword" }
```

For example, the following code creates an `email` property with the `keyword` data type.

Listing 4.14 Defining `email` as a `keyword` type for a faculty document

```
PUT faculty
{
  "mappings": {
    "properties": {          Defines the
      "email": {             email property
        "type": "keyword"          Declares email
      }                            as a keyword type
    }
  }
}
```

We can also declare numeric values as keywords: for example, `credit_card_number` may be declared as a `keyword` for efficient access rather than as a numeric type such as `long`. There's no way we can build range queries on such data. The rule of thumb is that if numerical fields are *not* used in range queries, declaring them as `keyword` types is advised as it helps with faster retrieval.

NOTE Sample code demonstrating the `keyword` data type is available with the book's files.

THE CONSTANT_KEYWORD TYPE

When the corpus of documents is expected to have the same value, regardless of number, the `constant_keyword` type comes in handy. Let's say the United Kingdom is carrying out a census in 2031, and for obvious reasons, the `country` field of each citizen's census document will be `"United Kingdom"` by default. There is no need to send the `country` field for each document when it is indexed into the `census` index. The mapping schema defines an index (`census`) with a field called `country` of type `constant_keyword`.

Listing 4.15 `census` index with `constant_keyword`

```
PUT census
{
  "mappings": {
    "properties": {
      "country":{
        "type": "constant_keyword",
        "value":"United Kingdom"
      }
    }
  }
}
```

Note that we set the default value for this field to `"United Kingdom"` when declaring the mapping definition. Now we index a document for John Doe, with just his name (no `country` field):

```
PUT census/_doc/1
{
  "name":"John Doe"
}
```

When we search for all residents of the UK, even though the document doesn't have that field during indexing, we receive a positive result that returns John's document:

```
GET census/_search
{
  "query": {
    "term": {
      "country": {
        "value": "United Kingdom"
      }
    }
  }
}
```

The `constant_keyword` field will have exactly the same value for every document in that index.

THE WILDCARD DATA TYPE

The `wildcard` data type is another special data type that belongs to the `keyword` family. It supports searching data using wildcards and regular expressions. We define a field as a `wildcard` type by declaring it as `"type": "wildcard"` in the mapping definition. We then query the field by issuing a `wildcard` query, as shown in listing 4.16.

> **NOTE** A document with `"description":"Null Pointer exception as object is null"` was indexed before this query.

> **Listing 4.16 A `wildcard` query with a wildcard value**

```
GET errors/_search
{
  "query": {
    "wildcard": {          ◁──┐ Uses a wildcard
      "description": {          query
        "value": "*obj*"   ◁──┐ Searches using
      }                        wildcards
    }
  }
}
```

Keyword fields are efficient and performant, so using them appropriately improves indexing and search query performance.

4.5.3 *The date data type*

Elasticsearch provides a `date` data type to support indexing and searching date-based operations. Date fields are considered structured data, so we can use them in sorting, filtering, and aggregations.

Elasticsearch parses a string value and infers that it is a date if the value conforms to the ISO 8601 date standard. That is, the date value is expected to be in the format `yyyy-MM-dd` or (with a time component) `yyyy-MM-ddTHH:mm:ss`.

JSON doesn't have a date type, so dates in incoming documents are expressed as strings. These are parsed by Elasticsearch and indexed appropriately. For example, a value such as

`"article_date":"2021-05-01"` or `"article_date":"2021-05-01T15:45:50"`

is considered a date and is indexed as a date type because the value conforms to the ISO standard.

As we did with other data types, we can create a field with the `date` type during the mapping definition. The next listing creates a `departure_date_time` field for a flight document.

> **Listing 4.17 Creating an index with a `date` type**

```
PUT flights
{
  "mappings": {
    "properties": {
      "departure_date_time":{
        "type": "date"
      }
    }
  }
}
```

When indexing a flight document, setting `"departure_date_time"` `:"2021-08-06"` (or `"2021-08-06T05:30:00"` with a time component) will index the document with the date as expected.

> **NOTE** When no mapping definition for a date field exists in an index, Elasticsearch parses a document successfully when the date format is either `yyyy-MM-dd` (ISO date format) or `yyyy/MM/dd` (non-ISO date format). However, once we've created the mapping definition for a date, the date format of the incoming document is expected based on the format defined in the mapping definition.

We can change the format of the date if we need to: instead of setting the date in ISO format (`yyyy-MM-dd`), we can customize the format based on our needs by setting it on the field during field creation:

```
PUT flights
{
  "mappings": {
    "properties": {
      "departure_date_time":{
        "type": "date",
```

```
            "format": "dd-MM-yyyy||dd-MM-yy"        ◁──┐  Date is set in either of
          }                                            │  these two formats.
        }
      }
    }
  }
}
```

Incoming documents can now have the departure field set as

```
"departure_date_time" :"06-08-2021"
```

or

```
"departure_date_time" :"06-08-21"
```

In addition to providing the date as a string value, we can provide it in a number for-mat—either seconds or milliseconds since the epoch (January 1, 1970). The following mapping definition sets three dates with three different formats:

```
{
  ...
  "properties": {
    "string_date":{ "type": "date", "format": "dd-MM-yyyy" },
    "millis_date":{ "type": "date", "format": "epoch_millis" },
    "seconds_date":{ "type": "date", "format": "epoch_second"}
  }
}
```

The given dates are converted internally to `long` values stored in milliseconds since the epoch, equivalent to `epoch_millis`.

We can use `range` queries to fetch dates. For example, the following snippet retrieves flights scheduled between 5:00 and 5:30 a.m. on a given date:

```
"range": {                              ◁──┐  A range query fetching
  "departure_date_time": {                   │  documents between two dates
    "gte": "2021-08-06T05:00:00",                ◁──┐  The time range is between
    "lte": "2021-08-06T05:30:00"                     │  5:00 and 5.30 a.m.
    }
}
```

Finally, we can accept multiple date formats on a single field by declaring the required formats:

```
                                                        Sets four different
                                                        formats on the field
"departure_date_time":{
  "type": "date",
  "format": "dd-MM-yyyy||dd/MM/yyyy||yyyy-MM-dd||yyyy/MM/dd"    ◁──┘
}
```

Refer to the documentation about Elasticsearch's `date` data type for more informa-tion, as we can't cover all the options in this chapter. Also refer to the book's files for complete examples.

4.5.4 Numeric data types

Elasticsearch supplies several numeric data types to handle integer and floating-point data. Table 4.2 lists the numeric types.

Table 4.2 Numeric data types

Integer types	`byte`	Signed 8-bit integer
	`short`	Signed 16-bit integer
	`integer`	Signed 32-bit integer
	`long`	Signed 64-bit integer
	`unsigned_long`	64-bit unsigned integer
Floating-point types	`float`	32-bit single-precision floating-point number
	`double`	64-bit double-precision floating-point number
	`half_float`	16-bit half-precision floating-point number
	`scaled_float`	Floating-point nmber backed by `long`

We declare the field and its data type as `"field_name":{ "type": "short"}`. The following snippet demonstrates how we can create a mapping schema with numeric fields:

```
"age":{
  "type": "short"
},
"grade":{
  "type": "half_float"
},
"roll_number":{
  "type": "long"
}
```

This example creates three fields with three different numeric data types.

4.5.5 The boolean data type

The `boolean` data type represents the binary value of a field: `true` or `false`. This example declares a field's type as `boolean`:

```
PUT blockbusters
{
  "mappings": {
    "properties": {
      "blockbuster":{
        "type": "boolean"
      }
    }
  }
}
```

We can then index a couple of movies—*Avatar* (2009) as a blockbuster and *The Matrix Resurrections* (2021) as a flop:

```
PUT blockbusters/_doc/1
{
  "title":"Avatar",
  "blockbuster":true
}

PUT blockbusters/_doc/2
{
  "title":"The Matrix Resurrections",
  "blockbuster":"false"
}
```

In addition to setting the field as JSON's `boolean` type (`true` or `false`), the field also accepts "stringified" Boolean values such as `"true"` and `"false"`, as shown in the second example.

We can use a `term` query (Booleans are classified as structured data) to fetch the results. For example, the following query fetches *Avatar* as a blockbuster:

```
GET blockbusters/_search
{
  "query": {
    "term": {
      "blockbuster": {
        "value": "true"
      }
    }
  }
}
```

We can also provide an empty string for a `false` value: `"blockbuster":""`.

4.5.6   *The range data types*

The range data types represent lower and upper bounds for a field. For example, if we want to select a group of volunteers for a vaccine trial, we can segregate volunteers based on categories such as age 25–50 or 51–70, demographics such as income level, city dwellers, and so on. Elasticsearch supplies a `range` data type to support search queries on range data. The range is defined by operators such as `lte` (less than or equal to) and `lt` (less than) for upper bounds and `gte` (greater than or equal to) and `gt` (greater than) for lower bounds.

Elasticsearch provides various range data types: `date_range`, `integer_range`, `float_range`, `ip_range`, and more. In the next section, we see the `date_range` type in action.

THE DATE_RANGE TYPE EXAMPLE

The `date_range` date type helps index a range of dates for a field. Then we can use `range` queries to match criteria based on the lower and upper bounds of the dates.

Let's code an example to demonstrate the `date_range` type. Venkat Subramaniam is an award-winning author who delivers training sessions on various subjects, from programming to design to testing. Let's consider a list of his training courses and the dates for our example. We create a `trainings` index with two fields—the name of the course and the training dates—that have the `text` and `date_range` type, respectively.

Listing 4.18 Index with a `date_range` type

```
PUT trainings
{
  "mappings": {
    "properties": {        Name of the
      "name":{          ◁─── training session
        "type": "text"
      },
      "training_dates":{   ◁─┐ The training_dates field is
        "type": "date_range"  │ declared as a date_range type.
      }
    }
  }
}
```

Now that the index is ready, let's index a few documents with Venkat's training courses and dates:

```
PUT trainings/_doc/1
{
  "name":"Functional Programming in Java",
  "training_dates":{
    "gte":"2021-08-07",
    "lte":"2021-08-10"
  }
}

PUT trainings/_doc/2
{
  "name":"Programming Kotlin",
  "training_dates":{
    "gte":"2021-08-09",
    "lte":"2021-08-12"
  }
}

PUT trainings/_doc/3
{
  "name":"Reactive Programming",
  "training_dates":{
    "gte":"2021-08-17",
    "lte":"2021-08-20"
  }
}
```

The `date_range` type field expects two values: an upper bound and a lower bound. These are usually represented by abbreviations like `gte` (greater than or equal to), `lt` (less than), and so on.

With the data prepped, let's issue a search request to find Venkat's courses between two dates.

Listing 4.19   Searching for courses between two dates

```
GET trainings/_search
{
  "query": {                      We use a range
    "range": {          ◁────     query to search.
      "training_dates": {       ◁──┐ Searches for courses
        "gt": "2021-08-10",       │ between these two dates
        "lt": "2021-08-12"
      }
    }
  }
}
```

In response to the query (the results are skipped for brevity), we learn that Venkat is delivering a "Programming Kotlin" training between the two dates (the second document matches the dates). The `date_range` made it easy to search a range of data. In addition to `date_range`, we can create other ranges including `ip_range`, `float_range`, `double_range`, `integer_range`, and so on.

4.5.7   *The IP address (ip) data type*

Elasticsearch provides a specific data type to support internet protocol (IP) addresses: the `ip` data type. This data type supports both IPv4 and IPv6 IP addresses. To create a field of `ip` type, use `"field":{"type": "ip"}` as the following example shows:

```
PUT networks
{
  "mappings": {
    "properties": {
      "router_ip":{ "type": "ip" }      ◁──┐ The field's data
    }                                       │ type is ip.
  }
}
```

Indexing the document is straightforward:

```
PUT networks/_doc/1
{                                     Indexes a document
  "router_ip":"35.177.57.111"   ◁──   with an IP address
}
```

Finally, we can use our search endpoint to search for IP addresses that match our query. The following query searches for data in the `networks` index to get the matching IP address:

```
GET networks/_search
{
  "query":{
    "term": {              Term-level search
                           for IP addresses
      "router_ip": { "value": "35.177.0.0/16" }    ⊲─┐ Searches for IP addresses
    }                                                 │ in this range
  }
}
```

The previous couple of sections have reviewed the core data types. Elasticsearch provides a rich set of data types for almost any use case we can think of. Some core data types are straightforward and intuitive to work with, while others, like `object`, `nested`, `join`, `completion`, and `search_as_you_type` require special attention. In the next section, we explore a few of these advanced data types.

4.6 Advanced data types

We've looked at core and common data types to represent data fields. Some can be classified as advanced types, including some specialized types. In the next few sections, we touch on these additional types with definitions and examples.

> **NOTE** Covering all the data types would bloat this book, and I am also not a big fan of overly long chapters. So, I've made the judicious call to include only the most important and useful advanced data types. The book's GitHub repository and website include examples of the types cited here as well as those omitted.

4.6.1 The geo_point data type

With the advent of smartphones and devices, location services and searching for nearby places have become common. Most of us have used a smart device to do things like find the location of the nearest restaurant or asked for GPS directions to our mother-in-law's house at Christmas. Elasticsearch has a specialized data type to capture a place's location.

Location data is expressed as a `geo_point` data type representing longitude and latitude. We can use this to pinpoint an address for a restaurant, school, golf course, and so on. Let's see it in action.

The following code shows the schema definition of a `restaurants` index: restaurants with `name` and `address` fields. The only notable point is that the `address` field is defined as a `geo_point` data type.

Listing 4.20 Mapping schema with a field declared as a `geo_point` type

```
PUT restaurants
{
  "mappings": {
    "properties": {
      "name":{
        "type": "text"
```

```
    },
    "address":{
      "type": "geo_point"
    }
  }
 }
}
```

Let's index a sample restaurant (fictitious London-based Sticky Fingers) with an address provided as a longitude and latitude.

Listing 4.21 Address represented by longitude and latitude

```
PUT restaurants/_doc/1
{
  "name":"Sticky Fingers",
  "address":{          ◁─┐  The address is provided as a pair
    "lon":"0.1278",       │  of longitude and latitude values.
    "lat":"51.5074"
  }
}
```

The restaurant's address is given in the form of a longitude (`lon`) and latitude (`lat`) pair. There are other ways to provide these inputs, as we see shortly; but first, let's fetch restaurants within the location perimeter.

We can fetch restaurants using a `geo_bounding_box` query to search data involving geographical addresses. The query takes inputs of `top_left` and `bottom_right` geopoints (provided as `lon` and `lat` pairs) to create a boxed area around our point of interest, as shown in figure 4.8.

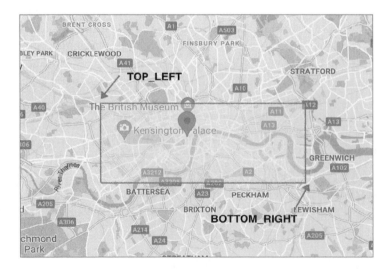

Figure 4.8 Geo-bounding box around a location in central London

Listing 4.22   Fetching restaurants around a geographical location

```
GET restaurants/_search
{
  "query": {
    "geo_bounding_box":{
      "address":{
        "top_left":{          ◁─┐  Top-left corner
          "lon":"0",             │  of the box
          "lat":"52"
        },
        "bottom_right":{      ◁─┐  Bottom-right corner
          "lon":"1",             │  of the box
          "lat":"50"
        }
      }
    }
  }
}
```

The query fetches our Sticky Fingers restaurant because it falls in the geo-bounding box represented by the two geopoints.

> **NOTE** When searching for an address using `geo_bounding_box`, a common mistake is providing incorrect inputs (`top_left` and `bottom_right`) to the query. Make sure the longitude and latitudes of these two inputs form the bounding box.

Earlier, I mentioned that we can provide location information in various formats, not just longitude and latitude, including as an array or a string. Table 4.3 lists these formats.

Table 4.3   Location information-related formats

Format	Explanation	Example
Array	Geopoint represented as an array. Note the order of the geopoint inputs: it takes `lon` and `lat`, not the other way around (unlike the string format—see the next row).	`"address":[0.12,51.5]`
String	Geopoint as string data with `lat` and `lon` inputs.	`"address":"51.5,0.12"`
Geohash	An encoded string formed by hashing the longitude and latitude coordinates. The alphanumeric string points to a place on earth.	`u10j4`
Point	A precise location on a map. Known as well-known text (WKT), a standard mechanism to represent geometrical data.	`POINT(51.5,-0.12)`

In this section, we have worked with geo-queries without prior knowledge about them. We cover this topic in detail in chapter 12.

4.6.2 *The object data type*

Often, data is hierarchical: for example, an `email` object consisting of top-level fields like `subject` as well as an inner object to hold attachments, which in turn may have properties such as the attachment file name, its type, and so on. JSON allows us to create hierarchical objects—objects wrapped in other objects. Elasticsearch has a special data type to represent a hierarchy of objects: the `object` type.

The data types for the top-level `subject` and `to` fields are `text` and `keyword`, respectively. Because an attachment is an object itself, its data type is `object`. The two properties `filename` and `filetype` in the `attachments` object can be modeled as `text` fields. With this information, we can create a mapping definition.

> **Listing 4.23 Schema definition with object data types**

```
PUT emails
{
  "mappings": {
    "properties": {        ◁──┐ Top-level properties
      "to":{                   │ for the emails index
        "type": "keyword"
      },
      "subject":{
        "type": "text"
      },
      "attachments":{    ◁──┐ Inner object consisting of
        "properties": {      │ second-level properties
          "filename":{
            "type":"text"
          },
          "filetype":{
            "type":"text"
          }
        }
      }
    }
  }
}
```

The `attachments` property is something we should draw attention to. The type of this field is `object` as it encapsulates two other fields. The two fields defined in the `attachments` inner object are no different from the `subject` and `to` fields declared at the top level, except that they are one level down.

Once the command is executed successfully, we can check the schema by invoking the `GET emails/_mapping` command.

> **Listing 4.24 The `GET emails/_mapping` response**

```
{
  "emails" : {
    "mappings" : {
```

```
        "properties" : {
          "attachments" : {                          attachments is an inner
            "properties" : {     The type is hidden   object with other fields.
              "filename" : {     here, but it is an
The field's type is   "type" : "text",   object by default.
shown, as expected.
          . . .
}
```

The response consists of `subject`, `to`, and `attachments` as top-level fields (not all properties are shown, for brevity). The `attachments` object has further fields encapsulated as properties with the appropriate fields and their definitions. When we fetch the mapping (`GET emails/_mapping`), while all other fields show their associated data types, `attachments` don't: by default, Elasticsearch infers the `object` type for inner objects.

Next, let's index a document.

Listing 4.25 Indexing an email document

```
PUT emails/_doc/1
{
  "to:":"johndoe@johndoe.com",
  "subject":"Testing Object Type",
  "attachments":{
    "filename":"file1.txt",
    "filetype":"confidential"
  }
}
```

Now that we have primed our `emails` index with one document, we can issue a simple `search` query on the inner object fields to fetch relevant documents (and prove our point).

Listing 4.26 Searching for emails with an attachment file

```
GET emails/_search
{
  "query": {
    "match": {
      "attachments.filename": "file1.txt"
    }
  }
}
```

This query returns the document from our store because the filename matches our document. Note that we use a `term` query on the `keyword` field as we wish to match an exact field value (file1.txt).

While object types are pretty straightforward, they have one limitation: inner objects are *flattened* out and not stored as individual documents. The downside of this action is that the relationship is lost between the objects indexed from an array. Let's review this limitation using a detailed example.

LIMITATIONS OF THE OBJECT TYPE

In our earlier email example, the `attachments` field was declared as an `object` type. While we created an email with just one attachment object, nothing stops us from creating multiple attachments (emails often have multiple files attached), as shown in the next listing.

Listing 4.27 Indexing a document with multiple attachments

```
PUT emails/_doc/2
{
  "to:":"mrs.doe@johndoe.com",
  "subject":"Multi attachments test",
  "attachments":[{
    "filename":"file2.txt",
    "filetype":"confidential"
  },{
    "filename":"file3.txt",
    "filetype":"private"
  }]
}
```

By default, the `attachments` field is the `object` type: an inner object composed of an array of attachment files. Notice that the classification type of the file file2.txt is `confidential` and of file3.txt is `private` (see table 4.4).

Table 4.4   Attachment filenames and classified types

Attachment name	File type
file2.txt	`confidential`
file3.txt	`private`

Our email document is indexed and has ID 1 and a couple of attachments. Let's work through a simple search requirement: matching documents given the filename file2.txt and file type `private`. Looking at the data in table 4.4, this query should return no results because file2.txt's classification is `confidential`, not `private`. Let's query and check the result.

To do so, we need to use an advanced query called a *compound query* that combines various leaf queries to create a complex query. One such compound query is the `bool` `search` query. Without going into detail about how the `bool` query is constructed, let's look at it in action. We write our `bool` query with two other query clauses:

- A `must` clause checking for all documents that match the attachment's filename using a `term` query
- A second `must` clause checking whether the file classification is `private`

The query is given in the following listing.

Listing 4.28 Advanced `bool` query with `term` queries

```
GET emails/_search          ◁─┐   A bool query that searches for a
{                             │   match with a filename and file type
  "query": {
    "bool": {                     must clause defining
      "must": [          ◁──────  the mandatory clauses
        {"term": { "attachments.filename.keyword": "file2.txt"}},
        {"term": { "attachments.filetype.keyword": "private" }}
      ]
    }
  }
}
```

Defines
the query
as a bool
query

When this query is executed, it returns the following document:

```
"hits" : [[
{
  ...
  "_source" : {
    "to:" : "mrs.doe@johndoe.com",
    "subject" : "Multi attachments test",
    "attachments" : [
      {
        "filename" : "file2.txt",
        "filetype" : "confidential"
      },
      ..
    ]
  }
}]
```

Unfortunately, this result is incorrect—no document exists with the combination of the name file2.txt and the type `private` (recheck table 4.4). This is where the `object` data type breaks down—it can't honor the relationships between the inner objects.

Ideally, the values `file2.txt` and `private` are in different objects, so the search shouldn't consider them a single entity. The reason is that inner objects are not stored as individual documents—they are flattened:

```
{
  ...
  "attachments.filename" :["file1.txt","file2.txt","file3.txt"]
  "attachments.filetype":["private","confidential"]
}
```

As you can see, `filenames` are collected as an array and stored in the `attachments .filename` field, so they are also file types. Unfortunately, because they are stored this way, their relationship is lost. We can't say if file1.txt is `private` or `confidential` because the array doesn't hold the state.

This is the limitation of indexing an array of objects for a field and trying to search the objects as individual documents. The good news is that a data type called `nested` solves this problem, as we discuss in the next section.

4.6.3   *The nested data type*

Our previous example showed that a search query didn't honor individual document integrity. We can fix this problem by introducing the nested data type. The nested type is a specialized form of an object type that maintains the relationship between arrays of objects in a document.

Continuing our example of emails and attachments, let's define the attachments field as the nested data type rather than letting Elasticsearch derive it as an object type. This calls for creating a schema by declaring the attachments field as a nested data type.

Listing 4.29   Mapping the schema definition for the nested type

```
PUT emails_nested
{
  "mappings": {
    "properties": {
      "attachments": {
        "type": "nested",          ◁──┤ Declares the attachments
        "properties": {                  field as a nested type
          "filename": {            ◁──┐
            "type": "keyword"          │ The filename field is declared as a
          },                           │ keyword type to avoid tokenizing.
          "filetype": {
            "type": "text"        ◁──┐
          }                          │ We can leave this
        }                            │ field as text.
      }
    }
  }
}
```

In addition to creating the attachments field as a nested type, we declared filename as a keyword type. This field's value is tokenized: for example, file1.txt is split into file1 and txt. As a result, a search query may be matched with txt and confidential or txt and private, as both records have txt as a common token. To avoid this, we can use filename as a keyword field. You can also see this method in listing 4.28, where we use attachments.filename.keyword in our search query.

Let's return to the problem at hand: we have a schema definition, so all we need to do is index a document.

Listing 4.30   Indexing a document with the nested property

```
PUT emails_nested/_doc/1
{                              ┐ Provides a couple of
  "attachments" : [       ◁──┘ objects as attachments
    {
      "filename" : "file1.txt",
      "filetype" :  "confidential"
    },
```

```
    {
      "filename" : "file2.txt",
      "filetype" :  "private"
    }
  ]
}
```

Once this document is successfully indexed, the final piece of the jigsaw is the search. Listing 4.31 shows the search query written to fetch documents. The criteria are emails with an attachment that has file1.txt and private as the filename and classification type, respectively. This combination doesn't exist, so the results must be empty, unlike in the case of an object where the data is searched across documents, leading to false positive results.

> **Listing 4.31   Fetching results matching a filename and classification**

```
GET emails_nested/_search
{
  "query": {                        ┌─ A nested query to fetch
    "nested": {         ◄───────────┘  data from nested fields
      "path": "attachments",  ◄──┐  The path points to the
      "query": {                 └─ name of the nested field.
        "bool": {                                      ┌─ Search clauses: must
          "must": [                          ◄─────────┘  match file1.txt and private
            { "match": { "attachments.filename": "file1.txt" }},
            { "match": { "attachments.filetype":  "private" }}
          ]
        }
      }
    }
  }
}
```

This query searches for a file named file1.txt with a private classification, which doesn't exist. No documents are returned for this query, which is exactly what we expect. The classification of file1.txt is confidential, not private, so it doesn't match. When a nested type represents an array of inner objects, the individual object is stored and indexed as a hidden document.

The nested data type is good at honoring associations and relationships. If you ever need to create an array of objects, each of which must be treated as an individual object, the nested data type may become your friend.

Elasticsearch has no array types

While we are on the subject of arrays, interestingly, there is no array data type in Elasticsearch. However, we can set any field with more than one value, thus representing the field as an array. For example, a document with one name field can be changed from a single value to an array simply by adding a list of data values to the field: "name": "John Doe" to "name": ["John Smith", "John Doe"].

> **(continued)**
>
> How does Elasticsearch deduce the data type when we provide the values as an array during dynamic mapping? The data type is derived from the type of the first element in the array. For example, `"John Smith"` is a string, so name is a `text` type despite its representation as an array.
>
> An important point to consider when creating arrays is that we cannot mix different types in an array. For example, we cannot declare the name field like this: `"name"`: `["John Smith", 13, "Neverland"]`. This is illegal because the field consists of multiple types.

4.6.4   *The flattened data type*

So far, we've looked at indexing fields parsed from a JSON document. Each field is treated as individual and independent when it is analyzed and stored. However, sometimes we may not need to index all the subfields as individual fields, thus avoiding the expensive analysis process. Think of a stream of chat messages on a chat system, the running commentary during a live football match, or a doctor taking notes about a patient's ailments. We can load this kind of data as one big blob rather than declaring each field explicitly (or deriving it dynamically). Elasticsearch provides a special data type called `flattened` for this purpose.

A `flattened` field holds information in the form of one or more subfields, and each subfield's value is indexed as a keyword. None of the values are treated as `text` fields, and thus they do not undergo the text analysis process.

Consider an example of a doctor taking running notes about their patient during a consultation. The mapping consists of two fields: the patient's name and the doctor's notes. The main point in this mapping is the declaration of the `doctor_notes` field as a `flattened` type.

Listing 4.32   Creating a mapping with the `flattened` data type

```
PUT consultations
{
  "mappings": {
    "properties": {
      "patient_name":{
        "type": "text"              This field can consist of
      },                            any number of subfields.
      "doctor_notes":{      ⬅──┘
        "type": "flattened"   ⬅──┐  The field is declared
      }                          │  as flattened.
    }
  }
}
```

The idea is that any field (and its subfields) declared `flattened` will not be analyzed; all the values are indexed as `keywords`. Let's create a patient consultation document and index it.

Listing 4.33 Indexing a consultation document with doctor notes

```
PUT consultations/_doc/1
{
  "patient_name":"John Doe",        ┐  The flattened field can hold
  "doctor_notes":{          ⟵──┘  any number of subfields.
    "temperature":103,
    "symptoms":["chills","fever","headache"],      ┐  All of these fields are
    "history":"none",           │  indexed as keywords.
    "medication":["Antibiotics","Paracetamol"]   ┘
  }
}
```

As you can see, `doctor_notes` holds a lot of information—but remember, we did not create these inner fields in our mapping definition. Because `doctor_notes` is a `flattened` type, all the values are indexed as is, as keywords.

Finally, we can search the index using any keywords from the doctor notes.

Listing 4.34 Searching the `flattened` data type field

```
GET consultations/_search
{
  "query": {
    "match": {
      "doctor_notes": "Paracetamol"    ⟵┐  Searching for a
    }                │  patient's medication
  }
}
```

Searching for `"Paracetamol"` returns John Doe's consultation document. You can experiment by changing the `match` query to any of the fields—for example, `doctor_notes:chills`—or write a complex query like the one shown next.

Listing 4.35 Advanced query on a `flattened` data type

```
GET consultations/_search
{
  "query": {
    "bool": {
      "must": [
          {"match": {"doctor_notes": "headache"}},
          {"match": {"doctor_notes": "Antibiotics"}}
        ],
      "must_not": [
          {"term": {"doctor_notes": {"value": "diabetes"}}}
        ]
    }
  }
}
```

In the query, we check for headaches and antibiotics, but the patient shouldn't be diabetic—the query returns John Doe as he isn't diabetic but has headaches and is on antibiotics.

The `flattened` data types come in handy, especially when we expect many fields on an ad hoc basis and defining mapping definitions for all of them beforehand isn't feasible. Keep in mind that the subfiles of a flattened field are always `keyword` types.

4.6.5   *The join data type*

If you are from a relational database world, you know the relationships between data—the joins that enable parent-child relationships. Every document indexed by Elasticsearch is independent and maintains no relationship with any other documents in that index. Elasticsearch denormalizes the data to achieve speed and gain performance during indexing and search operations. While we are advised to be cautious about maintaining and managing relationships in Elasticsearch, the `join` data type is available to create parent-child relationships if we need them.

Let's learn about `join` data by considering an example of doctor-patients relationships (one-to-many): one doctor can have multiple patients, and each patient is assigned to one doctor. To work with parent-child relationships using the `join` data type, we need to create a field that is the `join` type and add information via a `relations` object that mentions the relationship (in this case, the doctor-patient relationship). The following listing prepares the `doctors` index with a schema definition.

Listing 4.36   Mapping of the `doctors` schema definition

```
PUT doctors
{
  "mappings": {
    "properties": {
      "relationship":{              ◁─┐ Declares a property
        "type": "join",               │ as the join type
        "relations":{
          "doctor":"patient"        ◁─┐ Names of the
        }                             │ relations
      }
    }
  }
}
```

The query has two important points to note:

- We declare a `relationship` property of type `join`.
- We declare a `relations` attribute and give the names of the relations (in this case, only one `doctor:patient` relation).

Once the schema is ready and indexed, let's index two types of documents: one representing the doctor (parent) and the other representing two patients (children). Here's the doctor's document, with the relationship named `doctor`.

Listing 4.37 Indexing a doctor document

```
PUT doctors/_doc/1
{
  "name":"Dr. Mary Montgomery",
  "relationship":{
    "name":"doctor"          ◁────┐  The relationship attribute
  }                               │  must be one of the relations.
}
```

The `relationship` object declares that the type of the document is `doctor`. The `name` attribute must be the parent value (`doctor`) as declared in the mapping schema. Now that Dr. Mary Montgomery is ready, the next step is to associate two patients with her.

Listing 4.38 Creating two patients for our doctor

```
PUT doctors/_doc/2?routing=mary     ◁────┐  Documents must have
{                                        │  the routing flag set.
  "name":"John Doe",
  "relationship":{         ◁────┐  We define the type of
   "name":"patient",            │  relationship in this object.
   "parent":1         ◁────┐  The patient's parent (doctor)
  }                        │  is the document with ID 1.
}
```
The document is a patient. →

```
PUT doctors/_doc/3?routing=mary
{
  "name":"Mrs. Doe",
  "relationship":{
    "name":"patient",
    "parent":1
  }
}
```

The `relationship` object should have the value `patient` (remember the parent-child portion of the `relations` attribute in the schema?), and `parent` should be assigned a document identifier of the associated doctor (ID 1 in our example).

We need to understand one more thing when working with parent-child relationships. Parents and associated children are indexed into the *same shard* to avoid multi-shard search overheads. And as the documents coexist, we need to use a mandatory routing parameter in the URL. (Routing is a function that determines the shard where the document resides; we look at the routing algorithm in chapter 5.)

Finally, it's time to search for patients belonging to a doctor with ID 1. The following query searches for all the patients associated with Dr. Montgomery.

Listing 4.39 Fetching patients of Dr. Montgomery

```
GET doctors/_search
{
  "query": {
    "parent_id":{
```

```
      "type":"patient",
      "id":1
    }
  }
 }
}
```

To fetch the patients belonging to a doctor, we use a `search` query called `parent_id` that expects the child type (`patient`) and the parent's ID (Dr. Montgomery's document ID is 1). This query returns Dr. Montgomery's patients: Mr. and Mrs. Doe.

> **NOTE** Implementing parent-child relationships in Elasticsearch has performance implications. As we discussed in chapter 1, Elasticsearch may not be the right tool if you are considering document relationships, so use this feature judiciously.

4.6.6   *The search_as_you_type data type*

Most search engines suggest words and phrases as we type in a search bar. This feature has various names: search as you type, typeahead, autocomplete, or suggestions. Elasticsearch provides a convenient data type called `search_as_you_type` to support this feature. Behind the scenes, Elasticsearch works very hard to ensure that fields tagged as `search_as_you_type` are indexed to produce n-grams, which we see in action in this section.

Suppose we are asked to support typeahead queries on a `books` index: when the user starts typing a book's title letter by letter in a search bar, we should be able to suggest books based on the letters they type. First we need to create a schema with the field of type `search_as_you_type`.

Listing 4.40   Mapping schema with the `search_as_you_type` type

```
PUT tech_books4
{
  "mappings": {
    "properties": {
      "title": {
        "type": "search_as_you_type"      ⟵┐  The title supports the
      }                                      │  typeahead feature.
    }
  }
}
```

The notable point is that the title in the schema definition is declared as the `search_as_you_type` data type. Let's index a few documents with various titles (this book plus my—hopefully—future titles).

Listing 4.41   Indexing a few books

```
PUT tech_books4/_doc/1
{
  "title":"Elasticsearch in Action"
}
```

```
PUT tech_books4/_doc/2
{
  "title":"Elasticsearch for Java Developers"
}

PUT tech_books4/_doc/3
{
  "title":"Elastic Stack in Action"
}
```

Because the `title` field's data type is `search_as_you_type`, Elasticsearch creates a set of subfields called *n-grams* that partially match the user's search. The `_index_prefix` generates edge-n grams such as `[e, el, ela, elas, elast, elasti, elastic]` for the word *Elastic*. A 2-gram token is a shingle token filter producing two tokens, `["elasticsearch", "in"]` and `["in", "action"]"`, for the title *Elasticsearch in Action*. Similarly, a 3-gram is a shingled token filter generating tokens like `["elasticsearch for java", "for java developers"]` for the title *Elasticsearch for Java Developers.* (The source code is available with the book's files, if you want to try these examples.)

In addition to these n-grams, the root field (`title`) is indexed as is with the given or default analyzer. All other n-grams are produced by employing various shingle-token filters, as shown in table 4.5.

Table 4.5 Subfields created automatically by the engine

Fields	Explanation	Examples
title	The `title` field is indexed with either a chosen analyzer or the default analyzer if one is not chosen.	If a standard analyzer is used, the title is tokenized and normalized based on the standard analyzer's rules.
title._2gram	The `title` field's analyzer is customized with a shingle-token filter. The shingle size is set to 2 on this filter.	Generates two tokens for the given text. For example, the 2-grams for the title "*Elasticsearch in Action*" are `["elasticsearch", "in"]`, `["in", "action"]`.
title._3gram	The `title` field's analyzer is customized with a shingle-token filter. The shingle size is set to 3 on this filter.	Generates three tokens for the given text. For example, the 3-grams for the title "*Elasticsearch for Java developers*" are `["elasticsearch","for","java"]`, `["for","java","developers"]`
title._index prefix	The analyzer of `title._3gram` is applied along with an edge n-gram token filter	Generates edge n-grams for the field `title._3grams`. For example, the `_index_prefix` generates the following edge n-grams for the world "Elastic": `[e, el, ela, elas, elast, elasti, elastic]`

Because these fields are created for us, searching on the field should return type-ahead suggestions, because the n-grams help produce them effectively. Let's create the search query as shown in the next listing.

Listing 4.42 Searching in `search_as_you_type` and its subfields

```
GET tech_books4/_search
{
  "query": {
    "multi_match": {
      "query": "in",
      "type": "bool_prefix",
      "fields": ["title","title._2gram","title._3gram"]
    }
  }
}
```

As the query shows, we are creating a `multi_match` query (with a `bool_prefix` as the type) because the search is carried out across the main field and its subfields (`title` and subfields of `title`: `_2gram`, `_3gram`, etc.). This query should return the books *Elasticsearch in Action* and *Elastic Stack in Action*. We use a `multi-match` query because we are searching for a value across multiple fields: `title`, `title._2gram`, and `title._3gram`.

N-grams, edge n-grams, and shingles

If you are hearing about n-grams, edge n-grams, and shingles for the first time, these concepts may baffle you. I briefly explain them here, and we cover them in detail in chapter 7.

An *n-gram* is a sequence of words of a given size. We can have 2-grams, 3-grams, and so on. For example, if the word is *action*, the 3-grams (n-grams for size 3) are `["act", "cti", "tio", "ion"]`, the bi-grams (size 2) are `["ac", "ct", "ti", "io", "on"]`, and so on.

Edge n-grams are n-grams of every token, where the start of the n-gram is anchored to the beginning of the word. For *action*, the edge n-grams are `["a", "ac", "act", "acti", "actio", "action"]`.

Shingles are word n-grams. For example, the sentence "Elasticsearch in Action" outputs the shingles `["Elasticsearch", "Elasticsearch in", "Elasticsearch in Action", "in", "in Action", "Action"]`.

Sometimes we may want a field that we can declare as more than a single data type. For example, a movie title can be both `text` and `completion` data types. Fortunately, Elasticsearch allows us to declare a single field with multiple data types. Let's find out how we can create multi-typed fields.

4.7 *Fields with multiple data types*

We've seen that each field in a document is associated with a data type. However, Elasticsearch is flexible and also lets us define fields with multiple data types. For example, the `subject` field in our email data can be a `text`, `keyword`, or `completion` type, depending on our requirements. We can create multiple types in schema definitions using the `fields` object inside the main field definition. It has the following syntax:

```
"my_field1":{                    ┐  Declares the type
  "type": "text",          ◁──┘  of my_field1      ┐  Defines a fields object to
  "fields": {                                    ◁──┘  enclose more types
    "kw":{ "type":"keyword" }    ◁──┐  Declares an additional
  }                                 │  field with the label kw
}
```

Basically, `my_field1` is indexed as a `text` type as well as a `keyword` type. When we expect to use it as `text`, we can provide the field as `my_field1` in queries. We use the label `my_fields1.kw` (note the dot notation) as the field name when searching it as a `keyword`.

The following example schema definition creates our single field `subject` with multiple data types (`text`, `keyword`, and `completion`).

Listing 4.43 Schema definition with a multi-typed field

```
PUT emails_multi_type
{
  "mappings": {
    "properties": {
      "subject":{
        "type": "text",        ◁──┐  The text
        "fields": {                │  type
          "kw":{ "type":"keyword" },  ◁──┐  The subject is
          "comp":{ "type":"completion" }  │  also a keyword.
        }                          ◁──┐  The subject is a
      }                               │  completion type, too.
    }
  }
}
```

The `subject` field has three types associated with it: `text`, `keyword`, and `completion`. To access these, we have to use the format `subject.kw` for the `keyword`-type field or `subject.comp` for the completion type.

We have learned a lot about mapping concepts in this chapter. Let's wrap up and look forward to the next chapter, which discusses working with documents.

Summary

- Every document consists of fields with values, and each field has a data type. Elasticsearch provides a rich set of data types to represent these values.
- Elasticsearch consults a set of rules when indexing and searching data. These rules, called mapping rules, let Elasticsearch know how to deal with the varied data shapes.
- Mapping rules are formed by either dynamic or explicit mapping processes.

- Mapping is a mechanism for creating field schema definitions up front. Elasticsearch consults the schema definitions while indexing documents so the data is analyzed and stored for faster retrieval.
- Elasticsearch also has a default mapping feature: we can let Elasticsearch derive the mapping rather than providing it explicitly ourselves. Elasticsearch determines the schema based on the first time it sees a field.
- Although dynamic mapping is handy, especially in development, if we know more about the data model, it is best to create the mapping beforehand.
- Elasticsearch provides a wide range of data types for text, Booleans, numerical values, dates, and so on, stretching to complex fields like joins, completion, geopoints, nested, and others.

Working with documents

It is time to work with and understand operations on documents in Elasticsearch. Documents are indexed, fetched, updated, or deleted based on our requirements. We can load data into Elasticsearch from stores such as databases and files or from real-time streams. Similarly, we can update or modify data that exists in Elasticsearch. If needed, we can even delete and purge documents. For example, we may have a product catalog database that needs to be imported into Elasticsearch to enable search capabilities on products.

Elasticsearch exposes a set of APIs for working with our documents:

- *Document indexing APIs*—To index documents into Elasticsearch
- *Read and search APIs*—To allow clients to fetch/search documents

- *Update APIs*—To edit and modify the fields of a document
- *Delete APIs*—To remove documents from the store

Elasticsearch classifies these APIs into two categories: single-document APIs and multi-document APIs. As the name suggests, *single-document APIs* perform operations like indexing, fetching, modifying, and deleting documents one by one, using the appropriate endpoints. These APIs are useful when working with events such as orders generated by an e-commerce application or tweets from a set of Twitter handles. We use single-document APIs to operate on these documents individually.

Multi-document APIs, on the other hand, are geared toward working with documents in batches. For example, we may have a requirement to import a product catalog into Elasticsearch from a database consisting of millions of records. Elasticsearch exposes a bulk (`_bulk`) endpoint API for this purpose to help import data in batches.

Elasticsearch also exposes advanced query-based APIs to work with our documents. We can delete and update a number of documents that match certain criteria by developing a complex query if needed. We can also use sophisticated search queries to find and update or delete documents. Finally, we can move data from one index to another using reindexing APIs. Reindexing helps us migrate our data without any downtime in production, although we must consider the performance implications.

In this chapter, we discuss single- and multi-document APIs and various operations on documents. The first step in working with Elasticsearch is to get some data into the engine. Let's begin by looking at the indexing document APIs and the mechanics of indexing documents.

> **NOTE** The code for this chapter is available on GitHub (http://mng.bz/ MBr8) and on the book's website (https://www.manning.com/books/elastic search-in-action-second-edition). You can find the movie data set used in the examples at http://mng.bz/a1pX.

5.1   *Indexing documents*

Just as we insert records into a relational database, we add data (in the form of documents) to Elasticsearch. These documents sit in a logical bucket called an *index*. The act of persisting documents to these indexes is known as *indexing*. So, when we hear the term *indexing*, it means storing or persisting documents into Elasticsearch.

> **Text analysis**
>
> The documents undergo a process called *text analysis* in Elasticsearch before being stored. The analysis process prepares data to make it suitable for various search and analytical features. This analysis gives the search engine the ability to deliver relevancy and full-text search capabilities. Text analysis is discussed in depth in chapter 7.

As we mentioned in the opening paragraphs of this chapter, Elasticsearch provides APIs to index both single and multiple documents into Elasticsearch. We go over these document APIs in detail in the next section.

5.1.1 Document APIs

We communicate with Elasticsearch using RESTful APIs over HTTP. We can perform basic CRUD (create, read, update, and delete) operations using single-document APIs. There are also APIs designed to work with multiple documents instead of targeting a single document. We discuss both types in this chapter, but for now, let's focus on how to index documents using single-document APIs. To begin, there's an important concept to understand: document identifiers.

DOCUMENT IDENTIFIERS

Each document we index can have an identifier (ID), usually specified by the user. For example, the document for the movie *The Godfather* can be given an ID (say, id = 1), and the movie *The Shawshank Redemption* can be given another ID (id = 2). Similar to a primary key in a relational database, the ID is associated with that document for its lifetime (unless it is deliberately changed).

Sometimes the client (user) doesn't need to give a document an ID. Imagine an automatic car sending thousands of alerts and heartbeats to a server. Not every message needs a sequence of IDs; it can have a random ID, albeit a unique one. In this case, the system generates a random universally unique identifier (UUID) for the document that's being indexed.

Document APIs allow us to index documents with or without an ID. But there is a subtle difference when using HTTP verbs such as POST and PUT:

- If a document has an ID provided by the client, we use the HTTP PUT method to invoke a document API for indexing the document.
- If the document does not have an ID provided by the client, we use the HTTP POST method when indexing. In this case, once the document is indexed, it inherits the system-generated ID.

Let's check out the process of indexing documents using both methods.

INDEXING A DOCUMENT WITH AN IDENTIFIER (PUT)

When a document has an ID, we can use the single-document index (_doc) API with HTTP's PUT action to index the document. The syntax for this method is as follows:

```
PUT <index_name>/_doc/<identifier>
```

Here, <index_name> is the name of the index where the document will be housed, and _doc is the endpoint that must be present when indexing a document. The <identifier> is the document's identity (like a primary key in a database), which is a mandatory path parameter when using the HTTP PUT method.

Let's index a movie document using the API. Head to Kibana, and write and execute the following query.

> **Listing 5.1 Indexing a new document into the `movies` index**

```
PUT movies/_doc/1
{                          ◁─── |  Body of the request  |  Document
  "title":"The Godfather",                                indexing URL
  "synopsis":"The aging patriarch of an organized crime dynasty transfers
  ➥ control of his clandestine empire to his reluctant son"
}
```

The URL `PUT movies/_doc/1` is the RESTful method that invokes the document index API. This request has a body represented by the enclosing JSON document (with the movie data). The results are shown in figure 5.1. Let's quickly go over the parts of the URL, as listed in table 5.1.

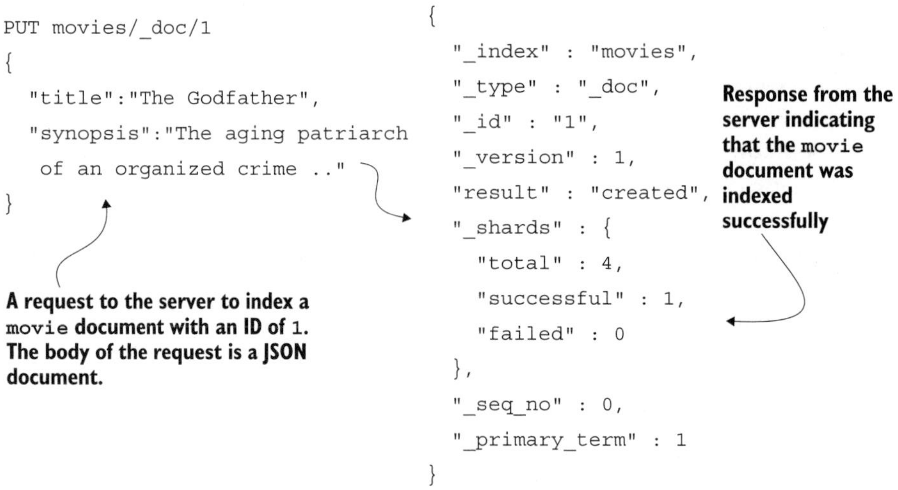

```
PUT movies/_doc/1                      {
{                                        "_index" : "movies",
                                         "_type" : "_doc",        Response from the
  "title":"The Godfather",               "_id" : "1",             server indicating
  "synopsis":"The aging patriarch        "_version" : 1,          that the movie
   of an organized crime .."                                      document was
                                         "result" : "created",    indexed
}                                        "_shards" : {            successfully
                                           "total" : 4,
                                           "successful" : 1,
   A request to the server to index a     "failed" : 0
   movie document with an ID of 1.      },
   The body of the request is a JSON     "_seq_no" : 0,
   document.                             "_primary_term" : 1
                                       }
```

Figure 5.1 Indexing a document with an ID

Table 5.1 `PUT` URL constituents

PUT	The HTTP verb indicates that we are asking the server to create a new resource. The usual convention for a `PUT` action is to send some data to the resource URL so the server will create the new resource in its store.
movies	The name of the index where we want our `movie` document to persist.
_doc	The endpoint of the service call. In earlier Elasticsearch versions (before 5.x), the URL had a type associated with it (something like `movies/movie/1`). The document type was deprecated, and a generic endpoint `_doc` was amended to the URL (making it `movies/_doc/1`).
1	The path parameter to indicate the resource's ID (the `movie` document's ID).

Request in cURL format

Kibana shortens the URL so it looks pretty. Behind the scenes, it expands the URL by adding the server details to the request. This is possible because every Kibana instance is implicitly connected to the Elasticsearch server (the kibana.yml configuration file defines the server's details). The URL in cURL format is

```
curl -XPUT "http://localhost:9200/movies/_doc/1"
-H 'Content-Type: application/json'
-d'{  "title":"The Godfather",  "synopsis":"The aging patriarch .."}')
```

You can fetch the cURL command from Kibana's Dev Tools—just click the wrench icon, and copy your request as a URL by choosing Copy as cURL as shown in the figure.

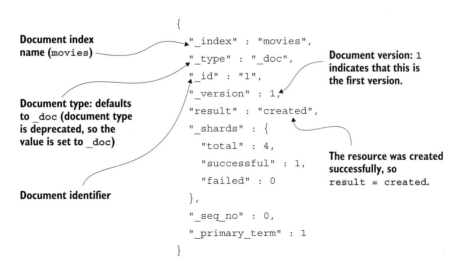

Exporting the query as cURL

TIP While you are here, click the Auto Indent link to indent your code the JSON way.

After executing the preceding script, we expect the response to appear in the pane on the right-hand side of Kibana (see figure 5.2). Let's dissect it briefly. The response is a JSON document with few attributes. The `result` attribute indicates the operation's

Figure 5.2 Response from the server when a document is indexed successfully

action: created indicates that we successfully indexed a new document in Elastic-search's store. The _index, _type, and _id attributes are derived from our incoming request and assigned to the document. _version indicates the current version of this document; the value 1 means the first version of the document. The number is incremented if we modify the document and reindex it. We visit the _shards information down the line, but all it's saying here is that the document's journey to the store was completed.

If you are curious, re-execute the same command and check the response. You'll notice that the result attribute changes to updated and the version number increments. Every time you execute the query, the version is updated.

When we first tried to insert the document, no movies index had been pre-created for us (if the index already exists, be sure you delete it by running the DELETE movies command). When the document was first seen by the server, the server realized the index didn't exist yet, and it created a movies index for us so our document indexing went smoothly. The schema of this index was also nonexistent, but the server derived the schema by analyzing the first incoming document. We learned about mapping definitions in chapter 4; refer to section 4.1.1 if needed.

We just indexed a document that has an ID. Not every document can or will have an identity with a business need. For example, while it's a good idea for a movie document to have an ID, traffic alerts from traffic lights received by a traffic management system don't need to be associated with an ID. Similarly, tweet streams, cricket match commentary messages, and so on don't need an identity—a random ID will suffice.

Indexing a document without an ID follows the same process as indexing one with an ID, except the HTTP verb changes from PUT to POST. Let's see this in action.

INDEXING A DOCUMENT WITHOUT AN IDENTIFIER (POST)

In the previous section, we indexed a document that had an ID associated with it. We used the HTTP PUT method to create the resource in Elasticsearch. But not every business model promotes data documents with IDs (for example, stock price ticks or tweets). In such cases, we can let Elasticsearch generate random IDs. To index these documents, instead of using the PUT method as we did earlier, we use the POST action.

The HTTP POST method follows a format similar to PUT, but the ID is not provided as part of the URL parameter.

> **Listing 5.2 Indexing a document with no ID using POST**

```
POST myindex/_doc                    ⟵┐  The URL has no ID
{                                     │  attached to it.
  "title":"Elasticsearch in Action"  ⟵┐  The request body is
}                                     │  a JSON document.
```

We invoke the _doc endpoint on the index *without an ID* but with a body. This POST request tells Elasticsearch that it needs to assign the documents newly generated random IDs during the indexing process.

NOTE The POST method doesn't expect the user to provide the document ID. Instead, it automatically generates a randomly created ID for the document when it is persisted. We can also use POST with an ID. For example, POST myindex/_doc/1 is a valid invocation. However, PUT without an ID is invalid; that is, invoking PUT myindex/_doc will throw an error.

As an example, let's consider users posting movie reviews. Each movie review is captured as a JSON document, which is sent to Elasticsearch from Kibana. We are not going to provide the document ID for this request.

Listing 5.3 Indexing a movie review without an ID

```
POST movies_reviews/_doc          ◁─┐  The URL
{                                    │  has no ID.
  "movie":"The Godfather",
  "user":"Peter Piper",
  "rating":4.5,
  "remarks":"The movie started with a ..."
}
```

Once the server executes the index request, the response is sent back to the Kibana console. Figure 5.3 illustrates this process.

```
{
    "_index" : "movies_reviews",        The ID is a UUID
    "_type" : "_doc",                   auto-generated
    "_id" : " 53NyfXoBW8A1B2amKR5j",    by the server and
    "_version" : 1,                     assigned to the
    "result" : "created",               movie review.
    "_shards" : {
      "total" : 4,
Response from   "successful" : 1,       The result
the server      "failed" : 0           indicates that
    },                                  the document
    "_seq_no" : 0,                      was indexed
    "_primary_term" : 1                 successfully.
}
```

Figure 5.3 The server creates and assigns a randomly auto-generated ID to the document.

In the response, the _id field is randomly generated data, while the rest of the information is the same as the earlier PUT request shown in listing 5.1. You may wonder how we decide which verb to consider when indexing the document—the PUT or POST method. The following sidebar provides an answer!

When to use PUT and/or POST

If we want to control the IDs or we already know the IDs of our documents, we use the PUT method to index the documents. They can be our domain objects with a pre-defined identity strategy (like primary keys) that we can adhere to. Retrieving documents using an ID may be a reason to consider which way to learn. If we know the document ID, we can use the document APIs to get the document (we discuss retrieval shortly). For example, here we provide an ID for a movie document:

```
POST movies/_doc/1
{
   "movie":"The Godfather",
}
```

On the other hand, using IDs for documents originating from streaming data or time-series events doesn't make sense (imagine price quotes originating from a pricing server, share price fluctuations, system alerts from a cloud service, tweets, or heart-beats from an automated car). Having a randomly generated UUID is good enough for these events and messages. But because the IDs are randomly generated, we may need to write a search query to retrieve documents rather than simply retrieving them using IDs as we do for PUTS.

In summary, use the HTTP POST action to index documents that don't have a business identity. For example, we don't provide an ID for a movie review document:

```
POST movies_reviews/_doc
{
   "review":"The Godfather movie is a masterpiece..",
}
```

When indexing a document, the document index API doesn't care if the document exists or not. If we index it for the first time, the document is created and stored as expected. If we index the same document again, it is saved even if the content is completely different than the earlier document. Does Elasticsearch block the operation of overwriting the document's content? Let's find out.

USING _CREATE TO AVOID OVERRIDING A DOCUMENT

Let's change course slightly and see what happens if we execute the following query.

> **Listing 5.4   Indexing the incorrect document content**

```
PUT movies/_doc/1
{
   "tweet":"Elasticsearch in Action 2e is here!"    ◁── Not a movie but a tweet
}
```

In the example, we are indexing a document with a tweet into a movies index with a document ID of 1. Hold on a second: don't we already have a movie document (*The God-father*) with that ID in our store? Yes, we do. Elasticsearch has no control over such over-writing operations. The responsibility is passed down to the application or the user.

Rather than depending on the user's discretion, which can lead to incorrect data due to accidental overwrites, Elasticsearch provides another endpoint: _create. This endpoint solves the overwrite situation. We can use the _create endpoint instead of _doc when indexing a document to avoid overriding the existing document. Let's look at this in action.

THE _CREATE API

Let's index the movie document with ID 100, but this time let's use the _create endpoint. The next listing shows the operation's invocation.

Listing 5.5 Indexing a new movie using the `_create` endpoint

```
PUT movies/_create/100
{
  "title":"Mission: Impossible",
  "director":"Brian De Palma"
}
```

We've indexed a new movie (*Mission: Impossible*), this time using the _create endpoint instead of _doc. The fundamental difference between these two methods is that the _create method does not let us reindex the document with the same ID, while _doc wouldn't mind.

Next, let's try to change the content of the document by sending a tweet message as the movie document. The query is shown in next.

Listing 5.6 Adding and updating a field

```
PUT movies/_create/100
{
  "tweet":"A movie with popcorn is so cool!"    ⟵⎯  Indexing a tweet in place
}                                                      of an existing movie
```

We are (maybe accidentally) overriding the contents of the movie document. However, Elasticsearch throws a version conflict error:

```
{
"type" : "version_conflict_engine_exception",
"reason":"[100]:version conflict,document already exists(current version[1])"
}
```

Elasticsearch doesn't let the data be overwritten. This is the _create API's way of indicating that the document cannot be updated because the version already exists.

> **NOTE** Although the _create endpoint does not allow us to update the document, we can swap the _create endpoint with _doc to perform the update if needed.

The takeaway for this section is that if we need to protect our documents by not allowing them to be overwritten accidentally, we should use the _create API.

Disabling index auto-creation

By default, Elasticsearch auto-creates a required index if the index doesn't already exist. If we want to restrict this feature, we need to set a flag called `action` `.auto_create_index` to `false`. This can be done two ways:

- Set the flag to `false` in the elasticsearch.yml config file.
- Explicitly set the flag by invoking the `_cluster/settings` endpoint:

```
PUT _cluster/settings
{
  "persistent": {
    "action.auto_create_index": "false"
  }
}
```

For example, the call `PUT my_new_index/_doc/1` fails if `action.auto_create_index` is set to `false`. You may want to do this if you have already created the index manually (most likely with predefined settings and mapping schema) and don't need to allow the creation of indexes on demand. We talk more about indexing operations in the next section.

Now that we understand how documents are persisted, let's examine the mechanics of how Elasticsearch stores them. The next section focuses on how the indexing process works.

5.1.2   *Mechanics of indexing*

We briefly looked at how indexing works in section 3.2.3. In this section, we go over the mechanics involved when a document is indexed (see figure 5.4). As we already

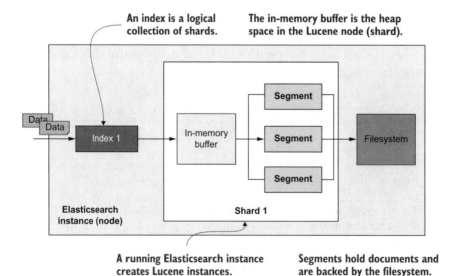

Figure 5.4   Mechanics of indexing documents

know, shards are Lucene instances that hold the physical data that's logically associated with an index.

When we index a document, the engine decides which shard the document will be housed in based on the routing algorithm (discussed in section 3.5). Each shard comes with heap memory, and when a document is indexed, the document is first pushed into the shard's in-memory buffer. The document is held in this in-memory buffer until a refresh occurs. Lucene's scheduler issues a refresh every second to collect all the documents available in the in-memory buffer, and then it creates a new segment with these documents. The segment consists of the document data and inverted indexes. Data is first written to the filesystem cache and then committed to the physical disk.

Because I/O operations are expensive, Lucene avoids frequent I/O operations when writing data to the disk. Hence, it waits for the refresh interval (one second), after which the documents are bundled to be pushed into segments. Once the documents are moved to segments, they are made available for searching.

Apache Lucene is an intelligent library when dealing with data writes and reads. After pushing the documents to a new segment (during the refresh operation), it waits until three segments are formed. It uses a three-segment-merge pattern to merge the segments to create new segments: whenever three segments are ready, Lucene instantiates a new one by merging them. Then it waits for three more segments to be created so it can create a new one, and so on. Every three segments merge to create another segment, as shown in figure 5.5.

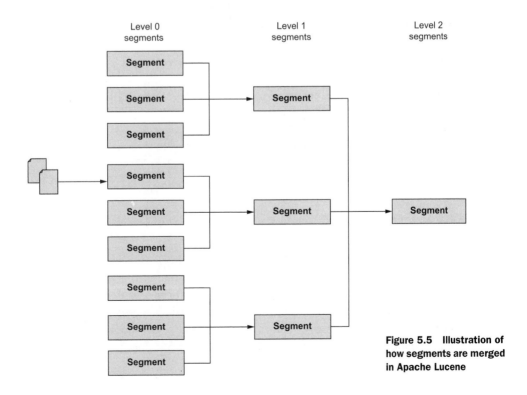

Figure 5.5 Illustration of how segments are merged in Apache Lucene

During the one-second refresh interval, a new segment is created to hold however many documents are collected in the in-memory buffer. The heap memory of the shard (Lucene instance) dictates the number of documents it can hold in an in-memory buffer before flushing them out to the file store. For all practical purposes, Lucene treats the segments as immutable resources. That is, once a segment is created with available documents from the buffer, no new documents will make their way into this existing segment. Instead, they're moved into a new segment. Similarly, deletes are not performed physically on documents in segments, but documents are marked for removal later. Lucene employs this strategy to provide high performance and throughput.

5.1.3 *Customizing the refresh process*

Indexed documents live in memory until the refresh cycle kicks in. This means we have uncommitted (non-durable) documents until the next refresh cycle. A server failure can trigger a data loss. The risk of data loss increases as the refresh period increases (a one-second refresh cycle time has a lower risk of losing data than a one-minute refresh cycle time). On the other hand, reducing the refresh time leads to more I/O operations, which can cause performance bottlenecks—so we must find the optimal refresh strategy for our organization.

Elasticsearch is an *eventually consistent* application—meaning documents are eventually written to the durable store. Documents are moved into the filesystem as segments during the refresh process and thus are available to search. The refresh process is expensive, especially if the engine is hammered with a large number of indexing requests.

CONFIGURING THE REFRESH CYCLE

The good news is that we can configure this refresh setup. We can reset the time interval from the default 1 second to, say, 60 seconds by tweaking the settings on an index level using the `_settings` endpoint.

> **Listing 5.7 Setting a custom refresh interval**

```
PUT movies/_settings
{
  "index":{
    "refresh_interval":"60s"
  }
}
```

This is a dynamic setting, which means we can change the refresh setting on a live index at any time. To switch off the refresh operation completely, set the value to `-1`. The in-memory buffer will accumulate incoming documents if the refresh operation is off. The use case for this scenario may be that we are migrating many documents from a database into Elasticsearch, and we don't want data to be searchable until the migration completes successfully. To manually re-enable refresh on the index, we simply issue a POST <index>/_refresh command.

CLIENT-SIDE REFRESH CONTROLS

We can also control the refresh operation from the client side for CRUD operations on documents by setting the refresh query parameter. The document APIs (index, delete, update, and _bulk) expect refresh as a query parameter. For example, the following snippet advises the engine to start the refresh once the document has been indexed as opposed to waiting for the refresh interval to expire:

```
PUT movies/_doc/1?refresh
```

The refresh query parameter can have three values:

- refresh=false *(default)*—Tells the engine not to force the refresh operation but instead to apply the default setting (one second). The engine makes the document available for search only after the predefined refresh interval. We can also not provide the query parameter, which achieves the same effect.

    Example: PUT movies/_doc/1?refresh=false

- refresh=true *(or empty string)*—Forces the refresh operation so the document is visible for searching immediately. If our refresh time interval is set to 60 seconds and we index 1,000 documents with refresh=true, all 1,000 documents should be available to search instantly rather than waiting for the 60-second refresh interval.

    Example: PUT movies/_doc/1?refresh=true

- refresh=wait_for—A blocking request that compels the client to wait until the refresh operation kicks in and completes before the request is returned. For example, if our refresh interval is 60 seconds, the request is blocked for 60 seconds until the refresh is performed. However, it can be manually started by invoking the POST <index>/_refresh endpoint.

    Example: PUT movies/_doc/1?refresh=wait_for

We also need to understand the mechanics of retrieving documents. Elasticsearch provides a GET API for reading documents, which is similar to the indexing APIs we saw previously. The next section looks at the mechanics of reading documents from the Elasticsearch stash.

5.2 *Retrieving documents*

Elasticsearch provides two types of document APIs for retrieving documents:

- A single-document API that returns one document, given an ID
- A multi-document API that returns multiple documents, given an array of IDs

If a document is not available, we receive a JSON response indicating that the document is not found. Let's see how to retrieve documents using both APIs.

5.2.1   *Using the single-document API*

Elasticsearch exposes a RESTful API to fetch a document given the document ID, similar to the indexing API we discussed in the previous section. The API definition for getting a single document is

```
GET <index_name>/_doc/<id>
```

GET is the HTTP method that indicates we are fetching a resource. The URL indicates the resource's endpoint—in this case, the index_name followed by _doc and the document ID.

As you may have noticed, the difference between indexing the document and fetching is just the HTTP verb: modifying PUT/POST to GET. There are no changes to the URL, following RESTful services best practices.

Let's retrieve the movie document with an ID of 1 that we indexed earlier. Executing a GET movies/_doc/1 command on the Kibana console fetches the previously indexed document. The JSON response is shown in figure 5.6.

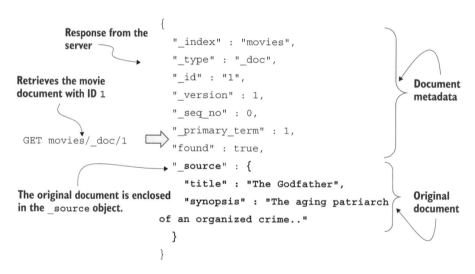

Figure 5.6   Retrieving a document using the GET API call

The response has two parts: the metadata and the original document. The metadata consists of _id, _type, _version, and so on. The original document is enclosed under the _source attribute. That's it! It is as simple as that to fetch a document if we know its ID.

The document may not exist in the store. If the document is not found, we get a response with the attribute found set to false. For example, trying to find a document with ID 999 (which doesn't exist in our system) returns the following response:

```
{
  "_index" : "movies",
  "_type" : "_doc",
  "_id" : "999",
  "found" : false
}
```

We can of course find out if the document exists in the store beforehand by using the read API but with the HTTP HEAD action on the resource URL. For example, the following query checks if the movie with ID 1 exists.

Listing 5.8 Checking if a document exists

```
HEAD movies/_doc/1
```

This query returns 200–OK if the document exists. If the document is unavailable in the store, a 404 Not Found error is returned to the client, as figure 5.7 shows.

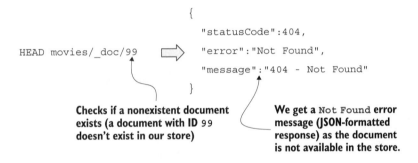

Figure 5.7 Fetching a nonexistent document returns a "Not Found" message.

We can send a HEAD request to the server to determine if the document exists before requesting it. If you think this incurs an additional round trip to the server, indeed it does. Based on the HEAD request's response, we may (or may not) have to send another request to fetch the actual object. Instead, we can use a GET request to start with, which returns the document if it exists or a Not Found message if not. Of course, the choice is yours.

So far, we've fetched only a single document for a single index. How can we satisfy the requirement of fetching multiple documents with IDs from either the same index or multiple indexes? For example, how can we fetch two documents with IDs 1 and 2 from the movies index? We can use a multi-document API called _mget, which is the topic of the next section.

5.2.2 Retrieving multiple documents

In the previous section, we used a single-document API to fetch one document at a time. However, we may have requirements like these:

- Retrieve a list of documents from an index, given the document IDs.
- Retrieve a list of documents from multiple indexes, given the document IDs.

Elasticsearch exposes a multi-document API (_mget) to satisfy these requirements. For example, to fetch a list of documents given IDs, we can use _mget API as shown in the following listing.

Listing 5.9 Fetching multiple documents at once

```
GET movies/_mget
{
  "ids" : ["1", "12", "19", "34"]
}
```

Figure 5.8 shows the format of the call to fetch multiple documents from various indexes. As you can see, the _mget endpoint is provided with a JSON-formatted request object. The docs key inside the request expects an array of document _index and _id pairs that we can use to fetch documents from multiple indexes. The code in the next listing fetches documents from three different indexes.

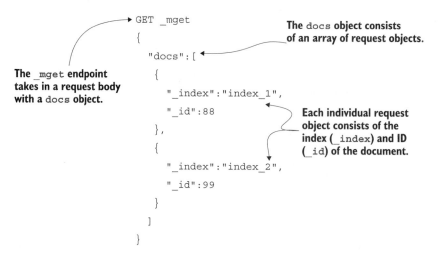

Figure 5.8   Fetching multiple documents using the _mget API

Listing 5.10 Fetching documents from three different indexes

```
GET _mget                   ◁──┐ _mget call with no index
{                              │ mentioned in the URL
  "docs":[
    {
      "_index":"classic_movies",   ◁──┐ The first index
      "_id":11                        │ is provided here.
    },
```

```
  {
    "_index":"international_movies",   ⊲——| Index 2
    "_id":22
  },
  {
    "_index":"top100_movies",   ⊲——| Index 3
    "_id":33
  }
 ]
}
```

The request is formed with the requirement of fetching three documents from three different indexes: `classic_movies`, `international_movies`, and `top100_movies`. Note that if the index doesn't exist, we will get an `index_not_found_exception`.

We can provide as many indexes as required, although this API has a downside: we have to create an individual `_index/_id` pair for each ID. Unfortunately, Elasticsearch does not yet allow the `_id` attribute to accept an array of IDs. We can hope that the Elastic folks implement this feature in the near future.

5.2.3   *The ids query*

We looked at using the `_mget` API to fetch multiple documents in the previous section. However, there is another route to fetch multiple documents: using an `ids` (short for IDs) query. This simple `search` query takes a set of document IDs to return the documents. The `ids` query is available as part of the search APIs. We discuss this API in detail in chapters 8 to 10, but here's the query in action if you are curious.

Listing 5.11   Using an `ids` query to fetch multiple documents

```
GET classic_movies/_search
{
  "query": {
    "ids": {
      "values": [1,2,3,4]
    }
  }
}
```

We can also fetch from multiple indexes by adding the indexes to the URL. Here's an example:

```
GET classic_movies,international_movies/_search
{
  # body
}
```

That wraps up how to retrieve multiple documents from a single or multiple indexes. Now, let's move our focus to the responses. Did you notice that our responses (see figure 5.6) get metadata along with the original source document? What if we want to fetch only the source without metadata? Or what if we want to hide some of the sensitive information in the source document when returning it to the client? We can manipulate the responses based on our requirements, as we discuss in the next section.

5.3   *Manipulating responses*

The response returned to the client can contain a lot of information, and the client may not be interested in receiving all of it. And sometimes there may be sensitive information that must not be exposed in the source sent back as the response. Also, sending a huge amount of data as a response (if the source has 500 attributes, for example) is a waste of bandwidth! There are ways to manipulate responses before sending them to the client. First, let's fetch the source of the document without metadata.

5.3.1   *Removing metadata from the response*

Usually, the response object consists of metadata and the original document (the source). The notable attribute in the response is the _source attribute, which encompasses the original input document. We can fetch just the source (original document) without the metadata by issuing the query like this:

```
GET <index_name>/_source/<id>
```

Notice that the _doc endpoint is replaced with _source; everything else in the invocation stays the same. Let's get the movie document by using this _source endpoint.

Listing 5.12   Fetching the original document with no metadata

```
GET movies/_source/1
```

As the response in figure 5.9 indicates, the document we indexed is returned with no additional information. There are no metadata fields like _version, _id, or _index; there's just the original source document.

```
                                          {
                                            "title" : "The Godfather",
GET movies/_source/1      ⇨                 "synopsis" : "The aging patriarch .."
                          ⬆                 }

The _source endpoint allows us                      Only the original document is
to fetch the original document                      returned; the metadata is
without metadata.                                   suppressed.
```

Figure 5.9   The _source endpoint returns the original document with no metadata.

What if we want to get the metadata but not the source document? Sure, we can do that too. Let's look at how we can suppress the source data.

5.3.2   Suppressing the source document

There may be instances where a document is loaded with hundreds of fields: for example, a full tweet (from the Twitter API) consists of more than just a tweet—it has dozens of attributes such as the tweet, author, timestamps, conversations, attachments, and so on. When retrieving data from Elasticsearch, sometimes we don't want to look at the source data at all—we want to suppress the source data completely and just return the metadata associated with the response. In that case, we can set the _source field to false as the request parameter in our query.

Listing 5.13   Suppressing the original source data

```
GET movies/_doc/1?_source=false
```

The response to this query is shown in figure 5.10. The command sets the _source flag to false, indicating to the server not to return the original document. As you can see from the response, only the metadata is returned, not the source document. Not fetching the original document also frees up bandwidth.

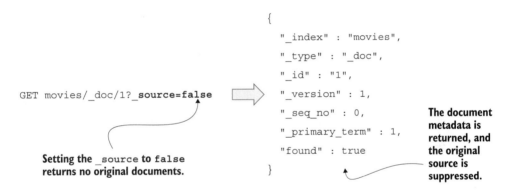

Figure 5.10   Returning metadata only

We now know how to avoid getting the whole document back, but how about returning a document with selective (inclusive or exclusive) fields? For example, we may want the title and rating of a movie to be returned, but not the synopsis. How can we customize what fields are included or excluded in the return list? We see how to do that in the next section.

5.3.3   Including and excluding fields

In addition to suppressing the _source field, we can include and/or exclude fields when retrieving documents. This is done using the _source_includes and _source_ excludes parameters, similar to the _source parameter we used previously. We can provide the _source_includes attribute with a comma-separated list of fields we want to return. Similarly, we can use `_source_excludes` to exclude the fields from the response; no surprise there.

We may need to enhance our `movie` documents for this example, as the current document has no more than two fields. Let's add a few extra fields for a third movie (*The Shawshank Redemption*).

Listing 5.14 New `movie` document with additional attributes

```
PUT movies/_doc/3                          ◄───┐ Indexing a new
{                                               │ document
  "title":"The Shawshank Redemption",
  "synopsis":"Two imprisoned men bond ..",   ┐ New field:
  "rating":9.3,                          ◄───┘ rating attribute
  "certificate":"15",                    ◄─────┐ New field:
  "genre":"drama",                             │ certificate attribute
  "actors":["Morgan Freeman","Tim Robbins"]
}
```

Once this document is indexed, we can experiment with fields that should or should not be returned in the response.

INCLUDING FIELDS USING _SOURCE_INCLUDES

To include a custom list of fields, append the `_source_includes` parameter with comma-separated fields. Say we want to fetch the `title`, `rating`, and `genre` fields from our `movies` index in our response and suppress the others. We can execute the following command.

Listing 5.15 Selectively including few fields

```
GET movies/_doc/3?_source_includes=title,rating,genre
```

This returns the document with these three fields, filtering out the rest:

```
{
  ...
  "_source" : {
    "rating" : 9.3,
    "genre" : "drama",
    "title" : "The Shawshank Redemption"
  }
}
```

This response has both the original document information (under the `_source` object) and the associated metadata. We can also rerun the query using the `_source` endpoint instead of `_doc` to eliminate the metadata and obtain a document with custom fields.

Listing 5.16 Returning selective fields with no metadata

```
GET movies/_source/3?_source_includes=title,rating,genre
```

In the same vein, we can exclude some fields while returning the response by using the _source_excludes parameter.

EXCLUDING FIELDS USING _SOURCE_EXCLUDES

We can exclude fields we don't want to be returned in the response using the _source_excludes parameter. It is a URL path parameter that accepts comma-separated fields. The response consists of all the document fields minus the fields mentioned in the _source_excludes parameter.

Listing 5.17 Excluding the fields in response

```
GET movies/_source/3?_source_excludes=actors,synopsis
```

Here, the actors and synopsis fields are excluded from the response. What if we want to include some fields and explicitly exclude some fields too? Can an Elasticsearch query support this functionality? Sure—we can ask Elasticsearch to satisfy these requirements, as discussed in the next section.

INCLUDING AND EXCLUDING FIELDS

We can mix and match the return attributes we want, because Elasticsearch allows us to fine-tune the response. To demonstrate, let's create a new movie document with various ratings (amazon, metacritic, and rotten_tomatoes).

Listing 5.18 New movie model with ratings

```
PUT movies/_doc/13
{
  "title":"Avatar",
  "rating":9.3,
  "rating_amazon":4.5,
  "rating_rotten_tomatoes":80,
  "rating_metacritic":90
}
```

How can we return all the ratings except amazon? Here's where the power shines of setting up _source_includes and _source_excludes with appropriate attributes.

Listing 5.19 Selectively ignoring certain fields

```
GET movies/_source/13?_source_includes=rating*&_source_excludes=rating_amazon
```

The query and response are shown in figure 5.11.

In this query, we enable a wildcard field, _source_includes=rating*, to fetch all the attributes prefixed with the word *rating* (rating, rating_amazon, rating_metacritic, rating_rotten_tomatoes). The _source_excludes parameter, on the other hand, suppresses a field (for example, _source_excludes=rating_amazon). The resultant document should consist of all the ratings except the Amazon rating.

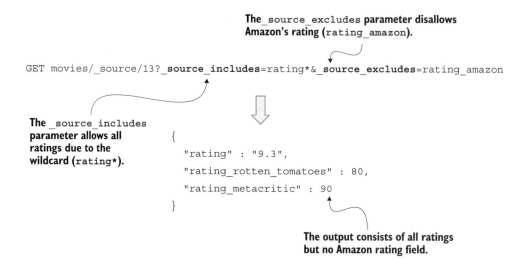

The `_source_excludes` **parameter disallows Amazon's rating (**`rating_amazon`**).**

```
GET movies/_source/13?_source_includes=rating*&_source_excludes=rating_amazon
```

The `_source_includes` **parameter allows all ratings due to the wildcard (**`rating*`**).**

```
{
    "rating" : "9.3",
    "rating_rotten_tomatoes" : 80,
    "rating_metacritic" : 90
}
```

The output consists of all ratings but no Amazon rating field.

Figure 5.11 Tweaking what attributes are and are not part of the return result

So far, we've seen how to create and read documents, including manipulating responses. We now understand the mechanics of updating the documents. There will always be a need to update existing documents by modifying an existing field's value or adding a new field. Elasticsearch provides a set of update APIs for this purpose, discussed in the next section.

5.4 *Updating documents*

Indexed documents sometimes need to be updated with modified values or additional fields, or the entire document may need to be replaced. Similar to indexing documents, Elasticsearch provides two types of update queries—one for working against single documents and the other for working on multiple documents:

- The `_update` API updates a single document.
- `_update_by_query` allows us to modify multiple documents at the same time.

Before we look at some examples, we need to understand the mechanics involved when updating documents. Let's do that next.

5.4.1 *Document update mechanics*

Elasticsearch requires a few steps when we update documents. Figure 5.12 illustrates the procedure: Elasticsearch first fetches the document, modifies it, and then reindexes it. Essentially, it *replaces* the old document with a new document. Behind the scenes, Elasticsearch creates a new document for updates. During this update, Elasticsearch increments the version of the document once the update operation completes. When the newer version of the document (with the modified values or new fields) is ready, it marks the older version for deletion.

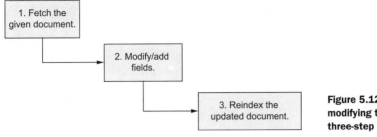

Figure 5.12 Updating or modifying the document is a three-step process.

If you think we can make the same updates by calling the GET, UPDATE, and POST methods on the document individually, you are absolutely right. In reality, this is what Elasticsearch does. As you can imagine, these are three different calls to the server, each resulting in a round trip to and from the client to the server. Elasticsearch avoids this round trip by cleverly executing the set of operations on the same shard, thus saving network traffic between client and server. By using the _update API, Elasticsearch avoids network calls, bandwidth, and coding errors.

5.4.2 The _update API

When we plan to update a document, we usually focus on one or more of the following scenarios:

- Adding more fields to an existing document
- Modifying existing field values
- Replacing the whole document

All of these operations are performed using the _update API. The format is simple:

```
POST <index_name>/_update/<id>
```

When managing our resources with the _update API, we use the POST method based on RESTful API conventions. The document ID is provided in the URL along with the index name to form the full URL.

> **NOTE** The previous update URL uses the _update endpoint, but we can also use POST <index_name>/_doc/<id>/_update. Because the types were deprecated and are removed from version 8, avoid using the _doc endpoint to update the document.

Now that we know the basics of the _update API, let's update our movie document (*The Godfather*) with a couple of additional attributes: actors and director.

ADDING NEW FIELDS

To amend a document with new fields, we pass a request body consisting of the new fields to the _update API. The new fields are wrapped in a doc object as the API expects. The code in the following listing amends the movie document with two additional fields. Noted that we are implicitly assuming that dynamic=true.

Listing 5.20   Adding fields to a document using the `_update` API

```
POST movies/_update/1
{
  "doc": {
    "actors":["Marlon Brando","Al Pacino","James Caan"],
    "director":"Francis Ford Coppola"
  }
}
```

This query adds `actors` and `director` fields to our `movie` document. If we fetch the document (`GET movies/_doc/1`), the additional fields are available in the return document.

MODIFYING EXISTING FIELDS

Sometimes we may need to change existing fields. Doing so isn't complicated; we just have to provide the new value to the field in a `doc` object as we did in the previous query. For example, to rename our `title` field, we write a query like the one shown in the next listing.

Listing 5.21   Updating the title of an existing document

```
POST movies/_update/1
{
  "doc": {
    "title":"The Godfather (Original)"
  }
}
```

When it comes to updating an element in an array (like adding a new actor to the list in the `actors` field), we must provide both the new and old values. For example, let's say we want to add another actor (Robert Duvall) to the `actors` field for our *The Godfather* document.

Listing 5.22   Updating an existing field with additional information

```
POST movies/_update/1          ◁───────────  We're updating the
{                                             document with ID 1.
  "doc": {                     ◁──┐  The updates must be
    "actors":["Marlon Brando",    │  enclosed in the doc object.
             "Al Pacino",
             "James Caan",
             "Robert Duvall"]  ◁──┐  Old and new
  }                               │  values together
}
```

The query updates the `actors` field to add Robert Duvall. Note that we provide the existing actors in the array along with our new actor. If we only included Robert Duvall in the `actors` array, Elasticsearch would replace the list with just his name.

We've seen in the last couple of sections how to amend an existing document. There are instances when we need to amend documents based on conditions. We do this using scripts, as discussed in the next section.

5.4.3   *Scripted updates*

We've been using the update API to modify the documents by to adding fields or updating existing ones. In addition to doing this on a field-by-field basis, we can execute updates using scripts. Scripted updates allow us to update the document based on conditions: for example, ranking a movie as a blockbuster if it crosses a certain threshold of box office earnings.

Scripts are provided in a request body using the same _update endpoint, with updates wrapped in a `script` object consisting of the `source` as the key. We provide updates as a value to this `source` key with the help of the context variable `ctx`, fetching the original document's attributes by calling `ctx._source.<field>`.

UPDATING ARRAYS USING A SCRIPT

Let's update our `movie` document by adding an actor to the existing array. This time, we don't use the method shown in listing 5.22, where we attached all the existing actors to the `actors` field along with the new actor. Instead, we simply use a script to update the `actors` field with another actor.

Listing 5.23   Adding an actor to the `actors` list via a script

```
POST movies/_update/1
{
  "script": {
    "source": "ctx._source.actors.add('Diane Keaton')"      ⊲—┤ Additional actor
  }
}
```

`ctx._source.actors` fetches the `actors` array and invokes the `add` method on that array to insert the new value (`Diane Keaton`) in the list. Similarly, we can delete a value from the list using a scripted update, although doing so is a bit involved.

REMOVING AN ELEMENT FROM THE ARRAY

Removing an element from an array using a script requires us to provide the index of the element. The `remove` method takes an integer that points to the index of the actor we want to remove. To fetch the index of an actor, we can invoke the `indexOf` method on the appropriate array object. Let's see this in action, removing Diane Keaton from the list.

Listing 5.24   Removing an actor from the list of actors

```
POST movies/_update/1
{
  "script":{
    "source":
```

```
    "ctx._source.actors.remove(ctx._source.actors.indexOf('Diane Keaton'))"   ◁─┐
  }
}
```
**The remove method expects the
integer position of the actor.**

`ctx._source.actors.indexOf('Diane Keaton')` returns an index of the element in
the `actors` array. This is *required* for the `remove` method.

ADDING A NEW FIELD

We can also add a new field to our document using a script like that in the following
listing. Here we add a new field, `imdb_user_rating`, with a value of `9.2`.

Listing 5.25   Adding a new field with a value using a script

```
POST movies/_update/1
{
  "script": {
    "source": "ctx._source.imdb_user_rating = 9.2"
  }
}
```

> **NOTE**   To add a new value to an array (as we did in listing 5.23), we invoke the
> `add` method on the array: `ctx._source.<array_object>.add('value')`

REMOVING A FIELD

Removing a field is also a straightforward job. The following listing removes a field
(`imdb_user_rating`) from our `movies` document.

Listing 5.26   Removing a field from the source document

```
POST movies/_update/1
{
  "script": {
    "source": "ctx._source.remove('imdb_user_rating')"
  }
}
```

> **NOTE**   If we try to remove a nonexistent field, we do not get an error message
> letting us know that we are trying to remove a field that doesn't exist on the
> schema. Instead, we get a response indicating that the document was updated
> and the field was incremented (which I consider a false positive).

ADDING MULTIPLE FIELDS

We can write a script that adds multiple fields at once.

Listing 5.27   Adding multiple new fields using a script

```
POST movies/_update/1
{
  "script": {
    "source": """
```

```
    ctx._source.runtime_in_minutes = 175;
    ctx._source.metacritic_rating= 100;
    ctx._source.tomatometer = 97;
    ctx._source.boxoffice_gross_in_millions = 134.8;
    """
  }
}
```

The notable thing in this listing is that the multiline updates are carried out in a triple-quote block. Each key-value pair is segregated with a semicolon (;).

ADDING A CONDITIONAL UPDATE SCRIPT

We can also implement logic that is a bit more complicated in the script block. Let's say we want to tag a movie as a blockbuster if the gross earnings are over $125 million. (I've made up this rule; in reality, other factors are involved, such as budget, stars, return on investment, and so on, to make a movie a blockbuster.) To do this, let's create a script with a condition that checks the movie's gross earnings; if the earnings cross the threshold, we label that movie a blockbuster. In the next listing, we write a simple if/else statement whose logic is based on earnings and sets a blockbuster flag accordingly.

Listing 5.28 Conditionally updating the document using an if/else block

```
POST movies/_update/1
{
  "script": {
    "source": """
    if(ctx._source.boxoffice_gross_in_millions > 125)
      {ctx._source.blockbuster = true}
    else
      {ctx._source.blockbuster = false}
    """
  }
}
```

The if clause checks for the value of the field boxoffice_gross_in_millions. It then automatically creates a new blockbuster field (we don't have that field yet on our schema) and sets the flag to true or false based on the outcome of the condition.

So far, we've been working with straightforward examples using scripts. However, scripts allow us to do more—from a simple update to a complex conditional modification on a data set. Understanding the nitty-gritty of scripting is out of scope for this book, but learning a few concepts is advised, so let's briefly discuss the anatomy of a script.

ANATOMY OF A SCRIPT

Let's pause to briefly examine the anatomy of a script. A script has three parts: source, language, and parameters, as shown in figure 5.13.

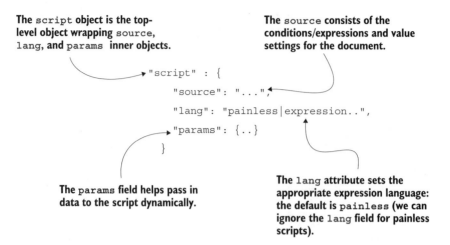

Figure 5.13   The anatomy of a script

The `source` field is where we provide the logic, while the `params` field contains the parameters that the script expects, separated by a vertical bar (or pipe) character. We can also provide the language our script is written in: for example, one of the languages `painless`, `expression`, `moustache`, or `java`, where `painless` is the default. Next, let's see how to update a document by passing values via the `params` attribute.

PASSING DATA TO A SCRIPT

One problem with the code in listing 5.27 is that we hardcoded the threshold earnings in the script (gross earnings as $150 million). Instead, we can set a threshold value in the script using the `params` property. Let's revisit our blockbuster script, but this time we pass the value of the gross earnings threshold to the script's logic via `params`.

Listing 5.29   Dynamically passing a parameter to the script

```
POST movies/_update/1
{
  "script": {                     ◁── Business logic goes here.
    "source": """
 if(ctx._source.boxoffice_gross_in_millions >     ◁── Checks the value against params
    params.gross_earnings_threshold)
  {ctx._source.blockbuster = true}
 else
  {ctx._source.blockbuster = false}
 """,
    "params": {                   ◁── Provides the parameter values
      "gross_earnings_threshold":150
    }
  }
}
```

The script has two notable changes from the previous version in listing 5.28:

- The `if` clause is now compared against a value read from the `params` object (`params.gross_earnings_threshold`).
- The `gross_earnings_threshold` is set to `150` via the `params` block.

When the script is executed, Elasticsearch consults the `params` object and replaces the attribute with the value from the `params` object. If we want to change the value of gross earnings for setting a blockbuster flag (perhaps the `params.gross_earnings_threshold` needs to be updated to $500 million), we can simply pass the new value in the `params` flag.

Did you notice the hardcoded `params` value in the script? You may wonder why we hardcode the `gross_earnings_threshold`'s value in the script in the `params` object. Well, there is much more to scripting functionality than we've seen here. Scripts are compiled when they are executed for the first time. The compilation of the script carries a performance cost, so it is considered an expensive operation in Elasticsearch. However, scripts associated with dynamically changing parameters (using the `params` object) avoid this compilation cost because the script is compiled the first time only and is updated with the variable's (`params`) value when invoked for the rest of the time. This is a significant benefit, so the general practice is to provide dynamic variables via the `params` object to the script (refer to listing 5.29).

SCRIPTING LANGUAGES
The scripts developed in this chapter are derived from Elasticsearch's special scripting language, called Painless, to decode the logic and execute the scripts. The default language is Painless (we didn't specify the language explicitly in our code earlier). We can plug into other scripting languages (Mustache, Expression, or even Java) by using a `lang` parameter. Regardless of the language we use, we must follow this set pattern:

```
"script": {
    "lang": "painless|mustache|expression|java",
    "source": "...",
    "params": { ... }
}
```

So far, we've updated individual documents using the `_update` API call or scripts. How about updating a bunch of documents that match a criterion? That's exactly what we learn in the next section.

5.4.4   Replacing documents

Let's say we need to replace an existing document with a new one. This is easy: we can use the same PUT request we performed earlier in the chapter when indexing a new document. Let's insert a new movie title (*Avatar*) in our `movies` document but associate it with an existing document (ID = 1).

Listing 5.30   Replacing the content of a document

```
PUT movies/_doc/1
{
  "title":"Avatar"
}
```

The existing movie, *The Godfather*, is replaced with the new data attributes (*Avatar*) after we execute this command.

> **NOTE**   If our intent is to replace existing content with something else, we use the _doc API on the same ID with a new request body. However, if we do not wish to replace the document, we must use the _create endpoint (discussed in section 5.1.1).

Sometimes, when we try to update a nonexistent document, we want Elasticsearch to index it as a new document rather than throw an error. This is what the *upsert* operation is all about.

5.4.5   *Upserts*

Upsert, short for update and insert, is an operation that either updates a document (if it exists) or indexes a new document with the data provided (if it does not exist). Figure 5.14 demonstrates this operation.

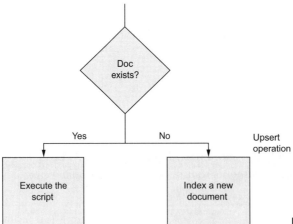

Figure 5.14   Upsert operation workflow

Let's say we want to update gross_earnings for the movie *Top Gun*. Remember, we don't have this movie in our store yet. We can develop a query to update the gross_earnings field and create a new document with this update.

The query has two parts: a `script` and an `upsert` block. The `script` part is where we update the field on an existing document, while the `upsert` block consists of the new `movie` document information.

Listing 5.31 Upsert block example

```
POST movies/_update/5
{
  "script": {
    "source": "ctx._source.gross_earnings = '357.1m'"
  },
  "upsert": {
    "title":"Top Gun",
    "gross_earnings":"357.5m"
  }
}
```

When we execute this query, we expect the script to run and update the `gross_earnings` field on a document with ID 5 (if the document is available). What happens if that document is not in our index? Well, that's where the `upsert` block comes into play.

The second part of the JSON request is interesting: the `upsert` block consists of fields constituting a new document. Because there is no document with that ID in the store, the `upsert` block creates a new document with the specified fields. So, an upsert action provides us with the facility of either updating an existing document or creating a new one if it's the first time we index it.

If we run the same query a second time, the `script` part is executed and changes the field `gross_earnings` to `357.1m` (from `357.5m` in the original document). This happens because the document already exists.

5.4.6 Updates as upserts

In section 5.4.2, we looked at partially updating a document using the `doc` object via the `_update` API. In the following listing, we update a movie with an additional field, `runtime_in_minutes`. If document 11 exists, this field is updated as expected; otherwise, an error is thrown, stating that the document does not exist.

Listing 5.32 Updating a nonexistent field (which will throw an error)

```
POST movies/_update/11
{
  "doc": {
    "runtime_in_minutes":110
  }
}
```

To avoid errors—maybe we want to create a new document if the document does not exist—we can use a `doc_as_upsert` flag. Setting this flag to `true` allows the contents of the `doc` object to be stored as a new document if the document (ID = 11) doesn't exist.

Listing 5.33   Updating the document if the field doesn't exist

```
POST movies/_update/11
{
  "doc": {
    "runtime_in_minutes":110
  },
  "doc_as_upsert":true
}
```

This time, if we don't have a document with ID 11 in our store, it's not a problem. The engine does not throw an error; instead, it creates a new document with ID 11 and fields extracted from the doc object (runtime_in_minutes, in this case).

5.4.7   *Updating with a query*

Sometimes we wish to update a set of documents matching a search criterion—for example, updating all movies with a rating greater than 4 stars to indicate that they are popular. We can run a query to search for such a set of documents and apply updates to them by using the _update_by_query endpoint. For example, let's update all movies with an actor name matching Al Pacino to say Oscar Winner Al Pacino, instead.

Listing 5.34   Updating a document using a query method

```
POST movies/_update_by_query          ◁─┐ Searches for documents
{                                        │ and updates the set
  "query": {            ◁────────┐ Search query: searches for
    "match": {          │ all movies with Al Pacino
      "actors": "Al Pacino"
    }
  },                    ┌─ Applies the following script logic
  "script": {    ◁──────┘ to the matching documents
    "source": """
    ctx._source.actors.add('Oscar Winner Al Pacino');
    ctx._source.actors.remove(ctx._source.actors.indexOf('Al Pacino'))
    """,
    "lang": "painless"
  }
}
```

In this listing, the match query executes first (we discuss match queries in chapter 10, but think of it as a type of query where we can fetch documents matching a given criterion) to fetch all movies with actor Al Pacino. When the match query returns its results, a script executes to change Al Pacino to Oscar Winner Al Pacino. Because we need to remove the old name, we also invoke a remove operation in the script.

_update_by_query is a handy mechanism to update many documents based on a criterion. However, there is a lot going on behind the scenes when we use this method; see the following sidebar to learn more.

> **Mechanics of update_by_query**
>
> Elasticsearch first parses the input query and identifies the shards that contain documents that could potentially match our query. For each of these shards, Elasticsearch executes the query and finds all documents that match it.
>
> Elasticsearch will run the script we've provided on each of these matched documents. Before updating the documents, Elasticsearch checks if the current document's version corresponds with the version when it was found during the query phase. If they match, the update proceeds; if not (perhaps, the document was updated due to another operation interim), Elasticsearch retries the operation. Each document is then updated in memory and re-indexed, marking the old document as deleted while a new one added to the index.
>
> When updating a particular document fails, the failure is logged but the rest of the documents will get updated as per the script. Any conflicts during the update process can be either retried a specific number of times or ignored completely as per the pre-configured settings. Once the operation is completed and the indexes are refreshed, so the changes are available for search.
>
> The `_update_by_query` operation returns a response that includes count of total processed documents, version conflicts, successfully updated ones and failed documents. As you can imagine, the `_update_by_query` operation is a resource-intensive operation, hence careful consideration of its affect on your cluster's performance needs to be considered. We can let Elasticsearch process the updates in batches if it's using too many resources. The batch size and throttling limits can be configured.

We now know the mechanism to update documents. It is time to discuss delete operations—specifically, how to delete a single document or multiple documents simultaneously. The next section is dedicated to deleting documents in multiple ways.

5.5   *Deleting documents*

When we want to delete documents, there are two methods: using an ID or a query. In the former case, we can delete a single document; and in the latter, we can delete multiple documents at once. When deleting by query, we can set filter criteria (for example, delete documents whose status field is unpublished or documents from last month). Let's see both of these methods in action.

5.5.1   *Deleting with an ID*

We can delete a single document from Elasticsearch by invoking the HTTP DELETE method on the indexing document API:

```
DELETE <index_name>/_doc/<id>
```

The URL is the same as the one we used for indexing and retrieving the document. Given the ID of the document to be deleted, we construct the URL by specifying the index, the _doc endpoint, and the document ID. For example, we can invoke the following query to delete the document with ID 1 from the movies index.

```
DELETE movies/_doc/1
```

The response received from the server indicates that the document was deleted successfully:

```
{
  ...
  "_id" : "1",
  "_version" : 2,
  "result" : "deleted"
}
```

The response returns a `result` attribute set to `deleted` to let the client know the object was deleted successfully. If the document isn't deleted (for instance, it doesn't exist in our store), we get a response with the `result` value set to `not_found` (status code 404). Interestingly, Elasticsearch increments the `_version` flag if the delete operation succeeds.

5.5.2   *Deleting by query (_delete_by_query)*

Deleting a single document is easy, as we just saw. But if we want to delete multiple documents based on a criterion, we can use `_delete_by_query` (similar to `_update_by_query` in section 5.4.7). If we want to delete all movies directed by James Cameron, for example, we can write this query.

```
POST movies/_delete_by_query
{
  "query":{
    "match":{
      "director":"James Cameron"
    }
  }
}
```

Here we create the query in the request body using as our criterion all movies directed by James Cameron. Documents that are matched with the criterion are then marked and deleted.

The body of this `POST` uses a special syntax called Query DSL (domain-specific language), which lets us pass in a variety of attributes like `term`, `range`, and `match` (as in this listing), similar to basic `search` queries. We learn more about search queries in later chapters, but for now, note that `_delete_by_query` is a powerful endpoint with sophisticated delete criteria. Let's see a few examples in the following sections.

5.5.3 Deleting with a range query

We may wish to delete records that fall in a certain range: movies with ratings between 3.5 and 4.5, flights canceled between two dates, and so on. We can use a `range` query to set a criterion for a range of values for such requirements. The following listing uses `_delete_by_query` to delete movies that earned between $350 million and $400 million.

Listing 5.37 Deleting all movies with a range of gross earnings

```
POST movies/_delete_by_query
{
  "query": {
    "range": {
      "gross_earnings_in_millions": {
        "gt": 350,
        "lt": 400
      }
    }
  }
}
```

Here, `_delete_by_query` accepts a `range` query with a match criterion: find documents whose gross earnings fall between $350 and $400 million dollars. As we expect, all matching documents are deleted.

We can also construct complex queries. For example, listing 5.38 shows a query that constructs criteria to delete movies directed by Steven Spielberg, where those movies are rated between 9 and 9.5 and earned less than $100 million. The listing uses a `bool` query as the request.

NOTE For the following query, you need to index the movies dataset from the book's files: http://mng.bz/zXeX.

Listing 5.38 Deleting movies with complicated query criteria

```
POST movies/_delete_by_query
{
  "query": {
    "bool": {                          Matches movies
      "must": [{          ⟵┘          directed by Spielberg
          "match": {
            "director": "Steven Spielberg"
          }
        }
      ],                               The rating should be greater
      "must_not": [{      ⟵┘          than 9 but less than 9.5.
          "range": {
            "imdb_rating": {
              "gte": 9,
              "lte": 9.5
```

```
          }
        }
      }
    ],                          Earning shouldn't fall
    "filter": [{        ⟵──┘   below $100 million
      "range": {
        "gross_earnings_in_millions": {
          "lt": 100
        }
      }
    }
  ]
}
}
}
```

The query uses complex query logic called a `bool` query that combines multiple smaller queries to work on a grand scale. Chapter 12 is dedicated to `bool` queries and digs deeper into how we can construct complicated queries.

5.5.4 *Deleting all documents*

WARNING Delete operations are irreversible! Be cautious before hitting Elasticsearch with a delete query.

You can delete a whole set of documents from an index using the `match_all` query.

Listing 5.39 Deleting all documents at once

```
POST movies/_delete_by_query
{
  "query": {
    "match_all": {}
  }
}
```

This code runs a `match_all` query. It matches all documents and deletes them simultaneously. This is a destructive operation, so be careful when deleting an entire set of documents! We can also delete the entire index by issuing the `DELETE movies` command—but remember, these are irreversible commands.

So far, we have deleted documents on a single index. We can also delete documents across multiple indexes by simply providing a comma-separated list of indexes in the API URL. The example format is shown here:

```
POST <index_1>,<index_2>,<index_3>/_delete_by_query
```

The following listing deletes all documents across multiple movie-related indexes. Note that we can use `GET _cat/indices` to list all indexes.

Listing 5.40 Deleting documents from three different movie indexes

```
POST old_movies,classics,movie_reviews/_delete_by_query
{
  "query": {
    "match_all": {}
  }
}
```

Again, be careful about issuing delete queries, because you may lose the whole data set! Unless you wish to purge a complete data set, exercise delete operations with caution in production.

We have been indexing the documents individually so far, but in the real world, there's always a case to index large sets of documents simultaneously. We may have 100,000 movies to read from a CSV file, or 500,000 currency foreign exchange rates fetched from a third-party service to be indexed into our engine. While we can usually use an ETL (extract-transform-load) tool like Logstash to extract, enrich, and publish data; Elasticsearch provides a bulk (_bulk) API to index messages in bulk. We discuss the bulk API in the next section.

5.6 Working with documents in bulk

So far, we've indexed documents individually using Kibana. Indexing a single document or handful of documents using the API methods is straightforward. This is well and good for development purposes, but we rarely do this in production. It is cumbersome and error-prone for a larger data set (for example, when extracting a larger number of records from a database).

Fortunately, Elasticsearch provides a _bulk API to index large quantities of data to index large data sets simultaneously. We can also use the _bulk API to manipulate documents, including deleting them.

The _bulk API accepts a POST request, which can perform index, create, delete, and update actions simultaneously. This saves bandwidth by avoiding multiple trips to the server. There is a special format for the _bulk API, which you may find a bit weird but is not difficult to get your head around. Let's look at the format first.

5.6.1 Format of the _bulk API

The _bulk API consists of a specific syntax with a POST method invoking the API call (see figure 5.15). The request body consists of two lines for every document that needs to be stored. The first indicates one of the actions to be performed on the document: index, create, delete, or update. The document is described in the second line, which we cover shortly.

Once we choose the action, we need to provide a value for this action key with metadata. The metadata is usually the name of the document's index and the document ID. For example, the metadata for a document with ID 100 in a movies index is "_index":"movies","_id":"100".

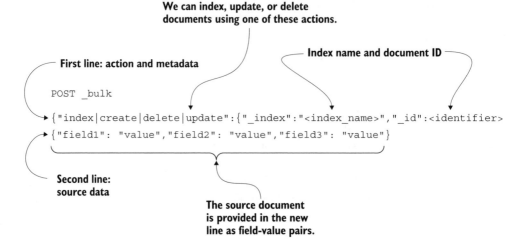

Figure 5.15   The _bulk API's generic format

The second line in figure 5.15 is the document's source, which is what we want to store the document. As expected, the document is formatted in JSON and added to the request in the new line. Both the metadata and source lines are delimited with new line (\n) separators expressed in JSON (that is, newline-delimited JSON [NDJSON, http://ndjson.org]—a convenient format for storing records to be consumed one by one).

> **NOTE**   The request attached to the _bulk API must adhere strictly to the NDJSON format; otherwise, the documents won't be bulk indexed. Each line must end with a newline delimiter because the bulk request is newline-sensitive. Make sure your document is formatted as NDJSON.

With this concept in mind, let's create a bulk request to index the movie document *Mission Impossible.*

5.6.2   *Bulk indexing documents*

We want to index documents using _bulk API, so let's check out the following example. The same request is shown in figure 5.16 with annotations.

Listing 5.41   Bulk indexing in action

```
                     The _bulk
                     API URL                         We want to "index"
POST _bulk        ⟵—┘                                this document.
{"index":{"_index":"movies","_id":"100"}}        ⟵—┘
{"title": "Mission Impossible","release_date": "1996-07-05"}   ⟵—┐  Our
                                                                     document
```

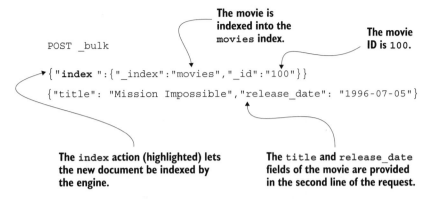

Figure 5.16 Indexing the new movie *Mission Impossible* using the `_bulk` API

If we execute this query, we have a document with ID 100 that is indexed into the `movies` document with the fields given in the second line. That is, the movie *Mission Impossible* is indexed into our store. The two lines make one request—we have to code two lines for each document we want to be acted on.

We can also shorten the metadata line. For example, we can remove the index and attach it to the URL, instead.

Listing 5.42 Bulk API with index embedded in the request URL

```
POST movies/_bulk
{"index":{"_id":"100"}}
{"title": "Mission Impossible","release_date": "1996-07-05"}
```

The URL includes the index.

The _index field has been removed.

We can also get rid of the `_id` field if we want system-generated random IDs for our movies. The following snippet demonstrates this approach.

Listing 5.43 Letting the system generate document IDs

```
POST movies/_bulk
{"index":{}}
{"title": "Mission Impossible","release_date": "1996-07-05"}
```

Both the _index and _id were removed

The system assigns the ID for this document, a random UUID.

Of course, you may wonder why we need to follow this bulk approach when we can index the same document using the document index API (`PUT movies/_doc/100`). That is a fair question, but we haven't yet unleashed the full power of the `_bulk` API. Suppose we have a requirement to index Tom Cruise's movies into our `movies` index. The request is written in the next listing.

Listing 5.44   Bulk indexing Tom Cruise's movies

```
POST movies/_bulk
{"index":{}}
{"title": "Mission Impossible","release_date": "1996-07-05"}
{"index":{}}
{"title": "Mission Impossible II","release_date": "2000-05-24"}
{"index":{}}
{"title": "Mission Impossible III","release_date": "2006-05-03"}
{"index":{}}
{"title": "Mission Impossible - Ghost Protocol","release_date": "2011-12-26"}
```

Because we've attached the index name in the URL (POST movies/_bulk) and are not concerned with a predefined ID, the query indexes four of Tom Cruise's movies successfully.

5.6.3   *Independent entities and multiple actions*

We only indexed the *Mission Impossible* movies, but we can index other entities in the same request. The notable thing is that the _bulk API helps to wrap up multiple entities—we can bundle not just movies, but any types, such as books, flights, logs, and so on, in a request. The following listing has a list of mutually exclusive requests.

Listing 5.45   Bulk request with mixed bag of requests

```
POST _bulk
{"index":{"_index":"books"}}            ⟵─  Indexes
{"title": "Elasticsearch in Action"}         a book
{"create":{"_index":"flights", "_id":"101"}}      ⟵─  Creates a flight
{"title": "London to Bucharest"}
{"index":{"_index":"pets"}}        ⟵
{"name": "Milly","age_months": 18}      Indexes a pet into
{"delete":{"_index":"movies", "_id":"101"}}   a pets index
{ "update" : {"_index":"movies", "_id":"1"} }    ⟵   Deletes a movie
{ "doc" : {"title" : "The Godfather (Original)"} }      Updates the title
                                                         of a movie
```

This bulk request includes almost all the actions possible when using the _bulk API. Let's drill down into these individual actions.

THE CREATE ACTION

We can swap the index action with create so we do not replace the document if it doesn't exist while indexing (see section 5.1.3). The following code shows the create operation in action.

Listing 5.46   _bulk API with the create operation

```
POST _bulk
{"create":{"_index":"movies","_id":"101"}}              ⟵─  Avoids accidental
{"title": "Mission Impossible II","release_date": "2000-05-24"}    overwrites
```

THE UPDATE ACTION

Updating a document follows a similar pattern, but we must wrap the fields to be updated in a `doc` object, as we learned in section 5.4.2. This example updates the movie with ID 200 (*Rush Hour*) with additional fields (`director` and `actors`).

Listing 5.47   Bulk updating the move *Rush Hour*

```
POST _bulk
{"update":{"_index":"movies","_id":"200"}}
{"doc": {"director":"Brett Ratner", "actors":["Jackie Chan","Chris Tucker"]}}
```

THE DELETE ACTION

Finally, let's use the `_bulk` API to delete a document. The format is slightly different, as shown next.

Listing 5.48   Bulk call with the `delete` action

```
POST _bulk
{"delete":{"_index":"movie_reviews","_id":"111"}}
```

As you can see, we don't need a second line for this operation. The query deletes the movie review with ID 111 from the `movie_reviews` index. Remember, you can lose your entire data set if you are not careful when issuing `delete` queries.

5.6.4   *Bulk requests using cURL*

We've been using Kibana to perform operations on documents using the `_bulk` API. We can also perform these actions using cURL. In fact, using cURL may be the preferred method if we have a larger chunk of records to deal with.

To use cURL, we need to create a JSON file containing all the data and pass that file to cURL with the flag `--data-binary`. The data used in listing 5.49 is available in the movie_bulk_data.json file available with the book's files; you can pass the file to cURL.

Listing 5.49   Using cURL to execute a bulk data operation

```
curl -H "Content-Type: application/x-ndjson"
  -XPOST localhost:9200/_bulk
  --data-binary "@movie_bulk_data.json"
```

The `localhost` is the address of our instance of Elasticsearch that is up and running on our local machine.

> **NOTE**   Be sure to give the `--data-binary` flag the name of your file (without the extension) with a `@` prefix.

We now know how to work with bulk requests. However, sometimes we want to move documents from one index to another (for example, from `blockbuster_movies` to classic_movies). The _bulk API may not be suitable for moving (or migrating) data between indexes. Elasticsearch provides a popular feature: the reindexing (_reindex) API. This is discussed in detail in the next section.

5.7   Reindexing documents

Depending on our application and business needs, we may need to move documents from one index to another from time to time. This is especially true when we need to migrate an older index to a newer one due to changes in our mapping schema or settings. We can use the _reindex API for such requirements, as this format shows:

```
POST _reindex
{
  "source": {"index": "<source_index>"},
  "dest": {"index": "<destination_index>"}
}
```

When would we put reindexing into action, you may ask? Suppose we want to update our movies index with schema modifications that may break the existing index if we implement them directly on it. In this case, the idea is to create a new index with the updated settings (say, a movies_new index with the updated schema) and move the data from the old movies index to the new one. The query in the following listing does exactly that.

Listing 5.50   Migrating data between indexes using the _reindex API

```
POST _reindex
{
  "source": {"index": "movies"},
  "dest": {"index": "movies_new"}
}
```

This query grabs a snapshot of the movies index and pushes the records into the new index. Data is migrated between these indexes as expected.

One of the important use cases of reindexing is zero-downtime migration in production if we use this approach with aliases. We go over this in chapter 6.

This has been a long chapter, and we've covered a lot. Let's wrap it up and jump to the next chapter, where we discuss indexing operations in detail.

Summary

- Elasticsearch provides a set of APIs that work on documents. We can use these APIs to execute CRUD actions (create, read, update, and delete) on individual documents.
- Our documents are held in the shard's in-memory buffer and pushed into a segment during the refresh process. Lucene employs a strategy of creating a new segment with the documents during the refresh. It then cumulatively merges three segments to form a new segment, and the process repeats.

- Documents with identifiers (IDs) use the HTTP PUT action when indexing (for example, PUT <index>/_doc/<ID>), whereas documents with no IDs invoke the POST method.
- Elasticsearch generates random unique identifiers (UUIDs) and assigns them to documents during the indexing process.
- To avoid overriding a document, we can issue the following commands:
  - _create—This API throws an error if the document already exists.
  - _mget—This API lets us retrieve multiple documents at once, given their IDs.
  - _bulk—This API performs document operations such as indexing, deleting, and updating multiple documents in one invocation call.
- We can tweak the source and the metadata retrieved as a result of query invocations and then customize the returned document source to include and/or exclude fields by setting the _source_includes and _source_excludes properties, respectively.
- The _update API lets us modify an existing document by updating and adding fields. The expected updates are wrapped in a doc object and passed as the request body.
- Multiple documents can be modified by constructing an _update_by_query query.
- Scripted updates allow us to modify documents based on conditions. If the conditional clause mentioned in the request body is evaluated to true, the script is put into action.
- Documents can be deleted using HTTP DELETE for a single document or by running a _delete_by_query method on multiple documents.
- Migrating data between indexes is performed by the reindexing API. The _reindex API call expects to be given the source and destination indexes to transfer data.

Indexing operations

This chapter covers

- Basic indexing operations
- Index templating
- Status management and monitoring
- Index lifecycle management (ILM)

In the last few chapters, we worked with indices without delving into intricate details. While that is adequate for getting started with Elasticsearch, it is far from ideal. Configuring an index with appropriate settings not only lets Elasticsearch run efficiently but also increases resiliency. A sound organizational indexing strategy creates a future-proof search engine and, hence, a smoother user experience.

For a healthy and performant Elasticsearch cluster, we need to work with indices at a lower level. Understanding index management in depth helps when setting up a resilient and coherent search system. This chapter is dedicated to indexing operations and understanding the mechanics, indexing APIs, and inner workings in detail.

We begin by exploring the configuration settings on an index. Indexes come with three sets of configurations: settings, mappings, and aliases. Each configuration modifies the index in one way or another. For example, we use settings to tweak the number of shards and replicas and to change other index properties. Shards and replicas allow scaling and high availability of data. Mappings define an effective schema for our data for indexing and querying data efficiently. Aliases (alternate names given to indices) let us query across multiple indexes easily and reindex data with zero downtime. We cover all these configurations in detail in the first part of the chapter.

Although it is possible to instantiate indexes manually, it is a tedious, ineffective, and sometimes erroneous process. Instead, organizations should strive for a strategy that develops indexes using index templates. With index templates, we can create indexes with a predefined configuration; and understanding the template mechanism lets us develop indexes for advanced operations such as rollover. Section 6.6 looks at these templates and templating processes in action.

Indexes grow over time along with data, which if unchecked may lead to the system becoming unresponsive. Elasticsearch provides a mechanism to create lifecycle policy definitions to help manage and monitor indexes productively. When an index ages or becomes a certain size, it can be rolled over to a new index, thus preventing unavoidable exceptions.

Similarly, larger indexes created in anticipation of more data can be retired automatically after a set period. Although, index lifecycle management is an advanced topic, it is both fun and engaging. We work through index lifecycle management options in section 6.9. This chapter digs deep into indexing management, index monitoring, and the index lifecycle, so let's jump right in.

NOTE The code for this chapter is available on GitHub (http://mng.bz/Pzyg) and on the book's website (https://www.manning.com/books/elasticsearch -in-action-second-edition).

6.1 Indexing operations

Let's quickly recap what an index is: it is a logical collection of our data backed up by shards (primary and replicas). Documents represented as JSON and having similar attributes (employees, orders, login audit data, news stories by region, and so on) are held in respective indexes. Any index consisting of shards is distributed across various nodes in the cluster. A newly created index is associated with a set number of shards, replicas, and other attributes by default.

We bring indexes to life with custom configurations. We can perform many operations when developing an index, from creating it to closing, shrinking, cloning, freezing, deleting, and other operations. Understanding these operations allows us to set up the system for efficient data storage and search retrieval. Let's begin by looking at creating indexes and the operations involved in instantiating them.

6.2 Creating indexes

When we indexed a document for the first time in earlier chapters, Elasticsearch also created the index *implicitly*. This is one of the ways we can create an index. An alternative is to create indexes *explicitly;* we have much more control over customizing indexes when we create them via that route. Let's look at both approaches:

- *Implicit (automatic) creation*—When indexing a document for the first time, if the index doesn't exist, Elasticsearch creates it implicitly with default settings. This method of index creation usually works well, but care should be taken when using this approach in production because incorrect or unoptimized indexes will bring unexpected consequences to the running system.

  Elasticsearch uses dynamic mapping to deduce field types when creating the mapping schema with this method. Unfortunately, the mapping definitions produced are not foolproof; for example, data in a non-ISO date format (dd-MM-yyyy or MM-dd-yyyy) is determined to be a text field rather than a date data type.

- *Explicit (manual) creation*—Choosing this approach lets us control index creation so we can customize the index as required. We can configure the index with a mapping schema doctored by resident data architects, allocate shards based on current and projected storage expectations, and so on.

  Elasticsearch provides a set of index creation APIs that help us create indexes with personalized configurations. We can take advantage of these APIs when creating indexes up front so the indexes are optimized for storage and data retrieval. The APIs provide great flexibility; for example, we can create an individual index with features such as appropriately sized shards, applicable mapping definitions, multiple aliases, and more.

> **NOTE** To control automatic index creation, we can turn off creating indexes by setting the action.auto_create_index flag to false via the cluster settings API or setting this property in config/elasticsearch.yml. By default, this flag is set to true. We use this feature shortly.

6.2.1 *Creating indexes implicitly (automatic creation)*

When we index a document for the first time, Elasticsearch doesn't complain about a nonexistent index; instead, it happily creates one for us. When an index is created this way, Elasticsearch uses default settings such as setting the number of primary and replica shards to one. To demonstrate, let's quickly index a document with car information using the document API. (We created the cars index in chapter 4. We delete and re-create it to start fresh in this chapter.)

Listing 6.1 First document containing car data

```
DELETE cars          ◁——┐  Deletes the cars index
                         │  so we start from scratch
PUT cars/_doc/1                        ◁————
{
  "make":"Maserati",
  "model":"GranTurismo Sport",
```

The index doesn't exist but is created the first time a document is indexed. By indexing a document, we create the cars index implicitly.

```
"speed_mph":186
}
```

Because this is the first document to be stored in the `cars` index, when we send this request to Elasticsearch, the server instantly creates an index called `cars` because that index doesn't exist in the store. The index is configured with the default settings and a document ID of 1. We can fetch the details of the newly created index by invoking the `GET cars` command, as figure 6.1 shows.

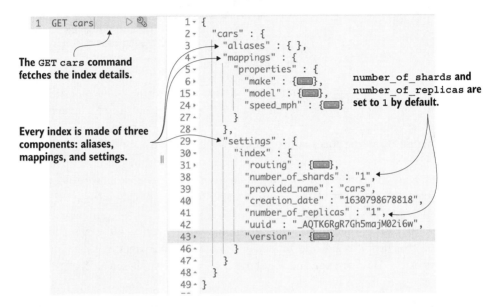

Figure 6.1 Fetching the details of the `cars` index

We should note a few important things from the response: each index is made of *mappings*, *settings*, and *aliases*. Elasticsearch creates the mappings schema automatically by determining each field's data type from the field's value. For example, because the `make` and `model` types seem to contain textual information, these fields are created as `text` fields. Also, Elasticsearch takes the liberty of allocating a primary shard and a replica shard by default.

Static settings can't be changed on an operational index

Not all default settings (`number_of_shards`, `number_of_replicas`, etc.) applied by the engine can be changed on an index that's operational. For example, the `number_of_replicas` setting can be modified on a live index, but `number_of_shards` can't. We need to take that shard offline to change the primary shard's number and other static settings.

DISABLING AUTO-CREATION FOR AN INDEX FEATURE

As mentioned earlier, Elasticsearch lets us block the automatic creation of indexes by setting the action.auto_create_index attribute to false (the default is true). We can tweak this setting to modify the flag's value by invoking a cluster-wide property change using the cluster settings API. The following listing disables the feature.

Listing 6.2   Disabling automatic creation of indexes

```
PUT _cluster/settings          ◁────┐   Updates the settings
{                                    │   across the whole cluster
  "persistent": {            ◁───────────┐
    "action.auto_create_index":false  ◁──┐   The changes can be
  }                                       │   persistent or transient.
}                          Shuts down auto-creation
```

The persistent property indicates that the settings will be permanent. On the other hand, using the transient property saves the settings only until the next reboot of the Elasticsearch server.

While disabling this feature sounds cool, in reality, doing so is not advisable. We are restricting automatic creation on *any* index, but an application or Kibana may need to create an index for administrative purposes; Kibana often creates hidden indexes. (A dot placed in front of an index name is treated as a hidden index: .user_profiles, .admin etc.)

Rather than switching off the automatic index creation altogether, there is a way to tweak this property beyond binary options. We can instead provide a selective set of indexes via comma-separated regular expressions that allow (or disallow) this change. Here's an example:

```
action.auto_create_index: [".admin*, cars*, "*books*", "-x*","-y*","+z*"]
```

This setting allows the automatic creation of hidden indexes with admin as the prefix, as well as any index prefixed with cars or books and those following the plus sign (+). However, this setting does not allow any index starting with x or y to be automatically created because the minus sign (-) indicates that automatic index creation is disallowed. It also means any other index that doesn't match this pattern will not be instantiated automatically. For example, if we try to index a document into the flights index, index creation will fail because the index name doesn't match the regular expressions we just defined (more on this in a bit). Here's the exception issued by the engine:

```
no such index [flights] and [action.auto_create_index]
([.admin*, cars*, *books*, -x*,-y*,+z*]) doesn't match
```

Allowing the server to create the index fosters a rapid development process. However, we rarely go into production without tweaking some of these properties. For example, we may decide to have a strategy of 10 primary shards with 2 replicas per shard, in which case we must change the settings (it would be disastrous to design a search service with just one primary shard). Also, as we learned in chapter 4, Elasticsearch may not derive the correct data types correctly based on the document's field values. Incorrect data types lead to setbacks during search operations.

Fortunately, Elasticsearch allows us to create indexes to meet our requirements by letting us configure and instantiate them explicitly as we require. Before we jump into developing custom indexes, we need to know about index configurations, discussed in the next section.

INDEX CONFIGURATIONS

Every index is made of a configuration consisting of mappings, settings, and aliases, regardless of whether it was created automatically or explicitly. We covered mappings in chapter 4; we recap here and present two other configurations:

- *Mappings*—Mapping is the process of creating a schema definition. Data that is stored usually has multiple data types associated with its fields, such as `text`, `keyword`, `long`, `date`, and so on. Elasticsearch consults the mapping definitions to apply appropriate rules for analyzing incoming data before storing it for efficient and effective searching. For example, the following snippet sets the mapping for the `cars_index_with_sample_mapping` index:

```
PUT cars_index_with_sample_mapping
{
  "mappings": {
    "properties": {
      "make":{
        "type": "text"
      }
    }
  }
}
```

We can issue the `GET cars_index_with_sample_mapping/_mapping` command to fetch the schema for our newly created `cars_index_with_sample_mapping` index.

- *Settings*—Every index comes with a set of configuration settings, such as number of shards and replicas, refresh rate, compression codec, and others. A few settings (called *dynamic settings*) can be tweaked on a live index at runtime. Other settings (*static settings*) are applied to an index in a non-operational mode. We look at these two types shortly. The next listing configures an index with a few settings.

Listing 6.3   Creating an index with custom settings

```
PUT cars_index_with_sample_settings          ◁─┐  Creates
{                                               │  the index
  "settings": {          ◁──────────┐  Applies
    "number_of_replicas": 3,        │  the settings
    "codec": "best_compression"
  }
}
```

Invoking GET cars_index_with_sample_settings/_settings fetches the settings for this index.

- *Aliases*—Aliases are alternate names given to indexes. An alias can point to a single or multiple indexes. For example, an alias named my_cars_aliases could point to all car indexes. We can also execute queries on aliases as if we are running them on individual aliases. This code shows how to create an alias.

Listing 6.4   Creating an index with an alias

```
PUT cars_index_with_sample_alias                    ◄─┐   Creates
{                                                     │   the index
  "aliases": {                         ◄──────────────────┐
    "alias_for_cars_index_with_sample_alias": {}  ◄──┐     Declares the aliases object
  }                                                  │     to configure the alias
}                                           The alias itself
```

We can issue GET cars_index_with_sample_alias/_alias to fetch the alias for this index.

When we explicitly create an index, we can set mappings, settings, and aliases up front. This way, the index is instantiated with all the required configurations in place. We can, of course, modify some of these configurations at runtime (we can tweak *closed* [non-operational] indexes, too). In the next section, we see how to set these configurations on explicitly created indexes.

6.2.2   *Creating indexes explicitly*

Indexes created implicitly are seldom ready for production configurations. Creating an index explicitly means we are expected to set custom configurations. We can direct Elasticsearch to configure an index with the required mappings and settings, as well as aliases, rather than depending on the defaults.

We already know that creating an index is easy: simply issue PUT <index_name>. This command creates a new index with the default configuration (similar to the index created when a document is indexed for the first time). For example, PUT cars creates a cars index, and issuing GET cars returns the index. Let's see how we can manage these indexes with custom configurations.

6.2.3   *Indexes with custom settings*

Every index can be instantiated with settings (default or custom) during creation. We can also change some settings when the index is still in operation. For this purpose, Elasticsearch exposes the _settings API to update the settings on a live index. However, as we mentioned, not all properties can be altered on a live index—only dynamic properties. That brings us to a brief discussion of the two types of index settings, static and dynamic:

- *Static settings*—Static settings are those that are (and can be) applied during index creation and cannot be changed while the index is in operation. These are properties like the number of shards, compression codec, data checks on startup, and so on. If we want to change the static settings of a live index, we must close the index to reapply the settings or re-create the index with new settings.

It is always best to instantiate an index with the required static settings because applying them as an afterthought requires the index to be shut down. Having said that, there are ways to manage index upgrades (reindexing is one form of an upgrade) with zero downtime (we looked at the re-indexing feature in the last chapter—section 5.7).

- *Dynamic settings*—Dynamic settings can be applied on a live (operational) index. For example, we can change properties like the number of replicas, allowing or disallowing writes, refresh intervals, and others on indexes that are in operation.

A handful of settings fall in both camps, so having a high-level understanding of each type helps in the long run. Let's see how we can instantiate an index with some static settings.

NOTE You can consult the official documentation to learn more about the static and dynamic settings Elasticsearch supports: http://mng.bz/1qXR.

We want to create an index with these properties: three shards with five replicas per shard, the compression codec, the maximum number of script fields, and the refresh interval. To apply these configuration settings to our index, we use a `settings` object.

Listing 6.5 Creating an index with custom settings

```
PUT cars_with_custom_settings          ◁──── Creates an index
{                                             with custom settings
    "settings":{                        ◁──── The settings object encloses
        "number_of_shards":3,                 the required properties.
        "number_of_replicas":5,           ──────> Sets the number
        "codec": "best_compression",              of replicas to 5
        "max_script_fields":128,        ◁──── Changes the compression
        "refresh_interval": "60s"       ◁──   from its default value
    }
}
```

Sets the number of shards to 3

Changes the refresh interval from its default of 1 second

Increases the maximum number of script fields from its default of 32

We instruct Elasticsearch to create an index with the settings we think are essential based on our requirements. Issuing the `GET cars_with_custom_settings` command fetches the details of the index, reflecting the custom settings for shards and replicas that we set a moment ago.

As mentioned, some settings are written in stone once the index is live (static settings), and others (dynamic settings) can be changed on a running index. If we try to change any of the static properties (for example, the `number_of_shards` property) on a live index, Elasticsearch throws an exception saying that it can't update non-dynamic settings. We can update the dynamic settings using the `_settings` endpoint, as shown in the following listing.

Listing 6.6   Updating dynamic property on an index

```
PUT cars_with_custom_settings/_settings
{
  "settings": {
    "number_of_replicas": 2
  }
}
```

The `number_of_replicas` property is dynamic, so it doesn't matter if the index is live; the property is applied instantly.

> **NOTE** Elasticsearch does not allow us to change the shard count once the index is operational. There is a simple, yet valid reason for this: a document's home is derived by this routing function: `shard_home = hash(doc_ID) % number_of_shards`. The routing function is dependent on the number of shards, so modifying the shard count (i.e., changing the `number_of_shards`) would break the routing function because existing documents might be misplaced or incorrectly assigned to a shard.

If we want to reconfigure indexes with new settings, we must carry out a few steps:

1. Close the current index (the index cannot support read/write operations).
2. Create a new index with the new settings.
3. Migrate the data from the old index to the new index (reindexing operation).
4. Repoint the alias to the new index (assuming the index has an existing alias).

We have seen reindexing operations in the last chapter (Section 5.7) in action. We also have a section on reindexing data with zero downtime discussed in section 6.2.3.

Fetching configurational settings is a straightforward job: simply issue a GET request.

Listing 6.7   Fetching the settings of an index

```
GET cars_with_custom_settings/_settings
```

We can also fetch settings of multiple indexes by using comma-separated indexes or wildcard patterns on the index names. The following listing shows how to do this (the code is available with the book's files).

Listing 6.8   Fetching the settings of multiple indexes at once

```
GET cars1,cars2,cars3/_settings        ⟵  Fetches multiple
GET cars*/_settings        ⟵              index settings

                                Fetches the settings for the index
                                identified with a wildcard (*)
```

We can also get a single attribute. For example, this listing shows a request that fetches the number of shards.

Listing 6.9   Fetching a single attribute

```
GET cars_with_custom_settings/_settings/index.number_of_shards
```

Here, the properties are enclosed in an inner object `index`, so we must prefix the attribute with the top-level object like this: `index.<attribute_name>`.

6.2.4   Indexes with mappings

In addition to settings, we can provide field mappings when creating an index. This is how we create a schema for our data model. The following listing shows the mechanism to create an index with a mapping definition for a `car` type (it's actually `cars_with_mappings` index, but for brevity, we can assume the index considers `car` entities) with `make`, `model`, and `registration_year` attributes.

Listing 6.10   Creating an index with field mappings for a `car` document

```
PUT cars_with_mappings
{
  "mappings": {              ◁──┐ The mappings object
    "properties": {                encloses the properties.  ◁── The fields with car data
      "make":{                                                    types are declared here.
        "type": "text"        ◁──┐ Declares make
      },                            as a text type
      "model":{
        "type": "text"
      },                                 ◁──┐ Declares registration_year as
      "registration_year":{                   a date type
        "type": "date",
        "format": "dd-MM-yyyy"     ◁──┐ The field's
      }                                 custom format
    }
  }
}
```

Of course, we can also combine settings and mappings. The next listing shows this approach.

Listing 6.11   Creating an index with both settings and mappings

```
PUT cars_with_settings_and_mappings     ◁──┐ Index with both
{                                            settings and mappings
  "settings": {                ◁──┐ Settings on
    "number_of_replicas": 3        the index
  },
  "mappings": {          ◁──┐ Mappings schema
    "properties": {            definition
      "make":{
```

```
      "type": "text"
    },
    "model":{
      "type": "text"
    },
    "registration_year":{
      "type": "date",
      "format": "dd-MM-yyyy"
    }
  }
 }
}
```

Now that we know how to set up an index with settings and mappings, the final piece in the jigsaw is to create an alias.

6.2.5   *Index with aliases*

Aliases are alternate names given to indexes for various purposes such as searching or aggregating data from multiple indexes (as a single alias) or enabling zero downtime during reindexing. Once we create an alias, we can use it for indexing, querying, and all other purposes as if it were an index. Aliases are handy during development as well as in production. We can also group multiple indexes and assign an alias to them so we can write queries against a single alias rather than a dozen indexes.

To create an index similar to the one we saw when configuring the index with settings and mappings (listing 6.11), we can set the alias information in an `aliases` object.

> **Listing 6.12   Creating an alias using an `aliases` object**

```
PUT cars_for_aliases          ◁──┐ Creates an index
{                                 │ with an alias
  "aliases": {
    "my_new_cars_alias": {}   ◁──┐ Points the alias
  }                               │ to the index
}
```

However, there's another way to create aliases, rather than using the index APIs: using an alias API. Elasticsearch exposes the alias API, and the syntax is as follows (check the `_alias` endpoint highlighted in bold):

```
PUT|POST <index_name>/_alias/<alias_name>
```

Let's create an alias called `my_cars_alias` that points to our `cars_for_aliases` index.

> **Listing 6.13   Creating an alias using an `_alias` endpoint**

```
PUT cars_for_aliases/_alias/my_cars_alias
```

As shown in figure 6.2, `my_cars_alias` is the alternate (second) name of the `cars_for_aliases` index. All query operations performed on the index so far can be redirected to `my_cars_alias` going forward. For example, we can index a document or search on this alias, as shown in the figure.

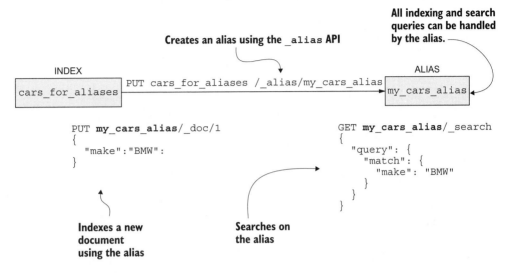

Figure 6.2   Creating an alias for an existing index

We can also create a single alias pointing to multiple indexes (see figure 6.3), including indexes provided with a wildcard. Listing 6.14 shows the code that creates an alias (`multi_cars_alias`). This, in turn, points to multiple indexes (`cars1, cars2, cars3`). Note that one of these indexes must be a write index.

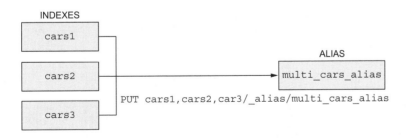

Figure 6.3   Creating an alias pointing to multiple indexes

Listing 6.14   Creating a single alias pointing to multiple indexes

```
PUT cars1,cars2,cars3/_alias/multi_cars_alias
```
◁── **Comma-separated indexes list**

When creating an alias pointing to multiple indexes, at least one index must have an `is_write_index` property set to `true`. For example, this snippet creates a `cars3` index with `is_write_index` enabled:

```
PUT cars3
{
  "aliases": {
    "cars_alias": {
    "is_write_index":true
    }
  }
}
```

Similarly, we can create an alias pointing to multiple indexes using a wildcard (we must make sure one of the indexes has an `is_write_index` property set to `true`).

Listing 6.15 Creating an alias with a wildcard

```
PUT cars*/_alias/wildcard_cars_alias        ◁─┐  All indexes prefixed
                                              │  with cars
```

Once the aliases are created, getting the index (`GET <alias_name>`) details will reflect the aliases defined on the index. `GET cars` returns the index with all aliases created on that index (in addition to all the mappings and settings).

Listing 6.16 Fetching aliases, settings, and mappings for an index

```
GET cars
```

Now that we understand the mechanism of creating aliases, let's see how to fetch the alias details. Similar to settings and mappings, we can send a `GET` request to the `_alias` endpoint to fetch the details of the aliases.

Listing 6.17 Getting an alias on a single index

```
GET my_cars_alias/_alias
```

Of course, we can also extend the same command to multiple aliases.

Listing 6.18 Fetching aliases associated with multiple indexes

```
GET all_cars_alias,my_cars_alias/_alias
```

MIGRATING DATA WITH ZERO DOWNTIME USING ALIASES

Configuration settings for indexes in production may have to be updated with newer properties, perhaps due to a new business requirement or a technical enhancement (or to fix a bug). The new properties may not be compatible with the existing data in that index, in which case we can create an index with new settings and migrate the data from the old index into the brand-new index.

This may sound well and good, but one potential problem is that queries that were written against the old index (GET cars/_search { .. }, for example) need to be updated because they now need to run against a new index (cars_new). If these queries are hardcoded in the application code, we may need a hotfix release to production.

Say we have an index called vintage_cars with data about vintage cars, and we are required to update the index. Here's where we can lean on aliasing; we can devise a strategy with an alias in mind. By executing the following steps (also illustrated in figure 6.4), we can probably achieve the migration with zero downtime:

1 Create an alias called vintage_cars_alias to refer to the current index vintage_cars.

2 Because the new properties are incompatible with the existing index, create a new index, vintage_cars_new, with the new settings.

3 Copy (i.e., reindex) the data from the old index (vintage_cars) to the new index (vintage_cars_new).

4 Re-create the existing alias (vintage_cars_alias), which pointed to the old index, to refer to the new index. (See the next section.) Thus, vintage_cars_alias now points to vintage_cars_new.

5 All queries that were executed against the vintage_cars_alias are now carried out on the new index.

6 Delete the old index (vintage_cars) when reindexing and releasing have been shown to work.

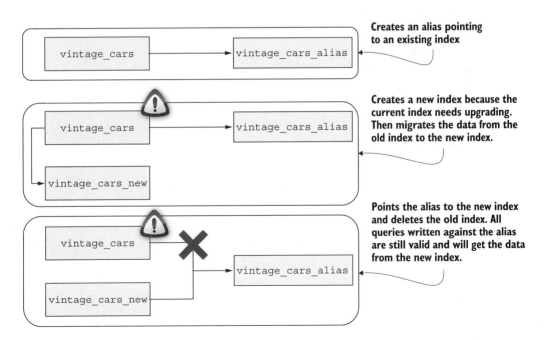

Figure 6.4 Achieving migration with zero downtime

Queries executed on the alias will now fetch data from the new index without the application being bounced. Thus, we've achieved zero downtime.

MULTIPLE ALIASING OPERATIONS USING THE _ALIASES API

In addition to working with aliases using the _alias API, we can use another API to work on multiple aliasing actions: the _aliases API. It combines several actions, such as adding and removing aliases and deleting the indexes. Whereas the _alias API is used to create an alias, the _aliases API helps create multiple actions on indexes related to aliasing.

The code in listing 6.19 performs two distinct aliasing operations on two indexes: it removes an alias pointing to an old index and repoints (via the add action) the same alias to a new index (see the previous section to understand the need for doing this).

Listing 6.19 Performing multiple aliasing operations

```
POST _aliases              ◁┐   Uses the _aliases API to
{                           │   execute multiple actions
  "actions": [         ◁┐        Lists the
    {                    │        individual actions
      "remove": {  ◁───────────  Removes the alias that
        "index": "vintage_cars",  │  points to an old index
        "alias": "vintage_cars_alias"
      }
    },
    {                    Adds an alias that
      "add": {  ◁─┘     points to a new index
        "index": "vintage_cars_new",
        "alias": "vintage_cars_alias"
      }
    }
  ]
}
```

We remove an alias, vintage_cars_alias, that was originally created for the vintage_cars index. We then reassign it to the vintage_cars_new index.

With the _aliases API, we can also delete the alias pointing to the existing index and assign it to a new index when the new index is ready after migrating the data. And we can create an alias for multiple indexes using the same _aliases API by using the indexes parameter to set up the list of indexes. The following listing shows how to do that.

Listing 6.20 Creating an alias pointing to multiple indexes

```
POST _aliases
{
  "actions": [
    {
      "add": {
```

```
            "indices": ["vintage_cars","power_cars","rare_cars","luxury_cars"],
            "alias": "high_end_cars_alias"
        }
      }
   ]
}
```

Here, `actions` creates an alias called `high_end_cars_alias` that points to four car indexes (`vintage_cars`, `power_cars`, `rare_cars`, and `luxury_cars`). Now that we've mastered the art of creating and aliasing indexes, let's look at how to read them.

6.3   Reading indexes

So far, the indexes we've looked at are *public* indexes—those usually created by users or applications to hold data. We discuss public indexes in the next section and then look at another type of index: the hidden index.

6.3.1   Reading public indexes

We can fetch the details of an index by simply issuing a GET command (like GET cars), as we've already seen. The response provides mappings, settings, and aliases as JSON objects. The response can also return the details of multiple indexes. Say we want to return the details of three indexes: `cars1`, `cars2`, and `cars3`. The following listing shows the way forward.

Listing 6.21   Getting index configurations for multiple indexes

```
GET cars1,cars2,cars3        ◁──┐  Retrieves details
                                 │  of three indexes
```

> **NOTE**   Kibana complains if the multiple-indexes URL has a space between the indexes. For example, GET `cars1,  cars2` will fail because there's a space after the comma. Be sure multiple indexes are separated by just a comma.

This command returns relevant information for all three indexes, but providing a long list of comma-separated indexes does not necessarily sit well with developers. Instead, we can use wildcards if our indexes have a pattern. For example, the code in the following listing fetches all indexes starting with the letters *ca*.

Listing 6.22   Getting multiple index configurations with a wildcard

```
GET ca*    ◁──┐  Returns all indexes
              │  prefixed with ca
```

Using the same principle with comma-separated indexes and wildcards, we can get the configurations for specific indexes. For example, the following listing gets all indexes prefixed with *mov* and *stu* (short for *movies* and *students*).

> **Listing 6.23 Fetching configurations for specific indexes**

```
GET mov*,stu*
```

Although all these GET commands fetch the aliases, mappings, and settings of the specified indexes, there is yet another way to return that information. Say we want to fetch an individual configuration for a specific index. We can use the relevant APIs to do so.

> **Listing 6.24 Getting individual configurations for an index**

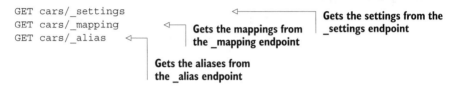

```
GET cars/_settings
GET cars/_mapping
GET cars/_alias
```
Gets the settings from the _settings endpoint

Gets the mappings from the _mapping endpoint

Gets the aliases from the _alias endpoint

These GET commands return the specified configurations for a public index. Let's look at retrieving this information for a hidden index next.

> **NOTE** To determine whether the index exists in the cluster, we can use the command HEAD <index_name>. For example, HEAD cars returns the error code 200–OK if the index exists and the error 404–Not Found if the index doesn't exist.

6.3.2 *Reading hidden indexes*

As mentioned, there are two types of indexes: the normal (public) indexes that we've worked with so far and hidden indexes. Similar to hidden folders in computer file systems, which are prefixed with a dot (.etc, .git, .bash, etc.), hidden indexes are usually reserved for system management. They are used for Kibana, application health, and so forth. For example we can create a hidden index by executing the command PUT .old_cars (note the dot in front of the index name).

> **NOTE** Although we can use hidden indexes mimicking public indexes for operational use (because Elasticsearch has no checks and balances in version 8 and earlier), this will change in future versions. All hidden indexes will be reserved for system-related work. With this change in mind, my advice is to be mindful of creating hidden indexes for business-related data.

The GET _all or GET * call fetches all indexes, including hidden indexes. For example, figure 6.5 shows the result of issuing a GET _all command: it returns the entire index list, including hidden indexes (indexes with a dot in front of the name).

Now that we know how to create and read indexes, we can, if the need arises, execute delete operations on them. This is discussed in detail in the next section.

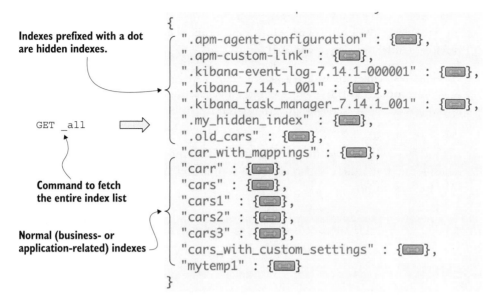

Figure 6.5   Fetching a list of all public and hidden indexes

6.4   *Deleting indexes*

Deleting an existing index is straightforward: a DELETE action on the index (like DELETE <index_name>) deletes the index permanently. For example, issuing a DELETE cars command deletes the cars index when the command is issued, meaning all the documents in that index are gone—forever—including any settings, mapping schemas, and aliases!

DELETING MULTIPLE INDEXES

We can also delete multiple indexes. Append a comma-separated list of indexes to delete them simultaneously.

Listing 6.25   Deleting multiple indexes

```
DELETE cars,movies,order
```

We can delete indexes using a wildcard pattern as well: DELETE *. However, if we also want to delete hidden indexes, we must use the _all endpoint: DELETE _all. Note that we must set the action.destructive_requires_name property to false when attempting to delete indexes with a wildcard or _all:

```
PUT _cluster/settings
{
 "transient": {
   "action.destructive_requires_name":false
 }
}
```

The `action.destructive_requires_name` property is set to `true` by default, so you may receive a "Wildcard expressions or all indices are not allowed" error when trying to delete indexes using a wildcard or `_all`.

> **WARNING**   Deleting indexes accidentally can result in permanent data loss. When you are working with DELETE APIs, caution is advised, because accidental invocations can destabilize the system.

DELETING ONLY ALIASES

In addition to deleting the whole index, which internally deletes mappings, settings, aliases, and data, there's also a mechanism to delete only aliases. We use the `_alias` API for this purpose.

Listing 6.26   Deleting an alias explicitly

```
DELETE cars/_alias/cars_alias        ◁──┐  Deletes
                                         │  cars_alias
```

Deleting an index is a destructive task because data is purged permanently. Needless to say, before issuing this operation, be certain you really want to delete the index and all its configurations and data. Next, let's look at some less destructive operations: closing and opening indexes.

6.5   *Closing and opening indexes*

Depending on the use case, we can close or open an index—the index is put on hold for further indexing or searching when it is closed. Let's look at the options for closing an index.

6.5.1   *Closing indexes*

Closing an index means exactly that: it is closed for business, and any operations on it will cease. There will be no indexing of documents or search and analytic queries.

> **NOTE**   Because closed indexes are not available for business operations, you must take care before closing an index. Doing so could break the system if indexes are closed but referenced in your code. This is one good reason to depend on aliases rather than real indexes!

The close index API (`_close`) shuts down the index. The syntax is POST `<index_name>/_close`. For example, the following listing closes the `cars` index (until further notice), and thus any operations on it result in errors.

Listing 6.27   Closing the `cars` index indefinitely

```
POST cars/_close
```

This code closes the index for business. No more read/write operations are allowed on it.

Closing all or multiple indexes

We can close multiple indexes by using comma-separated indexes (including wildcards).

Listing 6.28 Closing multiple indexes

```
POST cars1,*mov*,students*/_close
```

Finally, if we want to halt all live operations on indexes in a cluster, we can issue a close index API call (`_close`) with either `_all` or `*`, as shown in the next listing (be sure the `action.destructive_requires_name` propertyliases is set to `false` to avoid a "wildcard expression not allowed" error).

Listing 6.29 Closing all indexes

```
POST */_close
```

Closes all indexes in the cluster

Avoiding destabilizing the system

As you can imagine, closing (or opening) *all* indexes may destabilize the system. It's one of those super admin capabilities that, if executed without forethought, can lead to disastrous results, including taking down the system or making it irreparable. Closing indexes blocks read/write operations and thus minimizes the overhead of maintaining cluster shards. The resources are purged, and memory is reclaimed on the closed indexes.

Can we disable the ability to close indexes? Yes, we can disable the close feature if we never want to close any indexes. By disabling this functionality, we allow indexes to be operational forever (unless we delete them). To do this, we set the `cluster.indices.close.enable` property to `false` (it is `true` by default) on the cluster using the configuration settings.

Listing 6.30 Disabling the closing indexes feature

```
PUT _cluster/settings
{
  "persistent": {
    "cluster.indices.close.enable":false
  }
}
```

6.5.2 Opening indexes

Opening an index kick-starts the shards back into business; once they're ready, they are open for indexing and searching. We can open a closed index by simply calling the `_open` API.

Listing 6.31 Putting the index back into operation

```
POST cars/_open
```

Once the command is executed successfully, the `cars` index is available instantly. Similar to the `_close` API, the `_open` API can be invoked on multiple indexes, including specifying indexes using wildcards.

So far, we've worked with several index operations and created indexes with custom mappings and settings, albeit individually. While this method is effective in development, it is far from ideal in production environments—it can be cumbersome to create a set of indexes over and over. Also, we may not want engineers to create indexes with an unexpected number of shards or replicas, which could destabilize our cluster. This is where we can use index templates.

Tighter control and business standards are expected as part of an overall indexing strategy, so Elasticsearch provides index templates to assist in developing indexes with an organizational strategy in mind. We can use this feature to apply configurations at scale, as discussed in the next section.

6.6   *Index templates*

Copying the same settings across various indexes, especially one by one, is tedious and sometimes error-prone. If we define an indexing template with a schema up front, a new index will be implicitly molded from this schema if the index name matches the template. Thus, any new index will follow the same settings and be homogenous across the organization, and DevOps won't need to repeatedly advocate for optimal settings with individual teams in the organization.

One use case for an indexing template is creating a set of patterns based on environments. For example, indexes for a development environment may have 3 shards and 2 replicas, while indexes for a production environment have 10 shards with 5 replicas each.

With index templating, we can create a template with predefined patterns and configurations. We can have a set of mappings, settings, and aliases bundled up in this template, along with an index name. Then, when we create a new index, if the index name matches the pattern name, the template is applied. Additionally, we can create a template based on a *glob* (global command) pattern, such as wildcards, prefixes, and so on.

NOTE   The *glob* pattern is commonly used in computer software to represent filename extensions (*.txt, *.cmd, *.bat, and so on).

Elasticsearch upgraded its template functionality beginning with version 7.8, and this newer version is abstract and much more reusable. (If you are interested in index templates from prior versions, see the official documentation for details.) Index templates are classified into two categories: *composable* index templates (or simply *index templates*) and *component* templates. As the name indicates, composable index templates are composed of zero or more component templates. An index template can also exist on its own without being associated with any component templates. Such index templates can contain all the required template features (mappings, settings, and aliases). They are used as independent templates when creating an index with a pattern.

Although a component template is itself a template, it's not very useful if it's not associated with an index template. However, it can be associated with many index templates. Usually, we develop a component template (for example, specifying the codecs for a development environment) and attach it to various indexes via the composable index templates simultaneously. This is shown in figure 6.6.

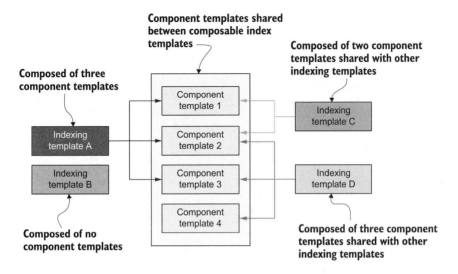

Figure 6.6   Composable (index) templates are composed of component templates.

In the figure, indexing templates A, C, and D share component templates between themselves (for example, component template 2 is used by all three indexing templates). Indexing template B is a standalone template with no component templates.

We can create an index template with no component templates. This brings us to certain rules when creating templates:

- An index created with configurations explicitly takes precedence over the configurations defined in the index or component templates. This means if you create an index with explicit settings, don't expect them to be overridden by the templates.
- Legacy templates carry a lower priority than composable templates.

6.6.1   Creating composable (index) templates

To create an index template, we use an `_index_template` endpoint, providing all the required mappings, settings, and aliases as an index pattern in this template. Let's say our requirement is to create a template for cars, represented with a pattern having wildcards: `*cars*`, as shown in listing 6.32 This template has certain properties and settings, such as `created_by` and `created_at` properties, as well as shards and replica numbers. Any index matched with this template during its creation inherits the configurations defined in the template. For example, new_cars, sports_cars, and vintage_cars indexes have created_by and created_at properties, as well as shards and replicas 1 and 3, respectively, if these are defined in the template.

Listing 6.32   Creating an index template

```
PUT _index_template/cars_template
{
  "index_patterns": ["*cars*"],
  "priority": 1,
  "template": {
    "mappings": {
      "properties":{
        "created_at":{
          "type":"date"
        },
        "created_by":{
          "type":"text"
        }
      }
    }
  }
}
```

When we execute this command (you may get a deprecation warning—ignore it for now), the template is created with the index pattern *cars*. When we create a new index, if the name of the new index (say, vintage_cars) matches the pattern (*cars*), the index is created with the configuration defined in the template. When the index matches the given pattern, the templated configurations are applied automatically.

Template priority

An index template carries a priority: a positive number defined when creating the template. The higher the priority, the higher the precedence. Priority is useful when we have similar or the same settings in two different templates. If an index matches more than one index template, the one with higher priority is used. For example, cars_template_feb21 overrides cars_template_mar21 in the following code (although the names suggest the other way around!):

```
POST _index_template/cars_template_mar21
{
  "index_patterns": ["*cars*"],
  "priority": 20,          ◁── Lower-priority
  "template": { ... }          index template
}
POST _index_template/cars_template_feb21
{
  "index_patterns": ["*cars*"],
```

```
    "priority": 30,          ◁─┐  Matching template, but
    "template": { ... }        │  with a higher priority
}
```

When multiple templates match the indexes being created, Elasticsearch applies all the settings from all matching templates, but the one with higher priority gets to the top. In the previous example, if `cars_template_mar21` has a codec that defines `best_compression`, it's overridden by a codec with a default value (defined in the `cars_template_feb21` template). That's because the latter template has a higher priority.

Now that we know more about index templates, let's look at reusable component templates.

6.6.2   *Creating component templates*

If you are from a DevOps background, at some point you've probably had a requirement to create indexes with a preset configuration for each environment. Rather than manually applying each configuration, you can create a component template for each environment.

A component template is nothing but a reusable block of configurations that we can use to make more index templates. However, component templates are of no value unless they are associated with index templates. They are exposed via a `_component_template` endpoint. Let's see how this fits together.

Let's say we need to create a template for a development environment that should have three primary shards with three replicas per shard. The first step is to declare and execute a component template with this configuration.

Listing 6.33   Developing a component template

```
POST _component_template/dev_settings_component_template
{
  "template":{
    "settings":{
      "number_of_shards":3,
      "number_of_replicas":3
    }
  }
}
```

In this listing, we use the `_component_template` endpoint to create a template. The body of the request holds the template information in a `template` object. Once executed, the `dev_settings_component_template` becomes available for use elsewhere in the index templates. Note that this template does not define an index pattern; it's simply a code block that configures some properties for us.

In the same way, let's create another template. This time, let's define a mapping schema.

Listing 6.34 Component template with a mapping schema

```
POST _component_template/dev_mapping_component_template
{
  "template": {
    "mappings": {
      "properties": {
        "created_by": {
          "type": "text"
        },
        "version": {
          "type": "float"
        }
      }
    }
  }
}
```

The `dev_mapping_component_template` consists of a mapping schema predefined with two properties, `created_by` and `version`.

Now that we have two component templates, the next step is to put them to use. We can do this by letting an index template for, say, `cars`, use them.

Listing 6.35 Index template composed of component templates

```
POST _index_template/composed_cars_template
{
  "index_patterns": ["*cars*"],
  "priority": 200,
  "composed_of": ["dev_settings_component_template",
                  "dev_mapping_component_template"]
}
```

The highlighted `composed_of` tag is a collection of all component templates we want to apply. In this case, we choose the settings and mappings component templates.

After the script is executed, if we create an index with *cars* in the index name (`vintage_cars`, `my_cars_old`, `cars_sold_in_feb`, etc.), the index is created with the configuration derived from both component templates. To create a similar pattern in a production environment, for example, we can create a composable template with a `prod_*` version of the component templates.

So far, we have worked with CRUD operations on indexes and instantiated those indexes using templates. However, we have no visibility on index performance. As the next section discusses, Elasticsearch provides statistics on data that's been indexed, deleted, and queried.

6.7 *Monitoring and managing indexes*

Elasticsearch provides detailed statistics on the data that goes into indexes as well as what is pulled out. It provides APIs to generate reports such as the number of documents an index holds, deleted documents, merge and flush statistics, and more. In the next couple of sections, we review APIs to fetch these statistics.

6.7.1   Index statistics

Every index generates statistics such as the total number of documents it has, a count of documents deleted, the shard's memory, get and search request data, and so on. The _stats API helps us retrieve index statistics for both primary and replica shards.

The following listing shows the mechanism to fetch statistics for a `cars` index by invoking the _stats endpoint. Figure 6.7 shows the statistics returned by this call.

> **Listing 6.36   Fetching the statistics of an index**

```
GET cars/_stats
```

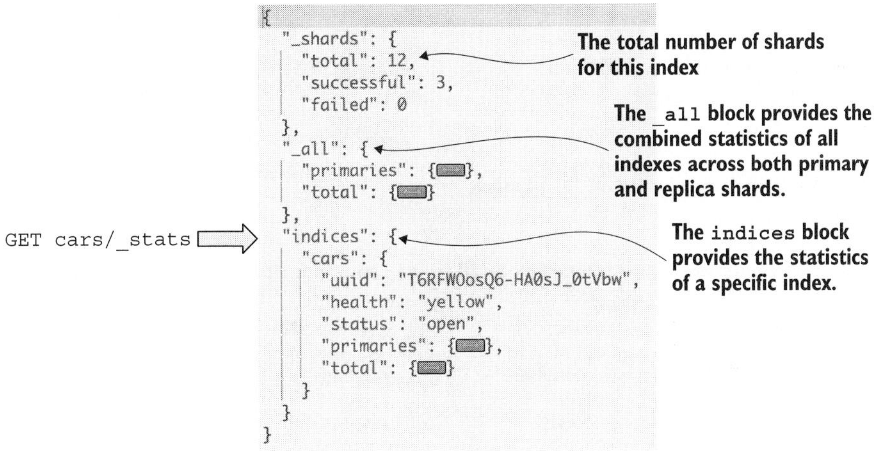

```
{
  "_shards": {
    "total": 12,              ◀——  The total number of shards
    "successful": 3,               for this index
    "failed": 0
  },
  "_all": {               ◀——  The _all block provides the
    "primaries": {▭},           combined statistics of all
    "total": {▭}                indexes across both primary
  },                            and replica shards.
  "indices": {            ◀——  The indices block
    "cars": {                   provides the statistics
      "uuid": "T6RFWOosQ6-HA0sJ_0tVbw",   of a specific index.
      "health": "yellow",
      "status": "open",
      "primaries": {▭},
      "total": {▭}
    }
  }
}
```

GET cars/_stats ▭⟹

Figure 6.7   Statistics for a `cars` index

The response includes a `total` attribute, which is the total number of shards (primary and replica) associated with this index. As we have only one primary shard, the `successful` attribute points to this shard count.

The response consists of two blocks:

- The _all block, with the aggregated statistics for all indexes combined
- The `indices` block, with statistics for individual indexes (each index in that cluster)

These blocks consist of two buckets of statistics: the `primaries` bucket contains statistics related to just the primary shards, while the `total` bucket indicates statistics for both primary and replica shards. Elasticsearch returns over a dozen statistics (see figure 6.8) that we can find in the response `primaries` and `total` buckets. Table 6.1 describes a few of these statistics.

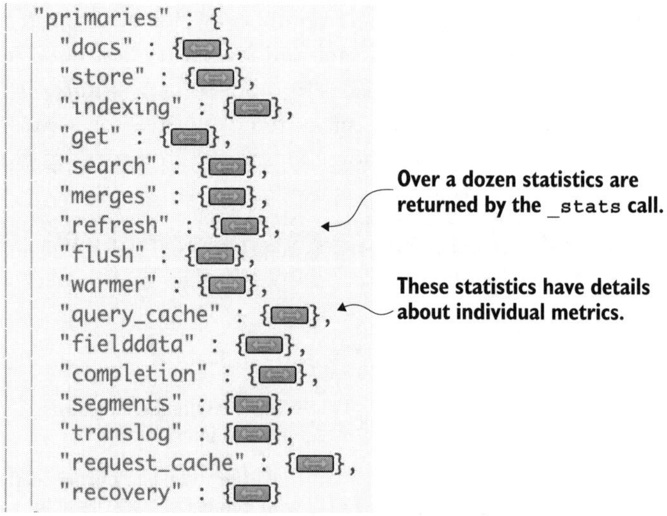

```
"primaries" : {
    "docs" : {▭},
    "store" : {▭},
    "indexing" : {▭},
    "get" : {▭},
    "search" : {▭},
    "merges" : {▭},
    "refresh" : {▭},
    "flush" : {▭},
    "warmer" : {▭},
    "query_cache" : {▭},
    "fielddata" : {▭},
    "completion" : {▭},
    "segments" : {▭},
    "translog" : {▭},
    "request_cache" : {▭},
    "recovery" : {▭}
```

Over a dozen statistics are returned by the `_stats` call.

These statistics have details about individual metrics.

Figure 6.8   Multiple statistics for an index

Table 6.1   Index statistics fetched by a call to the `_stats` endpoint (the list is shortened for brevity)

Statistic	Description
docs	Number of documents in the index and number of documents deleted
store	Size of the index (in bytes)
get	Number of GET operations on the index
search	Search operations including query, scroll, and suggest times.
refresh	Number of refresh operations

There are more statistics, such as indexing, merge, completion, field data, segments, and others, but we've omitted them here due to space constraints. See http://mng.bz/Pzd5 for a complete list of statistics that Elasticsearch exposes via the index statistics APIs.

6.7.2   *Multiple indexes and statistics*

Just as we fetch statistics data on an individual index, we can also fetch statistics on multiple indexes by providing comma-separated index names. The following listing shows the command.

Listing 6.37   Fetching statistics for multiple indexes

```
GET cars1,cars2,cars3/_stats
```

We can also use wildcards on indexes, as shown next.

Listing 6.38   Fetching statistics using wildcards

```
GET cars*/_stats
```

And here is how to get the stats for all the indexes in the cluster (including hidden indexes).

Listing 6.39   Fetching statistics for all indexes in the cluster

```
GET */_stats
```

We may not need to find all the statistics all the time, so we can, for example, find only the certain statistics about segments such as stored fields and terms memory, file size, document count, and so on. The following listing returns the statistics in segments.

Listing 6.40   Segment statistics

```
GET cars/_stats/segments
```

This command returns the following data:

```
"segments" : {
        "count" : 1,
        "memory_in_bytes" : 1564,
        "terms_memory_in_bytes" : 736,
        "stored_fields_memory_in_bytes" : 488,
        "term_vectors_memory_in_bytes" : 0,
        "norms_memory_in_bytes" : 64,
        "points_memory_in_bytes" : 0,
        "doc_values_memory_in_bytes" : 276,
        "index_writer_memory_in_bytes" : 0,
        "version_map_memory_in_bytes" : 0,
        "fixed_bit_set_memory_in_bytes" : 0,
        "max_unsafe_auto_id_timestamp" : -1,
        "file_sizes" : { }
    }
```

While we're on the subject, Elasticsearch provides an index segments API to peek into the lower-level details of segments. Invoking the code GET cars/_segments provides a detailed view of segments managed by Apache Lucene, such as the list of segments and the number of documents (including deleted documents) the segment holds, disk space, whether the segment is searchable, and so on (see figure 6.9). We can also get the segment information across the entire index by invoking the GET _segments call.

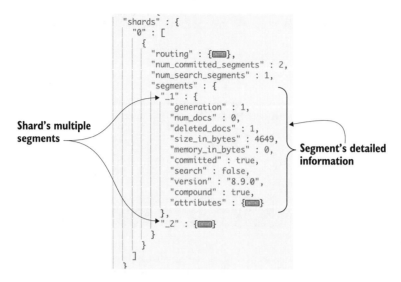

Figure 6.9   Detailed information about every segment in a shard

Sometimes we may need to manage an overgrown index to save space or reduce the infrastructure behind a predominantly dormant index. We can perform such operations using advanced tricks, discussed in detail in the next section.

6.8   Advanced operations

Earlier, we looked at CRUD operations such as creating, reading, and deleting indexes. In addition to such basic operations, we can perform advanced operations like splitting an index to add more shards or downsizing an index by shrinking it or rolling it over periodically (such as daily). Let's review a few advanced operations we can perform on our indices.

6.8.1   Splitting an index

Sometimes indexes are overloaded with data. To avoid the risk of losing data or mitigate slower search query responses, we can redistribute the data onto additional shards. Adding shards to the index optimizes memory and distributes documents evenly.

For example, if an index (cars) with 5 primary shards is overloaded, we can split the index into a new index with more primary shards: say, 15. Expanding an index from a small size to a larger size is called *splitting* the index. Splitting is nothing more than creating a new index with more shards and copying the data from the old index into the new index.

Elasticsearch provides a _split API for splitting an index. There are some rules, such as how many shards a new index can be created with, but first let's see how we can split an index.

Let's say our `all_cars` index was created with two shards, and because the data is growing exponentially, the index is now overloaded. To mitigate the risk of slow queries and degrading performance, we want to create a new index with more space. To do this, we can split the index into a new one with more room and additional primary shards.

Before we invoke the split operation on the `all_cars` index, we must make sure the index is disabled for indexing purposes—that is, we need to change the index to read-only. The following code helps by invoking the `_settings` API.

Listing 6.41   Making sure the index is read-only

```
PUT all_cars/_settings          ◁─┐ Uses the
{                                  │ _settings API
  "settings":{
    "index.blocks.write":"true"  ◁─┐ Closes the index for
  }                                │ writing operations
}
```

Now that the prerequisite of making the index non-operational is complete, we can split it by invoking the `_split` API. This API expects the source and target indexes:

```
POST <source_index>/_split/<target_index>
```

Now, let's split the index into a new index (`all_cars_new`).

Listing 6.42   Splitting the `all_cars` index

```
POST all_cars/_split/all_cars_new  ◁─┐ _split expects a
{                                    │ target index.
  "settings": {
    "index.number_of_shards": 12   ◁─┐ Sets the number of shards
  }                                  │ on the new index
}
```

This request kicks off the splitting process. The splitting operation is synchronous, meaning the client's request waits for a response until the process is completed. Once the split completes, the new index (`all_cars_new`) will have all the data as well as additional space because more shards were added to it.

As mentioned earlier, the splitting operation comes with certain rules and conditions. Let's look at some of those:

- *The target index must not exist before this operation.* In addition to the configuration we provide in the request object while splitting (listing 6.42), an exact copy of the source index is transferred to the target index.
- *The number of shards in the target index must be a multiple of the number of shards in the source index.* If the source index has three primary shards, the target index can be defined with a number of shards that is a multiple of three (three, six, nine, etc.).

- *The target index can never have fewer primary shards than the source's index has.* Remember, splitting allows more room for the index.
- *The target index's node must have adequate space.* Make sure the shards are allocated with the appropriate space.

During the splitting operation, all the configurations (settings, mappings, and aliases) are copied from the source index into the newly created target index. Elasticsearch then moves the source segment's hard links to the target index. Finally, all the documents are rehashed, because the documents' home has changed.

Target's index number must be multiple of source's index number

The target index's number of primary shards must be a multiple of the number of primary shards of the source index. To see what happens, provide a non-multiple number to reset `index.number_of_shards` (to 14: a non-multiple of source's primary shards number, which is 3) as the following query shows:

```
POST all_cars/_split/all_cars_new
{
  "settings": {
    "index.number_of_shards": 14
  }
}
```

Unfortunately, this query throws an exception because we violated the second rule in the previous list. Here's the exception:

```
"reason" : "the number of source shards [3] must be a factor of [14]"
```

Splitting indexes also helps resize a cluster by adding primaries to the original count. The configurations are copied across the source to the target shards. So, other than adding more shards, the split API can't change any settings on the target index. If we just need to increase the number of shards so the data is spread across the newly created indexes, splitting is the best way to go. Also, remember that target indexes must not exist before invoking a splitting operation. Now that we've worked on splitting indexes, let's look at another operation: shrinking an index.

6.8.2 *Shrinking an index*

While splitting an index expands it by adding additional shards for more space, shrinking is the opposite: it reduces the number of shards. Shrinking helps consolidate all the documents spread over various shards into fewer shards. Doing so can help in use cases like these:

- We had one or move indexes during a holiday period, with data spread across numerous shards. Now that the holiday period is over, we wish to reduce the shard count.
- To increase read speed (search throughput), we added data nodes. Once demand subsides, there is no reason to keep all those nodes active.

Let's say we have an index (all_cars) distributed among 50 shards and want to resize it to a single-digit shard count: say, 5 shards. Similar to what we did with a splitting operation, the first step is to ensure that our all_cars index is read-only, so we set the index.blocks.write property to true. We can then readjust the shards to a single node. The code in the following listing shows these actions as prerequisites before shrinking the index.

Listing 6.43   Prerequisites before shrinking the index

```
PUT all_cars/_settings
{
  "settings": {
    "index.blocks.write": true,
    "index.routing.allocation.require._name": "node1"
  }
}
```

Now that the source index is all set for shrinking, we can use the shrink operation. The format is as follows: PUT <source_index>/_shrink/<target_index>. Let's issue the shrink command to shrink the all_cars index.

Listing 6.44   Shrinking the index

```
PUT all_cars/_shrink/all_cars_new          ◁─── Shrinks the
{                                                source index
  "settings":{
    "index.blocks.write":null,             ◁─── Removes the
    "index.routing.allocation.require._name":null,   read-only instruction
    "index.number_of_shards":1,            ◁─── Reduces the
    "index.number_of_replicas":5                 number of shards
  }
}
```

Sets the node name to null ▷ (points to "index.routing.allocation.require._name":null,)

We need to point out a few things in this script. The source index was set with two properties: read-only and the allocation index node name. These settings will be carried over to the new target index if we do not reset them. In the script, we nullify these properties so the target index won't have these restrictions imposed when it's created. We also set the number of shards and replicas on the newly instantiated target index and create a hard link for the target index, pointing to the source index file segments.

> **NOTE** Keep in mind that the number of shards must be smaller than (or equal to) the source index's shard count (after all, we are shrinking the index!). And, yes, as you may have imagined, the target index's shard number must be a factor of the source index's shard number.

While we are here, we can also remove all replicas from the source index so the shrink operation is more manageable. We just need to set the index.number_of_replicas property to zero. Remember that the number_of_replicas property is dynamic, meaning it can be tweaked on a live index.

We must also perform the following actions before shrinking an index:

- *The source index must be switched off (made read-only) for indexing.* Although not mandatory, it is recommended that we also turn off the replicas before shrinking.
- *The target index must not be created or exist before the shrinking action.*
- *All index shards must reside on the same node.* We must set the `index.routing .allocation.require.<node_name>` property on the index with the node name to achieve this.
- *The target index's shard count must be a factor of the source index's shard number.* Our `all_cars` index with 50 shards can only be shrunk to 25, 10, 5, or 2 shards.
- *The target index's node must satisfy the memory requirements.*

We can use shrinking operations when we have many shards but the data is sparsely distributed. As the name suggests, the idea is to reduce the number of shards.

Splitting or shrinking indexes is a nice way to manage them as our data grows. Another advanced operation is to create indexes on a set pattern with the help of a rollover mechanism.

6.8.3 *Rolling over an index alias*

Indexes accumulate data over time. Yes, we can split an index to handle additional data, as we saw earlier. However, splitting simply readjusts the data into additional shards. Elasticsearch provides another mechanism called *rollover*, where the current index is automatically rolled over to a new blank index.

Unlike in a splitting operation, in a rollover, documents are not copied to the new index. The old index becomes read-only, and any new documents are indexed into this rolled-over index from now on. For example, if we have an index `app-000001`, rolling over creates a new index `app-000002`. If we roll over once again, another new index, `app-000003`, is instantiated, and so on.

The rollover operation is frequently used when dealing with time-series data. Time-series data—data generated for a specific period like every day, week, or month—is usually held in an index created for a particular period. Application logs, for example, are created based on the date: `logs-18-sept-21`, `logs-19-sept-21`, and so on.

This will be easy to understand when you see it in action. Let's say we have an index for cars: `cars_2021-000001`. Elasticsearch performs a few steps to roll over this index:

1. Elasticsearch creates an alias pointing to the index (in this case, `cars_2021-000001`). Before it creates the alias, we must ensure that the index is writable by setting `is_write_index` to `true`. The idea is that the alias must have at least one writable backing index.
2. Elasticsearch invokes a rollover command on the alias using the `_rollover` API. This creates a new rollover index (for example, `cars_2021-000002`).

NOTE The trailing suffix (such as `000001`) is a positive number, and Elasticsearch expects the index to be created with it. Elasticsearch can only increment from a positive number; it doesn't matter what the starting number is.

As long as we have a positive integer, Elasticsearch will increment the number and move forward. For example, if we provide my-index-04 or my-index-0004, the next rollover index will be my-index-000005. Elasticsearch automatically pads the suffix with zeros.

We go over these steps in the next couple of sections.

CREATING AN ALIAS FOR ROLLOVER OPERATIONS

The first thing we need to do before a rollover operation is to create an alias pointing to the index we want to roll over. We can use the rollover API for index or data stream aliases. For example, the following listing invokes the _aliases API to create an alias called latest_cars_a for the index cars_2021-000001 (make sure you create this index up front).

Listing 6.45 Creating an alias for an existing index

```
POST _aliases                          ◁─┐  Uses the _aliases API
{                                         │  to invoke an add action
  "actions": [                         ◁─┘
    {                                     ┌─ The add
      "add": {                        ◁─┘   action
        "index": "cars_2021-000001",  ◁─┐ The index we wish to create
        "alias": "latest_cars_a",     ◁─┐ for cars' rollover data
        "is_write_index": true        ◁─┐ Creates the alias
      }                                 │  to the cars index
    }                                   │
  ]                                   ◁─┘ Makes the
}                                         index writable
```

The set of actions ──▷ (points to "actions": [ )

The _aliases API request body expects the add action with an index and its alias defined. It creates the alias latest_cars_a pointing to an existing index, cars_2021-000001, with the POST command.

One important point to note: the alias must point to a writable index—hence we set is_write_index to true in the listing. If the alias points to multiple indexes, at least one must be a writable index. The next step is to roll over the index.

ISSUING A ROLLOVER OPERATION

Now that we have created an alias, the next step is to invoke the rollover API endpoint. Elasticsearch has defined a _rollover API for this purpose.

Listing 6.46 Rolling over the index

```
POST latest_cars_a/_rollover
```

The _rollover endpoint is invoked on the alias, not the index. Once the call is successful, a new index, cars_2021-000002, is created (*-000001 is incremented by 1). Here is the response to the call.

Listing 6.47   Response from a `_rollover` call

```
{
  "acknowledged" : true,
  "shards_acknowledged" : true,
  "old_index" : "latest_cars-000001",        Old index
                                              name
  "new_index" : "latest_cars-000002",        New index
  "rolled_over" : true,                       name
  "dry_run" : false,
  "conditions" : { }
}
```

As the response indicates, a new index (`latest_cars-000002`) was created as a rollover index. The old index was put into read-only mode to pave the way for indexing documents on the newly created rollover index.

> **NOTE** The rollover API is applied to the alias, but the index behind this alias is the one that is rolled over.

Behind the scenes, invoking the `_rollover` call on the alias does a couple of things:

- Creates a new index (`cars_2021-000002`) with the same configuration as the old one (the name prefix stays the same, but the suffix after the dash is incremented).
- Remaps the alias to point to the new index that was freshly generated (`cars_2021-000002`, in this case). Our queries are unaffected because all queries are written against an alias (not a physical index).
- Deletes the alias on the current index and repoints it to the newly created rollover index.

When we invoke a `_rollover` command, Elasticsearch performs a set of actions (remember, the current index must have an alias pointing to the index as a prerequisite):

- Makes the current index read-only (so only queries are executed)
- Creates a new index with the appropriate naming convention
- Repoints the alias to this new index

If we re-invoke the call in listing 6.47, a new index `cars_2021-000003` is created, and the alias is reassigned to this new index rather than the old `cars_2021-000002` index. When we need to roll over the data to a new index, simply invoking `_rollover` on the alias will suffice.

Naming conventions

Let's touch base with the naming conventions we use when rolling over indexes. The `_rollover` API has two formats—one where we can provide an index name

```
POST <index_alias>/_rollover
```

and another where the system determines it:

```
POST <index_alias>/_rollover/<target_index_name>
```

Specifying a target index name, as given in the second option, lets the rollover API create the index with the given parameter as the target index name. However, the first option, where we don't provide an index name, has a special convention: `<index_name>-00000N`. The number (after the dash) is always six digits with padded zeros. If our index follows this format, rolling over creates a new index with the same prefix, but the suffix is automatically incremented to the next number: `<index_name>-00000N +1`. The increment starts from wherever the original index number is: for example, `my_cars-000034` is incremented to `my_cars-000035`.

You may wonder when you would want to roll over an index. That is up to you. When you think the index is clogged, or you need to (re)move older data, you can invoke a rollover. However, first ask yourself:

- Can you we automatically roll over the index when the shard's size has crossed a certain threshold?
- Can you instantiate a new index for everyday logs?

Although we have seen the rollover mechanism in this section, we can satisfy these questions using the relatively new *index lifecycle management* (ILM) feature, which is discussed at length in the next section.

6.9 *Index lifecycle management (ILM)*

Indexes are expected to grow in size as data pours in over time. Sometimes an index is written too frequently, and the underlying shards run out of memory; other times, most of the shards are sparsely filled. Wouldn't it be ideal to automatically roll over the index in the former case and shrink it in the latter?

> **NOTE** Index lifecycle management (ILM) is an advanced topic, and you may not need it when starting with Elasticsearch. If that's the case, you can skip this section and return to it when you need to learn how Elasticsearch deals with time-series data and how to act on indexes by rolling them over, freezing or deleting them based on certain conditions "automagically" (well, based on defined policies), and more.

We also need to consider time-series data. Take an example of logs written to a file daily. These logs are then exported to indexes suffixed with a period, like `my-app-2021-10-24.log`. When a day is rolled off to the next day, the respective index should be rolled over, too: for example, `my-app-2021-10-24.log` to `my-app-2021-10-25.log` (the date is incremented by day), as figure 6.10 shows.

Figure 6.10 Rolling over to a new index when the new day dawns

We could write a scheduled job to do this for us. But fortunately, Elastic recently released a new feature called *index lifecycle management* (ILM). As the name suggests, ILM is about managing indexes based on a lifecycle *policy*. The policy is a definition declaring rules that are executed by the engine when the conditions of the rules are met. For example, we can define rules based on rolling over the current index to a new index when

- The index reaches a certain size (40 GB, for example)
- The number of documents in the index reaches, say, 10,000
- The day rolls over

Before we start scripting the policy, let's examine the lifecycle of an index: the phases an index progresses through based on criteria and conditions.

6.9.1 *Index lifecycle*

An index has five lifecycle phases: hot, warm, cold, frozen, and delete, as shown in figure 6.11. Let's briefly describe each of these phases:

- *Hot*—The index is in full operational mode. It is available for reads and writes, thus enabling the index for both indexing and querying.
- *Warm*—The index is in read-only mode. Indexing is switched off, but the index is open for querying so it can serve search and aggregation queries.
- *Cold*—The index is in read-only mode. Similar to the warm phase, indexing is switched off but the index is open for querying, although queries are expected to be infrequent. When the index is in this phase, search queries may result in slow response times.

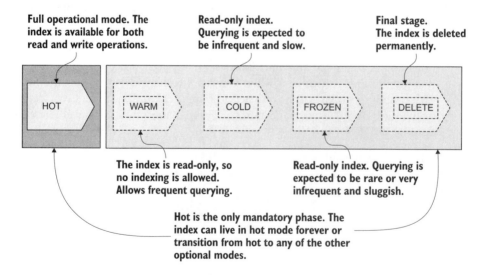

Figure 6.11 Lifecycle of an index

- *Frozen*—Similar to the cold phase, where the index is switched off for indexing but querying is allowed. However, queries are more infrequent or even rare. When the index is in this phase, users may notice longer query response times.
- *Delete*—This is the index's final stage, where it is deleted permanently. As such, the data is erased and resources are freed. Usually we take a snapshot of the index before deleting it so the data from the snapshot can be restored in the future.

Transitioning from the hot phase to every other phase is optional. That is, once created in the hot phase, an index can remain in that phase or transition to any of the other four phases. In the following sections, we check out a few examples that set an indexing lifecycle policy so the system can manage indexes automatically.

6.9.2 Managing the index lifecycle manually

So far, we've created or deleted an index on demand when needed (intervening manually). But we cannot delete, roll over, or shrink indexes based on conditions such as the size of the index exceeding a certain threshold, after a certain number of days, and so forth. We can use ILM to help us set up this feature.

Elasticsearch exposes an API for working with the index lifecycle policy with the `_ilm` endpoint. The format is `_ilm/policy/<index_policy_name>`. The process is split into two steps: defining a lifecycle policy and associating that policy with an index for execution.

STEP 1: DEFINING A LIFECYCLE POLICY

The first step is to define a lifecycle policy, where we provide the required phases and set the relevant actions on those phases.

Listing 6.48 Creating a policy with hot and delete phases

```
PUT _ilm/policy/hot_delete_policy          ◁────  The ILM
{                                                  API
   "policy": {          ◁──── Defines the policy
     "phases": {              and its phases            Defines the first
       "hot": {                                         phase (hot)
         "min_age": "1d",            ◁────  Sets the minimum age before
         "actions": {          ◁────        other actions are carried out
           "set_priority": {
Sets the    "priority": 250        Defines the actions that
priority  }                        must be carried out
         }
       }
     },
       "delete": {       ◁────  Defines the
         "actions": {           delete phase
           "delete" : { }
         }
       }
     }
   }
}
```

The hot_delete_policy defines a policy with two phases: hot and delete. Here's what the definition states:

- *Hot phase*—The index is expected to live for at least one day before carrying out the actions. The block defined in the actions object sets a priority (250, in this example). Indexes with a higher priority are considered first during node recovery.
- *Delete phase*—The index is deleted once the hot phase completes all the actions. As there is no min_age on the delete phase, the delete action kicks in immediately when the hot phase finishes.

How do we attach this policy to an index? That's what we discuss next.

Now that we have defined the policy, the next step is to associate an index with it. To see this in action, let's create an index and attach the policy from listing 6.48 to it.

> **Listing 6.49   Creating an index with an associated index lifecycle**

```
PUT hot_delete_policy_index
{                                        Uses the settings object
  "settings": {                          to set the property
    "index.lifecycle.name":"hot_delete_policy" # Name of the policy
  }
}
```

This script creates the hot_delete_policy_index index with a property setting on the index: index.lifecycle.name. The index is now associated with a lifecycle policy, as index.lifecycle.name points to our previously created policy (hot_delete_policy) from listing 6.48. This means the index undergoes a phase transition based on the policy definition. When the index is created, it first enters the hot phase and stays in that phase for a day (min_age=1d, as defined in our policy) before it applies a few actions (in this case, setting a priority on the index).

As soon as the hot phase completes (one day, based on the policy definition), the index transitions into the next stage: the delete phase, in this case. This is a straightforward phase where the index is deleted automatically.

> **NOTE** The hot_delete_policy policy defined in listing 6.48 deletes the index after one day based on the definition. Be aware that if you use this policy in production, you may find no index available after the delete phase (the delete phase purges everything).

To sum up, attaching an index lifecycle policy to an index transitions the index into given phases and executes certain actions defined in each phase. We could define an elaborate policy such as a hot phase for 45 days, a warm phase for one month, and then a cold phase for a year, and finally delete the index after a year.

Suppose we want to transition indexes based on conditions, such as every month or at a particular size. Fortunately, Elasticsearch provides automated and conditional index lifecycle rollovers.

6.9.3 Lifecycle with rollover

In this section, we set conditions on a time-series index to roll over when those conditions are met. Let's say we want the index to be rolled over based on the following conditions:

- On each new day
- When the number of documents hits 10,000
- When the index size reaches 10 GB

The following script defines a simple lifecycle policy declaring a hot phase where the shards are expected to roll over based on these conditions, with a few actions.

Listing 6.50   Simple policy definition for the hot phase

```
PUT _ilm/policy/hot_simple_policy
{
  "policy": {
    "phases": {                    Declares a
      "hot": {                     hot phase          The index enters this
        "min_age": "0ms",                             phase instantly.
        "actions": {
          "rollover": {                               The index rolls over if any
            "max_age": "1d",                          of the conditions are met.
            "max_docs": 10000,
            "max_size": "10gb"
          }
        }
      }
    }
  }
}
```

In our policy, we declare one phase—the hot phase—with rollover as the action to be performed when any of the conditions declared in the rollover actions are met: for example, if the number of documents reaches 10,000, the index size exceeds 10 GB, or the index is one day old, the index rolls over. Because we declare the minimum age (min_age) to be 0ms, as soon as the index is created, it is instantly moved into the hot phase and then rolled over.

The next step is to create an indexing template and attach the lifecycle policy to it. The following script declares an index template with an index pattern mysql-*.

Listing 6.51   Attaching a lifecycle policy to a template

```
PUT _index_template/mysql_logs_template
{                                                    Index pattern for
  "index_patterns": ["mysql-*"],                     all MySQL indexes
  "template":{
    "settings":{                                                    Attaches
      "index.lifecycle.name":"hot_simple_policy",                   the policy
```

```
        "index.lifecycle.rollover_alias":"mysql-logs-alias"    ◁──┐ Attaches
      }                                                            │ an alias
    }
  }
}
```

We need to note a couple of things from this script. We must associate our previously defined index policy by setting it as `index.lifecycle.name` with this index template. Also, as the policy's definition has a hot phase with rollover defined, we must provide the `index.lifecycle.rollover_alias` name when creating this index template.

The final step is to create an index matching the index pattern defined in the index template, with a number as a suffix so rollover indexes are generated correctly. Note that we must define the alias and declare that the current index is writeable by setting `is_write_index` to `true`.

Listing 6.52   Setting the index as writable for the alias

```
PUT mysql-index-000001       ◁──┐ Creates an index with
{                                │ the appropriate format
  "aliases": {
    "mysql-logs-alias": {    ◁──┤ Enables the alias
      "is_write_index":true  ◁──┐ The backing index
    }                            │ must be writable.
  }
}
```

Once we create the index, the policy kicks in. In our example, the index enters the hot phase, because `min_age` is set to 0 milliseconds, and then moves into the phase's `rollover` action. The index stays in this phase until one of the conditions (age, size of the index, or number of documents) is met. As soon as the condition is positive, the rollover phase is executed, and a new index `mysql-index-000002` is created (note the `index` suffix). The alias is remapped to point to this new index automatically. Then `mysql-index-000002` is rolled over to the `mysql-index-000003` index (again, if one of the conditions is met), and the cycle continues.

Policy scan interval

By default, policies are scanned every 10 minutes. To alter this scan period, we need to update the cluster settings using the `_cluster` endpoint.

When we are trying out lifecycle policies in development, a common problem is that none of the phases are executed. For example, although we set the phases' times (`min_age`, `max_age`) in milliseconds, none of the phases execute. If we are not aware of the scan interval, we may think the lifecycle policies are not being invoked—but the policies are waiting to be scanned.

We can reset the scan period by invoking the `_cluster/settings` endpoint with the appropriate period. For example, the following snippet resets the poll interval to 10 milliseconds:

```
PUT _cluster/settings
{
  "persistent": {
    "indices.lifecycle.poll_interval":"10ms"
  }
}
```

Now that we understand index rollover using lifecycle policies, let's script another policy with multiple phases.

Listing 6.53   Creating an advanced lifecycle policy

```
PUT _ilm/policy/hot_warm_delete_policy
{
  "policy": {
    "phases": {
      "hot": {
        "min_age": "1d",        ◁──┐ The index waits one day
        "actions": {                 │ before becoming hot.
          "rollover": {         ◁──┐ Rolls over when one of
            "max_size": "40gb",      │ the conditions is met
            "max_age": "6d"
          },
          "set_priority": {     ◁──┐ Sets the priority (an
            "priority": 50           │ additional action)
          }
        }
      },
      "warm": {
        "min_age": "7d",        ◁──┐ Waits seven days before
        "actions": {                 │ carrying out the actions
          "shrink": {           ◁──┐ Shrinks
            "number_of_shards": 1    │ the index
          }
        }
      },
      "delete": {               ◁──┐ Deletes the
        "min_age": "30d",       ◁──┐ index, but ...
        "actions": {                 │ ... first stays in this
          "delete": {}               │ phase for 30 days.
        }
      }
    }
  }
}
```

This policy consists of hot, warm, and delete phases. Let's look at what happens and what actions are executed in these phases:

- *Hot phase*—The index enters this phase after one day because the `min_age` attribute is set to `1d`. After one day, the index moves into the rollover stage and waits for the conditions to be satisfied: the maximum size is 40 GB (`"max_size":` `"40gb"`) or the age is older than six days (`"max_age": "6d"`). Once one of these conditions is met, the index transitions from the hot phase to the warm phase.

- *Warm phase*—When the index enters the warm phase, it stays there for a week (`"min_age": "7d"`) before any of its actions are implemented. After the seventh day, the index is shrunk to one node (`"number_of_shards": 1`), and then the index is deleted.

- *Delete phase*—The index stays in this phase for 30 days (`"min_age": "30d"`). After this time lapses, the index is deleted permanently. Be wary of this stage, because the delete operation is irreversible! My advice is to make a backup of the data before you delete the data permanently.

It's time to wrap up. In this chapter, we learned a lot about indexing operations and ILM. In the next chapter, we go over text analysis in detail, so stay tuned.

Summary

- Elasticsearch exposes index APIs to create, read, delete, and update indexes.
- Every index has three sets of configurations: aliases, settings, and mappings.
- Indexes can be created implicitly or explicitly:
  - Implicit creation kicks in when an index doesn't exist and a document is indexed for the first time. Default configurations (such as one replica and one shard) are applied on an index that's created implicitly.
  - Explicit creation occurs when we instantiate indexes with a custom set of configurations using the index API.
- An index template lets us create indexes with predetermined configuration settings that, based on a matching name, are applied during index creation.
- An index can be resized using a shrinking or splitting mechanism. Shrinking reduces the number of shards, while splitting adds more primary shards.
- An index can be conditionally rolled over as required.
- Index lifecycle management (ILM) helps transition indexes between these lifecycle phases: hot, warm, cold, frozen, and delete. In the hot phase, the index is fully operational and open for searching and indexing; but in the warm and cold phases, the index is read-only.

Text analysis

Elasticsearch does a lot of ground (and grunt) work behind the scenes on incoming textual data. It preps data to make it efficiently stored and searchable. In a nutshell, Elasticsearch cleans text fields, breaks text data into individual tokens, and enriches the tokens before storing them in inverted indexes. When a search query is carried out, the query string is searched against the stored tokens, and any matches are retrieved and scored. This process of breaking the text into individual tokens and storing it in internal memory structures is called *text analysis*.

The aim of text analysis is not just to return search results quickly and efficiently, but also to retrieve *relevant* results. The work is carried out using *analyzers*:

software components prebuilt to inspect the input text according to various rules. If the user searches for "K8s", for example, we should be able to fetch books on Kubernetes. Similarly, if search sentences include emojis such as ☕ (coffee), the search engine should be able to extract coffee-appropriate results. These and many more search criteria are honored by the engine due to the way we configure the analyzers.

In this chapter, we examine the mechanics of text extraction and analysis in detail. We begin by looking at one of the common analyzers—the `standard` analyzer—which is a default analyzer that lets us work easily on English text by tokenizing words using whitespace and punctuation as well as lowercasing the final tokens. It also has support for customization: that is, if we want to stop indexing a set of predefined values (maybe common words like *a, an, the, and, if,* and so on, or swear words), we can customize the analyzer to do so. In addition to working with the `standard` analyzer, later in the chapter, we look at prebuilt analyzers such as `keyword`, `simple`, `stop`, `whitespace`, `pattern`, and others. We also get our hands dirty with language-specific analyzers for English, German, Spanish, French, Hindi, and so on. We begin with an overview of what text analysis is all about.

NOTE The code for this chapter is available on GitHub (http://mng.bz/ JgYQ) and on the book's website (https://www.manning.com/books/elastic-search-in-action-second-edition).

7.1 Overview

Elasticsearch stores both structured and unstructured data. As we've seen in previous chapters, working with structured data is straightforward. We match documents for the given query and return the result: for example, retrieving a customer's information by their email address, finding canceled flights between dates, getting the sales figures for the last quarter, fetching a list of patients assigned to a surgeon on a given day, and so on. The results are definitive: results are returned if the query matches the documents or not if the query does not match.

Querying unstructured data, on the other hand, involves determining whether a document matches the query and how relevant the document is to the query (how well the document matches). For example, searching for "Konda" across book titles should fetch *Elasticsearch in Action* and other books I've written but not anaconda-related movies.

Analyzers applied during search

Text is analyzed when the data is indexed as well as at querying time. Just as a field is analyzed during indexing, a search query goes through the same process. The same analyzer is often used during search, but our requirements may make a different analyzer more appropriate. Section 7.5 discusses using different analyzers for search and specifying required analyzers for indexing.

7.1.1 Querying unstructured data

Unstructured data is information that doesn't neatly fit into typical tables or databases. It's usually filled with text, but can also include things like dates, numbers, or facts. Examples of unstructured data are emails, documents, photos, social media posts, and more.

Suppose our search engine contains this quote from Albert Einstein:

```
"quote": "Imagination is more important than knowledge"
```

Users get positive results with queries consisting of either an individual word or a combination of words ("imagination", "knowledge", etc.). Table 7.1 shows a set of search keywords users can search with in this case and the expected results.

Table 7.1 Possible search queries and expected results

Search keywords	Results	Notes
"imagination", "knowledge"	Yes	Individual keywords are exact matches, so positive results are returned.
"imagination knowledge", "knowledge important"	Yes	Combined keywords also match the document and so return results.

However, searching for other criteria may yield no results. For example, as shown in table 7.2, if the user searches for "passion", "importance", "passionate wisdom", "curious cognizance", or similar terms, the engine fails to return matching results with the default settings. Words such as *passion* and *cognizance* are synonyms in the quote. (Similarly, the default settings miss abbreviations.) We can tweak the analyzers to honor synonyms, stemming, spelling mistakes, and more, as we see later in the chapter.

Table 7.2 Possible search queries with no results

Search keywords	Results	Notes
"imagine", "passion", "curious", "importance", "cognizance", "wisdom", "passionate wisdom", "extra importance"	No	Synonyms and alternate names do not yield positive results.
"impartant", "knowlege", "imaginaton"	No	Spelling mistakes may result in poor or no matches.
Imp, KNWL, IMGN	No	Abbreviations do not return positive results.

We should expect users to query our engine with numerous combinations: synonyms, abbreviations, acronyms, emojis, lingo, and so on. A search engine that helps fetch relevant answers for a variety of search criteria always wins.

7.1.2 *Analyzers to the rescue*

To build an intelligent search engine that never disappoints, we give the engine extra assistance during data indexing by using *text analysis* carried out by software modules called *analyzers*. To serve many queries, we must prepare the search engine on the data it consumes during the indexing phase.

> **Only text fields are analyzed—the rest are not!**
>
> Elasticsearch analyzes only `text` fields before storing them in their respective inverted indexes. No other data types undergo text analysis. Elasticsearch also uses the same principle of analyzing the query's text fields when executing the search query.

Users don't often want to enter an exact search string—they may omit some common words, reverse the order, ignore correct spellings etc. The power of a search engine like Elasticsearch comes from the fact that it can search not only for individual words but also for synonyms, abbreviations, root words, and so on. We can attach different analyzers—including standard, language, and custom analyzers—based on our requirements.

Analyzing data during the indexing process and capturing it based on our requirements lets Elasticsearch satisfy a spectrum of search query variations. An analyzer consists of several other components that help analyze text.

7.2 *Analyzer modules*

An analyzer is a software module tasked with two functions: *tokenization* and *normalization*. Elasticsearch uses these processes so `text` fields are analyzed and stored in inverted indexes for query matching. Let's look at these concepts at a high level before drilling down into the anatomy of the analyzer.

7.2.1 *Tokenization*

Tokenization, as the name indicates, is a process of splitting sentences into individual words by following certain rules. For example, we can instruct the process to break sentences at a delimiter, such as whitespace, a letter, a pattern, or other criteria.

This process is carried out by a component called a *tokenizer*, whose sole job is to chop the sentence into individual words called *tokens* by following certain rules. A `whitespace` tokenizer is commonly employed during the tokenization process: it separates each word in the sentence with whitespace and removes any punctuation and other non-characters.

Words can also be split based on non-letters, colons, or other custom separators. For example, a movie reviewer's assessment saying "The movie was sick!!! Hilarious :) :)" can be split into individual words: *The, movie, was, sick, Hilarious,* and so on (note that the words are not yet lowercased). Similarly, *pickled-peppers* can be tokenized to *pickled* and *peppers, K8s* can be tokenized to *K* and *s*, and so on.

While this helps to search on words (individual or combined), it can only go so far in answering queries such as those with synonyms, plurals, and other elements mentioned earlier. The normalization process takes the analysis from here to the next stage.

7.2.2 Normalization

During *normalization,* tokens (words) are massaged, transformed, modified, and enriched using stemming, synonyms, and stop words. These features are added to the analysis process to ensure that the data is stored appropriately for searching purposes.

One such feature is *stemming:* an operation during which words are reduced (stemmed) to their root words. For example, *author* is a root word for *authors, authoring,* and *authored.* In addition to stemming, normalization also deals with finding appropriate synonyms before adding them to the inverted index. For example, *author* has synonyms such as *wordsmith, novelist,* and *writer.* And finally, each document will contain words such as *a, an, and, is, but,* and *the* that are called *stop words* because they do not have a place in finding relevant documents.

Both tokenization and normalization are carried out by the analyzer module. An analyzer does this by employing filters and a tokenizer. Let's dissect the analyzer module and see what it is made of.

7.2.3 Anatomy of an analyzer

Tokenization and normalization are carried out by three software components—character filters, tokenizers, and token filters—which essentially work together as an analyzer module. As figure 7.1 shows, an analyzer module consists of a set of filters and a tokenizer. Filters work on raw text (character filters) and tokenized text (token filters). The tokenizer's job is to split the sentence into individual words (tokens).

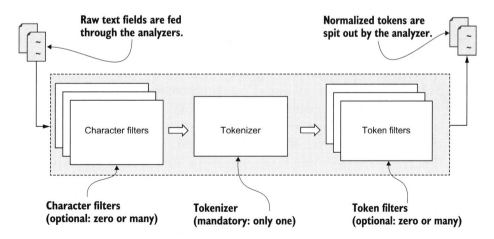

Figure 7.1   Anatomy of an analyzer module

All `text` fields go through this pipe: raw text is cleaned by character filters, and the resulting text is passed on to the tokenizer. The tokenizer splits the text into tokens (individual words). The tokens then pass through token filters, where they are modified, enriched, and enhanced. The finalized tokens are stored in the appropriate inverted indexes. Search queries are analyzed the same way.

Figure 7.2 shows an example of the analysis process. We saw this figure in chapter 3, and it is presented again here for completeness.

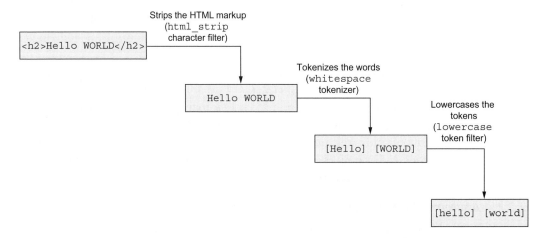

Figure 7.2   An example of text analysis in action

As we've mentioned, an analyzer is composed of three low-level building blocks:

- *Character filters*—Applied on the character level. Every character of the text goes through these filters. The filter's job is to remove unwanted characters from the text string. For example, this process can purge HTML tags like `<h1>`, `<href>`, and `<src>` from the input text. It also helps replace text with other text (e.g., Greek letters with the equivalent English words) or match text in a regular expression (regex) and replace it with its equivalent (e.g., match an email based on a regex and extract the domain of the organization). Character filters are optional; an analyzer can exist without a character filter. Elasticsearch provides three character filters out of the box: `html_strip`, `mapping`, and `pattern_replace`.
- *Tokenizers*—Split `text` fields into words using a delimiter such as whitespace, punctuation, or word boundaries. Every analyzer must have *one and only one* tokenizer. Elasticsearch provides a handful of tokenizers to help split incoming text into individual tokens that are then fed through the token filters for further normalization. Elasticsearch uses the `standard` tokenizer by default; it breaks words based on grammar and punctuation.

- *Token filters*—Perform further processing on tokens produced by tokenizers. For example, token filters can change case, create synonyms, provide root words (stem), produce n-grams and shingles, and so on. Token filters are optional. There can be either zero, one, or many associated with an analyzer module. Elasticsearch provides a long list of token filters out of the box.

Character and token filters are optional, but we *must* have one tokenizer. We look at these components in detail later in the chapter, but first let's find an API to help test the analyzers before we put them into production.

7.2.4 Testing analyzers

You may be curious how Elasticsearch breaks text, modifies it, and then plays with it. After all, knowing how the text is split and enhanced up front helps us to choose the appropriate analyzer and customize it if needed.

Elasticsearch exposes an endpoint just for testing the text analysis process: the `_analyze` endpoint helps us understand the process in detail. This handy API allows us to test how the engine treats text during indexing. It's easy to understand with an example.

> **The _analyze endpoint**
>
> The `_analyze` endpoint helps a lot in understanding how text is treated and indexed by the engine, as well as why a search query may not produce the desired output. We can use this as the first step in testing our text with the expected analyzers before putting the code into production.

Let's say we want to determine how Elasticsearch will deal with this piece of text when it's indexed: "James Bond 007".

Listing 7.1 Testing the analyzer using the `_analyze` endpoint

```
GET _analyze
{
  "text": "James Bond 007"
}
```

Executing this script produces the set of tokens shown in figure 7.3. The output of the query shows us how the analyzer treats the text field. In this case, the field is split into three tokens (`james`, `bond`, and `007`), all lowercase. Because we didn't specify an analyzer in the code, by default, it is assumed to be the `standard` analyzer. Each token has a type: `ALPHANUM` for a string, `NUM` for a numeric token, and so on. The token's position is also saved, as you can see in the results. That brings us to the next point: specifying the analyzer explicitly during the `_analyze` test.

```
{
  "tokens" : [
    {
      "token" : "james",
      "start_offset" : 0,
      "end_offset" : 5,
      "type" : "<ALPHANUM>",
      "position" : 0
    },
    {
      "token" : "bond",
      "start_offset" : 6,
      "end_offset" : 10,
      "type" : "<ALPHANUM>",
      "position" : 1
    },
    {
      "token" : "007",
      "start_offset" : 11,
      "end_offset" : 14,
      "type" : "<NUM>",
      "position" : 2
    }
  ]
}
```

- The `standard` analyzer is used by default as it was not specified in the query.

- The input text is broken into a set of tokens. There are three tokens in this case: "james", "bond", and "007".

- Elasticsearch deduces the type associated with each token: `ALPHANUM` for alphanumerics and `NUM` for numbers.

- `start_offset` and `end_offset` indicate the start and end character offset of the word.

- All tokens are lowercased.

Figure 7.3   Tokens produced by invoking the `_analyze` endpoint

EXPLICIT ANALYZER TESTS

In listing 7.1, we didn't mention the analyzer, although the engine applied the `standard` analyzer by default. However, we can also explicitly enable an analyzer. The code in the following listing enables the `simple` analyzer.

Listing 7.2   Explicitly enabling an analyzer

```
GET _analyze
{
  "text": "James Bond 007",
  "analyzer": "simple"
}
```

The `simple` analyzer (we learn about various types of analyzers in the next section) truncates text when a non-letter character is encountered. So this code produces only two tokens: "james" and "bond" ("007" is truncated), as opposed to the three tokens produced by the earlier script that used the `standard` analyzer.

If you are curious, change the analyzer to `english`. The output tokens are then "jame", "bond", and "007". The notable point is that "james" is stemmed to "jame" when the `english` analyzer is applied. (We discuss the `english` analyzer in section 7.3.7.)

CONFIGURING ANALYZERS ON THE FLY

We can also use the `_analyze` API to mix and match filters and tokenizers, essentially creating a custom analyzer on the fly (we are not really building or developing a new analyzer as such). An on-demand custom analyzer is shown in the following code.

Listing 7.3 Creating a custom analyzer

```
GET _analyze
{
  "tokenizer": "path_hierarchy",
  "filter": ["uppercase"],
  "text": "/Volumes/FILES/Dev"
}
```

This code uses a `path_hierarchy` tokenizer with an `uppercase` filter and produces three tokens from the given input text: "/VOLUMES", "/VOLUMES/FILES", and "/VOLUMES/FILES/DEV". The `path_hierarchy` tokenizer splits the text based on a path separator; so, three tokens tell us about the three folders in the hierarchy.

We've been talking about analyzer modules for the last few sections. Elasticsearch provides several of them; let's look at these built-in analyzers in detail.

7.3 Built-in analyzers

Elasticsearch provides eight out-of-the-box analyzers we can use in the text analysis phase. These analyzers usually suffice for basic cases, but if we need to create a custom one, we can do so by instantiating a new analyzer module with the required components. Table 7.3 lists the Elasticsearch analyzers.

Table 7.3 Built-in analyzers

Analyzer	Description
standard	The default analyzer that tokenizes input text based on grammar, punctuation, and whitespace. The output tokens are lowercased.
simple	Splits input text on any non-letters, such as whitespace, dashes, and numbers. Unlike the `standard` analyzer, the `simple` analyzer also lowercases the output tokens.
stop	A `simple` analyzer with English stop words enabled by default
whitespace	Tokenizes input text based on whitespace delimiters
keyword	Doesn't mutate the input text. The field's value is stored as is.
language	Helps work with human languages, as the name suggests. Elasticsearch provides dozens of analyzers for different language such as English, Spanish, French, Russian, Hindi, and so on.
pattern	Splits tokens based on a regular expression (regex). By default, all non-word characters help to split the sentence into tokens.
fingerprint	Sorts the tokens and removes duplicates to produce a single concatenated token

The `standard` analyzer is the default and is widely used during text analysis. Let's look at the `standard` analyzer with an example in the next section, after which we look at the other analyzers in turn.

NOTE   Elasticsearch lets us create a plethora of custom analyzers by mixing and matching filters and tokenizers. It would be too verbose and impractical to go over each of them, but I present as many examples as possible in this chapter. Refer to the official documentation for specific components and their integration into your application. I've also added more examples in the book's source code that you can use to experiment with analyzers.

7.3.1   *The standard analyzer*

The `standard` analyzer is the default analyzer used in Elasticsearch. Its job is to tokenize sentences based on whitespace, punctuation, and grammar. Suppose we want to build an index with a strange combination of snacks and drinks. Consider the following text that mentions coffee with popcorn:

Hot cup of ☕ and a 🍿 is a Weird Combo :(!!

We can index this text into a `weird_combos` index:

```
POST weird_combos/_doc
{
  "text": "Hot cup of ☕ and a 🍿 is a Weird Combo :(!!"
}
```

The text is tokenized, and the list of tokens is split (shown here in a condensed form):

```
["hot", "cup", "of", "☕", "and", "a", """🍿""", "is", "a", "weird", "combo"]
```

The tokens are lowercased, as you can see in the output. The standard tokenizer removes the smiley at the end and the exclamation marks, but the emojis are saved as if they were textual information. This is the default behavior of the `standard` analyzer, which tokenizes the words based on whitespace and strips out non-letter characters like punctuation. Figure 7.4 shows the workings of this example input text when passed through the analyzer.

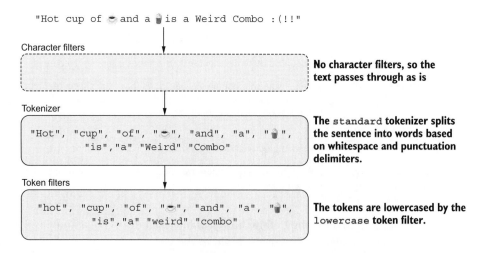

Figure 7.4   The `standard` (default) analyzer in action

Next, let's see how we can use the `_analyze` API to check the output before we index the text (again, we don't specify the analyzer because Elasticsearch uses the `standard` analyzer if we don't mention one explicitly):

```
GET _analyze
{
  "text": "Hot cup of ☕ and a 🍿 is a Weird Combo :(!!"
}
```

The output of this GET command is as follows (other than the first token, the rest are condensed for brevity):

```
{
  "tokens" : [
    {
      "token" : "hot",          ⊲──  The lowercase token filter
      "start_offset" : 0,            lowercases the words.
      "end_offset" : 3,
      "type" : "<ALPHANUM>",
      "position" : 0
    },
    { "token" : "cup", ... },       Stop words are not removed because
    { "token" : "of", ... },   ⊲──  the stop filter is disabled by default.
    { "token" : "☕", ... },   ⊲──  The coffee cup is indexed as
    { "token" : "and", ... },       is—the width is one character.
    { "token" : "a", ... },
    { "token" : """🍿""", ... },  ⊲── The popcorn emoji is indexed as
    { "token" : "is", ... },          is—the width is two characters.
    { "token" : "a", ... },
    { "token" : "weird", ... },
    { "token" : "combo", ... }  ⊲──  The smiley and exclamation marks are
  ]                                  removed by the standard tokenizer.
}
```

The words are split based on whitespace and non-letters (punctuation), which is the hallmark of the `standard` tokenizer. The tokens are then passed through the `lowercase` token filter. Figure 7.5 shows a condensed output of this command in Dev Tools.

Components of a built-in analyzer

As discussed, each of the built-in analyzers comes with a predefined set of components such as character filters, tokenizers, and token filters—for example, a `fingerprint` analyzer is composed of a `standard` tokenizer and several token filters (`fingerprint`, `lowercase`, `asciifolding`, and `stop`) but no character filters. It isn't easy to tell the anatomy of an analyzer unless you memorize them over time! So, my advice is to check the definition on the documentation page if you need to know the nitty-gritty details of an analyzer.

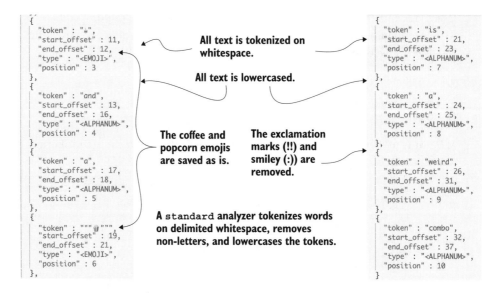

Figure 7.5   The output tokens from a `standard` analyzer

As you can see, the tokens for "coffee" and "popcorn" are stored as is, and non-letter characters such as ":(" and "!!" are removed. The "coffee" token has a width of one character (check the offsets), and the "popcorn" token is stored as two characters wide.

TESTING THE STANDARD ANALYZER

We can add a specific analyzer during our text analysis testing phase by adding an `analyzer` attribute in the code. The following listing demonstrates this.

Listing 7.4   Testing the `standard` analyzer with an explicit call

```
GET _analyze
{
  "analyzer": "standard",        ⟵  Specifies the analyzer (not really necessary
                                      here because standard is the default analyzer)
  "text": "Hot cup of ☕ and a 🍿 is a Weird Combo :(!!"
}
```

This code produces the result shown in figure 7.5. We can replace the value of the analyzer with a chosen one if we are testing the `text` field using a different analyzer: for example, `"analyzer": "whitespace"`.

The output indicates that the text was tokenized and lowercased.

Figure 7.6 illustrates the `standard` analyzer with its internal components and anatomy. It consists of a `standard` tokenizer and two token filters: `lowercase` and `stop`. No character filter is defined on the `standard` analyzer. Remember, analyzers consist of zero or more character filters, at least one tokenizer, and zero or more token filters.

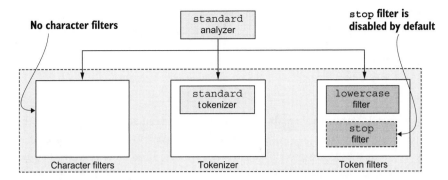

Figure 7.6   Anatomy of a `standard` **analyzer**

Although the `standard` analyzer is associated with a `stop` words token filter (as shown in figure 7.6), the filter is disabled by default. We can switch it on by configuring its properties, as discussed in the next section.

CONFIGURING THE STANDARD ANALYZER

Elasticsearch allows us to configure a few parameters such as the stop words filter, stop words path, and maximum token length on the `standard` analyzer, thus customizing the analyzer. The way to configure the properties is via the index settings. When we create an index, we can configure the analyzer through the `settings` component:

```
PUT <my_index>
{
  "settings": {
    "analysis": {          ⟵┘ The analysis object
      "analyzer": {        ⟵  sets the analyzer.
        ...                    The analyzer this index
      }                        is associated with
    }
  }
}
```

In the next few sections, we go over the mechanics of customizing this analyzer.

CONFIGURING STOP WORDS

Let's consider the example of enabling English stop words on the `standard` analyzer. We can do this by adding a filter during index creation, as the following listing shows.

> **Listing 7.5   The** `standard` **analyzer with a stop words filter enabled**

```
PUT my_index_with_stopwords
{
  "settings": {
    "analysis": {                              Sets the analyzer
      "analyzer": {              ⟵┘            for the index        Names the
        "standard_with_stopwords":{   ⟵┘                            analyzer
```

```
                              "type":"standard",
                              "stopwords":"_english_"
                           }
                        }
                     }
                  }
               }
            }
```

The standard
analyzer type ⌐⟶

Enables the English
stop words filter ⟵⌐

As we saw earlier, the stop words filter on the standard analyzer is disabled by default. Now that we've created the index with a standard analyzer configured with stop words, any text that is indexed goes through this *modified* analyzer. To test this, we can invoke the _analyze endpoint on the index.

Listing 7.6   The standard analyzer in action with stop words

```
POST my_index_with_stopwords/_analyze
{
   "text": ["Hot cup of ☕ and a 🍦 is a Weird Combo :(!!"],
   "analyzer": "standard_with_stopwords"
}
```

Invokes the _analyze
API on the index ⟵⌐

Analyzer we had
created in listing 7.5 ⟵⌐

The output of this call shows that common (English) stop words such as *of, a,* and *is* were removed:

```
["hot", "cup", "☕" "🍦","weird", "combo"]
```

We can change the stop words for a language of our choice. For example, the code in the next listing shows the index with Hindi stop words and the standard analyzer.

Listing 7.7   Standard analyzer enabling Hindi stop words

```
PUT my_index_with_stopwords_hindi
{
   "settings": {
     "analysis": {
       "analyzer": {
         "standard_with_stopwords_hindi":{
           "type":"standard",
           "stopwords":"_hindi_"
         }
       }
     }
   }
}
```

We can test the text using the standard_with_stopwords_hindi analyzer:

```
POST my_index_with_stopwords_hindi/_analyze
{
   "text": ["आप क्या कर रहे हो?"],
   "analyzer": "standard_with_stopwords_hindi"
}
```

If you are curious, the Hindi sentence in this example translates to "what are you doing?"

The output from the script is shown here:

```
"tokens" : [{
  "token" : "कैसी",
  "start_offset" : 3,
  "end_offset" : 7,
  "type" : "<ALPHANUM>",
  "position" : 1
}]
```

The only token that is output is कैसी (the second word) because the rest of the words were stop words. (They are common in the Hindi language.)

FILE-BASED STOP WORDS

In the previous examples, we provided a clue to the analyzer about which stop words it should use (English or Hindi) by specifying an off-the-shelf filter. If the built-in stop-word filters don't satisfy our requirements, we can provide stop words via an explicit file.

Let's say we don't want users to input swear words in our application. We can create a file with all the blacklisted swear words and add the path of the file as the parameter to the `standard` analyzer. The file path must be given relative to the config folder of Elasticsearch's installation. The next listing creates an index with an analyzer that accepts a stop-word file.

Listing 7.8 Creating an index with custom stop words in a file

```
PUT index_with_swear_stopwords
{
  "settings": {
    "analysis": {
      "analyzer": {
        "swearwords_analyzer":{         ◁──┐ Names the analyzer so it can be
          "type":"standard",               │ referenced when indexing/testing
          "stopwords_path":"swearwords.txt" ◁──┐ The file location must be
        }                                        │ relative to the config folder.
      }
    }
  }
}
```

Uses the standard analyzer ──▷

The `stopwords_path` attribute looks for a file (swearwords.txt, in this case) in a directory inside Elasticsearch's config folder. The following listing creates the file in the config folder. Be sure you change into the $ELASTICSEARCH_HOME/config directory and create a swearwords.txt file there. Notice that each blacklisted word goes on a new line.

Listing 7.9   Blacklisted words in the text file swearwords.txt

```
damn
bugger
bloody hell
what the hell
sucks
```

Once the file is created and the index is developed, we are ready to use the analyzer with our custom-defined swear words.

Listing 7.10   Putting the custom swear words to work

```
POST index_with_swear_stopwords/_analyze
{
  "text": ["Damn, that sucks!"],
  "analyzer": "swearwords_analyzer"
}
```

This code should stop the first and last words from going through the indexing process because they are on our swear words black list. The next attribute we can configure is the length of tokens: how long they should be as output.

CONFIGURING THE TOKEN LENGTH

We can configure the maximum token length to split tokens based on the length we request. For example, listing 7.11 creates an index with a `standard` analyzer. The analyzer is configured to have a maximum token length of seven characters. If we provide a word that is 13 characters long, it will be split into two tokens of seven and six characters (for example, "Elasticsearch" will become "Elastic", "search").

Listing 7.11   Creating an analyzer with a custom token length

```
PUT my_index_with_max_token_length
{
  "settings": {
    "analysis": {
      "analyzer": {
        "standard_max_token_length":{
          "type":"standard",
          "max_token_length":7
        }
      }
    }
  }
}
```

So far, we've worked with the `standard` analyzer. Next on the list of built-in analyzers is the `simple` analyzer, which has the single purpose of splitting text on non-letters. Let's discuss the details of using a `simple` analyzer.

7.3.2 *The simple analyzer*

While the `standard` analyzer breaks text into tokens when it encounters whitespace or punctuation, the `simple` analyzer tokenizes sentences at the occurrence of a non-letter like a number, space, apostrophe, or hyphen. It does this by using a `lowercase` tokenizer, which is not associated with any character or token filters (see figure 7.7).

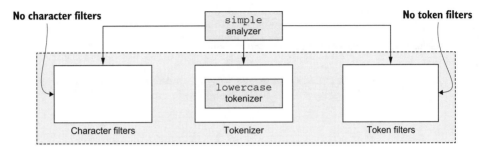

Figure 7.7 Anatomy of a `simple` analyzer

Let's consider an example of indexing the text "Lukša's K8s in Action".

Listing 7.12 Analyzing text using a `simple` analyzer

```
POST _analyze
{
  "text": ["Lukša's K8s in Action"],
  "analyzer": "simple"
}
```

This results in the following:

```
["lukša","s","k","s","in","action"]
```

The tokens were split when an apostrophe ("Lukša's" becomes "Lukša" and "s") or number ("K8s" becomes "k" and "s") was encountered, and the resulting tokens were lowercased.

A `simple` analyzer can't do much configuration, but if we want to add a filter (character or token), the easiest way to do so is to create a custom analyzer with the required filters and the `lowercase` tokenizer (the `simple` analyzer has a lone `lowercase` tokenizer). We see this in section 7.4.

7.3.3 *The whitespace analyzer*

As the name suggests, the `whitespace` analyzer splits the text into tokens when it encounters whitespace. There are no character or token filters on this analyzer except a `whitespace` tokenizer (see figure 7.8). The following listing shows a script using the `whitespace` analyzer.

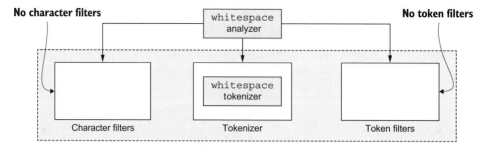

Figure 7.8   Anatomy of the `whitespace` **analyzer**

Listing 7.13   The `whitespace` **tokenizer in action**

```
POST _analyze
{
  "text":"Peter_Piper picked a peck of PICKLED-peppers!!",
  "analyzer": "whitespace"
}
```

If we test this script, we get this set of tokens:

```
["Peter_Piper", "picked", "a", "peck", "of", "PICKLED-peppers!!"]
```

Note these two points from the result: first, the text was tokenized only on whitespaces, not dashes, underscores, or punctuation. Second, case is preserved—the capitalization of the characters and words was kept intact.

As mentioned earlier, similar to the `simple` analyzer, the `whitespace` analyzer is not exposed to configurable parameters. If we need to modify the analyzer's behavior, we may need to create a modified custom version. We examine custom analyzers shortly.

7.3.4   *The keyword analyzer*

As the name suggests, the `keyword` analyzer stores text without any modifications or tokenization. That is, the analyzer does not tokenize the text, nor does the text undergo any further analysis via filters or tokenizers. Instead, it is stored as a string representing a `keyword` type. As figure 7.9 shows, the `keyword` analyzer is composed of a `noop` (no-operation) tokenizer and no character or token filters.

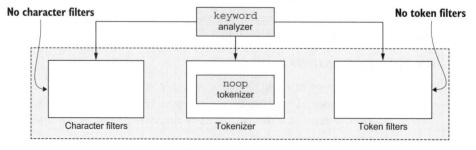

Figure 7.9   Anatomy of the `keyword` **analyzer**

Text passed through the analyzer is converted and stored as a keyword. For example, if we pass "Elasticsearch in Action" through the `keyword` analyzer, the whole text string is stored as is, unlike the way earlier analyzers split the text into tokens.

Listing 7.14   Using the `keyword` analyzer

```
POST _analyze
{
  "text":"Elasticsearch in Action",
  "analyzer": "keyword"
}
```

The output of this script is shown here:

```
"tokens" : [{
  "token" : "Elasticsearch in Action",
  "start_offset" : 0,
  "end_offset" : 23,
  "type" : "word",
  "position" : 0
}]
```

As you can see, only one token was produced as a result of processing the text via the `keyword` analyzer. There's also no lowercasing. However, there is a change in how we search if we use the `keyword` analyzer to process text. Searching for a single word will not match the text string—we must provide an exact match. In our example, we must provide the exact group of words as in the original sentence: "Elasticsearch in Action".

7.3.5   *The fingerprint analyzer*

The `fingerprint` analyzer removes duplicate words and extended characters and sorts the words alphabetically to create a single token. It consists of a `standard` tokenizer and four token filters: `fingerprint`, `lowercase`, `stop`, and ASCII folding (`asciifolding`) token filters (see figure 7.10).

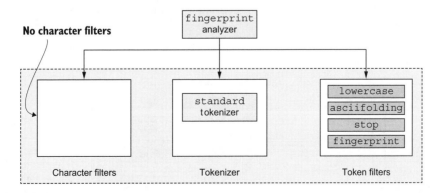

Figure 7.10   Anatomy of the `fingerprint` analyzer

For example, let's analyze the text shown in the next listing, which defines *dosa*—a South Indian savory pancake. The code analyzes a description of this dish using a `fingerprint` analyzer.

Listing 7.15 Analyzing text using a `fingerprint` analyzer

```
POST _analyze
{
  "text": "A dosa is a thin pancake or crepe originating from South India.
➥ It is made from a fermented batter consisting of lentils and rice.",
  "analyzer": "fingerprint"
}
```

When we execute this code, the output is as follows:

```
"tokens" : [{
  "token" : "a and batter consisting crepe dosa fermented from india is it
➥ lentils made of or originating pancake rice south thin",
  "start_offset" : 0,
  "end_offset" : 130,
  "type" : "fingerprint",
  "position" : 0
}]
```

When you look closely at the response, you see that the output consists of only one token. The words were lowercased and sorted, duplicate words (*a, of, from*) were removed, and the set of words was turned into a single token. Any time we have text that needs to be deduplicated, sorted, and concatenated, `fingerprint` is the logical choice.

7.3.6 *The pattern analyzer*

Sometimes we want to tokenize and analyze text based on a certain pattern—for example, removing the first *n* numbers of a phone number or removing the dash between every four digits of a credit card number. Elasticsearch provides a `pattern` analyzer for that purpose.

The default `pattern` analyzer splits sentences into tokens based on non-word characters. This pattern is represented as `\W+` internally. As figure 7.11 shows, the `pattern` tokenizer and the `lowercase` and `stop` filters form the `pattern` analyzer.

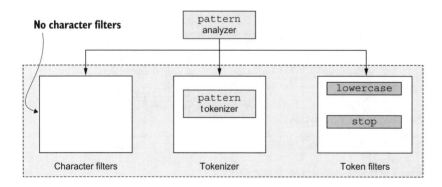

Figure 7.11
Anatomy of the
`pattern` analyzer

As the default (`standard`) analyzer only works on non-letter delimiters, we need to configure the analyzer to provide any other required patterns. *Patterns* are Java regular expressions provided as a string when configuring the analyzer.

> **NOTE** To learn more about Java regular expressions, go to http://mng.bz/ QPDe.

Let's say we have an application that authorizes e-commerce payments, and we receive payment authorization requests from various parties. A 16-digit card number is provided in the format 1234-5678-9000-0000. We want to tokenize this card data on a dash (-) and extract the four tokens individually. We can create a pattern that splits the field into tokens based on the dash delimiter.

To configure the `pattern` analyzer, we must create an index by setting `pattern_analyzer` as the analyzer in the `settings` object. The following listing shows the configuration.

Listing 7.16 Pattern that delimits tokens based on a dash

```
PUT index_with_dash_pattern_analyzer          ◁─┐ Creates an index with
{                                                │ the analyzer settings
  "settings": {
    "analysis": {
      "analyzer": {                        In settings, defines the
        "pattern_analyzer": {       ◁─┘    analyzer in the analysis object
          "type": "pattern",        ◁─┐ Specifies the type of
          "pattern": "[-]",           │ analyzer as pattern
          "lowercase": true   ◁─  Attaches a lowercase
        }                            token filter
      }
    }
  }
}
```

Regex representing the dash ─┐▷

In the code, we create an index with `pattern` analyzer settings. The `pattern` attribute indicates the regex, which follows Java's regular expression syntax. In this case, we set the dash as our delimiter, so the text is tokenized when it encounters that character. Now that we have the index, let's put this analyzer into action.

Listing 7.17 Testing the `pattern` analyzer

```
POST index_with_dash_pattern_analyzer/_analyze
{
  "text": "1234-5678-9000-0000",
  "analyzer": "pattern_analyzer"
}
```

The output of this command contains four tokens: `["1234","5678","9000","0000"]`.

Text can be tokenized based on a plethora of patterns. I suggest experimenting with regex patterns to get full benefit from the `pattern` analyzer.

7.3.7   *Language analyzers*

Elasticsearch provides language analyzers for working with the following languages: Arabic, Armenian, Basque, Bengali, Bulgarian, Catalan, Czech, Dutch, English, Finnish, French, Galician, German, Hindi, Hungarian, Indonesian, Irish, Italian, Latvian, Lithuanian, Norwegian, Portuguese, Romanian, Russian, Sorani, Spanish, Swedish, and Turkish. We can configure these out-of-the-box language analyzers to add a stopwords filter so we don't index a language's unnecessary (or common) words. The following listing demonstrates three language analyzers (English, German, and Hindi) in action.

Listing 7.18   English, German, and Hindi language analyzers

```
POST _analyze
{
  "text": "She sells Sea Shells on the Sea Shore",
  "analyzer": "english"
}
```
Uses the english language analyzer. The output is ["she", "sell", "sea", "shell", "sea", "shore"].

```
POST _analyze
{
  "text": "Guten Morgen",
  "analyzer": "german"
}
```
Uses the german language analyzer. The output is ["gut","morg"].

```
POST _analyze
{
  "text": "नमस्ते कैसी हो तुम",
  "analyzer": "hindi"
}
```
Uses the hindi language analyzer. The output is ["नमस्ते","कैसी","तुम"].

We can configure a language analyzer with a few additional parameters to provide our own list of stop words or ask the analyzer to exclude the stemming operation. For example, the stop token filter used by the english analyzer categorizes a handful of words as stop words. We can override this list based on our requirements. For example, if we only want to override *a, an, is, and,* and *for,* we can configure our stop words as the following listing shows.

Listing 7.19   Index with custom stop words on the english analyzer

```
PUT index_with_custom_english_analyzer
{                                              ◁──┐ Creates an index
  "settings": {                                    with analyzer settings
    "analysis": {
      "analyzer": {
        "index_with_custom_english_analyzer":{  ◁──  Provides a
          "type":"english",                          custom name
          "stopwords":["a","an","is","and","for"]  ◁──  Provides our set
        }                                               of stop words
```
The type of analyzer here is english.

```
        }
      }
    }
}
```

We create an index with a custom `english` analyzer and a set of user-defined stop words. When we test a piece of text with this analyzer, the stop words are honored.

Listing 7.20   Testing the custom stop words for the `english` analyzer

```
POST index_with_custom_english_analyzer/_analyze
{
  "text":"A dog is for a life",
  "analyzer":"index_with_custom_english_analyzer"
}
```

This code outputs just two tokens: "dog", and "life". The words *a*, *is*, and *for* were removed because they matched the stop words we specified.

Language analyzers have another feature that they are always eager to implement: stemming. *Stemming* is a mechanism to reduce words to their root form. For example, any form of the word *author* (*authors, authoring, authored*, etc.) is reduced to the single word *author*. The following listing shows this behavior.

Listing 7.21   Reducing all forms of `author` to the `author` keyword

```
POST index_with_custom_english_analyzer/_analyze
{
  "text":"author authors authoring authored",
  "analyzer":"english"
}
```

This code produces four tokens (based on the `whitespace` tokenizer), all of which are "author"—because the root word for any form of *author* is *author*!

But sometimes, stemming goes too far. If you add "authorization" or "authority" to the list of words in the previous listing, it is also stemmed and indexed as "author"! Obviously, we can't find pertinent answers when searching for "authority" or "authorization" because those words do not make it to the inverted index due to stemming.

All is not lost. We can configure our `english` analyzer, asking it to ignore certain words (such as *authorization* and *authority*, in this case) that do not need to get through the analyzer. We can use the `stem_exclusion` attribute to configure words to exclude from stemming. The next listing does this by creating an index with custom settings and passing the arguments to the `stem_exclusion` parameter.

Listing 7.22   Creating an index with custom stem-exclusion words

```
PUT index_with_stem_exclusion_english_analyzer
{
  "settings": {
```

```
    "analysis": {
      "analyzer": {
        "stem_exclusion_english_analyzer":{
          "type":"english",
          "stem_exclusion":["authority","authorization"]
        }
      }
    }
  }
}
```

Once we've created the index with these settings, the next step is to test the indexing request. The following listing uses the `english` analyzer to test a piece of text.

Listing 7.23   Stem exclusion in action

```
POST index_with_stem_exclusion_english_analyzer/_analyze
{
  "text": "No one can challenge my authority without my authorization",
  "analyzer": "stem_exclusion_english_analyzer"
}
```

The tokens created by this code are our usual tokens plus two untouched words: "authority" and "authorization". These two words will be output along with the other "stemmed" words.

We can also further customize the language analyzers. We discuss customizing analyzers in the next section.

While most analyzers do what we want in most cases, sometimes we need to implement text analysis for additional requirements. For example, we may want to remove special characters like HTML tags from incoming text or avoid specific stop words. The job of removing HTML tags is taken care of by the `html_strip` character filter, but unfortunately, not all analyzers have it. In such cases, we can customize the analyzer by configuring the required functionality: we can add a new character filter like `html_strip` and perhaps enable the `stop` token filter. Let's see how to configure the `standard` analyzer to suit advanced requirements.

7.4   *Custom analyzers*

Elasticsearch provides a lot of flexibility when it comes to analyzers: if off-the-shelf analyzers don't cut it for us, we can create our own custom analyzers. They can mix and match existing components from a large stash in Elasticsearch's component library.

Usual practice is to define a custom analyzer in `settings` when creating an index with the required filters and a tokenizer. We can provide any number of character and token filters but only one tokenizer (see figure 7.12).

As the figure shows, we define a custom analyzer on an index by setting the type to `custom`. Our custom analyzer is developed with an array of character filters represented by the `char_filter` object and an array of token filters represented by the `filter` attribute.

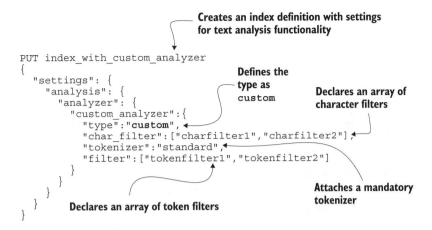

Figure 7.12 Anatomy of a custom analyzer

NOTE In my opinion, the developers of Elasticsearch should have named the `filter` object `token_filter`, instead, to match `char_filter`. And using plural names (`char_filters` and `token_filters`) also would have made more sense, because they expect an array of stringified filters!

We provide a tokenizer from the list of off-the-shelf tokenizers with our custom configuration. Let's look at an example. Listing 7.24 shows the script for developing a custom analyzer. It has the following:

- A character filter (`html_strip`) that strips HTML characters from the input field
- A `standard` tokenizer that tokenizes the field based on whitespace and punctuation
- A token filter for uppercasing words

Listing 7.24 Custom analyzer with filters and a tokenizer

```
PUT index_with_custom_analyzer
{
    "settings": {
      "analysis": {
        "analyzer": {
          "custom_analyzer":{            ⟵── Specifies the custom analyzer
            "type":"custom",             ⟵──── The type must be custom to let Elasticsearch know about our custom analyzer.
            "char_filter":["html_strip"],
            "tokenizer":"standard",      ⟵─┐ Declares a single tokenizer (standard, in this case)
            "filter":["uppercase"]       ⟵─┘
          }
        }                                      Token filter to uppercase incoming tokens
      }
    }
}
```

Array of character filters ──→ (points to `"char_filter":["html_strip"]`)

We can test the analyzer using the following code snippet:

```
POST index_with_custom_analyzer/_analyze
{
  "text": "<H1>HELLO, WoRLD</H1>",
  "analyzer": "custom_analyzer"
}
```

This program produces two tokens: ["HELLO", "WORLD"]. Our html_strip filter removed the H1 HTML tags before letting the standard tokenizer split the field into two tokens based on a whitespace delimiter. Finally, the tokens were uppercased as they passed through the uppercase token filter.

Customization helps satisfy a range of requirements, but we can achieve even more advanced results. Let's take a look.

7.4.1   *Advanced customization*

While the default configurations of the analyzer components work most of the time, sometimes we need to create analyzers with nondefault configurations for their components. For example, we may want to use a mapping character filter to map the character *&* to the word *and* and the characters *<* and *>* to *less than* and *greater than*, respectively.

Suppose our requirement is to develop a custom analyzer that parses text for Greek letters and produces a list of Greek letters. The following code creates an index with these analysis settings.

Listing 7.25   Extracting Greek letters with a custom analyzer

```
PUT index_with_parse_greek_letters_custom_analyzer
{
  "settings": {
    "analysis": {
      "analyzer": {
        "greek_letter_custom_analyzer":{        ◄── Creates a custom
          "type":"custom",                            Greek-letter-parser
          "char_filter":["greek_symbol_mapper"],   ◄── analyzer
          "tokenizer":"standard",                  ◄── The custom analyzer is made
          "filter":["lowercase", "greek_keep_words"]  of a custom char_filter.
        }                                        ◄── Supplies two token filters;
      },                                              greek_keep_words is
      "char_filter": {                                defined next.
        "greek_symbol_mapper":{   ◄── Defines the Greek letters and
          "type":"mapping",            maps them to English words
          "mappings":[           ◄── The actual mappings: a list of
            "α => alpha",             symbols and corresponding values
            "β => Beta",
            "γ => Gamma"
          ]
        }
      },
      "filter": {                    We don't want to index all
        "greek_keep_words":{   ◄──   the field values, only words
                                     that match the keep words.
```

A standard tokenizer tokenizes the text.

```
        "type":"keep",
        "keep_words":["alpha", "beta", "gamma"]
      }
    }
  }
 }
}
```
◁─┐ **Keep words; all other words are discarded.**

This code is a bit of a handful, but it's easy to understand. In the first part, where we define a custom analyzer, we provide a list of filters (both character and token filters, if needed) and a tokenizer. You can imagine this as the entry point to the analyzer definition.

The second part of the code defines the filters declared earlier. For example, `greek_symbol_mapper`, redeclared in the new `char_filter` section, uses `mapping` as the filter's type with a set of mappings. The same goes for the `filter` block, which defines the `keep_words` filter. This filter removes any words that aren't in the `keep_ words` list.

Now we can execute a test sample for analysis. The sentence in the following listing should be passed through the test analysis phase.

Listing 7.26 Parsing Greek letters from normal text

```
POST index_with_parse_greek_letters_custom_analyzer/_analyze
{
  "text": "α and β are roots of a quadratic equation. γ isn't",
  "analyzer": "greek_letter_custom_analyzer"
}
```

Greek letters (α, β, and γ, for example) are processed by the custom analyzer (`greek_letter_custom_analyzer`), which output the following:

```
"alpha","beta","gamma"
```

The rest of the words, like *roots* and *quadratic equation*, are removed.

So far, we have looked at the analyzers in detail, including built-in and custom ones. We can configure analyzers not just at the field level but also at the index or query level. And we can also specify a different analyzer for search queries if our requirements dictate. We discuss these points in the next section.

7.5 Specifying analyzers

Analyzers can be specified at the index, field, and query level. Declaring analyzers at the index level provides an index-wide default catch-all analyzer for all text fields. However, if further customization is required on a field level, we can also enable a different analyzer at that level. In addition, we can provide a different analyzer instead of the index-time analyzer while searching. Let's look at each of these options.

7.5.1 Analyzers for indexing

Sometimes we may have a requirement to set different fields with different analyzers—for example, associating a name field with a `simple` analyzer and a credit card number field with a `pattern` analyzer. Fortunately, Elasticsearch lets us set different analyzers on individual fields as required. Similarly, we can set a default analyzer per index so that any fields not explicitly associated with a specific analyzer during the mapping process inherit the index-level analyzer.

FIELD-LEVEL ANALYZERS

We can specify required analyzers at a field level while creating a mapping definition of an index. The following code shows how we can do this during index creation.

Listing 7.27   Setting field-level analyzers during index creation

```
PUT authors_with_field_level_analyzers
{
  "mappings": {
    "properties": {
      "name":{
        "type": "text"            ◁──┐ Uses the standard
      },                             │ analyzer
      "about":{
        "type": "text",
        "analyzer": "english"     ◁──┐ Explicitly sets the
      },                             │ english analyzer
      "description":{
        "type": "text",
        "fields": {
          "my":{
            "type": "text",
            "analyzer": "fingerprint"  ◁──┐ Fingerprint analyzer
          }                              │ on a multi-field
        }
      }
    }
  }
}
```

The `about` and `description` fields are specified with different analyzers except for the `name` field, which implicitly inherits the `standard` analyzer.

INDEX-LEVEL ANALYZERS

We can also set a default analyzer of our choice at the index level. The following listing demonstrates.

Listing 7.28   Creating an index with a default analyzer

```
PUT authors_with_default_analyzer
{
  "settings": {
    "analysis": {
      "analyzer": {              ┐ Setting this property sets
        "default":{        ◁──┘ the index's default analyzer.
          "type":"keyword"
```

```
            }
          }
        }
      }
    }
}
```

We are, in effect, replacing the `standard` analyzer, which is the default for a `keyword` analyzer. We can test the analyzer by invoking the `_analyze` endpoint on the index.

Listing 7.29 Testing the default analyzer

```
PUT authors_with_default_analyzer/_analyze
{
  "text":"John Doe"
}
```

This code outputs a single token `"John Doe"` with no lowercasing or tokenizing, indicating that our `keyword` analyzer has analyzed it. You can try the same code using a `standard` analyzer, and you'll notice the difference.

Setting analyzers at an index level or field level works during the indexing process. However, we can also use a different analyzer during the querying process—let's see why and how.

7.5.2 *Analyzers for searching*

Elasticsearch lets us specify a different analyzer during query time than during indexing. Let's see these two methods in this section as well as some rules that Elasticsearch follows when picking up an analyzer defined at various levels.

ANALYZER IN A QUERY

We haven't looked in depth at search yet, so don't worry if the following listing baffles you a bit (we discuss search in the next few chapters).

Listing 7.30 Setting the analyzer alongside a search query

```
GET authors_index_for_search_analyzer/_search
{
  "query": {              ┌─  Query to search all authors
    "match": {    ◁───────┘   with the given criteria
      "author_name": {
        "query": "M Konda",
        "analyzer": "simple"   ◁─┐  The analyzer is specified explicitly
      }                          │  and is usually different than the
    }                            │  one the field was indexed with.
  }
}
```

We specify the analyzer explicitly (the `author_name` field was probably indexed using a different type of analyzer!) while searching for an author.

SETTING THE ANALYZER AT A FIELD LEVEL

The second mechanism sets the search-specific analyzer at the field level. Just as we set an analyzer on a field for indexing purposes, we can add a property called `search_analzyer` on a field to specify the search analyzer.

Listing 7.31   Setting a search analyzer at the field level

```
PUT authors_index_with_both_analyzers_field_level
{
  "mappings": {
    "properties": {
      "author_name":{
        "type": "text",
        "analyzer": "stop",
        "search_analyzer": "simple"
      }
    }
  }
}
```

The `author_name` field is set with a `stop` analyzer for indexing and a `simple` analyzer for search time.

DEFAULT ANALYZER AT THE INDEX LEVEL

We can also set a default analyzer for search queries, just as we did for indexing time, by setting the required analyzer on the index at index-creation time.

Listing 7.32   Setting default analyzers for search and indexing

```
PUT authors_index_with_default_analyzer
{
  "settings": {
    "analysis": {
      "analyzer": {
        "default_search":{          ⟵——  Sets the default search
          "type":"simple"                 analyzer for the index using
        },                                the default_search property
        "default":{          ⟵——  Default analyzer
          "type":"standard"         for the index
        }
      }
    }
  }
}
```

We set the default analyzer for indexing and search at the same time. You may wonder if we can set a search analyzer at the field level during the indexing rather than at runtime during the query. The following listing demonstrates exactly that: it sets different analyzers for indexing and searching at a field level during the creation of an index.

> **Listing 7.33 Specifying index/search analyzers during index creation**

```
PUT authors_index_with_both_analyzers_field_level
{
  "mappings": {
    "properties": {
      "author_name":{
        "type": "text",
        "analyzer": "standard",
        "search_analyzer": "simple"
      }
    }
  }
}
```

The `author_name` field uses a `standard` analyzer for indexing and a `simple` analyzer during search.

ORDER OF PRECEDENCE

The engine begins to use the analyzers based on the following order of precedence when it finds analyzers at various levels (highest precedence first):

1. An analyzer defined at a query level
2. An analyzer defined by setting the `search_analyzer` property on a field when defining the index mappings
3. An analyzer defined at the index level
4. The indexing analyzer set on a field or an index

Now that we understand the built-in analyzers and how to create custom analyzers, it is time to look into the individual components of analyzers in detail. In the next three sections, we review the components that form an analyzer: tokenizers and character and token filters. Let's start with character filters.

7.6 Character filters

When a user searches for answers, the expectation is that they won't search with punctuation or special characters. For example, there is a high chance a user may search for "cant find my keys" (without punctuation) rather than "can't find my keys !!!". Similarly, the user should not search for the string "<h1>Where is my cheese?</h1>" (with the HTML tags). We also don't expect the user to search using XML tags like "<operation>callMe</operation>". Search criteria don't need to be polluted with unneeded characters. We also don't want users to search using symbols: ? instead of "alpha" or ? in place of "beta", for example.

Based on these assumptions, we can analyze and clean the incoming text using character filters. Character filters help purge unwanted characters from the input stream. Although they are optional, if they are used, they form the first component in the analyzer module.

An analyzer can have zero or more character filters. A character filter carries out the following specific functions:

- *Removes unwanted characters from an input stream*—For example, if the incoming text has HTML markup, as in "<h1>Where is my cheese?</h1>", the requirement is to drop the <h1> and </h1> tags.
- *Adds to or replaces additional characters in the existing stream*—If the input field contains 0s and 1s, we may want to replace them with "false" and "true", respectively. Or if the input stream includes the character ?, we can map it to the word "beta" and index the field.

We can use three character filters to construct an analyzer: the html_strip, mapping, and pattern filters. We saw these in action earlier, and in this section, we briefly review the semantics.

7.6.1 *HTML strip (hmtl_strip) filter*

As the name suggests, this filter strips unwanted HTML tags from the input fields. For example, when an input field with a value of <h1>Where is my cheese?</h1> is processed by the html_strip character filters, the <h1> and </h1> tags are purged, leaving "Where is my cheese?". We can test the html_strip character filter using the _analyze API.

Listing 7.34   The html_strip character filter in action

```
POST _analyze
{
  "text":"<h1>Where is my cheese?</h1>",
  "tokenizer": "standard",
  "char_filter": ["html_strip"]
}
```

The character filter simply strips the HTML tags from the input field and produces the tokens "Where", "is", "my", and "Cheese". However, we may need to avoid parsing the input field for certain HTML tags. For example, the business requirement may be to strip <h1> tags from the following input but preserve the preformatted (<pre>) tags:

```
<h1>Where is my cheese?</h1>
<pre>We are human beings who look out for cheese constantly!</pre>
```

We can configure the html_strip filter to add an escaped_tags array with a list of tags to leave unparsed. The first step is to create an index with the required custom analyzer.

Listing 7.35   Custom analyzer with an added filter configuration

```
PUT index_with_html_strip_filter
{
  "settings": {
    "analysis": {
      "analyzer": {
```

```
            "custom_html_strip_filter_analyzer":{
                "tokenizer":"keyword",
                "char_filter":["my_html_strip_filter"]          ◁─┐  Declares a custom
            }                                                       character filter
        },
        "char_filter": {
            "my_html_strip_filter":{
                "type":"html_strip",
                "escaped_tags":["h1"]        ◁─┐  The escaped_tags attribute ignores
            }                                    parsing <h1> tags in the input field.
        }
    }
  }
}
```

This index has a custom analyzer consisting of an `html_strip` character filter. The `html_strip` is extended in this example to use the `escaped_tags` option, which specifies that `<h1>` tags should be left untouched. To test this, we can run the following code.

Listing 7.36 Testing the custom analyzer

```
POST index_with_html_strip_filter/_analyze
{
  "text": "<h1>Hello,</h1> <h2>World!</h2>",
  "analyzer": "custom_html_strip_filter_analyzer"
}
```

This code leaves the word with the `<h1>` tags as is and strips the `<h2>` tags. It results in this output: `"<h1>Hello,</h1> World!"`.

7.6.2 *The mapping character filter*

The `mapping` character filter's sole job is to match a key and replace it with a value. In our earlier example of converting Greek letters to English words, the `mapping` filter parsed the symbols and replaced them with words: α as *alpha*, β as *beta*, and so on.

Let's test the `mapping` character filter. In the following listing, "UK" is replaced with the "United Kingdom" when parsed with the `mapping` filter.

Listing 7.37 The `mapping` character filter in action

```
POST _analyze
{
  "text": "I am from UK",
  "char_filter": [
    {
      "type": "mapping",
      "mappings": [
        "UK => United Kingdom"
      ]
    }
  ]
}
```

If we want to create a custom analyzer with a configured `mapping` character filter, we follow the same process as earlier to create an index with analyzer settings and required filters. This example shows the procedure for customizing a `keyword` analyzer to attach a `mapping` character filter.

Listing 7.38   A keyword analyzer with a `mapping` character filter

```
PUT index_with_mapping_char_filter
{
  "settings": {
    "analysis": {
      "analyzer": {
        "my_social_abbreviations_analyzer": {          Custom analyzer with a
          "tokenizer": "keyword",                       mapping character filter
          "char_filter": [
            "my_social_abbreviations"        Declares a
          ]                                   character filter
        }
      },
      "char_filter": {                        Expands the defined character
        "my_social_abbreviations": {          filter with mappings
          "type": "mapping",
          "mappings": [
            "LOL => laughing out loud",       Provides a set of mappings in the
            "BRB => be right back",           mappings object as name-value pairs
            "OMG => oh my god"
          ]
        }
      }
    }
  }
}
```

Specifies the name of the filter: mapping, in this case

We've created an index with custom analyzer settings and provided mappings in the character filter. Now we can test it using the `_analyze` API.

Listing 7.39   Testing the custom analyzer

```
POST index_with_mapping_char_filter/_analyze
{
  "text": "LOL",
  "analyzer": "my_social_abbreviations_analyzer"
}
```

The text results in `"token" : "laughing out loud"`, which indicates that "LOL" was replaced with the full form, "laughing out loud".

7.6.3   *Mappings via a file*

We can also provide a file containing mappings rather than specifying them in the definition. Listing 7.40 uses a character filter with mappings loaded from an external file, secret_organizations.txt (be sure to create this file if you don't have it the config folder). The file must be present in Elasticsearch's config directory (*<INSTALL_DIR>*/ elasticsearch/config) or input with an absolute path where it is located.

> **Listing 7.40 Loading external mappings via a file**

```
POST _analyze
{
  "text": "FBI and CIA are USA's security organizations",
  "char_filter": [
    {
      "type": "mapping",
      "mappings_path": "secret_organizations.txt"
    }
  ]
}
```

The secret_organizations.txt sample file should consist of the following data:

```
FBI=>Federal Bureau of Investigation
CIA=>Central Intelligence Agency
USA=>United States of America
```

7.6.4 *The pattern_replace character filter*

The `pattern_replace` character filter, as the name suggests, replaces a character with a new character when the field matches a regular expression (regex). Following the same code pattern as in listing 7.38, let's create an index with an analyzer associated with a `pattern_replace` character filter.

> **Listing 7.41 Using a `pattern_replace` character filter**

```
PUT index_with_pattern_replace_filter
{
  "settings": {
    "analysis": {
      "analyzer": {
        "my_pattern_replace_analyzer":{        ⟵┘ Custom analyzer with a
          "tokenizer":"keyword",                    pattern_replace character filter
          "char_filter":["pattern_replace_filter"]  ⟵┐ Declares the
        }                                              pattern_replace filter
      },
      "char_filter": {                    ┌─ Expands the defined
        "pattern_replace_filter":{      ⟵┘  pattern_replace filter with options
          "type":"pattern_replace",     ⟵┐ Indicates the type of the
          "pattern":"_",                    filter (pattern_replace)
          "replacement":"-"   ⟵┐ Defines the
        }                          replacement value
      }
    }
  }
}
```

Indicates the pattern to search and replace

This code tries to match and replace our input field, replacing the underscore (_) character with a dash (-). We can test the analyzer with the following code.

> **Listing 7.42   Testing a custom pattern replace character filter**

```
POST index_with_pattern_replace_filter/_analyze
{
  "text": "Apple_Boy_Cat",
  "analyzer": "my_pattern_replace_analyzer"
}
```

The output is "Apple-Boy-Cat" with all the underscores replaced with dashes.

The input text has been cleaned of unwanted characters, but there remains the job of splitting the text into individual tokens based on delimiters, patterns, and other criteria. That job is undertaken by a tokenizer component, discussed in the next section.

7.7   *Tokenizers*

The job of a tokenizer is to create tokens based on certain criteria. Tokenizers split incoming input fields into tokens that are usually the individual words of a sentence. Elasticsearch provides over a dozen tokenizers, each of which tokenizes fields based on the tokenizer's definition.

> **NOTE**   As you can imagine, discussing all the tokenizers in this book would be impractical (and also boring to read). I have chosen a few important and popular tokenizers here so you can understand the concept and mechanics. Example code is available with the book's files.

7.7.1   *The standard tokenizer*

A `standard` tokenizer splits text into tokens based on word boundaries (whitespace delimiters) as well as punctuation (commas, hyphens, colons, semicolons, etc.). The following code uses the `_analyze` API to execute the tokenizer on a field:

```
POST _analyze
{
  "text": "Hello,cruel world!",
  "tokenizer": "standard"
}
```

This results in three tokens: "Hello", "cruel", and "world". The comma and the whitespace act as delimiters to tokenize the field into individual tokens.

The `standard` analyzer has only one attribute that can be customized: `max_token_length`. This attribute produces tokens of the size it defines (the default size is 255). We can set this property by creating a custom analyzer with a custom tokenizer.

Listing 7.43 Index with a custom tokenizer

```
PUT index_with_custom_standard_tokenizer
{
  "settings": {
    "analysis": {
      "analyzer": {
        "custom_token_length_analyzer": {
          "tokenizer": "custom_token_length_tokenizer"
        }
      },
      "tokenizer": {
        "custom_token_length_tokenizer": {
          "type": "standard",
          "max_token_length": 2
        }
      }
    }
  }
}
```

Creates a custom analyzer with a pointer to the custom tokenizer

Custom tokenizer with max_token_length set to two characters

Similar to how we created an index with a custom component for types of character filters in section 7.7.1, we can create an index with a custom analyzer encompassing a `standard` tokenizer. The tokenizer is then extended by providing the `max_token_length` size (in listing 7.43, the length is set to 2). Once the index is created, we can use the `_analyze` API to test the field.

Listing 7.44 Testing a token size for the tokenizer

```
POST index_with_custom_standard_tokenizer/_analyze
{
  "text": "Bond",
  "analyzer": "custom_token_length_analyzer"
}
```

This code spits out two tokens: "Bo" and "nd", honoring our request for a token size of two characters.

7.7.2 *The ngram and edge_ngram tokenizers*

Before we jump into learning about n-gram tokenizers, let's recap n-grams, edge n-grams, and shingles. N-grams are sequences of words of a given size prepared from a given word. Take as an example the word *coffee*. The two-letter n-grams, usually called bi-grams, are "co", "of", "ff", "fe", and "ee". Similarly, the three-letter tri-grams are "cof", "off", "ffe", and "fee". As you can see, n-grams are generated by sliding the letter window.

On the other hand, edge n-grams are words with letters anchored at the beginning of the given word. Again using *coffee* as our example, the edge n-grams are "c", "co", "cof", "coff", "coffe", and "coffee". Figure 7.13 shows these n-grams and edge n-grams.

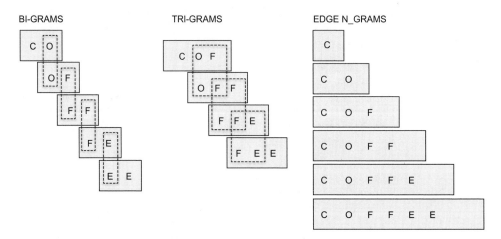

Figure 7.13   Pictorial representation of n-grams and edge n-grams

The `ngram` and `edge_ngram` tokenizers emit n-grams, as the names suggest. Let's look at them in action.

THE NGRAM TOKENIZER

To correct spelling and broken words, we usually use n-grams. The `ngram` tokenizer emits n-grams with a minimum size of 1 and a maximum size of 2 by default. For example, this code produces n-grams of the word "Bond":

```
POST _analyze
{
  "text": "Bond",
  "tokenizer": "ngram"
}
```

The output is [B, Bo, o, on, n, nd, d]. Each n-gram is made of one or two letters: this is the default behavior. We can customize the `min_gram` and `max_gram` sizes by specifying the configuration.

Listing 7.45   An `ngram` tokenizer

```
PUT index_with_ngram_tokenizer
{
  "settings": {
    "analysis": {
      "analyzer": {
        "ngram_analyzer":{
          "tokenizer":"ngram_tokenizer"
        }
      },
      "tokenizer": {
        "ngram_tokenizer":{
```

```
      "type":"ngram",
      "min_gram":2,
      "max_gram":3,
      "token_chars":[
        "letter"
      ]
    }
   }
  }
 }
}
```

Using the `min_gram` and `max_gram` attributes of this `ngram` tokenizer (set to `2` and `3`, respectively), we can configure the index to produce n-grams. Let's test this feature.

Listing 7.46 Testing the `ngram` tokenizer

```
POST index_with_ngram_tokenizer/_analyze
{
  "text": "bond",
  "analyzer": "ngram_analyzer"
}
```

This produces the following n-grams: "bo", "bon", "on", "ond", and "nd". The n-grams have two or three characters.

THE EDGE_NGRAM TOKENIZER

Following the same path, we can use the `edge_ngram` tokenizer to spit out edge n-grams. This is the code that creates an analyzer with the `edge_ngram` tokenizer:

```
..
"tokenizer": {
  "my_edge_ngram_tokenizer":{
    "type":"edge_ngram",
     "min_gram":2,
     "max_gram":6,
     "token_chars":["letter","digit"]
   }
}
```

Once the `edge_ngram` tokenizer is attached to a custom analyzer, we can test the field using the `_analyze` API:

```
POST index_with_edge_ngram/_analyze
{
  "text": "bond",
  "analyzer": "edge_ngram_analyzer"
}
```

This invocation spits out these edge n-grams: "b", "bo", "bon", and "bond." Note that all the words are anchored on the first letter.

7.7.3   *Other tokenizers*

As mentioned earlier, there are other tokenizers, and they are briefly described in table 7.4. You can find code examples with the book's files.

Table 7.4   Out-of-the-box tokenizers

Tokenizer	Description
`pattern`	Splits a field into tokens on a regex match. The default pattern is to split words when a non-word character is encountered.
`uax_url_email`	Parses fields and preserves URLs and emails. The URLs and emails are returned as they are, without any tokenization.
`whitespace`	Splits text into tokens when whitespace is encountered
`keyword`	Doesn't touch the tokens. This tokenizer returns the text as is.
`lowercase`	Splits text into tokens when a non-letter is encountered and lowercases the tokens
`path_hierarchy`	Splits hierarchical text such as filesystem folders into tokens based on path separators

The final component of an analyzer is a token filter. Its job is to work on the tokens spit out by the tokenizers. We briefly discuss the token filters in the next section.

7.8   *Token filters*

The tokens produced by tokenizers may need further enriching or enhancements such as lowercasing (or uppercasing) the tokens, providing synonyms, developing stemming words, removing apostrophes or other punctuation, and so on. Token filters work on tokens to perform such transformations.

Elasticsearch provides almost 50 token filters, and we can't discuss all of them here. We look at a few—feel free to reference the official documentation to learn about the rest of the token filters. We can test a token filter by simply attaching to a tokenizer and using it in the `_analyze` API call.

Listing 7.47   Adding a token filter with the tokenizer

```
GET _analyze
{
  "tokenizer" : "standard",
  "filter" : ["uppercase","reverse"],
  "text" : "bond"
}
```

The filter accepts an array of token filters; for example, here we provide the `uppercase` and `reverse` filters. The output is "DNOB" ("bond" is uppercased and reversed).

We can also attach filters to a custom analyzer, as the following listing shows. Then because we know how to attach token filters, we look at a few examples.

```
Listing 7.48  Custom analyzer with additional filters
```

```
PUT index_with_token_filters
{
  "settings": {
    "analysis": {
      "analyzer": {                          ┌─ Defines a
        "token_filter_analyzer": {     ◁──┘  custom analyzer
          "tokenizer": "standard",
          "filter": [ "uppercase","reverse"]    ◁─┐ Provides token filters
        }                                          │ as an array of filters
      }
    }
  }
}
```

7.8.1   The stemmer filter

As explained earlier in the chapter, *stemming* reduces the words to their root words (for example, *bark* is the root word for *barking*). Elasticsearch provides an out-of-the-box stemmer that reduces the words to their root form. The next listing shows an example.

```
Listing 7.49  Using a stemmer as the token filter
```

```
POST _analyze
{
  "tokenizer": "standard",
  "filter": ["stemmer"],
  "text": "barking is my life"
}
```

When executed, this code produces a list of tokens: "bark", "is", "my", and "life". The original word "barking" is transformed to "bark".

7.8.2   The shingle filter

Shingles are word n-grams generated at the token level (unlike n-grams and edge n-grams that emit n-grams at the letter level). For example, the text, "james bond" emits the shingles "james" and "james bond". Here's an example of a shingle filter:

```
POST _analyze
{
  "tokenizer": "standard",
  "filter": ["shingle"],
  "text": "java python go"
}
```

The result is [java, java python, python, python go, go]. The default behavior of the filter is to emit unigrams and two-word n-grams. We can change this default behavior by creating a custom analyzer with a custom shingle filter.

Listing 7.50 Creating a custom analyzer for shingles

```
PUT index_with_shingle
{
  "settings": {
    "analysis": {
      "analyzer": {
        "shingles_analyzer":{
          "tokenizer":"standard",              Creates a custom analyzer
          "filter":["shingles_filter"]         with a shingles filter
        }
      },
      "filter": {
        "shingles_filter":{              Attributes of the shingle filter
          "type":"shingle",             (for example, minimum and
          "min_shingle_size":2,          maximum shingle sizes)
          "max_shingle_size":3,
          "output_unigrams":false        Turns off the output
        }                                of single words
      }
    }
  }
}
```

Invoking this code on some text produces groups of two or three words.

Listing 7.51 Running the `shingle` analyzer

```
POST index_with_shingle/_analyze
{
  "text": "java python go",
  "analyzer": "shingles_analyzer"
}
```

The analyzer returns [java python, java python go, python go] because we configured the filter to produce only two- and three-word shingles. Unigrams (one-word
shingles) like "java", "python", and so forth are removed from the output because we
disabled their output in our filter.

7.8.3 The synonym filter

We worked with synonyms earlier without going into detail. *Synonyms* are different
words with the same meanings. For example, if a user searches for "football" or "soccer" (the latter being what football is called in America), either search should point to
a football game. The synonym filter creates a set of words to produce a richer user
experience while searching.

Elasticsearch expects us to provide a set of words and their synonyms by configuring the analyzer with a synonym token filter. We create the synonym filter on an index's
settings as the next listing shows.

Listing 7.52   Creating an index with a synonym filter

```
PUT index_with_synonyms
{
  "settings": {
    "analysis": {
      "filter": {
        "synonyms_filter":{
          "type":"synonym",
          "synonyms":[ "soccer => football"]
        }
      }
    }
  }
}
```

Here, we create a synonyms list (*soccer* is treated as an alternate name for *football*) associated with the synonym type. Once the index is configured with this filter, we can test the text field:

```
POST index_with_synonyms/_analyze
{
  "text": "What's soccer?",
  "tokenizer": "standard",
  "filter": ["synonyms_filter"]
}
```

This produces two tokens: "What's", and "football". The word *soccer* is replaced by the synonym.

We can provide synonyms via a file on a filesystem rather than hardcoding them as we did in listing 7.52. To do that, we provide the file path in the synonyms_path variable.

Listing 7.53   Synonyms loaded from a file

```
PUT index_with_synonyms_from_file_analyzer
{
  "settings": {
    "analysis": {
      "analyzer": {
        "synonyms_analyzer":{
          "type":"standard",
          "filter":["synonyms_from_file_filter"]
        }
      }
      ,"filter": {
        "synonyms_from_file_filter":{
          "type":"synonym",
          "synonyms_path":"synonyms.txt"          ◁──── **Relative path of
        }                                                the synonyms file**
      }
    }
  }
}
```

Be sure to create a file called synonyms.txt under $ELASTICSEARCH_HOME/config with the following contents.

Listing 7.54   synonyms.txt file with a set of synonyms

```
important=>imperative
beautiful=>gorgeous
```

We can call the file using a relative or absolute path; a relative path points to the config directory of Elasticsearch's installation folder. We can test this analyzer by invoking the _analyze API with the following input.

Listing 7.55   Testing the synonyms

```
POST index_with_synonyms_from_file_analyzer/_analyze
{
  "text": "important",
  "tokenizer": "standard",
  "filter": ["synonyms_from_file_filter"]
}
```

We get the token "imperative" as the response, proving that the synonyms are picked up from the synonyms.txt file we dropped in the config folder. You can add more values to this file while Elasticsearch is running and try them, too.

That's a wrap! This chapter is fundamental for the discussion of search that we embark on in the next chapter. We have completed all the necessary background to work with search functionality in depth.

Summary

- Elasticsearch analyzes `text` fields via the text analysis process. Text analysis is carried out using either built-in or custom analyzers. Non-text fields are not analyzed.
- Text analysis consists of two phases: tokenization and normalization. Tokenization splits the input field into individual words or tokens, and normalization enhances the word (for example, changing it to a synonym, stemming it, or removing it).
- Elasticsearch employs a software module called an analyzer to carry out text analysis. An analyzer is a package made of character filters, token filters, and a tokenizer.
- Elasticsearch uses a `standard` analyzer by default if no analyzer is given explicitly during indexing and searching. A `standard` analyzer employs no character filter, a `standard` tokenizer, and two token filters (`lowercase` and `stop`), although the `stop` filter is off by default.
- Every analyzer must have one (and only one) tokenizer, but it can have zero or more character or token filters.

- Character filters help strip unwanted characters from input fields. Tokenizers act on the fields processed by character filters (or on raw fields, since character filters are optional). Token filters work on the tokens emitted by the tokenizer.
- Elasticsearch provides several out-of-the-box analyzers. We can mix and match existing tokenizers with character or token filters to make custom analyzers that suit our requirements.

Introducing search 8

This chapter covers

- Fundamentals of search
- Types of search methods
- Introduction to Query DSL
- Common search features

It is time to enter the world of search. So far, we've looked at priming Elasticsearch with data, and the last chapter discussed the mechanics of how text fields are analyzed. We got a taste of searching data using a set of queries, but we didn't look at searching in depth or the nitty-gritty of search variants. Chapters 8 through 12 are dedicated to search.

Search is the core functionality of Elasticsearch and answers user queries efficiently and effectively. Once data is indexed and available for search, users can ask various questions. For example, if our fictitious online bookstore's website search is powered by Elasticsearch, we can expect many queries from clients. They may range from simple queries like finding a book based on a title search word to complex queries searching for books that match multiple criteria: a particular edition, published between a range of dates, hardbound, review rating higher than 4.5 out of 5, price less than a certain amount, and so on. The UI may support various widgets such as dropdowns, sliders, check boxes, and so forth to enable filtering the search even further.

This chapter introduces search and the fundamental features we can use while searching. We first discuss search mechanics: how a search request is processed and a response is created and sent to the client. We then look at fundamentals of search: the search API and contexts in which search queries are performed. We dissect a request and a response to dig deeper into their components.

We also look at types of searches, the URI request, and Query DSL, as well as why we prefer Query DSL over the URI request method. Finally, we examine crosscutting search features such as highlighting, pagination, explanation, and manipulating response fields.

NOTE The code for this chapter is available on GitHub (http://mng.bz/ e1yZ) and on the book's website (https://www.manning.com/books/elastic search-in-action-second-edition).

8.1 Overview

Elasticsearch supports simple search functionality and advanced searches that consider multiple criteria, including geospatial queries. Broadly speaking, Elasticsearch deals with two variants of search: *structured search* and *unstructured search*. We've gone over these variants in earlier chapters, so this is pretty much a recap; feel free to skip this section.

Structured search returns results with no associated *relevance* score. Elasticsearch fetches documents if they match exactly and doesn't worry about whether they are a close match or how well they match. Searches for flights between a set of dates, best-selling books during a particular sales promotion, and so on fall into this category. When the search is carried out, Elasticsearch checks whether the match is successful: for example, there are or are not flights that fall in the given date range, and there are or are not best-selling books. Nothing falls into a *maybe* category. This type of structured search is provided by *term-level queries* in Elasticsearch.

On the other hand, in an unstructured search, Elasticsearch retrieves results that are closely related to the query. Results are scored based on how relevant they are to the criteria: highly relevant results get higher scores and so are positioned at the top of the list. Searching on `text` fields yields relevant results, and Elasticsearch provides full-text search to search unstructured data.

We communicate with the Elasticsearch engine using a RESTful API to execute queries. A search query is written using a special query syntax called Query DSL (domain-specific language) or a URL standard called *query requests*. When a query is issued, any available node in the cluster picks the request and processes it. The response is returned as a JSON object, with an array of individual documents as results in the object.

If the query is executed on `text` fields, each individual result is returned with a relevancy score. The higher the score, the greater the relevancy (meaning the resultant document is a very close match). Results are sorted in descending order, with the result with the highest score at the top.

Not every result in a response is accurate. Just as we can expect an incorrect or irrelevant result sometimes when searching on Google, Elasticsearch may not return 100% relevant results. This is because Elasticsearch employs two internal strategies, precision and recall, that affect the relevancy of results.

Precision is the percentage of relevant documents retrieved over a set of documents available in the index, and *recall* is the percentage of relevant documents retrieved over a set of applicable (all relevant) documents. We discuss precision and recall in detail in chapter 10.

Many features are common to search regardless of the query type we choose (full-text, term-level, geospatial, etc.). We discuss these search features throughout the chapter and see applications of them in the next few chapters when we work with search and aggregations. The following section explains the mechanics of search: how Elasticsearch works on a search query to retrieve matching results.

8.2   How does search work?

A lot happens when a user invokes a search query against Elasticsearch. Although we touched on the mechanics earlier, let's recap. Figure 8.1 shows how the engine carries out a search in the background.

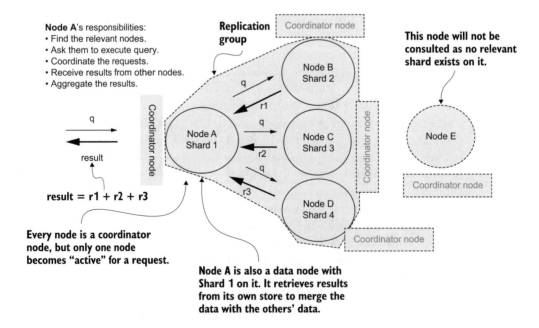

Figure 8.1   A typical search request, and the mechanics of how a search works

When a search request is received from a user or a client, the engine forwards that request to one of the available nodes in the cluster. By default, every node in the cluster is assigned to a *coordinator* role, so every node is eligible to pick up client requests on a round-robin basis. Once the request reaches the coordinator node, it determines the nodes on which shards of the applicable documents exist.

In figure 8.1, Node A is the *coordinator* node that receives the client's request. It was chosen as a coordinator node for no reason other than demonstration purposes. Once chosen for the (coordinator) active role, it selects a *replication group* with a set of shards and replicas on individual nodes in a cluster that consists of data. Remember, an index is made of shards, and each shard can exist independently on other nodes. In our example, the index is made of four shards (1, 2, 3, and 4) that exist on Nodes A to D, respectively.

Node A formulates the query request to send to other nodes, requesting them to carry out the search. Upon receiving the request, the respective node performs the search request on its shard. It then extracts the top set of results and responds to the active coordinator with those results. The active coordinator then merges and sorts the data before sending it to the client as a final result.

If the coordinator has a role as a data node, it also digs into its store to fetch results. Not every node that receives the request is necessarily a data node. Similarly, not every node is expected to be part of the replication group for this search query. Now, let's take a moment to load some movie data into our Elasticsearch engine.

8.3   Movie sample data

Let's create some movie test data and movie mappings for this chapter. Because we don't want Elasticsearch to deduce the field types, we provide the relevant data types for each field as mappings when we create the index (especially the `release_date` and `duration` fields, which can't be `text` fields). The following listing shows the `movies` index mapping (if this index exists already, delete it for this chapter's examples by issuing `DELETE movies`).

Listing 8.1   Mappings schema for the `movies` domain

```
PUT movies          ◁─┐  Movies   ┌  Mappings
{                      │  index  ◁─┘  schema
  "mappings": {
    "properties": {   ◁─┐ Fields and
      "title": {        │ their types
        "type": "text",
        "fields": {   ◁──────┐  Multi-field
          "original": {      │  construct
            "type": "keyword"
          }
        }
      }
    },
    "synopsis": {
```

```
        "type": "text"
      },
      "actors": {
        "type": "text"
      },
      "director": {
        "type": "text"
      },
      "rating": {
        "type": "half_float"
      },
      "release_date": {
        "type": "date",
        "format": "dd-MM-yyyy"
      },
      "certificate": {
        "type": "keyword"
      },
      "genre": {
        "type": "text"
      }
    }
  }
}
```

Table 8.1 shows a few notable elements from this mapping. The rest of the attributes are self-explanatory.

Table 8.1   Some `movies` fields and their respective data types

Field	Declared data types
title	text and keyword
release_date	date with the format dd-MM-yyyy
certificate	keyword

With the mapping in place for the `movies` domain, the next task is to index the sample data using the `_bulk` API. The next listing shows this API in action with a sample of data.

Listing 8.2   Listing 8.2 Indexing sample movie data using the `_bulk` API

```
PUT _bulk     ◁──┐ The _bulk
                    API
{"index":{"_index":"movies","_id":"1"}}    ◁──┐ Document with an
{"title":"The Shawshank Redemption","genre":"Drama",..}    ID of 1 for indexing    The document
{"index":{"_index":"movies","_id":"2"}}                                            itself
{"title":"The Godfather","genre":"Crime, Drama","...}    ◁──┐ Document with an
{"index":{"_index":"movies","_id":"3"}}                        ID of 2 for indexing
```

For brevity, we show only part of the script. The full script is available with the book's files.

> **NOTE**   To avoid having too many domain models and messing with sample data, we use the same movie data in chapters 8 and 9.

With an understanding of search mechanics and sample data in hand, let's turn to the fundamentals of search.

8.4   Search fundamentals

Now that we know the inner workings of search, let's look at the search API and how to invoke the engine to carry out search queries. Elasticsearch exposes a _search endpoint to communicate with it to execute search queries. Let's look at the endpoint in detail.

8.4.1   The _search endpoint

Elasticsearch provides RESTful APIs to query data: a _search endpoint, to be specific. We use GET/POST to invoke this endpoint, passing query parameters along with the request or a request body. The queries we construct depend on the type of data we are searching for. There are two ways of accessing the search endpoint:

- *URI request*—We pass the search query along with the endpoint as parameters to the query. For example, GET movies/_search?q=title:Godfather fetches all movies matching the word *Godfather* in the title (*The Godfather* trilogy, for example).
- *Query DSL*—Elasticsearch implements a DSL for search. Search criteria wrapped in a JSON body are sent to the server along with the request URL. The result is wrapped in a JSON object as well. We can provide a single query or combine multiple queries, depending on our requirements. (Query DSL is also the mechanism to send aggregate queries to the engine. We look more at aggregations later in the chapter.) Here's an example of the same requirement to fetch all movies with the word *Godfather* in the title field:

```
GET movies/_search
{
  "query": {
    "match": {
      "title": "Godfather"
    }
  }
}
```

Although both approaches are useful in their own ways, Query DSL is powerful and feature-rich. It is a first-class querying mechanism, and it's easier to write complex criteria using Query DSL than with the URI request mechanism. We look at various invocations in this chapter and chapters 9 through 12 and work more extensively with Query DSL than with the URI request method.

NOTE   Query DSL is like a Swiss Army knife when it comes to talking to Elasticsearch, and it is the preferred option. The Elasticsearch team developed this DSL specifically to work with the engine. Anything and everything we want to ask Elasticsearch can be retrieved using Query DSL.

Don't fret if you don't understand search queries and how they are coded. We work through several examples in this chapter and discuss them in detail in coming chapters.

8.4.2   Query vs. filter context

We need to examine another fundamental concept: the execution context. Internally, Elasticsearch uses an execution context when running searches. This execution context can be either a *filter* context or a *query* context. All queries issued to Elasticsearch are carried out in one of these contexts. We can't ask Elasticsearch to apply a certain type of context—our query lets Elasticsearch decide and apply the appropriate context. For example, if we are running a `match` query, it should be executed in a query context, whereas a `filter` query is executed in a filter context. Let's execute a couple of queries to understand the context in which the query is executed.

QUERY CONTEXT

We use a `match` query to search for documents by matching keywords with the field's values. The following listing is a simple `match` query that searches for "Godfather" in the `title` field.

```
Listing 8.3   Match query executed in a query context
```

```
GET movies/_search
{
  "query": {
    "match": {
      "title": "Godfather"
    }
  }
}
```

This code returns our two *Godfather* movies, as expected. However, if we look at the results closely, each movie has an associated relevancy score:

```
"hits" : [{
  ...
 "_score" : 2.879596
 "_source" : {
   "title" : "The Godfather"
   ...
 }
},
{
   ...
  "_score" : 2.261362
  "_source" : {
```

```
        "title" : "The Godfather: Part II"
        ...
    }
  }]
```

The output indicates that the query was executed in a query context because the query determined not only whether it matched a document but also how well the document was matched.

Why is the score for the second result (2.261362) slightly lower than the score for the first result (2.879596)? Because the engine's relevancy algorithm found "Godfather" in a title with two words ("the", "godfather"), and that match ranks higher than a match in a title of four words ("the","godfather","part","II").

NOTE Queries on full-text search fields run in a query context because they are expected to have a score associated with each matched document.

Although fetching the result with a relevancy score is fine for most use cases, sometimes we do not need to find out how well the document matched. Instead, we just want to know whether there's a match. This is where the filter context comes into play.

FILTER CONTEXT

Let's rewrite the query from listing 8.3, but this time wrap our `match` query in a `bool` query with a `filter` clause.

Listing 8.4   A `bool` query with no score

```
GET movies/_search
{
  "query": {
    "bool": {
      "filter": [{
          "match": {
            "title": "Godfather"
          }
        }
      ]
    }
  }
}
```

In this listing, the results do not have a score (`score` is set to 0.0) because our query gives Elasticsearch a clue that it must be run in a filter context. If we are not interested in scoring the document, we can ask Elasticsearch to run the query in a filter context by wrapping the query in a `filter` clause, as we did here.

The main benefit of running a query in this context is that because Elasticsearch doesn't need to calculate scores for the returned search results, it can save some computing cycles. These filter queries are more idempotent, so Elasticsearch caches them for better performance.

Compound queries

A `bool` query is a compound query with several clauses (`must`, `must_not`, `should`, and `filter`) to wrap leaf queries. The `must_not` clause contradicts the `must` query's intent. Both `filter` and `must_not` clauses are executed in a `filter` context. We can also use the `filter` context in a bool query, we can also use it in a `constant_score` (the name is a giveaway) query.

The `constant_score` query is another compound query in which we can attach a query in a `filter` clause. The following query shows this in action:

```
GET movies/_search
{
  "query": {
    "constant_score": {
      "filter": {
        "match": {
          "title": "Godfather"
        }
      }
    }
  }
}
```

We look at compound queries in chapter 11.

Knowing the execution context gets us one step closer to understanding the inner workings of the Elasticsearch engine. The filter execution context helps create performant queries because the additional effort of running the relevancy algorithm is not required. We look at examples that demonstrate these contexts in the following chapters.

Now that we've had an overview of search in general (and with search data at hand), let's look at what constitutes a search request and dissect the results (search response).

8.5   *Anatomy of a request and a response*

We had a quick glance at the search request and response in the last few chapters without worrying about attribute details and explanations. However, it is important to understand the request and response objects, to formulate the query object without errors and understand the meaning of the attributes featured in the response. In this section, we delve into the request and response objects.

8.5.1   *Search requests*

Search queries can be executed using a URI request method or Query DSL. As we discussed earlier, we focus on the Query DSL in this book as it is more powerful and expressive. Figure 8.2 shows the anatomy of a search request.

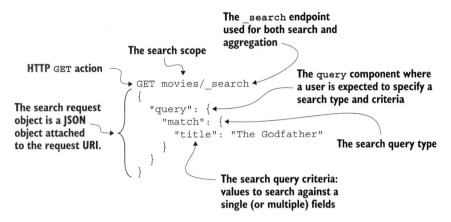

Figure 8.2 Components of a search request

The GET method is the HTTP action that specifies our intention: getting data from the server with the request details carried over in a body. There's a school of thought that the GET method in a RESTful architecture shouldn't send parameters using the body of the request and that instead, we should use a POST method if we are querying the server. But Elasticsearch implements the GET method request that accepts a body, which helps formulate the query parameters. We can replace GET with POST, as both GET or POST act on the resource the same way.

> **NOTE** The internet is full of hot debates about using GET with and without a payload. Elasticsearch takes the route of using GET with a payload. (If you want to understand the schools of thought, search for "HTTP get with body" on the internet). In this book, we use GET with a payload for search and aggregation queries, although you can replace GET with POST if you are not comfortable using the GET method with a body.

The search scope in the GET (or POST) action defines the index or an alias that the engine uses to carry out the search. We can also include multiple indexes, multiple aliases, or no index in this URL. To specify multiple indexes (or aliases), enter comma-separated index (or alias) names. Providing no index or alias on the search request tells the search to run against all the indexes across the cluster. For example, if we have a cluster with 10 indexes, running a search query like GET _search {...} without specifying index or alias names searches for all matching documents against all 10 indexes.

The search request object or payload is a JSON object enclosing the request details. The request details include the query component and can include other components such as pagination-related size and form attributes, a list that indicates which source fields to return in the response, sort criteria, highlighting, and so forth. We discuss individual features later in this chapter.

The main constituent of the request is the query. It's the query's job to compose the question that needs to be answered. It does so by creating a `query` object that defines a query type and its required input. We can select from many query types serving various search criteria. We learn about these query types in detail in the next few chapters.

We can create specific queries for specific use cases, ranging from match and term-level queries to special queries like geo-shapes. Query types can build a simple leaf query that targets a single search requirement or construct a complex requirement using compound queries to deal with advanced searching via logical clauses. Now that we are familiar with the anatomy of a search request, it's time to dissect the response.

8.5.2   *Search responses*

We looked at search responses earlier in the book but never covered the details. Figure 8.3 shows a typical response; let's discuss these attributes briefly to understand what they represent.

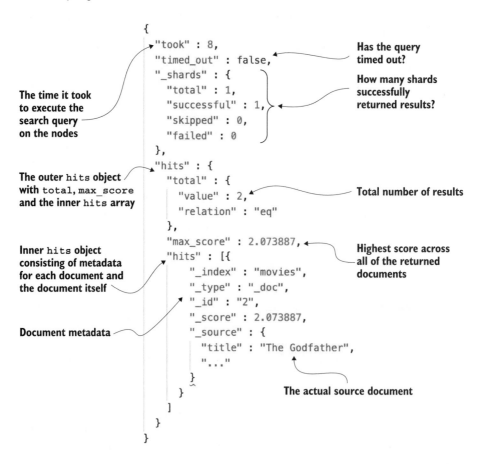

Figure 8.3   Constituents of a search response

The `took` attribute, measured in milliseconds, indicates the time it takes for the search request to complete. This time is measured from when a coordinator node receives the request to the time it aggregates the response before sending it back to the client. It doesn't include client-to-server marshaling/unmarshalling times.

The `timed_out` attribute is a Boolean flag that indicates whether the response has partial results, meaning whether any of the shards failed to respond in time. For example, if we have three shards and one fails to return results, the response consists of the results from the two shards but indicates the failed shard's state in the next object under the `_shards` attribute.

The `shards` attribute provides the number of shards that successfully executed the query and returned results and the number that failed. The `total` field is the number of shards expected to be searched, and the `successful` field denotes the shards that have returned data. A `failed` flag, on the other hand, indicates shards that failed during execution of the search query; the flag is denoted by the `failed` attribute.

The `hits` attribute (called *outer* `hits`) consists of information about the results. It contains another `hits` field (called *inner* `hits`). The outer `hits` object consists of the returned results, maximum score, and total results. The maximum score, represented by the `max_score` property, is the returned document with the highest score. The inner `hits` object consists of the results (the actual documents). This is an array of all the individual documents sorted by relevancy in descending order. Each document receives this `_score` attribute if the query is executed in a query context.

We've mentioned the two types of requests we can create for a query that asks a question: URI request and Query DSL. The next two sections discuss these in detail.

> **NOTE**   As stated earlier, because of the versatility and features of Query DSL, we use it as our search mechanism in this book. However, for completeness, we briefly discuss URI request search in the following section. This way, you can experiment by creating equivalent URI request methods if you want to create cross-function search queries.

8.6   URI request searches

The URI request method is an easy way to search for simple queries. We invoke the `_search` endpoint by passing required parameters. The following syntax shows how to implement this search:

```
GET|POST <your_index_name>/_search?q=<name:value> AND|OR <name:value>
```

The `_search` endpoint is invoked on our index (or multiple indexes) with a query in the form of `q=<name:value>`. Note that the query is appended after the `_search` endpoint with a question mark (?) delimiter. With this method, we pass in the query parameters attached to the URL as `name:value` pairs. Let's issue some search queries using this method.

8.6.1   *Searching for movies by title*

Let's say we want to find movies by searching for a word in the title field ("Godfather", for example). We use the `_search` endpoint on the `movies` index with the query parameter `Godfather` as the `title` attribute.

Listing 8.5   Search query to fetch movies matching "Godfather"

```
GET movies/_search?q=title:Godfather
```

The URL is composed of the `_search` endpoint followed by the query represented by the letter q. This query returns all movies with a title matching the word "Godfather" (we should get two movies in the response: *The Godfather Part I* and *Part II*).

To search for movies matching multiple words, we can add the titles as search keywords with a space between them. The following query searches for all movies matching the words "Godfather", "Knight", and "Shawshank".

Listing 8.6   Searching for movies by multiple words

```
GET movies/_search?q=title:Godfather Knight Shawshank
```

This query returns four movie titles: *The Shawshank Redemption, The Dark Knight, The Godfather Part I,* and *The Godfather Part II*. Note that by default, Elasticsearch uses the `OR` operator between the query inputs, so we don't need to specify it (it is assumed to be present implicitly).

If we check the relevancy scores, *The Shawshank Redemption* and *The Dark Knight* received the same score (3.085904), and *The Godfather Part I* scored a bit higher than *The Godfather Part II*. We can ask Elasticsearch to explain how it derived this scoring by passing an `explain` flag:

```
GET movies/_search?q=title:Godfather Knight Shawshank&explain=true
```

We discuss the `explain` flag in section 8.8.3.

---

cURL format

The cURL equivalent for the code in listing 8.6 is

```
curl -XGET "http://localhost:9200/movies/_search?q=title:Godfather
        Knight Shawshank"
```

You can generate a cURL command automatically by clicking the wrench icon next to the Play button in the Dev Tools UI, as shown in the figure.

8.6.2 Searching for a specific movie

To fetch a specific movie, we can combine criteria with the AND operator. The following query returns a single movie, *The Dark Knight*, matching the title and actors fields.

Listing 8.7 Fetching a movie by title *and* actor

```
GET movies/_search?q=title:Knight AND actors:Bale
```

The AND operator helps narrow the results. If we omit the AND operator and run the query as in the next listing, we get two more movies (both *Godfather* movies as well as *The Dark Knight*).

Listing 8.8 Fetching a title *or* an actor

```
GET movies/_search?q=title:Godfather actors:Bale
```

Here, we are searching for movies that match "Godfather" *or* movies that match the actor Christian Bale. (Remember that Elasticsearch uses the OR operator by default.) Alternatively, to specify the AND operator in a multi-fields search, we can simply append the default_operator parameter to the query.

Listing 8.9 Setting default_operator as AND

```
GET movies/_search?q=title:Godfather actors:Bale&default_operator=AND
```

This query does not return any results because there is no *Godfather* movie with Christian Bale (at least not so far). Be sure the default_operator parameter is prefixed with an ampersand (&), as shown in listing 8.9. But there shouldn't be a space after the & because Kibana doesn't like a space between the & and the default_operator attribute.

8.6.3 Additional parameters

We can pass more parameters with the URL and add multiple criteria to the query. For example, we can set two attributes, from and size, to fetch paginated results (we look at pagination later in this chapter). We can also sort the results using, for example, rating to sort by movie ratings. Again, we can ask Elasticsearch to explain how it calculates the scoring using the explain parameter. Let's write a query with all these requirements and a few others.

Listing 8.10 Expanding our query with additional parameters

```
GET movies/_search?q=title:Godfather actors:
(Brando OR Pacino) rating:(>=9.0 AND <=9.5)&from=0&size=10
&explain=true&sort=rating&default_operator=AND
```

This query is a mashup of parameters, but here is the gist. We are searching for *Godfather* movies (title) starring Marlon Brando OR Al Pacino (actors) with a rating between 9 AND 9.5. We also add pagination (from, size), sort by rating, and ask Elasticsearch to explain. We retrieve two movies (both *Godfathers*), although Brando is not in *The Godfather Part II* (we specify Brando OR Pacino in the actors field).

As you may have guessed, the URL request method of writing queries is crude and error-prone. Ideally, we should write queries using Query DSL. Fortunately, we can wrap a URL request in Query DSL to get the best of both worlds.

8.6.4   *Supporting URI requests with Query DSL*

Query DSL has a query_string method that allows us to wrap a URI request call (we look at Query DSL in the next section). We can send the URI query parameters to search for movies with multiple title keywords in the request body as a query_string.

Listing 8.11   Using a URI method wrapped in Query DSL

```
GET movies/_search
{
  "query": {
    "query_string": {
      "default_field": "title",
      "query": "Knight Redemption Lord Pulp",
      "default_operator": "OR"
    }
  }
}
```

The query_string is equivalent to the q parameter we used earlier in the URI search method. While it is much better than the URI request approach, the query_string method is strict with syntax and has some unforgiving characteristics. Unless there's a strong reason not to, use Query DSL queries rather than query_string. We can use query_string for quick testing, but relying on it for complicated and in-depth queries may be asking for trouble.

It's time to venture into the mighty kingdom of Query DSL. Because Query DSL is a Swiss Army knife for searching, it warrants a dedicated section.

8.7   *Query DSL*

The Elasticsearch team developed the search-specific, all-purpose language and syntax called Query DSL. It's a sophisticated, powerful, expressive language that can create a multitude of queries from basic to complex, in addition to nested and more complicated queries. It can also be extended for analytical queries. It is a JSON-based query language that can be constructed with queries for search and analytics. The syntax and format are as follows:

```
GET books/_search        ◁──┐   Invokes the _search endpoint
{                            │   on the books index
```

```
     "query": {                 ◁─┐  All queries are wrapped
Query ┌─▷  "match": {              │  in this object.
 type │          ...       ◁──┐  The query criteria
      │       }                 │  are enclosed here.
       }
   }
```

We invoke the _search endpoint with a query object, passed in as the body of the request. The query object consists of the logic for creating the required criteria.

8.7.1   Sample query

We have worked with a few queries written using the Query DSL format. For completeness, let's write a multi_match query that searches for a keyword, "Lord", across two fields, synopsis and title.

Listing 8.12   Query DSL sample query

```
GET movies/_search
{
  "query": {
    "multi_match": {
      "query": "Lord",
      "fields": ["synopsis","title"]
    }
  }
}
```

GET movies/_search is the shorthand search request from a client to the Elasticsearch server. The full request is something like this:

```
GET http://localhost:9200/movies/_search
```

My Elasticsearch server is running locally, of course, so localhost is the server's address. This request expects a JSON-formatted body that consists of the query.

8.7.2   Query DSL for cURL

The same query can be invoked via cURL. The following listing shows this invocation.

Listing 8.13   Query DSL via cURL

```
curl -XGET "http://localhost:9200/movies/_search" -H
'Content-Type: application/json' -d'
{
  "query": {
    "multi_match": {
      "query": "Lord",
      "fields": ["synopsis","title"]
    }
  }
}'
```

The query is provided as an argument to the -d parameter. Note that the entire query (beginning with Content-Type) is enclosed in single quotes when sending the request via cURL.

8.7.3   *Query DSL for aggregations*

Although we haven't yet introduced the analytics part of Elasticsearch, here's a quick primer. With Query DSL, we use a similar format for aggregations (analytics), with an aggs (short for *aggregations*) object instead of a query object. The following listing shows this format.

> **Listing 8.14   Aggregation query written in Query DSL format**

```
GET movies/_search
{
  "size": 0,
  "aggs": {
    "average_movie_rating": {
      "avg": {
        "field": "rating"
      }
    }
  }
}
```

This query fetches the average rating of all movies using a metric aggregation called avg (short for *average*). Now that we understand the overall form for Query DSL, let's look more at leaf and compound queries, which we touched on earlier.

8.7.4   *Leaf and compound queries*

Query DSL supports both leaf and compound queries. The body of the search query can accept simple or complex query criteria.

A *leaf query* is straightforward, with no clauses. Such queries fetch results based on certain criteria (for example, getting top-rated movies, movies released during a particular year, the gross earnings of a movie, and so on).

With leaf queries, we can find results for criteria against certain fields. The following listing shows an example. (Don't worry about the contents of the query; we discuss such queries in depth in the next few chapters.)

> **Listing 8.15   Leaf query that matches a phrase**

```
GET movies/_search
{
  "query": {
    "match_phrase": {
      "synopsis": "A meek hobbit from the shire and eight companions"
    }
  }
}
```

Leaf queries cannot fetch multiple `query` clauses. For example, they are not designed
to search for movies that match a title but must *not* match a particular actor *and* have
been released during a specific year *and* have a rating that is not below a certain number. The advanced requirement of logically combining certain clauses to serve a complex query is not possible with a leaf query, which leads to the introduction of
compound queries.

Compound queries allow us to create complex queries by combining leaf queries and
even other compound queries using logical operators. A Boolean (`bool`) query, for
example, is a popular compound query that supports clauses like `must`, `must_not`,
`should`, and `filter`. We can write significantly complex queries using compound queries, like this example.

> **Listing 8.16   Compound query**

```
GET movies/_search
{
  "query": {
    "bool": {
      "must": [{"match": {"title": "Godfather"}}],
      "must_not": [{"range": {"rating": {"lt": 9.0}}}],
      "should": [{"match": {"actors": "Pacino"}}],
      "filter": [{"match": {"actors": "Brando"}}]
    }
  }
}
```

This compound query combines a handful of leaf queries joined by logical operators.
It fetches all movies that *must* match the title *Godfather, and must not* have a rating less
than 9. The query *should* also consider movies with the actor Pacino. Finally, it filters
out everything except movies with the actor Brando. That's a lot! But fear not; we
work with advanced querying using compound queries in upcoming chapters.

Leaf queries (as well as advanced queries) are wrapped in the `query` object of the
search request. Other than implementing the advanced query's logic (which may
sometimes be too complex), we should see no significant difference when writing
compound queries.

There are several crosscutting features, such as sorting, pagination, and highlighting, that any type of a search query can use. They are not specific to `term` or `match`-
level queries, compound queries, or leaf queries. We discuss these features in detail in
the following section. We also use these features now and then during search and
aggregation.

8.8   *Search features*

Elasticsearch provides capabilities to add features to queries and results. We can manipulate source documents in the response by asking Elasticsearch to return a full document or only specific fields. We can sort documents based on one or more fields in
addition to sorting on the document's relevancy score. Elasticsearch lets us paginate

results: for example, we can specify that every page consists of 100 documents instead of the default 10 documents that Elasticsearch returns. There's also a function to high-light results with the search match words in the results. We can even ask the engine to grab results only from a specific set of shards using the shard routing function.

Additionally, most search queries support a handful of crosscutting functions, regardless of the type of query (term-level, full-text, geospatial query, etc.). Some are irrelevant to a specific type of query; for example, sorting isn't advisable on `text` fields, so it is limited to term-level queries. In the next few sections, we explore these features to understand their application in detail.

8.8.1   Pagination

More often than not, queries yields many results, possibly hundreds or even thou-sands. Sending all the results for a query simultaneously is asking for trouble because both the server side and client side need enough memory and processing capacity to deal with the data load.

By default, Elasticsearch sends the top 10 results, but we can change this number by setting the `size` parameter on the query. The maximum value is 10,000, but we can also change this limit, as discussed shortly. The query in the next listing sets `size` to 20, returning the top 20 results at once.

> **Listing 8.17   Query to fetch a specific number of results**

```
GET movies/_search
{
  "size": 20,
  "query": {
    "match_all": {}
  }
}
```

Setting `size` to 20 returns the top 20 results. If we have an index with 1 million docu-ments, setting size to 10,000 retrieves that many documents (ignore the performance considerations for a moment!).

> **Resetting the 10,000-document size limit**
>
> The maximum number of results we can fetch by setting the `size` attribute is 10,000. Suppose we set the size to, say, `10001` and execute the following query:
>
> ```
> GET movies/_search
> {
>   "size": 10001,
>   "query": {
>     "match_all": {}
>   }
> }
> ```

We get the following exception: "The result window is too large, from + size must be less than or equal to: [10000] but was [10001]."

Although 10,000 is fine for most searches, if we need to get more documents than that, we must reset `max_result_window` on the index. The `max_result_window` is a dynamic setting, so we can change it by executing the following query on a live index with the required changes:

```
PUT movies/_settings
{
  "max_result_window":20000    ⟵  Sets the maximum return
}                                   results size to 20000
```

Having said that, it is *not* advisable to use this form of search when fetching large data sets. Instead, it's best to use the `search_after` feature, which we discuss later in this section. Elasticsearch provides a `scroll` API to fetch large data sets, but I advise you to use the `search_after` feature over the `scroll` API.

In addition to the `size` parameter, which helps batch results, Elasticsearch has another parameter called `from` to offset results. As an offset, the `from` setting helps skip a given number of results. For example, if `from` is set to `200`, the first 200 results are ignored, and results will be returned starting with 201. The following listing shows how to paginate results by setting the `size` and `from` attributes.

Listing 8.18 Paginating results using `size` and `from`

```
GET movies/_search
{                            Fetches every page
  "size": 100,     ⟵        with 100 results
  "from": 3,       ⟵         Fetches from the third page (of 100
  "query": {                 results), ignoring the first two pages
    "match_all": {}
  }
}
```

In the listing, by setting `size` to 100, we fetch 100 documents in every page. In addition, we fetch results from the fourth page (as `from` is set to `3`).

If the result set is too large (more than 10,000), rather than working with the pagination using the `size` and `from` attributes, we need to use the `search_after` attribute. We see an example of this (deep pagination) in chapter 9. For now, let's look at another common search feature, highlighting.

8.8.2 Highlighting

When we search for a keyword on a website in our internet browser using Ctrl-F, the results are highlighted so they stand out. For example, the word *dummy* is highlighted in figure 8.4. Highlighting keywords in results for our clients is engaging and visually appealing.

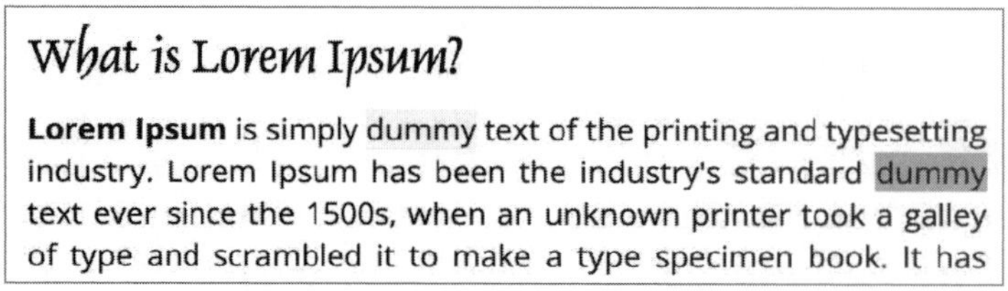

What is Lorem Ipsum?

Lorem Ipsum is simply dummy text of the printing and typesetting industry. Lorem Ipsum has been the industry's standard dummy text ever since the 1500s, when an unknown printer took a galley of type and scrambled it to make a type specimen book. It has

---

Figure 8.4   An example of highlighted text

In Query DSL, we can add a `highlight` object at the same level as the top-level `query` object:

```
GET books/_search
{
  "query": { ... },
  "highlight": { ... }
}
```

The `highlight` object expects a `fields` block, in which we provide the individual fields to highlight in the results:

```
GET books/_search
{
  "query": { ... },
  "highlight": {
    "fields": {
      "field1": {},
      "field2": {}
    }
  }
}
```

When results are returned from the server, we can ask Elasticsearch to highlight the matches with its default settings by enclosing the matched text in emphasis tags (`<em>match</em>`). The code in the next listing creates a `highlight` object, indicating the text to highlight in the `title` field of the results.

Listing 8.19   Highlighting results when matched

```
GET movies/_search
{
  "_source": false,           ⟵  Suppresses the source
  "query": {                       to be returned
    "term": {
      "title": {
        "value": "godfather"
      }
    }
  },"highlight": {            ⟵  Includes a highlight object along
    "fields": {                   with the fields to be highlighted
```

```
            "title": {}              ◁─────┐  The field we want
        }                                  │  to highlight
    }
}
```

The following code highlights the word *Godfather* with `<em>` tags. The source is suppressed in the results because we set `_source` to `false` in the query:

```
{
  ...
  "highlight" : { "title" : ["The <em>Godfather</em>"] }
},
{
  ...
  "highlight" : { "title" : ["The <em>Godfather</em> II"]}
}
```

We use `<em>` tags to emphasize the font in HTML-based browsers. We can also use custom tags. For example, this code creates a pair of curly braces (`{{` and `}}`) as a tag:

```
...
"highlight": {
    "pre_tags": "{{",
    "post_tags": "}}",
    "fields": {
      "title": {}
    }
  }
```

The result is `"The {{Godfather}}"` (with curly braces as the highlights). Now that we know how to highlight search results, let's turn our attention to relevancy scores in data.

8.8.3 *Explaining relevancy scores*

Elasticsearch provides a mechanism that tells us exactly how the engine calculates relevancy scores. This is achieved using an `explain` flag on a `_search` endpoint or an `explain` API. The `explain` API is also used to determine why a document has or has not matched a query. In this section, we look at both of these methods to understand their commonalities and subtle differences.

THE EXPLAIN FLAG

You may have noticed a positive number (a relevancy score value) in some of the earlier query results. Those values were computed and set by the engine, but we didn't explain how. If we are curious about the calculation, Elasticsearch provides a flag called `explain` that we can set in the body of the query. When we set the `explain` attribute to `true`, Elasticsearch returns the results with the details of how it arrived at that score. In other words, it explains the logic and calculations carried out by the engine behind the scenes.

The following listing shows a `match` query. Because we want to know how the scores are calculated, we set `explain` to `true`.

Listing 8.20   **Asking the engine to explain the score**

```
GET movies/_search
{
  "explain": true,
  "_source": false,
  "query": {
    "match": {
      "title": "Lord"
    }
  }
}
```

The `explain` attribute is set at the same level as the `query` object. The result of this query is interesting, as figure 8.5 shows.

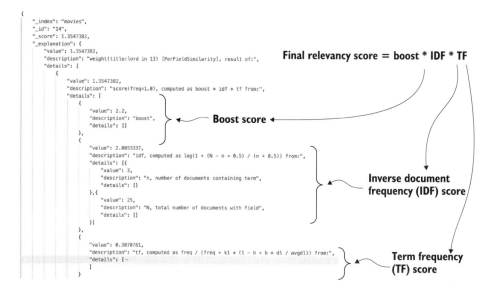

Figure 8.5   The explanation of how Elasticsearch calculates relevancy scores

The relevancy score is calculated by multiplying three components: the inverse document frequency (IDF), the term frequency (TF), and the boost factor. Elasticsearch goes into detail about how it evaluates and measures each of these components. For example, the `description` field in the return response shows that the IDF is computed as

```
log(1 + (N - n + 0.5) / (n + 0.5))
```

where

- *n* is the total number of documents containing the term (in figure 8.5, three documents contain the word *lord*).

- *N* is the total number of documents (figure 8.5 shows 25 documents in our index).

Similarly, the TF is calculated using this formula:

```
freq / (freq + k1 * (1 - b + b * dl / avgdl))
```

An explanation of how each variable is calculated is provided in the `details` section of the results. I recommend that you look at this section to check the application of the formulas by the engine to produce the score.

> **NOTE** What if there's no match? For example, what if we perform the search with "Lords" instead of "Lord"? We'd quickly find out that the results are empty. Try this in the code for yourself to view the results.

THE EXPLAIN API

Although we use the `explain` attribute to understand the mechanics of relevancy scoring, there's also an `_explain` API that provides insight into why a document matched (or not), in addition to providing scoring calculations. The query in the following listing uses an `_explain` endpoint with a document ID as the parameter to demonstrate this approach.

Listing 8.21 Explaining scores using the `_explain` endpoint

```
GET movies/_explain/14
{
  "query":{
    "match": {
      "title": "Lord"
    }
  }
}
```

This query is the same as that in listing 8.20, but this time, to explain the scores, we invoke the `_explain` endpoint instead of setting the `explain` flag on the `_search` endpoint.

Finally, let's misspell the word *Lord* as *Lords* in the `match` attribute in listing 8.21 and rerun the query. As you might expect, we don't get the same results. Instead, we get a clue:

```
{
  "_index" : "movies",
  "_type" : "_doc",
  "_id" : "14",
  "matched" : false,
  "explanation" : {
    "value" : 0.0,
    "description" : "no matching term",
    "details" : [ ]
  }
}
```

As the `explanation` object's `description` says, *Lords* does not match the indexed data. Understanding the reasons for a match (or lack of a match) helps us troubleshoot the status of queries (for example, in the previous example, we know that the matching term doesn't exist in our index). If you retry the query in listing 8.21 using the `explain` flag, you may not get any information back from the engine other than an empty array.

A search query built using the `explain` flag on the `_search` API can produce many results. In my opinion, asking for an explanation of all document scores at a query level is a waste of computing resources. Instead, pick one document and ask for an explanation using the `_explain` API.

8.8.4 Sorting

By default, results returned by the engine are sorted on the relevancy score (`_score`): the higher the score, the higher on the result list. However, Elasticsearch lets us manage the sort order of the relevancy score (ascending or descending), and we can also sort on other fields, including multiple fields.

SORTING RESULTS

To sort results, we must provide a `sort` object at the same level as `query`. The `sort` object consists of an array of fields, where each field contains a few tweakable parameters:

```
GET movies/_search
{
  "query": {
    "match": {
      "genre": "crime"
    }
  },
  "sort": [
      { "rating" :{ "order": "desc" } }
  ]
}
```

Here, the results of a `match` query that searches for all the movies in the crime genre are sorted by movie rating. The `sort` object defines the field (`rating`) and the order in which the results are expected to be sorted—in this case, descending order.

SORTING ON RELEVANCY SCORES

Documents with relevancy scores are sorted on `_score` in descending order by default if no sorting is specified in the query. For example, the query in the following listing sorts the results in descending order because a sort order is not mentioned.

> Listing 8.22 Default sorting of scores in descending order

```
GET movies/_search
{
  "size": 10,
  "query": {
    "match": {
```

```
        "title": "Godfather"
      }
    }
  }
}
```

This is equivalent to issuing the `sort` block in a query, as shown in the next listing.

Listing 8.23 Sorting on `_score`

```
GET movies/_search
{
  "size": 10,
  "query": {
    "match": {
      "title": "Godfather"
    }                          Enables sort by setting the
  },                           sort block at the same
  "sort": [                    level as the query block
    "_score"        No sort order is specified, so
  ]                 the results are sorted in
}                   descending order by default.
```

If we want to reverse the order with an ascending sort so lower-scored documents are at the top of the list, we simply add the `_score` field to specify the order. The following listing shows how to do this.

Listing 8.24 Sorting results in ascending order by score

```
GET movies/_search
{
  "size": 10,
  "query": {
    "match": {
      "title": "Godfather"
    }
  },
  "sort": [
    {"_score":{"order":"asc"}}
  ]
}
```

You have probably guessed the query to sort on a nonscoring document field. The next listing sorts data based on `rating` from highest to lowest.

Listing 8.25 Sorting results by a field

```
GET movies/_search
{
  "size": 10,
  "query": {
    "match": {
      "genre": "crime"
```

```
      }
    },
    "sort": [
      {"rating":{"order":"desc"}}
    ]
}
```

When we run this query, the results (omitted for brevity) are sorted with the highest-rated movie at the top of the list. If we look carefully at the results, we see that the score is set to null—when we use a field for sorting, Elasticsearch does not compute the score. However, we can ask Elasticsearch to compute the score even if we don't sort on _score. To do that, we can use the `track_scores` Boolean field. The following listing shows how to set `track_scores` so the engine calculates the scores.

Listing 8.26   Enabling scoring when sorting on fields

```
GET movies/_search
{
  "track_scores":true,
  "size": 10,
  "query": {
    "match": {
      "genre": "crime"
    }
  },
  "sort": [
    {"rating":{"order":"asc"}}
  ]
}
```

The highlighted `track_scores` attribute in the listing tells the engine to calculate the relevancy scores of documents. However, the documents are not sorted on the _score attribute, because a custom field is used for sorting.

We can also enable sorting on multiple fields. The next query enables sorting on the `rating` and `release_date` fields.

Listing 8.27   Sorting by multiple fields in ascending order

```
GET movies/_search
{
  "size": 10,
  "query": {
    "match": {
      "genre": "crime"
    }
  },
  "sort": [
    {"rating":{"order":"asc"}},
    {"release_date":{"order":"asc"}}
  ]
}
```

When we sort on multiple fields, the sort order is important! The results of this query are first sorted in ascending order on the `rating` field. If multiple movies have the same rating, the second field (`release_date`) is used to break the tie, so results with the same rating are sorted by `release_date` in ascending order.

> **NOTE** We look at *geosorting* in chapter 12. Understanding geoqueries and sorting on geopoints warrant a dedicated chapter.

8.8.5 *Manipulating results*

You may have observed that search queries return results from the original documents specified with the _source field. Occasionally, we may want to fetch only a subset of fields. For example, we may need just the title and rating of a movie when a user searches for a certain type of rating, or we may not need the document included in the engine's response. Elasticsearch lets us manipulate the response, whether fetching selected fields or suppressing the entire document.

SUPPRESSING DOCUMENTS

To suppress the document returned in the search response, we set the _source flag to `false` in the query. The following listing returns a response with just the metadata.

> **Listing 8.28 Suppressing the source document**

```
GET movies/_search
{
  "_source": false,      ◁──┐  Setting the _source flag to false removes
  "query": {                 │  the source document from the result.
    "match": {
      "certificate": "R"
    }
  }
}
```

The response does not mention the original document:

```
"hits" : [
      {
        "_index" : "movies",
        "_type" : "_doc",
        "_id" : "1",
        "_score" : 0.58394784
      },
      {
        "_index" : "movies",
        "_type" : "_doc",
        "_id" : "2",
        "_score" : 0.58394784
      },
      ...
]
```

FETCHING SELECTED FIELDS

We can fetch just a few selected fields rather than the entire document. Elasticsearch provides a `fields` object to indicate which fields should be returned. We define the fields explicitly in this object. For example, the following query fetches only the `title` and `rating` fields in the response:

```
GET movies/_search
{
  "_source": false,
  "query": {
    "match": {
      "certificate": "R"
    }
  },
  "fields": [
    "title",
    "rating"
  ]
}
```

The following snippet shows the response. The document is resorted with the `title` and `rating` fields, as expected:

```
{
  "_index" : "movies",
  "_type" : "_doc",
  "_id" : "1",
  "_score" : 0.58394784,
  "fields" : {
    "rating" : [
      9.296875
    ],
    "title" : [
      "The Shawshank Redemption"
    ]
  }
}
```

Note that each field is returned as an array instead of a single field. Because it could potentially have multiple values, the results are represented as a json array (Elasticsearch doesn't have an array type).

We can also use wildcards in the field's mapping. For example, setting `title*` retrieves `title`, `title.original`, `title_long_descripion`, `title_code`, and any other fields with the `title` prefix. (We do not have all these fields in our mapping, other than `title` and `title.original`, so you can add them to the mapping to experiment with the wildcard setting.)

SCRIPTED FIELDS

Sometimes we need to compute a field on the fly and add it to the response. For example, suppose we want to set a movie as top-rated if it falls within the range of the highest ratings returned (the rating is greater than, say, 9). We can use scripting features when adding such ad hoc fields on demand.

To use the scripting feature, append the query with the `script_fields` object at the same level with the required name of the new dynamic file and the logic to populate it. The following listing creates a new field, `top_rated_movie`, by setting a flag based on the ratings the movie receives.

Listing 8.29 Source filtering with a `script` field

```
GET movies/_search
{
  "_source": ["title*","synopsis", "rating"],
  "query": {
    "match": {
      "certificate": "R"
    }
  },
  "script_fields": {
    "top_rated_movie": {
      "script": {
        "lang": "painless",
        "source": "if (doc['rating'].value > 9.0) 'true'; else 'false'"
      }
    }
  }
}
```

The script consists of the `source` element where the logic of populating the new field (`top_rated_movie`) is defined: we stamp the movie as top-rated if its rating is greater than 9. For completeness, let's look at the output (edited for brevity) with the new `top_rated_movie` field:

```
"hits" : [{
  ...
  "_source" : {
    "rating" : "9.3",
    "synopsis" : "Two imprisoned men bond ...",
    "title" : "The Shawshank Redemption"
  },
  "fields" : {
    "top_rated_movie" : ["true"]
  }
}
...
```

SOURCE FILTERING

Earlier, we set the _source flag to `false` to suppress documents from being returned in the response. Although we showed all-or-nothing scenarios, there are a couple of use cases where we can implement the _source option to tweak the response further. For example, the following listing sets _source to ["title*", "synopsis", "rating"] so that the results return the `synopsis` and `rating` fields along with all fields with `title` as a prefix.

Listing 8.30   Using the `_source` tag to fetch custom fields

```
GET movies/_search
{
  "_source": ["title*","synopsis", "rating"],
  "query": {
    "match": {
      "certificate": "R"
    }
  }
}
```

We can take the `_source` option even further by setting a list of `includes` and `excludes` to control the return fields.

Listing 8.31   Source filtering using `includes` and `excludes`

```
GET movies/_search
{
  "_source": {
    "includes": ["title*","synopsis","genre"],
    "excludes": ["title.original"]
  },
  "query": {
    "match": {
      "certificate": "R"
    }
  }
}
```

The `_source` object expects two arrays:

- `includes`—All the fields that should be returned in the result
- `excludes`—Fields that must be excluded from the fields returned from the `includes` list

In listing 8.31, we expect all `title` fields (`title` and `title.original`), as well as the `synopsis` and `genre` fields, to be returned from the query. However, we can suppress `title.original` by including it in the `excludes` array. We can play with the `includes` and `excludes` arrays to gain finer control over what fields are returned and suppressed. For example, if we add an `"excludes": ["synopsis","actors"]` array to the `_source` object, all fields except `synopsis` and `actors` are returned.

8.8.6   *Searching across indexes and data streams*

Data is usually spread across indexes and data streams. Fortunately, Elasticsearch lets us search data across multiple indexes and data streams by appending the required indexes in the search request. For example, omitting the index name(s) on the search request tells the engine to search across all indexes:

```
GET _search
{
  "query": {
    "match": {
      "actors": "Pacino"
    }
  }
}
```

We can also use `GET */_search` or `GET _all/_search`, which is equivalent to the previous query. All these forms search across all indexes in the cluster.

When we search across multiple indexes, we may want a document found in one index to take precedence over the same document found in another index. That is, we may want to boost certain indexes over others when performing a search across multiple indexes. For that, we can attach an `indices_boost` object at the same level as the `query` object. We can input multiple indexes with the appropriate boost rating set on this `indices_boost` object.

To demonstrate, we can create two new indexes (`index_top` and `index_new`) and index the movie *The Shawshank Redemption* in them (the code is available with the book's files). Now that we have the same movie across three indexes, let's create the query with a requirement to enhance the document score obtained from `movies_top` so *The Shawshank Redemption* is the topmost result.

Listing 8.32 Boosting the score of a document

```
GET movies*/_search
{
  "indices_boost": [
    { "movies": 0.1},        ← Lowers indices_boost to 0.1
    { "movies_new": 0},      ← Lowers indices_boost to 0
    { "movies_top": 2.0}     ← Increases indices_boost to 2.0
  ],
  "query": {
    "match": {
      "title": "Redemption"
    }
  }
}
```

The query doubles the score if the document is found in Query DSL's `movies_top` and decreases it to 10% (0.1) of its original value for documents fetched from the `movies` index. Finally, we set `indices_boost` to 0 for `movies_new` documents which means effectively no boost is applied. If the document's original score is 0.2876821 in `movies_top`, for example, the new score is 0.5753642 (2 * 0.2876821). The other documents' scores are calculated based on the setting in the `indices_boost` object.

And that's a wrap! The next chapter discusses term-level queries now that we better understand Query DSL and URI search features.

Summary

- Searching can be categorized as structured and unstructured search types.
- Structured data works with non-text fields like numeric and date fields or fields that are not analyzed during indexing time and produce binary results (either they exist or they don't).
- Unstructured data deals with text fields expected to have a relevancy score. The engine scores the results based on how well the resultant documents match the criteria.
- We use term-level search for structured queries and full-text search for unstructured data.
- Every search request is processed by a coordinator node. Coordinator nodes are responsible for asking other nodes to execute the query, return partial data, aggregate it, and respond to the client with a final result.
- Elasticsearch exposes a `_search` endpoint for queries and aggregations. We can invoke the `_search` endpoint by either using a URI request with parameters or building a full request using a special syntax called Query DSL.
- Query DSL is the preferred choice for creating search queries. We can construct a plethora of queries, including advanced queries, using Query DSL.
- Query DSL allows us to create leaf and compound queries. Leaf queries are simple search queries with a single criterion. Compound queries are used for advanced queries built with conditional clauses.
- Crosscutting features are available for most types of queries: pagination, highlighting, explanation of the scoring, manipulation of the results, and so on.

Term-level search

Term-level searches are designed to work with structured data such as numbers, dates, IP addresses, enumerations, keyword types, and so on. They help us find the answers but don't look at relevance. That is, they search for exact matches rather than how well documents match the query. One fundamental difference between these queries and full-text searches is that term-level queries do not undergo text analysis.

This chapter focuses on term-level searches in detail and works through the various query types with examples. Let's begin with an overview and then look at specific queries.

> **NOTE** The code for this chapter is available on GitHub (http://mng.bz/Gyw8) and on the book's website (https://www.manning.com/books/elasticsearch-in-action-second-edition).

313

9.1   *Overview of term-level search*

Term-level search is structured: queries return results in exact matches. They search for structured data such as dates, numbers, and ranges. With this type of search, we don't care how well the results match (how well documents correspond to the query), just that the query returns data if the query is matched. Hence, we do not expect a relevancy score associated with the results of a term-level search.

A term-level search produces a yes or no binary option similar to a database's WHERE clause. Query results are fetched if the condition is met; otherwise, the query doesn't return any results.

Although documents have scores associated with them, the scores don't matter. Documents are returned if they match the query, but not with relevance. In fact, we can run term-level queries with a constant score. They can be cached by the server, thus providing a performance benefit if the same query is rerun. These queries are like traditional database searches.

9.1.1   *Term-level queries are not analyzed*

One important characteristic of term-level queries is that they are not analyzed and tokenized (unlike full-text queries). The exception to this rule is when we use normalizers. Terms are matched against words stored in the inverted index without applying analyzers to match the indexing pattern. This means the search words must match the fields indexed in the inverted index.

For example, if we search for "Java" in a title field using a term-level query, chances are documents won't match. This is because during indexing, assuming we are using a standard analyzer, the word *Java* is converted to lowercase (*java*) and inserted into the title's inverted index. Because term-level queries are not analyzed, the engine tries to match the search word "Java" with the word "java" in the inverted index, so the match fails. We can return the same results from the query (with "Java" capitalized) if we use a keyword type instead (we explain shortly, so hang tight).

Term-level queries are suitable for keyword searches, not text field searches, because we know any field identified as a keyword is added to the inverted index without being analyzed during the indexing process. Like keywords, numerics, Booleans, ranges, and so on are not analyzed and are added directly to the respective inverted indexes.

9.1.2   *Term-level query example*

Let's take a simple example from the movie *The Godfather*. Figure 9.1 illustrates indexing and the term-level search. The standard analyzer doesn't find a hit because "The Godfather" doesn't exist as a single token stored in the inverted index (it is split into two tokens by the analyzer). Similarly, using just "Godfather" as a search word in the term-level query doesn't return any results because the word *Godfather* does not match the lowercased *godfather*.

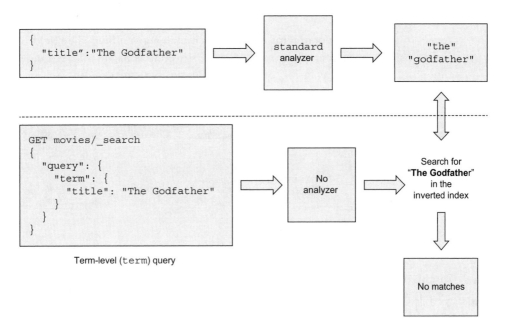

Figure 9.1 Indexing and term-level searching for the movie *The Godfather*

As the figure shows, there are two processes: indexing the document and searching for the document. If the field is a `text` field, assuming the `standard` analyzer is applied, the title is broken into two tokens and lowercased `["the" "godfather"]` during the indexing process.

On the other hand, during a term-level search, search terms are passed as is, without any text analysis. If a term-level query searches for "The Godfather", the engine attempts to search for the exact string "The Godfather" in the inverted index.

We can still run term-level queries on `text` fields, although it's not advisable on fields with lengthy text. We can also use term-level queries if the text has enumerations like days of the week, movie certificates, gender, and so on. If we are indexing gender, such as male and female, term-level queries must use "male" and "female" to successfully return any results because of the `standard` analyzer's activity during the indexing process. The takeaway is that term-level queries search for *exact* words.

Elasticsearch exposes several term-level queries, including `term`, `terms`, `ids`, `fuzzy`, `exists`, `range`, and others. We examine a few important ones in the next section and then present hands-on examples.

> **NOTE** We indexed the sample movie data in chapter 8, and we build all our queries based on that data. For completeness, the source code for this chapter provides the steps to index the movie mapping and sample data.

9.2   *The term query*

A `term` query fetches documents that exactly match a given field. The field is not analyzed. Instead, it is matched against the value stored as is in the inverted index during indexing. For example, using our movie dataset, we can develop a `term` query to search for R-rated movies.

Listing 9.1   Fetching movies with a given rating

```
GET movies/_search
{
  "query": {
    "term": {          The term query
      "certificate": "R"    declaration
    }
  }
}
```

The name of the query (`term` in this case) identifies that we are about to perform a term-level search. The object expects the field (`certificate`, in this case) and the search value. Keep in mind that the certificate is a `keyword` data type, so during the indexing process, the value "R" was not processed by any analyzer (actually, it's a `keyword` analyzer which doesn't alter the case); hence it's stored as is.

If you run this query, you'd get all R-rated movies (14 in our sample data set are R-rated). These are wrapped up in the return JSON response. In the next section, we observe the effect of running a term-level search on `text` fields (instead of keyword types).

9.2.1   *The term query on text fields*

Let's see what happens if we change the query with the rating value to "r" from "R" by lowercasing our search criteria (such as `"certificate": "r"`). Surprisingly, this query doesn't get any results. Can you guess the reason?

Recall from chapter 7 that Elasticsearch analyzes `text` fields during indexing and when searching. The `certificate` field is a `keyword` type, so the field never goes through the analysis process. This means it will always be matched with the contents of the inverted index. When indexing the document, the `certificate` value `"R"` is never tokenized or passed through filters; it's inserted into the inverted index as is.

The other side of the coin is searching: `term` queries are also not analyzed. Unlike a `standard` tokenizer that tokenizes the query's field into multiple tokens and lowercases them, the query field remains as is. If we search for "R", it is considered uppercase because no lowercase conversion (via the `standard` tokenizer) is applied behind the scenes. Therefore, when we search for a lowercase certificate as ("r", for example), there are no matches ("R" was indexed, not "r"), so there is no result.

This brings up an important point about working with `term` queries: `term` queries are unsuitable when working with `text` fields. Although nothing stops us from using them, they are intended for non-text fields like keywords, numericals, and dates. A term query still produces scores when invoked in the query context.

If you want to use a term query on a text field, be sure the text field is indexed like an enumeration or a constant. For example, an order status field with CREATED, CANCELLED, and FULFILLED states is a good candidate to use a term query even though it is a text field.

However, if text fields are populated with unstructured text like non-enumeration-styled values, we won't get the expected results when we run term queries. Let's check out an example of what happens when we run a term query on a text field.

9.2.2   Example term query

Let's see what happens if we search a text field called title using a term query. The following listing searches for "The Godfather" in the title of the movie using a term query. (Remember that in our movie mappings, the title field has an explicit text field mapping set.)

> **Listing 9.2   Using a term-level query on a text field**

```
GET movies/_search
{
  "query": {
    "term": {
      "title": "The Godfather"
    }
  }
}
```

When we run this code, we receive *no* results (see figure 9.1). This is because the title field is a text field, so it underwent an analysis process and was stored in the index before the search. *The Godfather* was broken down and stored as lowercase tokens (because we are using the standard analyzer by default) in the inverted index: ["the", "godfather"]. A search query is not analyzed for term queries; instead, it takes each word as is and compares it against the inverted index. In this case, the query criterion "The Godfather" does not match the tokens ("the" and "godfather") for the title field.

Rerunning the query using "the godfather" also does not return any results (try running the query, lowercasing the title like this). The term query tries to match the exact value "the godfather", which is not in the inverted index (remember, the title was tokenized and stored as two words: "the" and "godfather"). However, searching for "godfather" returns results because the word *godfather* was analyzed and inserted into the inverted index during data indexing, and hence a match is found.

The takeaway is that we need to run term queries on non-text fields. If you want to use a term query to search a text field, be sure the text field contains data in the form of enumerations or constants.

9.2.3 Shortened term-level queries

The `term` queries in listings 9.1 and 9.2 are shortened versions. While it is convenient to write the shortened version, let's take a moment to see the original full version of the query from listing 9.1.

Listing 9.3 Full syntax of a query

```
GET movies/_search
{
  "query": {
    "term": {
      "certificate": {        The certificate field
        "value": "R",         has values enclosed
        "boost": 2            in an object.         The certificate's
      }                                             search criteria
    }
  }                           In addition to the value, we can
}                             provide parameters like boost.
```

The `certificate` field expects an object with `value` and other parameters. `value`, which appears at the same level as the field in the shortened version, is one level lower than the field. The enclosed object can also host other attributes, such as `boost`, as in this example.

While the full version adds features to a query, the shortened version is straightforward and used extensively when a query is simple and needs no further tweaking. We use shortened versions throughout the book unless we are interested in working with other parameters.

So far, we have searched for words against a single field using a `term` query. A `term` query looks at exact matches for a single word, such as `"certificate":"R"`. But what if we want to search for multiple values in a single field? For example, how can we search for R-rated and PG-13 movies on the `certificate` field? That's where the `terms` query comes into the picture.

9.3 The terms query

As the name suggests, a `terms` (note the plural) query searches for multiple criteria against a single field. We can throw in all possible values of the field that we would like to search for. Say we want to search for all movies with multiple content ratings, such as PG-13 and R. We use a `terms` query for this purpose.

Listing 9.4 Searching for multiple search criteria in a field

```
GET movies/_search
{
  "query": {
    "terms": {                The terms query expects an
      "certificate": ["PG-13","R"]    array of search criteria.    Multiple search criteria
    }                                                               against a single field
  }
}
```

The `terms` query expects a list of search words to be queried against a field, passed in as an array to the `terms` object. The array values are searched against the existing documents one by one to fetch matches. Each word is matched exactly. In this listing, we search for all movies with a PG-13 or R rating in the `certificate` field. The resultant documents combine all PG-13 and R movies.

There's a limit to how many terms we can set in the array: a whopping 65,536 terms. If we need to modify this limit (to increase or decrease it), we can use the index's dynamic `index.max_terms_count` property setting to alter the limit. The following query sets `max_terms_count` to 10.

Listing 9.5 Resetting the maximum number of terms

```
PUT movies/_settings
{
  "index":{
    "max_terms_count":10
  }
}
```

This setting restricts a user setting no more than 10 values in the `terms` array. Remember, this is a dynamic setting on the index, so we can change it on a live index.

There's a slightly different version of the `terms` query: a `terms` lookup query. The idea is to create the `terms` array from an existing document's values rather than setting it specifically. The next section discusses it with an example.

9.3.1 Example terms query

So far, we have provided a list of values in an array as the search criteria for a `terms` query. A `terms` lookup query is a variation of a `terms` query that lets us set the terms by reading an existing document's field values. It is best understood with an example.

To explain this feature, we need to deviate from our movies data set, create a new index with appropriate schema, and index a few documents. The following listing creates a `classic_movies` index with two properties: `title` and `director`.

Listing 9.6 Creating a new index

```
PUT classic_movies
{
  "mappings": {
    "properties": {
      "title": {          ⟵─┐  The title field
        "type": "text"       │  is a text field.
      },
      "director": {       ⟵─┐  Declares the director
        "type": "keyword"    │  field as keyword type
      }
    }
  }
}
```

There is nothing special about this index—except we define the `director` field as a `keyword` type, to avoid complexity. Now, let's index a few movies.

Listing 9.7   Indexing three movies

```
PUT classic_movies/_doc/1
{
  "title":"Jaws",
  "director":"Steven Spielberg"
}

PUT classic_movies/_doc/2
{
  "title":"Jaws II",
  "director":"Jeannot Szwarc"
}

PUT classic_movies/_doc/3
{
  "title":"Ready Player One",
  "director":"Steven Spielberg"
}
```

The documents are self-explanatory.

9.3.2   *The terms lookup query*

Now that we have indexed these three documents, let's return to the `terms` lookup query discussion. Say we wish to fetch all movies directed by Spielberg. However, we don't want to construct a `terms` query and provide the terms directly up front. Instead, we let the `terms` query know to get the values of the terms from a document. The next listing does exactly this.

Listing 9.8   A `terms` lookup search

```
GET classic_movies/_search
{
  "query": {                          A terms query       The field that we          The index field denotes the
    "terms": {            ◁──┘        (with a twist!)     are interested in          name of the index where
      "director": {           ◁                           searching against          the document resides.
        "index":"classic_movies",                    ◁
        "id":"3",                      ◁─┐   Name of the field containing
        "path":"director"   ◁─┐        │   the terms for the query
      }                       │
    }                         │   Search field in the
  }                           │   current document
}
```

This code requires a bit of explanation. We create a `terms` query with `director` as the field in which we want to look for multiple search terms. In a regular `terms` query, we would provide an array with a list of names. But here, we ask the query to look up the `director` values in another document: the document with the `id` value 3.

The document with this ID should be picked up from the `classic_movies` index, because the `index` field mentions that ID in the query. And of course, the field from which to fetch the values is `director`, as declared as the `path` field. Running this query fetches two movies that were directed by Spielberg.

The `terms` lookup query helps build a query based on values obtained from another document rather than a set of values passed in the query. It offers greater flexibility when constructing query terms: we can easily swap the index with any other index from which to obtain a document. For example, say we have an index called `movie_search_terms_index` containing several documents of search terms (document 1 contains `director` terms, document 2 contains `actors` terms, and so on). We can reference this document with `director` terms from `movie_search_terms_index` in our main query and fetch the results. This way, the main query can be constant while the lookup documents are changed as required. Now that we understand `terms` queries, let's move on to a query type where we fetch documents given a set of IDs.

9.4 The ids query

Sometimes we want to obtain the documents that have those IDs from Elasticsearch. As the name suggests, the `ids` query fetches matching documents given a set of document IDs. It's a much simpler way to fetch multiple documents simultaneously. The following listing shows how to retrieve documents using a list of document IDs.

> **Listing 9.9 Fetching multiple documents using an `ids` query**

```
GET movies/_search
{
  "query": {
    "ids": {                      Name of
                                  the query
      "values": [10,4,6,8]            Provides the document
    }                                 IDs as an array
  }
}
```

This query returns four documents with the corresponding four IDs. Each document that is indexed has a mandatory `_id` field.

> **NOTE** Metadata fields are not allowed to be part of the schema definition. The `_id` field, along with other fields like `_source`, `_size`, `_routing`, and so on, are metadata fields and so cannot be part of the index mapping exercise.

We can also use a `terms` query to fetch documents with a set of document IDs, instead of using an `ids` query, as we saw in listing 9.4. The next listing shows another example.

> **Listing 9.10 A `terms` query using a set of IDs to fetch documents**

```
GET movies/_search
{
  "query": {
    "terms": {
```

```
      "_id":[10,4,6,8]
      }
    }
}
```

Here, we use a `terms` query and set the array of document IDs in the `_id` field as our search criteria. Now, let's look at another term-level query type: the `exists` query.

9.5   *The exists query*

Sometimes, project documents have hundreds of fields. Fetching all the fields in a response is a waste of bandwidth, and knowing whether a field exists before attempting to fetch it is a good precheck. An `exists` query fetches documents for a given field if the field exists. For example, if we run the following query, we get a response containing the document because the document with the `title` field exists.

Listing 9.11   Running an `exists` query to check whether a field exists

```
GET movies/_search
{
  "query": {
    "exists": {          ⟵┐ Defines the query
      "field": "title"      type as exists
    }               ⟵┐ Provides the field that we want
  }                    to check in the document
}
```

If the field doesn't exist, the query returns an empty `hits` array (`hits[]`). If you are curious, try this query with a nonexistent field like `title2`, and you'll see the empty array.

There's another subtle use case of an `exists` query: to retrieve all documents that *don't* have a particular field (a nonexistent field). For example, the next listing checks for all documents that aren't classified as confidential (assuming classified documents have a field called `confidential` set to `true`).

Listing 9.12   Finding non-confidential documents

```
PUT top_secret_files/_doc/1      ⟵┐
{
  "code":"Flying Bird",            Adds two documents, one
  "confidential":true              with a confidential flag
}

PUT top_secret_files/_doc/2      ⟵┘
{
  "code":"Cold Rock"
}
GET top_secret_files/_search     ⟵┐ Compound query that fetches
{                                   documents without a confidential field
  "query": {
    "bool": {
      "must_not": [{
```

```
        "exists": {
          "field": "confidential"
        }
      }
    ]
  }
 }
}
```

We add two documents to the `top_secret_files` index: one of the documents has an additional field called `confidential`. We then write an `exists` query in the `must_not` clause of a `bool` query to fetch all documents that are not categorized as confidential. (We discuss compound queries in chapter 11.)

Sometimes we want to work with data that falls in a certain predefined range: fetching movies from last month, sales in a quarter, highest grossers, etc. These queries are grouped under the heading of `range` queries, which we look at next.

9.6 *The range query*

Frequently, we need a set of data that falls within a range: flights delayed between certain dates, sales profits on a particular day, pupils of average height in a class, and so on. Elasticsearch provides a `range` query for these types of inquiries.

A `range` query returns documents for a range in a field. The query accepts lower and upper bounds on the field. For example, to fetch all movies with a rating between 9.0 and 9.5, we can execute the following `range` query.

> **Listing 9.13 Fetching movies with a specified range of ratings**

```
GET movies/_search
{
  "query": {
    "range": {
      "rating": {
        "gte": 9.0,
        "lte": 9.5
      }
    }
  }
}
```

This `range` query fetches movies within the specified `rating` limits. A `rating` field is an object that accepts bounds, defined as operators. Table 9.1 shows the operators we can use to specify the range.

We use `range` queries to search across a range of dates or numbers. For example, to fetch all movies made after 1970, we simply stitch together this query.

Table 9.1 Operators in a `range` query

Operator	Meaning
gt	Greater than
gte	Greater than or equal to
lt	Less than
lte	Less than or equal to

Listing 9.14   Fetching post-1970 movies using a `range` query

```
GET movies/_search
{
  "query": {
    "range": {
      "release_date": {
        "gte": "01-01-1970"
      }
    }
  },
  "sort": [
    {
      "release_date": {
        "order": "asc"
      }
    }
  ]
}
```

The `release_date` field declares a `gte` operator with the search requirement: in this case, the year 1970. Notice that we also *sort* the movies in ascending order on the release date using the `sort` attribute in the query. The movies returned are therefore sorted from oldest to newest.

Because we are discussing `range` queries, let's use this opportunity to review date math in a `range` query. We discuss this in the following section.

Data math in range queries

Elasticsearch supports sophisticated data math in queries. For example, we can ask the engine to perform tasks like these:

- Fetch book sales from two days ago (current day minus two days).
- Find access-denied errors in the last 10 minutes (current hour minus 10 minutes).
- Get tweets for particular search criteria from last year.

Elasticsearch expects a specific data expression that deals with data math. The first part of the expression is called an *anchor date*, followed by two vertical bars (||) indicating that the anchor date is being manipulated by adding or subtracting a certain number of time units (minutes, seconds, years, days, etc.) and then the time we want to add to or subtract from the anchor date.

Say we want to fetch movies released two days ago. We set the anchor date as today (at the time of writing, 22-05-2023) and subtract two days:

```
GET movies/_search
{
  "query": {
    "range": {
      "release_date": {
```

```
        "lte": "22-05-2023||-2d"      ◁─┐  The anchor date followed
      }                                   │  by || minus two days
    }
  }
}
```

The `range` query's `lte` operator takes a date value expressed as date math. In this case, 22-05-2023 is the anchor date, and we subtract two days from it (`-2d`). (Elasticsearch has a dictionary of letters for date math: *y* for years, *M* for months, *w* for weeks, *d* for days, *h* for hours, *m* for minutes, *s* for seconds, and so on.)

Instead of specifying the current date, Elasticsearch lets us use a keyword: `now`. The `now` keyword represents the current date. For example, using `now-1y` sets the date to one year ago:

```
GET movies/_search
{
  "query": {
    "range": {
      "release_date": {
        "gte": "now-1y"      ◁─┐  Fetches all the movies from last
      }                          │  year: the current date (represented
    }                            │  as now) minus one year
  }
}
```

We build the `release_date` expression by using `now` and subtracting one year from it.

There are many options to manipulate dates in Elasticsearch, and I advise you to consult the documentation to learn more. Note that Elasticsearch doesn't cache queries containing date math, so there are performance implications when using date math in `range` queries.

In the next section, we look at `wildcard` queries. These queries don't let us down if we provide partial search criteria, because we use wildcards to build up the expression.

9.7 *The wildcard query*

As their name implies, `wildcard` queries let us search for words with missing characters, suffixes, and prefixes. For example, suppose we want to search for all possible combinations of movies with titles ending in *father* or *god*, even if they are missing a single character like *god?ather*. This is where we can use a `wildcard` query. The `wildcard` query accepts an asterisk (`*`) or a question mark (`?`) in the search word, as described in table 9.2.

Table 9.2 Types of wildcards

Character	Description
* (asterisk)	Searches for zero or more characters
? (question mark)	Searches for a single character

Let's search for documents where the movie title contains a word starting with *god*.

Listing 9.15 Wildcard search in action

```
GET movies/_search
{
  "query": {                    The wildcard
    "wildcard": {        ◁——    query type
      "title": {
        "value": "god*"   ◁——┐  Searches the value field
      }                       │  with a wildcard operator
    }
  }
}
```

Three movies (*The Godfather, The Godfather II,* and *City of God*) should be returned for this `wildcard` query. Of course, any movie (*Godzilla, God's Waiting List,* etc.) can also be fetched because we expect all titles that have the prefix *god* (those movies are not in our index, but if they were, the query would return them, too).

> **Wildcard queries on text fields**
>
> The query in listing 9.15 is run on the `title` field, which is a `text` data type. Because term-level queries are not analyzed, we use lowercase "god". Also, the `title` field was indexed with the `standard` analyzer, which, by default, lowercased the word.
>
> If you want to use a `keyword` field instead of a `text` field, change `title` to `title.original` (the `title.original` field is defined as `keyword` in our `movies` schema) and run the query with the value "The God*". But if you omit "The" from "The God*" and run the query, you won't get any results. Because `title.original` is a `keyword` typed field, the value is persisted during indexing without any text analysis.

We can tweak our queries by placing wildcards anywhere in a word. For example, the query "g*d" fetches two movies from our stash: *The Good, the Bad, and the Ugly* and *City of God*. If we want to find the match of a given query criterion in a return document, we can use highlighting (discussed in chapter 8). The following listing shows this approach.

Listing 9.16 Searching with a wildcard operator in a word

```
GET movies/_search
{
  "_source": false,
  "query": {
    "wildcard": {
      "title": {                   Wildcard operator between
        "value": "g*d"   ◁——       the letters of a word
      }
    }
}
```

```
    },
    "highlight": {
      "fields": {
        "title": {}
      }
    }
}
```

The highlight block lets
us visualize the results.

The output shows us that two movies matched:

```
"title": [ "The <em>Good</em>, the Bad and the Ugly" ]
"title": [ "City of <em>God</em>"]
```

We use the `?` wildcard only if we want to match one character. For example, `"value": "go?ather"` searches for all the words that match the third character at the wildcard's position. We can also combine multiple `?` characters, such as "g???ather".

Expensive queries

Some queries are expensive for the engine to run because of how we implement them. The `wildcard` query is one, along with `range`, `prefix`, `fuzzy`, `regex`, and `join` queries. Using such a query occasionally may not impact server performance, but overusing these expensive queries may destabilize the cluster, leading to bad user experiences.

Elasticsearch allows us to execute expensive queries on the cluster at our discretion. However, if we want to stop the execution of these queries on the cluster, we can set the `allow_expensive_queries` attribute to `false` on the cluster settings:

```
PUT _cluster/settings
{
  "transient": {
    "search.allow_expensive_queries": "false"
  }
}
```

By switching off `allow_expensive_queries`, we protect the cluster from overload.

Note that if we set `allow_expensive_queries` to `false`, `wildcard` queries are not executed. The following error is thrown if we try: `"reason" : "[wildcard] queries cannot be executed when 'search.allow_expensive_queries' is set to false."`

Wildcards fetch results with missing characters in a word or a sentence. Sometimes we wish to query words with a prefix—that's when `prefix` queries come into the picture, as discussed next.

9.8   *The prefix query*

We may want to query for words using the beginning of a word (a prefix), like *Leo* for Leonardo or *Mar* for Marlon Brando, Mark Hamill, or Martin Balsam. We can use `prefix` queries to fetch records that match the prefix, as shown in the following listing.

Listing 9.17   Using a `prefix` query

```
GET movies/_search
{
  "query": {
    "prefix": {            ←──  Specifies the prefix
      "actors.original": {      type query
        "value": "Mar"     ←─┐
      }                       │ Queries for words
    }                         │ that start with "Mar"
  }
}
```

This query fetches three movies with actors named Marlon, Mark, and Martin when we search for the prefix "Mar". Note that we are running a `prefix` query on the `actors.original` field, which is the `keyword` data type.

> **NOTE** Prefix queries are expensive and can destabilize the cluster. See the "Expensive queries" sidebar in section 9.7 for how to prevent an overloaded cluster and section 9.8.2 to speed up `prefix` queries.

9.8.1 *Shortened queries*

As we discussed at the beginning of this chapter, we don't need to add an object consisting of values at the field block level. Instead, we can create a shortened version for brevity.

Listing 9.18   Shortening `prefix` query usage

```
GET movies/_search
{
  "query": {
    "prefix": {
      "actors.original":  "Leo"
    }
  }
}
```

As we wish to find the matching fields in the results, we add highlights to the query. Adding a `highlight` block to a `prefix` query accentuates one or more fields that match.

Listing 9.19   A `prefix` search with highlighting

```
GET movies/_search
{
  "_source": false,
  "query": {
    "prefix": {
      "actors.original": {
        "value": "Mar"
```

```
        }
      }
    },
    "highlight": {          ◁─┐  Highlights the matched
      "fields": {               actors in the results
        "actors.original": {}
      }
    }
  }
}
```

Because we don't want the source to be returned in the response (`"_source": false`), the following results highlight where the prefix matched with the word:

```
"hits" : [{
    ..
    "highlight" : {
      "actors.original" : ["<em>Marlon Brando</em>"]
    }
  },
  {
    ..
    "highlight" : {
      "actors.original" : ["<em>Martin Balsam</em>"]
    }
  },
  {
    ..
    "highlight" : {
      "actors.original" : ["<em>Mark Hamill</em>"]
    }
  }]
```

We mentioned earlier that running `prefix` queries exerts computation strain. Fortunately, there is a way to speed up such painstakingly ill-performant queries.

9.8.2 Speeding up prefix queries

A `prefix` query is slow to run because the engine must derive results based on a prefix (any lettered word). But there's a mechanism to speed them up: using the `index_prefixes` parameter on the field.

We can set `index_prefixes` when developing the mapping schema. For example, the mapping definition in the following listing sets the `title` field (remember, `title` is a `text` data type) with an additional parameter, `index_prefixes`, on a new index (`boxoffice_hit_movies`) that we are creating for this exercise.

> **Listing 9.20 New index with the `index_prefixes` parameter**

```
PUT boxoffice_hit_movies     ◁─┐  Creates a new index with
{                                just one property, title
  "mappings": {
    "properties": {
      "title":{
```

```
        "type": "text",
        "index_prefixes":{}        ◁─┐  Sets the index_prefixes
      }                               │  parameter on the title field
    }
  }
}
```

The sole `title` property includes an additional property, `index_prefixes`. This indicates to the engine that during the indexing process, it should create the field with prebuilt prefixes and store those values. For example, suppose we index a new document:

```
PUT boxoffice_hit_movies/_doc/1
{
  "title":"Gladiator"
}
```

Because we set `index_prefixes` on the `title` field in listing 9.20, Elasticsearch indexes prefixes with a minimum character size of 2 and a maximum character size of 5 by default. This way, when we run a `prefix` query, it doesn't need to calculate the prefixes. Instead, it gets them from storage.

We can also change the default `min` and `max` sizes of the prefixes that Elasticsearch creates during indexing. This is done by tweaking the sizes of the `index_prefixes` object.

Listing 9.21   Custom character lengths for `index_prefixes`

```
PUT boxoffice_hit_movies_custom_prefix_sizes
{
  "mappings": {
    "properties": {
      "title":{
        "type": "text",
        "index_prefixes":{                ┌─  Sets the minimum number
          "min_chars":4,        ◁─────────┘   of characters for the prefix
          "max_chars":10        ◁─┐  Sets the maximum number
        }                         │  of characters for the prefix
      }
    }
  }
}
```

In the listing, we ask the engine to pre-create prefixes with a minimum and maximum character length of 4 and 10 letters, respectively. Note that `min_chars` must be greater than 0, and `max_chars` should be less than 20 characters. This way, we can customize the prefixes that Elasticsearch should create beforehand during indexing.

9.9   *Fuzzy queries*

Spelling mistakes are common during searches. We may search for a word with an incorrect letter or letters: for example, searching for "rama" movies instead of "drama" movies. The search can correct this query and return "drama" movies instead of failing and returning nothing. The principle behind this type of query is called *fuzziness*, and Elasticsearch employs `fuzzy` queries to forgive spelling mistakes.

Fuzziness is a process of searching for similar terms based on the *Levenshtein distance algorithm* (also referred to as the *edit distance*). The Levenshtein distance is the number of characters that need to be swapped to fetch similar words. For example, searching for "cake" can fetch "take", "bake", "lake", "make", and so on if we use a `fuzzy` query with `fuzziness` (edit distance) set to 1. The following query should return all drama movies because applying a `fuzziness` of 1 to "rama" results in "drama".

Listing 9.22 A `fuzzy` query in action

```
GET movies/_search
{
  "query": {
    "fuzzy": {
      "genre": {
        "value": "rama",
        "fuzziness": 1
      }
    }
  },
  "highlight": {
    "fields": {
      "genre": {}
    }
  }
}
```

In this example, we use the edit distance of 1 (one character) to fetch similar words. You can also try removing a character from the middle of the word, like "dama" or "dram"; these queries also result in positive results when `fuzziness` is set to 1.

> **NOTE** Unlike a `wildcard` query, which uses a wildcard operator (* or ?), a `fuzzy` query doesn't use operators. Instead, it fetches similar words using the Levenshtein edit distance algorithm.

If we drop one more letter (for example, `"value": "ama"` with `fuzziness` set to 1), the `fuzzy` query in listing 9.22 does not return any results. Because we are missing two letters, we need to set the edit distance to 2 to solve this problem.

Listing 9.23 A `fuzzy` query with two letters missing in a word

```
GET movies/_search
{
  "query": {
    "fuzzy": {
      "genre": {
        "value": "ama",          ◁─┐ A word with
                                    │ missing letters
```

```
        "fuzziness": 2        ◁─────┐  Setting fuzziness to 2 forgives two-letter
      }                             │  substitutions/modifications.
    }
  }
}
```

This can be a clumsy way to handle things because we may not know if the user has mistyped one letter or a few letters. This is why Elasticsearch provides a default setting for `fuzziness`: the AUTO setting. If the `fuzziness` attribute is not supplied, the default setting of AUTO is assumed. The AUTO setting determines the edit distance based on the length of the word, as shown in table 9.3. Sticking to the default setting of AUTO for the `fuzziness` attribute is preferred unless we know the exact use case at hand.

Table 9.3   Using the AUTO `fuzziness` setting

Word length in characters	Fuzziness (edit distance)	Explanation
0 to 2	0	If the word is shorter than two characters, fuzziness is not applied. This means misspelled words cannot be corrected.
3 to 5	1	If the length of the word is 3 to 5 characters, an edit distance of 1 is applied.
More than 5	2	If the length of the word is longer than 5 characters, an edit distance of 2 is applied.

Let's wrap up here. We learned a lot about term-level searching in this chapter. While term-level search helps find answers in structured data, the real power of a search engine lies in its ability to search unstructured data. In Elasticsearch, unstructured data is associated with full-text searching—searching `text` fields and yielding results with relevance scores. We examine full-text queries in detail in the next chapter.

Summary

- Term-level searching is carried out on structured data such as numbers, keywords, Booleans, and dates.
- A term-level search produces a binary result: the search leads to a result or none. There is no *likely match* scenario.
- Term-level queries are not analyzed, meaning that when applied to `text` fields undergoing text analysis during indexing, they can yield incorrect or no results.
- There are many term-level search queries: `term`, `terms`, `prefix`, `range`, `fuzzy`, and others.
- A `term` query searches for a single term against a field, while a `terms` (plural) query search for multiple values against a single field.
- A `range` query helps search data within a set of bounds: for example, searching for crimes that happened in London in the last month.

- A `wildcard` query uses * and ? operators to fetch results.
- Fuzziness employs Levenshtein's edit distance to fetch similar-looking words. Elasticsearch employs `fuzzy` queries to support the user's spelling inconsistencies.
- A `prefix` query retrieves results given a prefix (no need to specify a wildcard operator). As prefix operations are expensive to execute on a live index, we can ask Elasticsearch to pre-create them at index time to avoid finding them during a live query phase.

Full-text searches

This chapter covers

- Overview of full-text queries
- Working through match queries
- Looking at match phrases, multi-match, and other queries
- Looking at query strings and simple query string queries

In the last chapter, we looked at term-level searching, the mechanism we use to search structured data. Although a structured data search is important, the power of modern search engines vests efficiently and effectively to run when we search unstructured data. Elasticsearch is one such modern search engine that stands as a front-runner in searching unstructured data with relevance.

Elasticsearch provides the capability to search unstructured data through full-text search queries. A full-text search is all about relevancy: fetching the relevant documents to the user's search. For example, when searching for the word *Java* in an online bookstore, one shouldn't expect to receive details about the Indonesian island of Java or the wet-pressed coffee grown on this island.

In this chapter, we review the mechanics of searching unstructured data by employing full-text search APIs. Elasticsearch provides a handful of full-text queries in the form of `match`, `query_string`, and others. As `match` queries are the most commonly used queries when working with full text, we dedicate a good chunk of the chapter to various `match` queries. We also work through query-string searches, which are equivalent to using an URI request search but with a request body similar to Query DSL.

10.1 Overview

When we search on a retail website such as Amazon or eBay, we see results close to what we are looking for. If the results are not what we expect, we express our frustration and vow never to return to that site or application, don't we? A user's search experience is crucial to retaining a happy customer.

Relevance is all about how appropriate search results are and how closely they are related to what the user is searching for. Elasticsearch thrives on producing relevant results with speed and accuracy by employing sophisticated relevance algorithms.

When we talk about relevance, two measures usually spring to mind: precision and recall. Relevance is measured using these two factors, and understanding them at a high level is important (although not crucial).

10.1.1 Precision

Precision is the percentage of relevant documents of the overall number of documents returned. When a query returns results, not all results are directly related to the query. There may be a few nonrelevant documents in the results.

For example, suppose we are searching for a 4K television from a particular manufacturer (say, LG), and we obtain 10 results. Not all of these results are relevant: a few are 4K cameras (see figure 10.1), and a couple are projectors, because LG also produces those.

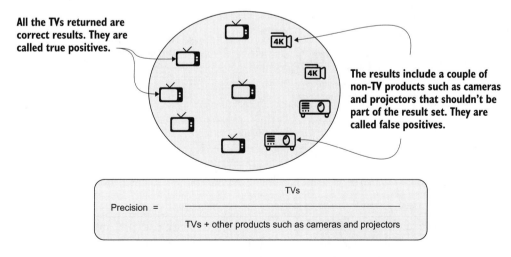

Precision = $\dfrac{\text{TVs}}{\text{TVs} + \text{other products such as cameras and projectors}}$

Figure 10.1   A precision example in action, returning search results for a 4K television

In the figure, the result consists of *true positives* (relevant documents) as well as *false positives* (irrelevant documents). Precision is about how many of the retrieved documents are relevant. In this case, we know 6 documents are TVs out of 10 resulting documents, so 6 documents are relevant, and the remaining 4 are irrelevant. Hence, the precision is

```
precision = 6 / 10 × 100% = 60%
```

This tells us that only 60% of the documents returned are relevant. Some documents not directly related to the query (irrelevant documents) also appear in the results, for various reasons.

10.1.2 *Recall*

Recall is the other side of the coin. It measures how many documents that were returned are relevant. For example, there may have been a few more relevant results (TVs) that were not returned (i.e., were omitted) as part of the results set. The percentage of relevant documents retrieved is called *recall* (see figure 10.2).

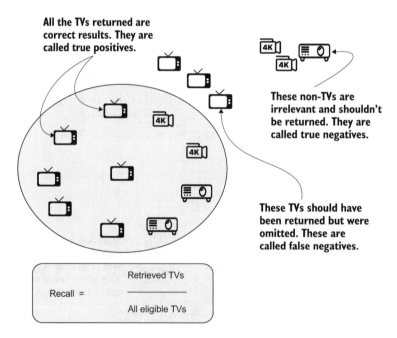

All the TVs returned are correct results. They are called true positives.

These non-TVs are irrelevant and shouldn't be returned. They are called true negatives.

These TVs should have been returned but were omitted. These are called false negatives.

$$\text{Recall} = \frac{\text{Retrieved TVs}}{\text{All eligible TVs}}$$

Figure 10.2   The recall measure in action for our 4K television example search

As the figure shows, three TVs fell into the search bucket but were not returned. These are called *false negatives*. On the other hand, a few products like cameras and projectors weren't returned that are genuinely irrelevant and, thus, not expected to be part of the result. These are *true negatives*. In the current scenario, recall is calculated as

```
Recall = 6 / (6+3) x 100% = 66.6%
```

Ideally, we want precision and recall to be a perfect match with no omissions (no relevant documents omitted). However, this is almost impossible because these measures always work against each other. They are inversely proportional: the higher the precision (number of best-match documents), the lower the recall (number of documents returned). Figure 10.3 shows the inverse relationship between these two factors.

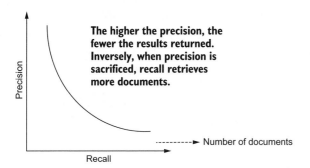

Figure 10.3 Precision and recall are always at odds with each other.

We need to make sure the returned results strike a balance between the precision and recall strategies. Figure 10.4 summarizes precision and recall.

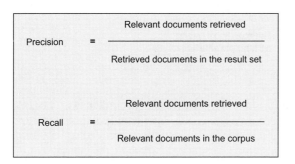

Figure 10.4 The formulas for precision and recall

We can tune results for precision and recall when designing and executing queries. We can also use `match` queries, filters, and `boost` to tweak precision and recall to fine-tune their balance. In this chapter we do not directly tune these parameters but rather work on queries to see how the results are affected. If you are interested in learning more about precision and recall in the information retrieval context, I suggest you check out this article from Google for Developers: http://mng.bz/a1eo.

Now that we understand the concept of relevance and the controlling factors (precision and recall), the rest of the chapter is dedicated to working with the full-text queries. We begin by getting some sample data.

10.2   Sample data

In this chapter, we work with a fictional book store. We index a set of 50 technical books into an index named `books` by invoking the `_bulk` API. We do not tweak the mapping for this part of the sample data, so you can index the books as is. The data for the books is available on GitHub at http://mng.bz/zX2g, and the script to index the books is at http://mng.bz/0KzW; the files are also available from the book's website (https://www.manning.com/books/elasticsearch-in-action-second-edition).

Elasticsearch provides a number of full-text queries. Because each query type has many implementation details, they are described in separate sections for ease of flow. The first query we look at is the `match_all` query, which returns everything.

10.3   The match_all query

As the name suggests, the match all (`match_all`) query fetches all the documents in the index. Because this query is expected to return all available documents, it is the perfect partner for honoring 100% recall.

10.3.1   Building the match_all query

We form the query with a `match_all` object, passing it no parameters. The code in the following listing shows how to build a `match_all` query.

Listing 10.1   Fetching all documents using `match_all`

```
GET books/_search
{
  "query": {
    "match_all": { }      ⊲──┐ The match_all query
  }                           with no parameters
}
```

This query returns all documents available in the `books` index. The notable point is that the response indicates each book has a score of 1.0 by default:

```
{
 "max_score" : 1.0,
 ...
 "hits" : [{
   "_index" : "books",
   "_type" : "_doc",
   "_id" : "2",
   "_score" : 1.0,
   "_source" : {
     "title" : "Effective Java",
       ...
     }
```

```
  },
  {
    ...
    "_score" : 1.0,
    "_source" : {
    "title" : "Java: A Beginner's Guide",
    ...
  },
  ...
}]
```

We can boost the score if needed by simply amending the query. The next listing shows how.

Listing 10.2 Boosting the query with a predefined score

```
GET books/_search
{
  "query": {
    "match_all": {          The match_all query sets a score
      "boost": 2      ◁─┘  of 2 for all returned documents.
    }
  }
}
```

We add a `boost` parameter to the query that returns all documents with a boosted score.

10.3.2 *Short form of a match_all query*

We wrote a `match_all` query with a query body in listing 10.1. However, providing the body is redundant. The same query can be rewritten in a shorter format like this:

```
GET books/_search
```

Behind the scenes, Elasticsearch executes a `match_all` query with a default `boost` of 1 when the query body is not provided. Unless we want to change the `boost` value, we can invoke the search endpoint without a body.

10.4 *The match_none query*

While the `match_all` query returns all the results from an index or multiple indexes, the opposite query, `match_none`, returns no results. The following listing shows the syntax.

Listing 10.3 The `match_none` query

```
GET books/_search
{
  "query": {           A query that
    "match_none": {}  ◁─┘ matches nothing
  }
}
```

The match_none query is more useful in scenarios where you want to conditionally exclude all documents, often based on some external logic in your application. For example, if a certain condition in our application is met, we might insert a match_none query into the must clause of your bool query to ensure that no documents are returned.

Let's say we have an application feature that allows administrators to "lock down" the movie database for maintenance or upgrades. When the database is locked, you want all search queries to return no results rather than throwing erroneous results. In this case, you could insert a match_none query based on the *lockdown* condition in your application. The bool query written in the snippet below demonstrates such use case:

```
{
  "query": {
    "bool": {
      "must": [{
          "match_none": {}
        }
      ]
    }
  }
}
```

The query gets a match_none inserted under specific conditions (database being upgraded) which means, no queries will return results.

In the next section, we learn about the match query. Most of the queries we use when working with Elasticsearch are match queries in one form or another.

10.5 *The match query*

The match query is the most common and powerful query for multiple use cases. It is a full-text search query returning documents that match the specified criteria. The match query can be modified to include many different options.

10.5.1 *Format of a match query*

Let's first look at the format of the match query:

```
GET books/_search
{
  "query": {
    "match": {           ← The query type is match.
      "FIELD": "SEARCH TEXT"   ← The query expects a criterion to be specified as a name-value pair.
    }
  }
}
```

The match query expects the search criterion to be defined as a field value. The field can be any text field in a document whose values are to be matched. The value can be a word or multiple words and can be uppercase, lowercase, or CamelCase.

We can also pass several additional parameters in the `match` query's full form. So far, we have discussed a shortened form of the `match` query. Here is an example of the full form:

```
GET books/_search
{
  "query": {
    "match": {                        Declares FIELD as an object
      "FIELD": {                      with additional parameters        The query attribute
        "query":"<SEARCH TEXT>",                                        holds the search text.
        "<parameter>":"<MY_PARAM>",            The parameter (analyzer,
      }                                        operator, prefix_length, fuzziness,
    }                                          etc.) expects a value to be set.
  }
}
```

We can search across multiple indexes by providing comma-separated indexes in the search URL:

```
GET new_books,classics,top_sellers, crime* /_search
{
  ...
}
```

Any number of indexes can be provided when invoking the `_search` endpoint, including wildcards.

> **NOTE** If we omit the index (or indexes) in the search request, we effectively search the entire index. For example, `GET _search { ... }` searches across all the indexes in the cluster.

10.5.2 Searching using a match query

Now that we know the format for a `match` query, let's look at an example where we want to search for Java books with *Java* in the `title` field. The following listing sets the `title` field to the word "Java" as the text to search.

Listing 10.4 Searching for Java books

```
GET books/_search
{
  "query": {                The match query
    "match": {              in action
      "title": "Java"          Sets the search criteria, searching for
    }                          the word "Java" in the title field
  }
}
```

We create a `match` query with the criterion of searching for a word in a `title` field. Elasticsearch fetches all documents that match the word *Java* in the `title` field, as expected.

10.5.3 *Analyzing match queries*

In chapter 9, we saw that term-level queries are not analyzed. On the other hand, `match` queries that work on text fields *are* analyzed. The same analyzers used during the indexing process (unless our search queries are explicitly defined with different analyzers) process the search words in `match` queries. If a `standard` analyzer (the default analyzer) is used during the indexing of a document, search words are analyzed using the same `standard` analyzer before the search is executed.

Additionally, the `standard` analyzer applies the same `lowercase` token filter (remember, the `lowercase` token filter is applied during indexing) to the search words. Thus, if we provide uppercase search keywords, they are converted to lowercase letters and searched against the inverted index. For example, if we change the `title` value to use uppercase criteria such as `"title"`: `"JAVA"` and rerun the query, the results are the same as for the search query in listing 10.4. If we change the `title` value to lowercase or modify it any other way (`java`, `jaVA`, etc.), the query still returns the same results.

10.5.4 *Searching for multiple words*

In listing 10.4, we use a single word ("Java") as the search criterion against a `title` field. We can expand this criterion to accommodate searching for multiple words or sentences in a single field. For example, we can search for the words "Java Complete Guide" in the `title` field, "Concurrency and Multithreading" in the `synopsis` field, and so on. Indeed, searching for a string of words (like a broken sentence) is more common than searching for a single word. The query in the following listing does exactly that.

Listing 10.5   A `match` query for a set of words

```
GET books/_search
{
  "query": {
    "match": {
      "title": {
        "query": "Java Complete Guide"
      }
    }
  },
  "highlight": {
    "fields": {
      "title": {}
    }
  }
}
```

Here, we intend to search for a specific title (*Java Complete Guide*). That is, we want to fetch a book titled *Java Complete Guide,* if available, and return nothing otherwise. But if you execute this query, you may be surprised to see more documents returned than the one that matches the search query exactly.

This is because Elasticsearch employs an OR Boolean operator by default for this query, fetching all documents that match any of the search words. The words are matched individually rather than as a phrase: in our example, Elasticsearch searches for "Java" and returns the relevant documents, followed by another search for "Complete" that adds those results to the list, and so on. The query returns "Java", "Complete", or "Guide", including combinations of the words, as its results. The same search can be rewritten (although the OR operator is redundant) as the next listing shows.

Listing 10.6 Specifying the OR operator explicitly

```
GET books/_search
{
  "query": {
    "match": {
      "title": {
        "query": "Java Complete Guide",
        "operator": "OR"          ◁──┐  Specifies the OR operator explicitly
      }                              │  (although it is set by default)
    }
  }
}
```

To change this behavior to find documents with all three words in the title, we need to enable the AND operator.

Listing 10.7 Specifying the AND operator explicitly

```
GET books/_search
{
  "query": {
    "match": {
      "title": {
        "query": "Java Complete Guide",
        "operator": "AND"         ◁──┐  Explicitly specifies
      }                              │  an AND clause
    }
  }
}
```

This query tries to find a book or books that match all three words (the title must include "Java" *and* "Complete" *and* "Guide"). However, our data set does not contain a book called *Java Complete Guide*, so no results are returned.

10.5.5 Matching at least a few words

The OR and AND operators are opposing conditions. The OR condition fetches either of the search words, and the AND condition gets matching documents for exactly all of the words. What if we want to find documents matching at least a few words from the given set? In the previous example, suppose we want at least two words out of three to match (say, *Java* and *Guide*). This is where the `minimum_should_match` attribute comes in handy.

The `minimum_should_match` attribute indicates the minimum number of words that should be used to match the documents. The next listing shows this in action.

Listing 10.8 Matching at least two words

```
GET books/_search
{
  "query": {
    "match": {
      "title": {
        "query": "Java Complete Guide",
        "operator": "OR",
        "minimum_should_match": 2        ◁── Sets the minimum number of
      }                                       words that should match
    }
  }
}
```

This query matches at least two words (the `minimum_should_match` attribute is set to 2) and fetches documents with a combination of two of the given three words. The OR operator is redundant here because it is applied by default.

NOTE Setting the value to 3 in the listing 10.8 is as good as changing the operator to AND: all the words must be matched.

10.5.6 *Fixing typos using the fuzziness keyword*

When searching for things, we sometimes incorrectly type the search criteria (we all have been there); for example, instead of searching for Java books, we may post a query with "Kava" as the search criterion. We know our intention is to search for Java books—and so does Elasticsearch.

Fuzziness makes character changes to the input string so it is the same as the string that may exist in the index. It employs the Levenshtein distance algorithm to fix incorrect spellings. We look at fuzziness further in section 10.12, but let's see how to use it with `match` queries.

A `match` query lets us add a `fuzziness` parameter to fix spelling mistakes. We can set it as a numeric value, where the expected value is 0, 1, or 2, meaning zero, one, or two character changes (insertions, deletions, modifications), respectively. In addition to setting these values, we can use the AUTO setting to let the engine deal with the changes. The following listing shows how we can use `fuzziness` (with a value of 1) to sort out our "Kava" typo.

Listing 10.9 Fixing a spelling mistake with the `fuzziness` parameter

```
GET books/_search
{
  "query": {
```

```
      "match": {
        "title": {
          "query": "Kava",
          "fuzziness": 1        ⟵—⟍  Setting fuzziness to 1 replaces one
        }                             letter with all other combinations.
      }
    }
  }
}
```

When searching for the text string "Java Complete Guide", we use a set of words to search for a book (or books) and usually expect the words to be treated individually (like a set of search words). However, we sometimes want to search for a phrase or sentence. That's when the match_phrase query is useful.

10.6   *The match_phrase query*

A matching phrase (match_phrase) query finds documents that exactly match a given phrase. The idea is to search for the phrase (group of words) in a given field in the given order. For example, if we are looking for the phrase "book for every Java programmer" in the synopsis of a book, documents are searched with those words in that order.

In our previous section (section 10.5) on match queries, we saw that words can be split individually and searched with an AND/OR operator when using a match query. The match_phrase query is the opposite. It returns results that match the search phrase exactly. The following listing illustrates the match_phrase query in action.

> **Listing 10.10   The `match_phrase` query in action**

```
GET books/_search
{
  "query": {                  ⟍  Specifies a
    "match_phrase": {        ⟵—⟍ match_phrase query
      "synopsis": "book for every Java programmer"   ⟵—⟍  Specifies the phrase (group
    }                                                      of words) to be matched
  }
}
```

The match_phrase query expects a phrase. It returns exactly one document because only one in our books index has that phrase in the synopsis field.

What if we drop a word or two in the search phrase? For example, suppose we remove *for* or *every* (or both) from the phrase "book for every Java programmer" and rerun the query. Unfortunately, the query won't return any results! This is because match_phrase expects the words in a search phrase to match the exact phrase, word by word. Searching for "book Java programmer" returns no results. But there is a fix to this problem: using the slop parameter.

The slop parameter allows us to ignore the number of words between the words in a phrase. We can drop the in-between words, but we must let the engine know how many words to drop. This is done by setting a value for the slop parameter. The slop attribute is an integer value indicating the number of words that can be ignored in a phrase during a `match_phrase` search. For example, `slop` with a value of 1 ignores one word missing from a phrase, `slop` with a value of 2 forgives two words, and so on. The default value of `slop` is 0, meaning we are not forgiven for providing a phrase with missing words.

Returning to our earlier example, let's drop the word *for* from the given phrase so that instead of "book for every Java programmer", we search for "book every Java programmer". Because we drop a single word, we need to set the `slop` parameter to 1. We also need to expand the query by providing two additional parameters in the `query` and `slop` objects for the `synopsis` field.

Listing 10.11   A `match_phrase` query with `slop` that drops one word

```
GET books/_search
{
  "query": {
    "match_phrase": {
      "synopsis": {          We expand this field to
                             include an object with
                             additional parameters.
        "query": "book every Java programmer",     Phrase with one
                                                    missing word: for
        "slop": 1      Sets slop to 1, meaning the
      }                query looks for phrases
    }                  with a single missing word
  }
}
```

If we want to use the `slop` parameter, both `query` and `slop` must be provided along with the field's object, as shown in listing 10.11 (the long form of the query). Because `slop` is set to 1, the query matches if one word is missing in an entire phrase in the `synopsis` field. This query returns the book matching our entire phrase. The takeaway is that a `match_phrase` query looks for an exact phrase, but if we are unsure about our search, we can use the `slop` parameter to indicate how forgiving our query should be.

The `match_phrase` query has a slight variation: the `match_phrase_prefix` query. In addition to matching an exact phrase, we can match the last word as a prefix. Let's discuss this next with an example.

10.7   *The match_phrase_prefix query*

A `match_phrase_prefix` query is like a `match_phrase` query in that, in addition to matching the exact phrase, the query matches all the words, using the last word in the search phrase as a prefix. This is easier to understand via an example. The following listing searches for the prefix "found" in the tags, which can apply to "foundation", "founded", and so on.

Listing 10.12   Using a `match_phrase_prefix` query

```
GET books/_search
{
  "query": {
```

```
        "match_phrase_prefix": {          ⟵───  Specifies the
          "tags": {                             match_phrase_prefix query
            "query": "concepts and found"
          }
        }
      },
      "highlight": {
        "fields": {
          "tags": {}
        }
      }
    }
}
```

Specifies the prefix to search for points to `"query": "concepts and found"`

This query fetches all books with tags matching "found". It matches "foundational" in our books index.

Similar to a `match_phrase` query, word order is also important in a `match_phrase_prefix` query. And again, `slop` comes to the rescue. For example, to retrieve books with the phrase *concepts and foundations* in the `tags` field, we can drop a word by adding the `slop` keyword.

Listing 10.13 Using a `match_phrase_prefix` query with `slop`

```
# Match phrase prefix
GET books/_search
{
  "query": {
    "match_phrase_prefix": {
      "tags": {
        "query": "concepts found",       ⟵─── The phrase omits one
        "slop":1     ⟵───                       word ("and") and has
      }                Sets slop to 1 because    a prefix ("found").
    }                  one word is dropped
  }                    from the phrase
}
```

Setting the `slop` keyword to 1 queries books with the tags `concepts` and `found*`, but it ignores the word *and*. The query should return the book *Kotlin Programming* as the result because the query matches the phrase "Kotlin concepts and foundational APIs" in the `tags` field.

So far, we've queried search criteria across a single field. However, let's say we want to find the words "Software Development" across the `title`, `synopsis`, and `tags` fields. That's what happens when we use a `multi_match` query, discussed in the next section.

10.8 The multi_match query

As the name suggests, a multi-match (`multi_match`) query searches across multiple fields. For example, to search for the word "Java" across the `title`, `synopsis`, and `tags` fields, a `multi_match` query is the answer. The following listing shows a query that searches for "Java" across these three fields.

Listing 10.14   Searching multiple fields using `multi_match`

```
GET books/_search
{
  "_source": false,          Suppresses the source document
  "query": {                 from appearing in the results
    "multi_match": {         Specifies the
      "query": "Java",       multi_match query
      "fields": [            Defines the search criterion
        "title",             as the word "Java"
        "synopsis",
        "tags"               Searches across multiple
      ]                      fields provided in an array
    }
  },
  "highlight": {             Highlights the matches
    "fields": {              returned in the results
      "title": {},
      "tags": {}
    }
  }
}
```

The `multi_match` query expects an array of fields along with the search criterion. We get the aggregated results by combining all the results for individual fields.

10.8.1   *Best fields*

You may wonder what the document's relevancy is when we search multiple fields. Fields where more words are matched score higher. If we search for "Java Collections" across multiple fields, a field (say, `synopsis`) where two words match is more relevant than a field with one (or no) matches. In this case, the document with this `synopsis` field is given a higher relevancy score.

   Fields that match all the search criteria are called the *best fields*. In the previous example, assuming `synopsis` contains both words, *Java* and *Collections*, we can say that `synopsis` is the best field. Multi-match uses a `best_fields` type under the hood when running queries. This type is the default for `multi_match` queries. Of course, there are other fields, as we see shortly.

   Let's rewrite the query from listing 10.14. This time, instead of letting Elasticsearch use the default setting (the `best_fields` type), we specifically override the `type` field.

Listing 10.15   Specifying the `best_fields` type explicitly

```
GET books/_search
{
  "_source": false,
  "query": {
    "multi_match": {
      "query": "Design Patterns",    Sets the type of multi_match
      "type": "best_fields",         query to best_fields
```

```
      "fields": ["title","synopsis"]
    }
  },
  "highlight": {
    "fields": {         ◁─────┐  Suppresses the source
      "tags": {},             │  but shows the highlights
      "title": {}
    }
  }
}
```

We query for "Design Patterns" across the `title` and `synopsis` fields. This time, we explicitly instruct the `multi_match` query to use the `best_fields` type.

> **NOTE** The default type for a `multi_match` query is `best_fields`. The `best_fields` algorithm ranks the field with the most words higher than that with the fewest.

If you look at the response and the scores (see the following code snippet), you'll see that the book *Head First Design Patterns* has a score of 6.9938974 compared to *Head First Object-Oriented Analysis Design,* which has a score of 2.9220228:

```
"hits" : [{
  "_index" : "books",
  "_id" : "10",
  "_score" : 6.9938974,
  "highlight" : {
    "title" : [
      "Head First <em>Design</em> <em>Patterns</em>"
    ]
  }
},
{
  "_index" : "books",
  "_id" : "8",
  "_score" : 2.9220228,
  "highlight" : {
    "title" : [
      "Head First Object-Oriented Analysis <em>Design</em>"
    ]
  }
}
...]
```

There are other types of `multi-match` queries, including `cross_fields`, `most_fields`, `phrase`, and `phrase_prefix`. We can use the `type` parameter to set the query type to search for the best match among multiple fields. However, we won't delve into all these types here; consult Elasticsearch's documentation for more information.

How does Elasticsearch carry out a `multi_match` query? It is rewritten using a disjunction max (`dis_max`) query behind the scenes. We discuss this query type next.

10.8.2 *The dis_max query*

In the previous section, we looked at the `multi_match` query, which searches for criteria in multiple fields. To execute this query type behind the scenes, Elasticsearch rewrites the `multi_match` query using a *disjunction max query* (`dis_max`). The `dis_max` query splits each field into a separate `match` query, as the following listing shows.

Listing 10.16   Disjunction max (`dis_max`) query in use

```
GET books/_search
{
  "_source": false,
  "query": {                          Specifies the dis_max      Defines the set of
    "dis_max": {          ◁───────    query type                 queries to include in a
      "queries": [                                    ◁───────   dis_max query block
        {"match": {"title": "Design Patterns"}},      ◁──────┐  Specifies a
        {"match": {"synopsis": "Design Patterns"}}]          │  match query
    }
  }
}
```

Multiple fields are split into two `match` queries under the `dis_max` query. The query returns documents with a high relevancy `_score` for the individual field.

> **NOTE**   The `dis_max` query is classified as a compound query: a query that wraps up other queries. We discuss compound queries in chapter 11.

In some situations, the relevancy scores of the fields in a `multi_match` query are the same. In that case, the scores end up in a tie. To break the tie, we use a tiebreaker.

10.8.3 *Tiebreakers*

The relevancy score is based on a single field's score, but if the scores are tied, we can specify `tie_breaker` to solve the tie. When we use `tie_breaker`, Elasticsearch calculates the overall score slightly differently, as we see shortly; first, let's check out an example.

The following listing queries two words against two fields: `title` and `tags`. However, the code also adds a `tie_breaker` parameter.

Listing 10.17   A `multi_match` query with a tiebreaker

```
GET books/_search
{
  "query": {                          Specifies a
    "multi_match": {      ◁───────    multi_match query     Queries for
      "query": "Design Patterns",                 ◁──────   "Design Patterns"
      "type": "best_fields",                      ◁────────────────────────┐  Sets the query's
      "fields": ["title","tags"],   ◁──────┐  Defines the set of            type to best_fields
      "tie_breaker": 0.9                    │  fields to search
    }
  }
}
```
Sets the tiebreaker

When we search for "Design Patterns" using the `best_fields` type and specify multiple fields (`title` and `synopsis`), we can provide a `tie_breaker` value to overcome any tie on equal scores. When we provide a tiebreaker, the overall scoring is calculated as follows:

```
Overall score = score of the best match field +
score of the other matching fields * tie_breaker
```

Earlier, we worked with a `dis_max` query. Elasticsearch converts all `multi_match` queries to the `dis_max` query. For example, the `multi_match` query from listing 10.17 can be rewritten as a `dis_max` query.

Listing 10.18 The `dis_max` query with a tiebreaker

```
GET books/_search
{
  "_source": false,
  "query": {
    "dis_max": {
      "queries": [
        {"match": {"title": "Design Patterns"}},
        {"match": {"synopsis": "Design Patterns"}}],
      "tie_breaker": 0.5        ⟵──┐  The tiebreaker
    }
  },
  "highlight": {
    "fields": {
      "title": {},
      "synopsis": {},
      "tags": {}
    }
  }
}
```

The `multi_match` query is now written as `dis_max` query. That's exactly what Elasticsearch does behind the scenes.

When we search multiple fields, we sometimes want to give additional weight to a particular field (for example, finding our search words in a title is more relevant than the same search words appearing in a lengthy `synopsis` or `tags` field). How do we let Elasticsearch know to give extra weight to the `title` field? We can boost individual queries, as discussed in the following section.

10.8.4 *Boosting individual fields*

Websites and applications usually provide a search bar for users to search for products, books, reviews, and so forth. When a user enters a few words, they don't mean they are interested in searching for only those words in a particular field. For example, when we search for "C# book" on Amazon, we don't ask Amazon to search only in a particular category, such as title or synopsis. We simply input the string in the text box and let Amazon figure out the result. That's what we can do using individual field boosts!

In a `multi_match` query, we can bump up (boost) the criteria for a specific field. Suppose that when searching for "C# Guide", we decide that finding the word in the title is more important than finding it in tags. In this case, we can boost the field's importance field by using a caret and a number: `title^2`, for example. The following listing shows the full query for this scenario.

Listing 10.19   Boosting the score for a field in a `multi_match` query

```
GET books/_search
{
  "query": {
    "multi_match": {
      "query": "C# Guide",
      "fields": ["title^2", "tags"]          ◁────  Doubles the importance
    }                                                of the title field
  }
}
```

In this listing, we double the `title` field's importance. So if the text "C# Guide" is found in the `title` field, that document has a higher score than a document with the text in the `tags` field.

Next, let's look at the `query_string` query. This type of query helps us build a request URL search, mimicking Kibana Query Language (KQL) in a Query DSL format. We review the need for the `query_string` query and work with it in the following section.

Query strings and KQL

In chapter 8, we looked at the URI search method (a search query approach in addition to Query DSL). We created a request by passing the `search` query and its parameters to the URL, rather than in a request body. We also saw that although the URI method is simple, it becomes error-prone as the complexity of the query criteria increases.

On Kibana's Discover tab, we usually use KQL to create search criteria using operators. For example, to search for "2nd edition Java book written by Bert, released after 2010", the equivalent query written in the Discover tab's KQL box is as follows:

```
title:Java and author :Bert and edition:2 and release_date>=2000-01-01
```

> ### Kibana's Discover tab showing a KQL query
>
> Elastic introduced KQL for querying logs and metrics in Elasticsearch indexes through Kibana. KQL is a flexible and intuitive language supporting a wide range of search capabilities, including field-level searches, logical operations, and complex queries. We can search using wildcards and, as shown in the example query, combine multiple search queries with logical operators such as AND, OR, and NOT. KQL also provides auto-completion and syntax highlighting, making it easier to construct and under-stand queries. The principle behind KQL uses the URI request API. It is handy to use URI-type queries without having to worry about constructing a query in Query DSL mode—if only there were an approach that gave us the best of both worlds.
>
> The good news is that we can achieve the same URI functionality using a special query called query_string. This query type lets us define a query using logical oper-ators in a request body.

10.9   The query_string query

The query_string type lets us construct a query using operators such as AND or OR, as well as logical operators such as > (greater than), <= (less than or equal to), * (con-tains in), and so on. This is easily understood with an example, so let's jump right into the code.

In the sidebar in the previous section, we fetched Bert's books using a long query on Kibana's Discover tab: title:Java and author :Bert and edition:2 and release_date>=2000-01-01. We can achieve this by writing a query_string query.

Listing 10.20   Creating a query string with operators

```
GET books/_search
{
  "query": {
    "query_string": {          <--| Specifies the
                                   | query_string query
      "query": "author:Bert AND edition:2 AND release_date>=2000-01-01"   <--|
    }                                                                        |
  }                                              Provides the search
}                                                criteria in the query
```

The query_string query expects a query parameter where we provide the criteria. The query is constructed as name-value pairs: in this example, author is the field, and Bert is the value. Looking at the code, notice the following:

- The search query is built using Query DSL syntax (the GET request has a body).
- The search criteria are written to concatenate the fields using operators.

The query is as simple as writing a question in plain English. We can create complex criteria using these operators (in plain English) and provide them to the engine to get results for us.

Sometimes we do not know which fields users want to search; they may want a query to focus on the `title` field, the `synopsis` or `tags` field, or all of them. In the next section, we go over ways to specify fields.

10.9.1 Fields in a query_string query

In a typical search box, the user does not need to specify a field when searching for something. For example, take a look at the following query.

Listing 10.21   Query string with no fields specified

```
GET books/_search
{
  "query": {
    "query_string": {
      "query": "Patterns"          ◁───  The query search word
    }                                     (fields are not mentioned)
  },
  "highlight": {            ◁───┐  Highlights
    "fields": {                 │  responses
      "title": {},
      "synopsis": {},
      "tags": {}
    }
  }
}
```

We want to search for the keyword "Patterns" in the previous query. Remember, the query does not ask us to search any fields. It is a generic query that should be executed across all fields. The response shows that some results are highlighted on a different field for individual documents:

```
"highlight" : {
    "synopsis" : ["Head First Design <em>Patterns</em> is one of ..."],
      "title" : ["Head First Design <em>Patterns</em>"]
},
...
"highlight" : {
 "synopsis" : [ "create .. using modern application <em>patterns</em>"]
},
...
```

Instead of letting the engine search query against all available fields, we can assist Elasticsearch by providing fields to run the search on. The next listing shows how to do this.

Listing 10.22   Specifying fields explicitly in a `query_string` query

```
GET books/_search
{
  "query": {
    "query_string": {
      "query": "Patterns",        ◁───  The query criterion with
                                         no fields mentioned
```

```
      "fields": ["title","synopsis","tags"]
    }
  }
}
```
← Explicitly declares the fields as an array of strings

Here, in an array in the `fields` parameter, we explicitly specify the fields against which this criterion should be searched. If we are unsure of the fields when constructing a query, we can use another parameter, `default_field`.

Listing 10.23   Query string with a default field

```
GET books/_search
{
  "query": {
    "query_string": {
      "query": "Patterns",
      "default_field": "title"
    }
  }
}
```
← Default field declaration

If a field is not mentioned in the query, the search is carried out against the `title` field. That's because the `title` field is declared the `default_field`.

10.9.2 *Default operators*

In listing 10.23, we searched for a single word, "Patterns". If we extend that search to include an additional word, such as "Design", we may get multiple books (two books, with the current data set) instead of the correct one: *Head First Design Patterns*. The reason is that Elasticsearch uses the OR operator by default when searching. Hence, it finds books with both words, "Design" *or* "Patterns", in the `title` field.

If this is not our intention (say, for example, we want to fetch a book with the exact phrase *Design Patterns* in the title), we can use the AND operator. The following `query_string` query has an additional parameter, `default_operator`, where we can set the operator to AND.

Listing 10.24   Query string with the AND operator

```
GET books/_search
{
  "query": {
    "query_string": {
      "query": "Design Patterns",
      "default_field": "title",
      "default_operator": "AND"
    }
  }
}
```
← Changes the operator from OR to AND

This `query_string` query is declared with the AND operator. Hence, we expect *Design Patterns* to be treated as a single word.

10.9.3 *The query_string query with a phrase*

If you are wondering whether there's support for phrase searches using `query_string`, indeed there is. We can rewrite the code in listing 10.24 using a phrase rather than changing the operator. The only thing we need to note is that phrases must be enclosed in quotes. That means the quotes that correspond to the phrase must be escaped: for example, `"query": "\"Design Patterns\""`. The next query searches for a phrase.

Listing 10.25 A `query_string` query with a phrase

```
GET books/_search
{
  "query": {
    "query_string": {
      "query": "\"making the code better\"",      ⟵——┐  Quotes around the sentence
      "default_field": "synopsis"                        make it a phrase query.
    }
  }
}
```

This code searches for the phrase `"making the code better"` in the `synopsis` field and fetches the book *Effective Java*. We can also use the `slop` parameter (discussed earlier in this chapter in section 10.5.2 and in chapter 8) if we are missing one or two words from the phrase. For example, the following listing shows how the `phrase_slop` parameter allows for a missing word in the phrase (*the* is dropped from the phrase) and still gets a successful result.

Listing 10.26 A `query_string` query with a phrase and `phrase_slop`

```
GET books/_search
{
  "query": {
    "query_string": {                              ┌  The phrase with
      "query": "\"making code better\"",      ⟵——┘  one word removed
      "default_field": "synopsis",
      "phrase_slop": 1        ⟵——┐  Sets phrase_slop to 1 to honor
    }                               the phrase with one missing
  }
}
```

The query is missing a word, but the `phrase_slop` setting forgives the omission, and we get the desired result.

When building a search service, we must consider supporting spelling mistakes. Applications should handle these mistakes gracefully and, instead of returning incorrect or no results, identify the spelling issue to enhance and accommodate the results. This improves the user search experience. Elasticsearch provides support for handling incorrect spelling through *fuzzy queries*.

10.10 *Fuzzy queries*

We can ask Elasticsearch to forgive spelling mistakes using fuzzy queries with `query_string` queries. All we need to do is suffix the query criteria with a tilde (~) operator. This is best understood with an example.

Listing 10.27   A fuzzy query string query

```
GET books/_search
{
  "query": {
    "query_string": {
      "query": "Pattenrs~",        ⟵┐  Incorrectly spelled "Pattenrs"
      "default_field": "title"        │  as the search word
    }
  }
}
```

By setting the suffix with the ~ operator, we ask the engine to consider the query fuzzy. By default, an edit distance of 2 is used when working with fuzzy queries. The *edit distance* is the number of mutations required to transform a string into another string. For example, the words *cat* and *cap* only differ by a single letter. Hence, we require an edit distance of 1 to transform *cat* into *cap*.

   In chapter 9, we learned about fuzzy queries in the term-level context, which utilize the Levenshtein distance algorithm. Another type of edit distance algorithm is the Damerau–Levenshtein distance algorithm, which is used to support fuzzy queries in the full-text context. It supports insertions, deletions, or substitutions of a maximum of two characters as well as transposition of adjacent characters.

> **NOTE** The Levenshtein distance algorithm defines the minimum number of mutations required for a string to be transformed into another string. These mutations include insertions, deletions, and substitutions. The Damerau–Levenshtein distance algorithm goes one step further. In addition to having all the mutations defined by Levenshtein, the Damerau-Levenshtein algorithm considers transposition of adjacent characters (for example, *TB > BT > BAT*).

By default, the edit distance in a `query_string` query is 2, but we can reduce it if needed by setting it to `1` after the tilde: `"Pattenrs~1"`. In the next two sections, we look at some simpler queries.

10.11 *Simple string queries*

The `query_string` query is strict on syntax, and errors in the input are not forgiven. For example, the following query throws an error because the input has parsing problems (on purpose—we added a quote to the input criterion).

Listing 10.28   A `query_string` query with an illegal quote character

```
GET books/_search
{
  "query": {
    "query_string": {
      "query": "title:Java\""      ◁──┐ Query with a syntax error
    }                                   │ (no corresponding quote)
  }
}
```

This query is not parsed. Elasticsearch throws an exception stating that the syntax was violated (`"reason": "Cannot parse 'title:Java\"': Lexical error at line 1, column 12. Encountered: <EOF> after : \"\"\""`). Throwing this JSON parse exception to the user validates stricter syntax for `query_string` queries. However, if we want Elasticsearch to ignore syntactical errors and continue with the job, there's an alternative: a `simple_query_string` query, discussed in the following section.

10.12 *The simple_query_string query*

As the name suggests, the `simple_query_string` query is a variant of the `query_string` query with a simple, limited syntax. We can use operators such as +, -, |, *, and ~ to construct the query. For example, searching for "Java + Cay" produces a Java book written by Cay, as the next listing shows.

Listing 10.29   A simple_query_string query

```
GET books/_search
{
  "query": {
    "simple_query_string": {      ◁──┐ Specifies the type of the query
      "query": "Java + Cay"           │ as simple_query_string
    }                             ◁──┐ Searches the query
  }                                   │ with the AND operator
}
```

The + operator in the query allows the query to search for "Java" *and* "Cay" across all fields. We can specify the fields if we want to check a set of fields instead of all the fields by setting the `fields` array. Table 10.1 describes the operators we can use in `simple_query_string`.

Table 10.1   Operators for a `simple_query_string` query

Operator	Description
|	OR
+	AND
-	NOT
~	Fuzzy query

Table 10.1 Operators for a `simple_query_string` query *(continued)*

Operator	Description
*	Prefix query
"	Phrase query

Unlike the `query_string` query, the `simple_query_string` query doesn't respond with errors if there's a syntax error in the input criteria. It takes a quieter approach of not returning anything if there is a syntactic error in the query, as the next listing shows.

Listing 10.30 No issue with incorrect syntax

```
GET books/_search
{
  "query": {
    "simple_query_string": {          ⟵─┐ A simple_query_string
      "query": "title:Java\""           │ query
    }                                  ⟵─┐ Query with
  }                                       │ incorrect syntax
}
```

Although we issue the same query with incorrect syntax (an extra quote at the end), no error is returned to the user other than no documents being returned. The `simple_query_string` query is helpful in such situations.

And that's a wrap! This chapter has been all about full-text queries: queries on unstructured data. In chapter 11, we look at compound queries in detail. Compound queries are advanced search queries that wrap leaf queries such as term-level and full-text queries.

Summary

- Elasticsearch is big on searching unstructured data using full-text queries. Full-text queries yield relevancy, meaning the documents matched and returned have a positive relevancy score.
- Elasticsearch provides a `_search` API for querying purposes.
- Several kinds of `match` queries work for various use cases when searching full text with relevance. The most common query is the `match` query.
- The `match` query searches on text fields for search criteria and scores documents using the relevance algorithm.
- Match all (`match_all`) queries search across all indexes and do not require a body.
- To search for a phrase, we use a `match_phrase` query or its variant, `match_phrase_prefix`. Both types of queries let us search for specific words in a defined order. Additionally, we can use the `phrase_slop` parameter if the phrase is missing words.

- Searching for user criteria across multiple fields is enabled by using a `multi_match` query.

- A query string (`query_string`) query uses logical operators such as AND, OR, and NOT. However, the `query_string` query is strict on syntax, so we receive an exception if the input syntax is incorrect.

- If we need Elasticsearch to be less strict about the query string syntax, then instead of using a `query_string` query, we can use a `simple_query_string` query. With that query type, all syntactical errors are suppressed by the engine.

Compound queries

This chapter covers

- Working with compound queries
- Boolean search queries
- Constant score queries
- Boosting queries
- Disjunction maximum queries
- Function score queries

In the last two chapters, we looked at term-level and full-text queries. We discussed searching structured and unstructured data using queries, some producing relevance scores and others working in a filter context where scores are irrelevant. Most queries allow setting simple search criteria and working on a limited set of fields, such as finding books written by an author or searching for best-selling books.

In addition to providing queries for complex criteria, we sometimes need to boost scores based on certain criteria while at the same time negating scores for negative matches (for example, all books launched during a training program may get a positive boost while simultaneously, expensive books are suppressed

361

[negated]). Or maybe we want to set scores based on custom requirements rather than using Elasticsearch's built-in relevance algorithms.

The individual leaf queries we've worked with so far are limited in that they can search based on one or several criteria but not based on more complex requirements (for example, searching for books written by a specific author, published between certain dates, listed as a best-seller or rated 4.5 out of 5, with a specific number of pages). Such advanced queries require advanced searching query capabilities. We look at these compound queries in this chapters.

Compound queries are advanced search constructs to query complex search criteria in Elasticsearch. They are made of individual leaf queries wrapped in conditional clauses and other constructs to provide capabilities such as letting the user set custom scores using predefined functions, boosting positive search matches while suppressing negative clauses, developing scores using scripts, and so on. They allow us to use individual leaf queries to develop fully fledged advanced queries of various types.

In this chapter, we examine the requirements that compound queries satisfy, and their semantics and usage. We look at Boolean queries, where multiple leaf queries are cast in a few conditional clauses to design an advanced search query, and we use clauses like `must`, `must_not`, `should`, and `filter` to arrange the leaf queries into a compound query. We look at `boosting` queries to enhance the query's score when a positive match occurs while simultaneously lowering the score for negations. We then learn about a predefined static scoring query called `constant_score`, which helps set a static score on the returned results.

We also run through function score queries to help set user-defined custom scoring algorithms using a set of functions. We look at the mechanics of setting scores using scripts and weights based on other field values present in the document, as well as random numbers. But first, let's get some sample data.

11.1 Sample product data

In this chapter's examples, we work with a data set of electrical and electronic products such as televisions (TVs), laptops, mobile phones, refrigerators (fridges), and so on. The product data is available on GitHub (http://mng.bz/Rxwa) and on the book's website (https://www.manning.com/books/elasticsearch-in-action-second-edition). In this section, we review the definition and indexing processes.

11.1.1 The products schema

The first step in developing the `products` index is to create a data schema defining the fields and their data types. The following listing shows the schema at a glance (the full schema is available with the book's files).

Listing 11.1 Defining the `products` schema

```
PUT products
{
  "mappings": {
```

```
    "properties": {
      "brand": {
        "type": "text"
      },
      "colour": {
        "type": "text"
      },
      "energy_rating": {
        "type": "text"
      },
      ...
      "user_ratings": {
        "type": "double"
      },
      "price": {
        "type": "double"
      }

    }
  }
}
```

There are no surprises in the `products` definition except that a couple of attributes (`price` and `user_ratings`) are defined as `double` but the rest are declared as `text` fields. Most fields are declared as multiple data types (e.g., `text` and `keyword`) to accommodate working with term-level queries on data (e.g., energy rating or color).

The mapping in listing 11.1 creates an empty `products` index with the relevant schema for the e-commerce electrical products we are about to index. Next, we index a set of sample products.

11.1.2 Indexing products

Now that the schema is ready, let's index our product data set for Elasticsearch, which is available with the book's files. Copy the contents of products.txt and paste them into Kibana. We use the `_bulk` API to index this data. This code snippet shows a sample of the data:

```
PUT _bulk
{"index":{"_index":"products","_id":"1"}}
{"product": "TV", "brand": "Samsung", "model": "UE75TU7020", "size": "75",
"resolution": "4k", "type": "smart tv", "price": 799, "colour": "silver",
"energy_rating": "A+", "overview": "Settle in for an epic..",
"user_ratings": 4.5, "images": ""}
{"index":{"_index":"products","_id":"2"}}
{"product": "TV", "brand": "Samsung", "model": "QE65Q700TA", "size": "65",
"resolution": "8k", "type": "QLED", "price": 1799, "colour": "black",
"energy_rating": "A+", "overview": "This outstanding 65-inch ..",
"user_ratings": 5, "images": ""}
{"index":{"_index":"products","_id":"3"}}
...
```

Now that we've indexed our products data set, let's set the scene by discussing the need for compound queries and why and how they help build advanced queries.

11.2   *Compound queries*

We worked with leaf queries in the last two chapters (term-level and full-text queries): queries that work on single (individual) fields. If our requirement is to find the top-selling books from a period, we can use a leaf query to fetch those results. Leaf queries help find answers to simple questions without support for conditional clauses. However, the real world seldom involves simple query requirements.

Most requirements demand developing complex queries with multiple clauses and conditions. For example, a complex query may consist of finding best-selling books written by a particular author and published during a specific period, or a particular edition; or returning all books categorized by various geographical zones except a specific country, ordered by the highest grosser.

Here's where compound queries shine: they help develop complex search queries by combining one or more leaf queries. Fortunately, we can use Query DSL (discussed in chapter 8) to write compound queries: we use the same _search endpoint with a request body that consists of a query object. Figure 11.1 shows the syntax for a compound query.

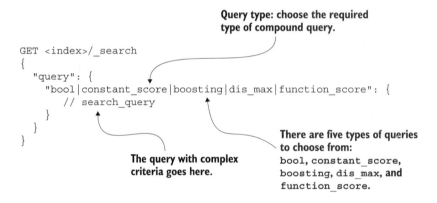

Figure 11.1   Compound query syntax

The basic syntax for compound queries is no different from other queries. However, the body of the query object is made of different components, depending on the type of compound query we want to use.

Elasticsearch provides five such queries for varied search requirements: Boolean (bool), constant score, function score, boosting, and disjunction max. Table 11.1 briefly describes these five compound queries. For example, if our requirement is to develop an advanced query using conditional clauses, we can use a Boolean query encompassing multiple leaf queries using AND, OR, and other conditions. Similarly, if the requirement is to set a static score across all results, a constant-score query is what we need. We apply these five types of queries in different use cases in this chapter.

Table 11.1 Types of compound queries

Compound query	Description
Boolean (bool) query	A combination of conditional clauses that wraps individual leaf (term and full-text) queries. Works similarly to the AND, OR, and NOT operators.
	Example: products= TV AND color = silver NOT rating < 4.5 AND brand = Samsung OR LG
Constant score (constant_score) query	Wraps a filter query to set constant scores on results. Also helps boost the score.
	Example: Search for all TVs with user ratings higher than 5 but set a constant score of 5 for each result regardless of the search engine's calculated score.
Function score (function_score) query	User-defined functions to assign custom scores to result documents
	Example: Search for products, and if the product is from LG and is a TV, boost the score by three (via a script or weight function).
Boosting (boosting) query	Boosts the score for positive matches while negating the score for non-matches
	Example: Fetch all TVs but lower the score of those that are expensive.
Disjunction max (dis_max) query	Wraps several queries to search for multiple words in multiple fields (similar to a multi_match query)
	Example: Search for smart TVs in two fields (say, overview and description) and return the best match.

Of these types, the bool query is the most commonly used compound query due to its flexibility and support for multiple conditional clauses. We have a lot to cover when discussing the bool query, so it deserves a dedicated section. But before we proceed with the rest of the chapter, we must set up our sandbox to experiment with compound queries.

11.3 The Boolean (bool) query

The Boolean (bool) query is the most popular and flexible compound query to create complex criteria for searching data. As the name indicates, it combines Boolean clauses, each with a leaf query made of term-level or full-text queries. Each clause has a typed occurrence of must, must_not, should, or filter clauses, briefly explained in table 11.2.

Table 11.2 Boolean clauses

Clause	Description
must	An AND query where all the documents must match the query criteria
	Example: Fetch TVs (product = TV) that fall within a specific price range
must_not	A NOT query where none of the documents match the query criteria
	Example: Fetch TVs (product = TV) that fall within a specific price range *but* with an exception, such as not being a certain color

Table 11.2   Boolean clauses *(continued)*

Clause	Description
should	An OR query where one of the documents must match the query criteria
	Example: Search for fridges that are frost-free *or* energy rated above C grade.
filter	A filter query where the documents must match the query criteria (similar to the must clause), but the filter clause does not score the matches
	Example: Fetch TVs (product = TV) that fall within a specific price range (but the score of the documents returned will be zero)

A compound query consisting of these clauses can contain multiple leaf queries or even additional compound queries. We can create advanced, complicated search queries by combining the leaf and compound queries. Let's discuss the bool query syntax and structure.

11.3.1   *The bool query structure*

As mentioned earlier, a bool query is a combination of Boolean clauses producing unified output. Figure 11.2 illustrates the basic structure of a bool query with empty clauses.

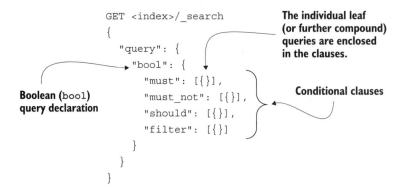

Figure 11.2   Syntax of a sample Boolean (bool) query with four conditional clauses

As you can see, a bool query is configured with a set of conditions captured in the clauses. A bool query can accept at least one of the queries embedded in a clause. Each clause can then host one or more leaf or compound queries as an array of queries. As the following code snippet shows, we can provide multiple term-level and full-text queries (shown in bold) inside any clause (in italics):

```
GET books/_search
{
  "query": {
    "bool": {
```

```
      "must": [
          { "match": {"FIELD": "TEXT"}},
{ "term": {"FIELD": {"value": "VALUE"}}}
      ],
      "must_not": [
          {"bool": { "must": [{}]}}}
      ]
      "should": [
          { "range": { "FIELD": {"gte": 10,"lte": 20}}},
{ "terms": { "FIELD": [ "VALUE1", "VALUE2" ]}}
      ]
    }
  }
}
```

Here, we have three clauses, and each clause holds leaf queries such as match, term, range, and so on. We also have a compound clause in the must_not clause, where we can further expand our criteria using the same set of clauses. These individual queries joined in clauses let us write a search query that satisfies advanced query requirements.

While you may understand the previous query from a theoretical perspective, unless you write and execute queries, you can't appreciate their full potential. Let's examine the bool query from the ground up, building a query one clause at a time and evolving it as we go. We start our sprint with the must clause.

11.3.2 *The must clause*

The criterion we declare in a bool query's must clause yields positive results when the queries defined in the (clause) block satisfy the criterion. That is, the output contains all the documents that match the conditions in the must clause.

Let's explore a simple query to begin with. Suppose our requirement is to find all TVs in the products index. For that, we write a bool query with a must clause. Because we are looking only for TVs, we can put the search criterion in a match query, matching products that are TVs. The following listing provides the code.

Listing 11.2 A bool query's must clause with a match query

```
GET products/_search
{
  "query": {
    "bool": {            ⟵── A bool query      The must
      "must": [          ⟵──                   clause
        {
          "match": {     ⟵──
            "product": "TV"    A match query that
          }                    queries by author
        }
      ]
    }
  }
}
```

Search criterion ⟶ (points to "product": "TV")

Let's dissect this query. The `bool` declaration inside the `query` object indicates that this is a `bool` query. The `bool` object is then wrapped with a `must` clause with the criterion to match the given search word, `TV`. When we execute this query, a few TVs are returned, as expected (the output is omitted here for brevity).

A match query is a bool query

The `match` query we've worked with so far is a type of Boolean query. For example, the `bool` query in listing 11.2 can be rewritten as a `match` (full-text) query to fetch TVs. The following leaf query returns the same TVs returned by the previous `bool` query:

```
GET books/_search
{
  "query": {
    "match": {
      "author": "Joshua"
    }
  }
}
```

You may be inclined to use a `match` query for a simple (single) criterion, but alas, there's more complexity in the real world; so, you may have to lean on the `bool` query.

11.3.3 *Enhancing the must clause*

Fetching TVs isn't that exciting, is it? Let's make our query a bit more interesting. In addition to fetching TVs, let's add a condition: fetch only TVs whose value is in a certain price range. We need to join two queries to achieve what we want.

This requirement asks us to use a `must` clause with two `match` queries: one to match on the `product` field and another to match on `price`. Remember, the `must` clause accepts an array of leaf-level queries. While a `match` query is sufficient to search on the type of product, we can add a `range` query to a `bool` query to fetch all TVs in a certain price range.

Listing 11.3   Finding TVs within a price range

```
GET products/_search
{
  "query": {
    "bool": {
      "must": [          ⟵─  The must query with two
        {                    individual leaf queries
          "match": {    ⟵┐  A match query
            "product": "TV"  │  to find TVs
          }
        },
        {                    A range query with
          "range": {    ⟵─  a price range
```

```
      "price": {
        "gte": 700,
        "lte": 800
      }
    }
  }
]
}
}
}
```

Here, we create two leaf queries with a conditional AND between the match and range queries. The queries go like this: search for TVs *and* fetch those in a specified price range. The result is one TV, because our data set contains only one TV with a price in the range ($799).

Of course, we can add further criteria to the query. For example, the query in the next listing searches for all silver or black TVs with 4K resolution.

Listing 11.4 Three leaf queries wrapped in a `must` clause

```
GET products/_search
{
  "query": {
    "bool": {                    The must query with
      "must": [         ⬅┘      three leaf queries
        {
          "match": {       ⬅┐   The match leaf query
            "product": "TV"      to search for TVs
          }
        },
        {
          "term": {        ⬅┐   The term query to find
            "resolution": "4k"   TVs with 4K resolution
          }
        },
        {
          "terms": {       ⬅    The terms query to
            "colour": [          fetch silver or black TVs
              "silver",
              "black"
            ]
          }
        }
      ]
    }
  }
}
```

As you can imagine, we can combine multiple full-text and term-level queries (or other leaf queries) to develop a search solution for complex and complicated criteria using a bool query—we have just scratched the surface. We can build even more advanced queries using other clauses; we discuss the must_not clause next.

11.3.4 *The must_not clause*

The opposite of `must`, as you can guess, is the `must_not` query clause. For example, on a shopping site, we may want to search for products with specific details, asking the retailer to *ignore* products that are not available. Figure 11.3 shows an example (from a UK retailer, John Lewis).

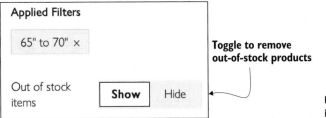

Figure 11.3   Hiding out-of-stock items during search

The search engine hides all out-of-stock items before showing the search results. This is the sort of functionality the `must_not` clause can satisfy.

Like the `must` clause, `must_not` accepts an array of leaf queries to build advanced search criteria. The query's sole aim is to filter out matches that do *not* meet the criteria specified. The best way to understand this is with an example. The query in the following listing searches for all TVs that are not a specific brand (in this case, Samsung or Philips).

> **Listing 11.5   Fetching TVs using `must_not` to exclude certain brands**

```
GET products/_search
{
  "query": {
    "bool": {
      "must_not": [            A must_not clause to
        {                      host a terms query
          "terms": {           The terms query that searches
            "brand.keyword": [ for specific brands
              "Samsung",
              "Philips"
            ]
          }
        }
      ]
    }
  }
}
```

This listing shows the `bool` query provided with a `must_not` clause that holds a `terms` query. At first, as expected, the `terms` query fetches products that are Samsung or Philips. As this `terms` query exists under a `must_not` clause, the effect is to negate what the query does. That is, the results "must not match what's matched to the query in the clause". Hence, because the `terms` query is wrapped in a `must_not` clause, the result is the opposite: it fetches all products that are *not* manufactured by Samsung and Philips.

The problem with the query is that it fetches *all* products (TVs, fridges, monitors, and so on). But, remember, our requirement is to get *TVs only* that are *not* manufactured by Samsung or Philips. We should modify the query to fetch TVs, omitting those particular brands.

If you are thinking we should add a `must` clause to the `must_not` clause in listing 11.5, you are correct. We can create a `term` query wrapped in a `must` clause to fetch all TVs and then remove (filter out) the specific brands from the results using `must_not`. Let's update the query to reflect this.

Listing 11.6   Filtering out certain brands

```
GET products/_search
{
  "query": {
    "bool": {
      "must_not": [          ◁──┐  The must_not clause that
        {                        │  ignores a set of brands
          "terms": {
            "brand.keyword": [
              "Philips",
              "Samsung"
            ]
          }
        }
      ],
      "must": [              ◁──┐  A must clause that
        {                        │  looks for (matches) TVs
          "match": {
            "product": "TV"
          }
        }
      ]
    }
  }
}
```

We have two query clauses: a `must` and a `must_not`, both wrapped in a single `bool` compound query. Now we are searching for TVs that are not the two specific brands. Can we add more to the `must_not` clause? Yes; it can be enhanced with multiple leaf queries, as we discuss in the following section.

11.3.5 Enhancing the must_not clause

Similar to how we enhanced the query for `must` clauses (section 11.3.3), it's a no-brainer to provide multiple query criteria inside the `must_not` clause. For example, in addition to fetching products that are not manufactured by Philips and Samsung, we can query for only TVs that have four-star ratings or above (the `must_not` query uses a range query that filters out TVs with user ratings below 4.0).

Listing 11.7   Enhancing the `must_not` query

```
GET products/_search
{
  "query": {
    "bool": {
      "must_not": [                    ◁── The must_not clause with
        {                                   two individual queries
          "terms": {                  ◁── The terms query that matches the
            "brand.keyword": [             given values in the brand field
              "Philips",
              "Samsung"
            ]
          }
        },
        {
          "range": {                  ◁── The range query that fetches TVs
            "user_ratings": {              rated less than or equal to 4 stars
              "lte": 4.0
            }
          }
        }
      ],
      "must": [                       ◁── The must clause with
        {                                  a few leaf queries
          "match": {
            "product": "TV"
          }
        },
        {
          "term": {
            "resolution": {
              "value": "4k"
            }
          }
        },
        {
          "range": {
            "price": {
              "gte": 500,
              "lte": 700
            }
          }
        }
      ]
    }
  }
}
```

Although the query in listing 11.7 is verbose, dissecting it helps understand its crux. This `bool` query is composed of two clauses: `must` and `must_not`. The `must` clause searches for all 4K resolution TVs with a price tag between $500 and $700. This list is then fed into to the `must_not` clause, which has two leaf queries that work on the list of TVs produced by the `must` clause. The first query filters out all Philips or Samsung TVs (keeping TVs from all other brands). The second leaf query further filters this list with a `range` query that drops all TVs whose ratings are less than 4.0.

> **NOTE** The `must_not` clause does not influence the relevance score of the returned results. This is because `must_not` queries are executed in a filter context. Queries executed in a filter context *do not* produce a score; they give binary results (yes or no). Hence, the score generated by other clauses, such as `must` and `should`, are not modified by the queries declared in the `must_not` clause.

So far, we've looked at `must` and `must_not` clauses to construct our compound queries. The queries from these clauses are located on either side of the scale: the `must` clause is particular about criteria matching exactly, whereas the `must_not` clause does the opposite—it provides results that do not match any of the criteria.

Our examples fetched all TVs that matched a certain condition while dropping certain brands. Suppose we want to fetch results for a partial match: for example, fetching TVs that are larger than 85 inches *or* manufactured by a specific company. This type of query is supported by the third clause of the `bool` query: the `should` clause.

11.3.6 *The should clause*

Simply put, the `should` clause is an OR clause that evaluates the search based on an OR condition (whereas the `must` clause is based on the AND operator). For example, look at the following query.

> **Listing 11.8   Using a `should` query with a few criteria to fetch TVs**

```
GET products/_search
{
  "_source": ["product","brand", "overview","price"],
  "query": {
    "bool": {                        The should clause with
      "should": [        ⟵          two individual queries
        {
          "range": {      ⟵┐       Query to match products
            "price": {      │       within a specific price range
              "gte": 500,
              "lte": 1000
            }
          }
        },
        {
          "match_phrase_prefix": {   ⟵┐  Query to search products matching
            "overview": "4K Ultra HD"  │  a phrase in the overview field
          }
        }
      ]
    }
  }
}
```

The should clause is made of two queries that search for products in the price range $500 to $1,000 *or* products with the phrase "4K Ultra HD" in the overview field. We get more results than you may expect (remember the OR condition):

```
{
  ...
  "_score" : 12.059638,
  "_source" : {
    "overview" : ".. 4K Ultra HD display ...",
    "product" : "TV",
    "price" : 799,
    "brand" : "Samsung"
  }
},
{
  ...
  "_score" : 11.199882,
  "_source" : {
    "overview" : ".. 4K Ultra HD ...",,
    "product" : "TV",
    "price" : 639,
    "brand" : "Panasonic"
  }
},
{
  ...
  "_score" : 10.471219,
  "_source" : {
    "overview" : ".. 4K Ultra HD screen.. ",
    "product" : "TV",
    "price" : 1599,
    "brand" : "LG"
  }
}
...
```

The results include products that are not in the specified price range (for example, the third product in the returned result is $1,599 (way beyond what we've asked for); however, it is a match because the second criterion, 4K Ultra HD, matched. This indicates that the should clause operates on the OR condition.

There's more than using the OR condition on queries when executing the search for a should clause. Although we only ran the should query, usually it's joined with other clauses like must and must_not. The advantage of using a should clause with a must clause is that the results that match the query in the should clause get a boosted score. Let's discuss this in detail in the next section, using an example.

BOOSTING THE SCORE WITH A SHOULD CLAUSE
The query in listing 11.8 has a should clause, which returns positive results using an OR condition. When used with the must clause, the should clause adds weight to the relevance scoring. Let's say we issue a must clause that matches an LG TV.

Listing 11.9 Fetching TVs using a must query

```
GET products/_search
{
  "_source": ["product","brand"],
  "query": {
    "bool": {
      "must": [          ◁─── The must clause with two
        {                      individual match queries
          "match": {
            "product": "TV"
          }
        },
        {
          "match": {
            "brand": "LG"
          }
        }

      ]
    }
  }
}
```

There's not much to dissect in this query except the _score mentioned in the result, which is 4.4325914:

```
"hits" : [
  {
    "_index" : "products",
    "_id" : "5",
    "_score" : 4.4325914,
    "_ignored" : [
      "overview.keyword"
    ],
    "_source" : {
      "product" : "TV",
      "brand" : "LG"
    }
  }
]
```

Now, let's add a should clause to this query. The following listing shows the effect on the score.

Listing 11.10 Adding a should clause to boost the score

```
GET products/_search
{
  "_source": ["product","brand"],
  "query": {
    "bool": {          │ The must clause that
      "must": [   ◁──┘ searches for LG TVs
```

```
      {
        "match": {
          "product": "TV"
        }
      },
      {
        "match": {
          "brand": "LG"
        }
      }
    ],
    "should": [
      {
        "range": {
          "price": {
            "gte": 500,
            "lte": 1000
          }
        }
      },
      {
        "match_phrase_prefix": {
          "overview": "4K Ultra HD"
        }
      }
    ]
  }
 }
}
```

The should clause that checks the price range or match phrase of the resulting TVs

This query, using a `must` clause with a `should` clause, boosts the score of the matching documents. The earlier score of 4.4325914 is now a whopping 14.9038105:

```
"hits" : [
    {
      "_index" : "products",
      "_id" : "5",
      "_score" : 14.9038105,
      "_ignored" : [
        "overview.keyword"
      ],
      "_source" : {
        "product" : "TV",
        "brand" : "LG"
      }
    }
  ]
```

The score increased because the query was successful in the `must` clause and also matched in the `should` clause. The takeaway is that if the query in a `should` clause matches (in addition to positive matches in the `must` clause), the score increases. Having said that, how many queries should it match? There can be several leaf queries in a `should` clause, right? Do all the leaf queries need to match, or can we ask Elasticsearch

to check if at least one of the leaf queries matches? This can be achieved with the
`minimum_should_match` attribute, discussed next.

THE MINIMUM_SHOULD_MATCH SETTING

When we run a set of queries in a `must` clause along with queries in a `should` clause,
the following rules are applied implicitly:

- All the results must match the query criteria declared in the `must` clause (the
  query will not return positive search results if one of the `must` queries fails to
  match the criteria).

- There is no need for any of the results to match the criteria declared in the
  `should` clause. If they match, the `_score` is boosted; otherwise, there's no effect
  on the score.

Sometimes, however, we may need at least one of the `should` criteria to be matched
before sending the results to the client. We want the score to be boosted based on these
`should` query matches. We can do this using the `minimum_should_match` attribute.

For example, we can declare the query from listing 11.10 successful *if and only if at
least one* of the matches is positive; it returns positive results (with a boosted score)
only if one of the many queries matches. The following listing shows this.

> **Listing 11.11   Using the `minimum_should_match` parameter**

```
GET products/_search
{
  "_source": ["product","brand","overview", "price","colour"],
  "query": {
    "bool": {
      "must": [{
          "match": {
            "product": "TV"
          }
        },
        {
          "match": {
            "brand": "LG"
          }
        }],
      "should": [{
          "range": {
            "price": {
               "gte": 500,
               "lte": 2000
            }
          }
        },
        {
          "match": {
            "colour": "silver"
          }
        },
```

```
    {
      "match_phrase_prefix": {
        "overview": "4K Ultra HD"
      }
    }],
    "minimum_should_match": 1        ◁────
  }
  }
}
```

Matches at least one leaf query in the should clause

In the listing, we set `minimum_should_match` to 1. This means the query tries to match the criteria defined in the leaf queries of the `should` clause but with the condition that at least one of the queries must be a positive match: if a product is silver *or* the product is 4K Ultra HD *or* the price is between $500 and $2,000. However, if none of the criteria in the `should` clause match, the query fails, as we are asking the query to satisfy the `minumum_should_match` parameter.

As you may have guessed, a `bool` query can be declared with a `should` clause on its own—that is, without a `must` clause. Based on whether a `bool` query consists of a `must` clause along with the `should` clause, the default value of `minimum_should_match` varies. The default value of `minimum_should_match` is set to 0 if the `bool` query consists of a `should` with a `must` clause; it is set to 1 with only a `should` clause (see table 11.3).

Table 11.3 Default values of the `minimum_should_match` attribute

Clauses	Default value of minimum_should_match
should clause only (no must clause)	1
should with a must clause	0

So far, we've looked at `must`, `must_not`, and `should` clauses. Although `must_not` runs in a filter context, `must` and `should` run in a query context. We discussed the query context versus filter context in chapter 8, but for completeness, let's touch base on these concepts here. Queries run in a query context execute the appropriate relevancy algorithm, so we can expect relevancy scores associated with the resultant documents. Queries in a filter context do not output scores and are performant because execution of the scoring algorithm isn't needed. That leads to a clause that doesn't use relevance scoring but works in a filter context: the `filter` clause.

11.3.7 *The filter clause*

The `filter` clause fetches all documents that match the criteria, similar to the `must` clause. The only difference is that the `filter` clause runs in a filter context, so the results are not scored. Remember, running a query in a filter context speeds up query performance because it caches the query results returned by Elasticsearch. The following listing shows a `filter` query in action.

Listing 11.12   The `filter` clause

```
GET products/_search
{
  "query": {
    "bool": {                     Executes the query in a
      "filter": [{       ⟵─────   filter context implicitly
          "term": {
            "product.keyword": "TV"
          },
          {
            "range": {
              "price": {
                "gte": 500,
                "lte": 1000
              }
            }
          }
        }
      ]
    }
  }
}
```

The following snippet shows the results of this query. Note that the result scores are zero:

```
"hits" : [{
    ...
    "_score" : 0.0,
    "_source" : {
      "product" : "TV",
      "colour" : "silver",
      "brand" : "Samsung"
    }
  },
  {
    ...
    "_score" : 0.0,
    "_source" : {
      "product" : "TV",
      "colour" : "black",
      "brand" : "Samsung"
    }
  }
  ...
]
```

The `filter` clause provides no scoring. Because scoring is not required for the output, Elasticsearch can cache the query/results, which benefits the application's performance.

We usually combine a `filter` clause with a `must` clause. The results of the `must` clause are fed through the `filter` clause, which filters non-fitting data. The next example shows this approach.

Listing 11.13   A `filter` clause with a `must` clause

```
GET products/_search
{
  "_source": ["brand","product","colour","price"],
  "query": {
    "bool": {
      "must": [{
          "match": {
            "brand": "LG"
          }
        }
      ],
      "filter": [{
          "range": {
            "price": {
              "gte": 500,
              "lte": 1000
            }
          }
        }
      ]
    }
  }
}
```

Here, we fetch all LG products (we have one TV and three fridges manufactured by LG in our stash). Then we filter them by price, leaving only two fridges that fall in our price range (both are $900):

```
"hits" : [{
        ..
        "_score" : 2.6820748,
        "_source" : {
          "product" : "Fridge",
          "colour" : "Matte Black",
          "price" : 900,
          "brand" : "LG"
        }
      },{
        ..
        "_score" : 2.6820748,
        "_source" : {
          "product" : "Fridge",
          "colour" : "Matte Black",
          "price" : 900,
          "brand" : "LG"
        }
      }]
```

Note that both of the returned documents now carry a score, meaning the query was executed in the query context. As we discussed, a `filter` query is similar to a `must` query except that it's not run in a query context (the `filter` query is run in a filter context). Therefore, adding filters does not affect the scoring of the documents.

So far, we've worked with `bool` queries employing individual clauses with leaf queries. We can combine all these clauses to construct a complex advanced query. Let's look at that in the next section.

11.3.8 *Combining all the clauses*

Let's combine the `must`, `must_not`, `should`, and `filter` clauses. The requirement is to find products manufactured by LG that are not silver, that either are fridge freezers or have an energy rating of A++, and that are in a specific price range.

The query in listing 11.14 fetches LG products with a `match` query in a `must` clause, ignores the color silver in a `must_not` clause, and queries for a fridge freezer *or* a certain energy rating using a `should` clause. Finally, we use a `filter` clause to check the price of the products to see if they fit in a specific price range.

Listing 11.14 All the clauses combined

```
GET products/_search
{
  "query": {
    "bool": {
      "must": [{
          "match": {
            "brand": "LG"
          }
        }],
      "must_not": [{
          "term": {
            "colour": "silver"
          }
        }],
      "should": [{
          "match": {
            "energy_rating": "A++"
          }
        },
        {
          "term": {
            "type": "Fridge Freezer"
          }
        }],
      "filter": [{
          "range": {
            "price": {
              "gte": 500,
              "lte": 1000
            }
          }
        }
      ]
    }
  }
}
```

This listing combines the four clauses using a `must` query, matching LG TVs but not silver ones (`must_not` clause). If a product has an A++ energy rating or is a fridge freezer (`should` clause), that's even better. Finally, we filter the products by price (`filter` clause).

We can enhance the query with further clauses and leaf queries as more complex requirements are added to the list. There is no restriction on how many queries a clause can contain; it is entirely up to our discretion. But how do we know which leaf queries in the various clauses matched to get results? Were any of the queries omitted based on our requirements? Knowing the exact leaf query that obtained the final outcome (aka results) is a great way to identify queries that were executed and produced results. We can do this by naming every query.

11.3.9 Named queries

We may build dozens of queries for a complex query; however, we have no clue how many are used in a match to get the final results. We can name our queries so that Elasticsearch outputs the results along with the names of the queries used during the query match. Let's look at an example. The next listing shows a complex query with all the clauses and a few leaf queries.

Listing 11.15 Complex queries given individual names

```
GET products/_search
{
  "_source": ["product", "brand"],
  "query": {
    "bool": {
      "must": [
        {
          "match": {
            "brand": {
              "query": "LG",
              "_name": "must_match_brand_query"    ⟵──┘ Query name to match the
            }                                              brand in a must clause
          }
        }
      ],
      "must_not": [
        {
          "match": {
            "colour.keyword": {
              "query":"black",
              "_name":"must_not_colour_query"     ⟵──┘ Query name to not
            }                                              match a particular color
          }
        }
      ],
      "should": [
        {
          "term": {
```

```
          "type.keyword": {
            "value": "Frost Free Fridge Freezer",
            "_name":"should_term_type_query"        ◁─┐   Query name to match the
          }                                            │   type in a should clause
        }
      },
      {
        "match": {
          "energy_rating": {
            "query": "A++",
            "_name":"should_match_energy_rating_query"  ◁─┐  Query name to match
          }                                                 │  the energy rating in
        }                                                   │  a should clause
      }
    ],
    "filter": [
      {
        "range": {
          "price": {
            "gte": 500,
            "lte": 1000,
            "_name":"filter_range_price_query"    ◁─┐   Query name to match
          }                                          │   the price range in
        }                                            │   a filter clause
      }
    ]
  }
 }
}
```

The individual leaf queries are tagged with the `_name` property with a value of our choice. Once the query is executed, the response includes a `matched_queries` object attached to each result. Enclosed in this `matched_queries` is the set of queries matched to fetch the document:

```
"hits" : [
    {
      ...
      "_source" : {
        "product" : "Fridge",
        "brand" : "LG"
      },
      "matched_queries" : [
        "filter_range_price_query",
        "should_match_energy_rating_query",
        "must_match_brand_query",
        "should_term_type_query"
      ]
    },
    {
      ...
      "_source" : {
        "product" : "Fridge",
        "brand" : "LG"
```

```
    },
    "matched_queries" : [
      "filter_range_price_query",
      "should_match_energy_rating_query",
      "must_match_brand_query",
      "should_term_type_query"
    ]
  }
]
```

The results are matched on the four queries mentioned in the `matched_queries` block. The real benefit of naming queries is removing redundant queries not associated with the outcome. This way, we can reduce the query size and concentrate on tweaking the queries that are part of fetching the results.

This concludes our look at the `bool` query, which is one of the most important and sophisticated compound queries. In the next few sections, we look at other compound queries, starting with constant scores.

11.4　Constant scores

Previously, we looked at a `filter` query within a `bool` clause. For completeness, let's rerun a sample `filter` query to fetch products with a user rating between 4 and 5.

> **Listing 11.16　The `filter` clause declared in a `bool` query**

```
GET products/_search
{
  "query": {
    "bool": {
      "filter": [
        {
          "range": {
            "user_ratings": {
              "gte": 4,
              "lte": 5
            }
          }
        }
      ]
    }
  }
}
```

The query results in all products matching the criteria for user ratings. The only point of interest is that the query is executed in a filter context; so, no score (zero) is associated with the results. However, we may need to set a nonzero score, especially when we want to boost a particular search criterion. This is where a new query type, `constant_score`, enters the picture.

As the name suggests, `constant_score` wraps a `filter` query and produces the results with a predefined (boosted) score. The query in the following listing shows this in action.

```
GET products/_search
{
  "query": {
    "constant_score": {        ◁——  Declares the
      "filter": {                    constant_score query
        "range": {          ◁——  Wraps a
          "user_ratings": {        filter query
            "gte": 4,
            "lte": 5
          }
        }
      },
      "boost": 5.0    ◁——  Boosts the results using
    }                       a predefined score
  }
}
```

The `constant_score` query in this listing wraps a `filter` query. It also has another attribute, `boost`, which enhances the score with the given value. Therefore, all the resulting documents are stamped with a score of 5 rather than 0.

If you are wondering about the practical use of `constant_score`, look no further. The following listing shows a `bool` query where we wrap a `constant_score` function into a `must` query alongside a `match` query.

```
GET products/_search
{
  "query": {
    "bool": {              The must clause with two queries:
      "must": [{    ◁——  match and constant_score
        "match": {      ◁——  The match query that
          "product": "TV"       searches for TVs
        }
      },
      {
        "constant_score": {    ◁——  The constant_score that
          "filter": {                boosts the score by 3.5 if
            "term": {                the color of the TV is black
              "colour": "black"
            }
          },
          "boost": 3.5
        }
      }
    ]
  }
}
```

The must clause in this bool query holds two queries: a match and a constant_score. The constant_score query filters all TVs based on color, but with a tweak: it boosts the score by 3.5 for all black TVs. Here, we ask the Elasticsearch engine to take our input when scoring the result by setting the boost value to our choice in a filtered query wrapped under constant_score.

In this section, we saw query results assigned a static score using the constant_score function. But what if we want some results scored higher and others at the bottom of the results page? That's what a boosting query does, as we discuss next.

11.5   *The boosting query*

Sometimes we want biased answers. For example, we may want the result list to have LG TVs at the top and Sony at the bottom. This sort of biased manipulation of scoring so the list has favored items at the top is done with a boosting query. A boosting query works with two sets of queries: a positive part, where any number of queries produce a positive match; and a negative part, which matches queries to negate the score with a negative boost.

Let's consider an example. We want to search for LG TVs, but if the price is greater than $2,500, we drop them to the bottom of the list using a score calculated by the value specified by the negative boost of the negative query. Let's see how this is done.

Listing 11.19   A boosting query in action

```
GET products/_search
{
  "size": 50,
  "_source": ["product", "price","colour"],
  "query": {
    "boosting": {                      The boosting query's
      "positive": {        ←──┘        positive part
        "term": {
          "product":"tv"
        }
      },
      "negative": {        ←──┘        The boosting query's
        "range": {                     negative part
          "price": {
            "gte": 2500
          }
        }
      },
      "negative_boost": 0.5    ←──┐    The negative
    }                              │    boost
  }
}
```

A boosting query in action

As shown, the boosting query has two parts: positive and negative. In the positive part, we simply create a query (a term query, in this case) to fetch TVs. On the other hand, we don't want TVs that are too expensive, so we suppress expensive TVs from the results (move them to the bottom of the list) by negating the scores of those matched in the `negative` part of the query. The value set by the `negative_boost` attribute is used to recalculate the score of those matched in the `negative` part. This pushes the results from the `negative` part down the list.

The `boosting` query in listing 11.19 is simple: it uses leaf queries in the `positive` and `negative` parts. However, we can also script a compound query like a `boosting` query with other compound queries. We can declare the `boosting` query with `bool`, `constant_score`, or other compound queries, including top-level leaf queries. The query in the next listing shows this: a `boosting` query with embedded `bool` queries.

Listing 11.20   A `bool` query with a constant score

```
GET products/_search
{
  "size": 40,
  "_source": ["product", "price","colour","brand"],
  "query": {
    "boosting": {                      ◁──┐ Declares a
      "positive": {                        │ boosting query
        "bool": {              ◁──┐ Defines the positive part of the boosting
          "must": [                │ query in a bool query, which also has a
            {                      │ must clause within a match query
              "match": {
                "product": "TV"
              }
            }
          ]
        }
      },
      "negative": {        ◁──┐ Defines the negative part
        "bool": {              │ of the query with an
          "must": [            │ embedded  bool query
            {
              "match": {
                "brand": "Sony"
              }
            }
          ]
        }
      },
      "negative_boost": 0.5  ◁──┐ Sets negative_boost to 0.5 on
    }                            │ successful matches for queries
  }                              │ from the negative part
}
```

This `boosting` query consists of both `positive` and `negative` parts, as expected, and the negative part has a `negative_boost` value set to `0.5`. The query works as follows: it searches for TVs (as shown in the `positive` block), and if the TV brand is Sony, its score is reduced by 0.5. Although Sony TVs may be excellent, they are sent to the bottom of the result set because we manipulated their score using the `negative_boost` setting.

A `boosting` query therefore helps us downplay a certain type of document by using a negative score. We can prepare the results by manipulating the score based on the negative query and negative boost. Let's now jump to another compound query: disjunction max (`dis_max`).

11.6   *The disjunction max (dis_max) query*

In chapter 10, we worked with a query called `multi_match`, which searched for words across multiple fields. To search for a smart TV across two fields, `type` and `overview`, we can use `multi_match`. For completeness, here's the resulting `multi_match` query.

Listing 11.21   Searching multiple fields using a `multi_match` query

```
GET products/_search
{
  "query": {
    "multi_match": {
      "query": "smart tv",
      "fields": ["type","overview"]
    }
  }
}
```

We bring up the `multi_match` query under the heading of a disjunction max (`dis_max`) query because `multi_match` uses the `dis_max` query behind the scenes. The `dis_max` query wraps several queries and expects at least one of them to match. If more than one query matches, the `dis_max` query returns the document(s) with the highest relevance score. Let's revisit the query from listing 11.21 but this time use `dis_max` to search for the words "smart tv" in the `type` and `overview` fields.

Listing 11.22   The `dis_max` query in action

```
GET products/_search
{
  "_source": ["type","overview"],
  "query": {
    "dis_max": {                          ◁─────   Declares the dis_max query
      "queries": [{               ◁──┐            that wraps a set of queries
        "match": {                   │  Declares a set of queries
          "type": "smart tv"         │  with match conditions
        }
      },
      {
        "match": {
          "overview": "smart tv"
        }
      }]
    }
  }
}
```

The dis_max query is a compound query that expects a number of leaf queries defined in the queries object. Here, we declare two match queries, searching for multiple words in two different fields: type and overview.

When searching for multiple words across multiple fields, Elasticsearch uses the *best-fields strategy*, which favors a document with all the words in the given fields. For example, suppose we are searching for "smart TV" across two fields, overview and type. We can expect that a document with this phrase in both fields is more relevant than a document with "smart" in the overview field and "TV" in the type field.

When executing a dis_max query on multiple fields, we can also consider scores from other matching queries. In this case, we use a tiebreaker to add the scores from other field matches, not just the best fields. Let's add the tie_breaker attribute to the following query.

Listing 11.23   A dis_max query with a tiebreaker

```
GET products/_search
{
  "_source": ["type","overview"],
  "query": {
    "dis_max": {
      "queries": [{
        "match": {
          "type": "smart tv"
        }
      },
      {
        "match": {
          "overview": "smart TV"
        }
      },
      {
        "match": {
          "product": "smart TV"
        }
      }],"tie_breaker": 0.5
    }
  }
}
```

The tie_breaker value is a positive floating-point number between 0.0 and 1.0 (the default is 0.0). In this case, we multiply the non-best fields' scores by the tiebreaker and add the result to the score of each document that matches multiple fields.

The final compound query we look at in this chapter is the function score query. It gives us much more flexibility when assigning scores based on our needs using predefined functions.

11.7   The function_score query

Sometimes we want to assign a score to a returned document from a search query based on in-house requirements, such as giving weight to a particular field or displaying a sponsor's advertisement based on a random relevance score. Function score (`function_score`) queries help create a score based on user-defined functions, including random, script-based, or decay functions (Gauss, linear, etc.).

Before we start working with the `function_score` query, let's execute the query in the following listing. It is a straightforward `term` query that returns documents.

Listing 11.24   Term search with a standard `term` query

```
GET products/_search
{
  "query": {
    "term": {
      "product": {
        "value": "TV"
      }
    }
  }
}
```

The query doesn't do much other than search for a TV using a standard `term` query. The only point to note is the score of the top document returned by this query: 1.6376086.

Although this query is purposely simple, some queries require heavy processing to compute a relevance score. Maybe we aren't interested in fetching the score computed by Elasticsearch's Best Match 25 (BM25) relevance algorithm (or any custom algorithm) because we want to create a score based on our own requirements. In such a case, we can wrap a query in a `function_score` construct to generate a score based on user-defined functions.

Listing 11.25   A `term` search wrapped in a `function_score`

```
GET products/_search
{
  "query": {
    "function_score": {          ◁──┐  A function_score wraps a query to
      "query": {                     │  generate a user-defined score.
        "term": {
          "product": "tv"
        }
      }
    }
  }
}
```

The `function_score` query expects a few attributes: a query, functions, how the score should be applied to the documents, and so on. Rather than learning about them in theory, we see these in the hands-on examples in this section.

User-defined functions let us modify and replace the score with our custom score. We can do so by plugging in a function that tweaks the score based on our requirements. For example, if we want a randomly generated score, there's a simple random_score function query for that purpose. Or we may want to compute the score based on field values and parameters, in which case we can use a script_score function query. We also look at a couple other functions in this section, but let's start with random_score.

11.7.1   *The random_score function*

As the name suggests, the random_score function creates a randomly generated score for the resulting documents. We can run the query from listing 11.25, wrapped in a function_score query, but this time specifically assign a random_score function to the query.

Listing 11.26   Term search wrapped in a random_score **function**

```
GET products/_search
{
  "query": {
    "function_score": {            A function_score with a
      "query": {                   term query and a function
        "term": {
          "product": "TV"
        }
      },
      "random_score": {}           A random_score function
    }                              that generates and assigns a
  }                                random score for each call
}
```

This function_score query is made of a term query and a random_score function. Every time we execute this query, we get a different score for the same returned document. The random scores are, well, random and can't be reproduced. When you re-execute the query, expect the score to change.

What if we have a requirement to reproduce the random score so that no matter how many times we execute the same query, the randomly generated score is always the same? For this purpose, we can tweak the random_score function by priming it with seed and field values. The following listing shows the query with a random_score function initialized with a seed.

Listing 11.27   Tweaking random scores by setting a seed

```
GET products/_search
{
  "query": {
    "function_score": {
      "query": {
        "term": {
          "product": "TV"
        }
```

```
        },
        "random_score": {              Initializes the customized
          "seed": 10,          ◁──┘    random_score with a seed
          "field":"user_ratings"          ◁──┐ Computes the
        }                                      │ random score
      }
    }
  }
```

As you can see, `random_score` is initialized with a `seed` value and a `user_ratings` `field` value. If we execute this query more than once, we are guaranteed to get the same (albeit random) score. The algorithm and mechanics to determine the random score are beyond the scope of this book; consult the Elasticsearch documentation if you want to understand more about random scoring mechanics.

While the `random_score` function is one way to generate a random score, generating a static score using a scripting function is also interesting. In the next section, let's look at how we can use the `script_score` function.

11.7.2   The script_score function

Suppose we want to triple-boost the document score (multiply the field's value by a factor of 3) based on a field's value (for example, the `user_rating` of a product). In this instance, we can use a `script_score` function to compute the score based on the values of other fields (such as `user_ratings`) in the document.

Listing 11.28   Multiplying the field's value by an external parameter

```
GET products/_search
{
  "query": {
    "function_score": {
      "query": {
        "term": {
          "product": "tv"
        }                         The script_score function holds
      },                          the key to generating a score
      "script_score": {    ◁──┘   based on its defined script.
        "script": { #B
          "source":"_score * doc['user_ratings'].value * params['factor']", ◁──┐
          "params": {    ◁──┐ Passes the external
            "factor":3          │ parameters to the script        The source is where
          }                                                        we define our logic.
        }
      }
    }
  }
}
```

The script
object ┌──▷

The `script_score` function produces a score, and in this example it calculates that score based on a simple script calculation: find `user_ratings` and multiply the value by the original score and `factor` (passed via external `params`). We can construct a complicated query based on a fully fledged script if needed.

Scripts can create a complex scenario with parameters, field values, and mathematical functions (for example, the square root of the average user ratings multiplied by a given `boosting` factor). However, not every requirement needs such a complicated script. If our requirement is just to use a field's value, a simple way to get the result is to use a function called `field_value_factor`.

11.7.3   The field_value_factor function

The `field_value_factor` function helps achieve scoring by using fields without the complexity of scripting. The following listing shows the mechanism.

Listing 11.29   Deriving the score from a field without scripting

```
GET products/_search
{
  "query": {
    "function_score": {
      "query": {
        "term": {
          "product": "tv"
        }
      },
      "field_value_factor": {
        "field": "user_ratings"
      }
    }
  }
}
```

The field_value_factor object
that declares the field
(user_ratings, in this case)

The script shows that the `field_value_factor` function works on a field (`user_ratings` in this listing) to produce a new relevancy score.

We can add attributes to the `field_value_score` function. For example, we can multiply the score by using a `factor` attribute and applying a mathematical function such as a square root or a logarithmic calculation. The next listing shows this in action.

Listing 11.30   Additional attributes on `field_value_factor`

```
GET products/_search
{
  "query": {
    "function_score": {
      "query": {
        "term": {
          "product": "tv"
        }
      },
      "field_value_factor": {
```

```
          "field": "user_ratings",
          "factor": 2,
          "modifier": "square"
        }
      }
    }
  }
}
```

This script fetches the value of user_ratings from the document. It then multiplies the value by a factor of 2 and squares it.

11.7.4   *Combining function scores*

We looked at individual functions in the last few sections, but we can also combine functions to produce an even better score. For example, the following listing shows a function_score query that produces a score employing two functions: weight and field_value_factor.

> **Listing 11.31   Two functions producing a unified score**

```
GET products/_search
{
  "query": {
    "function_score": {
      "query": {
        "term": {
          "product": "TV"
        }
      },
      "functions": [          ◁─────┐  The functions object,
        {                            │  which expects an
          "filter": {                │  array of leaf functions
            "term": {
              "brand": "LG"
            }
          },
          "weight": 3       ◁────┐  The weight
        },                       │  function
        {
          "filter": {
            "range": {
              "user_ratings": {
                "gte": 4.5,
                "lte": 5
              }
            }
          },
          "field_value_factor": {    ◁────┐  The field_value_factor is based
            "field": "user_ratings",      │  on the user_ratings field.
            "factor": 5,
            "modifier": "square"
          }
        }
```

```
    ],
    "score_mode": "avg",
    "boost_mode": "sum"
  }
 }
}
```

The `functions` object in this query expects multiple functions (such as `weight` and `field_value_factor`), which combine to produce a unified score. The `weight` field (the weighting function) expects a positive integer, which is used in further calculations. The original score of fetching a TV using a `term` query is complemented by the following:

- If the brand is LG, increase the score by a weight of 3.
- If user ratings are in the range 4.5 to 5, use the `user_rating` field's value and square it by a factor of 5.

As more functions match, the score's final value increases. Thus the document may appear at the top of the list.

Function scoring modes

Did you notice the `score_mode` and `boost_mode` fields at the end of the script? These two attributes of the `function_score` query allow us to achieve a combined score from the original query and the score emitted by a single or many functions.

By default, the scores produced by these functions are all multiplied to get to a single, final score. However, we can change that behavior by setting the `score_mode` attribute in the `function_score` query. The `score_mode` attribute defines how individual scores are computed. For example, if the `score_mode` of a query is set to `sum`, the scores emitted by the individual functions are all summed up. The `score_mode` attribute can be any mode, such as `multiply` (default), `sum`, `avg`, `max`, `min`, or `first`.

The score from these functions will then be added to (or multiplied by, or averaged with, etc.) the original score of the query (in the example, the `term` query that finds TVs) from the document based on the `boost_mode` parameter. The `boost_mode` parameter can be `multiply` (default), `min`, `max`, `replace`, `avg`, or `sum`. To learn more about the modes and the mechanics involved in function scoring, consult Elasticsearch's official documentation.

That's a wrap! This chapter introduced compound queries that are advanced, useful, and practical. The `bool` query is the Swiss Army knife of all queries, and it helps build complex search queries. In the next chapter, we look at other advanced searches, such as geospatial searches and join queries.

Summary

- Compound queries combine leaf queries to create advanced queries that satisfy multiple search criteria.

- The `bool` query is the most popular compound query, consisting of four clauses: `must`, `must_not`, `should`, and `filter`.

- The queries in `must_not` and `filter` clauses do not contribute to the overall relevance score. On the other hand, queries in `must` and `should` clauses always improve the scoring.

- The `constant_score` query wraps a `filter` query and produces a constant score set by the user.

- The `boosting` query increases the score of a `positive` clause while suppressing the score on the queries that aren't a match (the `negative` clause).

- The `dis_max` query, used by the `multi_match` query, wraps queries and executes them individually.

- The `function_score` query sets a custom score based on a user-defined function, such as a field's value or weight or a random value.

Advanced search

This chapter covers

- Geo data types
- Searching locations and addresses with geoqueries
- Using `geo_shape` to search for 2D shapes
- Using `span` queries to work with low-level positional tokens
- Specialized queries such as percolators

Earlier chapters have covered searching data using term-level and full-text queries. We've also looked at advanced queries like `bool`, `boosting`, and others. To continue building on what we've discussed and advance the query landscape, this chapter introduces several kinds of specialized queries.

We begin by looking at searches aimed at geolocations. Common use cases involving *geoqueries* include searching nearby restaurants for a delivery order, finding directions to a friend's house, locating popular schools within a 10 km range, and so on. Elasticsearch has first-class support for satisfying such location-related searches. It also provides several geospatial queries: `geo_bounding_box`, `geo_distance`, and `geo_shape`.

Next, we examine how to search two-dimensional (2D) shapes using *shape queries*. Design engineers, game developers, and others can search in an index of 2D shapes. Then we look at low-level positional queries called `span` *queries*. Although full-text and term-level leaf queries help us search for data, they can't find words in a particular order, their position, the exact (or approximate) distance between words, and so on. This is where `span` queries come into play.

Finally, we wrap up the chapter by looking at specialized queries such as `distance_feature`, `percolator`, `more_like_this`, and `pinned`. The `distance_feature` query boosts results that are nearer to a particular location: for example, searching for schools within a 10 km radius, but giving schools with nearby parks higher priority. To append organically found search results to a list of sponsored results, we use `pinned` queries. The `more_like_this` queries find similar-looking documents. The final specialized query we discuss is the `percolator` query, which helps notify users when data is available for queries that didn't yield results in the past.

Let's begin by discussing the need for geospatial queries and the data types that support them. We then look at the queries provided by Elasticsearch out of the box for such search criteria.

NOTE The code for this chapter is available on GitHub (http://mng.bz/ 2D6w) and on the book's website (https://www.manning.com/books/elastic search-in-action-second-edition).

NOTE Unlike other chapters, this chapter examines multiple types of queries including geospatial, shape, span, and specialized queries. Due to the nature of these queries, I prepared multiple data sets to satisfy their requirements. So, the examples shift between data sets (indexes) in this chapter.

12.1 *Introducing location search*

In this day and age of the internet, it is a common requirement to enable location-based search in apps and applications. Location-based search fetches venues or places based on proximity, such as nearby restaurants, houses for sale within a 1 km radius, and so on. We also use location-based searches to find directions to a place of interest.

The good news is that geospatial support is a first-class citizen in Elasticsearch. Dedicated data types allow us to define a schema for indexing geospatial data, thus enabling focused search. The out-of-the-box data types that support geospatial data are `geo_point` and `geo_shape`.

Elasticsearch also provides geospatial search queries that suffice for most use cases, such as `bounding_box`, `geo_distance`, and `geo_shape`. Each of these queries satisfies a set of requirements that we discuss briefly in this section and at greater length later in the chapter.

12.1.1 *The bounding_box query*

We sometimes want to find a list of locations such as restaurants, schools, or universities in a surrounding area—let's say in a square or rectangle. We can construct a rectangle, often called a *georectangle*, by taking the coordinates of the top-left and bottom-right corners. These coordinates consist of a pair of longitude and latitude measurements representing the corners.

Elasticsearch provides a `bounding_box` query that lets us search for required addresses in a georectangle. This query fetches the points of interest (as query criteria) inside the georectangle constructed by our set of coordinates. For example, figure 12.1 shows the addresses in central London enclosed in one such georectangle. Addresses intersecting this rectangle are returned as positive results. We run through some `bounding_box` queries in detail shortly.

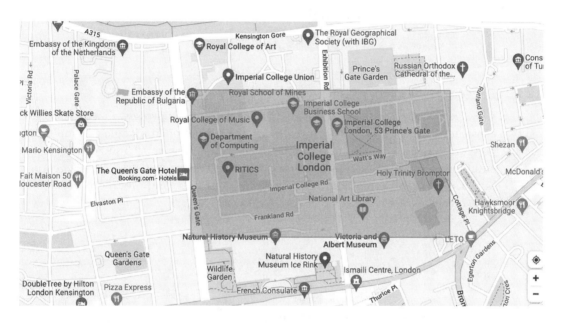

Figure 12.1   A georectangle constructed with a set of longitude and latitude coordinates

12.1.2   The geo_distance query

You may have seen Hollywood movies where an FBI agent tries to pin down a fugitive in an area drawn as a circle around a central focal point. That's what the `geo_distance` query does!

Elasticsearch provides the `geo_distance` query to fetch addresses in an area enclosed by a circle. The center is defined by the longitude, the latitude, and a radius as the distance. In figure 12.2, we have a central location (shown as the dropped pin on the map) and a circular area covering the addresses we are looking for. The focus (or central location) is a point on the map dictated by latitude and longitude coordinates.

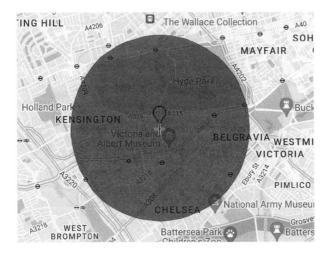

Figure 12.2   Addresses enclosed in a circular area constructed by a `geo_distance` query

12.1.3 *The geo_shape query*

A `geo_shape` query fetches a list of geographical points (addresses) in a geometrically constructed geo-envelope. The envelope can be a three-sided triangle or a multisided polygon (but the envelope must not be open-ended). Figure 12.3 shows a hexagonal envelope constructed on a map with six pairs of coordinates (each pair is a geopoint with latitude and longitude). The `geo_shape` search finds locations inside this polygon.

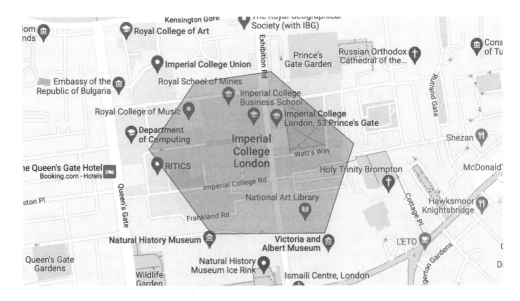

Figure 12.3   Finding addresses in a polygonal shape with a `geo_shape` query

Before we jump into experimenting with geospatial queries, we need to understand the mapping schema of geospatial data: the data types that support geodata and the mechanics for indexing that data. In the next section, we examine the `geo_point` type first and then `geo_shape`.

12.2 Geospatial data types

Similar to how the `text` data type represents textual data, Elasticsearch provides two dedicated data types to work with spatial data: `geo_point` and `geo_shape`. The `geo_point` data type expresses a longitude and latitude and works on location-based queries. The `geo_shape` type, on the other hand, lets us index geoshapes such as points, multi-lines, polygons, and a few others. Let's look at these spatial data types.

12.2.1 The geo_point data type

A location on a map is expressed universally by longitude and latitude. Elasticsearch supports representing such location data using a dedicated `geo_point` data type. We looked at the `geo_point` data type briefly in chapter 4; let's recap how we can define a field as a `geo_point` in our mapping schema. Once the mapping is ready, we can index a document. The following listing creates a data schema for a `bus_stops` index with a couple of fields.

Listing 12.1 Creating a mapping with `geo_point`

```
PUT bus_stops
{
  "mappings": {
    "properties": {
      "name":{
        "type": "text"
      },
      "location":{
        "type": "geo_point"          ⟵⎤ Defines the location attribute
      }                                  ⎦ as a geo_point data type
    }
  }
}
```

The `bus_stops` index is defined with two properties: `name` and `location`. The `location` property is represented by a `geo_point` data type, which means it should be set with latitude and longitude values when indexing the document. The following query indexes the London Bridge Station bus stop.

Listing 12.2 Indexing a bus stop with a location defined as a string

```
POST bus_stops/_doc
{
  "name":"London Bridge Station",       ⎤ Inputs the location as a string
  "location":"51.07, 0.08"          ⟵⎦ with latitude and longitude values
}
```

As the query shows, the `location` field has stringified latitude and longitude values separated by a comma: "51.07, 0.08". Providing the coordinates in this string format is not the only way to set the `location` field; we can use several other formats to input the `location` geographic coordinates, such as an array, a well-known-text (WKT) point, or a geohash.

Listing 12.3   Indexing in various formats for the `geo_point` data type

```
POST bus_stops/_doc
{
  "text": "London Victoria Station",
  "location" : "POINT (51.49 0.14)"      ◁─┐  Inputs the geo_point as
}                                             a WKT point (lat, lon)

POST bus_stops/_doc
{
  "text": "Leicester Square Station",
  "location" : {        ◁─┐  Inputs the geo_point
    "lon":-0.12,              as a location object
    "lat":51.50
  }
}

POST bus_stops/_doc
{
  "text": "Westminster Station",
  "location" : [51.54, 0.23]      ◁─┐  Inputs the geo_point
}                                      as an array (lon, lat)

POST bus_stops/_doc
{
  "text": "Hyde Park Station",         ┐  Inputs the geo_point
  "location" : "gcpvh2bg7sff"      ◁─┘  as a geohash
}
```

These queries index various bus stop locations using multiple formats. We can use a string with the latitude and longitude, as in listing 12.2, or an object, an array, a geohash, or a WKT-formatted POINT shape, as in listing 12.3.

Now it's time to learn about the `geo_shape` data type. As the name indicates, the `geo_shape` type helps index and search data using a particular shape: for example, a polygon. Let's see how we can index data for geoshapes.

12.2.2 *The geo_shape data type*

Like the `geo_point` type, which represents a point on the map, Elasticsearch provides a `geo_shape` data type to represent shapes such as points, multipoints, lines, and polygons. The shapes are represented by an open standard called GeoJSON (http://geojson.org) and are written in JSON format. The geometric shapes are mapped to the `geo_shape` data type.

Let's create the mapping for an index of `cafes` with a couple of fields. One of them is the `address` field, which points to the location of a cafe, represented as a `geo_shape` type.

Listing 12.4 Creating a mapping with the `geo_shape` field type

```
PUT cafes
{
  "mappings": {
    "properties": {
      "name":{
        "type": "text"
      },
      "address": {
        "type": "geo_shape"          Sets the address
      }                              type as geo_shape
    }
  }
}
```

The code creates an index called `cafes` to house local restaurants. The notable field is `address`, defined as a `geo_shape` type. This type now expects inputs of shapes in GeoJSON or WKT. For example, to represent a point on a map, we can input the field using `Point` in GeoJSON or `POINT` in WKT.

Listing 12.5 Inputting a `geo_shape` using WKT and GeoJSON formats

```
PUT cafes/_doc/1          Inputs the address
{                         in GeoJSON format
  "name":"Costa Coffee",
  "address" : {           Sets the address
    "type" : "Point",     type as geo_shape
    "coordinates" : [0.17, 51.57]    Coordinates (longitude and
  }                                  latitude) representing the Point
}

                          Inputs the address
PUT /cafes/_doc/2         in WKT format
{                                   Sets the address type as
  "address" : "POINT (0.17 51.57)"  POINT in WKT format
}
```

This code declares two ways to input a `geo_shape` field: GeoJSON and WKT. GeoJSON expects a `type` attribute of an appropriate shape (`"type":"Point"`) and the corresponding coordinates (`"coordinates":[0.17, 51.57]`), as in the first example. The second example in listing 12.5 shows the mechanics of creating a point using a WKT format (`"address": "POINT (0.17 51.57)"`).

NOTE There is a subtle difference when representing coordinates using a string format versus other formats. The string format expects the values in the order latitude followed by longitude, separated by a comma: for example,

"(51.57, 0.17)". However, the coordinates are interchanged for the Geo-JSON and WKT formats as longitude followed by latitude: for example, "POINT (0.17 51.57)".

We can build various shapes using these formats. Table 12.1 provides a brief description of a few of them. See the Elasticsearch documentation on how to index and search documents to understand the concepts and examples in detail.

Table 12.1   Shapes supported by the `geo_shape` data type

Shape	Description	GeoJSON representation	WKT representation
Point	A point represented by latitude and longitude	`Point`	`POINT`
Multipoint	An array of points	`MultiPoint`	`MULTIPOINT`
Polygon	A multi-edge shape	`Polygon`	`POLYGON`
Multipolygon	A list of multiple polygons	`MultiPolygon`	`MULTIPOLYGON`
Line string	A line between two points	`LineString`	`LINESTRING`
Multiline string	A list of multiline strings	`MultiLineString`	`MULTILINESTRING`

Now that we know how to work with the indexing side of geodata using the `geo_point` and `geo_shape` fields, we're ready to search our documents. We discuss this in the next section.

12.3   *Geospatial queries*

We need to index London restaurant data for the examples in this section. The data is available in the datasets folder on GitHub (http://mng.bz/1q5R) and on the book's website.

To locate geospatial data, our next task is to search documents for a given geocriterion. For example, the place where you get your coffee is represented by a longitude and latitude, which, in turn, is called a *point* on the map.

As another example, I can search for the restaurants nearest my house, which returns each matching cafe represented as a point. Or a plot of land on a map can be represented by a shape representing a country or your local school's playground.

Elasticsearch provides a set of geospatial queries specifically suited to search for these use cases (such as finding nearby addresses or searching for all the interesting spots in a given area). We examine the following queries in the following sections:

- `geo_bounding_box` *query*—Finds documents enclosed in a rectangle constructed by geopoints; for example, all restaurants located inside a georectangle
- `geo_distance` *query*—Finds addresses within a certain distance from a point; for example, all ATMs within 1 km of London Bridge

- `geo_shape` *query*—Finds addresses represented as shapes within a shape constructed by a set of coordinates; for example, agricultural farms contained in a green belt, where the farms and the green belt are represented by individual shapes as well as the green belt

We discuss queries for both geopoints and geoshapes in detail in the following sections. Let's begin with queries executed on `geo_point` fields.

12.4   The geo_bounding_box query

When we search for a list of addresses, we can use an area of interest. This area can be represented by a circle of a certain radius, an area enclosed by a shape such as a rectangle, or a polygon from a central point (a landmark).

Elasticsearch provides a `geo_bounding_box` query that lets us search for locations inside these areas. For example, as figure 12.4 shows, we can construct a rectangle using latitude and longitude coordinates and search to see if our address exists in that area.

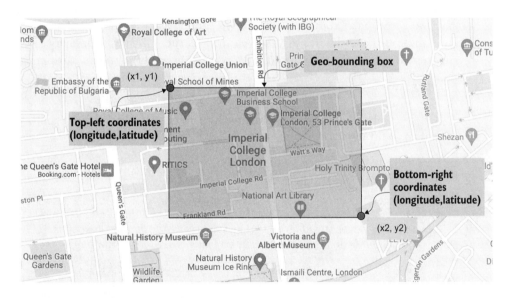

Figure 12.4   Georectangle from latitude and longitude coordinates

The `top_left` and `bottom_right` fields are the coordinates of latitude and longitude that make up our georectangle. Once we define a georectangle, we can check if the points of interest (the Imperial College London, for example) are present inside this rectangle.

Before we discuss the `geo_bounding_box` query in detail, let's write the query; then we can dissect it. The following query searches for all documents (locations) that fit in the rectangle constructed with `top_left` and `bottom_right` coordinates.

Listing 12.6   Matching restaurant locations in a georectangle

```
GET restaurants/_search
{
  "query": {
    "geo_bounding_box": {          Constructs a
      "location": {                georectangle        Sets the document's
        "top_left": {                                  geo_point field
          "lat": 52,               Defines the top_left
          "lon": 0.2               point, formed by a
        },                         latitude/longitude pair
        "bottom_right": {          Defines the bottom_right
          "lat": 49,               point, formed by a
          "lon": 0.1               latitude/longitude pair
        }
      }
    }
  }
}
```

The query searches for all documents that intersect (fit in) a georectangle made by
the two coordinates `top_left` and `bottom_right`, as in figure 12.4. The user can provide these two coordinates so that we can construct a rectangular shape. Restaurants
inside this rectangle are returned as search results, and the rest are dropped.

> **NOTE** We can also represent the vertices of the bounded rectangle as
> `top_right` and `bottom_left` (as opposed to `top_left` and `bottom_right`).
> Or we can break it down even further by using coordinates named `top`, `left`,
> `bottom`, and `right`.

Working with geoshape data

We executed the `geo_bounding_box` query in listing 12.6 on the schema with fields
declared as `geo_point` data types. But can we use the same query if our document
consists of a field defined as `geo_shape`, instead? We learned in section 12.3.3 that
geospatial data can also be represented using a `geo_shape` data type, remember?

We can use the query from listing 12.6 for geoshape data, except we must swap the
URL pointing to the appropriate index. For example, with the `cafes` index and geoshape data at hand, all we need to do is construct the same `geo_bounding_box`
query but change the URL to reflect the geoshapes index (`cafes`):

```
GET cafes/_search             The cafes index with
{                             geo_shape data type fields
  "query": {
    "geo_bounding_box": {
      "address": {            The address field is defined
        "top_left": {         as a geo_shape data type.
          "lat": 52,
          "lon": 0.04
        },
        "bottom_right": {
```

```
        "lat": 49,
        "lon": 0.2
      }
    }
  }
 }
}
```

This query searches for cafes in a given georectangle constructed with `top_left` and `bottom_right` parameters. Here, we use the `cafes` index in the URL (`GET`) when invoking the `geo_bounding_box` query. Other than swapping the geopoints index (`restaurants`) with an index consisting of geoshapes (`cafes`), there's no difference in the query!

We provide the longitude and latitude values as objects in listing 12.6. However, latitude and longitude can be set with multiple formats: as an array or WKT values. For example, the earlier `geo_bounding_box` queries provided `top_left` and `bottom_right` attributes as `"lat"` and `"lon"` objects:

```
"top_left": {
  "lat": 52.00,
  "lon": 0.20
}
```

Instead, we can set longitude and latitude as an array. But here's one gotcha to consider: the values in the array *must be reversed*. They should be `lon` and then `lat` (as opposed to `lat` and then `lon` in the previous examples).

NOTE For more information on this `lon`-`lat` inconsistency in geospatial software modules, see the article by Tom MacWright at https://macwright.com/lonlat.

The following listing shows the same `geo_bounding_box` query, but this time with longitude and latitude (highlighted in bold) provided as an array.

Listing 12.7 Geoquery with a geopoint specified as an array

```
GET restaurants/_search
{
  "query": {
    "bool": {
      "must": [
        {
          "match_all": {}
        }
      ],
      "filter": [
        {
          "geo_bounding_box": {
            "location": {
              "top_left": [0, 52.00],    ◁─── The top_left attribute
                                              with lon and lat values
```

```
            "bottom_right": [0.10, 49]
        }
      }
    }
  ]
}
}
}
}
```

⊲─┐ **The bottom_right attribute**
  │ **with lon and lat values**

We define the `top_left` and `bottom_right` attributes as an array of two geopoints: longitude and latitude.

We can also provide the longitude and latitude as a vector object. WKT is a standard text markup language for representing vector objects on a map. For example, to represent a point in WKT, we write `POINT(10, 20)`, which represents a point on a map with x- and y-coordinates 10 and 20, respectively. Elasticsearch provides WKT markup for bounding-box queries as `BBOX` with the respective values. The following query shows this.

Listing 12.8   Geoquery with a location represented as WKT

```
GET restaurants/_search
{
  "query": {
    "bool": {
      "must": [
        {
          "match_all": {}
        }
      ],
      "filter": [
        {
          "geo_bounding_box": {
            "location": {
              "wkt":"BBOX(0.08, 0.04, 52.00, 49.00)"
            }
          }
        }
      ]
    }
  }
}
```

⊲─┐ **Sets the coordinates**
  │ **in WKT format**

The `geo_bounding_box` filter's `location` field accepts the coordinates as `BBOX` with the corresponding longitude and latitude values. `BBOX` creates a georectangle from the pair to make the top-left and bottom-right points.

Other than your own preference, there's no difference between the WKT and array formats. If you are building an application that uses WKT standards for geodata, it makes sense to use WKT-based indexing and searching in Elasticsearch.

In this section, we learned how to find locations inside a georectangle using the `geo_bounding_box` query. Sometimes we may want to find restaurants near a central location: say, all restaurants 10 km from the city's center. This is where we can employ the `geo_distance` query. This query fetches all the available locations within a circle with a central focal point. We discuss the `geo_distance` query in detail next.

12.5   *The geo_distance query*

When we want to find a list of addresses surrounding a central point, the `geo_distance` query comes in handy. It works by circling an area with a radius of a given distance from a focal point. For example, as figure 12.5 shows, we may want to find nearby schools within a 10 km radius.

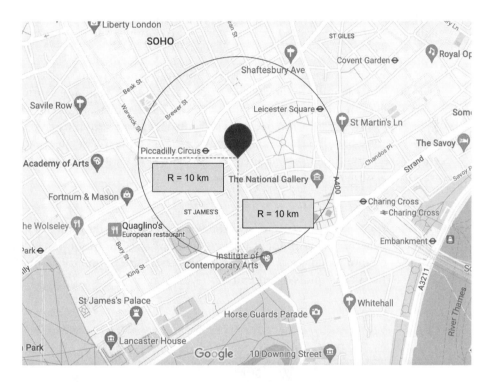

Figure 12.5   Returning schools with a `geo_distance` **query**

Let's look at the `geo_distance` query in action. The following listing defines a `geo_distance` query that fetches all the restaurants within 175 km of the given central coordinates.

Listing 12.9   Searching for restaurants within a given radius

```
GET restaurants/_search
{
  "query": {
    "geo_distance": {        ⟵  Declares the
      "distance": "175 km",        geo_distance query
```

Declares the
geo_distance query

Sets the vicinity of an
area to search (distance
from a central point)

```
        "location": {          ◁──┐   Sets the central location,
          "lat": 50.00,           │   defined as a point on the map
          "lon": 0.10
        }
      }
    }
  }
}
```

As the listing shows, the `geo_distance` query expects two attributes: `distance`, which provides the radius of the geocircle, and `location`, which defines the central point of the geocircle. The query returns all restaurants within 175 km of the defined point.

> **NOTE** The `distance` field accepts the distance measured in kilometers or miles as `km` or `mi`, respectively. Elasticsearch also honors a value given as `"350 mi"` as well as `"350mi"` (with the space removed).

It shouldn't surprise you that the field for defining the central point can be input using the latitude and longitude in the form of strings, arrays, WKT, and other formats. Queries can also be run on geoshapes, although I leave it to you to experiment with them.

The `geo_bounding_box` and `geo_distance` queries let us search for addresses represented as point-based locations in rectangular shapes and circles. However, we often need to search for an address defined as a shape inside another shape, preferably a polygon. This is where we use a `geo_shape` query.

12.6   *The geo_shape query*

Not all locations are point-based (coordinates with latitude and longitude values). Sometimes we want to determine whether shapes are present inside (or outside) the boundaries of another shape or whether they intersect the boundaries. For example, figure 12.6 shows some plots of land on our London map.

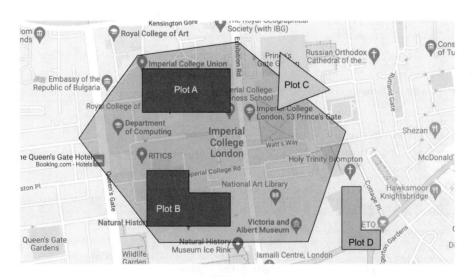

Figure 12.6   Plots of farmland in an area of London

In the figure, our geoshape is represented by the hexagon. Plots A and B are *within* the boundaries of this shape, plot C intersects the hexagon, and plot D is outside the boundaries of the geoshape. Elasticsearch provides the geo_shape query to search these plots of various shapes in an envelope built by coordinates.

The geo_shape query retrieves locations or addresses represented as shapes in another shape, such as the hexagon in figure 12.6. We construct this hexagonal shape by providing the coordinates as values to an envelope field.

Our cafes index contains a couple of documents with point-based shapes, so let's write a query to see how to retrieve this data. (If you are curious, index a few more documents with other shapes, too.) The query in the following listing searches for all cafes within the shape defined by the envelope field with longitude and latitude pairs.

Listing 12.10 Searching for cafes within a given shape

```
GET cafes/_search
{
  "query": {
    "geo_shape": {                    Defines a geo_shape query that
      "address": {                    expects a field and a shape
        "shape": {
          "type": "envelope",         Sets the shape attribute type
          "coordinates": [            that expects an envelope
            [0.1,55],                 built using coordinates
            [1,45]
          ]
        },
        "relation": "within"          Defines the relationship
      }                               between the envelope and
    }                                 the resulting geoshape
  }
}
```

The query fetches the documents (cafes) that fall within the envelope constructed by the given pair of longitude and latitude values. In this case, the search returns the Costa Coffee cafe found in the envelope.

One last thing we need to understand is the relation attribute. The relation attribute defines the relationship of the documents to be found for the given shape. The default value of relation is intersects, which means the query returns documents that intersect the given shape. Table 12.2 describes the possible values for the relation attribute.

Table 12.2 Relationships between documents and the envelope shape

Value of relation	Description
intersects (default)	Returns documents that intersect the given geometrical shape
within	Matches documents if they exist within the boundaries of the given geometrical shape

Table 12.2   Relationships between documents and the envelope shape *(continued)*

Value of `relation`	Description
`contains`	Returns documents if they contain the geometrical shape
`disjoint`	Returns documents that do not exist in the given geometrical shape

In figure 12.6, if we specifically set `relation=intersects`, the expected plots are A, B, and C (as C intersects the main envelope). If we set `relation=within`, plots A and B are returned because they are within the bounded envelope. Setting `relation=contains` returns plots A and B because they are contained in the envelope; and it should not be a surprise that plot D results from `relation=disjoint`.

So far, we've looked at geospatial queries: queries on geodata represented by `geo_point` and `geo_shape` fields. These queries enable us to search for data on a map for various use cases. Now, let's shift gears and discuss queries to search two-dimensional (2D) shapes. In the next section, we explore `shape` queries in detail.

12.7   *The shape query*

We build 2D shapes such as lines, points, and polygons using x and y Cartesian coordinates. Elasticsearch provides indexing and searching of 2D objects using `shape` queries. For example, a civil engineer's blueprint data, a machine operator's CAD (computer-aided designs) designs, and others fit this criterion. In this section, we briefly index and search geoshapes.

When we work with 2D data, we use the dedicated `shape` data type. We create fields of this `shape` type for indexing and searching 2D data. This is easy to understand by going over the following examples.

The following query shows the mapping for the `myshapes` index with two properties, `name` and `myshape`. As you may notice, the `myshape` attribute is defined as the `shape` data type.

Listing 12.11   Index mapping with a shape type

```
PUT myshapes
{
  "mappings": {
    "properties": {
      "name":{
        "type": "text"
      },
      "myshape":{
        "type": "shape"
      }
    }
  }
}
```

Now that we have the mapping, the next step is to index documents with different shapes. The following query indexes two documents with point and line shapes.

> **Listing 12.12   Indexing point and multipoint shapes**

```
PUT myshapes/_doc/1          ◁─┐  Indexes
{                              │  a point
  "name":"A point shape",
  "myshape":{
    "type":"point",
    "coordinates":[12,14]
  }
}

PUT myshapes/_doc/2          ◁─┐  Indexes
{                              │  a multipoint
  "name":"A multipoint shape",
  "myshape":{
    "type":"multipoint",
    "coordinates":[[10,13],[13,16]]
  }
}
```

The code places a point and a multipoint, both 2D shapes, into the `myshapes` index.
Figure 12.7 shows the two shapes: the line and the point.

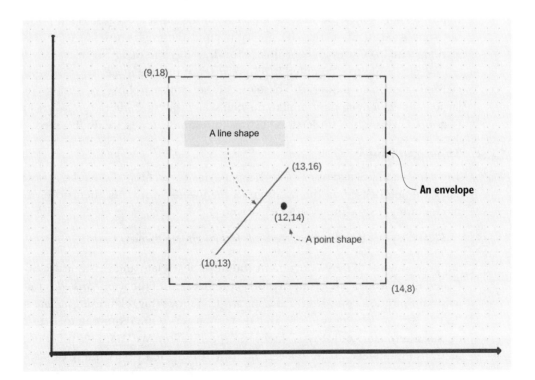

Figure 12.7   Searching for 2D shapes in a bounded envelope

We can search all the documents for shapes that fall in the geoshape enclosed in the envelope. The following query shows the code for this search.

Listing 12.13   Searching for all the shapes in a given envelope

```
GET myshapes/_search
{
  "query": {
    "shape":{                  ← Specifies a
      "myshape": {                shape query    ← Field on which
        "shape": {                                  the query is run
          "type":"envelope",
          "coordinates":[[10,16],[14,10]]   ← The envelope constructed
        }                                       by the given coordinates
      }
    }
  }
}
```

Shape we want to construct →

The shape query defined in the listing searches for documents contained in the envelope created from the given coordinates `[10,16],[14,10]`. (Refer to figure 12.7 to see the bounded envelope created by this query and the shapes contained within it.)

As the query in listing 12.13 shows, we can create a polygonal envelope using the required coordinates (be sure the end coordinates meet, because open polygons are not supported in Elasticsearch). Keep in mind that shape queries are useful when working with 2D Cartesian coordinates for drawings and designs.

We now jump to a completely different set of queries under the umbrella of specialized queries: span queries. These queries support searching for terms at a particular location in a document, unlike normal search queries, where the token's position is ignored. This is best understood by running some queries; we do this next.

12.8   *The span query*

Term-level and full-text queries work the magic of searching at the token (word) level. They are not focused on the positions of the tokens (words) or their order. Consider the following text, a quote by Isaac Newton:

> *Plato is my friend. Aristotle is my friend. But my greatest friend is truth.*

Suppose we want to find a document (quote) where Plato and Aristotle are both mentioned in the same order (not Aristotle and Plato), and the word *Aristotle* should be at least four positions away from *Plato*. Figure 12.8 shows this relationship: *Plato* is at position 1, *Aristotle* is at position 5, and their span is 5. Our requirement is to fetch all quotes where *Plato* and *Aristotle* meet this specification. We cannot satisfy this requirement using full-text (or term-level) queries. Although a prefix query can do a bit of justice to this requirement, it cannot satisfy other sophisticated criteria that we look at in the coming sections.

Plato is my friend. Aristotle is my friend. But my greatest friend is truth
Isaac Newton

| Plato | ~~is my friend~~ | Aristotle |

Position 1 ———————— Span = 5 ———————— **Position 5**

**Figure 12.8
Finding a quote using
a positional query**

This example shows why `span` queries come in handy. They are low-level queries that help us find documents with tokens specified by positions. When working with legal documents, research articles, or technical books, where sentences with the words' exact positions are required, we can use `span` queries. There are several kinds of `span` queries—`span_first`, `span_within`, `span_near`, and so on—and we take a peek at a few of them here; as always, refer to the documentation to learn more.

12.8.1   *Sample data*

Before we work with `span` queries, let's prime Elasticsearch with a `quotes` index and a couple of documents.

Listing 12.14   Priming Elasticsearch for a `span` query

```
PUT quotes          ◁─┐  Creates a quotes index with
{                      │  a couple of properties
  "mappings": {
    "properties": {
      "author":{
        "type": "text"
      },
      "quote":{
        "type": "text"
      }
    }
  }
}
                          Indexes
                          Newton's quote
PUT quotes/_doc/1   ◁─┘
{
  "author":"Isaac Newton",
  "quote":"Plato is my friend. Aristotle is my friend.
  ➧ But my greatest friend is the truth."
}
```

We create the `quotes` index with a couple of properties: `author` and `quote`, which are both text fields (`"type": "text"`). We also index the quote by Isaac Newton as defined in the listing. Now that we have primed the `quotes` index, let's see some `span` queries in action, beginning with the `span_first` query.

12.8.2   *The span_first query*

Suppose we want to find a particular word in the first n number of tokens. For example, we want to know if *Aristotle* exists in the first five positions of our documents (see figure 12.9).

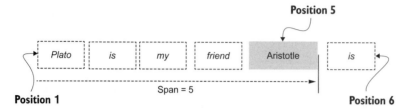

Figure 12.9   Searching for a document with a term in the first *n* number of tokens

As you can deduce from the figure, Aristotle is in the fifth position and therefore exists in the first five positions. This sort of use case can be satisfied by the span_first query. We see the query in action in the following listing.

Listing 12.15   Searching for the given term in the first five positions

```
GET quotes/_search
{
  "query": {
    "span_first": {              Fetches the document in the
      "match": {                 first n number of spans
        "span_term": {           The term we want
          "quote": "aristotle"   to search for
        }
      },
      "end": 5                   The first of n positions
    }                            to find a match
  }
}
```

The span_first query expects a match query where we provide other span queries. Here, the span_term query is wrapped in a span_first query. Although the span_term query is equivalent to a term query, it is commonly wrapped in other span query blocks. The end attribute indicates the maximum number of positions permitted when searching for the match term from the beginning of the field (in this case, end is 5).

> **NOTE**   The end attribute's name is a bit confusing. It is the end position of the token allowed when searching for match terms. I think the name n_position_from_beginning would be better suited.

In listing 12.15, we search for *Aristotle* in the first five positions from the start of the quote (see figure 12.9). Because *Aristotle*'s position is fifth, the document consisting of the quote is successfully returned. If we change the `end` attribute to anything less than 5, the query will not return the search term. The query returns successfully if the value for the `end` attribute is anything greater than 5 (6, 7, 10, and so on).

12.8.3 *The span_near query*

In the `span_first` query, the query word is always counted from the starting position (position 1). Instead of finding the word if it exists in the first *n* positions, sometimes we want to find words that are nearer to each other. For example, continuing with Newton's quote, suppose we want to determine whether the words *Plato* and *Aristotle* are next to each other or no further than three or four positions apart. As figure 12.10 illustrates, we obtain positive results if we are searching for a quote where Plato and Aristotle differ by three positions.

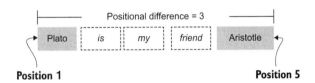

Figure 12.10   Words expected to be at a specified distance apart

In addition to finding the difference in distance between these words, we may want them to exist in the same order. The next listing shows a query to determine if *Plato* and *Aristotle* are near each other (about three positions from each other).

> **Listing 12.16   Searching for documents with terms near each other**

```
GET quotes/_search
{
  "query": {
    "span_near": {              ⟵  The span_near query definition
      "clauses": [              ⟵  with a couple of clauses
        {
                               The clauses consisting of two
          "span_term": {       independent span_terms to
            "quote": "plato"   search for individual words
          }
        },
        {
          "span_term": {
            "quote":  "aristotle"
          }
        }                      The slop attribute gives the
      ],                       acceptable number of
      "slop": 3,         ⟵     positions between the words.
      "in_order": true   ⟵     The in_order attribute sets
    }                          the order of the attributes.
  }
}
```

The span_near query accepts multiple clauses; we also have span_term queries trying to match our terms. Additionally, because we know these two words are three positions apart, we can provide this difference in the form of the slop attribute. The slop attribute permits the acceptable maximum positional difference between the words. For example, the query specifies that the two words can be separated by a maximum of three positions. We can increase the slop (say, "slop": 10) to reduce the strict constraints so the query has a greater chance of success. However, span queries are good at finding exact words at exact positions, so increase the slop attribute judiciously.

In addition to using the slop attribute, we can define the order of the words. Continuing with the same example, if order is unimportant, we can return a positive result even if we request span_near between *Aristotle* and *Plato* (instead of *Plato* and *Aristotle*). If order is important, we can set a Boolean for the in_order flag. The in_order attribute can be set to *true* or *false*; when it's set to *true*, as in listing 12.16, the order in which the words are indexed is taken into account.

12.8.4 *The span_within query*

The next use case for span queries is when we want to find a word between two words. For example, suppose we want to find documents where *Aristotle* is between two words: *friend* and *friend*, as shown in figure 12.11.

Figure 12.11   Finding a word if it exists between other words

We can use the span_within query type for this purpose. Let's look at the query in the following listing and then dissect it.

Listing 12.17   Searching for a word between other words

```
GET quotes/_search
{
  "query": {
    "span_within": {          ⟵──┐ A span_within query consisting
      "little": {                 └─ of two blocks: little and big
        "span_term": {       ⟵──┐ Defines the
          "quote": "aristotle"   │ search word
        }
      },
      "big": {               ⟵──┐ Encloses the
        "span_near": {           │ little block
          "clauses": [
            {
```

```
            "span_term": {
              "quote": "friend"
            }
          },
          {
            "span_term": {
              "quote": "friend"
            }
          }
        ],
        "slop": 4,
        "in_order": true
      }
    }
  }
}
```

This `span_within` query consists of two blocks, `little` and `big`. The `little` block within the search expects to be enclosed in the `big` block. In this query, we want to find documents where *Aristotle* is enclosed between the two words *friend* and *friend*, defined in the `big` block.

Remember, the `big` block is nothing but a `span_near` query (we discussed this query in the previous section). There are no restrictions on how many clauses we can have in the `big` block. For example, we can extend the query in listing 12.17 with the next listing, which has three clauses, each looking for the word *friend*.

Listing 12.18   Checking if a word exists in a set of words

```
GET quotes/_search
{
  "query": {
    "span_within": {
      "little": {
        "span_term": {
          "quote": "aristotle"
        }
      },
      "big": {
        "span_near": {
          "clauses": [
            {
              "span_term": {
                "quote": "friend"
              }
            },
            {
              "span_term": {
                "quote": "friend"
              }
            },
            {
```

```
            "span_term": {
              "quote": "friend"
            }
          }
        ],
        "slop": 10,          ◁─┐  Bumps up the slop
        "in_order": true        │  attribute's value
      }
    }
   }
  }
}
```

This query now tries to determine whether *Aristotle* is between a set of words (all *friend*) defined in the `big` block. The notable change is to bump up the `slop` value. Thus, `span_within` queries help us identify a query within another query.

12.8.5 *The span_or query*

The last `span` query we look at satisfies the OR condition, returning results matching one *or* more input criteria. Elasticsearch provides the `span_or` query for this. It finds documents matching one or more `span` queries from a given set of clauses. For example, the following query finds documents matching *Plato* or *Aristotle* but ignores the word *friends* (note the plural; our document contains the word *friend* in the `quote` field, not *friends*).

Listing 12.19 Searching for any matching word

```
GET quotes/_search
{
  "query": {
    "span_or": {          ◁─┐  Defines the
      "clauses": [           │  span_or query
        {                 ◁─┐  Lists multiple
          "span_term": {     │  clauses
            "quote": "plato"
          }
        },
        {
          "span_term": {
            "quote": "friends"
          }
        },
        {
          "span_term": {
            "quote": "aristotle"
          }
        }
      ]
    }
  }
}
```

This `span_or` query fetches the document with Newton's quote because it matches both Plato and Aristotle. Note that the friends query is not a match, but because the operator is `OR`, the query is happy to proceed because at least one of the words queried was a match. The query does not fail, although the word *friends* is not a match.

Elastic search has other `span` queries such as `span_not`, `span_containing`, `span_multi_term`, and others, but unfortunately, we cannot discuss all of these types here. I advise you to consult the documentation to better understand these queries. The documentation is available here: http://mng.bz/QPa4.

The next section deals with specialized queries such as `distance_feature`, `percolator`, and others. Let's turn our attention to those now.

12.9 *Specialized queries*

In addition to the types of queries we have seen so far, Elasticsearch has several advanced queries dedicated to serving specialized functions: for example, boosting the score for cafes serving chilled drinks at a specified location (`distance_feature` query), alerting the user when an item is back in stock (`percolate` query), finding similar-looking documents (`more_like_this` query), giving documents more importance (`pinned` query), and so on. We dedicate the final section of this chapter to looking at these specialized queries in detail.

12.9.1 *The distance_feature query*

When searching for classic literature, suppose we want to add a clause to find books published in 1813. Along with returning all books that are literature classics, we expect to find *Pride and Prejudice* (Jane Austen's classic), but we want to put *Pride and Prejudice* at the top of the list because it was printed in 1813. Topping the list means boosting the relevance score of the query results based on a particular clause; in this case, we specifically want books published in 1813 to be given higher importance. This functionality is available in Elasticsearch by using the `distance_feature` query. The query fetches results and marks them with a higher relevancy score if they are nearer to an origin date (1813, in this example).

The `distance_feature` query provides similar support for locations. We can highlight the locations nearer a particular address and boost them to the top of the list if we desire. Say that we want to find all restaurants serving fish and chips, but those topping the list should be near Borough Market by London Bridge. (Borough Market is a world-renowned thirteenth-century artisan food market; see https://boroughmarket.org.uk.)

We can use the `distance_feature` query for such use cases, to find results near an origin location or date. The dates and locations are fields declared as `date` (or `date_nanos`) and `geo_point` data types, respectively. Results closer to the given date or location are rated higher in relevance scores. Let's look at some examples to understand the concept in detail.

BOOSTING SCORES FOR NEARBY UNIVERSITIES USING GEOLOCATIONS

Let's say we are searching for universities in the United Kingdom. While searching, we want to give preference to universities within a 10 km radius of London Bridge. We boost the score for them.

To try this scenario, let's create a mapping for the university index with a location declared as a `geo_point` field. The following listing creates the mapping and the indexes for four universities: two in London and two elsewhere in the country.

Listing 12.20 Creating a `universities` index

```
PUT universities
{
  "mappings": {
    "properties": {
      "name":{
        "type": "text"
      },
      "location":{
        "type": "geo_point"
      }
    }
  }
}

PUT universities/_doc/1
{
  "name":"London School of Economics (LSE)",
  "location":[0.1165, 51.5144]
}

PUT universities/_doc/2
{
  "name":"Imperial College London",
  "location":[0.1749, 51.4988]
}

PUT universities/_doc/3
{
  "name":"University of Oxford",
  "location":[1.2544, 51.7548]
}

PUT universities/_doc/4
{
  "name":"University of Cambridge",
  "location":[0.1132, 52.2054]
}
```

Now that the index and data are prepped, let's fetch universities, boosting the relevance scores so those closer to London Bridge are at the top of the list. The map of London in figure 12.12 shows the approximate distances of these universities from London Bridge and Knightsbridge. We use the `distance_feature` query for this purpose, which matches the query criteria but boosts the relevance score based on the additional parameters provided.

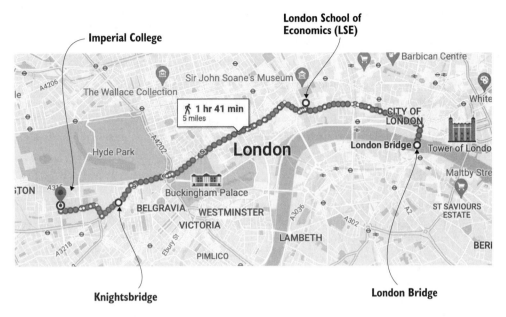

Figure 12.12   Map of London showing universities near London Bridge

Let's write the query and then dig into it to learn the details. The following listing uses a `distance_feature` query within a `bool` query to fetch universities.

Listing 12.21   Boosting scores of universities closer to London Bridge

```
GET universities/_search
{
  "query": {
    "distance_feature": {          ◁── The distance_feature
                                       query declaration
      "field": "location",
      "origin": [-0.0860, 51.5048],   ◁── Focal point where the distance
                                          is measured from an origin
      "pivot": "10 km"    ◁── Distance from
                              the focal point
    }
  }
}
```

The location to search for → `"field": "location"`

The query searches for all universities and returns two: the London School of Economics and Imperial College London. Additionally, if any universities are in the vicinity of 10 km around the origin (`-0.0860, 51.5048` represents London Bridge in the UK), they are scored higher than the others.

The `distance_feature` query, as defined in the listing, expects these properties:

- `field`—The `geo_point` field in the document

- `origin`—The focal point (in longitude and latitude) from which to measure the distance
- `pivot`—The distance from the focal point

In listing 12.21, London School of Economics is closer to London Bridge than Imperial College, so London School of Economics is returned at the top of the results with a higher score. Now let's look at using the `distance_feature` query with dates.

BOOSTING THE SCORE USING DATES

In the previous section, a `distance_feature` query helped us search for universities, boosting the score for those nearer to a certain geolocation. A similar requirement can also be satisfied with `distance_feature`: boosting the score of results if they are close to a date.

Suppose we want to search for all iPhone release dates, topping the list with iPhones released within 30 days around December 1, 2020 (for no particular reason other than trying out the concept). We can write a query similar to listing 12.21, except the `field` attribute is based on a date. Let's first create an `iphones` mapping and index a few iPhones.

Listing 12.22   Creating an `iphones` index and priming it with documents

```
PUT iphones
{
  "mappings": {
    "properties": {
      "name":{
        "type": "text"
      },
      "release_date":{
        "type": "date",
        "format": "dd-MM-yyyy"
      }
    }
  }
}
```

Indexes a few documents

```
PUT iphones/_doc/1    ⟵──┘
{
  "name":"iPhone",
  "release_date":"29-06-2007"
}

PUT iphones/_doc/2
{
  "name":"iPhone 12",
  "release_date":"23-10-2020"
}
PUT iphones/_doc/3
{
  "name":"iPhone 13",
  "release_date":"24-09-2021"
}
```

```
PUT iphones/_doc/4
{
  "name":"iPhone 12 Mini",
  "release_date":"13-11-2020"
}
```

Now that we have an index containing several iPhones, let's develop a query to satisfy our requirement: we want to fetch all iPhones but prioritize those released 30 days around December 1, 2020. The query in the next listing does this.

Listing 12.23 Fetching iPhones and boosting the ratings

```
GET iphones/_search
{
  "query": {
    "bool": {
      "must": [
        {
          "match": {
            "name": "12"
          }
        }
      ],
      "should": [
        {
          "distance_feature": {
            "field": "release_date",        ◁── The field against which our query executes
            "origin": "1-12-2020",           ──▷ Defines the focal date
            "pivot": "30 d"                  ◁── Pivots the number of days to boost scores
          }
        }
      ]
    }
  }
}
```

In this query, we wrap a `distance_feature` in a `bool` query with a `must` clause and a `should` clause (we discussed the `bool` query in chapter 11). The `must` clause searches for all documents with 12 in the `name` field and returns the iPhone 12 and iPhone 12 mini documents from our index. Our requirement is to prioritize phones released 30 days around the first of December (potentially, all phones released in November and December 2020).

To satisfy this requirement, the `should` clause uses the `distance_feature` query to enhance the scores of matching documents closest to the pivot date. The query fetches all the documents from the `iphones` index. Any iPhone released 30 days before or after December 1, 2020 (the origin) is returned with a higher relevance score.

Remember that the matches the `should` clause returns add to the overall score. So, the iPhone 12 Mini should top the list because the release date (`"release_date":` `"13-11-2020"`) of this iPhone is closer to the pivot date (`"origin":"01-12-2020"` ± 30 days). The results of the query are shown here for completeness:

```
"hits" : [
    {
        "_index" : "iphones",
        "_id" : "4",
        "_score" : 1.1876879,
        "_source" : {
            "name" : "iPhone 12 Mini",
            "release_date" : "13-11-2020"
        }
    },
    {
        "_index" : "iphones",
        "_id" : "2",
        "_score" : 1.1217185,
        "_source" : {
            "name" : "iPhone 12",
            "release_date" : "23-10-2020"
        }
    }
]
```

The iPhone 12 Mini scores higher than the iPhone 12 because it was released 17 days before our pivot date, while the iPhone 12 was released almost five weeks earlier.

12.9.2 *The pinned query*

You may have seen sponsored search results at the top of the result set when querying your favorite e-commerce website, such as Amazon. Suppose we want to implement such functionality in our application using Elasticsearch. Fret not: the `pinned` query is at hand.

The `pinned` query adds chosen documents to the result set so they appear at the top of the list. It does so by making their relevance scores higher than the others. The example query in the following listing shows this functionality.

Listing 12.24   Modifying search results by adding sponsored results

```
GET iphones/_search
{
    "query": {                         Specifies the
        "pinned":{          ◁──────    pinned query    List of document IDs scored higher
            "ids":["1","3"],                  ◁──────  than the rest of the results
            "organic":{
                "match":{                     ◁──────  A match query that searches
                    "name":"iPhone 12"                 for the iPhone 12
                }
            }
        }
    }
}
```
Carries out the query search ─▷

This `pinned` query has several moving parts. Let's look at the `organic` block first. The query block holds the search query; in this case, we are searching for the iPhone 12 in our `iphones` index. Ideally, this query should return the iPhone 12 and iPhone 12 Mini documents. However, the output incudes two documents (iPhone and iPhone 13) in addition to the iPhone 12 and iPhone 12 Mini. The reason is the `ids` field. This field encloses the additional documents that must be appended to the results and shown at the top of the list (the sponsored results), thus creating higher relevance scores synthetically.

The `pinned` query adds high-priority documents to results sets. These documents trump others in the list position to create sponsored results.

You may wonder if pinned results have scores: can one or more pinned results be prioritized over the other(s)? Unfortunately, the answer is no. These documents are presented in ID order as input in the query: `"ids":["1","3"]`, for example.

12.9.3 The more_like_this query

You may have noticed Netflix or Amazon Prime Video (or your favorite streaming app) showing you More Like This movies when you browse. For example, figure 12.13 shows the More Like This movies when I visit Paddington 2.

One of the requirements for users is searching for "similar" or "like" in documents: for example, finding quotes similar to Newton's "Friends and Truth," researching papers about COVID and SARS, or querying movies like *The Godfather*. Let's jump into an example to better understand the use case.

Let's say we are collecting a list of profiles about various people. To create profiles, we index sample documents into the `profiles` index.

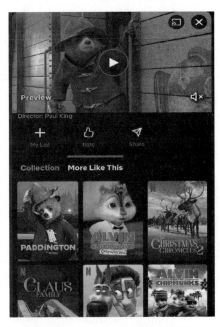

Figure 12.13 Viewing More Like This movies

Listing 12.25 Indexing sample profiles

```
PUT profiles/_doc/1
{
  "name":"John Smith",
  "profile":"John Smith is a capable carpenter"
}

PUT profiles/_doc/2
{
  "name":"John Smith Patterson",
  "profile":"John Smith Patterson is a pretty plumber"
}
```

```
PUT profiles/_doc/3
{
  "name":"Smith Sotherby",
  "profile":"Smith Sotherby is a gentle painter"
}
PUT profiles/_doc/4
{
  "name":"Frances Sotherby",
  "profile":"Frances Sotherby is a gentleman"
}
```

There's nothing surprising about these documents; they're just profiles of routine people. Now that these documents are indexed, let's find out how we can ask Elasticsearch to fetch documents similar to the text "gentle painter" or "capable carpenter", or even retrieve documents with a name similar to Sotherby. That's what the `more_like_this` query helps us do. The next listing creates a query to search profiles more like Sotherby.

Listing 12.26   Searching for More Like This documents

```
GET profiles/_search
{
  "query": {
    "more_like_this": {          ◁──┘  Defines the
      "fields": ["name", "profile"],   more_like_this query   │ Searches the given
      "like": "Sotherby",                              ◁──┘    input in fields
      "min_term_freq": 1,
      "max_query_terms": 12,     ◁──┐  Sets the term frequency
      "min_doc_freq":1              │  (defaults to 2)
    }                               │
  }                           Sets the number of
}                           terms to be selected
```

Defines the query criterion ┌▷

The `more_like_this` query accepts text in a `like` parameter, and this input text is matched against the fields included in the `fields` parameter. The query accepts a few tuning parameters, such as minimum term and document frequencies (`min_term`) and the maximum number of terms (`max_query_terms`) that the query should select. If we want to give the user a better experience when showing similar documents, the `more_like_this` query is the right choice.

12.9.4 *The percolate query*

Searching for documents given an input is straightforward. All we need to do is return search results from the index if there are any matches to the given criterion. This satisfies the requirement of searching for the user's criterion, and this is what we've done so far when querying for results.

There's another requirement that Elasticsearch satisfies: notifying the user when their current search yields negative results but the outcome will become available at a future date. Say, for example, that a user searches for a *Python in Action* book on our e-commerce bookseller site, but unfortunately, we do not have the book in stock. The dissatisfied customer leaves the site. However, we get new stock after a day or two, and the book is added to the inventory. Now, because the book reappears in our inventory, we want to notify the user so they can purchase it.

Elasticsearch supports this use case by providing a special `percolate` query, which uses the `percolator` field type. The `percolate` query is the opposite of our normal search query mechanism in that instead of running the query against documents, we search for a query given a document. This is a strange concept at first glance, but we demystify it in this section. Figure 12.14 shows the differences between a normal query and a `percolate` query.

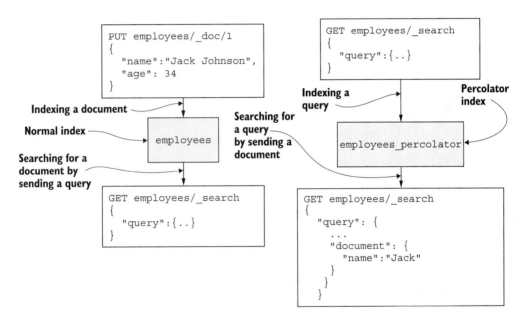

Figure 12.14 Normal vs. `percolate` queries

Let's see `percolate` queries in action by first indexing some documents. The following listing indexes three technical books into the `tech_books` index. Note that we do not include a Python book yet.

Listing 12.27 Indexing technical books

```
PUT tech_books/_doc/1
{
  "name":"Effective Java",
  "tags":["Java","Software engineering", "Programming"]
}

PUT tech_books/_doc/2
{
```

```
  "name":"Elasticsearch crash course",
  "tags":["Elasticsearch","Software engineering", "Programming"]
}

PUT tech_books/_doc/3
{
  "name":"Java Core Fundamentals",
  "tags":["Java","Software"]
}
```

Now that we've seeded our book inventory index, users can search for books using simple `match`/`term` queries. (I'm omitting these queries here because we've already mastered them.) However, not all user queries yield results; for example, someone searching for *Python in Action* won't find it. The following listing shows this.

Listing 12.28 **Searching for a nonexistent book**

```
GET tech_books/_search
{
  "query": {
    "match": {
      "name": "Python"
    }
  }
}
```

From the user's perspective, the search ends with a disappointing result: not returning the book they searched for. We can take our queries to the next level by notifying the user when the out-of-stock Python book becomes available. This is where we can put percolators to work.

Just as we index documents into an index, a percolator can have an index for a set of queries and expect the queries to be indexed. We need to define a schema for a `percolator` index. Let's call it `tech_books_percolator`.

Listing 12.29 **Creating a `percolator` index**

```
PUT tech_books_percolator
{
  "mappings": {
    "properties": {            Sets the field
      "query": {          ◁── name to query    Sets the query field's
        "type": "percolator"      ◁── data type to percolator
      },
      "name": {          ◁──┐  Sets the name field as it appears
        "type": "text"       │  in the tech_books index
      },
      "tags": {          ◁──┐  Sets the tags field as it appears
        "type": "text"       │  in the tech_books index
      }
    }
  }
}
```

This listing defines the index for holding percolator queries. Note the following:

- It contains a `query` field to hold users' (failed) queries.
- The data type of the `query` field must be `percolator`.

The rest of the schema consists of the definition borrowed from the original `tech_books` index.

Just as we define fields with data types such as `text`, `long`, `double`, `keyword`, and so on, Elasticsearch provides a `percolator` type. The `query` field is defined as `percolator` in listing 12.29, and it expects a query as the field value, which we see shortly.

Now that our percolator index (`tech_books_percolator`) mapping is ready, the next step is to store queries. These queries usually don't return results to users (like the Python example).

In the real world, a user query that doesn't yield a result will be indexed into this `percolator` index. The process of collating users' failed queries into a `percolator` index can be done inside the search application, but unfortunately, discussing it is out of scope here. Just imagine that the query in listing 12.29 doesn't yield a result and is now sent to the `percolator` index to be stored. The next listing provides the code to store the query.

Listing 12.30 Storing the query to search for a book

```
PUT tech_books_percolator/_doc/1
{
  "query" : {
    "match":{
      "name":"Python"       ◁──┐ The same query the user tried
    }                           │ to search with but that failed
  }                             │ to get a positive result
}
```

The listing shows the indexing of a query, which is unlike indexing a normal document. If you remember the document/indexing operations from earlier chapters, any time we index a document, we use a JSON-formatted document with name-value pairs. This code, however, has a `match` query.

The query in listing 12.30 is stored in the `tech_books_percolator` index with document ID 1. As you can imagine, this index keeps growing with failed searches. The JSON document consists of query(ies) issued by users that don't return positive results.

The final piece of the puzzle is to search the `tech_books_percolator` index when our stock is updated. As a bookshop owner, we are expected to stock up; the next time we receive new stock, let's assume the Python book is included. We can now index it into our `tech_books` index for users to search for and buy.

Listing 12.31 Stocking up (indexing) a Python book

```
PUT tech_books/_doc/4
{
  "name":"Python in Action",
```

```
    "tags":["Python","Software Programming"]
}
```

Now that the Python book is indexed, we need to rerun the user's failed query. But this time, instead of running the query on the `tech_books` index, let's run it against the `tech_books_percolator` index. The query against the `percolator` index has the following special syntax.

Listing 12.32   Searching for queries in the `percolator` index

```
GET tech_books_percolator/_search
{
  "query": {
    "percolate": {            ⟵──  Specifies the
      "field": "query",       ⟵──  percolate query  │  Sets the field's
      "document": {                                  │  name to query
        "name":"Python in Action",        ⟵──  Specifies the document
        "tags":["Python","Software Programming"]  │  consisting of the original book
      }                                             │  indexed into tech_books
    }
  }
}
```

The `percolate` query expects two bits of input: a `field` with a value of `query` (this coincides with the property defined in the percolator mapping in listing 12.28) and a document, which is the same document we indexed in our `tech_books` index. All we need to do is check for any query that matches the given `document`. Fortunately, *Python in Action* is a match (we indexed a query into our `percolator` index earlier).

Given the Python document defined in listing 12.31, we can return a query from the `tech_books_percolator` index. This lets us inform the user that the book they were looking for is back in stock! Note that we can extended the query stored in the `tech_books_percolator` index with a specific user ID.

Percolators are a little tricky to understand, but once you understand the use case, they aren't difficult to implement. Keep in mind that there must always be an automated, semi-automated, or manual process to sync the operations a user performs against the data stored in the `percolator` index.

That's a wrap! By discussing advanced queries in this chapter, we've covered the search part of Elasticsearch. The final part is aggregating data, which is the next chapter's subject. Stay tuned to learn more about how we can find intelligence in our data by analyzing it with various mathematical and statistical functions.

Summary

- Elasticsearch supports the `geo_point` and `geo_shape` data types to work with geodata.
- Geospatial queries fetch locations and addresses using coordinates formed from longitude and latitude values.

- A `geo_bounding_box` query fetches the addresses in a georectangle, which is constructed using a pair of longitude and latitude values as the top-left and bottom-right coordinates.
- A `geo_distance` query finds locations inside a circular area with a center provided as a pivot and the radius as the distance from the pivot.
- A `geo_shape` query fetches all suitable locations inside a given envelope formed by coordinates.
- A `geo_shape` query searches 2D shapes in a rectangular coordinate system (Cartesian plane).
- Span queries are advanced queries that work with lower-level positions of individual tokens or words. Elasticsearch supports several `span` queries: `span_first`, `span_within`, `span_near`, and more.
- A `distance_feature` query is a specialized query where the proximity of documents to a given focal point increases the relevance score and, thus, gives the documents higher priority.
- A `pinned` query lets us bundle additional (even unmatched) documents with the original result set, potentially creating sponsored search results.
- A `more_like_this` query finds related or similar-looking results.
- A `percolate` query lets us notify users about their negative searches at a future date.

Aggregations

Search and analytics are two sides of a coin, and Elasticsearch delivers absolute detail and countless features. Elasticsearch is a market leader in analytics by providing feature-rich functions for querying and analyzing data, thus enabling organizations to find insights and deep intelligence from their data. Whereas a search finds results for certain criteria, analytics, on the other hand, helps organizations derive statistics and metrics from it. So far, we've looked at searching for documents from a given corpus of documents. With analytics, we take a step back and examine the data from a high level to draw conclusions about it.

In this chapter, we look at Elasticsearch's aggregations in detail. Elasticsearch boasts many aggregations, predominantly categorized as one of these types: metric, bucket, and pipeline. Metric aggregations allow us to use analytical functions such as sum, min, max, and avg to perform calculations on data. Bucket aggregations help us categorize data into buckets or ranges. Finally, pipeline aggregations permit us to chain aggregations: that is take metric or bucket aggregations and create new aggregations.

Elasticsearch provides a lot of aggregations out of the box. We get familiar with each type before jumping into a few to get our hands dirty. Note that it is impractical to look at them individually due to space restrictions, but learning the concepts and applying them to several common aggregations is more important than documenting every one of them. That said, the book's source code contains as many aggregations as possible, especially those not discussed in this chapter.

NOTE The code for this chapter is available on GitHub (http://mng.bz/wvZg) and on the book's website (https://www.manning.com/books/elastic search-in-action-second-edition).

13.1 Overview

Aggregations let companies understand their amassed data. They help understand customers and their relationships, evaluate product performance, forecast sales, and answer a wide range of questions about application performance over time, security threats, and more. Aggregations in Elasticsearch primarily fall into three categories:

- *Metric aggregations*—These aggregations generate metrics such as sum, average, minimum, maximum, top hits, mode, and many others. They include popular, single-value metrics that help understand data over a large set of documents by answering questions like: What is the sum of all product sales in the last month? What is the minimum number of API errors? and What are the top search hits?
- *Bucket aggregations*—Bucketing is a process of collecting data into interval buckets. These aggregations split the data into given sets: for example, splitting cars into years of registration, students into various grades, and so on. Histograms, ranges, terms, filters, and others fall into this category.
- *Pipeline aggregations*—These aggregations work on the output of other aggregations to provide a complex set of statistical analytics such as moving averages, derivatives, and others.

We discuss these aggregations with examples in the following sections. First, let's look at the syntax and endpoint used to carry out the aggregations.

13.1.1 The endpoint and syntax

After working with search queries, you should be pretty familiar with the _search endpoint. The good news is that we can use the same _search endpoint to run aggregations. However, the body of the request uses a new object: aggregations (aggs for short) instead of the usual query object. The following snippet shows the aggregation query syntax:

```
GET <index_name>/_search
{
  "aggregations|aggs": {
    "NAME": {
      "AGG_TYPE": {}
    }
  }
}
```

The `aggs` object tells Elasticsearch that the query invocation is an aggregation type. The `NAME` attribute, provided by the user, gives a suitable name for the aggregation. Finally, `AGG_TYPE` is the type of aggregation: `sum`, `min`, `max`, `range`, `terms`, `histogram`, and so on.

13.1.2 *Combining searches and aggregations*

We can also combine aggregations with queries. For example, we can run a query to fetch results and then run aggregations on that result set. These are called *scoped aggregations* because the input is the query's result. The syntax is slightly extended from the previous aggregation query:

```
GET <index_name>/_search
{
  "query": {
    "QUERY_TYPE": {
      "FIELD": "TEXT"
    }
  },
  "aggs": {
    "NAME": {
      "AGG_TYPE": {}
    }
  }
}
```

The scope of the aggregation is defined by the query's output. If we don't associate a query with an aggregation request, it is assumed that it will work on all the documents of the index (or indexes) defined in the request URL.

13.1.3 *Multiple and nested aggregations*

In addition to running solo aggregations, we can execute multiple aggregations on the given data set. This feature is extremely handy if we need to extract analytics on various fields with multiple conditions. For example, we may want to create a histogram of iPhone 14 sales per day as well as a `sum` aggregation of total sales for the month. To do this, we can employ the `histogram` bucketing aggregation and the `sum` metric aggregation.

Additionally, sometimes we need to nest aggregations; for example, the bucketed data in a histogram may need further categorizing (bucketing) of data by date or by finding the minimum and maximum for each bucket. In this case, the aggregated data in each top-level bucket is fed into the next-level bucket for further aggregation. Nested aggregations can be further categorized using more buckets or single-value metrics (`sum`, `avg`, etc.). We look at nested aggregations with examples in the coming sections.

13.1.4 Ignoring results

Search (or aggregation) queries tend to return source documents in the response if not asked to suppress them in the query. We looked at how to manipulate responses in chapter 8, where we configured the `_source`, `_source_includes`, and `_source_excludes` parameters with appropriate settings.

When working with aggregations, the documents in the response are usually unimportant because we're more interested in the aggregations than the source. Under normal circumstances, unfortunately, the source documents are tagged along with the aggregations even when we run the `aggregation` query. If this is not our intention (and usually it is not, when running aggregations), we can tweak the query by setting the `size` parameter to zero. The following snippet shows this approach:

```
GET tv_sales/_search
{
  size = 0          Sets the size
                    parameter to zero
  "aggs": {
      <<your query goes here>>
    }
  }
}
```

We use this handy parameter (`size=0`) throughout this chapter to suppress source documents as we execute aggregation queries.

As pointed out earlier, aggregations are broadly classified as metric, bucket, or pipeline. In the next section, we look at metric aggregations with sample data specifically tailored for metric calculations. Subsequent sections discuss the remaining aggregations.

13.2 Metric aggregations

Metric aggregations are the simple aggregations we use often in daily life. For example,

- What are the average height and weight of the students in a class?
- What is the minimum hedge trade?
- What are the gross earnings of a best-selling book?

Elasticsearch provides metric functions to calculate most single- and multi-value metrics. If you are wondering what we mean by single- versus multi-value aggregations, this is a simple concept based on the number of outputs.

A single-value metric aggregation is an aggregation on a set of data that outputs a single value, such as `min`, `max`, or `average`. These aggregations work on input documents to produce single-value output data. On the other hand, the `stats` and extended_stats aggregations produce multiple values as output. For example, the stats aggregation output consists of min, max, sum, avg, and a couple more for the same set of documents.

Most metric aggregations are self-explanatory. For instance, a sum aggregation sums up all the given values, and avg averages the values. If you need to work with metrics not discussed in this chapter, see the documentation on the Elasticsearch site for their usage: http://mng.bz/qrRz.

13.2.1 Sample data

In the next few sections, we discuss popular aggregations. Before we do that, let's prime Elasticsearch with a few documents. The following listing primes our data store with a list of TV sales by creating a new index, tv_sales. You can also download the same sample set from GitHub (http://mng.bz/7DQ4) or the book's website.

Listing 13.1   Indexing TV sales data

```
PUT tv_sales/_bulk
{"index":{"_id":"1"}}
{"brand": "Samsung","name":"UHD TV","size_inches":65,"price_gbp":1400,
➡ "sales":17}
{"index":{"_id":"2"}}
{"brand":"Samsung","name":"UHD TV","size_inches":45,"price_gbp":1000,
➡ "sales":11}
{"index":{"_id":"3"}}
{"brand":"Samsung","name":"UHD TV","size_inches":23,"price_gbp":999,
➡ "sales":14}
{"index":{"_id":"4"}}
{"brand":"LG","name":"8K TV","size_inches":65,"price_gbp":1499,"sales":13}
{"index":{"_id":"5"}}
{ "brand":"LG","name":"4K TV","size_inches":55,"price_gbp":1100,"sales":31}
{"index":{"_id":"6"}}
{"brand":"Philips","name":"8K TV","size_inches":65,"price_gbp":1800,
➡ "sales":23}
{"index":{"_id":"7"}}
{"name":"8K TV","size_inches":65,"price_gbp":2000,"sales":23}
{"index":{"_id":"9"}}
{"name":"8K TV","size_inches":65,"price_gbp":2000,"sales":23,
➡ "best_seller":true}
{"index":{"_id":"10"}}
{"name":"4K TV","size_inches":75,"price_gbp":2200,"sales":14,
➡ "best_seller":false}
```

This listing indexes documents with various attributes to a tv_sales index. Take particular note of the best_seller field: it is only set on the last two records. Now that we have a sample data set, let's run a few common metric aggregations.

13.2.2 The value_count metric

The value_count metric counts the number of values present for a field in a set of documents. If our requirement is to fetch the number of values in Elasticsearch for a given field, the `value_count` aggregation does what we need. For example, running the following query returns the number of values in our stash for the `best_seller` field.

Listing 13.2 Finding the number of values for a field

```
GET tv_sales/_search
{
  size = 0
  "aggs": {                                    ┐ Names the
    "total-number-of-values": {  ◁─────────────┘ aggregation results
      "value_count": {           ◁───────┐
        "field": "best_seller"   ◁────┐  │ Names the aggregation
      }                               │  │ (value_count)
    }                                 │
  }                                   │ Field on which the
}                                     │ value_count is performed
```

The `value_count` aggregation is carried out on the `best_seller` field. Note that by default, aggregations are not executed on `text` fields. In our sample data, the `best_seller` field is a `boolean` data type and a good candidate for the `value_count` metric aggregation. Running the query in listing 13.2 outputs the following:

```
"aggregations" : {
    "total-values" : {
       "value" : 2
    }
  }
```

There are two values (two documents) for the `best_seller` field. Note that `value_count` doesn't pick unique values; it does not remove duplicate values for the specified field across the document set.

Aggregations on text fields are not optimized

Text fields do not support sorting, scripting, and aggregations. Aggregations are ideally carried out on nontext fields such as `number`, `keyword`, `boolean`, and so on. Because `text` fields are not optimized for aggregations, by default, Elasticsearch stops us from creating aggregation queries on them. If you are curious, try an aggregation on a `text` field like the name field, and see what exception Elasticsearch throws:

```
"root_cause" : [
{
   "type" : "illegal_argument_exception",
   "reason" : "Text fields are not optimised for operations that require
   ➥ per-document field data like aggregations and sorting, so these
   ➥ operations are disabled by default. Please use a keyword field
   ➥ instead. Alternatively, set fielddata=true on [name] in order to
   ➥ load field data by uninverting the inverted index. Note that this
   ➥ can use significant memory."
}
```

(continued)

As the error says, running aggregations on a `text` field is prohibited by default, so if we want to perform aggregations on `text` fields, we need to enable `fielddata` on the respective fields. We can set `"fielddata": true` when defining the mapping:

```
PUT tv_sales_with_field_data
{
  "mappings": {
    "properties": {
      "name":{
        "type": "text",
        "fielddata": true
      }
    }
  }
}
```

Note that enabling `fielddata` may lead to performance problems because data is stored in memory on the nodes. Rather than taking a performance hit by enabling `fielddata`, we can instead create a multi-field data type with `keyword` as the second type. This works because `keyword` data types are allowed for aggregations.

Finding the average of a set of numbers is a frequent operation in analytics. As expected, Elasticsearch provides a handy function called `avg` to find averages, which is the topic of the next section.

13.2.3 *The avg metric*

Finding the average of a set of numbers is a basic statistical function that we often require. Elasticsearch provides the `avg` metric aggregation out of the box for running an average calculation. For example, the next query fetches the average TV price using `avg`.

Listing 13.3   Average price of all TVs

```
GET tv_sales/_search
{
  "size": 0,
  "aggs": {                              Names the
    "tv_average_price": {                aggregation
      "avg": {                           Calculates the
        "field": "price_gbp"             average price
      }
    }                                    Field on which the
  }                                      average is calculated
}
```

`tv_average_price` is a user-defined name given to this average aggregation. The `avg` declaration in the code represents the average function. The data field on which we want to run our single-field `avg` metric is called `field`. When the query is executed, we get the following results:

```
"aggregations" : {
  "tv_average_price" : {
    "value" : 1555.3333333333333
  }
}
```

The engine calculates the average price of all TVs and returns it to the user. The average TV price across all six documents is about £1555.

13.2.4 *The sum metric*

The single-value `sum` metric adds the values of the field in question and produces an end result. For example, to find the total value of all TVs sold, we can issue the following query.

Listing 13.4   Total sum of all TVs sold

```
GET tv_sales/_search
{
  "size": 0,
  "aggs": {
    "tv_total_price": {
      "sum": {
        "field": "price_gbp"
      }
    }
  }
}
```

The `sum` metric adds all the prices and produces a single figure of £13,998 when we run the query. Similarly, let's look at the minimum and maximum metric functions next.

13.2.5 *The min and max metrics*

Sometimes we need to find the minimum and maximum quantities from a set of values, such as the *minimum* number of available speakers for a conference or the session with the most attendees. Elasticsearch exposes the corresponding metrics in the form of `min` and `max` to produce these extremes of a data set. The metrics are self-explanatory, but in the interest of completeness, let's look at them briefly.

MINIMUM METRIC

Suppose we want to find the cheapest TV in our stock. This clearly is a candidate for using the `min` metric on the data values.

Listing 13.5   Cheapest price for the TVs

```
GET tv_sales/_search
{
  "size": 0,
  "aggs": {
    "cheapest_tv_price": {          Calculates the
      "min": {            ◁──────   minimum value
        "field": "price_gbp"   ◁───┐
      }                            │  Applies the min
    }                              │  function to this field
  }
}
```

The `min` keyword fetches the metric, which works on the `price_gbp` field to produce the expected result: the field's minimum value derived from all the documents. We fetch the lowest-priced TV (£999) in our stock by executing the query.

MAXIMUM METRIC

We can use similar logic to fetch the best-selling TV: the TV with the *maximum* number of sales.

Listing 13.6   Best-selling TV

```
GET tv_sales/_search
{
  "size": 0,
  "aggs": {
    "best_seller_tv_by_sales": {
      "max": {
        "field": "sales"
      }
    }
  }
}
```

When we execute the query, it returns a TV that sells very quickly (maximum sales). From the results, it is LG's 8K TV with 48 sales.

13.2.6 *The stats metric*

While the previous metrics are single-value (meaning they work only on a single field), the `stats` metric fetches all common statistical functions. It is a multi-value aggregation that fetches several metrics (`avg`, `min`, `max`, `count`, and `sum`) simultaneously. The query in the next listing applies the `stats` aggregations to the `price_gbp` field.

Listing 13.7   All the common stats at once

```
GET tv_sales/_search
{
  "size": 0,
  "aggs": {
```

```
"common_stats":{          The stats
  "stats": {        ◁──┘  function
    "field": "price_gbp"   ◁──┐  Applies stats
  }                           │  to this field
}
    }
  }
}
```

Once executed, this query returns the following results:

```
"aggregations" : {
  "common_stats" : {
    "count" : 6,
    "min" : 999.0,
    "max" : 1800.0,
    "avg" : 1299.6666666666667,
    "sum" : 7798.0
  }
}
```

The `stats` metric returns all five metrics simultaneously. This makes it handy if we want to see the basic aggregations all in one place.

13.2.7   *The extended_stats metric*

Although `stats` is a useful, common metric, it doesn't provide advanced analytics such as variance, standard deviation, and other statistical functions. Elasticsearch includes another metric called `extended_stats` out of the box, which is the cousin of `stats` and deals with advanced statistical metrics.

The `extended_stats` metric provides three stats in addition to the standard statistical metrics: `sum_of_squares`, `variance`, and `standard_deviation`. The following listing demonstrates.

> **Listing 13.8   Advanced (extended) stats on the `price_gbp` field**

```
GET tv_sales/_search
{
  "size": 0,
  "aggs": {                      Applying the extended_stats
    "additional_stats":{         function fetches advanced
      "extended_stats": {   ◁──┘ statistical measures.
        "field": "price_gbp"   ◁──┐  Uses extended_stats
      }                           │  on this field
    }
  }
}
```

We invoke the `extended_stats` function on the `price_gbp` field. Doing so retrieves all the statistical data shown in figure 13.1. The query calculates a lot of advanced statistical information on `price_gbp` as well as common metrics (`avg`, `min`, `max`, etc.) and various variances and standard deviations.

```
"aggregations" : {
  "extended_stats" : {
    "count" : 6,
    "min" : 999.0,
    "max" : 1800.0,
    "avg" : 1299.6666666666667,
    "sum" : 7798.0,
    "sum_of_squares" : 1.0655002E7,
    "variance" : 86700.22222222232,
    "variance_population" : 86700.22222222232,
    "variance_sampling" : 104040.2666666668,
    "std_deviation" : 294.4490146395846,
    "std_deviation_population" : 294.4490146395846,
    "std_deviation_sampling" : 322.5527347065388,
    "std_deviation_bounds" : {
      "upper" : 1888.5646959458359,
      "lower" : 710.7686373874975,
      "upper_population" : 1888.5646959458359,
      "lower_population" : 710.7686373874975,
      "upper_sampling" : 1944.7721360797443,
      "lower_sampling" : 654.5611972535892
    }
  }
}
```

Figure 13.1   The extended statistics on the `price_gbp` field

13.2.8 *The cardinality metric*

The `cardinality` metric returns unique values for the given set of documents. A single-value metric fetches occurrences of distinct values from our data. For example, the query in the next listing retrieves the number of unique TV brands in our `tv_sales` index.

Listing 13.9   Fetching unique TV brands

```
GET tv_sales/_search
{
  "size": 0,
  "aggs": {
    "unique_tvs": {            The cardinality metric
      "cardinality": {    ◁──┘ fetches unique values.
        "field": "brand.keyword"   ◁──┐ Applies cardinality to the
      }                               └ brand.keyword field
    }
  }
}
```

Because we have four unique brands (Samsung, LG, Philips, and Panasonic), the query result has 4 in the `unique_tvs` aggregation:

```
"aggregations" : {
  "unique_tvs" : {
    "value" : 4
  }
}
```

Data is distributed in Elasticsearch, so trying to fetch exact counts of cardinality may lead to performance problems. To fetch an exact number, data must be retrieved and loaded into a hashset in the in-memory cache. And because this is an expensive operation, the cardinality runs as an approximation. So, counts for unique values may not be exact, but they are close.

In addition to the metric aggregations we've discussed, Elasticsearch exposes a few others. Going over all of them in this chapter is not practical, so I strongly recommend that you look at the Elasticsearch documentation to learn about those not covered here.

The next type of metric produces a bucket of documents rather than creating a metric across all documents. These are called *bucket aggregations*, a subject discussed in the next section.

13.3 Bucket aggregations

One requirement for data is running grouping operations. Elasticsearch calls these grouping actions *bucket aggregations*. Their sole aim is to categorize data into groups, commonly called *buckets*.

Bucketing is a process of collecting data into interval buckets. For example,

- Grouping runners for a marathon according to their age bracket (21–30, 31–40, 41–50, etc.)
- Categorizing schools based on their inspection ratings (good, outstanding, exceptional)
- Getting the number of new houses constructed each month or year

To play with bucketing aggregations, we reuse a data set we've worked with in the past: the book data. Pick up the data set from GitHub (http://mng.bz/mVZ0) or the book's website, and index it. This sample snippet provides a quick reminder (this is not the full data set):

```
POST _bulk
{"index":{"_index":"books","_id":"1"}}
{"title": "Core Java Volume I â€" Fundamentals","author": "Cay S. Horstmann",
➥ "edition": 11, "synopsis": "Java reference book that offers a detailed
➥ explanation of various features of Core Java, including exception
➥ handling, interfaces, and lambda expressions. Significant highlights
➥ of the book include simple language, conciseness, and detailed
➥ examples.","amazon_rating": 4.6,"release_date": "2018-08-27",
➥ "tags": ["Programming Languages, Java Programming"]}
{"index":{"_index":"books","_id":"2"}}
{"title": "Effective Java","author": "Joshua Bloch", "edition": 3,"synopsis":
➥  "A must-have book for every Java programmer and Java aspirant,
➥ Effective Java makes up for an excellent complementary read with other
➥ Java books or learning material. The book offers 78 best practices to
➥ follow for making the code better.", "amazon_rating": 4.7,
➥ "release_date": "2017-12-27", "tags": ["Object Oriented Software Design"]}
```

Now that we've primed our server with book data, let's run some common bucketing aggregations. There are at least two dozen aggregations out of the box, each with its own bucketing strategy. As I mentioned earlier, it would be boring and repetitive to document all the aggregations in this book. But once you understand the concept and get the idea of working with bucketing from our examples, you should be good to go with the other aggregations by following the documentation. Let's start with a common bucket aggregation: histograms.

13.3.1 *Histograms*

Histograms are neat bar charts representing grouped data. Most analytical software tools provide visual as well as data representation of histograms. Elasticsearch exposes a `histogram` bucket aggregation out of the box.

You may have worked with histograms where data is split into multiple categories based on the appropriate interval. The histograms in Elasticsearch are no different: they create a set of buckets over all the documents at a predetermined interval.

Let's take an example of categorizing books by ratings. We want to find the number of books in each rating category: 2 to 3, 3 to 4, 4 to 5, and so on. We can create a `histogram` aggregation using a set `interval` value of 1 so books fall into one-step buckets of ratings.

Listing 13.10   A `histogram` aggregation for books

```
GET books/_search
{
  "size": 0,
  "aggs": {                              Names our
    "ratings_histogram": {    ⟵——       aggregation
      "histogram": {                         Applies the aggregation
        "field": "amazon_rating",    ⟵——    on this field
        "interval": 1    ⟵——
      }                              Specifies the bucket
    }                                interval (one unit)
  }
}
```

Categorizes data into buckets ——▷ *(annotation pointing to the `histogram` block)*

The `histogram` aggregation expects the field on which we want to aggregate the buckets as well as the interval for the buckets. In this listing, we split the books based on the `amazon_rating` field with an interval of 1. This fetches all books that fall between 3 and 4, 4 and 5, and so on. Figure 13.2 shows the response.

As you can see, running the query fetches 2 books that fall in the bucket of ratings 2 to 3, 35 books with ratings 3 to 4, and so on. The response in figure 13.2 shows that the buckets have two fields: `key` and `doc_count`. The `key` field represents the bucket classification, and the `doc_count` field indicates the number of documents that fit in the bucket.

```
"aggregations" : {
  "ratings_histogram" : {
    "buckets" : [
      {
        "key" : 3.5,
        "doc_count" : 2
      },
      {
        "key" : 4.0,
        "doc_count" : 9
      },
      {
        "key" : 4.5,
        "doc_count" : 26
      },
      {
        "key" : 5.0,
        "doc_count" : 2
      }
    ]
  }
}
```

Figure 13.2   Book rating aggregation as a histogram

Histogram aggregation with Kibana

In listing 13.10, we developed an aggregation query and executed it in the Kibana Console. The results in JSON format aren't visually appealing, as shown in figure 13.2. It is up to the client who receives that data to represent it as a visual chart. However, Kibana has a rich set of visualizations to aggregate data. Working with the Kibana visualizations is out of scope for this chapter, but this figure shows the same data represented as a histogram in Kibana's Dashboard, this time with an interval of 0.5.

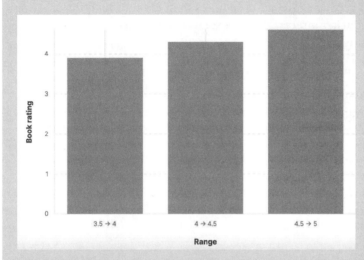

A histogram categorizing books by ratings viewed as a bar chart in Kibana's Dashboard

As you can see, the data is categorized into buckets based on the interval 0.5, and the buckets are filled with the documents that fit in them. To learn about Kibana visualizations, refer to the documentation at https://www.elastic.co/guide/en/kibana/current/dashboard.html.

THE DATE HISTOGRAM

Sometimes we want to group data based on dates rather than numbers. For example, we may want to find all the books released each year, get the weekly sales of an iPhone product, determine the number of server threat attempts every hour, and so forth. This is where the `date_histogram` aggregation comes in handy.

The histogram bucketing strategy we looked at in the last section is based on numerical intervals, but Elasticsearch also provides a histogram based on dates, aptly called `date_histogram`. Let's say we want to categorize books based on their release dates. Here's the query that applies bucketing to do this.

Listing 13.11   A `date_histogram` query

```
GET books/_search
{
  "size":0,
```

```
"aggs": {
  "release_year_histogram": {        Declares the histogram
    "date_histogram": {        ◄──┘   type (date_histogram)      Applies the aggregation
      "field": "release_date",                              ◄──  to this field
      "calendar_interval": "year"    ◄──┐ Defines the
    }                                    │ bucket interval
  }
}
}
```

The `date_histogram` aggregation requires the field on which the aggregation should run and the bucket interval. In the example, we use `release_date` as the date field with a `year` interval.

> **NOTE** We can set the bucket's interval value to `year`, `quarter`, `month`, `week`, `day`, `hour`, `minute`, `second`, or `millisecond`, based on our requirements.

Running the query in listing 13.11 produces the individual buckets for each year and the number of documents in that bucket. The following snippet shows the results at a glance:

```
...
{
  "key_as_string" : "2020-01-01T00:00:00.000Z",
  "key" : 1577836800000,
  "doc_count" : 5
},
{
  "key_as_string" : "2021-01-01T00:00:00.000Z",
  "key" : 1609459200000,
  "doc_count" : 6
},
{
  "key_as_string" : "2022-01-01T00:00:00.000Z",
  "key" : 1640995200000,
  "doc_count" : 3
}
...
```

Each key (expressed as `key_as_string`) represents a year: 2020, 2021, and 2022. As the results show, five books were released in 2020, six in 2021, and three in 2022.

INTERVAL SETUP FOR THE DATE HISTOGRAM

In listing 13.11, we set the interval to `year` in the `calendar_interval` attribute. In addition to `calendar_interval`, there's another type of interval: `fixed_interval`. We can set it as a calendar interval or a fixed interval.

The *calendar interval* (declared as `calendar_interval`) is calendar-aware, meaning the hours and days in a month are adjusted according to the daylight settings of the calendar. The following units are acceptable values: `year`, `quarter`, `month`, `week`, `day`, `hour`, `minute`, `second`, and `millisecond`. They can also be represented as single units like `1y`, `1q`, `1M`, `1w`, `1d`, `1h`, and `1m`, respectively. For example, we can write the query in listing 13.11 as `"calendar_interval": "1y"` instead of using `"year"`.

Note that we can't use multiples like 5y (five years) or 4q (four quarters) when setting the interval using calendar_interval. For example, setting the interval as "calendar_interval": "4q" results in a parser exception: "The supplied interval [4q] can not be parsed as a calendar interval".

The *fixed interval* (fixed_interval) lets us set time intervals as a fixed number of units, such as 365d (365 days) or 12h (12 hours). We can use these fixed intervals when we don't need to worry about calendar settings. The accepted values are days (d), hours (h), minutes (m), seconds (s), and milliseconds (ms).

Because fixed_interval does not know about the calendar, unlike calendar_interval, there are no units to support month, year, quarter, and so on. These attributes depend on the calendar (every month has a certain number of days). For example, the following listing fetches all the documents for 730 days (2 years).

Listing 13.12   Histogram with a fixed interval of 2 years (730 days)

```
GET books/_search
{
  "size":0,
  "aggs": {
    "release_date_histogram": {
      "date_histogram": {
        "field": "release_date",
        "fixed_interval": "730d"          ◁──┐ Sets a fixed interval
      }                                       │ of 2 years (730 days)
    }
  }
}
```

The query uses a fixed_interval of 730d (2 years). The results show all books in buckets of exactly 730 days:

```
{
  "key_as_string" : "2017-12-20T00:00:00.000Z",
  "key" : 1513728000000,
  "doc_count" : 11
},
{
  "key_as_string" : "2019-12-20T00:00:00.000Z",
  "key" : 1576800000000,
  "doc_count" : 11
},
{
  "key_as_string" : "2021-12-19T00:00:00.000Z",
  "key" : 1639872000000,
  "doc_count" : 3
}
```

If you are curious, run the same query with two different settings: "calendar_interval": "1y" and "fixed_interval": "365d". (The executable code is available with the book's file if you want to experiment with these settings.) After the queries run successfully, check the keys. In the first set of results (with fixed_interval: 730d), the keys start on January 1, 2005 (`"key_as_string"` : `"2005-01-01"`); in the latter (`fixed_interval: 365d`), they start on the first release date, December 23, 2004 (`"key_as_string"` : `"2004-12-23"`). The second bucket adds 365 days from the first release date, yielding December 23, 2005 (`"key_as_string"` : `"2005-12-23"`).

> **NOTE** When we use `fixed_interval`, the range starts from the first docu-
> ment's available date. Going forward, the `fixed_interval` is added to that.
> For example, if the `publish_date` of a document is 25-12-2020 and we set the
> interval as "`month`", the range starts with 25-12-2020 and goes to 25-01-2021,
> 25-02-2021, and so on.

13.3.2 *Child-level aggregations*

We looked at categorizing data into date buckets in the last section. In addition to creating buckets with the respective ranges, we may want to aggregate data inside those
buckets. For example, we may want to find the average rating of a book for each
bucket.

To satisfy such requirements, we can use a *sub-aggregation*: an aggregation that
works on the bucket's data. With bucketing aggregations, support for both metric and
bucket aggregations is applied at the child level. The following listing fetches books
released yearly plus the average rating for each bucket.

Listing 13.13   Average metric on books categorized per year

```
GET books/_search
{
  "size":0,
  "aggs": {
    "release_date_histogram": {          ◁──   The bucketing histogram that
      "date_histogram": {                      categorizes books by year
        "field": "release_date",
        "calendar_interval": "1y"
      },
      "aggs": {                                Names the sub-aggregation
        "avg_rating_per_bucket": {
          "avg": {                     ◁──     Applies a single-value metric
            "field": "amazon_rating"           across individual buckets
          }
        }
      }
    }
  }
}
```

There are two blocks of aggregation, one woven inside the other. The outer aggregation (`release_date_histogram`) produces the data as a histogram based on the calendar interval of one year. The results of this aggregation are then fed to the next level
of aggregation: the inner aggregation (`avg_rating_per_bucket`). The inner aggregation considers each bucket as its scope and runs the average (`avg`) aggregation on that

data. This produces the average rating of a book per bucket. Figure 13.3 shows the expected result from the aggregation execution.

```
{
  "key_as_string" : "2013-01-01T00:00:00.000Z",
  "key" : 1356998400000,
  "doc_count" : 2,
  "avg_rating_per_bucket" : {
    "value" : 4.200000047683716
  }
},
{
  "key_as_string" : "2014-01-01T00:00:00.000Z",
  "key" : 1388534400000,
  "doc_count" : 6,
  "avg_rating_per_bucket" : {
    "value" : 4.383333285649617
  }
}
```

Figure 13.3 **Finding the average rating per bucket (sub-aggregation)**

The keys are the dates that correspond to the calendar year for documents in that bucket. The notable thing about this query is that an additional object in the bucket, avg_rating_per_bucket, consists of the average book rating.

13.3.3 *Custom range aggregations*

A histogram provides an automatic set of ranges for given intervals. Sometimes we want to segregate data into a range that is not dictated by a strict interval (for example, classifying people into three groups by age: 18 to 21, 22 to 49, and 50+). The standardized interval does not meet this requirement. All we need is a mechanism to customize the ranges—and that's what we use the range aggregation for.

The range aggregation aggregates documents in a user-defined range. Let's look at it in action by writing a query to fetch books that fall in two categories of ratings: above and below the value 4 (1 to 4 and 4 to 5).

Listing 13.14 Classifying books into two baskets

```
GET books/_search
{
  "size": 0,
  "aggs": {
    "book_ratings_range": {          Declares the range
      "range": {                  ⟵  aggregation
        "field": "amazon_rating",  ⟵──┐ Applies the aggregation
        "ranges": [                     to this field
          {
            "from": 1,
            "to": 4
          },
          {
```

Sets the customized ranges ⟶

```
            "from": 4,
            "to":  5
        }

    ]
  }
 }
 }
 }
}
```

The query constructs an aggregation with a custom range defined by an array (`ranges`) with only two buckets: from 1 to 4 and from 4 to 5. The following response indicates that two books fall into the 1 to 4 rating and the rest into the 4 to 5 rating:

```
"aggregations" : {
  "book_ratings_range" : {
    "buckets" : [
    {
      "key" : "1.0-4.0",
      "from" : 1.0,
      "to" : 4.0,
      "doc_count" : 2
    },
    {
      "key" : "4.0-5.0",
      "from" : 4.0,
      "to" : 5.0,
      "doc_count" : 35
    }
   ]
  }
 }
```

The `range` aggregation is a slight variation of the `histogram` aggregation and well-suited for special or custom ranges that a user may need. Of course, if you want to go with the system-provided categories and don't need customization, a histogram is suitable.

> **NOTE** The `range` aggregation is made up of `from` and `to` attributes. The `from` value is included and the `to` value is excluded when calculating the bucket items that fit this range.

By the same principle, we can classify IP addresses in a custom range using a dedicated `ip_range` aggregation. The next listing shows that. (Note that this code is for demonstrative purposes only—we do not have a `networks` index primed with data consisting of the `localhost_ip_address` field.)

Listing 13.15   Classifying IP addresses in to two baskets

```
GET networks/_search
{
  "aggs": {
```

```
                   "my_ip_addresses_custom_range": {
                     "ip_range": {
                       "field": "localhost_ip_address",
                       "ranges": [
                         {
                           "to": "192.168.0.10",
                           "from": "192.168.0.20"
                         },
                     {
                           "to": "192.168.0.20",
                           "from": "192.168.0.100"


                         }
                       ]
                     }
                   }
                 }
               }
```

The ip_range bucketing segregates certain IPs into given buckets.

Defines the custom range of IP addresses that are expected to be categorized

Runs the range aggregation on this field (must be of type ip)

As you can see from this sample aggregation, we can segregate IP addresses based on our custom ranges. The query produces two ranges: one that includes `192.168.0.10` to `192.168.0.20` and the second with `192.168.0.20` to `192.168.0.100`.

13.3.4 The terms aggregation

When we want to retrieve an aggregated count of a certain field, such as authors and their book count, the `terms` aggregations comes in handy. The `terms` aggregation collects data in buckets for each occurrence of the term. For example, in the following query, the `terms` aggregation creates a bucket for each author and the number of books they've written.

Listing 13.16 Aggregated count of books by author

```
GET books/_search?size=0
{
  "aggs": {
    "author_book_count": {
      "terms": {
        "field": "author.keyword"
      }
    }
  }
}
```

Declares the terms aggregation type

Applies the aggregation to this field

The query uses the `terms` aggregation to fetch the list of authors in the `books` index and their book count. The response indicates that `key` is the author, and `doc_count` shows the number of books for each author:

```
"buckets" : [
  {
    "key" : "Herbert Schildt",
    "doc_count" : 2
  },
```

```
{
  "key" : "Mike McGrath",
  "doc_count" : 2
},
{
  "key" : "Terry Norton",
  "doc_count" : 2
},
{
  "key" : "Adam Scott",
  "doc_count" : 1
}
..
]}
```

Each bucket represents an author with the number of books the author wrote. By default, the `terms` aggregation only returns the top 10 aggregations, but we can tweak this return size by setting the `size` parameter, as the following listing shows.

Listing 13.17 A `terms` query with a custom size

```
GET books/_search?size=0
{
  "aggs": {
    "author_book_count": {
      "terms": {
        "field": "author.keyword",
        "size": 25      ◁─────┐  Sets the
      }                       │  aggregation size
    }
  }
}
```

Here, setting `size` to 25 fetches 25 aggregations (25 authors and their book counts).

13.3.5 *The multi-terms aggregation*

The `multi_terms` aggregation resembles the `terms` aggregation with an additional feature: it aggregates data based on multiple keys. For example, rather than just finding the number of books written by an author, we can find the number of books with a specific title and author. The following listing gets the author and their book's title(s) as a map.

Listing 13.18 Aggregation for authors and their book titles as a map

```
GET books/_search?size=0
{
  "aggs": {
    "author_title_map": {    │  Declares the
      "multi_terms": {   ◁───┘  aggregation type        The set of terms with which
        "terms": [                       ◁──────────────  to form the author/title map
          {
```

```
          "field": "author.keyword"
        },
        {
          "field": "title.keyword"
        }
      ]
    }
  }
}
```

As you can see, `multi_terms` accepts a set of terms. In the example, we expect Elasticsearch to return a book count using `author/title` keys. The response indicates that we were able to retrieve this information:

```
{
  "key" : [
    "Adam Scott",
    "JavaScript Everywhere"
  ],
  "key_as_string" : "Adam Scott|JavaScript Everywhere",
  "doc_count" : 1
},
{
  "key" : [
    "Al Sweigart",
    "Automate The Boring Stuff With Python"
  ],
  "key_as_string" : "Al Sweigart|Automate The Boring Stuff With Python",
  "doc_count" : 1
},
...
```

This response shows two variations of the `key` representation: as a set of fields (both `author` and `title`) and as a string (`key_as_string`), which simply stitches together the fields with a pipe (`|`) delimiter. The `doc_count` indicates the number of documents (books) in the index for that key.

If you are curious, rerun the query in listing 13.18, this time using the tags and the title as terms. You should get multiple books under the same tags (the code is available with the book's files).

Before we discuss the third type of aggregations—pipeline aggregations—we need to understand the concept of parent and sibling aggregations. These form the basis of pipeline aggregations. We discuss parent and sibling aggregations in the next section and then jump to pipeline aggregations.

13.4 Parent and sibling aggregations

Broadly speaking, we can group aggregations into two types: *parent* and *sibling* aggregations. You may find them a bit confusing, so let's see what they are and how they can be used.

13.4.1 Parent aggregations

Parent aggregations work on input from the child aggregation to produce new buckets, which are then added to the existing buckets. Take a look at the following code listing.

Listing 13.19 Parent aggregations

```
GET coffee_sales/_search
{
  "size": 0,
  "aggs": {
    "coffee_sales_by_day": {
      "date_histogram": {
        "field": "date",
        "calendar_interval": "1d"
      },
      "aggs": {
        "cappuccino_sales": {
          "sum": {
            "field": "sales.cappuccino"
          }
        }
      }
    }
  }
}
```

As figure 13.4 shows, the cappuccino_sales aggregation is created as a child of the parent coffee_sales_by_day aggregation. It is at the same level as date_histogram.

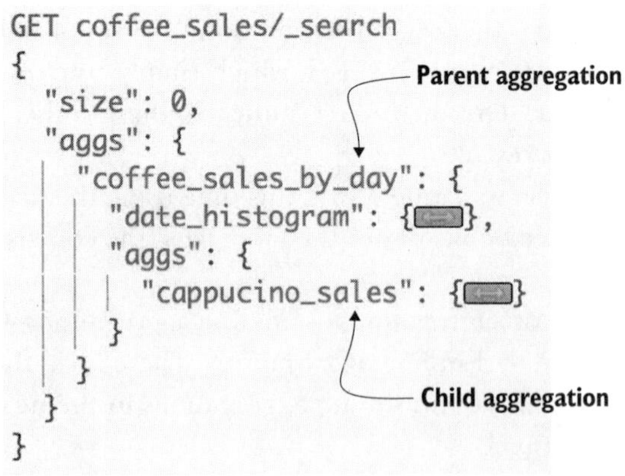

Figure 13.4 Parent aggregations visualized

Such an aggregation produces buckets inside the existing bucket. Figure 13.5 shows this result: the cappuccino_sales aggregation produces new buckets that are tucked under the main date_histogram bucket.

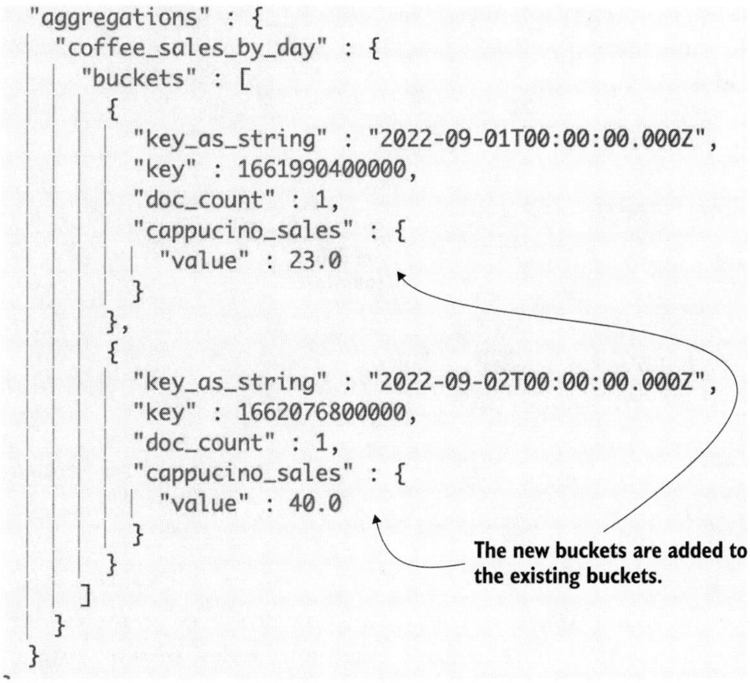

```
"aggregations" : {
  "coffee_sales_by_day" : {
    "buckets" : [
      {
        "key_as_string" : "2022-09-01T00:00:00.000Z",
        "key" : 1661990400000,
        "doc_count" : 1,
        "cappucino_sales" : {
          "value" : 23.0
        }
      },
      {
        "key_as_string" : "2022-09-02T00:00:00.000Z",
        "key" : 1662076800000,
        "doc_count" : 1,
        "cappucino_sales" : {
          "value" : 40.0
        }
      }
    ]
  }
}
```

The new buckets are added to
the existing buckets.

Figure 13.5 New buckets created inside existing buckets

13.4.2 Sibling aggregations

Sibling aggregations produce a new aggregation at the same level. The following listing creates an aggregation with two queries at the same level (thus, we call them
siblings).

Listing 13.20 Sibling aggregation in action

```
GET coffee_sales/_search
{
  "size": 0,
  "aggs": {
    "coffee_date_histogram": {
      "date_histogram": {
        "field": "date",
        "calendar_interval": "1d"
      }
    },
    "total_sale_of_americanos":{
      "sum": {
        "field": "sales.americano"
      }
    }
  }
}
```

The `coffee_date_histogram` and `total_sale_of_americanos` aggregations are defined at the same level. If we take a snapshot of the query with the aggregations collapsed, they look like figure 13.6.

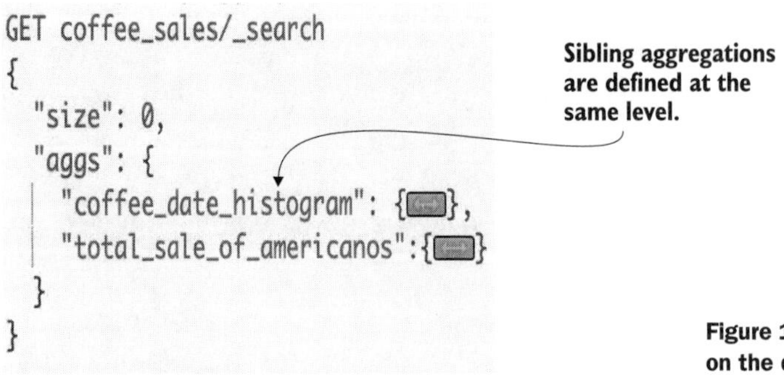

```
GET coffee_sales/_search
{
  "size": 0,
  "aggs": {
    "coffee_date_histogram": {▢},
    "total_sale_of_americanos":{▢}
  }
}
```

Sibling aggregations are defined at the same level.

Figure 13.6   Sibling aggregations on the query side

When we execute sibling queries, new buckets are produced; however, unlike with parent aggregations, where buckets are created and added to the existing buckets, with sibling aggregations, new aggregations or new buckets are created at the root aggregation level. The query in listing 13.20 produces the aggregated results in figure 13.7 with newly created buckets for each sibling aggregator.

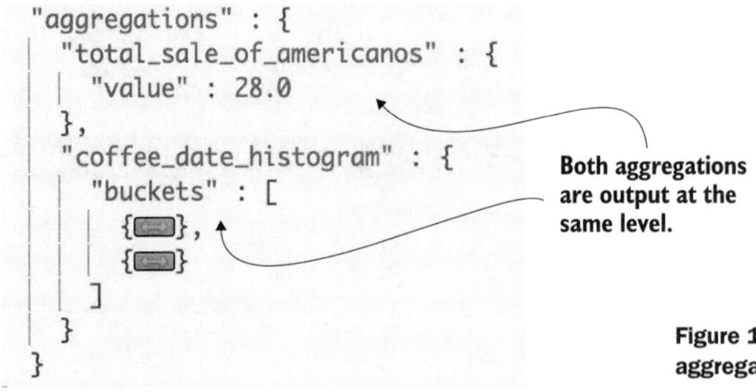

```
"aggregations" : {
  "total_sale_of_americanos" : {
    "value" : 28.0
  },
  "coffee_date_histogram" : {
    "buckets" : [
      {▢},
      {▢}
    ]
  }
}
```

Both aggregations are output at the same level.

Figure 13.7   Sibling queries output aggregations at the same level

13.5   *Pipeline aggregations*

In the last few sections, we looked at creating aggregations by generating metrics on data, bucketing data, or both. But sometimes we want to chain multiple aggregations to produce another metric level or a bucket. For example, say that we want to find the maximum and minimum of all the buckets produced during an aggregation or find the moving average of a sliding window of data, such as the hourly average sales during a cyber-Monday sale. Metric and bucket aggregations won't allow us to chain aggregations.

Elasticsearch provides a third set of aggregations called *pipeline aggregations* that permit aggregation chaining. These aggregations work on the output of other aggregations rather than individual documents or fields of documents. That is, we create a pipeline aggregation by passing the output of a bucket or metric aggregation. Before we get our hands dirty, let's look at the types of pipelines, their syntax, and other details.

13.5.1 Pipeline aggregation types

Broadly speaking, we can group pipeline aggregations into two types: *parent* and *sibling*. As explained in section 13.4, parent pipeline aggregations work on the input from the child aggregation to produce new buckets or new aggregations, which are then added to existing buckets. Sibling pipeline aggregations produce a new aggregation at the same level.

13.5.2 Sample data

We look at the parent and sibling aggregation types in detail as we execute some examples in this section. We use the `coffee_sales` data set for running pipeline aggregations. Follow the usual process of indexing data using the `_bulk` API, as in the following listing. You can fetch the sample data from the book's repository on GitHub (http://mng.bz/6D45) or the book's website.

Listing 13.21 Indexing data using the `_bulk` API

```
PUT coffee_sales/_bulk
{"index":{"_id":"1"}}
{"date":"2022-09-01","sales":{"cappuccino":23,"latte":12,"americano":9,
➡ "tea":7},"price":{"cappuccino":2.50,"latte":2.40,"americano":2.10,
➡ "tea":1.50}}
{"index":{"_id":"2"}}
{ "date":"2022-09-02","sales":{"cappuccino":40,"latte":16,"americano":19,
➡ "tea":15},"price":{"cappuccino":2.50,"latte":2.40,"americano":2.10,
➡ "tea":1.50}}
```

Executing this query indexes two sales documents into our `coffee_sales` index. The next step is to create pipeline aggregations to help us understand them in detail.

13.5.3 Syntax for pipeline aggregations

As mentioned earlier, pipeline aggregations work on the input from other aggregations. So, when declaring a pipeline, we must provide a reference to those metric or bucket aggregations. For our example, we can set a reference as `buckets_path`, which consists of aggregation names with an appropriate separator in the query. The `buckets_path` variable is a mechanism to identify the input to the pipeline query.

Figure 13.8 shows the parent aggregation `cappuccino_sales`. The pipeline aggregation `cumulative_sum`, as defined by `total_cappuccinos`, refers to the parent aggregation via `buckets_path`, which is set with a value referring to the name of the parent aggregation.

```
GET coffee_sales/_search
{
  "size": 0,
  "aggs": {
    "sales_by_coffee": {
      "date_histogram": {▭},
      "aggs": {
        "cappuccino_sales": {
          "sum": {▭}
        },
        "total_cappuccinos": {
          "cumulative_sum": {
            "buckets_path": "cappuccino_sales"
          }
        }
      }
    }
  }
}
```

The `cumulative_sum` **refers to the**
parent aggregation (defined by
`cappuccino_sales`**) by setting**
`buckets_path` **to** `cappuccino_sales`

Figure 13.8   Parent pipeline
aggregation `buckets_path` **setting**

The `buckets_path` setting becomes a bit more involved if the aggregation in play is a sibling aggregation. The `max_bucket` in the aggregation in figure 13.9 is a sibling pipeline aggregation (defined under the `highest_cappuccino_sales_bucket`

```
GET coffee_sales/_search
{▭}
```

```
GET coffee_sales/_search
{
  "size": 0,                    Sibling aggregations
  "aggs": {
    "sales_by_coffee": {
      "date_histogram": {▭},
      "aggs": {
        "cappuccino_sales": {▭}
      }
    },
    "highest_cappuccino_sales_bucket":{
      "max_bucket": {
        "buckets_path": "sales_by_coffee>cappuccino_sales"
      }
    }
  }
}
```

The `max_bucket` **(a sibling aggregation) refers to**
the constituents of sibling aggregations (defined by
`sales_by_coffee` **and** `cappuccino_sales`**) by**
setting `buckets_path` **to**
`sales_by_coffee>cappuccino_sales.`

The **">" operator is the aggregation**
separator.

The `buckets_path` **for a**
sibling pipeline aggregation

Figure 13.9
Sibling pipeline
aggregation
`buckets_path`
setting

aggregation), which calculates the result by taking input from the other aggregations set by the `buckets_path` variable. In this case, it is fed by the aggregation called `cappuccino_sales`, which lives under the `sales_by_coffee` sibling aggregation.

If you are puzzled about `buckets_path` or pipeline aggregations, hang in there. We look at them in practice in the next few sections.

13.5.4 Available pipeline aggregations

Knowing whether a pipeline aggregation is a parent or sibling helps us easily develop these aggregations. Tables 13.1 and 13.2 list the pipeline aggregations and their definitions.

Table 13.1 Parent pipeline aggregations

Name	Description
Buckets script (`buckets_script`)	Executes a script on multi-bucket aggregations
Bucket selector (`bucket_selector`)	Executes a script to select the current bucket for its place in the multi-bucket aggregation
Bucket sort (`bucket_sort`)	Sorts the buckets
Cumulative cardinality (`cumulative_cardinality`)	Checks recently added unique (cumulative cardinality) values
Cumulative sum (`cumulative_sum`)	Finds the cumulative sum of a metric
Derivative (`derivative`)	Finds the derivative of a metric in a histogram or date histogram
Inference (`inference`)	Finds the inference on a pretrained model
Moving function (`moving_function`)	Executes a custom script on a sliding window
Moving percentiles (`moving_percentiles`)	Similar to `moving_function`, except it calculates in percentiles
Normalize (`normalize`)	Calculates the normalized value of a given bucket
Serial difference (`serial_diff`)	Calculates the serial difference on a metric

Table 13.2 Sibling pipeline aggregations

Name	Description
Average (`avg_bucket`)	Calculates the average value of the sibling metric
Bucket count (`bucket_count_ks_test`)	Calculates the Kolmogorov–Smirnov statistic over a distribution
Bucket correlation (`bucket_correlation`)	Executes a correlation function
Change point (`change_point`)	Detects the dips and changes in a metric
Extended stats (`extended_stats`)	Calculates multiple statistical functions

Table 13.2 Sibling pipeline aggregations *(continued)*

Name	Description
Max bucket (`max_bucket`)	Finds the maximum-valued bucket
Min bucket (`min_bucket`)	Finds the minimum-valued bucket
Percentiles bucket (`percentiles_bucket`)	Calculates the percentiles of a metric
Stats bucket (`stats_bucket`)	Calculates common stats for a metric
Sum bucket (`sum_bucket`)	Calculates the sum of a metric

We can't look at all of the pipeline aggregations in this section, but we can review the basics of pipeline aggregations by working through a few common ones. To begin, suppose we want to find cumulative coffee sales: how many cappuccinos are sold daily, for example. Instead of a daily score, we want the total number of cappuccinos sold from the first day of operation, accumulated daily. The `cumulative_sum` aggregation is a handy parent pipeline aggregation that keeps a sum total for the current day, tracks the sum for the next day, and so on. Let's see it in action.

13.5.5 *The cumulative_sum parent aggregation*

To collect the cumulative sum of coffees sold, we can chain coffee sales by day and pass the results to the `cumulative_sum` pipeline aggregation. The following listing fetches the cumulative sum of cappuccinos sold.

Listing 13.22 Cumulative sales (sum) of cappuccinos sold daily

```
GET coffee_sales/_search
{
  "size": 0,
  "aggs": {
    "sales_by_coffee": {
      "date_histogram": {
        "field": "date",
        "calendar_interval": "1d"
      },
      "aggs": {
        "cappuccino_sales": {
          "sum": {
            "field": "sales.cappuccino"
          }
        },
        "total_cappuccinos": {
          "cumulative_sum": {          ◁──┐ Parent aggregation that
            "buckets_path": "cappuccino_sales"   calculates the cumulative
          }                                      total of cappuccino sales
        }
      }
    }
  }
}
```

The `sales_by_coffee` aggregation is a `date_histogram` that provides all the dates and documents that fall within those dates (so far, we only have two dates). We also have a sub-aggregation (`cappuccino_sales`) that sums the sales figures for cappuccinos for that bucket.

The bold portion of the code is the parent pipeline aggregation (`total_cappuccinos`). It fetches the cumulative cappuccino sales per day. This is called a parent pipeline aggregation because it is applied in the scope of its parent, the `cappuccino_sales` aggregation. Here is the result of the aggregation:

```
"aggregations" : {
    "sales_by_coffee" : {
        "buckets" : [
            {
                "key_as_string" : "2022-09-01T00:00:00.000Z",
                "key" : 1661990400000,
                "doc_count" : 1,
                "cappuccino_sales" : {
                    "value" : 23.0
                },
                "total_cappuccinos" : {
                    "value" : 23.0
                }
            },
            {
                "key_as_string" : "2022-09-02T00:00:00.000Z",
                "key" : 1662076800000,
                "doc_count" : 1,
                "cappuccino_sales" : {
                    "value" : 40.0
                },
                "total_cappuccinos" : {
                    "value" : 63.0
                }
            }
        ]
    }
}
```

Let's look at the result for a moment. The buckets are segregated by dates (check `key_as_string`) due to the `date_histogram` aggregation at the top of the query. We also created a sub-aggregation (`cappuccino_sales`) that fetches the number of cappuccinos sold daily (per bucket). The final part of the result is the cumulatively totaled sum of cappuccinos (`total_cappuccinos`) added to the existing bucket. Notice that on day 2, the total cappuccinos were 63 (23 from the first day and 40 from the second day).

While the cumulative sum total of cappuccinos is at an existing parent bucket level, finding the maximum or minimum coffees sold in buckets is at a sibling level. For that, we need to create an aggregation at the same level as the main aggregation, which is why the aggregation is called a sibling. Suppose we want to determine the day when the most cappuccinos were sold or, conversely, the fewest cappuccinos were sold. To do this, we need the pipeline aggregation's `max_bucket` and `min_bucket` aggregations, which the next section covers.

13.5.6 *The max_bucket and min_bucket sibling pipeline aggregations*

Elasticsearch provides a pipeline aggregation called `max_bucket` to fetch the top bucket from the set of buckets fetched from the other aggregations. Remember, a pipeline aggregation takes the input of other aggregations to calculate its own aggregation.

THE MAX_BUCKET AGGREGATION

The query in the following listing enhances the aggregation we performed in the last section. It does this by adding a `max_bucket` function.

Listing 13.23   Pipeline aggregation to find to sales of cappuccinos

```
GET coffee_sales/_search
{
  "size": 0,
  "aggs": {
    "sales_by_coffee": {
      "date_histogram": {
        "field": "date",
        "calendar_interval": "1d"
      },
      "aggs": {
        "cappuccino_sales": {
          "sum": {
            "field": "sales.cappuccino"
          }
        }
      }
    },
    "highest_cappuccino_sales_bucket":{
      "max_bucket": {
        "buckets_path": "sales_by_coffee>cappuccino_sales"
      }
    }
  }
}
```

As you can see in the bold code, `highest_cappuccino_sales_bucket` is the custom name given to the sibling pipeline aggregation we are about to perform. We declare the `max_bucket` aggregation at the same level as the `sales_by_coffee` aggregation, so it is called a sibling aggregation. This expects a `buckets_path`, which combines the aggregations `sales_by_coffee` and `cappuccino_sales`. (These two resulted from bucket and metric aggregations on the data.) When the query is executed, we get this response:

```
"aggregations" : {
  "sales_by_coffee" : {
  "buckets" : [{
    "key_as_string" : "2022-09-01T00:00:00.000Z",
```

```
            "key" : 1661990400000,
            "doc_count" : 1,
            "cappuccino_sales" : {
            "value" : 23.0
        },{
            "key_as_string" : "2022-09-02T00:00:00.000Z",
            "key" : 1662076800000,
            "doc_count" : 1,
            "cappuccino_sales" : {
                "value" : 40.0
            }
        }]
    },
    "highest_cappuccino_sales_bucket" : {
        "value" : 40.0,
        "keys" : [
            "2022-09-02T00:00:00.000Z"
        ]
    }
}
```

The bold portion contains the `highest_cappuccino_sales_bucket` information. The date `2022-09-02` (September 2, 2022) is when the most cappuccinos were sold.

THE MIN_BUCKET AGGREGATION

We can also fetch the days when fewer cappuccinos were sold. To do this, we need to use the `min_bucket` pipeline aggregation. Replace the highlighted code in listing 13.23 with the code in the following snippet:

```
..
"lowest_cappuccino_sales_bucket":{
    "min_bucket": {
        "buckets_path": "sales_by_coffee>cappuccino_sales"
    }
}
```

The result shows that the fewest cappuccinos were sold on September 1, 2022:

```
"lowest_cappuccino_sales_bucket" : {
    "value" : 23.0,
    "keys" : [
        "2022-09-01T00:00:00.000Z"
    ]
}
```

There are several other pipeline aggregations like the metric and bucket aggregations. Although it is impractical to discuss all of them in this chapter, the book's code samples include most of the aggregations. Also check the official documentation when you work with a particular aggregation. Here's the link to pipeline aggregations: http://mng.bz/XNzE.

And that's it for aggregations! Let's wrap it up here.

Summary

- Whereas a search finds answers in the amassed data based on a search criterion, an aggregation compiles patterns, insights, and information for data collected by organizations.
- Elasticsearch allows us to perform nested and sibling aggregations on data.
- Elasticsearch classifies aggregations into three types: metrics, buckets, and pipelines.
- Metric aggregations fetch single-value metrics such as `avg`, `min` and `max`, `sum`, and so on.
- Bucket aggregations classify data into various buckets based on a bucketing strategy. With a bucketing strategy, we can ask Elasticsearch to split data into buckets as needed.
- We can either let Elasticsearch create predefined buckets based on the interval we provide or create custom ranges:
  - If the interval is 10 for an age group, for example, Elasticsearch splits data into steps of 10.
  - If we want to create a range like 10 to 30 or 30 to 100, where the interval differs, we can create a custom range.
- Pipeline aggregations work on the output from other metric and bucket aggregations to create new aggregations or new buckets.

Administration 14

This chapter covers

- Horizontally scaling the cluster
- Internode communication
- Shards and replica sizing
- Working with snapshots and restoration
- Advanced configuration
- Understanding the master role in a cluster

So far, we've seen the inner workings of Elasticsearch, including its excellent queries and other features. We haven't bothered with advanced configurations like how nodes communicate with each other, how big shards need to be, and what settings to change to modify the Kibana port. In this chapter, we discuss these administrative features. We address some of them by using the queries we created while running the search server.

One powerful feature of Elasticsearch is its ability to scale up the server to provide petabytes of data. There is no complexity in setting this up other than procuring additional nodes. We cover how to scale the cluster in the first part of this chapter. We also experiment with the sizing of shards and see why allocating more replicas alleviates read performance problems.

We then move on to discuss how nodes communicate internally and form a cluster. We look at network settings and their importance in the second section of the chapter.

Any server with transactional and configuration data should be backed up regularly to avoid losing data in unforeseen circumstances. Elasticsearch provides functionalities to snapshot data at any time or as regularly as we wish and restore it as needed. We discuss the sophisticated snapshot and restoration functionalities in detail.

We also look at the advanced configuration for tweaking Elasticsearch properties. We examine the commonly used elasticsearch.yml configuration file and its contents, and we discuss how to change network settings, bump up the heap memory, and check the logs of a component at a trace level.

Finally, we discuss the role of the cluster master and how the cluster makes decisions based on a quorum, along with other details. We look at the split-brain scenario to understand the minimum number of master-eligible nodes required in a healthy cluster.

Productionizing Elasticsearch is an involved and expert task. Elasticsearch has many moving parts, and getting a handle on each is a huge task—but not impossible. While most of the features of Elasticsearch work out of the box, it is not enough to move the application to production; administrative tasks must also be taken care of. Many options must be tweaked and tuned to get Elasticsearch (or Elastic Stack) to a production state. Covering all these administrative tasks in one chapter would be tedious and impractical. However, I've included the common and important administrative functions that most developers and administrators must understand. Refer to the appropriate documentation for deep dives into functions not covered in this chapter. Let's start by learning about the scaling of clusters.

14.1 Scaling the cluster

Elasticsearch clusters can scale up to any number of nodes, from a single node to hundreds, based on the use case, data, and business requirements. Although we may work with a single-node cluster on a personal machine when learning about Elasticsearch, we seldom have a single-node cluster in production.

One reason we chose Elasticsearch is its resilience and fault-tolerance capabilities. We don't want to lose data when a node crashes. Fortunately, Elasticsearch can cope with hardware failures and recover from them as soon as the hardware is back online.

Choosing the cluster size is an important IT strategy for any organization, and multiple variables, factors, and inputs go into sizing Elasticsearch clusters for our data needs. Although we can add resources (memory or new nodes) to an existing cluster, it is important to forecast such demands.

In this section, we learn how to size and scale the cluster. We can add nodes to an existing cluster to increase read throughput or indexing performance. We can also downsize clusters by removing nodes, perhaps because the demand for indexing or read throughput has declined.

14.1.1 *Adding nodes to the cluster*

Each node in a cluster essentially runs an instance of Elasticsearch on a dedicated server. Nothing is stopping you from creating multiple nodes on a single server, but doing so defeats the purpose of data resiliency: if that server crashes, you'll lose all nodes on that server.

> **NOTE** It is advisable to deploy and run Elasticsearch on a dedicated server with as much computing power as your requirements demand, rather than bundling it with other applications—especially applications that are resource hungry.

When we launch an Elasticsearch server for the first time, a cluster is formed with a single node. This *single-node cluster* is the typical setup in development environments for testing and trying out products. Figure 14.1 shows a single-node cluster.

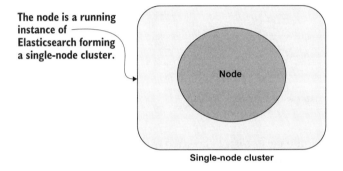

The node is a running instance of Elasticsearch forming a single-node cluster.

Single-node cluster

Figure 14.1 Single-node cluster

When we bring up more nodes (provided all nodes are christened with the same cluster name), they all join to make a *multi-node cluster*. Let's see how shards are created and distributed across the cluster as we keep adding nodes, from a single node to, say, three nodes.

Suppose we want to create an index called `chats` with one shard and one replica each. To do this, we need to define the number of shards and replicas during index creation by configuring the settings on the index.

Listing 14.1 Creating the `chats` index

```
PUT chats
{
  "settings": {
    "number_of_shards": 1,
    "number_of_replicas": 1
  }
}
```

This script creates the chats index with one primary shard on a single node. Elastic-search doesn't create the replica of this index on the same node where the primary shard exists. Indeed, there's no point in creating a backup drive in the same location as the main drive. Figure 14.2 shows this (a shard is created, but a replica isn't).

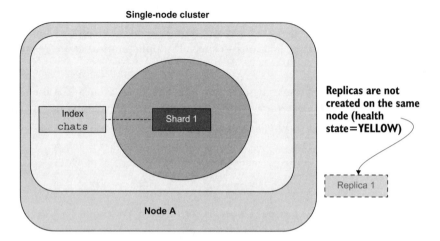

Figure 14.2   Single-node cluster with no replica created

If replicas aren't created, the cluster isn't classified as being in a healthy state. We can use the cluster health API to get a high-level view of the cluster state. The GET _cluster/health call fetches the health of the cluster and outputs it in a JSON format that details the unassigned shards, the state of the cluster, the number of nodes and data nodes, and so on. But what do we mean by cluster health?

14.1.2 *Cluster health*

As we discussed in chapter 3, Elasticsearch uses a simple traffic light system to let us know the state of the cluster: GREEN, RED, and YELLOW. When we first create an index on a single-node server, its health is YELLOW because the replica shards are not yet assigned (unless we purposely set replicas to zero on all indexes on this node, which is possible but is an anti-pattern). If needed, refer to section 3.2.5 for a refresher on the shard traffic light health system. Figure 14.3 is repeated from chapter 3 and defines the health of a cluster based on the shard assignments.

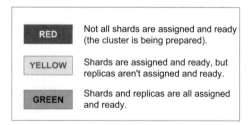

Figure 14.3   Representing the health of a cluster using traffic lights

Understanding this, we can ask Elasticsearch to explain why the cluster is unhealthy (or why shards are unassigned). We can query the server using the cluster allocation API for an explanation of why a shard is in its current state. The following query, for example, asks for an explanation about the `chats` index.

Listing 14.2 Asking the cluster for a shard failure explanation

```
GET _cluster/allocation/explain
{
  "index": "chats",
  "shard": 0,
  "primary": false
}
```

This query returns a detailed explanation of the state of this index. We already know the replica won't be created or assigned in a single-node server, right? To verify, let's ask the cluster if that's the case. The following snippet shows a condensed response from the server for the query in listing 14.2:

```
{
  "index" : "chats",
  "shard" : 0,
  "primary" : false,
  "current_state" : "unassigned",
  "allocate_explanation" : "cannot allocate because
➥ allocation is not permitted to any of the nodes",
  "node_allocation_decisions" : [{
    ...
    "deciders" : [{
      "decider" : "same_shard",
      "explanation" : "a copy of this shard is already allocated to
      ➥ this node ..]"}
    ]
  ...
}
```

The `current_state` of the `chats` index mentioned in the returned response says it is `unassigned`. The response explains that the server can't allocate a copy of the shard because of the `same_shard` decider. (Check the value of the `deciders` array in the previous snippet.)

The node in the cluster must fill different roles by default: `master`, `ingest`, `data`, `ml`, `transform`, and others. We can, however, specify the node's roles by setting the `node.roles` property with the appropriate roles in the elasticsearch.yml file.

We can index data into our `chats` index and perform search queries on this single node instance. Because there are no replicas, the risk of losing data and creating performance bottlenecks arises. To mitigate this risk, we can add node(s) to expand the cluster.

Adding a node is as simple as booting up Elasticsearch on a different machine but in the same network with the same `cluster.name` (a property in the elasticsearch.yml file), provided security is disabled.

> **WARNING** Since version 8.0, by default, Elasticsearch installations enable security, where `xpack.security.enabled` is `true`. When you bring up the Elasticsearch server for the first time, it generates the required keys and tokens and instructs you about the steps to be followed to obtain successful Kibana connectivity. If you are experimenting with Elasticsearch on your local machine, you can disable security, but I strongly recommend not jumping into production with an unsecured setup by setting the property `xpack.security.enabled` to `false` in the elasticsearch.yml file. An unsecured setup is very dangerous, and you are asking for trouble.

Bringing up a second node helps Elasticsearch create the replica shard on it. As figure 14.4 shows, Elasticsearch instantly creates the replica 1 shard, which is an exact copy of shard 1, when the second node starts and joins the cluster. The contents of shard 1 are synced up to replica 1 immediately, and once they are in sync, any write operations on shard 1 are replicated to replica 1 going forward. The same applies for multiple shards and multiple replicas.

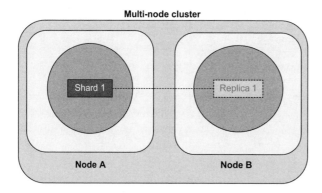

Figure 14.4   The replica shard is created on a second node.

If we add more nodes to the cluster, Elasticsearch scales the cluster elegantly with additional nodes. It automatically distributes the shards and replicas with the addition (or removal) of nodes. Elasticsearch manages everything transparently behind the scenes such that we—ordinary users or administrators—don't have to worry about the mechanics of communication between nodes, how the shards and their data are distributed, and so forth. Figure 14.5 illustrates how a shard (shard 2) is moved to a newly joined second node (thus making a multi-node cluster) and replicas are created.

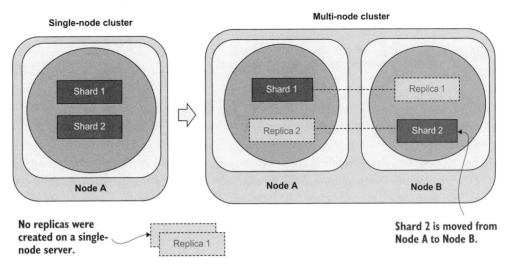

Figure 14.5 A newly joined node gets new shards moved from the single-node cluster.

Should node A crash, replica 1 on node B is instantly promoted to shard 1 and thus goes back to the single-node cluster until the second node is back online. We can keep adding new nodes to the cluster when necessary by bringing up the Elasticsearch server on the new node.

14.1.3 *Increasing read throughput*

Increasing the number of replicas has an added performance benefit. The replicas increase read throughput: reads (queries) can be served by the replicas while the shards do the indexing operations. If an application is read-intensive (that is, an application gets higher volumes of search queries than volumes of data that it indexes, typically an e-commerce application), increasing the number of replicas alleviates the load on the application.

As each replica is an exact copy of the shard, we can split the application's shards into two categories: *primary shards* deal with data, and *replica shards* deal with the read side of data. When a query comes from the client, the coordinator node diverts that request onto the read nodes for an answer. Thus, adding more replicas to the index helps improve read throughputs. Note the memory implications, however: because each replica is an exact copy of the shard, we need to size the cluster accordingly (see section 14.3).

To increase the replicas (and thus read throughput) to counter read-query performance bottlenecks, one strategy is to update the `number_of_replicas` setting on the live index. This is a dynamic setting that we can tweak even when the index is live and in production. For example, suppose we add 10 nodes to our 5-node cluster, with five shards to counteract read-query performance problems that are bringing the server to its knees. As the following listing shows, we can increase the replica count to increase the replica setting on the live index.

Listing 14.3   Increasing the replica count on a live index

```
PUT chats/_settings
{
  "number_of_replicas": 10
}
```

These additional replicas are per shard and are created on the newly formed nodes with data copied over to them. Now that we have additional replicas in our armory, they handle any read queries efficiently. It is Elasticsearch's responsibility to route client requests to the replicas, thus improving the application's search and query performance.

> **NOTE** A quick recap about resizing primary shards: once an index is created and live, we cannot resize it because `number_of_shards` is a static property of the index. If we must change this setting, we must *close* the index, create a new index with the new size, and *re-index* our data from the old index to our new index.

Although increasing read replicas increases read throughput, it strains the cluster's memory and disk space. That's because each replica consumes as many resources as its counterpart (primary shard).

14.2 *Node communication*

Elasticsearch hides the nitty-gritty details of what goes on behind the scenes, from starting the node to creating a cluster, indexing data, backups and snapshots, and querying. Adding nodes scales up the cluster and gives us the benefit of resilience from the start. We worked through a lot of APIs in earlier chapters, and those APIs enable communication between the client and the server. The expected communication medium in this case is an HTTP interface over RESTful APIs. The other side of the coin is communication between nodes: how each node talks to other nodes, how the master makes cluster-wide decisions, and so on. For this, Elasticsearch uses two types of communication:

- The HTTP interface for interactions between clients and nodes using RESTful APIs. (We looked at these when running queries.)
- The transport layer interface for node-to-node communications.

The cluster is exposed on port 9200 for HTTP (or HTTPS) communication by default, although we can change this by tweaking the configuration file (elastic-search.yml). On the other hand, the transport layer is set to port 9300, meaning node-to-node communications happen on that port. Both interfaces are set in the configuration file for individual nodes under the `network` attribute, but we can change this based on our requirements.

When we start Elasticsearch on a machine, it binds to the localhost by default. We can change this binding to a specific network address by changing `network.host` and `network.port` (as well as `transport.port` for node-to-node networking) if needed.

Changing these settings on a farm of computers is a pain, especially when you need to set up a cluster with hundreds of nodes. Be sure you have housekeeping scripts handy to alleviate this nuisance. One ideal way is to create configurations in a central folder and point the `ES_PATH_CONF` variable to those settings. (We can also use Ansible, Azure Pipelines, GitOps, etc., for such purposes.) Exporting this variable lets Elasticsearch choose the configuration from this directory.

Coming back to setting up the network properties, we can use special values in the config file to set the network host rather than configuring the host manually. Setting the `network.host` property to `_local_` lets Elasticsearch set its address automatically. This sets the loopback address (127.0.0.1) as the network host. The `_local_` special value is the default for the `network.host` attribute. My suggestion is to leave it untouched.

There's also a `_site_` value that sets the `network.host` attribute to site-local addresses (192.168.0.1, for example). We can set `network.host`, defaulting to these to special values by setting `network.host: [_local_, _site_]` in the configuration.

14.3 Shard sizing

One question that always arises when we talk about shards is sizing. Look at shard sizing in detail, especially the memory footprint we need to consider and other variables, to better understand this topic. For argument's sake, we focus on a use case with one index on a five-node cluster and then find the shard sizing with multi-indexes on the cluster.

14.3.1 Setting up a single index

Let's say we have a 5-node cluster with one index comprising 10 primary shards and 2 replicas. This means each shard has 2 replicas, and the total number of shards is 30 for both primary nodes and replicas. Figure 14.6 shows this configuration.

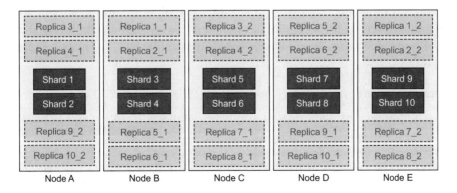

Figure 14.6   Shards and replicas spread across a multi-node cluster

Let's also assume that the primary shards comprise a few million documents occupying 300 GB of memory. We therefore create a 10-shard index, with each shard allocated about 50 GB of memory. Elasticsearch distributes the 300 GB of data among 10 shards, so each shard gets about 30 GB of documents. We also have 2 replicas for each shard, for a total of 20 replicas.

Replicas need to be set up with the same memory as the main shard because they are copies of the shard. Thus, 20 replicas consume 20 times 50 GB, or 1000 GB. And don't forget to add the memory allocated to the primary shards: 10 shards times 50 GB is 500 GB. We need at least 1500 GB (1.5 TB) to run this cluster with *one* index. Figure 14.7 shows these calculations.

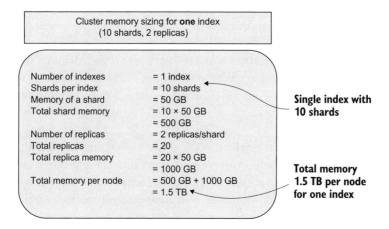

Figure 14.7   Memory sizing of a single index with 10 shards and 2 replicas

This cluster is made of individual nodes. Remember, these nodes need additional memory for operational purposes, including system indexes, in-memory data structures, and other operations. So, it is always advisable to add memory in addition to that allocated to shard sizing. As we mentioned, we are building a five-node cluster, so each node with 400 GB would make the cluster with 2000 GB. This will suffice for the current use case.

14.3.2   Setting up multiple indexes

In our example, we have only one index to manage, so we try to calculate memory costs based on that lone index. This is rarely the case in the real world. Any number of indexes can exist on the server, and at the very least, we need to provision servers to create several indexes in the future. If we extrapolate the cost calculations for five indexes, with each index having 10 shards and 2 replicas per index, figure 14.8 indicates our total memory.

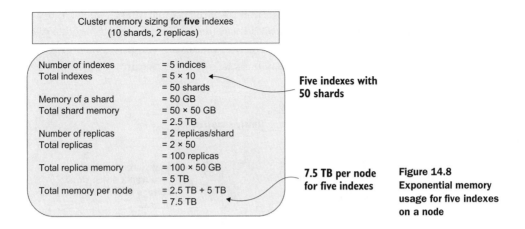

As you can see, memory increases exponentially when we consider additional indexes. In the earlier case of one index with 10 shards and 20 replicas (figure 14.7), we commissioned a 5-node cluster to handle 2000 GB of space requirements. In this new case with multiple indexes (figure 14.8), we need a massive cluster that can handle about 10 TB of space. We can deal with this in two ways: vertical scaling or horizontal scaling.

VERTICAL SCALING

We can use the same cluster that serves the 2 TB memory requirements and prop up the additional memory to handle new memory requirements: for example, increasing each server to 2 TB (five nodes with 2 TB = 10 TB). This is a vertical scaling activity. Although this is not a problem on a technical level, we may need to take the server down to upgrade it.

HORIZONTAL SCALING

The alternate (and probably preferred) approach is to add nodes to the cluster. For example, we can add 20 more nodes to the server, for a total of 25 nodes. We then have a newly formed cluster with 25 nodes, where each node has 400 GB of memory: the total can handle our 10 TB memory requirements.

While there is no one-size-fits-all solution, having a forward-thinking strategy with a tried-and-tested approach works well for most organizations. Shard sizing is tedious, and we need to exercise extreme caution to size them appropriately.

Because a major administrative requirement is making backups of indexes or the entire cluster from time to time, we cover this in the next section. Additionally, we look at restoring backups when needed. Elasticsearch provides a sleek mechanism for backing up and restoring—the snapshot.

14.4 Snapshots

Running applications in production without backup and restore functionality is risky. Data in our clusters should be stored in durable storage somewhere off-cluster. Fortunately, Elasticsearch provides easy snapshot and restore functionality for backing up our data and restoring it when needed.

Snapshots help to store incremental backups regularly. We can store the snapshots in a repository, usually mounted on a local filesystem or a cloud-based service such as AWS S3, Microsoft Azure, or Google Cloud Platform. As figure 14.9 shows, administrators snapshot clusters on a regular basis to a storage medium and then restore them on demand.

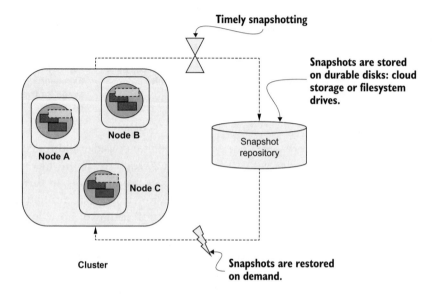

Figure 14.9   Mechanics of snapshot and restore on a cluster

A regular cluster snapshot is an administrative task that ideally should be automated with in-house scripts or handy tools. However, before we start backing up snapshots, we must ensure that our snapshot repository is a particular type and registered. This section discusses the mechanics to set up a repository and how to snapshot and restore data from the repository to a cluster.

14.4.1 Getting started

A few steps are required before we can use the snapshot and restore functionality. Broadly speaking, we need to perform the following three activities:

- *Register a snapshot repository.* Snapshots are stored on durable storage areas such as a filesystem, a Hadoop Distributed File System (HDFS), or cloud storage such as Amazon S3 buckets.
- *Snapshot the data.* Once we have a repository registered with the cluster, we can snapshot the data to back it up.
- *Restore from the store.* When we need to restore data, we simply pick the index, set of indexes, or full cluster that needs to be restored and start the restore operation from the previously registered snapshot repository.

As part of snapshotting, all indexes, all data streams, and the entire cluster state are backed up. Note that after the first snapshot is performed, subsequent backups will be incremental updates, not full copies. There are two ways we can work with snapshots:

- Snapshot and restore RESTful APIs
- The Kibana snapshot and restore feature

The first step is to choose a repository type and register it. Let's use both approaches to register a snapshot repository, as discussed in the next section.

14.4.2 Registering a snapshot repository

To keep things simple, let's pick the filesystem as our repository type: we want to store our snapshots on a disk mounted on a shared filesystem. We begin by mounting the filesystem with available memory on all the master and data nodes in the cluster. Once the server has this filesystem mounted, we need to let Elasticsearch know its location by specifying that in the configuration file.

Edit the elasticsearch.yml configuration file to amend the `path.repo` property, pointing it to the location of the mount. For example, if the mount path is /volumes/es_snapshots, `path.repo` looks like this: `path.repo: /volumes/es_snapshots`. After adding the mount path, we need to restart the respective nodes for this mount to be available for the nodes.

REGISTERING THE REPOSITORY USING SNAPSHOT APIS

When the nodes are back online after the restart, the final step is to invoke the snapshot repository API. The following listing shows the code.

> **Listing 14.4 Registering a filesystem-based snapshot repository**

```
PUT _snapshot/es_cluster_snapshot_repository        ◁── Names the repository
{                                                        provided to the
  "type": "fs",     ◁── Sets the type of repository       _snapshot API endpoint
  "settings": {          to filesystem ("fs")
    "location": "/volumes/es_snapshots"      ◁── Defines the location
  }                                               of the repository as a
}                                                 mounted filesystem
```

Elasticsearch provides the `_snapshot` API for carrying out actions related to snapshots and restores. In listing 14.4, we create a snapshot repository called `es_cluster_snapshot_repository`. The body of the request expects the type of repository we are creating and the properties required to set the repository type. In our example, we set `"fs"` (for filesystem) as our repository type and provide the filesystem path as the `"location"` in the `settings` object.

Because we've already added the mount point in the configuration file and, of course, restarted the node, the code in listing 14.4 should execute successfully to register our first repository. Issuing a `GET _snapshot` command returns the registered snapshot:

```
{
  "es_cluster_snapshot_repository" : {
    "type" : "fs",
    "settings" : {
      "location" : "/volumes/es_snapshots"
    }
  }
}
```

The response shows that one snapshot repository is registered and available for our snapshots.

> **NOTE** If you are running Elasticsearch on your local machine, you can set a temp folder as your repository location. For example, you can use /tmp/es_snapshots for *nix-based operating systems or c:/temp/es_snapshots for Windows.

As mentioned, we can use Kibana's Console to work with the snapshot and restore feature. As we did with the APIs, we can register the repository, too. Although the details of working with Kibana are outside the scope of this book, I provide a few pointers so you can work with the snapshot and restore functionality on Kibana.

REGISTERING A SNAPSHOT REPOSITORY ON KIBANA

Kibana has extensive support for working with the snapshot and restore feature, including registering snapshots, executing them, and restoring them. Let's see how we can register the repository on Kibana.

Head to the top-left menu of the Kibana Console and expand the Management menu, where you'll see, along with Dev Tools, a Stack Management navigation link (see figure 14.10). Click the link to navigate to the Stack Management page. Then, choose the Data > Snapshot and Restore menu item. The resulting page provides current repositories, snapshots, and their states.

The snapshot and restore functionality is tucked away under Stack Management link.

Figure 14.10 Accessing the Stack Management page for snapshot functionality

Go to the second tab, Repositories, and click Register a Repository. The next page is shown in figure 14.11.

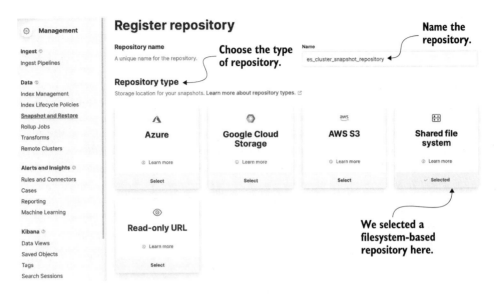

Figure 14.11   Naming the repository and choosing its type

Naming the repository is mandatory, followed by choosing a type: shared file system (fs), AWS S3, Azure's blob storage, and so on. Continuing with the example of choosing a local filesystem as our repository, click Shared File System to navigate to the next page. There, input the filesystem location and other requested properties (maximum and minimum bytes per second for snapshots and restores, chunk size, etc.). Click the Register button at the bottom of the page to create this repository.

14.4.3   Creating snapshots

Now that we've gone through the process of registering a snapshot repository, the next step is to create snapshots so the data is backed up to the repository we just created. There are a couple of ways to create a snapshot. Let's start with a simple manual technique: using the `_snapshot` API.

Listing 14.5   Creating a snapshot manually

```
PUT _snapshot/es_cluster_snapshot_repository/prod_snapshot_oct22
```

We ask the `_snapshot` API to create a snapshot named `prod_snapshot_oct22` under the repository `es_cluster_snapshot_repository`. This one-off manual snapshot backs up all the data (indexes, data streams, and cluster information) to the snapshot on the disk in the repository's filesystem.

We can also take a custom snapshot of a few indexes, rather than all the data as we just did. Attaching a request body to listing 14.5 specifies a set of indexes: say, all movies and all reviews.

Listing 14.6 Creating snapshots with specific indexes

```
PUT _snapshot/es_cluster_snapshot_repository/custom_prod_snapshots
{
    "indices": ["*movies*","*reviews*"]        ◁─┐ Backs up all movies and
}                                                 │ review-related indexes
```

The indices attribute takes a string or array of strings representing the set of specific indexes we want to back up. In our example, we back up any index with a glob pattern of *movies* and *reviews*. By default, all the indexes and data streams are included ([*]) if we don't specify what we want to back up. To omit some, we can use the pattern with a minus sign (or dash), like this: -*.old. This pattern, in our case, omits all indexes ending with .old.

We can also attach user-defined properties in a metadata attribute. Say, for example, we want to note the incident details of a user's request when taking the snapshot. The following listing shows this as a query.

Listing 14.7 Adding custom details to the snapshot

```
PUT _snapshot/es_cluster_snapshot_repository/prod_snapshots_with_metadata
{
    "indices": ["*movies*","*reviews*", "-*.old"],  ◁─┐ Includes or excludes these
    "metadata":{              ◁─┐ Defines the block of   │ indexes in the snapshot
        "reason":"user request",  │ custom information under
        "incident_id":"ID12345",  │ the metadata object
        "user":"mkonda"
    }
}
```

We enhance the list of indexes by removing "old" indexes as part of the snapshot process. We also add metadata with the user request information, and we can create as many details as possible in this object. The final step in the lifecycle of Elasticsearch's snapshot and restore functionality is to restore the snapshots, as we discuss in the next section.

14.4.4 *Restoring snapshots*

Restoring a snapshot is relatively straightforward. All we need to do is to invoke _restore on the _snapshot API.

Listing 14.8 Restoring data from a snapshot

```
PUT _snapshot/es_cluster_snapshot_repository/custom_prod_snapshots/_restore
```

The `_restore` endpoint copies data from the repository to the cluster. Of course, we can attach a JSON object to specify further details of which indexes or data streams we want to restore. The following query provides an example of such a request.

Listing 14.9   Restoring indexes from a snapshot

```
POST _snapshot/es_cluster_snapshot_repository/custom_prod_snapshots/_restore
{
  "indices":["new_movies"]        ◁────┐ Lists the indexes to be
}                                       │ restored from the snapshot
```

14.4.5   Deleting snapshots

We don't need to keep snapshots on disk all the time. One strategy most organizations follow is to create snapshots for individual indexes based on user requests. We may need to update our mapping or change the primary shards of a given index. Unfortunately, we can't do this as long as the index is in a live state.

The best approach is to create a new index with the appropriate shards and mapping and then take a snapshot of the current index, restore that to the newly created index from the snapshot, and delete the snapshot. Figure 14.12 shows this activity.

We can migrate data from an old index to a new one with the snapshot and restore functionality. Once we use the snapshots, we can delete them to free up storage space.

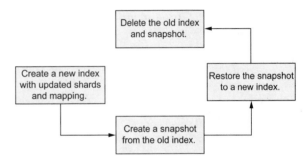

Figure 14.12   Snapshot lifecycle, from creation to deletion

Deleting snapshots is fairly straightforward: we use the HTTP `DELETE` action, providing the snapshot ID. The following listing deletes the snapshot we created earlier.

Listing 14.10   Deleting a snapshot

```
DELETE _snapshot/es_cluster_snapshot_repository/custom_prod_snapshots
```

If we issue the HTTP `DELETE` action command while the snapshot is in progress, Elasticsearch instantly halts the activity, deletes the snapshot, and removes the contents from the repository.

14.4.6   Automating snapshots

We've just seen the mechanism for creating snapshots, but these are ad hoc snapshots: we create them on demand (for example, when migrating data, rolling out a production hotfix release, etc.). However, we can automate this process to regularly back up and take snapshots using the snapshot lifecycle management (SLM) feature. Elasticsearch provides the `_slm` API to manage the lifecycle of snapshots and create lifecycle policies that are executed on a predefined schedule.

To do this, we can create a policy using the `_slm` API. This policy contains information such as the indexes it should back up, the schedule (cron job), the retention period, and so on. We must have registered a repository (see section 14.3.2), because it is a prerequisite for snapshot lifecycle management.

Suppose we want to back up all our movie indexes at midnight every night to a given repository. We also need to keep these snapshots for a week. We can write a policy and create the automation using the `_slm` API.

Listing 14.11   Creating a policy for scheduled snapshots

```
PUT _slm/policy/prod_cluster_daily_backups        ⟵───  The _slm API expects
{                                                          a policy identifier.
  "name":"<prod_daily_backups-{now/d}>",     ⟵───  Unique name given
  "schedule": "0 0 0 * * ?",              ⟵───        to a snapshot
  "repository": "es_cluster_snapshot_repository",   Cron job schedule
  "config": {                                        for midnight
    "indices":["*movies*", "*reviews*"],   ⟵───  Indexes to snapshot
    "include_global_state": false     ⟵───  Adds a cluster state
  },                                         to the snapshot
  "retention":{
    "Expire_after":"7d"      ⟵───  Retains the snapshot
  }                                 for a week (7d)
}
```

Registered repository ⟶ (points to `"repository"` line)

The `_slm` API creates a policy that is stored in the cluster for execution when the schedule kicks in. We must provide three parts: a unique name, the schedule, and the repository we registered earlier to store the snapshots. Let's look at these bits in detail.

The unique name (`<prod_daily_backups-{now/d}>` in listing 14.11) is a name constructed with data math in it. In this case, `<prod_daily_backups-{now/d}>` is parsed to `prod_daily_backups-5.10.2022` if it is run on October 5, 2022, because `{now/d}` indicates the current date. Every time the schedule kicks in, a new unique name is generated with the current date: `prod_daily_backups-6.10.2022`, `prod_daily_backups-7.10.2022`, and so on. Because we use date math in the name, we must enclose the name using angle brackets (`< >`) so the parser parses without any problems. Consult the Elasticsearch documentation (http://mng.bz/QPwe) for further details on date math in names.

As listing 14.11 shows, we provided a schedule in the form of a cron job: `"schedule": 0 0 0 * * ?`. This cron expression states that the job should be executed precisely at midnight. We can therefore expect our snapshot process to begin at midnight every night.

The `config` block in listing 14.11 consists of the indexes and cluster state we want to back up (in this example, all movies and review-related indexes). If we do not include the `config` block, all indexes and data streams are included in snapshot backups by default. The `include_global_state` attribute indicates that we want to include the cluster state in the snapshot. In the listing, we ignore the cluster state (`include_global_state` is set to `false`) as part of the snapshot.

The final piece is the retention information (`"retention":`), which specifies how long we want to keep the snapshots in the repository. We set the current snapshot's lifetime as one week by setting the `expire_after` attribute to `7d`.

When we execute this query, the automatic snapshot facility remains in place until we delete the policy. It is executed based on the schedule. This is the easier and preferred way to back up the entire cluster without manual intervention.

SLM USING KIBANA

We can also create an SLM policy using Kibana. Let's see briefly how to do this:

1 In Kibana, navigate to the Management > Snapshot and Restore feature link.
2 Click the Policies tab, and invoke the creation of a new policy by clicking the Create Policy button.
3 Fill in the details of this page as shown in figure 14.13.

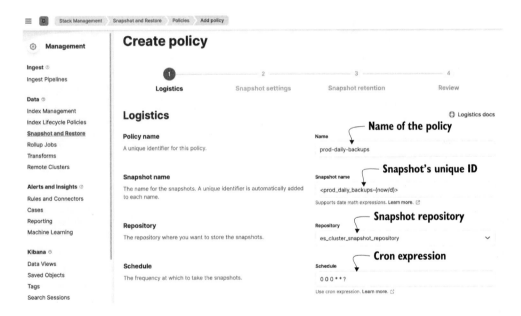

Figure 14.13   Creating an SLM policy using the Kibana Console

4 Navigate to the next page by clicking the Next button. Fill in the details related to the `config` block of the query in listing 14.11, including any specific indexes and data streams (or all), the global cluster state (or not), and so on. Figure 14.14 shows the Snapshot Settings configurations.

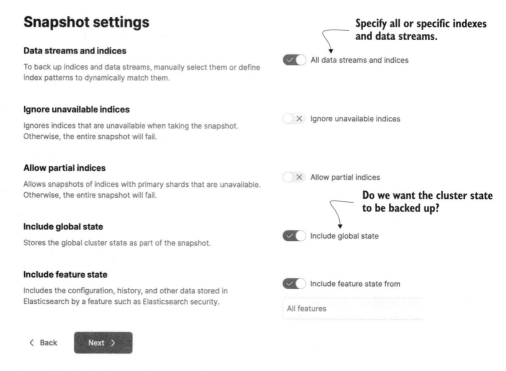

Figure 14.14   Configuring the snapshot's settings

5   Click Next, and fill in the retention details. We can provide three (all optional) pieces of information to clean up snapshots based on the retention policy. In figure 14.15, we ask the snapshot manager to delete this snapshot after a week (seven days). We also specify that at least three snapshots must always be

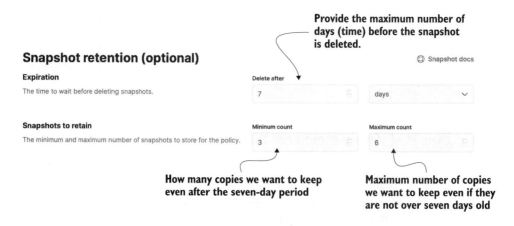

Figure 14.15   Configuring the snapshot's retention settings

available in our repository, so they are never all cleared. This `minimum_count` setting ensures that those three snapshots are never deleted, even if they are older than one week. Similarly, the `maximum_count` setting ensures that we have no more than the given number of snapshot copies (6, in this case), even if they are younger than seven days.

6 Review the options, and create the SLM policy.

MANUALLY EXECUTING SLM

We don't need to wait until the scheduled time in the policy to kick-start the snapshot action. If we have weekly snapshots scheduled in the policy and need to make a backup due to a production hotfix, we can use a manual start. The following listing shows how to manually execute the SLM policy by invoking the `_execute` endpoint on the API.

> **Listing 14.12 Manually executing scheduled snapshots**

```
POST _slm/policy/prod_cluster_daily_backups/_execute
```

Running this command starts the previously created `prod_cluster_daily_backups` policy instantly. We don't need to wait for its scheduled time.

> ### Searchable snapshots (Enterprise edition)
>
> In version 7.12, Elasticsearch introduced a brand-new feature called *searchable snapshots*. This functionality helps run search queries against snapshots. The idea is to use backups as indexes for certain queries. Because snapshots can be written to low-cost archival stores, not just using them to restore data but also mounting them effectively as indexes to run search queries is a big win.
>
> We know that adding replicas to the cluster is one way to improve read performance, but there is an associated cost: replicas cost time and money due to the extra space they require. By making snapshots mountable (using the `_mount` API), they are available for searches, effectively replacing replicas and thus reducing our costs by almost half.
>
> The searchable snapshots feature is available only for Enterprise licenses and is not free with the basic license. For this reason, we don't cover them in this book. If you're interested, check out the documentation for details on how to implement searchable snapshots (http://mng.bz/XN7M).
>
> Elasticsearch works by convention over configuration, leaving us with fewer decisions to make when working with the setup or running Elasticsearch and its operational side. However, running the system on defaults is asking for trouble. We must tweak the configuration when needed to provide additional memory or improve performance. We discuss high-level settings, what they mean, and how we can change them in the next section.

14.5   *Advanced configurations*

Elasticsearch has many settings and configurations that may baffle even expert engineers. Although it uses the *convention over configuration* paradigm and works with defaults most of the time, it is imperative to customize the configuration before taking the application to production.

In this section, we walk through some properties that fall under various categories and discuss their importance and how to tweak them. We can modify three configuration files:

- *elasticsearch.yml*—The most commonly edited configuration file, where we can set the cluster name, node information, data and log paths, and network and security settings
- *log4j2.properties*—Where we can set the logging levels of the Elasticsearch node
- *jvm.options*—Where we can set the heap memory of the running node

These files are read by the Elasticsearch node from the config directory, which is a folder under Elasticsearch's installation directory. This directory defaults to $ES_HOME/config for binary (zip or tar.gz) installations (the ES_HOME variable points to Elasticsearch's installation directory). If we install with a package manager like Debian or RPM distributions, it defaults to /etc/elasticsearch/config.

If we expect to access our configuration files from a different directory, we can set and export a path variable called ES_PATH_CONF, which points to the new configuration file location. In the next few subsections, we look at some settings that are important for both administrators developers to understand.

14.5.1   *The main configuration file*

Although the folks at Elastic developed Elasticsearch to run with defaults (convention over configuration), we are highly unlikely to rely on defaults when taking the node into production. We should tweak the properties to set specific network information, data or log paths, security aspects, and so on. To do so, we can amend the elasticsearch.yml file to set most of the required properties for our running applications.

We briefly touched on networking properties earlier in this chapter when discussing node communication. Elasticsearch exposes network properties as `network.*` attributes. We can set the host names and port numbers using this property. For example, we can change the port number of Elasticsearch to 9900 rather than holding on to default port 9200: `http.port :9900`. We can also set `transport.port` to change the port on which nodes communicate internally.

You may need to alter many properties, depending on your requirements. Refer to the official documentation to find more about these properties in detail: http://mng.bz/yQNE.

14.5.2   *Logging options*

Elasticsearch is developed in Java, and like most Java applications, it uses Log4j 2 as its logging library. A running node spits out logging information at the INFO level to the console and a file (using Kibana Console and rolling file appenders, respectively).

The Log4j properties file (log4j2.properties) consists of system variables (`sys:es.logs.base_path`, `sys:es.logs.cluster_name`, etc.) that are resolved at application runtime. Because Elasticsearch exposes these properties, they are available to Log4j, which lets Log4j set up its log file directory location, log file pattern, and other properties. For example, `sys:es.logs.base_path` points to the path where Elasticsearch writes the logs, which resolves to the $ES_HOME/logs directory.

By default, most of Elasticsearch runs at the INFO level, but we can customize the setting based on individual packages. For example, we can edit the log4j2.properties file and add a logger for the `index` package, as the following listing shows.

> **Listing 14.13   Setting the logging level for a specific package**

```
logger.index.name = org.elasticsearch.index
logger.index.level = DEBUG
```

Doing this allows the `index` package to output logs at the DEBUG level. Rather than editing this file on a specific node and restarting that node (we may need to do this for every node if we haven't done so before creating a farmed cluster), we can set the DEBUG log level at the cluster level for this package.

> **Listing 14.14   Setting the transient log level globally**

```
PUT _cluster/settings
{                                    The transient
  "transient": {          ⟵───┘     setting
    "logger.org.elasticsearch.index":"DEBUG"    ⟵───┘  Sets this index package's
  }                                                     logging level to DEBUG
}
```

As the query shows, we set the logger-level property for the `index` package to DEBUG in the `transient` block. The `transient` block indicates that the property is not durable (only available while the cluster is up and running). If we restart the cluster or it crashes, the setting is lost because it is not stored permanently on the disk.

We can set this property with a call to the cluster settings API (`_cluster/settings`), as listing 14.14 shows. Once this property is set, any further logging info related to the `index` in the `org.elasticsearch.index` source package is output at the DEBUG level.

Elasticsearch also provides a means of storing cluster properties durably. To store the properties permanently, we can use the `persistent` block. The following listing replaces the `transient` block with a `persistent` block.

> **Listing 14.15   Setting the log level permanently**

```
PUT _cluster/settings
{
  "persistent": {
    "logger.org.elasticsearch.index":"DEBUG",
```

```
    "logger.org.elasticsearch.http":"TRACE"
  }
}
```

This code sets the DEBUG level on the org.elasticsearch.index package and the TRACE level on the org.elasticsearch.http package. Because both are *persistent* properties, the logger writes detailed logs at these levels as set on the packages, the properties survive cluster restarts (or crashes).

Be careful about setting such properties permanently using the persistent property. I suggest enabling the DEBUG or TRACE logging level when troubleshooting or during a debugging episode. When you finish dealing with the episode in production, reset the level to INFO to avoid writing reams of requests to disk.

14.5.3 *Java virtual machine options*

Because Elasticsearch uses the Java programming language, many optimization tweaks can be done at the Java virtual machine (JVM) level. For obvious reasons, discussing such a huge topic in this book would not do it justice. However, if you are curious and want to understand the JVM or fine-tune performance at a lower level, refer to a book like *Optimizing Java* (Ben Evan and Jame Gough, 2018, O'Reilly) or *Java Performance* (Scott Oaks, 2020, O'Reilly). I highly recommend them as they provide the fundamentals along with operational tips and tricks.

Elasticsearch provides a jvm.options file in the /config directory with the JVM settings. However, this file is only for reference purposes (to check the node's memory settings, for example) and never to be edited. Heap memory is automatically set for the Elasticsearch server based on the node's available memory.

> **WARNING** Never edit the jvm.options file under any circumstances. Doing so may corrupt Elasticsearch's internal workings.

To upgrade memory or change JVM settings, we must create a new file with .options as the filename extension, provide the appropriate tuning parameters, and place the file in a directory called jvm.options.d under the config folder for archive installations (tar or zip). We can give any name to the custom file, but we must include the fixed .options extension.

For RPM/Debian package installations, this file should be under the /etc/elastic search/jvm.options.d/ directory. Similarly, mount the options file under the /usr/ share/elasticsearch/config folder for Docker installations.

We can edit the settings in this custom JVM options file. For example, to upgrade heap memory in a file called jvm_custom.options, we can use the following code.

Listing 14.16   Upgrading heap memory

```
-Xms4g
-Xmx8g
```

The -Xms flag sets the initial heap memory, and the -Xmx adjusts the maximum heap memory. The unwritten rule is not to let the -Xms and -Xmx settings exceed 50% of the node's total RAM. Apache Lucene running under the hood uses the second half of the memory for its segmentation, caching, and other processes.

As we now know, Elasticsearch is a distributed cluster with a master node controlling the cluster while the rest of the nodes perform their individual jobs. A great deal of thought has gone into designing and developing the master node and its features, and we discuss it in its own section next.

14.6   Cluster masters

Every node in a cluster can have multiple roles assigned: master, data, ingest, ml (machine learning), and others. Assigning the master role indicates that this node is a *master-eligible* node. Before we discuss master eligibility, let's look at the importance of a master node.

14.6.1   Master nodes

The master node is responsible for cluster-wide operations such as allocating shards to nodes, index management, and other lightweight operations. The master node is a critical component responsible for keeping the cluster healthy. It strives to keep the state of the cluster and node community intact. Only one master node exists for a cluster, and its sole job is to worry about cluster operations—nothing more, nothing less.

Master-eligible nodes are nodes that are tagged with the master role. Assigning a master role to a node doesn't mean the node becomes the cluster master, but it is one step closer to becoming one, should the elected master crash. The other master-eligible nodes are also in line to become a master, given an opportunity, so they are also one step closer to becoming the master.

What's the use of a master-eligible node, you may ask? Every master-eligible node exercises its vote to select a cluster's master. Behind the scenes, when we boot up nodes for the first time to form a cluster or when the master dies, one of the first steps is to elect a master. We examine elections for the master cluster in the following section.

14.6.2   Master elections

The cluster master is chosen democratically by election! An election is held to choose a master when the cluster is formed for the first time or when the current master dies. If the master crashes for whatever reason, the master-eligible nodes call for an election. Members cast their vote to elect a new master. Once elected, the master node takes over the duties of cluster management.

Not all days are happy days—circumstances beyond its control that can knock off a master node. Therefore, the master-eligible nodes communicate constantly with the master node to be sure it is alive and notify the master of their status. When the master node is gone, the immediate job of the master-eligible nodes is to call for elections to elect a new master.

A few properties, such as `cluster.election.duration` and `cluster.election` `.initial_timeout`, help us configure the frequency of elections and how long to wait before master-eligible nodes call for an election. The `initial_timeout` attribute, for example, is the amount of time a master-eligible node waits before calling for an election. By default, this value is set to 500 ms. For example, let's say master-eligible node A does not receive a heartbeat from the master node in 500 ms. It then calls for an election because it thinks the master has crashed.

In addition to electing a master, master-eligible nodes work together to get cluster operations rolling. Although the master is the king of the cluster, it needs support and buy-in from the master-eligible nodes. The master's job is maintaining and managing cluster state, as we see next.

14.6.3 *Cluster state*

The cluster state consists of all the metadata about shards, replicas, schemas, mappings, field information, and more. These details are stored as the global state in the cluster and are also written to each node. The master is the only node that can commit the cluster state. It has the responsibility to maintain the cluster with up-to-date information. Master nodes commit the cluster data in phases (similar to the two-phase commit transaction in a distributed architecture):

1   The master computes the cluster changes, publishes them to the individual nodes, and then waits for acknowledgments.

2   Each node receives the cluster updates, but the updates aren't applied to the nodes' local state yet. On receipt, they send an acknowledgment to the master.

3   When the master receives a quorum of acknowledgments from the master-eligible nodes, it commits the changes to update the cluster state (the master doesn't need to wait for acknowledgments from every node, just master-eligible nodes).

4   After successfully committing the cluster changes, the master node broadcasts a final message to individual nodes instructing them to commit the previously received cluster changes.

5   The individual nodes commit the cluster updates.

The `cluster.publish.timeout` attribute sets a time limit (30 s by default) to commit each batch of cluster updates successfully. This period runs from the time of posting the publication of the first cluster update messages to the nodes until the cluster state is committed. If the global cluster updates are committed successfully within the default 30 s, the master waits until this time elapses before starting the next batch of cluster updates. However, the story doesn't end here.

If the cluster updates are not committed in 30 s, the master may have died. The election for a new master begins as a result.

Although the global cluster updates are committed, the master still waits for nodes that haven't returned acknowledgments. Unless it receives acknowledgments, the master can't mark this cluster update a success. In such cases, the master keeps track of these nodes and waits for a grace period set by the `cluster.follower_lag.timeout` attribute, which defaults to 90 s. If the node(s) do not respond in this 90 s grace period, they are marked as failed nodes, and the master removes them from the cluster.

As you may have gathered, a lot goes on under the hood in Elasticsearch. Cluster updates happen frequently, and the master is responsible for maintaining the moving parts. In the previous cluster updates scenario, the master awaits acknowledgments from a group of master-eligible nodes called a quorum before committing the state, rather than waiting for the rest of the nodes. A quorum is the minimum number of master nodes required for a master to operate effectively, as discussed in the next section.

14.6.4   A quorum

The master is in control of maintaining and managing the cluster. However, it consults a quorum of master-eligible nodes for cluster state updates and master elections. A quorum is a carefully selected subset of master-eligible nodes required for a master to operate the cluster effectively. This is the majority of the nodes consulted by the master to reach a consensus on matters of cluster state and other problems.

Although we are learning about a quorum, the good news is that we (users/administrators) don't have to worry about how to form one. Clusters automatically formulate a quorum based on the available master-eligible nodes. There's a simple formula to find the minimum number of master-eligible nodes (quorum) required, given a set of master-eligible nodes:

```
Minimum number of master-eligible nodes = (number of master-eligible nodes /
    2) + 1
```

Suppose we have a 20-node cluster and 8 nodes assigned as master-eligible nodes (the node role is set to `master`). By applying this formula, our cluster creates a quorum with five (carefully chosen) master-eligible nodes (8 / 2 + 1 = 5). The idea is that we need at least five master-eligible nodes to form a quorum.

The rule of thumb is that the recommended minimum number of master-eligible members in any node cluster is three. Setting three master-eligible nodes as a minimum is a surefire way to manage the cluster. Another big advantage of having at least three nodes in a cluster quorum is that this alleviates the split-brain problem, which we look at in the following section.

14.6.5   *The split-brain problem*

Elasticsearch's cluster health heavily relies on multiple factors: network, memory, JVM garbage collection, and so on. In some instances, the cluster is split into two clusters with some nodes in one cluster and some in the other. For example, figure 14.16 shows a cluster with two master-eligible nodes, but one (Node A) is elected to be the master node. As long as we are in a happy state, the cluster is healthy, and the master carries out its responsibilities diligently.

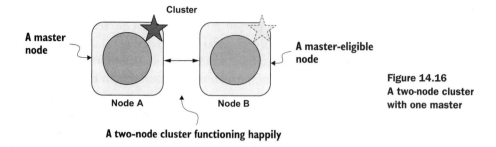

Figure 14.16
A two-node cluster
with one master

Now, let's throw a wrench in the works. Let's say Node B dies due to a hardware problem. Because Node A is the master, it continues working to service queries with one node: we effectively have a one-node cluster while we wait for another Node B to boot up to join the cluster.

Here's where things can get tricky. While Node B is booting up, suppose network connectivity is severed, making Node B unable to see the existence of Node A. This leads to Node B assuming a master role because it thinks there's no master in the cluster, even though Node A exists as the master. This leads to a *split-brain* situation (see figure 14.17).

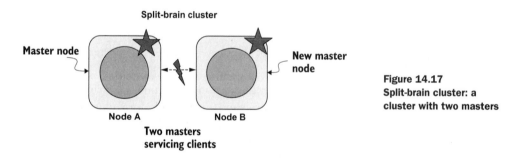

Figure 14.17
Split-brain cluster: a
cluster with two masters

The two nodes do not communicate due to network problems, so they work happily as part of the cluster. But because both nodes are masters, any requests coming to either one are carried out only by the receiving node. However, data in one node is not visible to the other node, which raises data discrepancies. This is one of the reasons to have at least three master-eligible nodes in a cluster. Having three such nodes avoids split-brain cluster formation.

14.6.6 *Dedicated master nodes*

Because a node can be assigned multiple roles, it's not a surprise to see a cluster with 20 nodes where all nodes are performing all roles. There is no harm in creating this type of cluster architecture; however, such a setting works only for lightweight cluster needs. As we already saw, the master node is the critical node in the cluster and keeps the cluster ticking.

If data is indexed or searched at an exponential growth rate, every node, including the master nodes, takes a performance hit. A slow-performing master node is asking for trouble: cluster operations run slower or can even stall. For this reason, it is always advisable to create a dedicated machine to host the master node. Having a dedicated master node lets clusters run smoothly and mitigates data loss and application downtime.

As mentioned, the rule of thumb is to have at least three dedicated master-eligible nodes in a cluster. When forming a cluster, be sure to set `node.roles` to `master`, as shown in the following snippet, to designate the node-dedicated master:

```
node.roles: [ master ]
```

This way, the dedicated `master` role is not overloaded by performing data- or ingest-related operations and just manages the cluster full time.

That's a wrap! We looked at the administrative part of Elasticsearch in this chapter. In the next chapter, we look at performance tuning.

Summary

- Elasticsearch horizontally scales when adding new nodes to the cluster. The new nodes join the cluster as long as they are associated with the same cluster name and network settings.
- One way to improve read throughput and, thus, performance is to add replicas to the cluster. The replicas take the read hits and serve data quickly.
- Nodes communicate with each other on a transport port, set to 9300 by default. This can be modified by adjusting the `transport.port` property in the elasticsearch.yml file.
- HTTP clients communicate with Elasticsearch on an http.port (set to 9200 by default) using RESTFul endpoints.
- A node can consist of multiple indexes, and each index can consist of multiple shards. The ideal size of a shard should be not more than 50 GB of memory.
- Shards and replicas occupy space, so our organizational strategy should define the appropriate sizes based on current requirements and future use.
- Although adding replicas improves the client's read/query performance, it comes with a cost. We must be sure to carry out appropriate trials and watch for spikes before assigning a standard size for each shard.
- Elasticsearch allows backing up and restoring data using its snapshot and restore feature. Snapshots let us make backups of the cluster to a repository.
- A repository can be a local filesystem or a cloud-based object store such as AWS S3.
- A snapshot can consist of indexes, data streams (as well as the cluster state, such as persistent or transient), indexing templates, index lifecycle management (ILM) policies, and more.

- A snapshot lifecycle management (SLM) endpoint declared as _slm creates a policy that defines the snapshot along with its schedule and other attributes.

- We can initiate restoring data from a snapshot manually by invoking the _restore API.

- We can use Kibana's rich interface to define snapshots and policies and restore them. The policies are available under the Stack Management navigation menu.

- Elasticsearch exposes various settings via its elasticsearch.yml, jvm.options, and log4j2.properties files.

- We can tweak many attributes, such as changing the cluster name, moving the log and data path, adding network settings, and so on, by editing the elastic-search.yml file.

- The config/jvm.options file defines JVM-related data for the node, but we must never edit this file.

- To customize the settings for JVM options, we need to create a new file ending with *.options (like custom_settings.options) and drop it in a folder called jvm.options.d, which should be present in the config folder for archived installations (tar or zip).

- We can set the required heap memory using the -Xms and -Xmx flags, where -Xms sets the maximum heap and -Xmx sets the minimum heap size. As a rule of thumb, never set heap size over 50% of available RAM.

- The master node in a cluster is a critical node that looks after managing and maintaining cluster-related operations and updating the distributed cluster state.

- The master node consults a quorum of nodes to commit the cluster state or elect a new master.

- A quorum is a minimum number of master-eligible nodes carefully selected by the cluster to alleviate node failures when making decisions.

- We should provide a minimum of three master-eligible nodes when forming a cluster, to avoid a split-brain cluster.

Performance and troubleshooting

This chapter covers

- Understanding the reasons for slow searches and indexing queries
- Tuning and improving the performance of slow queries and indexing
- Troubleshooting unstable clusters

Once the Elasticsearch cluster is ready for production, umpteen things can go wrong, from users complaining about slow searches to unstable nodes, network problems, over-sharding troubles, memory problems, and more. Maintaining the cluster's health in a GREEN (healthy) state is paramount. Constantly keeping an eye on the cluster's health and performance is one of the primary jobs of an administrator.

Troubleshooting an unstable cluster requires a good understanding of the inner workings of Elasticsearch, networking concepts, node communication, memory settings, and many APIs for nodes, clusters, cluster allocation, and other uses. Similarly, tweaking configurations to understand the document models, appropriate refresh times, and so forth helps tune the cluster for greater performance.

In this chapter, we look at common problems such as slow query and ingestion speeds to understand the reasons behind them. Because Elasticsearch is a complex distributed architecture, there are several places to look for fixes. We discuss the most obvious and commonly applied solutions in this chapter.

We also look at problems arising from unstable clusters and troubleshoot them with the help of cluster health, cluster allocation, and node APIs. Then we discuss how Elasticsearch sets memory and disk usage thresholds to keep the cluster alive and kicking. Let's begin by seeing why our search queries do not yield faster results and what troubleshooting options are available.

> **NOTE** As mentioned in chapter 14, similar to administration of Elasticsearch, performance tuning is an advanced topic that requires expert hands on the deck. Before tweaking your app for performance, consult the experts, read the documentation, and experiment in your lab environment. This chapter presents a helicopter view of the performance landscape.

15.1 Search and speed problems

Although Elasticsearch is a near-real-time search engine, we must carefully tame the beast to make sure it works as expected in various scenarios. Over time, Elasticsearch's performance may degrade if not architected well with future data requirements in mind and if not constantly maintained. Degradation of the server's performance is detrimental to overall cluster health, which affects search query and indexing performance.

The major problems that Elasticsearch users report most commonly are slow serving of search queries and slow indexing speeds. A unique selling point for Elasticsearch is its blazingly fast queries. However, we can't expect the out-of-the-box solution to fit all our needs. A multitude of variables such as sensible distribution of nodes, shards, and replicas depending on memory management and hardware availability allow us to create a healthy cluster as we prepare and productionize the infrastructure and applications.

Often, Elasticsearch is incorrectly set up for the search scenario at hand. For example, some applications are intensive on the search side, whereas others need to serve less-frequent searches.

15.1.1 Modern hardware

Elasticsearch uses Lucene under the hood for indexing and storing data. Data is stored in the filesystem, and although Lucene does this efficiently, additional help such as providing solid state drives (SSDs) rather than hard disk drives (HDDs), allocating abundant memory, assisting in infrequent merges, and so on goes a long way.

Each node consists of shards and replicas as well as other cluster data, including internal data structures that Elasticsearch maintains. Because Elasticsearch is developed in Java, allocating sizable heap memory overall helps with the smooth running of the application. The *heap* is the memory location where new objects are stored in the young generation space. As this space fills up, any objects surviving minor garbage collector (GC) runs are moved to the old generation space. Providing a larger heap for Elasticsearch helps avoid filling up the young generation space quickly, subsequently avoiding garbage collection runs.

A general rule of thumb is to provide at least half of the memory as heap memory to the application. For example, if your machine is configured with 16 GB RAM, be sure the heap is set to at least 8 GB. We can set this by configuring the .options file with the -Xmx setting (see section 14.5.3).

Also, attaching a local storage disk enables better performance when writing to disk rather than using a network-based filesystem and disk. Ultimately, provisioning individual nodes with local volumes is a better strategy.

Remember that we must understand the indexing and shard requirements to allocate initial memory. For example, based on how many shards and replicas we intend to hold on the node, we may need to calculate and provide physical disk memory.

Optimal shard numbers help avoid building a cluster with too many small shards. As the number of shards increases, so does communication between the nodes. Thus, performance also relies on network capacity and bandwidth. Adding replicas increases search query read throughput, but having too many replicas quickly consumes memory, and a larger number of replicas is difficult to manage.

15.1.2 Document modeling

Elasticsearch is a NoSQL database; data should be denormalized, unlike in relational databases, where data is normalized. For example, if an employee is created, the record consists of the full information about the employee.

Every document in Elasticsearch is self-contained, so no joins are expected on the data. If your data is predominantly parent-child, you may want to rethink using Elasticsearch. Nested and parent-child operations are slow and degrade performance from the outset. If you come from a relational database world, be sure you understand the NoSQL data modeling principles.

In addition, we should aim to limit searching multiple fields because searching queries across multiple fields slows the query response time. Instead, combine multiple fields into a single field and search against this single field. Fortunately, Elasticsearch provides a `copy_to` attribute on fields, which helps in this scenario.

Let's look at an example. Suppose we have a couple of fields (`title` and `synopsis`) in our `book` document, and they are indexed in our `programming_books1` index. When we write queries to search in `title` and `synopsis`, we usually search against these two individual fields.

Listing 15.1 A non-performant search across multiple fields

```
PUT programming_books1/_doc/1        ⊲─┐  Indexes a sample document
{                                       │  before issuing a search
  "title":"Elasticsearch in Action",
  "synopsis":"A straightforward, hands-on, example driven, action book"
}
```

```
GET programming_books1/_search
{
  "query": {                          Invokes a multi_match     Searches for the document
    "multi_match": {                   query to search across    using a multi_match query
      "query": "Elasticsearch hands-on example driven",
      "fields": ["title","synopsis"]     The fields
    }                                      to search
  }
}
```

This query searches for the criteria across multiple fields. It is an expensive query, based on the number of fields and documents (imagine searching over a dozen fields in numerous books). We can put a combined field pattern into action using the `copy_to` attribute on individual fields to alleviate such problems.

The following listing creates a mapping for the `programming_books2` index. The notable thing is the addition of a separate field called `title_synopsis`, which is a `text` data type.

Listing 15.2   Enhanced schema definition with a `copy_to` attribute

```
PUT programming_books2
{
  "mappings": {
    "properties": {
      "title":{
        "type": "text",
        "copy_to": "title_synopsis"       Copies the title info
      },                                   to title_synopsis
      "synopsis":{                         Copies the synopsis
        "type": "text",                    info to title_synopsis
        "copy_to": "title_synopsis"
      },
      "title_synopsis":{        Denotes title_synopsis
        "type": "text"          as a text field
      }
    }
  }
}
```

As you can gather from the schema definition in this listing, each of the two fields has an additional `copy_to` attribute with a value pointing to a third field, `title_synopsis`. Any data indexed into the `title` and `synopsis` fields is copied into `title_synopsis` behind the scenes. The next listing shows the indexing of a sample book document into the `programming_books2` index.

Listing 15.3   Indexing a sample document

```
PUT programming_books2/_doc/1
{
  "title":"Elasticsearch in Action",
  "synopsis":"A straightforward, hands-on, example-driven, action book"
}
```

We index the book with the two fields without mentioning the `title_synopsis` field in the document. How does it get indexed?

During the indexing process, Elasticsearch fills this third field (`title_synopsis`) by combining the `title` and `synopsis` fields (remember the `copy_to` attribute on these fields?). Thus, a combined field called `title_synopsis` holds the full data from the other fields.

Because we enhanced the schema with this `copy_to` functionality, we can rewrite the search query to become a simple `match` query rather than a `multi-match`.

Listing 15.4 A `match` query against the `title_synopsis` field

```
GET programming_books2/_search
{
  "query": {
    "match": {                          Specifies the title_synopsis
      "title_synopsis": {        ⬅——┘  field for the match query
        "query": "Elasticsearch hands-on example driven",
        "operator": "OR"
      }
    }
  }
}
```

We now use a simple `match` query (as opposed to the expensive `multi_match` query described in listing 15.1) to fetch our results. Because the grunt work of copying data to a combined field was done at the indexing time, the search simply queries against this already-available field.

Searching through multiple fields using `multi_match` (or even a `query_string` query, as discussed in chapter 9) is an expensive operation. Instead, we used the combined fields method with the `copy_to` construct. Matching a few fields rather than searching across dozens of them is a good candidate for performance enhancement.

15.1.3 Choosing keyword types over text types

Full-text searches undergo a text analysis phase: they are normalized and tokenized just like indexing, before the results are fetched. This is a computing-intensive operation, and we can avoid it on fields that are the `keyword` type. Keyword fields do not undergo text analysis, thus saving us time and effort when searching.

Consider declaring a `keyword` type for any `text` field if the use case allows searching on keywords. For example, we can create a book with a title defined as a `text` data type as well as a `keyword` field using the multi-fields feature.

Listing 15.5 A multi-field query using the `keyword` type

```
PUT programming_books3
{
  "mappings": {
    "properties": {
```

```
    "title":{
      "type": "text",
      "fields": {
        "raw":{
          "type":"keyword"        ◁──┐  Defines the title.raw
        }                            │  field as a keyword type
      }
    }
  }
 }
}
```

In addition to declaring the `title` field as `text` type, we also declare it as a `keyword` type under the name `title.raw`. This way, when we index the document, the `title` field is stored both as a `text` type (thus undergoing text analysis) and as a `keyword` type (with no text analysis). The search can be carried over the `title.raw` field (`keyword` type) to avoid analysis. The following listing shows this; we also index a sample doc before running the query.

Listing 15.6   A `match` query to minimize analysis overhead

```
PUT programming_books3/_doc/1      ◁──┐  Indexes a
{                                     │  sample book
  "title":"Elasticsearch in Action"
}

GET programming_books3/_search     ◁──┐  Searches on a
{                                     │  keyword field
  "query": {
    "match": {
      "title.raw": "Elasticsearch in Action"
    }
  }
}
```

Because we run the search against the `keyword` field, we have to make sure the `title.raw` value is spelled exactly like what was indexed. We cannot fetch the results if even a single letter is different from the original (for example, if the first letter is lowercase). Try the same query again, but this time with lowercase "elasticsearch". You will not receive any results.

There are a few other general recommendations such as using search filters, pre-indexing data, avoiding wildcard queries, and so on. Consult the official documentation for details: http://mng.bz/MBwm.

Whereas slower search speed impacts search-related performance, slower ingestion speed affects the write part of the application. We discuss these indexing speed problems in the following section.

15.2 Index speed problems

Although we predominantly encounter search problems when users search the data, the other side of the coin is problems while indexing the data. In this section, we look at several reasons indexing operations can underperform and tips for improving indexing performance.

15.2.1 System-generated identifiers

When we use user-supplied IDs, Elasticsearch has to perform an additional step: checking whether the supplied ID already exists in the index. If the answer is no, indexing the document with that ID goes ahead. This is an unnecessary network call that takes a toll when we have thousands or millions of documents to index.

Sometimes, however, we don't need to worry about the document ID; we can let Elasticsearch create randomly generated IDs for documents. This way, a node that gets a request to index a document creates a globally unique ID and assigns it to the document instantly.

If your organization can live with random IDs, using them instead of user-defined IDs benefits performance. There's a downside, though: indexing documents without a primary key breeds duplication.

15.2.2 Bulk requests

Indexing documents using single-document APIs (indexing one by one) is asking for trouble, especially if we need to index many data documents. Fortunately, Elasticsearch provides a `_bulk` API that helps index documents in batches. (We discussed the `_bulk` API in chapter 5.) Because there isn't a batch size written in stone, my advice is to try out performance on the cluster to find an optimal size.

For example, if you need to ingest large amounts of data overnight, try increasing the refresh setting for potential benefits from the perspective of disk-usage performance. During the indexing operation, especially bulk inserts, increasing the refresh time is another tweak that most administrators use. We learn about increasing refresh times next.

15.2.3 Adjusting the refresh rate

When a document is indexed, usually it's available for search in under a second, but various operations happen under the hood. Initially, documents in the in-memory buffer are moved to segments before being stored in the filesystem cache. They then are finally flushed to disk.

All operations carried out on an index are committed once a refresh is called. If we have a large influx of documents to index, refreshing ensures that they are written to disk as well as being available for searches. We need to know whether the freshly indexed documents are available for searching instantly.

If we pause the refresh, we exclude any of the latest indexed documents: they are not available for searches. We essentially minimize the resource-intensive operation of disk I/O. For example, if we pause the refresh operation for 1 minute, we potentially stop 60 rounds of disk sync. The downside is that any search queries during this period do not pick up the new documents indexed during this minute.

For example, if our use case allows holding the refresh for a defined period of time, we can reset the default refresh period by invoking the setting on the index. The following listing shows the code.

Listing 15.7   Customizing the refresh setting

```
PUT programming_books3/_settings
{
  "index":{
    "refresh_interval":"1m"        ◁─┐  Sets a custom value (here, 1
  }                                   │  minute) for the refresh cycle
}
```

Here, we set a one-minute interval for the refresh, so any books added during this minute aren't available for searching. A usual practice is to turn off the refresh operation before indexing. The next listing shows how we can turn off refresh completely.

Listing 15.8   Disabling refresh

```
PUT programming_books3/_settings
{
  "index":{
    "refresh_interval":-1
  }
}
```

By setting `refresh_interval` to `-1`, we essentially disable the refresh operation. Any documents that are indexed after we disable refresh are not available for searches. If you are curious about this setting's side effects, index a document and issue a search, as the following listing shows. The search should yield no results.

Listing 15.9   Searching with a disabled refresh index

```
PUT programming_books3/_doc/10          ◁─────────┐  Indexes a sample
{                                                  │  document
  "title":"Elasticsearch for Java Developers",
  "synopsis":"Elasticsearch meets Java"
}

GET programming_books3/_search          ◁─┐  Searching when refresh is
{                                          │  disabled returns no result.
  "query": {
    "match": {
```

```
      "title": "Elasticsearch Java"
    }
  }
}
```

A couple of things are going on here. We index a document into the same index (programming_books3) and then search for it. Because we canceled the refresh activity in listing 15.8, the match query doesn't yield any results.

Once indexing is complete, be sure to turn on refresh. (If refresh activity is disabled, no search queries will fetch the documents indexed during that refresh period.) We can reinstate the refresh interval by invoking this code.

Listing 15.10   Forcing a refresh on the index

```
POST programming_books3/_refresh
```

Invoking the _refresh endpoint at the end of the indexing operation (or periodically) ensures that indexed documents are available for searching. We can also allocate additional threads when working with bulk requests. To do so, we set the thread_pool attribute with additional writer threads in the elasticsearch.yml file, as the next listing shows.

Listing 15.11   Amending the writer threads' size

```
thread_pool:
  write:
    size: 50
    queue_size: 5000
```

Elasticsearch has many thread pools that we can change or modify according to our requirements. For example, in listing 15.11, the write (index) size of the pool is set to 50. This means we have 50 threads to help index data in multiple threads. The queue_size attribute holds the requests in a queue until a thread is available to process the next request.

We can fetch the current thread pool by invoking this command: GET _nodes/thread_pool. It fetches the various thread pools created as part of the node configuration. The following snippet shows the search and write thread pool sizes when executing this command:

```
# GET _nodes/thread_pool
"thread_pool": {
  ....
  "search": {
    "type": "fixed",
    "size": 7,
    "queue_size": 1000
  },
```

```
  "write": {
    "type": "fixed",
    "size": 4,
    "queue_size": 10000
  },
  ..
}
```

As you can see, Elasticsearch assigned seven and then four threads for searching and writing operations automatically, based on my computer's available number of processors. These settings are static, so we must edit the configuration file and restart the server for them to take effect.

In addition to the previous recommendations, there are a few others, such as increasing the indexing buffer size, switching off replicas during indexing, disabling swapping, and so forth. You can find a list of recommendations for improving the performance of indexing operations at http://mng.bz/a19Y.

15.3 *Unstable clusters*

A common problem when working with Elasticsearch is the stability of the cluster. Keeping the cluster healthy helps when servicing clients' requests. Many things can go wrong with the cluster! In this section, we look at some of the most common concerns.

15.3.1 *Cluster is not GREEN*

A cluster's health is represented by an effective, high-level traffic light status. Issuing GET _cluster/health provides the real-time status of the cluster: RED, YELLOW, or GREEN. An administrator's primary job is to make the cluster's status always GREEN.

If the status is RED, it must be addressed at any cost because part of the cluster is either not functioning or down. This unhealthy state of the cluster (indicated by the RED status) may be due to any number of problems such as hardware failures, network outages, corrupted filesystem, and others, leading to a loss of cluster nodes. In such a situation, DevOps engineers stop everything they are doing to fix this problem.

A YELLOW status indicates that the cluster is unhealthy but can run with manageable risk. This can indicate a loss of a few nodes, unassigned shards and replicas, or other problems. Although the cluster is available for business, it may soon go into the RED state if we don't fix the problem. The YELLOW state means trouble is waiting to happen.

Regular heartbeats originating from masters to nodes and vice versa establish the overall health of the cluster; the heartbeats from a master node to other nodes in the cluster provide a mechanism to find disconnected or nonresponsive nodes. In the same way, all nodes ping the master node regularly to check if it is alive and running.

The master node takes appropriate actions such as cluster data redistribution, cross-cluster replications, index management, shard rearrangement, and so on when members of the cluster appear or disappear. When they are deemed unfit for the purpose at hand, node(s) are removed from the cluster by the master.

A stable master is an important feature of a healthy cluster. If any ping from the nodes returns a negative response (meaning the master is probably down!), the nodes do not wait for another timed call but instead call for an election immediately. The master is elected instantly from the list of master-eligible nodes.

15.3.2   *Unassigned shards*

When we create an index with a set number of shards, Elasticsearch works out a strategy to allocate shards to available nodes. In a hypothetical example of 5 nodes with an index having 10 shards, each node is allocated 2 shards to balance shard assignment. Replicas are balanced similarly, although they are never allocated on the same node as their partners.

In some instances, shards cannot be assigned. For example, if we have a newly created index with 10 shards on a 5-node cluster and one or all of the shards are unassigned (unallocated) to any of these 5 nodes, the cluster will complain about unassigned shards.

However, we are talking about a hypothetical situation where one or all shards aren't allocated to any of the nodes. Unassigned or unallocated shards are a production incident. This usually happens during rebalancing of the shards due to a node (or a few nodes) failing for whatever reason. The unassigned shards have operational consequences on indexes that are newly created (fresh indexes) or already live after being created earlier.

If shards are unassigned for an *existing* index (most likely during the rebalancing phase after one or a few nodes die), read operations (searches) are halted because that shard's share of documents may have disappeared. Write operations also halt because of the same problem of unassigned shards. If this is true for a newly created index with unassigned shards, write operations pause until the shard allocation is fixed.

Elasticsearch provides a convenient `allocation` API to check the unassigned nature of shards. Issuing the following command fetches a detailed explanation of why Elasticsearch can't assign the shards to relevant nodes.

> **Listing 15.12   Getting an explanation for unassigned shards**

```
GET _cluster/allocation/explain
```

Because we didn't specify any shards with this request, Elasticsearch chooses an unassigned shard randomly and explains why the allocation wasn't successful. For example, on my single-node development cluster, invoking this command produces the response shown in figure 15.1.

There's a lot of information to digest in the output of the allocation explanation call. Figure 15.1 shows that the `programming_books2` index is unassigned (look at the `current_state` attribute). The `allocate_explanation` attribute explains the reason

Index that was unassigned

Unassignment reasons

Allocation detailed explanation

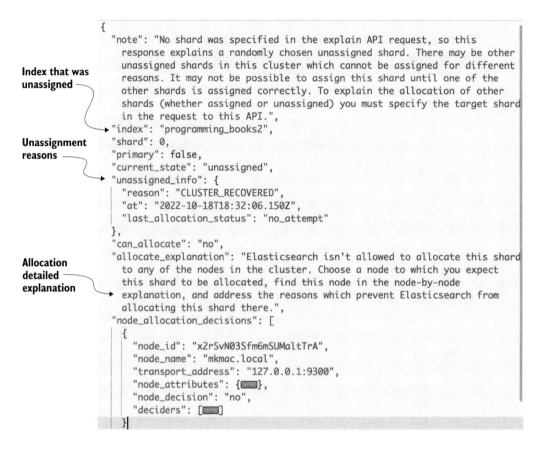

```
{
    "note": "No shard was specified in the explain API request, so this
        response explains a randomly chosen unassigned shard. There may be other
        unassigned shards in this cluster which cannot be assigned for different
        reasons. It may not be possible to assign this shard until one of the
        other shards is assigned correctly. To explain the allocation of other
        shards (whether assigned or unassigned) you must specify the target shard
        in the request to this API.",
    "index": "programming_books2",
    "shard": 0,
    "primary": false,
    "current_state": "unassigned",
    "unassigned_info": {
        "reason": "CLUSTER_RECOVERED",
        "at": "2022-10-18T18:32:06.150Z",
        "last_allocation_status": "no_attempt"
    },
    "can_allocate": "no",
    "allocate_explanation": "Elasticsearch isn't allowed to allocate this shard
        to any of the nodes in the cluster. Choose a node to which you expect
        this shard to be allocated, find this node in the node-by-node
        explanation, and address the reasons which prevent Elasticsearch from
        allocating this shard there.",
    "node_allocation_decisions": [
        {
            "node_id": "x2rSvN03Sfm6mSUMaltTrA",
            "node_name": "mkmac.local",
            "transport_address": "127.0.0.1:9300",
            "node_attributes": {...},
            "node_decision": "no",
            "deciders": [...]
        }
```

Figure 15.1 Reasons for unassigned shards

for this, and `node_allocation_decisions` contains `deciders` to provide the exact explanation. The following snippet shows these deciders:

```
"deciders": [{
  "decider": "same_shard",
  "decision": "NO",
  "explanation": "a copy of this shard is already
allocated to this node [[programming_books2][0],
    node[x2rSvN03Sfm6mSUMaltTrA],
[P], s[STARTED], a[id=eu1qh4I5THKRmD_7OcmWYw]]"
},
{
  "decider": "disk_threshold",
  "decision": "NO",
  "explanation": "the node is above the low watermark cluster
setting [cluster.routing.allocation.disk.watermark.low=85%],
having less than the minimum required [35gb] free space,
actual free: [24.9gb], actual used: [89.3%]"
}]
```

The `deciders` explanations reveal why the allocation fails. We can also fetch the details of a single unassigned shard using the same API by providing the index and the shard.

Listing 15.13   Getting an explanation for a single unassigned shard

```
GET _cluster/allocation/explain
{
  "index": "programming_books2",
  "shard": 0,
  "primary": true,
  "current_node": "mkmac.local"
}
```

This query fetches the allocation explanation for the given index. Based on the explanations, we can start troubleshooting to resolve unassigned shards and return the cluster to a GREEN state.

15.3.3   *Disk-usage thresholds*

Elasticsearch protects clusters from low disk memory by enabling disk-usage thresholds on the cluster. These thresholds are put in place to prevent nodes from running out of disk space and thus creating a failed cluster. Three thresholds are provided as low, high, and flood-stage disk watermarks for administrators to use accordingly.

LOW-DISK WATERMARK

The low-disk watermark is an 85% barrier threshold that kicks in if disk memory falls below 85% of total memory. If this threshold is crossed on a particular node, Elasticsearch does not allocate any new shards on that node until the node's memory drops below this setting. For example, if we have allocated 1 TB of disk memory to a node and 850 GB is already consumed, Elasticsearch raises this alert and takes measures to prevent node failures related to insufficient disk free space. The watermark can also be an absolute value, such as setting 200 GB instead of a memory threshold represented as a percentage.

Although this watermark threshold is set at 85% by default, we can use the cluster settings API to change it if needed. The following code shows the mechanism to change this. We decrease the low-disk-space watermark to 80%, which is a bit lower than the default.

Listing 15.14   Setting the low-disk watermark on the cluster

```
PUT _cluster/settings
{
  "transient": {
    "cluster.routing.allocation.disk.watermark.low":"80%"
  }
}
```

HIGH-DISK WATERMARK

The high-disk watermark threshold is set to 90% by default, which protects the node's memory from falling lower than 90% of available disk memory. When this watermark hits, Elasticsearch makes every effort to move (relocate) shards from this failing node to other nodes where the memory is adequate.

Similar to the low-disk watermark, this is a dynamic setting, so we can use the cluster settings API to amend the threshold. The next listing decreases the high-disk-space watermark to 85% from the default 90% to make sure an alert is published when the line is crossed. Note that we use an alternate way of expressing 85%: 0.85.

Listing 15.15   Setting the high-disk watermark on the cluster

```
PUT _cluster/settings
{
  "transient": {
    "cluster.routing.allocation.disk.watermark.high":"0.85"
  }
}
```

FLOOD-STAGE-DISK WATERMARK

When the high-disk watermark is crossed, Elasticsearch waits for one more threshold, the flood-stage-disk watermark, before it enters panic mode. The default flood-stage watermark is 95%: if disk memory on the node falls below 95%, Elasticsearch raises this alert and makes all the indexes on this node non-writable. Any shards allocated on the node with the flood-stage watermark enabled turn into read-only shards.

As soon as disk space is available and disk usage doesn't tip the watermark threshold, the flood-stage watermark is reset. As with the other watermarks, we can (re)set the flood-stage watermark's default threshold to suit our requirements. In this listing, we turn down the knob on the flood-stage watermark.

Listing 15.16   Setting the flood-stage-disk watermark on the cluster

```
PUT _cluster/settings
{
  "transient": {
    "cluster.routing.allocation.disk.watermark.flood_stage":"90%"
  }
}
```

We can invoke GET _cluster/settings to fetch all the watermark settings to make sure they are set on the cluster:

```
"transient": {
    "cluster": {
      "routing": {
        "allocation": {
          "disk": {
            "watermark": {
              "low": "80%",
```

```
            "flood_stage": "90%",
            "high": "85%"
        }
      }
    }
  }
 }
}
...
```

We can also provide all these settings simultaneously. I'll leave it up to you to experiment (or see the book's files for the solution).

Unresponsive server calls are always a problem in distributed systems. Users sometimes have to wait longer than needed only to realize that their call failed, but the server didn't return quickly enough to notify them. To avoid such error conditions, software systems implement circuit breakers. Elasticsearch has them too, as we discuss in the following section.

15.4   Circuit breakers

In distributed architectures and applications, failure of remote calls from nonresponsive services is a given, although it shouldn't be taken for granted. It is a common problem in a microservices world for a client to wait longer than usual only to receive an error. Fortunately, there is a circuit-breaker pattern to alleviate this problem.

A *circuit breaker* is a fallback method that is triggered when a response crosses a threshold time due to server-side problems such as being out of memory, resource locks, and so forth. It's like waiting a long time in a queue for a new iPhone, only to be disappointed when the store runs out—but they give you a gift certificate.

Elasticsearch is no different. It's a distributed application that's expected to throw errors and exceptions for many reasons. Elasticsearch implements circuit breakers to counteract problems that hamper a client's progress. It throws meaningful errors to the client if the circuit breakers are triggered.

Elasticsearch has six circuit breakers for various scenarios, including a parent-level catch-all circuit breaker. For example, if overall memory on the node increases due to the overall consumption of the current inflight requests, the inflight-requests circuit breaker kicks in to save the node from failure. The following query uses the nodes API to fetch the current memory limits set on various circuit breakers.

Listing 15.17   Fetching circuit breaker memory settings

```
GET _nodes/stats/breaker
```

Elasticsearch throws errors when the memory required to carry out an operation is inadequate (or action), and it triggers the circuit breakers. Clients get an "Out of Memory" error instantly from these circuit breakers. Table 15.1 lists the various types of circuit breakers, their limits, and the associated properties.

Table 15.1 Types of circuit breakers and their memory settings

Circuit breaker	Description and minimum memory limit	Property
Parent	The total memory that can be used across all the other circuit breakers. Defaults to 70% of JVM heap memory if real-time memory is taken into account (`indices.breaker.total.use_real_memory=true`); otherwise, it is 95% of JVM heap memory.	`indices.breaker.total.limit`
Inflight requests	The sum total of memory of all inflight requests, which is not to be exceeded by a threshold. The default is 100% of JVM heap memory, although it derives the actual percentage from the parent circuit breaker.	`network.breaker.inflight_requests.limit`
Request	Helps prevent exceeding the heap memory to serve a single request. The default is 60% of the JVM heap.	`indices.breaker.request.limit`
Field data	Helps prevent exceeding memory when loading fields into the `fields` cache. The default limit is 40% of heap memory.	`indices.breaker.fielddata.limit`
Accounting requests	Avoids accumulating memory after the request is served. The default is 100%, which means it inherits the threshold from the parent.	`indices.breaker.accounting.limit`
Script compilation	While all other circuit breakers look after memory, this circuit breaker limits the number of inline compilations in a fixed time period. The default is 150/5 min (150 script compilations in a period of 5 minutes).	`script.max_compilations_rate`

Circuit breakers help avoid using excess memory for few operations that occur frequently. This helps to maintain a stable cluster.

15.5 *Final words*

Because a huge number of things can go wrong on a production cluster, it is not only impractical but impossible to cover all performance and troubleshooting problems in this chapter. Those we have looked at barely scratch the surface. Most problems require a detailed investigation, profiling of the application, sifting through logs, trial-and-erroring a few options, and so on. A word of advice: stay calm and be methodical in your journey of maintaining a healthy and stable cluster.

I also advise you to take your Elasticsearch cluster for a drive so you understand it thoroughly inside and out. Experimenting with larger (future-proof) data sets in a nonfunctional environment ensures that you not only get a grip on the infrastructure side of things but also understand the search and file I/O performance metrics in detail.

Official documentation, discussion forums (Stack Overflow), and blog posts for engineers are available to help you manage and monitor clusters. You can follow their guidance to tweak the memory configuration for optimal performance, disk usage, and smooth running of the cluster.

This chapter concludes our journey through learning, understanding, and working with Elasticsearch. Elasticsearch is a complex beast; it requires dedicated knowledge and committed expertise to maintain and run production farms. The good news is that the Elastic folks have produced rich documentation about the product over the years (although it's a bit dry and overwhelming sometimes), which can help you when you're lost—and of course, you can refer to this book!

Summary

- Elasticsearch is a complex search engine, and maintaining and managing healthy clusters requires expertise.
- Slower search speeds are a common problem that clients complain about when searching for data with Elasticsearch. Provisioning modern hardware with appropriate allocation of memory and computing resources helps alleviate speed problems. Options like choosing keyword data types and tweaking the document data model also help increase search speed.
- Indexing speeds are a concern as well, especially when the system is ingestion heavy. If allowed, measures like using system-generated IDs for documents can speed up the indexing process. Loading data using bulk APIs (rather than single-document APIs) is a surefire way to improve ingestion performance.
- We can turn off or increase the refresh rate during indexing and then switch it on when indexing completes. Doing so makes the documents unavailable instantly for searches but improves indexing performance by reducing I/O hits.
- Due to the distributed nature of Elasticsearch, things can go wrong in many areas, from the cluster to the filesystem, node communication, memory, and so on. Keeping a healthy cluster is paramount, and administrators must strive to maintain a GREEN cluster state. Religiously following the traffic light management-based cluster health system helps with smooth running of the cluster.
- Occasionally, shards are left unassigned, and troubleshooting to find the exact cause helps us reattach nodes if necessary or take the appropriate action.
- Elasticsearch provides thresholds on the available disk memory, including low-, high-, and flood-stage-disk watermarks. The low- and high-disk watermarks allow Elasticsearch to manage shard reallocation and alert the administrator about upcoming cluster problems. The flood-stage watermark is a dire warning

about an out-of-disk memory problem on the node. To keep the cluster alive when this happens, Elasticsearch makes all shards read-only and does not allow any indexing operations on the shards of that node.

- Elasticsearch is a memory-hungry application, and appropriate controls should be implemented so that errors are instantly propagated to the client. It uses circuit-breaker patterns to create circuit breakers so the client doesn't need to wait longer than necessary. Each circuit breaker triggers Elasticsearch if the memory for a certain action grabs more memory than expected. A child circuit breaker inherits the memory thresholds from a parent circuit breaker.

appendix A
Installation

The first step in working with any product is downloading and installing it. In this appendix, we download, install, configure, and run Elasticsearch and Kibana. The installation instructions are available on the book's GitHub repository (http://mng.bz/gBmn) and on the book's website (https://www.manning.com/books/elasticsearch-in-action-second-edition)

By default, the 8.x version of Elasticsearch comes with security enabled. For simplicity, and so security doesn't get in our way, we disable this feature in this appendix. However, *do not* disable security in production. Edit config/elasticsearch.yml to add the following property at the end of the file:

```
xpack.security.enabled: false
```

A.1 Installing Elasticsearch

Installing Elasticsearch is a breeze. The folks at Elastic have put in a lot of effort to let us install the products in whatever fashion we want—using a binary, package manager, Docker, or even the cloud. The next few sections detail these options. Our preferred approach for this book is installing the software by downloading binaries, but there is no reason you can't try other options. The instructions on the Elastic site are informative; visit the website for details of installation methods we don't discuss.

A.1.1 Downloading the Elasticsearch binary

The easiest way to set up the Elasticsearch server on your computer is simply to download the compressed artifact, uncompress it, and execute the run script. Head to the Elasticsearch download page at https://elastic.co/downloads/elasticsearch and download the respective binary for your operating system. The website has downloadable artifacts for almost all operating systems, including Docker support.

We try Windows and macOS here, but the instructions for other operating systems follow the same pattern and are straightforward.

> **NOTE** We use a simple path of installing from a binary and running on a local machine, but it is usually handled differently in the real world. A separate team (DevOps, perhaps) may take ownership of installing and configuring the required setup and providing developers with preconfigured instances. The software can be on premises or in the cloud, depending on your organization's IT infrastructure strategy. Most cloud providers like AWS and Azure provide managed services. Elastic also has a managed cloud offering, which deploys the software in AWS, Azure, or Google Cloud.

Follow the instructions here to set up your personal development environment. Choose the right binary, and download it onto your computer. You can download it to any directory you choose. For example, I usually download software to the platform folder at <*my_home*>/DEV/platform for convenience. The current version of Elasticsearch is 8.6 as of writing this book, but be mindful that Elastic releases newer versions pretty quickly.

> **NOTE** The Elasticsearch binary is bundled with the Java JDK. This way, if you do not have Java installed (or it is not compatible), Elasticsearch does not moan about it; it goes about its business, referring to the packaged Java JDK. If you wish to install a non-bundled version, check out the download page, click the appropriate link that says non-JDK binary, and be sure JAVA_HOME is set and pointing to your local installation.

Now that you have downloaded the binary, the next step is to unpack the binary to install it on your local machine in your chosen folder. We discuss this in the next two sections for Windows and macOS operating systems: choose whichever section applies to your needs, and skip the other.

A.1.2   *Starting up on Windows*

After the file has downloaded successfully, uncompress the zip file to your installation folder. Table A.1 explains the folder structure Elasticsearch adheres to.

Table A.1   Elasticsearch folder structure

Folder name	Details
bin	The binary folder holding all the scripts to start the server as well as many other utilities. We usually don't need to touch the other executables, except the one to start the server: elasticsearch.bat (or .sh, depending on the OS).
config	Folder where the configuration for our server lives, especially the elasticsearch.yml file. Most properties are set for us so the server starts with sensible defaults.
plugins	A directory for hosting plugins—additional software modules that can be used to bring in new Elasticsearch features, such as creating a new text analyzer
modules	Contains modules

Table A.1 Elasticsearch folder structure *(continued)*

Folder name	Details
logs	Directory where our running Elasticsearch instance spits out logging data, including server and garbage collection logs
data	Folder to which data is written, like a persistence store. All documents are stored here on the computer's filesystem.

Once the binary is extracted to your folder, start a command prompt with administrative privileges. At the command prompt, issue a change directory (`cd`) command to move into Elasticsearch's bin folder:

```
cmd>cd <INSTALL_DIR>\elasticsearch\bin
Execute the elasticsearch.bat to start up the server:
cmd> elasticsearch.bat
```

If all goes well, you should see output like "Server Started" printed on the console. Here, we started our server as a single-node instance. Once it is started up, it joins a cluster automatically with one node (itself). The server is available by default at https://localhost:9200 (default settings).

Open your web browser, and visit the Elasticsearch home page at https://localhost:9200. If the server is running happily, a JSON response will come back from the server, as shown in figure A.1. This simple "success" message from Elasticsearch indicates that the server is alive and running.

```json
{
    "name": "mkmac.local",
    "cluster_name": "elasticsearch",
    "cluster_uuid": "h1KA7SGER-qKS31821YA1Q",
    "version": {
        "number": "8.4.2",
        "build_flavor": "default",
        "build_type": "tar",
        "build_hash": "89f8c6d8429db93b816403ee75e5c270b43a940a",
        "build_date": "2022-09-14T16:26:04.382547801Z",
        "build_snapshot": false,
        "lucene_version": "9.3.0",
        "minimum_wire_compatibility_version": "7.17.0",
        "minimum_index_compatibility_version": "7.0.0"
    },
    "tagline": "You Know, for Search"
}
```

Figure A.1 The Elasticsearch server's home page

A couple of attributes may need your attention. The `name` is the instance's name, which defaults to your computer's name. You can change by tweaking the configuration (as shown later).

The second property of importance is `cluster_name`, indicating the name of the cluster this node has joined. Again, Elasticsearch provides defaults, so the current cluster's name is `elasticsearch`, set by default.

A.1.3   *Starting up on macOS*

Download the macOS binary (tar.gz) and uncompress it to your preferred location, say /Users/*<username>*/DEV/platform. Open a terminal, and navigate to the bin directory in your installation folder:

```
$>cd ~/DEV/platform/elasticsearch/bin
```

Execute the `elasticsearch` run script:

```
$>./elasticsearch
```

This brings up the Elasticsearch server in a single-node cluster. The output to the console with the message "Server Started" indicates that the server was started successfully. Navigate to http://localhost:9200 on your favorite browser once the server is up and running. You should see the response shown in figure A.2.

```
mkonda@mkmac bin % curl http://localhost:9200
{
  "name" : "mkmac.local",
  "cluster_name" : "elasticsearch",
  "cluster_uuid" : "0a_3154xTjW9m-NELJE4fA",
  "version" : {
    "number" : "7.11.2",
    "build_flavor" : "default",
    "build_type" : "tar",
    "build_hash" : "3e5a16cfec50876d20ea77b075070932c6464c7d",
    "build_date" : "2021-03-06T05:54:38.141101Z",
    "build_snapshot" : false,
    "lucene_version" : "8.7.0",
    "minimum_wire_compatibility_version" : "6.8.0",
    "minimum_index_compatibility_version" : "6.0.0-beta1"
  },
  "tagline" : "You Know, for Search"
}
```

Figure A.2
Server response using
cURL on macOS

Accessing the server using cURL

In addition to accessing Elasticsearch's URL via browser, you can use cURL (command-line URL invocation utility) to interact with the server. Unix users love using cURL for hitting HTTP URLs. It's a very popular and useful command-line utility to talk to servers over HTTP. Most Unix-based systems have the utility installed by default

> (or you can download it online). You can also download the binary for Windows OS from https://curl.se/windows.
>
> Open a new terminal window, and type in the following:
>
> ```
> $>curl http://localhost:9200
> ```

The response indicates that the Elasticsearch server is working well (obviously, the version number will be different when you run on your local setup). The most important property is `cluster_name`. The default value is `"elasticsearch"`. If you are starting up a new node and wish to join this cluster (`elasticsearch`), all you have to do is to set `cluster_name` in the properties file to match the first server's `cluster_name` property.

A.1.4 Installing via Docker

If you are going the route of using Docker, you can do so two ways, as described here.

USING THE DOCKER IMAGE

Elastic publishes its Docker images in the docker.elastic.co repository. Pull the image from Elastic's docker repo:

```
docker pull docker.elastic.co/elasticsearch/elasticsearch:8.6.2
```

This fetches the image (which is based on CentOS) to your local machine. Once the image is downloaded, you can start your server by invoking the `docker run` command:

```
docker run -p 9200:9200 -p 9300:9300 -e "discovery.type=single-node"
    docker.elastic.co/elasticsearch/elasticsearch:8.6.2
```

This command starts the server in single-node mode, exposing the server at 9200 on your localhost.

After the command executes successfully, visit http://localhost:9200 on your browser (or issue a `curl` command) to receive a positive response from the server.

USING DOCKER-COMPOSE

The book's files include Docker files in the docker folder at http://mng.bz/5wvD or on the book's website. Copy (or check out to your local machine) the elasticsearch-docker-8-6-2.yml file. Issue the following command at the terminal:

```
docker-compose up -f elasticsearch-docker-8-6-2.yml
```

This command kick-starts your Docker container with both Elasticsearch and Kibana services.

A.1.5 Testing the server with the _cat API

Elasticsearch is a RESTful web server, meaning communicating with it is very easy. Elasticsearch exposes a special API called cat (compact and aligned text) with the _cat endpoint. While JSON formats are computer friendly, it would be uncomfortable for humans to read data in that format. The _cat API is not for programmatic consumption but is designed to produce output in a tabular (columnar) format that is easy on the human eye.

You can find the list of endpoints exposed by the _cat API by visiting http://local host:9200/_cat in your browser or executing this curl command:

```
curl 'localhost:9200/_cat'
```

Doing so returns over three dozen endpoints (we show only a few for brevity):

```
/_cat/shards
/_cat/shards/{index}
/_cat/nodes
/_cat/indices
/_cat/indices/{index}
/_cat/count
/_cat/count/{index}
/_cat/health
/_cat/aliases
...
```

Let's determine the cluster's health using the _cat API. Visit http://localhost:9200/ _cat/health or issue this curl command:

```
curl 'localhost:9200/_cat/health'
```

The /_cat/health endpoint exposes the cluster's health. The response to this query is something like the following:

```
1615669944 21:12:24 elasticsearch yellow 1 1 1 1 0 0 1 0 - 50.0%
```

This is a columnar representation of data, but as you can see, there are no column headings to identify the values. You can ask for output with column headings by adding a v (for *verbose*) at the end of the query:

```
curl 'localhost:9200/_cat/health?v'
```

This yields the following:

```
epoch      timestamp cluster       status node.total node.data shards pri
    relo init unassign pending_tasks max_task_wait_time
    active_shards_percent
1615669875 21:11:15  elasticsearch yellow          1         1      1   1
    0    0       1             0                 -                   50.0%
```

The response indicates that the cluster name is elasticsearch (third field), its status is YELLOW (fourth field), and so on.

A.2   *Installing Kibana*

Now that Elasticsearch is installed and up and running, you need to install Kibana. The installation follows the same path as for Elasticsearch, and we briefly go through the process for Windows and Mac.

A.2.1   *Downloading the Kibana binary*

Visit Kibana's download page (https://elastic.co/downloads/kibana) to download the latest version (8.6.2 at the writing of this book) of Kibana for your favorite operating system. Extract the archive to your installation folder.

A.2.2   *Kibana on Windows*

Issue a change directory (`cd`) command to move to the bin folder, and execute (or double-click) the kibana.bat file:

```
cmd:>cd <KIBANA_INSTALL_DIR>\bin          ⊲┐ Changes to the bin directory
                                            │ of the installation
cmd:>kibana.bat      ⊲┐ Starts the Kibana dashboard
                      │ by executing the script
```

Kibana should be running on your local machine on port 5601.

Be sure the Elasticsearch server is still up and running in the other command window. (When Kibana starts up, it looks for an instance of Elasticsearch to connect to. So, it is important to keep Elasticsearch running from the previous installation.) This will kick-start the Kibana server, as you can see in the logs:

```
Status changed from yellow to green - Ready
log [23:17:16.980] [info][listening] Server running at http://localhost:5601
log  [23:17:16.987] [info][server][Kibana][http] http server running at
http://localhost:5601
```

The application starts up and connects to your Elasticsearch server. Once you see a positive response in the command window, open your web browser and visit http://localhost:5601, where you will see the web application shown in figure A.3.

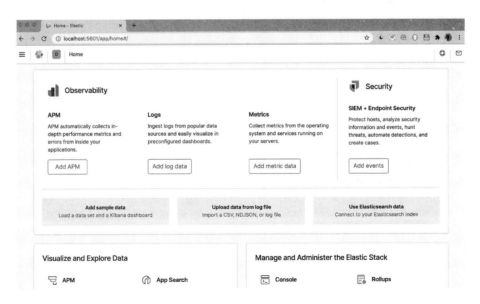

Figure A.3   Kibana web application running on localhost

A.2.3 *Kibana on macOS*

Once the binary is extracted, execute the Kibana shell script to run it:

```
$>cd <KIBANA_INSTALL_DIR>/bin        ◁─┐ Changes to the bin directory
                                         of the installation
$>./kibana    ◁─┐ Starts the Kibana dashboard
                  by executing the script
```

This starts your Kibana dashboard on default port 5601. You should see the following output in the terminal:

```
Status changed from yellow to green - Ready
log [23:17:16.980] [info][listening] Server running at http://localhost:5601
log  [23:17:16.987] [info][server][Kibana][http] http server running at
http://localhost:5601
```

As the log indicates, visiting http://localhost:5601 will land on Kibana's home page (see figure A.3) by default.

A.2.4 *Installing via Docker*

Similar to the installation of Elasticsearch, there are two ways to work with Docker, as described here.

USING THE DOCKER IMAGE

Elastic publishes its Docker images in the https://www.docker.elastic.co repository. Pull the image from Elastic's docker repo:

```
docker pull docker.elastic.co/elasticsearch/elasticsearch:8.6.2
```

This fetches the image to your local machine. Once the image is downloaded, you can start your engine by running the following commands:

```
docker network create elastic                                    ◁───────┐
docker run --name es01-test --net elastic -p 9200:9200 -p 9300:9300 -e   │
"discovery.type=single-node"                                    Creates  │
docker.elastic.co/elasticsearch/elasticsearch:7.14.0  ◁─┐ Runs the  a local│
                                                          container network│
```

This command starts the web server on port 5601, connecting to Elasticsearch search on 9200. Once the command executes successfully, visit http://localhost:5601 on your browser to see the web application in action.

USING DOCKER-COMPOSE

The book's files include Docker files in the docker folder at http://mng.bz/5wvD or on the book's website. Copy (or check out to your local machine) the elasticsearch-docker-8-6-2.yml file. Issue the following command at the terminal:

```
docker-compose up -f elasticsearch-docker-8-6-2.yml
```

This starts both Elasticsearch and Kibana in the Docker container.

appendix B
Ingest pipelines

Data that makes its way into Elasticsearch is not always clean. Usually, data requires transformation, enrichment, or formatting. There are options for cleaning data before bringing it into Elasticsearch for ingestion, such as writing custom transformers or using ETL (extract, transform, load) tools. Elasticsearch allows these capabilities via ingest pipelines that provide first-class support for manipulating data—we can split, remove, modify, and enhance data before it is ingested.

B.1   *Overview*

Data to be indexed into Elasticsearch may need to undergo transformation and manipulation. Consider an example of loading millions of legal documents represented as PDF files into Elasticsearch for searching. Although bulk loading them is one approach, it is inadequate, cumbersome, and error-prone.

If you are thinking we can use ETL tools for such data-manipulation tasks, you are absolutely right. A plethora of such tools are available, including Logstash. Logstash manipulates our data before it is indexed into Elasticsearch or persisted to a database or other destinations. However, it is not lightweight, and it requires an elaborate setup, preferably on a different machine.

Just as we write search queries using Query DSL, we can develop ingest pipelines with processors using the same syntax and apply them to incoming data to ETL the data. The workflow is straightforward:

1 Create one or more pipelines with the expected logic based on the business requirements regarding transformations, enhancements, or enrichments to be carried out on the data.
2 Invoke the pipelines on the incoming data. The data goes through the series of processors in a pipeline and is manipulated at every stage.
3 Index the processed data.

Figure B.1 shows the workings of two independent pipelines with different sets of processors. These pipelines are hosted/created on an ingest node. The data is massaged while going through these processors before indexing. We can invoke these pipelines during a bulk load or when indexing individual documents.

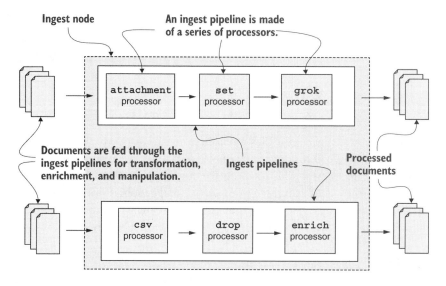

Figure B.1   Two independent pipelines processing data

A *processor* is a software component that performs one transformation activity on the incoming data. A *pipeline* is made of a series of processors. Each processor is dedicated to performing its one task. It processes the input based on its logic and spits out the processed data for the next stage. We can chain as many processors as our requirements dictate.

Elasticsearch provides over three dozen processors out of the box. Let's look at the mechanics of creating and using pipelines.

B.2   *Mechanics of ingest pipelines*

Ingest pipelines help us transform and manipulate data with minimal or no costly setup. A pipeline is made of a chain of processors, each performing a specific operation on the incoming data. These ingest processors are loaded onto nodes that are assigned an `ingest` role; remember from chapter 14 that each node in a cluster can be assigned a role—`master`, `data`, `ingest`, `ml`, and so on.

Let's take an example of MI5's top secret operations data being loaded from a database into Elasticsearch to integrate the search feature. The data extracted from the database must be stamped "confidential" using a `category` field (we can extend this example with further features later) before being indexed into Elasticsearch..

The first step in meeting this requirement is creating a pipeline with a processor. We need to add a field called `category` with the value `"confidential"` using a set processor. Elasticsearch exposes the `_ingest` API to create and test pipelines. We can create a new pipeline using the _ingest/pipeline/*<pipeline_name>* URL. The following code creates a new pipeline with one processor called `set`.

Listing B.1   Creating a confidential-stamping pipeline

```
PUT _ingest/pipeline/confidential_files_pipeline
{
  "description": "Stamp confidential on the file (document)",
  "processors": [                              We provide multiple
    {                                          processors as a chain.
      "set": {              A set processor
        "field": "category",   sets a new field.
        "value": "confidential"
      }
    }
  ]
}
```

We create an ingest pipeline called `confidential_files_pipeline` pipeline with a single `set` processor. The `set` processor's job is to create a new `category` field with the value `"confidential"`. When a new document is passed through this pipeline, the `set` processor will add a field called `category` to the document on the fly.

Once the pipeline definition is created, executing it stores the pipeline definitions in a cluster state. It is now ready to be put to use. However, we can use a `_simulate` API call to do a dry run before we start indexing the data.

Listing B.2   Creating a top-secret-stamper pipeline

```
POST _ingest/pipeline/confidential_files_pipeline/_simulate
{
  "docs": [{                       The docs array expects    Pipeline URL with
      "_source": {                 the set of documents.     the _simulate API
        "op_name": "Operation Cobra"
      }                            The _source field consists of
    }                              the additional field.
  ]
}
```

This code simulates the pipeline execution. We execute a document with one field-value pair on the `confidential_files_pipeline` pipeline. Executing the code does not index the document; instead, it tests the pipeline's logic. This is the response when we simulate the pipeline:

```
{
  "docs": [
    {
      "doc": {
```

```
        "_index": "_index",
        "_id": "_id",
        "_version": "-3",
        "_source": {
          "category": "confidential",
          "op_name": "Operation Cobra"
        },
        "_ingest": {
          "timestamp": "2022-11-03T23:42:33.379569Z"
        }
      }
    }
  ]
}
```

The _source object consists of our modified document: the pipeline adds the category field. This is the magic of the set processor.

As we discussed earlier, we can chain processors. Say we wish to uppercase the stamp ("CONFIDENTIAL"); all we need to do is add another processor—aptly called uppercase—to the pipeline and rerun the query.

Listing B.3 Chaining a second processor to uppercase a field

```
PUT _ingest/pipeline/confidential_files_pipeline
{
  "description": "Stamp confidential on the file (document)",
  "processors": [
    {
      "set": {
        "field": "category",
        "value": "confidential"
      },
      "uppercase": {            ◁─┐  The uppercase processor
        "field": "category"       │  is the new addition.
      }
    }
  ]
}
```

We added an uppercase processor so the two processors are chained: the output from the first processor becomes the input to the second processor. The result is as follows:

```
"_source": {
  "category": "CONFIDENTIAL",
  "op_name": "Operation Cobra"
}
```

The category field is added by the set processor, and the field is uppercased by the uppercase processor, yielding the CONFIDENTIAL stamp on the final document. In the next section, let's look at a practical example of loading PDFs using an ingest pipeline.

B.3   Loading PDFs into Elasticsearch

Let's say our business requirement is to load PDF files (such as legal documents or medical journals in PDF format) into Elasticsearch, enabling clients to conduct searches on them. Elasticsearch lets us index PDF files using a dedicated ingest processor called `attachment`.

The `attachment` processor is used in the ingest pipeline to load attachments: PDF files, Word documents, emails, and so on. It uses the Apache Tika (https:// tika.apache.org) library to extract the file data. The source data should be converted into Base64 format before being loading into the pipeline. Let's see this in action.

Continuing our MI5 example, we are expected to load all the secret data presented in PDF files into Elasticsearch. The following steps help visualize the process:

1   Define a pipeline with an `attachment` processor. The file's Base64 content is indexed into a field (for our example, we define the field as `secret_file_data`).

2   Convert the PDF file content into bytes, and feed it to the Base64 encoding utility (using any toolset at your disposal).

3   Invoke the pipeline for the incoming data so the `attachment` processor processes the data.

The following code creates a pipeline with an `attachment` processor.

Listing B.4   Pipeline with an attachment processor

```
PUT _ingest/pipeline/confidential_pdf_files_pipeline
{
  "description": "Pipeline to load PDF documents",
  "processors": [
    {
      "set": {
        "field": "category",
        "value": "confidential"
      },
      "attachment": {          ◁──┐  The attachment processor
        "field": "secret_file_data"   │  with a secret_file_data field
      }
    }
  ]
}
```

When we execute this code, the `confidential_pdf_files_pipeline` is created on the cluster. The `attachment` processor expects the Base64-encoded data from a file set in the `secret_file_data` field during pipeline ingestion.

Now that we have created the pipeline, let's test it. Suppose the file data is "Sunday Lunch at Konda's" (perhaps this is code for getting rid of Mr. Konda!), and we run the Base64 encoder to produce the data in a Base64-encoded form. (I'll leave it up to you to apply an encoder—see the sidebar "Base64 encoding" for more information.)

We can simulate the pipeline by passing the Base64 string and checking whether the output is what we expect (it should spit out "Sunday Lunch at Konda's"). The following code tests the pipeline in action. Note that `U3VuZGF5IEx1bmNoIGF0IEtvbm-RhJ3M=` is the Base64-encoded PDF file with a secret message ("Sunday Lunch at Konda's").

Listing B.5   Simulating the pipeline

```
POST _ingest/pipeline/confidential_pdf_files_pipeline/_simulate
{
  "docs": [
    {
      "_source": {
        "op_name": "Op Konda",
        "secret_file_data":"U3VuZGF5IEx1bmNoIGF0IEtvbmRhJ3M="
      }
    }
  ]
}
```

The `secret_file_data` field value is manually set with the Base64-encoded string, which is then fed to the pipeline.

Base64 encoding

Java has a `java.util.Base64` encoder class; similarly, Python has a `base64` module. There's most likely Base64 support in your choice of programming/scripting language. Note that we must convert the input into bytes before Base64 encoding can be applied.

We can use any programming language or scripting framework to locate and load files, convert them into bytes, and feed them to the processor. Listing B.5 includes a code snippet for the Java and Python languages. The full code is available with the book's files: Python (http://mng.bz/6D46) and Java (http://mng.bz/o1Zv).

Based on the pipeline definition (listing B.4), the `attachment` processor expects the `secret_file_data` field with the encoded data, and we provided it when simulating the pipeline. Here is the response from the test:

```
...
    "doc": {
      "_index": "_index",
      "_id": "_id",
      "_version": "-3",
      "_source": {
        "op_name": "Op Konda",
        "category": "confidential",
        "attachment": {
          "content_type": "text/plain; charset=ISO-8859-1",
          "language": "et",
```

```
          "content": "Sunday Lunch at Konda's",
          "content_length": 24
        },
        "secret_file_data": "U3VuZGF5IEx1bmNoIGF0IEtvbmRhJ3M="
      },
      "_ingest": {
        "timestamp": "2022-11-04T23:19:05.772094Z"
      }
    }
  }
...
```

The response creates an additional object called `attachment` with a few fields—
`content` is the decoded form of the PDF file. Additional metadata is available for the
attachment in `content_length`, `language`, and other fields; the original encoded data
is available in the `secret_file_data` field. We can choose what fields we wish to persist as part of the metadata. The following code, for example, sets only `content`, dropping the other metadata values:

```
PUT _ingest/pipeline/only_content_pdf_files_pipeline
{
  "description": "Pipeline to load PDF documents",
  "processors": [
    {
      "set": {
        "field": "category",
        "value": "confidential"
      },
      "attachment": {
        "field": "secret_file_data",
        "properties":["content"]          ◁────  Sets only the content
      }                                          field to be indexed
    }
  ]
}
```

Elasticsearch provides many ingest processors, and they suit a lot of requirements. As
you can imagine, going over all of them in this appendix would be impractical. My
advice is to check out the documentation at http://mng.bz/nWZ4 and experiment
with the code.

appendix C
Clients

One of the strengths of Elasticsearch is the rich interfacing mechanisms provided out of the box for many clients to perform search and aggregations. Whether we use a Java, Python, C#, JavaScript, or other main programming language client that supports the RESTful API over HTTP protocol, there's always first-class support.

Exposing APIs over a RESTful interface is a modern architectural decision that helps to create language-agnostic products. Elastic embraced this path to create a product that can be integrated with multi-language landscapes.

Currently, Elasticsearch can be integrated with these clients: Java, Python, .NET, Ruby, Go, JavaScript, Perl, and PHP, as well as community-contributed clients such as C++, Kotlin, Scala, Swift, Rust, Haskell, Erlang, and a few others. Elasticsearch is more than happy to consider a request for a bespoke client should the need arise. Put in a pull request to the team, and get it in motion.

Discussing all these clients is impractical (and I do not have enough experience with languages other than Java, Kotlin, Scala, Python, Go, JavaScript, and a couple of others). So, this appendix provides high-level query mechanics for Java, JavaScript, and Python.

C.1   *Java client*

Elasticsearch is written in Java, and as you may expect, Elasticsearch offers native support for invoking Elasticsearch APIs using the Java Client library. It is built using fluent API builder patterns and supports both synchronous and asynchronous (blocking and nonblocking) API invocations. It requires Java 8 at minimum, so make sure your applications are at least on Java 8.

In the next couple of sections, we look at Elasticsearch integration from a Maven/Gradle Java-based application as well as a Spring-based Java application.

> ### Spring Data Elasticsearch
> If you are working on a Spring framework-based Java application, there's another route to integrate it with Elasticsearch: Spring Data Elasticsearch. This project helps us connect and query Elasticsearch using familiar and well-proven Spring patterns such as templates and repositories. Just as we'd create a repository to represent a database layer, Spring Data Elasticsearch lets us use the repository layer to query Elasticsearch. Refer to the documentation for more on the Spring Data Elasticsearch project: http://mng.bz/vnyr.

C.2 Background

Elasticsearch released a new forward-compatible Java client, Java API Client, from version 7.17. The Java API client is a modern client that follows a decent pattern of feature clients with strongly typed requests and responses. The earlier incarnation of the client was Java High-Level REST Client (see notes below)—which attracted a fair amount of criticism as well as became a headache to maintain and manage for elastic folks due to its inherent nature of how it was designed by having a dependency on the shared common code with Elasticsearch server.

Elastic folks recognized the need for a modern client—independent of the server's code base, with its client API code generated based on the server's API schema and providing a "feature client" pattern (we see this in action shortly). This led to the creation of a Java API client. It is the next-generation lightweight client whose code is pretty much (99%!) generated, embracing fluent API builder patterns and auto marshaling and unmarshalling Java Objects to JSON and vice versa.

> ### Java High-Level REST Client
> Elasticsearch re-engineered to get away with Java High-Level REST client (let me put an acronym on this for easier reference later on JHLRC) and introduced an API-based client called Java API client. There are a few problems with the JHLRC. In particular, it is coupled with specific versions of the Elasticsearch server because it shares common code with the Elasticsearch server. APIs are all manually handwritten, which means a lot of maintenance over time, leading to it becoming error-prone. The dependency on the server codebase means backward/forward compatibility is compromised.

C.3 Maven/Gradle project setup

The `ElasticsearchClient`-related classes are provided in a jar artifact that can be downloaded as part of the dependencies in our project. For convenience, I've created a Maven-based project that is available on GitHub (http://mng.bz/4Dmv) and the book's website.

Usually, two dependencies required to bring in related classes. They are declared in the pom file.

Listing C.1   Maven dependencies

```
<dependencies>
 <dependency>
   <groupId>co.elastic.clients</groupId>
   <artifactId>elasticsearch-java</artifactId>
   <version>8.5.3</version>
 </dependency>
 <dependency>
   <groupId>com.fasterxml.jackson.core</groupId>
   <artifactId>jackson-databind</artifactId>
   <version>2.12.7</version>
 </dependency>
 ...
</dependencies>
```

I am using the latest and greatest library versions at the time of writing this section: the 8.5.3 version of the elasticsearch-java client artifact and the 2.12.7 version of the Jackson core library. You may need to upgrade these libraries based on your needs.

   If you use Gradle, add the following artifacts as dependencies in your Gradle build file.

Listing C.2   Gradle dependencies

```
dependencies {
  implementation 'co.elastic.clients:elasticsearch-java:8.5.3'
  implementation 'com.fasterxml.jackson.core:jackson-databind:2.12.7'
}
```

Once we set up the project, the next step is to initialize the client and get it to work for us.

C.4   *Initialization*

Let's look at the client initialization and how we can put it to work. The client class is co.elastic.clients.elasticsearch.ElasticsearchClient and is initialized by providing the transport object (co.elastic.clients.transport.ElasticsearchTransport) to its constructor. This transport object, in turn, needs the restClient and JSON mapper objects. Let's look at the steps:

1   Create a RestClient object that encapsulates Apache's HttpHost, pointing to the URL of the Elasticsearch server.

Listing C.3   Instantiating RestClient

```
RestClient restClient = RestClient.builder(
      new HttpHost("localhost", 9200)).build();
```

The RestClient builder is created and accepts our Elasticsearch endpoint exposed on localhost at port 9200.

2 Create the transport object using the code in listing C.4. The `Elastic-searchTransport` object is constructed with the previously instantiated `rest-Client` instance and a JSON mapper (we use the Jackson JSON mapper in this instance).

Listing C.4 Construct Transport object

```
JacksonJsonpMapper jsonMapper = new JacksonJsonpMapper();
```
Creates a new
JacksonJsonpMapper
object
```
ElasticsearchTransport elasticsearchTransport =
    new RestClientTransport(restClient, jsonMapper);
```
Creates the
transport object

We pass the `restClient` and `jsonMapper`, which were instantiated before creating the transport object.

1 Bring `ElasticsearchClient` to life with the following code.

Listing C.5 Construct the client

```
ElasticsearchClient elasticsearchClient =
       new ElasticsearchClient(elasticsearchTransport);
```

All `ElasticsearchClient` needs is the transport object created a moment ago. That's pretty much it—we have a client, and it's time to use it to interact with Elasticsearch.

C.5   *Namespace clients*

Earlier, we mentioned that the Java API client follows a pattern of requests, responses, and "feature" clients. Elasticsearch has a concept of package names and namespaces for each feature it exposes—for example, cluster-related APIs are available in the `*.cluster` package, indexing operations-related APIs in `*.index`, and so on. The Java API client follows the same pattern: a "client" is provided for every feature, as shown in figure C.1.

For example, all index-related classes such as requests, responses, and an indexing client exist under the `co.elastic.clients.elasticsearch.indices` package. The client for this namespace is `ElasticsearchIndicesClient` and is obtained from the main `ElasticsearchClient` (we see it working in a moment). All index operations are expected to be performed by this `ElasticsearchIndicesClient`. Similarly, all the other features follow the same pattern—a "folder" per feature (namespace), with each feature having a client named `ElasticsearchFEATUREClient`.

It may be overwhelming to see the number of classes, but the following examples of using the Java API client to fetch a feature/namespace client to support the feature clarify that the rest of the client specification follows the same approach. Let's see how to create an index.

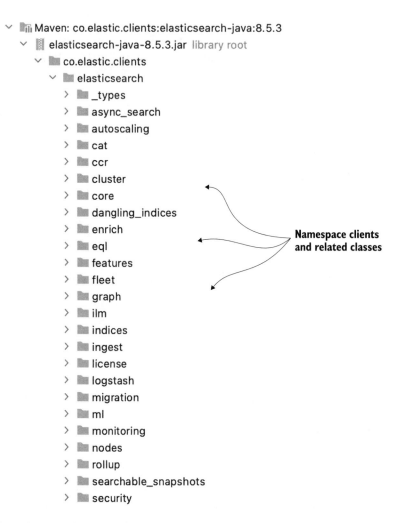

Figure C.1   Elasticsearch Java namespace clients

C.6   *Creating an index*

Let's create a `flights` index using this Java API client. All index-related operations form a namespace called `indices`, so classes and a client related to operations on indexes are in the `co.elastic.clients.elasticsearch.indices` package. As expected, the client supporting index operations is `ElasticsearchIndicesClient`. To obtain this client, we must ask the main Java API client (`ElasticsearchClient`) to provide an instance of the client:

```
ElasticsearchIndicesClient elasticsearchIndicesClient =
        this.elasticsearchClient.indices();
```

Calling the `indices()` function on the `elasticsearchClient` instance returns `Elas-ticsearchIndicesClient`. Once we have the client, we can invoke the `create()` method to create an index. The `create()` method expects a `CreateIndexRequest` object. This pattern leads to our next request/response pattern.

All methods on the client are expected to be passed in with a request object. There are many request classes, and each request object is instantiated using the builder pattern.

Suppose we need to create an index. This requires a `CreateIndexRequest` to be instantiated with the arguments needed to create an index. The following code creates the `CreateIndexRequest` using a builder:

```
CreateIndexRequest createIndexRequest =
  new CreateIndexRequest.Builder().index("flights").build();
```

The `index()` method accepts a string as the name of the index. Once the index is created, we can invoke the `create()` method on the client by passing this request:

```
CreateIndexResponse createIndexResponse =
        elasticsearchIndicesClient.create(createIndexRequest);
```

This call invokes the `create()` method on `elasticsearchIndicesClient`, which sends a query to the Elasticsearch server to create the index.

The result of this invocation is captured in the response object: `CreateIndex-Response`, in this case. Again, any invocation will return a response following the same pattern—for example, `CreateIndexRequest`'s response is a `CreateIndexResponse` object. The response object has all the required information about the newly created index.

The full method is given in listing C.6. The source code for the entire class along with the project is available with the book's files.

> **Listing C.6   Creating an index using `ElasticsearchIndicesClient`**

```
/**
* Method to create an index using bog-standard ElasticsearchIndicesClient
*
* @param indexName
* @throws IOException
*/
public void createIndexUsingClient(String indexName) throws IOException {
    ElasticsearchIndicesClient elasticsearchIndicesClient =
            this.elasticsearchClient.indices();
    CreateIndexRequest createIndexRequest =
new CreateIndexRequest.Builder().index(indexName).build();

CreateIndexResponse createIndexResponse =
        elasticsearchIndicesClient.create(createIndexRequest);
System.out.println("Index created successfully: "+createIndexResponse);
}
```

We can improve this code. Rather than instantiating `ElasticsearchIndicesClient` separately, we can instead use a builder, as shown in the following listing.

Listing C.7 Creating an index using the builder pattern

```
/**
* A method to create the index using Builder pattern
* @param indexName
* @throws IOException
*/
public void createIndexUsingBuilder(String indexName) throws IOException {

CreateIndexResponse createIndexResponse  = this.elasticsearchClient
  .indices().create(new CreateIndexRequest.Builder()
  .index(indexName)
  .build());

System.out.println("Index created successfully using
        Builder"+createIndexResponse);
}
```

We do not create `ElasticsearchIndicesClient` in this method. Instead, we pass in the request object (as a builder) to the `create()` method (the `indices()` method fetches the `ElasticsearchIndicesClient` on which the `create()` method is called behind the scenes).

We can go further—we can use a lambda function to make the code even more concise.

Listing C.8 Creating an index using Lambda expressions

```
/**
* A method to create an index using Lambda expression
* @param indexName
* @throws IOException
*/
public void createIndexUsingLambda(String indexName) throws IOException {

CreateIndexResponse createIndexResponse =
this.elasticsearchClient.indices().create(
                request -> request.index(indexName)
        );

System.out.println("Index created successfully using Lambda"
        +createIndexResponse);
}
```

The bold portion of the code is the lambda expression. It says that given a request (which is a `CreateIndexRequest.Builder()` type object), create an index using the `ElasticsearchIndicesClient` client.

As an index can be created using a schema, with settings as well as aliases, we can chain those methods in the request:

```
CreateIndexRequest createIndexRequest =
        new CreateIndexRequest.Builder()          Creates an index with
            .index(indexName)                     the given name
            .mappings(..)
            .settings(..)                         Creates a set
            .aliases(..)                          of mappings
            .build();                             Creates aliases
                                                  to the index
```

Adds settings
to the index

Next, let's see how to index a flight document into our index.

C.7   *Indexing documents*

In chapter 13, we discussed indexing documents using Query DSL in the Kibana Console (or cURL). For example, this code indexes the flight document with a random ID as the primary key.

Listing C.9   Indexing a document using Query DSL

```
POST flights/_doc
{
  "route":"London to New York",
  "name":"BA123",
  "airline":"British Airways",
  "duration_hours":5
}
```

Here, we invoke a `_doc` endpoint using the POST method with document details enclosed as a JSON object. The document ID is generated automatically by Elasticsearch. We can retrieve this document by issuing GET flights/_doc/_search.

Let's index the same document, but this time using the Java API client. Remember, we created the `flights` index in the previous section, so all we need to do is use the fluent API to build the query.

Listing C.10   Indexing a document with the Java API client

```
public void indexDocument(String indexName, Flight flight) throws IOException
    {
  IndexResponse indexResponse = this.elasticsearchClient.index(
    i -> i.index(indexName)
          .document(flight)
  );
    System.out.println("Document indexed successfully"+indexResponse);
}
```

Executing this query indexes a flight into our `flights` index. The `elasticsearchClient` exposes an `index` method that can be combined with other methods such as `id` and `document`. In this case, we don't use the ID because we let the system generate it.

The document method expects the flight object; did you notice we didn't transform the flight Java object to JSON? That's because we've delegated the responsibility of marshaling and unmarshaling to the JacksonJasonpMapper class that we associated with the transport object earlier.

The elasticsearchClient.index() method takes an IndexRequest object and spits out IndexResponse (this aligns with what we've discussed about requests and responses).

C.8   Searching

Searching data using queries with the Java API client follows a similar path: invoking the search() method in the ElasticsearchClient class by passing the required query. There's one subtle difference, though—the other features expose a client per namespace, but the search feature does not. Let's see this in action.

Suppose we wish to search for a route from London to New York. We create a match query, providing "London New York" as the search criterion against the route field in a nicely formed DSL when working with Kibana.

Listing C.11   Searching for a route using a match query

```
GET flights/_search
{
  "query": {
    "match": {
      "route": "London New York"
    }
  }
}
```

This simple match query checks for a route with the keywords "London New York". We may get one or two results depending on how many records we've indexed. This query can also be written in Java using the Java API client.

Listing C.12   Searching using the Java API client

```
this.elasticsearchClient.search(searchRequest -> searchRequest
    .index(indexName)
    .query(queryBuilder ->
        queryBuilder.match(matchQBuilder->
            matchQBuilder.field("route")
                .query(searchText)))
     ,Flight.class
);
```

The search() method expects a search request, which is provided as a lambda expression to the method. The query is written using another lambda function—given a query request (Query.Builder object), we invoke the match function with the Match-Query.Builder object. The JSON is converted to a Flight Java object, which is why Flight.class is provided as the argument to the query method.

The response from the `search()` method is a `SearchResponse`—so we can capture the results as shown here:

```
SearchResponse searchResponse =
    this.elasticsearchClient.search(..)
```

The `searchResponse` consists of results as `hits`, which we can iterate through to get the list of flights that were returned. The following listing shows the entire search request, including the flights returned in the response.

Listing C.13 Searching using the Java API client with hits

```
public void search(String indexName, String field, String searchText) throws
    IOException {

SearchResponse searchResponse =
  this.elasticsearchClient.search(searchRequest -> searchRequest
      .index(indexName)
      .query(queryBuilder -> queryBuilder
              .match(matchQueryBuilder ->
          matchQueryBuilder
                              .field("route")
                              .query(searchText)))
          ,Flight.class
  );

List<Flight> flights =                 ← Capture flights ...
  (List<Flight>) searchResponse.hits().hits()
    .stream().collect(Collectors.toList());

searchResponse.hits().hits()                      ← ... or print them to the console.
  .stream().forEach(System.out::println);

}
```

The `searchResponse` object has the results in the `hits` array—we just need to be sure to cast the hits to appropriate domain objects (`Flight`, in this case). The full source code of this example is available with the book's files. You can learn about the other clients in the documentation here: http://mng.bz/QPMQ.

index